WORKS ISSUED BY
THE HAKLUYT SOCIETY

THE JOURNAL OF
JEAN-FRANÇOIS DE GALAUP DE LA PÉROUSE

VOLUME I

SECOND SERIES
NO. 179

View of Port des Français, Northwest Coast, 'drawn from nature by Duché de Vancy in July 1786'. SHM 352:9.

The Journal
of
Jean-François de Galaup de la Pérouse
1785–1788

VOLUME I

Translated and edited by
JOHN DUNMORE

THE HAKLUYT SOCIETY
LONDON
1994

ISBN 0 904180 38 7
ISSN 0072 9396

Typeset by Waveney Typesetters, Norwich
Printed in Great Britain at
the University Press, Cambridge

SERIES EDITORS
W. F. RYAN and SARAH TYACKE

British Library Cataloguing-in-Publication Data
A catalogue record for this book is
available from the British Library

Published by the Hakluyt Society
c/o The Map Library
British Library, Great Russell Street
London WC1B 3DG

CONTENTS

LIST OF ILLUSTRATIONS AND MAPS

PREFACE

The quest for La Pérouse's journal goes back many years. During the 1960s while I was covering the broad field of French Pacific exploration, it struck me as strange that his journals were not listed in the records of the French Archives Nationales nor in those of the Service Historique de la Marine in the same manner as those of Bougainville, Surville or D'Entrecasteaux. The thought lingered nevertheless that they must be kept somewhere among the vast store of journals, correspondence, muster rolls and sundry papers of every kind that fill the seemingly endless shelves of the Archives. The French are creditably proud of their historical heritage and endeavour to preserve all the official documents that the ravages of wars and revolutions have spared. Having simply expressed the wish to read La Pérouse's original journal one day, I left it to the administrators' goodwill and the workings of chance, confident that one day the journal would emerge.

An expedition of such importance deserved recognition in the form of an annotated edition. James Cook had received the painstaking and devoted attention of J. C. Beaglehole, Bougainville's journal was about to appear in a fine commemorative edition, Surville's and J. R. Forster's journals would soon follow: La Pérouse could hardly be ignored.

There was, of course, Milet-Mureau's official publication of 1797, but there was no way to compare it with La Pérouse's own writings. Even if Milet-Mureau had not taken the kind of liberties with the content and style that Hawkesworth had taken with Cook's original journal, there was a dearth of acceptable footnotes. Milet-Mureau was neither a naval man nor a geographer; he was an army officer who had accepted the task of getting the manuscript ready for publication after several others, more qualified than him, had turned it down. He did his best, and the result was a credit to him, but his own style and indeed his own conclusions and preconceptions were everywhere apparent; the political situation in France as he worked on the journal had clearly compelled him to make a number of changes, such as eliminating references to Louis XVI. But one thing remained clear: Milet-Mureau had had access to the original documents which, one felt, must still exist somewhere.

Time went by as from the other side of the world one waited for advice from Paris that the manuscripts had been found. Alas, the only news that came was a formal notification that the search had been fruitless. It was quite possible that, in the turmoil that followed the blackest years of the French Revolution, the journals had been lost, or that they had been discarded as no longer needed once the Milet-Mureau was on sale. Nevertheless, on occasional visits to Paris, I delved further into the possibility that the manuscript had remained with the printers, the Imprimerie de la République, now the Imprimerie Nationale, that it had been returned to some local or regional naval archives, that it had been handed over to La Pérouse's widow or kept by Milet-Mureau and perhaps was still extant among the family papers of some distant descendant. I spent some of the summer months of 1978 idly looking through semi-relevant records or along shelves, watched over with a mixture of suspicion and commiseration by a variety of minor officials. But however protracted a search may be through stores and archives, it cannot bear fruit if the documents sought lie elsewhere. The clue that the journal had been in the Archives nationales all along was revealed by a post-graduate student from the Ecole Nationale des Chartes, Mlle Catherine Gaziello (now Mme Hustache) who reported, with the modesty of the true scholar, that she believed she might have found the La Pérouse manuscripts bound inside other material and simply listed as 'Scientific Documents'. Even a cursory examination of these old volumes left no doubt that they were the pages Milet-Mureau had worked on and it is these which form the text of La Pérouse's journal published for the first time in English translation.

Therefore, first in a list of acknowledgement must be Catherine Hustache, without whose help little could have been accomplished. Her own thesis, concentrating mainly on the origins of the voyage and the preparations made before the ships sailed, was subsequently published as *L'Expédition de Lapérouse 1785–1788: réplique française aux voyages de Cook* (Comité des Travaux Historiques et Scientifiques, Paris, September 1984).

The next person whose assistance must be acknowledged is

Rear-Admiral Maurice de Brossard, who had not only written several books on La Pérouse and the history of French naval exploration in the Pacific, but had a first-hand knowledge of the island – Vanikoro – on which the ships had been wrecked in 1788. His role in assisting with the recovery of valuable items from the reef and in solving the questions that still remained unanswered was of major importance. His help in dealing with the problem of the expedition's last few weeks and its loss on Vanikoro, with matters relating to navigation and with tracing, with an ease and a skill born of long familiarity with the files of the French navy, the background of several of the minor officers, deserves the fullest acknowledgement. His friend, the prominent historian, Michel Mollat du Jourdin, a member of the Institute and the Academy of Marine, was in charge of a series of prestigious publications of original journals being organised by the Imprimerie Nationale, Paris, in which the journals of Louis de Bougainville's 1766–1769 expedition and of Giovanni Verrazano's 1524 voyage had already appeared. He proved a tactful and helpful friend, especially when the proposal was made to publish a substantial annotated and illustrated edition of the La Pérouse journal in time for the two hundredth anniversary of the departure of the *Boussole* and *Astrolabe* in 1785, a task which, because of typographical and design complexities, required the completed transcription, variants, references and introductory material, to be in the hands of the printers in less than four years.

In the course of the preparation of that edition, a number of specialists contributed their knowledge, and their assistance has also been of considerable value to the present work. Others joined them in the meantime, and the help provided by all of them needs to be gratefully acknowledged: Dr Pierre Amalric, President of the Association Lapérouse-Albi-France; Professor Glynn Barratt, University of Ottawa; Dr Sandy Bartle, Museum of New Zealand; Frank Carleton, Père Receveur Commemoration Committee, Kensington, New South Wales, Australia; Jennifer Carter, Curator, Lapérouse Museum, Sydney; Dr John Dawson, Victoria University, Wellington, New Zealand; Professor Kerry Howe, Massey University, New Zealand; Ian McLaren, University of Melbourne; Mr Jacques Thomas, La Pérouse Boomerang Club de France. Over the years, the staff of various institutions have provided help and information, and thanks are due in particular to the Alexander Turnbull Library, Wellington, New Zealand; the Bibliothèque

Nationale, Paris; the Archives Nationales, Paris; and the Service Historique de la Marine, Vincennes, France, for their assistance and for kindly granting permission to reproduce illustrations and maps.

Not least, gratitude is due to the Council and Honorary Secretaries of the Hakluyt Society for making available to English readers this account of what is recognised as the greatest voyage of Pacific exploration organised by the French government in the period preceding the French Revolution.

Finally I acknowledge the kindness of the Service historique de la Marine Vincennes for permission to reproduce the seven illustrations and likewise the Archives nationales for authorising the reproduction of the maps and charts.

Waikanae, 1994 JOHN DUNMORE

EDITORIAL NOTE

The Choice of a Name

Anyone writing on La Pérouse is forced to make a choice between two widely used forms of the name: Lapérouse and La Pérouse.

Official reports, the instructions issued to him, the medal struck for the expedition in 1785, the *Almanach Royal*, letters and reports written by his collaborators, the influential Milet-Mureau edition of the *Voyage* published in 1797, all use the spelling La Pérouse; roughly three-quarters of the books and articles written about the expedition follow this practice. Paris has a Rue La Pérouse; Noumea, in New Caledonia, its Lycée La Pérouse; Australia has its La Pérouse district (but a Lapérouse Museum) in Sydney; New Zealand has a Mt La Pérouse, 3080 m high, close to Mt Cook; there is a Bahia La Pérouse in Easter Island, and Maui in the Hawaiian Islands has its La Pérouse Bay; the strait between the island of Sakhalin and Hokkaido is called La Pérouse Strait. The French navy keeps to this spelling when it names its vessels after the explorer: the cruiser *La Pérouse* was launched in 1877, the hydrographic ship *La Pérouse* was well known in the Pacific and the Indian Ocean in the 1960s.[1]

However, the explorer's home town of Albi has its Lycée Lapérouse, its Place Lapérouse and an imposing monument to the memory of Lapérouse, as well as an Association Lapérouse Albi. The Paris Musée de la Marine uses this spelling.[2] The Société de

[1] The cruiser *La Pérouse* was launched at Brest on 5 November 1877, see *L'Illustration*, LXX, No. 1812 (1877), pp. 309–10. On the naval survey ship *La Pérouse*, see Jacques Fourney, 'Le *La Pérouse* à Mayotte', *La Revue Maritime*, 200 (July 1963), pp. 679–89, and 'Une Mission Hydrogaphique Exceptionnelle: Le *La Pérouse* à Mururoa', *La Revue Maritime*, 245 (July 1967), pp. 869–91. This question has been the subject of articles by Jacques Thomas in the *Nouvelle Revue Maritime* and elsewhere, see below.

[2] Cf *La Généreuse et Tragique Expédition Lapérouse*, by François Bellec, the director of the Musée de la Marine, Paris, published in 1985. However, the problem of the navigator's name is revealed in some of the illustrations, such as a reproduction of the 'Décret de l'Assemblée Nationale' of 24 February 1791 relative to the 'recherche de M. de la Pérouse' (endpapers) and one of the list of the officers of the *Boussole* 'aux ordres de M. de la Pérouse' (p. 10).

Geographie published an important collection of articles in 1888 under the title *Centenaire de la mort de Lapérouse.*[1] The official bi-centennial edition of the journals, published by the Imprimerie Nationale – the lineal descendant of the Imprimerie de la République which published Milet-Mureau's *Voyage de la Pérouse* – adopted the spelling Lapérouse.

The matter is further complicated by the fact that the navigator was the first of his family to bear the name, and that since he had no children it died with him. Once his wife died in 1807, there were no Galaup de La Pérouse left. It was not until 21 February 1815 that a decree from Louis XVIII authorised the families of his two sisters to add 'La Peyrouse' to their own name.[2] A year later, on 18 March 1816, in Vannes, Brittany, the first birth certificate with the new name – now including the nobiliary particle – was issued, recording the birth of 'Alphonse Dalmas de la Peyrouse'. The spelling was erroneous, and the Dalmas family soon requested it to be amended to 'Pérouse'. This was not officially done until 1839, when a notice published in the *Bulletin des Lois* modified the 1815 decree and allowed the navigator's descendants 'to add to their names that of Lapérouse'.[3] Not only was the 'y' removed, but the name was now spelt in one word – and this in spite of the fact that letters had been signed prior to this date by 'Léon Dalmas de la Pérouse'.

The name had been created by the navigator's father when Jean-François de Galaup was about to enter the navy, a particularly class-conscious institution. The family's claim to the status of nobles was not under challenge, but in the eyes of some members of the older landed aristocracy, the Galaups could be regarded as relatively recent upstarts. A more resounding patronymic would be a help in his career and in his relations with other young officers. It was still possible at the time to change it by adding a more imposing surname to one's family name, a practice that sometimes incurred some criticism and even ridicule. The coming Revolution would put an end to it, laws passed in 1794 and 1803 requiring any such changes to go through lengthy legal processes.

The Galaups owned a farm known as La Pérouse (La Peyrouse, according to local spelling) meaning in the Occitan language, 'the

[1] But the title page included a reproduction of the 1785 medal with its reference to the ships under the command of La Pérouse.

[2] *Bulletin des Lois*, 5th series, No. 84, 2 March 1815.

[3] Ibid. No. 675, 29 August 1839.

stoney place'. They transferred it to the young man who was then able to call himself Jean-François de Galaup de la Pérouse, the last three words implying 'owner or lord of the (land and farm of) La Pe[y]rouse.'[1] The documents recording this transfer have not been found, but in 1772, when he was 31, Jean-François became godfather to his sister Jacquette's son, François-Marie-Léon Dalmas, and he is recorded in the baptism certificate as 'de Galaup de la Peyrouse'. The spelling 'Pérouse', however, appears in the great majority of official documents in which he is mentioned, thus avoiding confusion with the great Peyrouse family whose history in south-west France went back to St Louis and the Crusades.

The two-word spelling was used in official correspondence: from the Minister of Marine, from the Naval Commander at Brest, from Fleurieu, his friend and supporter, Director of Ports and Arsenals, from his subordinates, such as Fleuriot de Langle, and significantly by his wife in her appeals for assistance following his disappearance.

Evidence supporting the spelling 'Lapérouse' comes from two main sources. One is the nineteenth-century decrees allowing his sisters' descendants to add the name to their own patronym. In view of the original error of 1815, when the decree referred to 'Lapeyrouse', it is not impossible that the one-word spelling is another administrative error. The fact remains that today, surviving family members call themselves Lapérouse. Admittedly, they could not do otherwise without further tiresome administrative appeals.

Far more important is La Pérouse's own signature. He signed his letter 'Lapérouse' – as in fact did Eléonore, even though she separated the article from the noun in the body of her letters. The point has been made, with some emphasis, that his signature was an indication of his wish to be known as Lapérouse, but there is no record that he ever requested others, including his friends, to use this in preference to La Pérouse. The fact is that he used a highly

[1] From a legal opinion dated 30 September 1987 by Philippe Lemelletier, a legal consultant, genealogist and lecturer in law of Bordeaux, obtained by Jacques Thomas, of Paris, whose research on the background of the names Lapérouse/La Pérouse is hereby acknowledged. Further reference may be made to his article 'Lapérouse ou La Pérouse: légitimité d'une orthographe' in *Nouvelle Revue maritime*, Nos 2129–408 (January-February 1988), pp. 58–62, and in *Bulletin de la Société d'études historiques de la Nouvelle-Calédonie*, 71 (1987), pp. 67–71.

cursive form of writing and he often linked words together, omitting breaks or apostrophes. Thus we find 'delangle', 'Le Comte Dartois', 'Lamerique', 'Leurope'. A signature which linked the article to the following noun was quite common; well-known examples include the fabulist Jean de la Fontaine, the moralist François de la Rochefoucauld, the military leader Marie-Joseph de la Fayette (thus known in France, but normally referred to as Lafayette in the United States).

The evidence supporting the spelling Lapérouse thus seems to be outweighed by contrary evidence. Accordingly, in this work, unless the name used in the original text was Lapérouse, the form La Pérouse has been used.

Abbreviations used

The following simplified titles have been used for sources quoted in the text and footnotes:

Bulletin de la Société de Géographie 1888
Centenaire de la mort de Lapérouse, célébré le 20 avril 1888 en séance solennelle à la Sorbonne, [Bulletin de la] Société de Géographie, Series 7, vol. 9 (Paris, 1888), reprinted Albi, 1985.

Colloque Lapérouse Albi 1985
Colloque Lapérouse Albi, Mars 1985: Bicentenaire du voyage de Lapérouse 1785–1788. Actes du Colloque d'Albi. Association Lapérouse Albi-France, (Albi, 1988).

Cook, *Journals*
The Journals of Captain James Cook on his Voyages of Discovery. Edited by J.C. Beaglehole. 3 vols in 4, (Cambridge 1955–69): vol. I, *The Voyage of the* Endeavour, *1768–1771* (1955), vol. II, *The Voyage of the* Resolution *and* Adventure *1772–1775* (1961), vol. III, *The Voyage of the* Resolution *and* Discovery *1776–1780* (1967), with addenda and corrigenda (1961–69). (Hakluyt Society, Extra Series xxxiv-xxxvi).

Dunmore & Brossard
John Dunmore and Maurice de Brossard, *Le voyage de Lapérouse 1785–1788.* 2 vols (Paris, 1985).

Milet-Mureau, *Voyage*
M.L.A. Milet-Mureau, Voyage de La Pérouse autour du monde publié conformément au décret du 22 avril 1791. 4 vols (Paris, 1797).

Gaziello, *L'Expédition de Lapérouse 1785–1788*
Catherine Gaziello, *L'Expédition de Lapérouse 1785–1788: réplique française aux voyages de Cook.* Mémoires de la section d'histoire des sciences et des techniques, Comité des travaux historiques et scientifiques (Paris, 1984).

Taillemitte, *Bougainville*
Etienne Taillemitte, Bougainville et ses compagnons autour du monde 1766–1769. 2 vols (Paris, 1977).

Dunmore, *Who's Who*
John Dunmore, *Who's Who in Pacific Navigation*, (Honolulu, 1991).

Abbreviations are used as follows:

AN	Archives Nationales, Paris
AN.M.	Archives Nationales, Section Marine, Paris
BN	Bibliothèque Nationale, Paris
NAF	Nouvelles Acquisitions Françaises (at BN)
PRO	Public Record Office
SHM	Service Historique de la Marine, Vincennes

Measurements

Under the Old Regime, measurements had not been standardised and could vary from one country to another and from one district to the next. It is possible to translate some French terms into English: a *brasse*, for instance, is normally translated as a fathom, a *lieue* as a league, and an *encablure* as a cablelength, but these are forms of usage and are not truly equivalent. Measures in use prior to the introduction of the metric system included:

Lieue de Paris : 2000 *toises* (1674–1737)
Lieue (for road travel) : 2000 *toises;* (for transport of grain) : 2400 *toises* (from 1737); for postal services: 2200 *toises* (from 1737)
Lieue marine : 1/20 of a degree (5.55km.)
Toise : 6 *pieds* or feet (1.949m.)
Pied de roi : 12 *pouces* or inches (0.325m.)

Pouce : 12 *lignes* (2.7cm.)
Ligne : 12 *points* (2.26mm)
Point : equivalent to 0.188mm.
Brasse : 5 *pieds* (1.624m.). English fathom: 6 feet (1.82m.)
Encablure : Cablelength, one-tenth of a mile (185.2m.). English cablelength: 120 fathoms or 720 feet (219.45m.)

Personal Names and Place Names

Names of individuals and places appear in their accepted French or English spelling in introductory material, in appendices and in footnotes. In the translation of the journal and letters, they have been left as spelt, even though La Pérouse and others spell them variously in their MSS. Place names, however, have been standardised in their most common form where variants occur, to avoid unnecessary confusion. The English form has been used for well-known places or translated into English when the name is a descriptive one. Thus Cape Beau-Temps becomes Cape Fairweather. In other cases, La Pérouse's spelling has been retained, usually in italics with, if necessary, the English equivalent between square brackets.

INTRODUCTION

THE BACKGROUND

The expedition of the *Boussole* and *Astrolabe* must be set in the context of the Age of Enlightenment, but also against a background of Anglo-French rivalry expressed in a series of wars waged in many parts of the world. As the influence of Spain waned and Dutch interests remained centered on the islands of South-East Asia, the exploration of the Pacific, outwardly motivated by a thirst for knowledge, was affected by an undercurrent of political and strategic manoeuvrings. Perhaps nothing illustrates this more clearly than the expedition of Louis de Bougainville in 1767–69, which had its genesis in France's loss of its Canadian possessions and in Bougainville's attempt to set up a French colony on the Falkland Islands, which could be viewed – and indeed was viewed by London – as a move to establish a French base at or near the south-eastern entrance to the Pacific Ocean; Spain felt concerned that this challenged its own claims to the South American continent and its off-lying islands; Britain, even more worried that the French might gain control of an important sea route, intervened; France stepped back – and Bougainville won, as a sort of consolation prize, the right to sail on a major voyage of Pacific exploration of considerable geographical and hydrographical value.[1]

The moves and counter-moves of politicians and diplomats should not, however, obscure the strength and influence of the scientific world in the eighteenth century. In England, the Royal Society had been active since 1660, but the spirit of scientific enquiry had spread through Europe. It reached into such distant courts as those of Catherine the Great of Russian, Frederick the Great in Prussia and Louis XV the Well-Beloved in France; minor

[1] See Taillemitte, *Bougainville*, I, pp. 11–18.

rulers such as the Landgrave of Hesse-Cassel and the Stadtholder of the Netherlands had their own minor museums of science, and members of the nobility and wealthy bankers and merchants had their own collections, and in many cases their laboratories where they carried out – or had carried out on their behalf – experiments in chemistry and physics, their botanical gardens, their libraries. They were not only rich enough, but enthusiastic enough to subsidise scientific expeditions, the work of instrument makers and the publication of scientific papers.

Knowledge was spread to a wider audience, among the middle classes and into the provinces, by the great encyclopedias: Chambers' *Cyclopaedia* of 1728 in England, the *Enclyclopaedia Britannica* of 1768 in Scotland, and the influential *Encyclopédie* which appeared in France between 1751 and 1772. The French *Encyclopédistes* were typical of an age that had become passionately interested in knowledge and social philosophy; they included the most eminent minds of France: Diderot, d'Alembert, Voltaire, Montesquieu, Rousseau, Marmontel, Quesnay and Turgot. Their interests ranged into politics and trade: Quesnay, although a medical man, became the leader of the *Physiocrates* or *Economistes* who were seeking a formula that might solve France's problems and form the basis of a general economic theory. From there, their discussions extended into political theory and, dangerously for their times, into the rationale for a constitutional monarchy. They theorised about the social evolution of mankind, wondered whether the complexities of modern civilisation had not corrupted the innate goodness of human beings, and whether proof of this could not be found in unknown region where uncorrupted *bons sauvages* might yet have survived.

Parts of the world which Europeans had not yet explored held a great fascination for scientists of all kinds and for the educated public as well. Buffon's monumental *Histoire naturelle*, which began to appear in 1748 and was destined to reach 44 volumes, described in vivid detail what was known of the animal kingdom, but he began his work with a volume on the 'theory of the earth'. The question remained: what new species of animals and plants were there still in distant corners of the globe, waiting to be discovered.[1]

[1] Georges-Louis Leclerc de Buffon (1707–88). The final volumes were published after his death, the last one appearing in 1804. His views on the history of the earth were condemned by the Sorbonne in 1751 as modernist and counter to biblical revelation.

In an age of encyclopaedic collections, voyages of discoveries to the Pacific were not overlooked. The most influential work of the period was Charles de Brosses's two-volume *Histoire des navigations aux terres australes*, published in 1756 and reprinted in an English translation, without acknowledgment, by John Callander, in 1766–8 under the title *Terra Australia Cognita.*[1] This was followed in 1770–1 by Alexander Dalrymple's *An Historical Collection of the Several Voyages & Discoveries in the South Pacific Ocean*. The groundwork was now done, the problems stated and the potential for further discoveries and eventual colonisation laid out.

A major point of argument had been the possibility that, in southern oceans, might be found a vast southern continent. As enthusiasts speculated on its existence, they dreamed of the great wealth it might contain, and especially of untapped resources of gold and silver. More realistically, government ministers, aware that gold mines eventually become exhausted, saw its value in geostrategic terms: whoever controlled the southern continent would in turn control the seas. Navigators venturing into unknown seas found no solid evidence that it existed, and as the Pacific Ocean became better known so the hazy boundaries of the continent vanished into the distance. Alexander Dalrymple remained a firm believer, but James Cook swept vast tracts of ocean on his first voyage without coming upon any sign of its existence. The Frenchman Jean-François de Surville, sailing east from New Zealand to South America in 1770, cut another swathe across empty seas. When Cook returned, in 1773, he completed the work by sailing deep into the Antarctic.[2]

France, by then, was exploring the South Indian Ocean. Hopes had been raised in 1772 when Yves-Joseph de Kerguelen reported that he had had 'the good fortune to discover the southern continent.'[3] What he had done was to come upon the island which now bears his name, and which he should have reported as rocky,

[1] Callander's aim was not merely the advocacy of further Pacific exploration, but the extension of the British empire to regions where France planned to establish her own claims. See J. Dunmore, 'Rivalités franco-anglaises dans le Pacifique', *Le Colloque d'Akaroa*, Wellington, 1991, pp. 88–93.

[2] 'I had now made the circuit of the Southern Ocean in a high Latitude and traversed it in such a manner as to leave not the least room for the Possibility of there being a continent, unless near the Pole and out of the reach of Navigation.' Cook, *Journals*, II, p. 643.

[3] Quoted in A. Dupouy, *Le Breton Yves de Kerguelen*, Paris, 1929, p. 131.

dangerous and snow-covered. The enthusiasm which his glowing reports understandably aroused in government circles led to a second expedition being sent under his command which ended in bitter disappointment and disgrace. One positive result from this sad affair was that France would ensure, when another voyage of exploration was planned, that the man placed at its head would be experienced and reliable, and that the campaign would be carefully laid out in advance.

Nothing could be done until the great powers were at peace. Between 1778 and 1783, France was involved in the American War of Independence. French prestige, which had greatly suffered after the losses sustained in the Seven Years War, was restored by successful participation in the anti-colonial struggle. The French Navy, especially, which had gained from major reforms carried out from 1775–6, had proved itself in a number of engagements against the Royal Navy. Political and strategic considerations, new openings for trade, the need to maintain France's improved standing on the world scene, all these factors contributed to the move towards a major voyage of exploration. James Cook had been the dominant figure since 1770, but he had been killed on Hawaii in 1779. It was not entirely a matter of honour that a Frenchman should take up his mantle and complete his work, but it fitted neatly into the pattern of Anglo-French rivalry at a moment in history when England was suffering from the after-effects of an unfortunate conflict in which France had found itself on the winning side. It would be, as Catherine Gaziello expressed it in her study of the genesis and planning of La Pérouse's voyage, 'a French counter-stroke to the voyages of Cook.'[1]

The mood in France was favourable to some action being taken. Louis XVI, who had come to he throne in 1774, was interested in geography and a keen student of the literature of exploration. So were the philosophers, merchants, *littérateurs*, and ordinary Parisians who knew, or thought they knew, a great deal about the world's

[1] Gaziello, *L'Expédition de Lapérouse 1785–1788: réplique française aux voyages de Cook*, Paris, 1984, a major study of the voyage, based on a most exhaustive examination of the sources. The word *réplique* has subtleties that are not easy to render into English: 'answer' sounds too weak, 'counter-stroke' has a semi-belligerent undertone which is probably not wholly appropriate; 'riposte' or 'response' is no better for a set of actions which were intended to restore the balance and ensure that a Frenchman would also stand tall in the Pacific exploration's Hall of Fame.

largest ocean. Many were familiar with Bougainville's and Cook's voyages, accounts of which had been best-sellers. Merchants in particular were interested in the possibility of trade and above all in the fur trade. John Ledyard, the ambitious American who had sailed with Cook and a man of great if not always practical enthusiasm, even persuaded a group of Lorient traders to plan the fitting out of a ship for this purpose in February 1785.[1] The scheme fell through, but it illustrated one facet of French interest: the commercial one.

Although there can be little doubt that a French voyage of exploration had been in the mind of French officials for some time, and that some kind of plans were being discussed in high places during 1784, and probably as early as the second half of 1783 when the war was in its final stages, no document has been found in French archives with an earlier date than 2 February 1785. It is a receipt for 600 *livres*, relating to a payment made to William Bolts from the Ministry of Marine's secret funds – and Bolts was particularly knowledgeable about the Northwest Coast and the rich fur trade.

William Bolts born in the Netherlands in 1735, had moved to England in 1749 and worked variously for an English merchant, the East India Company, Austria and on his own account.[2] He had made contacts with the French in Mauritius in 1780 and appears to have been invited to travel from London to Paris towards the end of 1784, where he met the Directeur des Ports et Arsenaux de la Marine, Claret de Fleurieu, who was working closely with the Minister of Marine, the Maréchal de Castries. The plan suggested by Bolts, inspired by James Cook's third voyage, was to send ships to the Northwest Coast, purchase otter skins, take these to China and barter them for Asian goods which would be finally sold in Europe, thus making a profit at each stage of the journey. This scheme would form part of the first proposal for a combined voyage of exploration and trade which was submitted for the king's approval. Bolts overlooked the complications that would arise out of an official naval expedition trading on the coast or even, as the first French draft envisaged, sailing in concert with a merchant

[1] See J. Sparks, *Memoirs of the Life and Travels of John Ledyard*, Boston, 1847, pp. 195–201.

[2] See on this fairly elusive character, N. L. Hallward, *William Bolts, a Dutch Adventurer under John Company*, Cambridge, 1920.

vessel; but Fleurieu was fully aware of his government's policy of watching any moves England was making to establish trading footholds in distant lands and, if possible, anticipating them.[1]

It is highly likely that La Pérouse was involved at an early stage in the planning. During the summer of 1784, he had been held back in Lorient by the possibility that the Battle of the Saints, back in April 1782, when Admiral Rodney defeated the French fleet, might be the subject of a court-martial; but he then went to Paris and worked closely, if unofficially, with Fleurieu. Assisting them were the Marquis de Chabert-Cogolin,[2] a naval man and a member of the Académie des Sciences who specialised in the problem of longitudes, and Jean-Nicolas Buache de la Neuville, a leading hydrographer and geographer.[3] By January 1785, the project was sufficiently crystallised for Fleurieu to obtain estimates from the naval treasury for an expedition consisting of two ships. La Pérouse, however, was not sure that he would be appointed to head it, and on 8 February he wrote to his wife that he was 'still in the same state of uncertainty.... nothing has been decided.'[4] He no doubt expressed the same unease to Fleurieu who, the next day, told him that he was shortly to be given a major appointment. In view of the commercial orientation of the draft proposal, La Pérouse may have felt that such a command might not be entirely appropriate for a senior officer of the king's navy. Tempering his possible dissatisfaction was the fact that 1784 had been a year during which many naval units had been decommissioned and a considerable number of unemployed officers with good war records had been looking for whatever appointment might come their way.

He need not have worried. Louis XVI turned down the suggestion of combining trade with exploration. It would not only have been infra dig for the king's ships to take part in a commercial

[1] Gaziello, in *L'Expédition de Lapérouse 1785–1788* , pp. 50–1, shows how Bolts's plan fitted in with French policies and quotes a note by Fleurieu which makes it clear that La Pérouse himself 'considered it important to forestall the English on the Northwest Coast of America.' (AN. M. 3JJ 386, f.30.)

[2] Joseph de Chabert-Cogolin (1724–1805) had worked on charts of Newfoundland and the Canadian coast and supervised work on the navigational guide *Le Neptune de la Méditerranée.*

[3] Born in 1741, he was the nephew of the famous geographer Philippe Buache and became curator-hydrographer at the Dépôt des Cartes of the hydrographic service. He died in 1825.

[4] AN. M. C7 165, f. 37.

enterprise, it could also create awkward incidents. In this his instinct was right, for within a very few years rivalry on the Northwest Coast would give rise to the Nootka Incident which led the major powers to the brink of war; other problems of a like nature could easily arise in other parts of the world if royal units found themselves forced to defend the interests of an accompanying merchantman.

What would have been a relatively narrow undertaking was accordingly rapidly broadened into a major voyage of exploration. Commercial possibilities were still to be investigated, for instance around Japan and in eastern seas, but hydrography and scientific work became dominant. And underlying it all were political considerations added by government officials.

The king's role in deciding the form which the voyage was to take is hard to assess. For some, the expedition was Louis XVI's own, carefully planned by him, with La Pérouse commanding it, as it were, as a proxy.[1] In fact, it was planned by a number of people, with additional elements being contributed between March and May by naval specialists, including La Pérouse, by individual scientists and learned societies. The programme grew as planning proceeded. It had been hatched in secrecy, but by late March 1785 it became common knowledge and it aroused considerable enthusiasm among geographers and specialists of all kind. The *philosophes* found in an undertaking that was to carry on the work of James Cook a vehicle for research into a wide range of subjects, from chemistry to ethnology.

Undeniably, Louis XVI's intervention occurred at a very early stage. There is no evidence that he initiated the project, but he may have been informally approached in 1784 by Castries, the Minister of Marine, and encouraged him to proceed with preliminary planning. He responded to Fleurieu's draft proposal with enthusiasm. He had a genuine interest in geography and had been trained by the older Buache, Philippe, appointed to the offical post of Hydrographer in 1730. In 1769, at the age of 15, the future king had drawn a map, in colour, of the environs of Versailles, now held in the Bibliothèque Nationale, Paris.[2] It includes blank spaces such as

[1] For a view which stresses the role Louis XVI may have played, see Paul and Pierrette de Coursac, *Le Voyage de Louis XVI autour du monde: l'expédition Lapérouse*, Paris, 1985.

[2] BN, Cartes et Plans, ref. C.4349.

are found on explorers' charts, labelled 'Places which have not been surveyed'. Familiar with the accounts of navigators' voyages, he was also well advised on international problems. All this is reflected in the marginal comments he made on Fleurieu's *Projet*. He tersely rejects some suggestions as useless; in other cases he advises caution; he shows awareness of the danger of sailing at certain times of the year in stormy seas and of allowing the ships to sail separately; he does not rule out the benefits which new knowledge might bring to traders and whalers.

Once the king had formally approved the project, planning could go ahead. Louis XVI had commented on the overall programme, interested himself in the safety of his officers and men, and probably took a major role in drafting the instructions outlining to La Pérouse how he should behave towards native peoples. The next stages were the detailed planning of the itinerary and, finally, outlining the scientific work the expedition should undertake. This was done under Fleurieu's general supervision by officials in the Ministry of Marine, the Dépôt des Cartes et Plans and his own Direction des Ports et Arsenaux. Fleurieu reported to Castries, and through him, or possibly on some occasions directly, kept the king advised of progress.

The plan of navigation was to a large extent based on what James Cook had left unfinished. An inventory had been drawn up of what remained to be done. This had to be fitted in with the changing seasons, sea currents and the prevailing winds, ports of call – a broad rule was to avoid spending more than four months at sea without touching land – which were suitable politically and for the resources they could offer, and the commercial and scientific aims of the campaign. Essential features of any itinerary were the North-west Coast and the North-East Pacific.

The broad lines were probably agreed in April. In their final version, dated 25 July 1785, they outlined a complex voyage across the southern and northern Pacific. From Brest La Pérouse was to sail to Funchal and across to South America, continuing south in the hope of finding the Ile Grande, supposedly discovered by a Frenchman named Roche in the South Atlantic, thence to South Georgia Island and on to Sandwich Land, Staten Land and Cape Horn. Alternatively, he could touch at the Falkland Islands for refreshments and go through Le Maire's Strait to Christmas Sound and Tierra del Fuego.

There were various questions to settle in the South-West Pacific once La Pérouse had entered the ocean, such as the existence of Drake's Land and a supposed discovery made in 1714 by a Spanish captain, which was now believed to be unsubstantiated. A call at Easter Island would enable the French to rest their crews and prepare them for the crossing to Tahiti. La Pérouse would sail among the Society Islands, leaving seeds and shrubs which might be of value to Europeans navigating in these distant seas, and follow Bougainville's tracks through the Samoan and Tongan archipelagoes. He would then veer slightly north of west to survey the western coast of New Caledonia. The next stage would take him to Vanuatu and the Solomons, to the Louisiades, to Cook's Endeavour Strait, north of Cape York Peninsula, into the Gulf of Carpentaria, to begin an anti-clockwise navigation of the Australian continent, ending at Van Diemen's Land and finally across the Tasman Sea to New Zealand for refreshments and repairs. This, it was calculated, would take twenty months – he was to leave Queen Charlotte Sound, New Zealand, in March 1787.

This part of his instructions La Pérouse almost completely ignored. He had been clearly told that 'His Majesty did not intend that he should be compelled to adhere in all respects to this plan'.[1] He was left in no doubt that the itinerary had been drawn up as a broad guide: what mattered was to complete Cook's great work. There was little left to be done among the Society Islands, not much in Tonga and very little indeed around New Zealand. To spend the first year of a major and costly expedition revisiting places Cook had already surveyed and written about seems a strange priority. If one goes back to the earliest plan and the Bolt-inspired *projet*, one wonders why the French officials did not invite La Pérouse to sail to the Northwest Coast and across to China as soon as he had rounded Cape Horn – which is precisely what he did do. It is possible that the official instructions were calculated, in part, to throw the English off the scent, and that he was told privately that an early survey of the Northwest Coast and a report on the fur trade were the real priorities. William Pitt and Lord Howe, back in London, had no doubt learned some time in April, through their network of spies, that the French were planning a

[1] Concluding note to the main instructions: 'Sa Majesté n'a point entendu qu'il dût s'assujétir invariablement à ce Plan'. See 'Instructions', below.

major voyage, and at a time when British traders were setting out for the Northwest Coast they would have been more concerned about the French muscling in on the fur trade than about a voyage of exploration which, in its way, was a tribute to James Cook. The French, in fact, had representatives in London looking for instruments and information for the La Pérouse voyage: official sympathy and understanding would be helpful, and indeed it was forthcoming, for La Pérouse had proved a gallant and humane enemy during the recent war and the official aims of his voyage in no way threatened Britain's interest. The great sweep around the southern Pacific was therefore not a matter for concern and, for instance in the case of New Caledonia, it could be seen as sensibly complementing some of Cook's work. If there was a strategic or a political subplot – and any statesman or diplomat worth his salt would expect there to be one – it was not too sinister. Lord Dorset, the British ambassador in Paris, wrote to the Foreign Secretary on 5 May what he thought the French might be up to:

> I have the honour to inform your Lorship that Mons. de la Pérouse will shortly sail from Brest, and it is reported, with some degree of authority, that he has orders to visit New Zealand, with a view to examine into the quality of the timber of that country, which it is supposed, by the account given of it in Captain Cook's voyage, may be an object worthy of attention.
>
> This plan is recommended by Mons. de Suffrein, who says that ships may with little difficulty go from Mauritius to that country. It is believed that the French have a design of establishing some kind of settlement there; if it shall be found practicable, as it will be necessary to tap the trees at least six months before they fell them, in order to lighten the wood, which has no other defect, as is said, than that of being too heavy to use in its natural state.[1]

Dorset, however, had no great reputation as a political analyst and the Foreign Secretary relied more on other sources of information; but keeping London guessing would have been part of Versailles strategy.

Be that as it may, La Pérouse decided to invert the programme and begin with the second part. The instructions proposed that,

[1] In O. Browning (ed.), *Despatches from Paris 1784–1790*, Royal Historical Society, Camden Series III, vol. xvi, London, 1909, pp. 52–3. La Pérouse's instructions in fact required him to report on the possibility of a British settlement having already been established or being planned in New Zealand.

from New Zealand, he would proceed to Hawaii and Spanish California, then towards the Northwest Coast to seek a passage, if there was one, that might lead from the Pacific to Hudson Bay. If he found no sign of this famed North-West Passage, he was to continue north to within sight of the St Elias Mountains, and along the Aleutian chain to Kamchatka. He could then explore the Kuriles, the east coast of Japan, the Ryukyus and Formosa before putting in at Canton, Macao or Manila as circumstances dictated. This section of the voyage, it was optimistically predicted, would be completed in nine months – by the end of 1787.

The third section would take the expedition north again, to Korea, the Sea of Japan, along the west coast of Hokkaido and back to Kamchatka for a period of rest and refitting before sailing south to the Mariana Islands, to Mindanao, the Moluccas and through the Indonesian group to the Indian Ocean and the Ile de Fance. The homeward journey would take the ships into the Atlantic where there was an opportunity to avoid boredom by checking the positions of a number of islands – Gough, Diego Alvarez, Tristan da Cunha, Saxemberg, Dos Picos – which would add zest to the final stage of the expedition since it was doubtful that they all actually existed and only a throrough search and luck could settle the issue. It was expected that the ships would be back in Brest in the late summer of 1789, four years after their departure.

This massive undertaking could no longer be seen as a voyage aimed at discovering new openings for French merchants and fishermen and forestalling British moves in the post-war period. It was a voyage of exploration, cast in the traditional mould, a grandiose version of all that had gone before. When La Pérouse returned, the Pacific Ocean and some of the southern seas would have shed their last shreds of mystery. All that was needed to round off the great expedition was a comprehensive programme of scientific research.

Once the plan of navigation had been decided, approaches could be made to the many scientific bodies that were eager to benefit from the voyage. This was done towards the end of April. The Maréchal de Castries wrote formally to Condorcet, the permanent secretary of the Académie des Sciences, and La Pérouse called on him shortly after. No time was lost: on 25 and 27 May, drafts prepared by its various sections were read to members of the Académie, and the final *mémoires* were sent to Castries on 8 June. The Société Royale de Médecine was consulted at much the same time, and its report was ready by 31 May. La Pérouse went to see Buffon at the beginning of May, obtaining his advice on natural history and through him on work to be carried out by the expedition's gardener.

The scientists were not given a detailed itinerary. Fleurieu and La Pérouse agreed between them that a broad indication of the latitudes to be visited would suffice. As a result, the responses are remarkably broad and all-embracing: better information might have produced more specific requests for investigations and reports in localities of particular interest. However, it must be remembered that the expedition was being planned at a time when scientists were rarely specialists working in mutually exclusive areas of knowledge; theirs was the age of encyclopaedic curiosity, and the response to Castries might have been no different had he appended copies of the itinerary to his letter.

The list of those who collaborated in the preparation of these scientific summaries and questionnaires reads like a *Who's Who* of the eighteenth-century French world of science. The Marquis de Condorcet was a renowned mathematician elected to the Académie des Sciences in 1769 at the age of 26; he became its secretary in 1777 and was elected to the Académie Française in 1782; a biographer, he had already written a life of the economist and politician Turgot, and was at work on a biography of Voltaire; active during the French Revolution, he published a theory on the intellectual progress of mankind, *Esquisse d'un tableau historique des progrès de l'esprit humain*, but lost his life in the upheaval of the Terror. Antoine-Laurent Lavoisier is considered the founder of modern chemistry; an active member of the Académie des Sciences, he helped Condorcet to contact his colleagues and was probably the author of the chemistry section of the main *mémoire* on scientific problems. Jean-Charles de Borda and Jean-Sylvain Bailly wrote the section dealing with mathematics and astronomy – Borda was a noted naval astronomer and Bailly, a member of the Académie Française and of the Académie des Sciences, as well as of the Académie des Beaux-Arts, was also an astronomer. Louis Daubenton and Haüy prepared the section on physics – the former was a reputed naturalist, but Haüy eclipsed him as the author of a major work on crystallography. Leclerc de Buffon's renown as the author of the great, and at the time still incomplete *Histoire complète et scientifique de la nature* extended far beyond France's frontiers. In his shadow, but an important guide in the field of ornithology, stood H.J. Brisson, author of an influential *Ornithologia* in seven volumes; and André Thouin, Buffon's assistant and a professor at the Royal Botanical Garden, who wrote at length on botanical issues and the preservation of plants. All were men of wide interests, and these included the economic and political situation in France: not merely Condorcet, but Lavoisier and Bailly lost their lives during the Revolution.

While the scientific memoirs were being drawn up and argued over, Fleurieu and La Pérouse were discussing the choice of those scientists who were to be invited to join the expedition and the instruments they would need. Up-to-date charts were also essential. Two men acted as their advisers: Borda and Buache.

Borda had seagoing experience; he had been associated with the navy since 1767 and had sailed in the *Flore* in 1771 to test Berthoud's new chronometers. He recommended Monge and Dagelet for the La Pérouse expedition and possibly others. Fleurieu and the Minister, Castries, both consulted him on other points, and especially on the scientific instruments that would be required – his own reflecting circle was included among the items taken on the voyage. His precise role is not minuted among the documents relating to the expdition; its importance, however, is apparent from a letter addrssed by the Minister to Fleurieu as early as 29 March: 'I should like you to call on Friday; I should also like the Chevalier de Borda to attend with these gentlemen; after which we shall remain alone with Mr de Borda.'[1]

Jean-Nicolas Buache de Neuville belonged to a dynasty of geographers and cartographers, the Delisles and the Buaches. The Royal Geographer and a member of the Académie des Sciences, he had worked at the Dépôt des Cartes et Plans since 1773. Undoubtedly, Fleurieu consulted him informally while the campaign was being planned; once this was done, it fell to him to draw the charts. This involved a great deal of work under considerable pressure. He prepared three large maps of the Pacific Ocan, divided into northern, central and southern sectors, made five copies and appended tables of latitudes and longitudes. He drew 27 detailed maps and charts to accompany Fleurieu's instructions, making two copies of each so that both La Pérouse and Langle would have one. His aim was to present a cartographic summary of all that was known about

[1] AN. M. 2JJ 103. A biography was written by J. Mascart, *La Vie et les travaux du chevalier Jean-Charles de Borda (1733–1799)*, and published in Lyons in 1919.

the regions the expedition would visit, and like the various *mémoires* drawn up for La Pérouse by scientists and philosophers his work displays an encyclopaedic knowledge and an eagerness to have a vast array of questions answered. The task was completed on 13 June; it had taken six weeks of unremitting toil. Assisting him was his young cousin, Charles-François Beautemps-Beaupré, who would one day become the official geographer and cartographer on D'Entrecasteaux's great expedition.

One of the five copies of Buache's great map of the Pacific Ocean was reserved for Louis XVI. The king had played a significant part in the planning of the expedition: he would follow its progress on his map as reports came in from the various ports of call, and the eventual fate of La Pérouse's two ships would concern him until the very eve of his execution when, as he had done on many occasions before, he enquired: 'Is there any news of La Pérouse?'

THE NORTH-WEST PASSAGE

For centuries, symmetry was the chimera of geographers. In the sixth century B.C., the Greek Anaximander had not only split the world into four hemispheres, but drawn each one surrounded by water. This concept of symmetry combined with a circumfluent ocean was adopted by the Romans and copied by medieval cosmographers. It not only had the advantage of balance, but by then it could easily be defended by referring to the authority of the Ancients.

In the same frame of mind, closet geographers sought to prove the existence of a southern continent by using the equilibrium theory, arguing that the land masses of the northern hemisphere needed to be balanced by similar masses in the south, lest the globe topple over; and a corresponding argument was brought out to justify the belief that a strait must cut through northern America because the Strait of Magellan existed in the south.

Some held the view that a North-East Passage would be found in northern Asia, and some indeed looked for it, although this was a more difficult and dangerous undertaking. Northern America, however, looked at from across the Atlantic, offered the promise of deep inlets and unexplored bays: the greatest of these was Hudson Bay, a real inland sea, almost empty and scarcely explored, where rivers came to their final rest from some even more mysterious and promising hinterland.

The northern Pacific was less explored, but what few reports there had been, coming from Spanish sources, mentioned deep inlets curving inland towards vast lakes which might well be those of Upper Canada, known by then to stretch inland from the great St Lawrence River. This alternative was far more tempting than the Hudson Bay region into which some claim Sebastian Cabot had sailed in 1509, almost a century before Henry Hudson himself was sent by the Muscovy Company to seek a passage to Cathay through northern waters, because the obstacle which had destroyed the hopes of these men and of all their successors, namely impassable ice, would not be found, at least in such frightening masses, further south.

The Spaniards, owing to their early domination of the Pacific, were the first to build up theories about a northern passage leading from the Pacific to the Atlantic. Not only were small expeditions making their way cautiously up the coast from Mexico, but the discovery of the Japan Current, the *Vuelta de Poniente*, which flowed from west to east in the northern Pacific, turned their attention to a possible route back to Spain across the northern Atlantic for their galleons from Manila. Such a route would cut months from the voyage home.

In the 1560s, maps originating from Italy began to show a mysterious *Streto de Anian* around 63–66° of northern latitude, penetrating deep into the American continent and temptingly inching its way towards the areas which were to become Great Slave Lake and Hudson Bay. When Francis Drake appeared on the Pacific coast, began to raid Spanish possessions, and then mysteriously vanished, the Spanish speculated that he might well have entered the Pacific through this Strait of Anian.[1]

At the same time as Drake's voyage Sir Humphrey Gilbert's *Discourse for the Discoverie of a New Passage to Cataia*, published in

[1] The mysterious Anian may be a corruption of 'Aniu', a name given by Marco Polo to a land believed to lie to the east of China, see Ronald Latham (ed.) *The Travels of Marco Polo*, New York, 1982, p. 217. It may be worth pointing out that the aboriginal people of Japan are called the Ainus – in which case the story of the Strait of Anian transposed them to another continent.

London in 1576, expounded the benefits and practicality of what he had been seeking for ten years: an expedition to open up an alternative route to the East. He eventually sailed himself to Newfoundland where bases could be set up for further exploration, and at much the same period, Martin Frobisher's expeditions were being organised. These British attempts to find a North-West Passage would continue for many years, causing constant disquiet at the Spanish Court and giving rise in turn to Spanish voyages along the northern coast.[1]

In 1596, Apostolos Valerianos, a Greek from Cephalonia, better known as Juan de Fuca, met two Englishmen in Venice, Michael Lok and John Dowlass, and told them of a voyage he had made in 1592 to search for the Strait of Anian; he had found an inlet in 47–48° N. and had sailed through it to the Atlantic, this requiring twenty days. He was now endeavouring to find sponsors for a return voyage, which he estimated could take thirty days.[2] More serious evidence of the existence of deep inlets which might conceivably lead inland and, through rivers and lakes, into the Atlantic, was obtained from reports by Sebastián Vizcaíno who sailed north from Acapulco in 1602. A few years later, strange claims came from one Lorenzo Ferrer Maldonado that he had actually sailed west through the Strait of Anian in 1588 and met German traders on the way who spoke to him in Latin.[3]

Although the Spaniards were anxious to secure this strait in order to maintain their predominance in the Pacific Ocean, and were, to some extent, tempted by fanciful reports of wealthy lands through which the strait was supposed to pass, occasional attempts to discover it ended in failure. A new element came into play in 1624, when Abraham Goos published a map in Amsterdam, which

[1] See Henry R. Wagner, *The Cartography of the Northwest Coast of America to the Year 1800*, Berkeley, 1937, and the same author's *Spanish Voyages to the Northwest Coast of America in the Sixteenth Century*, San Francisco, 1929. Glyndwr Williams has dealt with British voyages in *The British Search for the Northwest Passage in the Eighteenth Century*, London, 1962 and in 'Myth and Reality: James Cook and the Theoretical Geography of Northwest America' in Robin Fisher and Hugh Johnston (eds), *James Cook and his Times*, Seattle, 1979, which he has updated in the same editors' *From Maps to Metaphors: The Pacific World of George Vancouver*, Vancouver, 1993. The literature on this topic is rapidly expanding.

[2] Pedro Novo y Colson, *Sobre los viajes apócrifos de Juan de Fuca y Lorenzo Ferrer Maldonado*, Madrid, 1881.

[3] W.M. Mathes, *Sebastian Vizcaíno y la Expansión Española en el Oceáno Pacífico 1580–1630*, Mexico, 1973, pp. 81–2.

showed California as a great island. A great offshore island implies a range of inlets, passages and straits: a new location for the Strait of Anian became available.

The Goos map was followed by another, a year later, the work of the Englishman Henry Briggs, and soon a tradition became established which dominated seventeenth-century cartography.[1] It took explorations by land, at the end of the century, to destroy the myth and return California to its peninsular state. Once it ceased to be regarded as an island, California could no longer conceal a mysterious strait. But the belief lingered on that somewhere, now obviously much further north, there was an opening which, however tortuous it might be, led from the Pacific to the Atlantic.

The belief was revived in England, where successive failures by explorers of northern Canada to find any real trace of a North-West Passage had bred discouragement among investors. The tenacious Strait of Anian reappeared and, since English merchant adventurers had not sailed along the Northwest Coast, nothing had yet been disproved in British eyes.

In 1708, the *Monthly Miscellany, or Memoirs for the Curious* published a letter by Bartolomé de Fonte, 'then Admiral of New Spain and Peru and now Prince of Chili', in which he stated that, to forestall a possible discovery by the English of the North-West Passage, he had been sent with four ships, sailing north from Callao in April 1640. Somewhere north of Cape Blanco, he had discovered an entrance he named Río de los Reyes, which led him into a great lake, and thence by smaller lakes and rivers he had been able to sail north-east, meeting on the way a ship commanded by a captain from Boston. At this point, the two captains stopped, exchanged courtesies and turned back. Fonte had not actually sailed right through the strait, but by deduction he could easily have done and visited his fellow-captain in New England.

The article aroused little interest. It contained interesting details about the shores along which he claimed to have sailed and the abundance of fish he found in the lakes and rivers, but it did not provide the solid information any English merchant adventurer would have needed, and in particular the location of the strait's Atlantic opening.

It eventually proved of value to a tireless promoter of the North-

[1] Wagner, *Cartography*, pp. 114, 128–9.

West Passage theory, Arthur Dobbs, an Ulster landowner who was instrumental in promoting the expedition of Christopher Middleton in 1741–2. For this he needed every shred of semi-evidence he could lay his hands on, and although he favoured Juca de Fuca's story, since the latitude was closer to that of Hudson Bay which was the route he proposed, he later added Fonte's for good measure. The Middleton expedition was an unmitigated failure – like others before him, he was defeated by ice and scurvy. Another expedition organised in 1746 by Dodds also ended in total failure.

Dodds publicised Fonte's voyage through the publication of his *Account of the Countries Adjoining to Hudson's Bay* (London, 1744). It struck a chord in English hearts, encouraged the British Parliament to offer a reward of £20,000 to whoever discovered the strait, gave rise to a disastrous voyage led by William Moor and Francis Smith, and led one Theodore Swaine Drage to publish a map in 1748 on which the strait was clearly shown.[1]

French geographers of good repute were taken in. Joseph-Nicholas Delisle and Philippe Buache – the latter, the Royal Geographer – addressed the *Académie Royale des Sciences* in 1750 presenting the Fonte voyage as fact, and followed this up with a map that gained wide acceptance. Buache's map of 1752 was not without value in summarising contemporary knowledge of the north Pacific region, but his outline of northern America is full of speculative blanks and dotted outlines, with a great western sea opening out towards the Great Lakes and a wide Strait of St Lazarus going east and north to the edge of Hudson Bay.[2]

This led the Spanish to advance counter-evidence: Fr Andrés Marcos Burriel's 1757 *Noticia de la California* poured scorn on the Fonte story – but his work was dismissed by others as an attempt by the Spanish to conceal the existence of a real strait which would benefit Spain, but endanger her South American possessions should other nations discover it. When it was translated into English a couple of years later, the pages dealing with the Fonte expedition

[1] John Barrow, *A Chronological History of Voyages into the Arctic Regions; Undertaken Chiefly for the Purpose of Discovering a North-East, North-west or Polar Passage between the Atlantic the Pacific*, London, 1818, pp. 278–96.

[2] Philippe Buache, *Considérations géographiques et physiques sur les nouvelles découvertes au nord de la Grande Mer appelée vulgairement la Mer du Sud, avec les cartes qui y sont relatives*, 2 vols, Paris, 1752–3. These and related geographical theories and attitudes in the eighteenth century have been ably analysed by Numa Broc in *La Géographie des philosophes*, Paris, 1972.

were omitted, allowing the editor to comment that the existence of a strait was 'a very probable thing'.[1]

A British expedition, properly organised, with scientific as well as less lofty aims, was needed to find the answer. The end of the Seven Years War made such an undertaking possible and John Byron was despatched in 1764 with the *Dolphin* and the *Tamar* to explore, among other parts of the Pacific, the Northwest Coast of America 'with great care and diligence', being advised in his instructions that 'mariners of great Experience...have thought it probable that a passage might be found' and requested to follow any such passage 'to the Eastern side of North America through Hudson's Bay...and return to England that way'.[2] Byron's ships were in no condition to attempt such a navigation and he wisely ignored the request. Britain's first real attempt to solve the northwest puzzle came to nothing.

By then, in spite of immense logistic problems, Russian explorers were beginning to reach the coast of Alaska. French cartographers succeeded in incorporating the voyages of Bering, Chirikov and others into their maps of the northern Pacific, combining them with Fonte and de Fuca's supposed voyages. In Müller's *Voyages from Asia to America* of 1761, in a map based on Delisle's work, Chirikov's discoveries are shown as reaching just to the edge of Fonte's Río de los Reyes, opposite the St Lazarus Archipelago.[3] In another, less influenced by the French, one finds attempts to find room for Francis Drake's New Albion and the even more elusive Port of Fancis Drake, 'wrongly named Port St Francisco'.

There was now too much doubt in official minds in London and Paris. The focus had shifted towards other Pacific puzzles, especially the perennial mystery of the southern continent. The Spanish continued to assert their claims to the Northwest Coast, particularly as Russian fur traders were starting to encroach on it, but efforts to defend what Spain regarded as her northern possessions were not closely linked to a belief in the existence of some elusive North-West Passage.[4]

[1] [Miguel Venegas] *A Natural and Civil History of California*, 2 vols, London, 1759.

[2] Robert E. Gallagher, *Byron's Journal of his Circumnavigation*, Cambridge, 1964 quoting PRO, Adm. 2/1332.

[3] Gerhardt Friedrich Müller, *Voyages from Asia to America*, London, 1761.

[4] James R. Gibson analysed Russian activities in 'A Notable Absence: The Lateness and Lameness of Russian Discovery and Exploration in the North Pacific 1639–1803', in Fisher and Johnston, *From Maps to Metaphors*, Vancouver, 1993.

James Cook's first voyage of 1768–71 was restricted to the central and southern Pacific, and his next expedition took him towards the Antarctic. By the time he was back in England, in 1775, the likelihood of a North-West Passage had been greatly lessened by explorations made overland by Samuel Hearne in 1771–2, but the arguments could only be laid finally to rest by a detailed survey of the North American coast. This would not be easy, because it was so indented and so cluttered by offshore islands, and much of the time fogbound, but it needed to be done. The task was assigned to Cook.

Men like Daines Barrington, a lawyer, antiquary and amateur geographer, had been gathering evidence since the early 1770s. Arguments over the practicality of a passage situated in high latitudes hinged on the issue of impassable ice fields; although it was accepted that ice formed readily in lakes and rivers, the view that salt prevented freezing and that accordingly sea water would not freeze – or do so only in very high latitudes – was widely held. Exploratory voyages showed that this did not necessarily mean that ships could find a satisfactory route in polar seas, but it did allow for the claim that a North-West Passage might still be practicable if it were found in northern Alaska. Daines Barrington was influential in persuading Parliament to renew its offer of a substantial reward for anyone who found this passage. The year 1775 was a particularly active one for all promoters of an expedition to get to the North-West Passage before either the Russians, or the Spanish, or the French discovered it. And in July 1776, Cook's instructions were handed to him.

They required him to sail to the Northwest Coast and 'carefully to search for, and to explore, such Rivers or Inlets as may appear to be of a considerable extent and pointing towards Hudsons or Baffins Bays, and if....there shall appear to be a certainty, or even a probability, of a Water Passage into the aforementioned Bays, or either of them, you are, in such case to use your utmost endeavours to pass through with one or both of the Sloops.'[1] Cook found no passage, unless the ice-choked Bering Strait far to the north could be considered such. He found no trace of Juan de Fuca Strait and bad weather kept him far from shore when he reached the latitude of 'the pretended Strait of Admiral de Fonte'. In fact, he belonged

[1] Cook, *Journals*, III, I, p. ccxxii.

to that substantial group of experienced and realistically minded mariners who had little faith in these straits: 'I give no credet to such vague and improbable stories, that carry their own confutation along with them.'[1]

Cook was followed on the Northwest Coast by another experienced and realistically-minded mariner, La Pérouse. The leading French geographers of his day were still reluctant to relegate Fuca and Fonte to the realm of imaginary voyagers – but too much evidence was now piling up to make their earlier position tenable. La Pérouse was still enjoined in the instructions he received to seek, on the Northwest Coast, a river or narrow inlet that might lead, by way of lakes, to Hudson Bay; but there was more emphasis on the potential offered by the fur trade, and on the possibility of Spanish, Russian and English settlements. However tempted the current Royal Geographer, Buache de la Neuville, the earlier Buache's nephew, might have been to mention the hypothetical western sea or the Strait of St Lazarus, he kept strictly to what was known at the time of La Pérouse's proposed expedition and set aside what was guesswork. As far as the North-West Passage was concerned, La Pérouse's function was to verify and complete the work which fog, storms and ice had prevented James Cook from carrying out to his satisfaction. His masters, just as the British Lords of the Admiralty had done with Cook, urged him to explore any passage which looked truly promising, but there was no urging to go forward into sounds and narrow waterways simply to discover something which geographers believed should exist.

La Pérouse had little faith in the speculations of these closet geographers. Fables or frauds, it mattered little: they were essentially a waste of time for navigators who had so much to do in the real world of uncharted waters, looming cliffs and dangerous shoals. Others, equally down-to-earth – men like Vancouver – were soon to follow him. The British Admiralty did not cling to any firm belief that the Passage existed, but it added it to Vancouver's instructions all the same;[2] after all, there were so many inlets, so many rivermouths still inadequately surveyed: one never knew what might be found. Vancouver found nothing, beyond

[1] Ibid., I, p. 335.

[2] W. Kaye Lamb (ed.), *The Voyage of George Vancouver 1791–1795*, London, 1984, I, 84, 283–4.

evidence that there were numerous deep inlets which Spanish explorers might have entered and more than enough for their sailors to use as the basis of plausible yarns. Juan de Fuca Strait might not lead all the way to the Atlantic, or even to some great inland sea, but at least it existed.

The myth lingered on for a few years. But published accounts of Cook's and Vancouver's voyages, and of La Pérouse's in France, the steady advance of the Russians and the arrival of the fur traders, put an end to the centuries-old speculation. The Strait of Anian vanished into the mists and Admiral de Fonte returned to the world of fantasy that had spawned him, and after so many hardships endured by explorers along the coast and across the land the North-West Passage finally faded away.

THE PARTICIPANTS

I. The Officers

Jean-François de Galaup was born at Le Gô, just outside Albi in south-west France, on 23 August 1741.[1] The family was influential and respected. The earliest Galaup to appear in local records was Huc Galaup who became a member of the Albi town council – a *consul* – in 1487; it began a family tradition: the Galaups provided *consuls* for next two centuries. The family fortunes grew steadily through the years, and in 1558 a Jean Galaup appears as 'Seigneur et Baron de Brens', at which date the Galaups acquired the yearned-for nobiliary particle and henceforth were known as 'de Galaup'. Their sons became magistrates, priests and army officers; they were careful to marry into families of distinction and to ensure that they rose slowly but surely towards the status of nobles. La Pérouse in no way followed the family pattern, although he was to acquire a fame far greater than any of his ancestors or relatives. He entered the navy, married beneath him, for love and not for advancement, and showed little interest in the niceties of Versailles and court life.

His paternal grandmother was the daughter of an army captain,

[1] See John Dunmore, *Pacific Explorer: The Life of Jean-François de la Pérouse 1741–1788*, Palmerston North and Annapolis, 1985.

his mother, Marguerite de Rességuier was the daughter of a colonel. The only link with sea life was a longstanding friendship between the Galaups and their distant relatives, the La Jonquières. Pierre-Jacques Taffanel de la Jonquière, born in 1680, had joined the navy, risen to the rank of commodore and ended his life as governor of French Canada; his nephew Clément Taffanel de la Jonquière also joined the navy and in the 1740s was beginning a distinguished if less brilliant career.[1]

Clément visited the Galaups and on at least one occasion brought with him a friend, another navy man, Charles d'Arsac de Ternay. It is reasonable to assume that their tales and their influence inspired the young Jean-François to seek a similar career. He had probably never seen the sea when he set out in November 1756 for Brest and the cadet school, the Hôtel de Saint-Pierre which housed the corps of the *Gardes de la Marine*.

His father, Victor-Joseph, no doubt after overcoming his surprise and a feeling of disappointment that the family pattern was being broken, decided that his son would have every chance of success. The first step was a change of name. Galaup, even with the nobiliary 'de', sounded inadequate beside such names as Taffanel de la Jonquière and D'Arsac de Ternay. The navy was very class-conscious and there were constant strains in wartime when 'temporary gentlemen' had to be given commissions; the distinction between the two castes was illustrated by a difference in the colour of their uniforms: officers from the aristocracy were known as the 'Reds' to distinguish them from those who had been recruited from the merchant service whose uniform was predominantly blue. One way of protecting his son from the petty innuendoes of his fellow cadets was to add an extra landed title to his name.

The Galaups owned a tenanted farm close to Albi, the Domaine de La Peyrouse. The name, which roughly translates as 'the rocky one', is not uncommon in south-west France, and there was a powerful and well-known aristocratic family, the La Peyrouse, who owned extensive lands in Périgord and Languedoc. If his new name became associated in people's minds with the La Peyrouse family, it would do Jean-François no harm. The property itself was

[1] On the links between La Jonquière and La Pérouse, see H. Manavit, 'Ce que Lapérouse doit à La Jonquière', *Revue du Tarn*, III, 1969, pp. 163–72, and H. and C. de la Jonquière, 'Une Famille Tarnaise: Les Taffanel de la Jonquière', *Colloque Lapérouse Albi 1985*, pp. 35–40.

not formally transferred to him until 1782, but the income seems to have been. So, when he left for Brest the young man became Jean-François de Galaup de la Pérouse (although he invariably signed letters and reports with the single word 'Lapérouse') and in time, when he began to move in government and court circles, he was referred to as the Comte de la Pérouse.[1]

He had joined the *Gardes* at the height of the Seven Years War. There was little time for formal study. On 3 May, he sailed from Brest in the *Célèbre* with the squadron of Dubois de la Motte, with reinforcements for Louisbourg on Cape Breton Island in what is now known as Nova Scotia. Commanding the *Célèbre* was Taffanel de la Jonquière, who would with Ternay be the young man's guide and mentor during his formative years. The *Célèbre* sailed back to France in October, and after a brief period of shore leave La Pérouse joined Ternay's frigate *Pomone*, then followed him onto the *Zéphire* and once more sailed to Canada. Back in Brest he was able to resume his studies before joining the *Formidable* in June 1759, to become part of an expedition intended to effect a landing in England. Admiral Hawke neutralised this French threat at the Battle of Quiberon Bay, during which the *Formidable* was captured and La Pérouse slightly wounded and taken prisoner. Released on parole, he was given leave and sent home to Albi to recuperate.[2]

He later resumed his studies in Brest, but was back in North American waters in 1762, sailing to Newfoundland in the *Robuste*, still under Ternay. The return journey, in September, was dangerous, with an English squadron lying in wait for them near Ushant. Ternay tried to find a port further south, on the Atlantic coast, but he was compelled to sail all the way to La Coruña in northern Spain. He remained there until 9 January 1763. By then the war was drawing to a close. French Canada and French India were lost, among other overseas colonies, and the treasury was empty. Now 21, still a *garde de la marine*, La Pérouse was sent home to Albi. It was a bleak time. His future depended on the government's policies: if

[1] On this, see Editorial Note, 'The Choice of a Name'. It should be borne in mind that 'comte de la Pérouse' is a courtesy title which usage would have confirmed with the passing in time; there is no record of any 'raising to the peerage' as some commentators have assumed.

[2] The early career of La Pérouse is detailed in M. de Brossard, *Lapérouse: des combats à la découverte*, Paris, 1978, pp. 15–96, and Dunmore, *Pacific Explorer*, pp. 37–61.

Versailles decided to retrench, his career in the navy would vegetate; it might even come to an end.

A number of young officers, those who had other prospects, went back on permanent leave to their families, effectively leaving the navy. Others, La Pérouse among them, declared themselves ready to accept whatever might become available. He returned to Brest, completed his formal studies and, on 1 October 1764, was promoted to the rank of *enseigne*. He then served on various *gabares* – little more than coastal storeships – sailing down to Bayonne to load timber from the Pyrenees and back to Brest. In 1768 he was able to join Ternay in the *Turquoise*, carrying out hydrographic work around the Brittany coast. It marked the end of three years of dreary work, not very different from what a merchant marine officer would be doing. (One cannot resist, at this point, thinking of James Cook's time on the coal run and in the Baltic trade.)

His period with the *Turquoise* was a valuable learning experience, though a brief one, followed by a spell in the *Belle-Poule*, an impressive frigate. This was interrupted for a few months when he was sent in command of a *bugalet* – an ammunition lighter – to check on English shipping movements and set up signalling stations on the coast. Back in the *Belle-Poule* at the end of 1770, he sailed to the West Indies and a year later, the frigate having been placed under Ternay's command, he sailed with his protector to the Ile de France in the Indian Ocean. Ternay had been appointed governor of the Ile de France (now known as Mauritius). He was to keep La Pérouse with him until 1776 when both returned to France.[1]

The Indian Ocean opened up a new opportunities for him. It did more: it introduced him to the exciting world of exploration. The Ile de France was the outpost from which expeditions like those of Marion du Fresne and Kerguelen set out for unknown seas, and it was there that men like Bougainville put in on the penultimate stage of their homeward voyage after crossing the Pacific Ocean. Geographers and cartographers back home might speculate about the existence of a southern continent and argue theory: here men and women knew at first hand of the problems and the dangers involved and argued over the benefits which would derive if one of the navigators the distant ocean should come upon a new land.

It was an exciting period. While the *Belle-Poule* was on her way

[1] On Ternay, see M. Linyer de la Barbée, *Le Chevalier de Ternay*, Grenoble, 1972.

across the Indian Ocean, somewhere between the Cape of Good Hope and the Ile de France, in July 1772, James Cook was setting out from Plymouth on his second voyage. When Ternay and La Pérouse arrived at Port-Louis, Ile de France, in August, they found the island in a state of ferment over the Kerguelen discovery. Yves de Kerguelen in the *Fortune* had sailed south from the island on 16 January, acccompanied by the *Gros-Ventre* commanded by François de St Allouarn; on 12 February he had discovered a stretch of land which he hastened back to Port-Louis to report about, having lost touch with the *Gros-Ventre* in thick fog. On 16 March, a mere five months before La Pérouse's arrival, Kerguelen reached Port-Louis, went to see the governor and the civil administrator and gave a glowing account of his discoveries that led the governor to write at once to the Minister in France that '[everything] seems to indicate a country that is inhabited and carefully cultivated'[1] and the administrator to write separately and with even greater enthusiasm that 'M. de Kerguelen has discovered for France, in the space of two months, a new world....It is not possible that so immense a discovery, so close to the Ile de France, since one can get there in three weeks, should fail to procure great advantages to the colony.'[2] Kerguelen had sailed back to France on 27 March to press for an immediate expedition to complete his explorations. By the time Ternay and La Pérouse reached Port-Louis, the excitement had cooled somewhat: it all seemed too good to be true – and what had happened to the *Gros-Ventre*?

Ternay took over from Des Roches as governor, while Maillard du Mesle, an administrator more concerned to balance the island's precarious budget than with grandiose schemes for new colonies, replaced Poivre. Within a few days, the *Gros-Ventre* appeared. St Allouarn had followed the original instructions, which were to sail east from the South Indian Ocean; he had reached Cape Leeuwin in Australia, explored the western coast of the continent as far as Shark Bay and then turned back for Timor and the Ile de France. St Allouarn was brought ashore in very poor health and died within a short time. The expedition brought with it the startling news that there was no pleasant inhabitable land in the South Indian Ocean, no sign of any continent, nothing but bleak islands, snow and

[1] Des Roches to the Minister, 20 March 1772. BN, NAF 9439–90.

[2] Poivre to the Minister, 21 March 1772. BN, NAF 9439–91.

storms. The existence of a southern continent was looking increasingly doubtful, for 1772 was also the year when the first French-language account of James Cook's *Endeavour* voyage was published, avidly read and promptly reprinted – and Cook's voyage had made deadly inroads into the continental theory.

Kerguelen meanwhile was granted his request for a second expedition. It was to be far grander, far more costly than the first. The official approval came on 16 September 1772, just eleven days after St Allouarn's return to the Ile de France. Since Versailles knew nothing of the *Gros-Ventre*'s reports, plans went ahead. When Kerguelen sailed in March 1773, with the *Oiseau* and the *Rolland*, a report of St Allouarn's voyage was about to reach France, but Kerguelen could not be called back. His two ships met with various mishaps and eventually separated, with the *Oiseau* going to Madagascar for supplies. Kerguelen did not reach the Ile de France until August. Ternay, but especially Maillard, were unco-operative; they made it difficult for Kerguelen to obtain replacements for the 34 sick he had to leave behind and to get a small corvette for coastal reconnaissance. Nevertheless, he had orders from the Minister and the officials were forced to help him, albeit ungraciously. Kerguelen sailed south on 8 November, reached Kerguelen Island on 14 December, carried out some surveys in appalling weather, had to admit that the place was of no value to anyone and sailed back to Madagascar and France in mid-January 1774. A year later, back in France, he was arrested, court-martialled on a number of charges and sentenced to six years' imprisonment, some of his incompetent and insubordinate officers being dismissed from the service or imprisoned.[1]

The year 1773 was marked by more bad news. In May the *Marquis-de-Castries* and the *Mascarin* limped into Port-Louis. They had sailed from the island with high hopes in October 1771 under Marc-Joseph Marion du Fresne.[2] The plan was to return to Tahiti a

[1] Kerguelen has had his defenders, notably M. de Brossard, *Kerguelen le découvreur*, Paris, 1970. He was ambitious and reckless, foolishly eager to undertake tasks the magnitude of which he failed to appreciate and all too easily given the means to attempt them; he was then unscrupulously fierce in his endeavours to justify himself. '[He] had resilience and unbounded self-confidence', but '[his] expeditions typified the drawbacks of the old class structure of the Navy'. Dunmore, *French Explorers in the Pacific*, I, 1965, pp. 248–9.

[2] On Marion du Fresne, see Dunmore, *French Explorers*, I, 1965, pp. 166–95, and Isabel Ollivier (transl.), *Extracts from the Journals of the Ships*, Mascarin *and* Marquis de Castries, Wellington, 1985.

Polynesian taken to France by Louis de Bougainville and sail in search of the southern continent. The expedition had met with some success in the South Indian Ocean, discovering some small groups of islands, stopped briefly in Tasmania and gone on to New Zealand where Marion du Fresne and a number of officers and men had been killed. Under a new commander the expedition had sailed north towards the Tongan archipelago, but no one had any enthusiasm left for any further exploring, the Polynesian had died of smallpox, the ships were in a bad state of repair, and the French made for Guam and Manila. Now, after some overhaul but many desertions in the Spanish colony, the ships were back, the officers and crew totally dispirited.

Consequently in his years in the Ile de France, La Pérouse was subjected to conflicting influences. On the one hand, there were news of discoveries James Cook was making throughout the Pacific, showing what could be achieved by a well-led and well-planned expedition, and there remained among the residents of the island a substantial and vocal number who had been impressed by what Bougainville had done and who still felt the French could and should organise their own expedition; and on the other hand, there was Maillard, the powerful *Intendant*, who was firmly opposed to any venture that might further strain the island's resources, and who was seconded in his views by Ternay who was concerned about the need to strengthen the island's defences and self-reliance. Supplies were often inadequate, and ships from France arrived only at irregular intervals and they needed to be refitted and revictualled in order to continue their voyage to the French Indian settlements or to start back on the journey home. So La Pérouse learned caution and realism, but he also acquired a yearning to sail one day towards that vast ocean about which so much had been written and which, from Port-Louis, looked tantalising near.

Ternay's instructions, like Maillard, were to carry out economies, to eschew grand schemes and to build up the island as a staging post to the east, and to do this he needed to strengthen the French presence in the Indian Ocean. He used La Pérouse's talents to develop this strategy, but first he needed to take prompt action to deal with a serious food shortage resulting from cyclones which had devastated the island in March and April. La Pérouse was transferred to *L'Africaine*, commanded by Claude-Joseph du Chayla, and sent to Madagascar in early September. The *Africaine*, a storeship carrying 40 guns – needed to impress the tribes of Madagascar who were almost constantly at war – made several expeditions to the east coast of Madagascar and to the nearby island of Bourbon (present-day Reunion), bringing back supplies of rice and bullocks. Then on 21 April 1773, La Pérouse took over command of the *Seine*, a ship of 700 tons, carrying 30 guns, with a complement of 110 officers and men.

His instructions were to sail to India by way of Bourbon and the Seychelles, following a route suggested some years earlier by Jacques-Raymond de Géron de Grenier and partly investigated in 1771 by Kerguelen. The practicality of the route was still not established, and there was speculation about the existence of an island called St John of Lisbon which the British might occupy and use as a base in the Indian Ocean. Ternay's long-term plan was to lessen dependence on the call at the Dutch-held Cape settlements for French ships on their way to the east by building up the Ile de France as the centre of a series of French bases including the Seychelles and the Amirantes in the north, Madagascar in the west, Rodriguez in the east, plus any other islands as yet undiscovered. If rumours about St John of Lisbon were even partly true, it was important to ensure that it fell into French hands; but rumours have a tendency to mushroom, and in the case of St John of Lisbon a cloud along the horizon or an erroneous longitude recorded for Rodriguez had been transformed into an island of economic and strategic significance. So La Pérouse would help to banish it from the maps, but he achieved a great deal more than that.

On 18 May 1773, he sailed with the *Seine*. He followed Grenier's route, keeping a wary eye for unknown dangers along the way. He had no chronometer and depended on dead reckoning, on constant soundings and on signs traditionally used by sailors: flights of birds, cloud formations, the colour of the sea. He made his way towards the Seychelles which he reached on 5 June. His longitude was 150 miles out but, making allowance for his lack of instruments, unreliable charts, unexpected currents and the general unawareness of the problem of compass deviation, it was a creditable result.

The islands were idyllic, but life ashore belied the promise of nature. The small European settlement on the island of Mahé was in total disarray; twenty or so squabbling settlers huddled in huts or squatted on the beach, leaving the weeds to take over their struggling plantations. La Pérouse had instructions to reorganise the colony, a task which took him three weeks. He then went on to Pondicherry, a French port in south-east India, spent a month there and sailed for Bengal on 27 August. He reached the mouth of the Ganges on 3 September and continued upriver to Chandernagore, the French settlement near Calcutta. He took on a cargo of comestibles for the Ile de France and began the slow voyage down the Hooghly to the Bay of Bengal in mid-December, watched suspiciously by a British guardship. He proceeded down the coast to Masulipatnam and Pondicherry, taking on more supplies for Mauritius, and sailed home on 3 February 1774, dropping anchor at Port-Louis on 24 March.[1]

The *Seine* had completed a useful voyage, during which he had gained a great deal of experience. Ternay granted him a respite of five months ashore while the ship was repaired. La Pérouse spent much of his time in the navy's offices, poring over charts and journals, writing a detailed report and catching up with news from France. He was now 32, an age when promotion begins to assume an importance coloured by anxiety. France had been at peace for more than ten years. Advancement was slow and La Pérouse was still an *enseigne* surrounded by others of his own age, all competing for the attention of the naval authorities. Under the Ancient Regime, birth and connections mattered greatly. La Pérouse had protectors like La Jonquière and Ternay, but others had well placed relatives. A 'red' officers he might be, but he lacked the uncle at court, the well-connected cousin, the sister married into the old nobility which others could call upon to place a good word in the influential ear at the right moment. And the Indian Ocean was far away from Versailles where beat France's administrative heart.

Ternay sent him back to India. The *Seine* reached Pondicherry on 20 September 1774 and after nearly a month there was sent to the French port of Mahé and then along the Malabar coast to Mangalore. This was the northernmost limit of the area controlled by Haydar Ali, the Mysore leader who was fiercely defending his independence against the British India Company and whom the French were supplying with arms. Not unexpectedly Haydar Ali welcomed him like an official representative of France and put on

[1] La Pérouse's 'Journal de la flûte du Roi *La Seine*' is held at the Archives Nationales, AN.M. C7 165, pp. 123–45.

the kind of display at which Indian princes excelled. La Pérouse continued north to Goa where the Portuguese were far from welcoming and on to Surat.

At last La Pérouse encountered action. On 5 January 1775 a Mahratta fleet hove into sight – three ships of 40 guns and over 20 smaller vessels. The fight lasted two hours, the Mahrattas fleeing back to their home base. This was a welcome change from carrying rice and trade goods. La Pérouse spent a fortnight at Surat, returned to Goa and arrived off Mahé at the end of February. To his surprise he found the port besieged by a force of ten thousand men led by the Malabar prince Cherikal. Not improbably, in view of the complex and constantly shifting political pattern in India, it included a fair number of the sepoys who had welcomed him ashore three months earlier.

As the senior officer he took over command of the town's small garrison of 60 Europeans and 200 Indians and reorganised the defences. Two night attacks were repelled, but La Pérouse realised that he needed a counter-attack to get Cherikal to lift the siege. He disposed of two other small ships, the *Trois-Amis*, a trading vessel, and the *Expérience*, a small galliot that was at anchor in the port and which he placed in charge of Robert de Clonard – with whom one day he would sail to the Pacific. Several sorties were made against Cherikal's camp, during one of which Clonard was wounded, and two further attacks by the besiegers were beaten back. Fortunately, Haydar Ali and the French were negotiating for peace with the British and their allies. An agreement was signed on 25 April and three days later La Pérouse sailed for the Ile de France. He limped into Port-Louis almost sinking, with two pumps going night and day.[1]

Now came the opportunity for a lengthy spell on land. La Pérouse had no objection. With his friend Mengault de la Hague he had bought a small property in the country, some distance from Port-Louis. There were other attractive homes not too far away: Ternay's own Le Réduit, Du Chayla's country house, and the residence of the Broudou family on Wilhems Plains. The Broudous came originally from Picardy, but had moved to the port of

[1] 'Précis de ma dernière campagne à la côte de Coromandel et à celle de Malabar jusqu'à Surate', AN.M. B4:125. An unsigned article 'La Campagne de Lapérouse dans l'Inde' appeared in the *Revue de l'Histoire des Colonies Françaises*, XXXII, 1929, pp. 301–6.

Nantes; then in 1768, Abraham Broudou had been sent to the Ile de France to manage the naval storeyards and supervise the hospital. He had two daughters, Elisabeth and Louise-Eléonore who was born in Nantes on 15 May 1755. La Pérouse became attracted to Eléonore and in June 1775 he hinted in a letter to his sister Jacquette that he was 'a little in love with a young person from this island and this could end in a marriage.'[1]

Jacquette Galaup, as no doubt her brother had intended her to, relayed the information to her mother and then to her father. Galaup's reaction was immediate: he had no wish to see his son married into some lower middle-class family, to the daughter of a senior clerk in the administrative service, as it turned out; this was still the age of arranged marriage, and children were expected to accept the bride their parents chose for them, not to give way to romantic attachments. The Galaups did not marry young – Victor-Joseph had taken a wife at the age of 31 – but La Pérouse was now 34 and his parents had been planning a suitable match for him for when he returned home. So old Galaup sent a message to Ternay, formally appointing him his son's guardian and expressing his firm opposition to what he regarded as a misalliance. By then La Pérouse had proposed to Eléonore and been accepted, but the marriage was blocked from two directions – a parental objection and an officer's obligation not to marry against the wishes of his superiors. And for good measure there was the strong bond of mutual respect and friendship between Ternay and Jean-François. Unrecorded, but adding to the obstacles, was an interview which Abraham Broudou undoubtedly had with his own superiors, either Maillard or Ternay, expressing their opposition to the proposed match.

Mengault de la Hague and La Pérouse sold their house on 23 May 1776. Outwardly, it marked a break with the Broudous, but the ties remained. Jean-François met Eléonore only on rare formal occasions, but letters were exchanged and promises made. Eléonore was to sail for France a mere fortnight after La Pérouse's turn of duty on the island came to an end in December 1776.

He still had one expedition ahead of him. In August 1776 the frigate *Consolante* put in at Port-Louis, on her way to Pondicherry

[1] From correspondence reprinted in *Bulletin de la Société de Géographie*, 1888, pp. 159–60.

with a new governor, the Maréchal de Bellecombe. The French government and Ternay were concerned about the situation in Madagascar where a French settlement had been made in 1774, led by a colourful character known as Maurice de Benyowski. Ternay and Bellecombe agreed that the *Consolante* would call at Madagascar and see how the small colony was faring. Since Bellecombe would be going on to India, Ternay needed someone who would go with him to Madagascar and report back to him. He chose La Pérouse, providing him with a small locally-built coastal vessel, the *Iphigénie*.

The two vessels sailed from Port-Louis on 10 September 1776, reaching Foulpointe on the 17th. The settlement was in a parlous state: the colonists had fallen out, Benyowski was behaving like a tyrant, the natives were at war with each other and against the French. Bellecombe, advised by La Pérouse who knew the island, arranged a truce and cemented it with a ceremony of reconciliation which included drinking a mixture of brandy, gunpowder and sea-water. Beniowsky asked Bellecombe to urge his government to send him military and financial support, but he had to be told that this was most unlikely. The Marshall had to admit that, even in his jungle village, Beniowsky was an impressive personage. 'It is hard to find a more extraordinary man', he wrote. In fact, Beniowsky was about to proclaim himself king of the province of Mananara and sail to France as the representative of an independent state; still impressive, he was welcomed at Versailles, showered with honours and given back a family castle in distant Poland by the Empress of Austria; but an adventurer to the end he would be killed in Madagascar in 1786.

All this took time. Eventually, Bellecombe went on his way and La Pérouse started back for the Ile de France. The *Iphigénie* had not been careened for five years, she was slow and leaky, and La Pérouse struggled against contrary winds and cross-currents, patching the vessel and pumping day and night. On 22 November, Maillard was writing to Paris that the *Iphigénie* was feared lost, as she was badly overdue; he was about the seal his letter when someone sighted a sail on the horizon. La Pérouse's last voyage in the Indian Ocean was over.[1]

[1] La Pérouse's reports to Ternay, dated November 1776, are held at the AN, Colonies C5 A6, nos. 12 and 13.

His time at the Ile de France was over as well. On 16 December, he sailed from Port-Louis with Ternay in the *Belle-Poule*.

In May, a few days after they reached Lorient, Ternay took La Pérouse to Paris and Versailles. As far as one can ascertain, this was Jean-François' first visit to the capital. He was promoted to the rank of lieutenant, effective back to 4 April, made a knight of the Order of St Louis and, in July, granted a pension of 300 *livres*. These rewards were tangible marks of appreciation which he hoped his family back in Albi would appreciate. La Pérouse, however, had not heard from his father – who admittedly was now losing his eyesight – and had only received a few letters from his sister during his years in the Indian Ocean. Ternay served as a substitute father, piloting him through the offices and drawing-rooms of Versailles, and introducing him to useful acquaintances. He brought him once more into contact with La Jonquière and presented him to the influential administrator, Claret de Fleurieu.

Returning to Brittany, La Pérouse once again met Eléonore who was now living with her mother in Nantes and would soon move to Brest where he lived when he was not in Paris. His family was planning his eventual marriage to a daughter of the Vésian family, but he was not consulted. And anyhow, rumours of an impending war with England were rife. Ternay needed his assistance over a plan to attack English shipping and outposts in the Indian Ocean; others, such as Mengault and Grenier, joined them, forming a group of specialists on eastern affairs whose knowledge the authorities could draw on if the need arose. Eléonore went to live in a Paris convent to be near Jean-François, but both realised that a combination of war and family opposition would force their hoped-for union into the background.

Claret de Fleurieu, who had supported La Pérouse and welcomed his draft plan for a campaign in the Indian Ocean,[1] warned the 'Indian Ocean lobby' that the main effort would be directed towards the Atlantic Ocean and the North American coastline, but he did not discourage them from continuing their planning. The European powers were jockeying for position while was effectively a 'phoney war' went on between them. The year 1778 opened with the standard British raid on French shipping. As many as 155 merchant ships, large and small, were seized in British ports. On 6

[1] Now held at the AN.M. C7 165.

February France signed a secret treaty of friendship with Benjamin Franklin, the representative of the Thirteen Colonies, and on 21 March the British Ambassador left for London. War was now official. On 24 February La Pérouse had taken over command of the *Serin*, a corvette of 14 guns, a slow, ill-equipped vessel which he sailed down to Bordeaux as part of a convoy and then to Ushant for inglorious coastguard duties. He left the *Serin* on 15 May and spent a month ashore – giving him an opportunity to go down to Nantes where Eléonore had now returned. Formal hostilities broke out with a battle between the *Arethusa* and his old ship, the *Belle-Poule*. La Pérouse was sent to St Malo to take command of a brand-new frigate, the *Amazone*.

He had to wait until August before the *Amazone* was ready to sail, thus missing the Battle of Ushant of 27 July. He went with Mengault, commanding the *Gentille*, and the cutter *Guèpe* on a raid against British shipping in the North Sea, capturing 12 prizes without loss. Meantime, Ternay, supplied with a brand-new ship of the line, the *Annibal*, was organising a large squadron for the Indian Ocean, which La Pérouse and Mengault both expected to join, but on 9 January 1779 it was learned that Pondicherry, likely to be a key base for French operations in India, had already fallen to the British; on 6 February La Fayette arrived from America seeking greater help for the American colonists; then came news that the French island of St Lucia in the West Indies had fallen and that other French-held islands were threatened. Everything now confirmed that the real theatre of war would be the Atlantic and that the East could only be a costly sideshow. Orders were sent to Ternay's ships to abort their plans to sail to the Indian Ocean and to prepare to join Vice-Admiral d'Estaing fleet in the Caribbean.

This meant delays and a change of leader. Ternay had to make room for La Motte-Picquet. La Pérouse in the *Amazone* sailed from Brest on 1 May 1779 with a convoy which, including the merchant ships, amounted to some 60 vessels. Within days of his arrival in the West Indies he was involved in action, taking part in the capture of Grenada and in the sea fight against Byron's fleet on 6 July. He sailed with the French squadron to Savannah in September when they were assailed by a four-day storm. Soon after, he captured an English frigate, the *Ariel*, losing 12 of his men and suffering considerable damage to sails and shrouds in the engagement. He limped into Charleston, towing the *Ariel*, took part in the land operations, but the French ships were forced to leave in late october, only to be scattered by another gale. La Pérouse sailed to Cadiz, capturing the privateer *Tiger* on the way, accompanied by the *Sagittaire* and her prize, the *Experiment* in which had been found General Garth and £650,000 in silver. After a period of rest, he went to Lorient, where he arrived on 28 February 1780. Ternay was waiting for him, impatient to set out on a new campaign.[1]

The plan was to escort a French army to America, led by Jean-Baptiste, Comte de Rochambeau. There were to be 5,000 soldiers, plus their officers and artillery support. Ternay sent La Pérouse to Versailles to discuss the massive logistical problems with Fleurieu. The navy's stores were depleted by the war, the merchant ships needed as transports were scattered in various ports, there was a shortage of men, naval vessels would be needed to escort the convoy; all these problems had to be explained to army officers unused to the problems of the sea. La Pérouse travelled to Nantes, to Lorient and back to Brest where the Comte d'Hector, the director of the arsenals and shore installations, was struggling in a tidal wave of orders and counter-orders. finally, on 2 May, the Ternay squadron was ready to sail, escorting 28 transport ships. The crossing took two months, which was not unexpected with such slow clumsy merchantment and with the constant risk of an unwelcome meeting with prowling units of the Royal Navy. The French reached Rhode Island on 9 July and, not without difficulty, the soldiers, many of them suffering from scurvy, were landed at Newport.

On 28 October, the *Amazone* sailed back to France, having on board Rochambeau's son, a colonel in his father's expeditionary force, who was going to Versailles to ask for more men. It was a speedy crossing – 39 days – and both men hastened to Versailles as soon as they reached Brest. La Pérouse found a new Minister of Marine in charge, the Marquis de Castries, who had close links with his native Albi.[2] He handed over Ternay's reports, left Rochambeau to his lobbying and closeted himself with Fleurieu to discuss a plan to raid British outposts on the northern American

[1] For details of the American campaigns, see M. de Brossard, *Lapérouse: des combats à la découverte*, Paris, 1978, pp. 299–445.

[2] Charles, Marquis de Castris, was born at Castries in south-west France, approximately 100 miles from Albi. He was, as he wrote to La Pérouse, 'a former resident of Albi', AN.M. C7 197, 25 August 1783.

coast. On 25 December, back in Brest, he took over command of a new frigate, the *Astrée*, and sailed for Boston escorting a small convoy. The weather was appalling and they did not reach Boston until 27 February 1781. There he learned that Ternay had died. 'The greatest friend I had in the world,' he wrote. 'He had been a father to me since I joined the navy.'

The *Astrée* was next engaged on convoy escorting and raids against privateers around the coast of Massachusetts. La Pérouse was impatient to set out on the northern raid he had planned, hoping to leave from Boston in April, but the Comte de Barras who had taken over command of the French squadron at Rhode Island was aiming to combine it with a fleet led by the Comte de Grasse and Washington and Rochambeau's land forces for a major offensive against the English redcoats. All these schemes were affected by the seesawing of the fortunes of war on the continent, and by the need to defend the French West Indies from a possible English attack. La Pérouse, now a *capitaine de vaisseau*, was sent to cruise off the Canadian coast, where he was joined by the *Hermione*, commanded by La Touche. On 21 July, of Aspy Bay, Cape Breton Island, they sighted a convoy of 20 sail escorted by several warships. Two frigates and a corvette veered towards the French to give the transport ships a chance to make their escape and a battle ensued which lasted until darkness forced an end to the engagement. There was heavy damage on both sides. With three killed and a dozen wounded, his ship badly damaged, La Pérouse had to return to Boston for repairs. This caused him to miss the Chesapeake campaign that ended in Cornwallis's surrender at Yorktown.

Barras sailed from Newport on 25 August and left La Pérouse in charge. The area became relatively quiet, with only one major incident in Boston Bay when La Pérouse unsuccessfully but gallantly tried to save the frigate *Magicienne* from the larger *Chatham*. Castries wrote him a letter of appreciation from Versailles, but it was a small consolation for missing the chance to carry out the hoped-for raid against the northern outposts or taking part of the Chesapeake campaign. In early December he received instructions from De Grasse to sail to the Caribbean with a fleet of transports bringing timber from Boston. He reached Martinique on 5 January 1782 and left a week later to join De Grasse's fleet at St Kitts. There followed a period of manoeuvrings, part of De Grasse's preparations for an attack on Jamaica. On the English side, Hood and

Rodney did their best to shadow the French and foil their plans. De Grasse captured Montserrat and sailed down to Martinique for the final marshalling of his forces; they would then sail to Santo Domingo where Spanish and French forces would unite for the assault on neighbouring Jamaica.

The fleet sailed north on 8 April, followed by Admiral Rodney's ships. The French got as far as Dominica without trouble, but calms and currents made manoeuvring difficult. The *Zélé* and the *Ville-de-Paris* collided, and La Pérouse was ordered to escort the damaged *Zélé* to Guadeloupe: as a result he missed the Battle of the Saints of 12 April in which the *Ville-de-Paris*, with De Grasse on board, was captured. The rest of the fleet managed to reach Santo Domingo and link up with the Spanish fleet. La Pérouse's lone *Astrée* succeeded in evading watching units of the British fleet and joined the French squadron. No attack on Jamaica was possible until the damage the French had sustained at the Saints was repaired; there were moreover growing reports of an imminent peace settlement. De Grasse's replacement, the Comte de Vaudreuil, decided he had no immediate need of La Pérouse's services, and he agreed to release him for a campaign in northern Canada. He gave him a solid warship of 74 guns, the *Sceptre*, which was only two years old. The *Astrée* was taken over by his friend Fleuriot de Langle, a third ship being added, the frigate *Engageante*, commanded by the young Marquis de la Jaille.

La Pérouse sailed on 31 May 1782, taking with him 300 soldiers and adequate supplies, although the need for secrecy had prevented him from taking any winter clothing. Even Langle and La Jaille were forbidden to open their sealed orders until they reached the latitude of Nova Scotia. All began to feel the cold once they reached Newfoundland. Heavy fog made the navigation particularly hazardous, especially when icefloes and then icebergs began to appear. It cleared on 18 July, revealing the entrance to Hudson Strait.

La Pérouse's plan, worked out with Fleurieu,[1] was to destroy the prosperous Hudson's Bay Company fur trade which was largely

[1] This is made clear in a letter dated 1 December 1780 from La Pérouse to Fleurieu, mentioning 'the expedition of which we have spoken' and outlining his plan for the proposed raid into Hudson Bay. AN.M. B4:183, 111–29. See also Fleuriot de Langle, *La Tragique Expédition de La Pérouse et Langle*, Paris, 1954, pp. 80ff, and P. Bonnichon, 'L'Expédition de Lapérouse en 1782 à la Baie d'Hudson', in *Colloque Lapérouse Albi 1985*, pp. 55–65.

based on two forts situated on the furthest shore of the bay, protected, so the English believed, by their isolation and the difficulty of navigating during a relatively short season through a labyrinth of islands and ice. The distance he had to cover was great indeed: 1900 miles from Santo Domingo, including 420 miles through the twisting strait and a further 450 miles to cross the bay to the forts.

The lack of winter clothing was relieved when the French met the Inuit from whom they bought furs and bearskins, but they were sailing past a desolate world. Baffin Island, the northern limit of Hudson Strait, offered nothing but a stony arid shore barren of trees, with only occasional patches of green visible in the shelter of the grey rocks. There was more ice ahead when on 1 August they reached the end of the strait and began to veer south into Hudson Bay, but at least the bitter cold wind began to drop. Their main target was Prince of Wales Fort, to the south-west across the bay, on the Churchill River; defended by stone walls 18 feet high with 42 guns, it looked formidable indeed as La Pérouse surveyed it on 8 August. It was only when the French landed, on the 9th, that they realised how ill-defended it was: there were fewer men than there were guns, and most were only traders and clerks. There was no need to fire a shot. After the surrender terms had been settled, La Pérouse dined with the British commander, Samuel Hearne, a man famous for his explorations of the bay and his discovery of the Coppermine River in the far north; he was 'a handsome man, well educated and with a wide knowledge'. La Pérouse was to allow him to sail back to England in a small vessel, the *Severn,* and was glad to hear in due course that he had safely reached England.

The plan had been to destroy, not to conquer, and accordingly only the traders and employees were taken on board and the stocks of furs safely stowed, the guns were spiked and the fort was blown up. It was all over in a few days, and La Pérouse sailed on to the other Company post, York Factory.

Without charts and with no help from his English prisoners, who quite properly refused to co-operate, the French found it hard to make their way in stormy weather through shallow water and dangerous rocks. York Factory was 150 miles away, on the Hayes River to the south. La Pérouse reached it on 20 August. There was no time for a surprise landing: it took three days of manoeuvring through shoals and rocks in perilous seas, and one longboat capsized with heavy loss of life. Guns could not be unloaded in the swampy ground around the fort, but fortunately the defenders had decided to surrender. Most of the furs traded that year had just been shipped to England in the *King George*; this meant there was little booty left for the French to carry off, but once the French had blown up the fort: 'The French Commander order'd a kind of Tent to be erected at the sloops creek to put provisions and stores in for the distressed Indians to prevent them from starving should any come to this place'. La Pérouse had done the same at Prince of Wales Fort for the men who were away hunting. 'If the King were here,' he wrote, 'He would approve of my conduct.'[1] Louis XVI was indeed impressed, and so were the British who would also remember his sympathetic treatment of Samuel Hearne and offer him help in return when the great voyage to the Pacific was being planned.

The return voyage began on 1 September. The English prisoners were as eager to get away as the French and they guided them out of the bay. In mid-September they reached the open sea. Hearne and 32 others took their leave off Resolution Island and began their journey to Stromness in the Orkneys. Langle took the *Astrée* direct to France to report on the successful raid and land the furs they had taken, while La Pérouse made his way to Cadiz where his men could recover in a mild climate and *Sceptre* could be repaired. It had been, as he reported to his mother, 'the hardest campaign ever undertaken'.[2]

The Hudson Bay raid astonished England and especially the London merchants who believed that the inaccessibility of their outposts was enough to protect them; but it was only a raid, a symbol of French strength and determination, with only a slight psychological value in the peace negotiations that had already begun. And it had been costly: when the *Sceptre* reached Cadiz on 13 October 1782, La Pérouse had 400 sick on board and 70 had died of scurvy and related illnesses; La Jaille's *Engageante* which was still with him had also suffered losses through scurvy and drownings, and only a few dozen were fit enough to work his ship.

La Pérouse had hopes of joining a force being readied for an attack on Gibraltar,[3] but the war was ending. An effective armistice

[1] Glyndwr Williams, ed., *Hudson's Bay Miscellany 1670–1870*, Winnipeg, p. 88 n.1; correspondence in BN, NAF 9424:389.

[2] Letter reprinted in Fleuriot de Langle, *La Tragique Expédition*, pp. 56–7.

[3] AN.M. B4:206, 68–9.

was agreed upon in November between Britain and the American colonies, formal discussions between France and Britain began in January and the peace treaty was formally signed on 3 September 1783. La Pérouse took the *Sceptre* to Brest in April 1783. He had been granted a pension of 800 *livres* in the previous November, and in 1784 he was to be appointed a member of the Society of the Cincinnati by the United States Congress.

He settled in Paris and began to work with Fleurieu and Castries. Ternay's death had given him greater independence, but the power of his father over his private life remained. The Galaups had completed their agreement with the aristocratic and well-to-do Vésian family of Albi: once the American war was over, Jean-François would marry Mademoiselle de Vésian. He was now 42, but traditional practices still ruled. From Cadiz he wrote to the girl's mother, tactfully agreeing to marry her daughter on condition that she was in favour of the match, but he added that he had loved another whom he had hoped to marry. A letter to Mr de Vésian was somewhat more straightforward: if his daughter was willing to marry a man almost 25 years her senior who spent most of his life at sea, the wedding could proceed as soon as he had freed himself from some other attachment. The warning signals were clear, creating perplexity on the Vésian side and anxiety among the Galaups – not without justification, for within three weeks of his arrival in Paris, La Pérouse had gone to see Eléonore Broudou and married her in the presence of a single witness on 8 July at the Church of St Marguerite.

The Vésians accepted his action with relative good grace and promptly found another suitor for their daughter. The Galaups decided that wagging tongues should be silenced by an appropriate ceremony. The newly-weds were invited to Albi and their union was formally consecrated at the cathedral with all the pomp expected of a leading local family. They bore no grudge against Eléonore, who was gentle and well-mannered, and closed ranks against a gossiping world.

However, an officer still needed his superiors' permission to marry. La Pérouse had not sought it, so he wrote direct to the Minister, apologising for his omission, detailing his romantic odyssey and the years of waiting, and offering to make amends by sailing around the world 'for six years if you order it'. Castries replied with a friendly letter, adding that as a former resident of

Albi he joined in the good wishes showered on the couple by relatives and friends. It had all suddenly come right.[1]

La Pérouse's hint about sailing around the world reveals the tenor of the discussions that had already begun between him, Fleurieu and Castries. It is not unlikely that the exchange of letters was no more than a formality, and that both men knew about La Pérouse's long attachment to Eléonore. What had been in fact a kind of reverse elopement could not be officially condoned, but there was nothing harmful or disgraceful in it and whether La Pérouse spent his summer leave down at Albi with Eléonore or some other bride was of no great moment to them. If anything, it was better for their plans that La Pérouse should be happily married than otherwise. Uppermost in their minds was the voyage of Pacific exploration which France could now begin to organise.

The first two years of La Pérouse's married life were still marked by long periods of separation. Eléonore remained in Albi, while he went back to Paris, working on plans that were being kept secret but evolving day by day towards a great undertaking which he would eventually be asked to lead. When he was formally told about his appointment, in February 1785, it was an occasion for both rejoicing and sadness, for they would again be separated

The expedition was expected back in mid-1789. Anxiety grew during the summer and autumn. It became clear by the end of the year that something had gone seriously wrong. Adding to the emotional strain were financial worries; the government helped to some extent, but France was going through a series of economic and political upheavals the like of which had never been experienced. When the Milet-Mureau account of the voyage was published in 1797 it was agreed than profits accruing from the sale would go to Mme de la Pérouse, but sales were disappointing. When Napoleon came to power he granted her a pension of 2400 francs and allocated her an appartment at the Château de Vincennes, which she decided not to use.[2] She preferred to live in Paris, where she had moved in 1789 to wait for her husband. She usually

[1] Correspondence relating to this episode in La Pérouse's life was reprinted in N. Barthès de Lapérouse, 'La Vie Privée de Lapérouse', *Bulletin de la Société de Géographie*, pp. 7–30. This romantic story was the subject of a fictionalised account by C. Péru, *Le Mariage de Lapérouse*, Albi, 1947.

[2] Sundry correspondence in AN.M. C7 165 72–89.

stayed with friends or relatives, a sad, dignified figure, living quietly until her death on 4 April 1807.

Paul-Antoine-Marie Fleuriot de Langle[1] was born on 1 August 1744 at the Château de Kerlouet in western Brittany of a noble family with a long tradition of naval service. He joined the navy at Brest in June 1758 and soon found himself in action, sailing in the *Diadème* to the West Indies and being wounded in a battle of Ushant on the return voyage in May 1760. He returned to the West Indies in the *Diadème* in February 1762, escorting a fleet transporting 5000 soldiers to reinforce the defences of Santo Domingo.

On both these occasions he went with the young Toussaint-Guillaume de la Motte-Picquet who was to have a great career in the navy, and it was under his command that Fleuriot de Langle sailed on 22 October 1763 in the frigate *Malicieuse* for a campaign directed against privateers which were harassing French shipping. Peace, however, was near and like all junior officers he went through a period of inaction and concern about his future prospects. He devoted himself to scientific study, for which he was particularly gifted. He nevertheless found a number of opportunities to go to sea – in the *Etoile* to Guiana in May-October 1764, in the storeship *Porteuse* on various short campaigns in 1765–66, in the *Biche* to the Mediterranean in 1766, and in the *Ecluse* for a short campaign in 1769.

He was promoted *garde du pavillon* in 1765 and *enseigne* in 1770. A year later he was served on the *Belle-Poule* where he met La Pérouse. In 1772 he joined the *Dédaigneuse* and in 1775 the *Tserpichore*. His reputation as a mathematician and scientist was growing rapidly. He was elected an associate member of the Académie Royale de Marine at the beginning of 1771 and invited to contribute to the *Dictionnaire de la Marine*. In March 1772 he was appointed secretary of a committee set up to evaluate a new compass devised by the instrument maker Levallois; this was to be the first of a series of commissions of enquiry on which he served. He became a full member of the Académie Royale de Marine in April 1775, and its secretary a year later. Several of his scientific papers, on longitudes

[1] On De Langle, see Fleuriot de Langle, *La Tragique Expédition*; Dunmore and Brossard, *Le Voyage de Lapérouse 1785–1788*, 1985, I, pp. 93–6, 99; Gaziello, *L'Expédition de Lapérouse 1785–1788*, pp. 127–8.

and on lunar distances, were read at meetings of the academy and published. In 1777 he was appointed supervisor of the *cadranerie* which made the navy's compasses.

The American war was beginning and Fleuriot de Langle returned to regular active service. He was promoted to *lieutenant de vaisseau* in July 1778. The Duc de Chartres who was the brother-in-law of Admiral of the Fleet the Duc de Penthièvre had befriended him since the time when they had served together in the *Solitaire* and he invited him to act as the executive officer of the *Saint-Esprit*, a ship of 80 guns, which took part in the Battle of Ushant of 27 July 1778. The French fleet under D'Orvilliers held Admiral Keppel's Western Squadron at bay, but there was confusion on both sides – Keppel was accused of incompetence on the British side and eventually lost his command, while Chartres was criticised for not acting speedily enough in response to D'Orvilliers' signals and thereby preventing the French from exploiting their victory. Chartres returned to Brest and La Motte-Picquet took over the *Saint-Esprit*. No blame was attached to Fleuriot de Langle, however, and he received the Cross of St Louis in November; his protector remained loyal as well and granted him the position of First Gentleman of the Bedchamber with an allowance of 2000 *livres* a year. The life of a courtier did not appeal to him, especially in wartime, and he went back to sea, commanding the *Hussard*, admittedly a mere cutter, escorting coastal vessels between St Malo and Bayonne. He did however capture an English privateer in June 1779, only to be himself captured in July.

After several months as a prisoner he was exchanged, returned to France and obtained the command of the frigate *Aigrette*. In April 1781 he transferred to the *Résolue* and sailed to America. With him went the smaller *Cybèle* which was loaded with munitions for the rebel colonists, and among his passengers were Colonel John Laurens, Washington's aide-de-camp and the son of Henry Laurens, the President of Congress who had been taken prisoner and was being held in the Tower of London. Even more important was Fleuriot de Langle's cargo of gold and silver totalling 4,300,000 *livres* which Louis XVI was sending to help the Americans. The ships arrived at Boston on 25 August, where he met his old friend La Pérouse. Since the latter was shortly after appointed to command the Boston-Newport bases, De Langle served under him for a while, helping to organise convoys for the West Indies. They met again in Martinique in December 1781. In March he took command of the *Experiment* in which he took part in the Battle of the Saints of 12 April.

When the French squadron gathered in Santo Domingo and the Comte de Vaudreuil began to reorganise his forces, Fleuriot de Langle was given the *Astrée* to join La Pérouse and La Jaille for the raid on the English forts in Hudson Bay. It was a hard and difficult campaign, involving careful navigation with inadequate charts through ice-strewn waters and along a rocky coast, and La Pérouse had an excellent opportunity to appreciate De Langle's skill as a navigator. After the raid, La Pérouse sailed to Cadiz while the *Astrée* went straight to Brest where Fleuriot de Langle dropped anchor in December 1782; he received a pension of 1200 *livres* and was promoted *capitaine de vaisseau*. In 1784 he was elected to the Society of the Cincinnati by the United States Congress for his services during the War of Independence.

Still a protégé of the Duc de Chartres, he spent some time at Versailles, but he yearned for a period of rest and for the peace of his country estates in Brittany. He went home and, on 9 December 1783, in Brest, he married Georgette-Marie-Françoise de Kérouartz, the niece and ward of the Comte Charles-Jean d'Hector, who held the rank of lieutenant-general in the navy and had commanded the Brest naval establishments since 1781. Hector, who had chaired Kerguelen's court-martial in 1775, was well aware of what an expedition in distant seas required and would be of considerable assistance to La Pérouse when the voyage to the Pacific was being organised.

When it was officially announced that La Pérouse had been appointed to head the expedition, rumours spread that Fleuriot de Langle had been the first choice. The main source for this is Louis de Bachaumont, a tireless recorder of court gossip, whose *Mémoires secrètes pour servir à l'histoire de la République des Lettres en France depuis 1762* appeared between 1777 and 1789; a letter by the botanist Lamartinière and a similar comment in the *Mémoires du Chevalier de Cotignon*[1] seem to add substance to the claim, but real evidence is lacking. One suspects that there was nothing more to it than snobbery – the feeling among some courtiers that a member of the

[1] Edited by A. Carré and first published in Grenoble in 1974. The reference appears on p. 389.

nobility should have been selected – and gossip twice repeated is still only rumour. There is no indication that De Langle felt that he should have been asked, and indeed he had already served under La Pérouse during the Hudson Bay raid. Furthermore, La Pérouse was the close collaborator of Fleurieu when the expedition was being planned, he worked under Castries, a fellow Albigeois, he was experienced and had proved his quality of leadership on a number of occasions before, and it would have been unreasonable and slighting to look elsewhere for a commander. Both men got on well although their characters were quite different: La Pérouse was plump, ebullient, a southerner who no doubt retained a trace of local accent, whereas De Langle was reserved, somewhat prim and tight-lipped to judge from a miniature portrait.

Both men had to sacrifice the prospect of family life. They had married within six months of each other. Fleuriot de Langle now had a boy whom he had to leave and might never see again. 'I cannot look at a child without thinking of my son,' he wrote to his sister from Macao in January 1787. 'Take all the care you can of my wife and child. My absence constantly increases my love for them'.[1] In March 1785 he had to leave home and start getting the frigates ready. Apart from a brief visit to Paris, he spent most of the time in Brest, assisted by Clonard who was mostly working on La Pérouse's frigate and by the Comte d'Hector with whom he was in almost daily contact.

During the voyage, he wrote to his family whenever the expedition put into a European-controlled port. Family affairs, property matters, these formed the main subject of his letters, but he often expressed concern for the families of his crew. After the drownings in Lituya Bay, on the Northwest Coast of America, he asked his sister to reassure the people of Lannion that no one from there had been drowned.

Physical exhaustion began to affect him after the calls in China and at Manila, and he left the astronomical observations to Law de Lauriston so as to concentrate on the task of navigation through the little-known waters of the north-east. The exploration of the Tartary coast and Kamchatka he found wearying, and the call at Petropavlosvk was too brief to help him regain his strength. Sailing

[1] Quoted by his descendant Fleuriot de Langle in *Colloque Lapérouse Albi 1985*, p. 73.

south towards the Samoan archipelago, with an abrupt change of climate, affected his health and his equanimity. The Langles were at times noted for their sharp temper, and relations between him and La Pérouse clearly became strained. There were differences of opinions on the character of the islanders and on the relatively minor issue of the preservation of drinking water. De Langle was sharp-tongued and insistent over the need to obtain fresh water, even though the watering place was in a small bay the French knew little about. La Pérouse, to avoid arguments, allowed him to go ashore, with tragic results.

Consequently, on 11 December 1787, De Langle went out with a watering party. He apparently had warned La Pérouse that he would hold him responsible should scurvy or some other sickness caused by old putrid water affected his men. La Pérouse kept to the traditional view that water kept in casks eventually improved in quality and that fresh water obtained from some watercourse near the shore was less safe – from the scientific point of view he was wrong, but there was some basis for this old sailors' tale because, especially in Europe, brooks and rivers close to human habitations doubled as outfalls for refuse. As it turned out, on the voyage to Botany Bay the expedition did not suffer from any illnesses that could be blamed on the drinking water.

The frigates found it difficult to come too close to the shore because of the lack of wind, and Fleuriot de Langle had cover quite some distance with the longboats. The watering cove was hidden from the vessels and the tide was ebbing, making it difficult to bring the boats further in. Seven or eight hundred islanders were gathered along the shore, and wisdom would have suggested that the French turn around or wait for more favourable conditions, but time was pressing and Langle was obviously reluctant to concede that la Pérouse had been right in opposing the attempt to get fresh water. Rolling the water casks over the seaweed and water pools was difficult; once the Samoans realised that the French were at a disadvantage, the situation became dangerous. Stones were thrown with a strength and an accuracy that astonished the sailors; some of the muskets had been carelessly handled and the priming was damp, so that several would not fire, and reloading was always a comparatively slow affair, especially in a longboat with men trying to scramble back into them; wielding their few swords or using their muskets as clubs, the French could do little more than fight a desperate defensive action. Fleuriot de Langle was killed, together with Lamanon and ten others. Of the 61 who had set out to get water, only 49 returned, a number of whom were wounded, some seriously.

There were no reprisals. La Pérouse stopped his men running to man their guns. The king had issued clear instructions to treat all native peoples with generosity and La Pérouse, unable to tell which were the attackers and which had been mere bystanders, was not prepared to order an indiscriminate revenge. His conscience, he wrote, called on him to stop. He did, however, reproach himself for having given in to De Langle's insistence. Ordering him not to go ashore would have widened the breach which had begun to develop between the two friends, and relations between them would probably have remained strained for the remainder of the voyage, but at least De Langle would have been saved.

The reason for the attack remains obscure. According to Vaujuas, a member of the expedition, gifts were made to some of the natives and not to others, causing jealousy and resentment. As is often the case in such situations, the Europeans would have found it difficult to identify the leaders and chiefs in such a large and jostling crowd. Other commentators tried to exonerate the islanders: Jacques Moerenhout, a trader from Antwerp who settled in Tahiti and eventually became French consul, reported to the Société de Géographie in 1836 that the attackers were not locals but a group of warriors from Apia who exercised a kind of overlordship over Tutuila and were determined to keep out any interlopers.[1] French missionaries later attempted to question the natives and discover the real motives for the attack, but the participants had long since died, memories fade and above all embarrassment about the whole tragic affair produces evasiveness.[2] The truth is probably less complex. Fear of the strange visitors and a concern that they might be attempting to land and conquer would be perfectly normal reactions to the appearance of the two ships along the Samoan coast, and seizing the opportunity to attack when the white men were at a clear disadvantage would also be understandable. All too often one tries to find complex cultural motives for such sudden attacks,

[1] Mentioned in M. de Brossard's chapter 'Les Hommes', Dunmore and Brossard, *Le Voyage de Lapérouse 1785–1788*, I, p. 96.

[2] An attempt to evaluate the various theories was made by P. Fleuriot de Langle in *La Tragique Expédition*, pp. 232–3.

but one forgets that in earlier times armed strangers landing on an isolated stretch of coast anywhere would have met with a similar response from the locals.

In 1882, the victims' remains were discovered in Aasu Bay, which still bore the name of Massacre Bay. A small monument was erected, surrounded by railings, which visiting French warships kept in good repair. In 1887, Captain Bénier, commanding the *Fabert*, was presented by the local chief with the skull and several bones of 'the great French chief'. Fleuriot de Langle's remains were taken back to France in 1889 and placed in the Church of St Louis in Brest. This church was destroyed during World War II and the cask containing the relics now rests in the chapel of the Ecole Navale near Brest.[8]

*Most of the officers bore a double name. They appear in the following list in alphabetical order by the patronymic most commonly found in the narrative and the records.

Prosper-Philippe d'Aigremont Pépinvast was born in Normandy, the son of a naval captain who had once served in the *Formidable* at the same time as La Pérouse, both being taken prisoner, with La Pérouse wounded, in Quiberon Bay on 14 November 1759. The young man joined the navy as a *garde de la marine* at Brest on 12 March 1778, served in the *Alexandre* from 1 May to 19 October 1778 and in the *Bien-Aimé* from 14 November 1778 to 14 November 1779. Promoted to *enseigne de vaisseau* on 16 February 1780, he joined the *Neptune* a couple of weeks later and sailed as part of Ternay's squadron escorting Rochambeau's troops to America. Aigremont Pépinvast took part in a battle off Bermuda on 20 April and when Ternay's death in December led to a reorganisation of commands, he followed his captain, Sochet-Destouches, onto the *Duc-de-Bourgogne*. La Pérouse, who was commanding the *Amazone* and later the *Astrée* met him on several occasions.

Returning to the *Neptune*, Aigremont Pépinvast was involved in various operations around Yorktown in September 1781, then transferred to the *Glorieux*, taking part in three sea fights before the Battle of the Saints of 12 April 1782 when the *Glorieux* was dismasted. La Pérouse who had helped the *Zélé* to reach Guadeloupe

[8] Brossard, loc. cit.

endeavoured to come to the assistance of the *Glorieux* but contrary winds held him back; as night fell he signalled several other French vessels making their way from Basse-Terre to join him in a rescue attempt, but in the darkness they saw fire across the sea and became concerned that the *Glorieux* was being destroyed. As it turned out, the ship was captured by the British and Aigremont Pépinvast was taken prisoner and sent to England. He was freed and returned to Brest in September 1782; he was given a period of recuperative leave and a grant of 1000 *livres* in consideration of all his belongings being lost with the *Glorieux*. He joined the storeship *Lamproie* on 2 April 1783, stayed with her until 28 May 1784 when he transferred to the *Désirée*, being discharged on 9 August. He received a grant of 800 *livres* for his services during the American War of Independence but saw no further service until the beginning of July 1785 when he was appointed to the *Astrolabe*. He was promoted to *lieutenant de vaisseau* on 1 May 1786. The Cross of St Louis had been promised him on his return from the La Pérouse expedition subject to his services being satisfactory; there is no doubt that he would have qualified for it, but he was struck down by dysentery in the Philippines; he declined the surgeon's help and chose self-cures, including strong stimulants. He died at Cavite on 25 March 1787.[1]

Blondela (sometimes found as Blondelas) is described in the records of the navy at the Archives Nationales as 'an excellent officer with a modesty which makes him quite interesting'.[2] The lack of information about his early years suggests a modest background, probably that of a 'blue' officer who kept at a deferential distance from his aristocratic fellow-officers. He distinguished himself during the American War of Independence, serving from March 1777 to the end of October 1782 almost without interruption, in the *Bien-Aimé*, the *Conquérant*, the *Palmier*, the *Triton*, the *Auguste* and again in the *Palmier*, taking part in nine seafights. The Comte de Vaudreuil had taken him under his protection and ensured that he was accepted into the navy on a permanent basis; on 1 September 1784 Blondela was promoted to *lieutenant de frégate*. He served in the

[1] Much of the information about the careers of La Pérouse's officers was obtained by Admiral de Brossard from service records at the Service Historique de la Marine, and forms the basis of his section in Dunmore and Brossard, *Le Voyage de Lapérouse 1785–1788*, I, pp. 101–25.

[2] AN.M. 4JJ 389, 22:12.

corvette *Levrette* from 29 October 1784 to 25 April 1785, and on 26 June he was granted a pension of 400 *livres*. A fortnight later he was appointed to the *Astrolabe*. He was promoted to *sous-lieutenant de frégate* on 1 May 1786. He was a gifted draughstman and La Pérouse was highly appreciative of the landscapes he drew during the voyage.

Charles-Marie Fantin de Boutin, the son of an administrator in the French Finance Ministry, joined the navy as a *garde de la marine* at Brest and went to sea almost at once in the *Dauphin Royal* in which he served from June to November 1777. Promoted to *enseigne* on 1 April 1778 he joined the *Magnifique* in which he remained until February 1781. He took part in a number of engagements, including the capture of Grenada and the siege of Savannah. He then transferred to the *Sibylle*, part of La Motte-Picquet's squadron and in October to the *Ceres* which had been captured from the English and was recaptured by them on 19 April 1782. He was freed after a few months as a prisoner, returned to France and granted a period of leave, the hostilities having come to an end. He took over command of the corvette *Vigilante* on 10 February 1784 and the transport ship *Désirée* on 28 September. He was discharged at Rochefort on 2 May 1785, appointed to the *Boussole* and arrived in Brest on 15 June. A few weeks earlier he had been made a knight of St Louis. He was promoted to *lieutenant de vaisseau* on 1 May 1786.

Pierre de Brossard joined the *Astrolabe* as assistant pilot. He appears in the muster roll as Pierre Brossard, born in Morlaix. He belonged to a respected Breton family and had sailed for over three years as a *volontaire* during the War of Independence. Fleuriot de Langle soon learned to appreciate his knowledge of astronomy and his reliability and he recommended him for early promotion.[1] He was effectively raised to the rank of *sous-lieutenant de vaisseau* second class from 14 April 1788, but by then the expedition had sailed from Botany Bay on the final stage of the voyage.

Frédéric Broudou was La Pérouse's brother-in-law, Eléonore's older brother. He had sailed on a privateer during the American War of Independence, but was a turbulent and a times violent youth. In 1782 he was arrested for threatening his sister Elzire with a pistol;

[1] Langle to Minister, letter of 25 September 1787, Petropavlovsk.

in 1784 his mother sought his incarceration at Mt Saint-Michel by means of a *lettre de cachet*, a form of warrant that could lead to imprisonment without trial under the Ancien Regime. This drastic move was not acted upon, going to sea under La Pérouse's supervision being a better alternative, and indeed there appears to have been no complaints about him during the voyage. Broudou sailed as a *volontaire*, but justified La Pérouse's faith in him to the extent that he was soon promoted to *lieutenant de frégate* and on 1 August 1786 to *sous-lieutenant de vaisseau.*[1]

Robert Sutton, Chevalier de Clonard, was born on 14 August 1751. One finds a John Sutton from Wexford among the officers of the Walsh Regiment, part of the brigades serving Louis XVI, and it seems likely that the family had Irish ancestry. Robert's father worked for the French India Company and his uncle Jean was one of the company's captains; his mother was still alive at the time the La Pérouse expedition was being organised and lived in Perigord, not far therefore from La Pérouse's home district. Robert de Clonard joined the *gardes de la marine* at Rochefort in 1767 and first served in ships of the India Company: the *Laverdy* in 1768 and the *Duc-de-Praslin* in 1770. He had transferred to the *Etoile* by 1773 when, sailing up the Ganges, he first met La Pérouse who was in command of the *Seine*. Clonard had just been promoted to *enseigne*. He was again associated with La Pérouse in February 1775 when the latter came to the defence of Mahé; Clonard was given the command of the small *Expérience* and was wounded during one of the battles. The two men remained together for much of their time in the Indian Ocean and sailed back to France together in the *Belle-Poule* in December 1776.

In the following year, Clonard received the cross of St Louis and was released from naval service for a time to sail to India in the *Etoile*. In May 1778 he joined the *Saint-Esprit* and took part in the Battle of Ushant. The *Saint-Esprit* was commanded by the Duc de Chartres whose executive officer was Fleuriot de Langle. Clonard stayed with this ship until the end of the year and shortly after took over command of the cutter *Pilote*. Promoted *lieutenant de vaisseau* on 13 March, he carried out coastguard duties until 10 December 1779 when he was taken prisoner. After his release, in 1780, he

[1] La Pérouse to Minister, letters of 17 and 19 September 1786, Monterey, 18 January 1787, Macau, and 25 September 1787, Petropavlovsk.

commanded the *Comte d'Artois* from May to December, and in the following year joined the *Glorieux*, sailing to the West Indies and taking part in the Battle of Tobago of 30 May. He was given the command of the *Diligente* in September, but his ship was wrecked in 1782. He went back to France and commanded in turn the storeships *Guyane* and *Lourde*. On 29 April 1785 he was appointed to the *Boussole* as La Pérouse's senior officer. There is no solid evidence that La Pérouse asked for him specifically, but he had been asked to suggest names and Clonard was a man he knew well and appreciated; their destinies had been linked since their days in the Indian Ocean.[1]

Clonard was promoted to *capitaine de vaisseau* from 1 January 1787. After the death of Fleuriot de Langle in Samoa, he took over the *Astrolabe* for the remainder of the voyage to Botany Bay and sailed as her captain from New South Wales on 10 March 1788. He does not appear to have married; after his death, his property was inherited by his brothers.[2]

Collinet (also found as Colinet). Little is recorded about him, except that he was a native of Rochefort, probably of middle-class origins. He served as an auxiliary during the American War of Independence and for a time under the Comte de Latouche-Tréville, who was also from Rochefort and a friend of La Pérouse. Latouche-Tréville was himself interested in Pacific exploration and had once submitted a proposal to the Minister of Marine, Sartines, for a voyage to the southern ocean; turned down, he sought the advice of James Cook and corresponded with the Englishman; the outbreak of the War of Independence put an end to his hopes.[3] Collinet took part in a number of engagements and was seriously wounded while serving in the *Aigle* in September 1782. He was promoted to *lieutenant de frégate* on 22 November 1782 and granted a pension of 1200 *livres*. He was serving in the storeship *Pérou* in 1783 when illness forced him to seek his discharge. He was later appointed to the *Portefaix* in which he remained until the end of 1784; this vessel

[1] 'He has a knowledge of navigation well beyond his years and his zeal is beyond praise,' La Pérouse had written of him as he returned to France in 1776. (BN, NAF, 9425:227).

[2] File in AN.M. C7 68.

[3] See J. Dunmore, *French Explorers in the Pacific*, Oxford, 1965, I, pp. 250–2, and J. Forsyth, 'Latouche-Tréville and his Proposal to Explore the South Coast of New Holland', *The Mariner's Mirror*, 45, 2, May 1959, pp. 118–19.

was to be renamed the *Boussole* and Colinet was chosen to join the La Pérouse expedition. He was given the rank of *sous-lieutenant de vaisseau* on 1 May 1786 with a pension of 400 *livres*.

Roux d'Arbaud was a student at the Ecole Militaire in Paris when he was selected for the *Boussole* as a *volontaire* – he was formally appointed a *garde de la marine* on 1 January 1786. His promotion to *lieutenant de vaisseau* from 14 April 1788 was something he never knew about, for by then the expedition had sailed from Botany Bay on its final voyage.

D'Arbaud's inclusion brings up the fascinating question of whether Napoleon Bonaparte narrowly missed out on being appointed to the *Boussole*. A book published in 1954 mentions a recollection by another student at the Ecole Militaire, Alexandre-Jean des Mazis: 'Buonaparte was in the mathematics class.... During 1784 the question arose of Mr de la Pérouse's voyage.... Buonaparte would have liked this opportunity of displaying his energy in such a fine enterprise, but Darbaud was the only one selected: they could not accept a greater number of pupils.'[1] The comment is not invalidated by Mazis getting the date wrong. It is not unlikely that the ambitious young Corsican expressed the wish to sail on such a prestigious expedition, but a decision against a naval career had been made at least two years earlier by Napoleon's mother when the youth was at the military school at Brienne and a report from his teachers advised her that he was 'highly suitable to become a naval officer'. There were greater prospects for a young man of his modest background in the army, and the formidable Letizia Bonaparte had made up her mind that a naval career was out of the question.[2]

Charles-Gabriel Morel d'Escures was born at Alençon in Normandy on 3 January 1751. His family were related to Vice-Admiral Comte d'Aché de Serquigny. He joined the navy first as a *volontaire*, and in 1772 served in the *Belle-Poule* when he no doubt met La Pérouse. He entered the Gardes de la Marine school at Brest in 1775, served in the corvette *Boussole* in 1776 and 1777. In July 1777 he was transferred to the *Fendant* and promoted *enseigne* on 1 August. Other transfers followed until 1781: the *Chasseur*, the frigate *Aigrette*, the frigate *Fortunée*, the *Amphion* in which he served from

[1] In P. Bartle, *La Jeunesse inédite de Napoléon*, Paris, 1954, p. 257.
[2] See on this episode, H.N. Williams, *The Women Bonaparte*, London, 1908, I, p. 52.

February 1779 to January 1781, taking part in the capture of Grenada and the siege of Savannah. He rose to *lieutenant de compagnie* in 1778 and *lieutenant de fusiliers* in 1779. He returned to the *Fendant* in May 1781 until April 1782 when he was promoted to *lieutenant de vaisseau* and joined the *Sibylle*, taking over command on 2 January 1783 when her captain, the Comte de Kergariou, was wounded in a battle; three weeks later, set upon by an English vessel, the *Centurion*, and outgunned, the *Sibylle* was captured. D'Escures spent a couple of months as a prisoner and after his release was given the transport ship *Dorade* which he commanded until the end of 1783.

He was appointed to the *Boussole* in July 1785, being granted a pension of 800 *livres*. His services in the recent war had also been recognised by the Cross of St Louis. He was drowned at Lituya Bay, Northwest Coast of America, on 13 July 1786, aged 35.[1]

Gabriel-Jean, Chevalier Dupac de Bellegarde, was born at Bellegarde in the Aude, southern France. He served as a cadet based on the port of Toulon in 1781 and joined the *gardes de la marine* there on 1 June 1782. From 12 November 1782 to 19 June 1783 and again from 13 July 1783 he served in the *Précieuse*. After a period ashore, he joined the storeship *Maréchal-de-Castries*, bound for the Indian Ocean. His ship was at Macao when La Pérouse arrived, and Richery, the *Maréchal-de-Castries*' captain, offered him Dupac de Bellegarde's services to compensate in part for the losses suffered at Lituya Bay; this transfer was effected on 1 January 1787, Dupac joining the *Astrolabe*. He proved himself a useful addition and was to be promoted to *lieutenant de vaisseau* effective from 4 August 1788, by which date the expedition had probably already been lost.[2]

Joseph-Ignace Raxi de Flassan had joined the *gardes de la marine* at Toulon on 1 July 1780; on 29 July he went to sea in the frigate *Flore*, transferring to the *Sultane* on 16 October 1781 where he remained until 24 January 1782. His next appointment came on 1 August 1782 when he joined the *Danaë*; he was discharged from this ship at Brest on 16 June 1783 and returned to his studies, at the completion of which he received a prize of an octant for his achievements in

[1] Langle requested the transfer of D'Escures pension to Vaujuas who came from an impoverished family. Letter to Minister, 25 September 1787, Kamchatka. D'Escures' file is in AN.M. C7 220.

[2] AN.M. C7 29.

mathematics, navigation and astronomy. He served in the *Levrette* from 27 October 1784 until 25 April 1785 and after a brief period of leave was appointed to the *Astrolabe*. He was promoted to *lieutenant de vaisseau* on 1 May 1786, but was drowned at Lituya Bay, Northwest Coast of America, on 13 July of the same year.

Pierre-Louis Guyet de la Villeneuve embarked as a youth in the *Bien-Aimé* which was commanded by François Huon de Kermadec, the uncle of the Kermadec who was to sail with D'Entrecasteaux a few years later on the voyage in search for the lost La Pérouse expedition. A few weeks later, on 1 July 1780, he was formally appointed a *garde de la marine* at Brest. On 1 March 1871 he joined the *Glorieux* and was involved in a number of sea fights: against Admiral Hood off Martinique on 29 April, at the capture of Tobago on 2 June and of St Kitts on 11 January 1782, against Hood's fleet on 25 and 26 January and at the Battle of the Saints on 9 and 12 April – on which day the *Glorieux* was captured and Guyet de Villeneuve taken prisoner. He was freed after a few months and returned to Brest in November 1782. He served in the *Astrée* from 27 January 1783, the *Bayonnaise* from 29 September 1783 to 16 July 1784, and the *Subtile* from 11 August 1784. He had by then been promoted to *enseigne de vaisseau* and he rose to *lieutenant de vaisseau* 2nd class in April 1786. The *Subtile*, commanded by La Croix de Vagnas de Castries, sailed to the East with the *Résolution*, commanded by D'Entrecasteaux. The plan was to meet up with La Pérouse at Macao, but the two expeditions missed each other; D'Entrecasteaux caught up with La Pérouse at Cavite where Guyet de Villeneuve was discharged on 7 April 1787 and transferred to the *Boussole*.[1]

Ange-Auguste-Joseph de la Borde de Boutervilliers was born on 7 July 1766, the third son of the Marquis de la Borde, a prominent financier linked to the Court who was to die on the scaffold during the French Revolution. He joined the *gardes de la marine* at Brest on 11 July 1781 and served until 5 April 1784 in the frigate *Iphigénie*. On 13 June 1784 he served in the *Séduisant* which was decommissioned at Toulon on 1 January 1785. He had already been granted a period of leave and did not return to the navy until May 1785; on 11 July he joined the *Astrolabe*. He was promoted to *enseigne* on 1 January 1786 and lieutenant de vaisseau on 1 May. He was

[1] Letter from La Pérouse to Minister, 25 September 1787, Petropavlovsk.

drowned in Lituya Bay, Northwest Coast of America on 13 July 1786.

Edouard-Jean-Joseph de la Borde Marchainville was born on 26 June 1762, the second son of the Marquis de la Borde and the brother of La Borde de Boutervilliers. He joined the *gardes de la marine* at Brest on 1 June 1776 and served in the *Bien-Aimé* from 18 February to 28 November 1777. Promoted to *enseigne* on 1 April 1778, he sailed in the *Guerrier*, part of the D'Estaing squadron, and took part in the capture of Grenada and the campaign around Savannah of August-October 1779. He was discharged at Rochefort on 28 November and on 14 April 1780 joined the *Bretagne*, commanded by Admiral Du Chaffault, part of the Brest squadron. He later transferred to the *Aigrette* as Fleuriot de Langle's first officer; when De Langle was given command of the *Résolue* he joined him for the campaign to the West Indies and the coast of America, and returned to France in April 1782 in the *Concorde*. After a brief period of leave, he returned to Rochefort to supervise the fitting out of the corvette *Fauvette* which he commanded from 9 November 1783 to 19 November 1784 and in which he sailed to North America. There was little demand for his services as the American war was over, and he had no difficulty in obtaining a period of leave, firstly to see to private affairs, then to travel to England and Holland to further his education – these travels lasted from March to June 1785, at which time he received his appoinment to the *Astrolabe*, this as the result of De Langle's request. He was described as 'gentle and highly knowledgeable in naval science' and had won a prize in August 1777 when completing his studies at Brest. He was promoted to *lieutenant de vaisseau* on 1 April 1786 and was due to receive the Cross of St Louis on 1 July 1787, but he lost his life at Lituya Bay, Northwest Coast of America on 13 July 1786.[1]

Jérôme Laprise-Mouton sailed as senior pilot at 70 *livres* and received a supplementary pay of 20 *livres* for secretarial duties. He had previously served in the *Northumberland*, a prize captured during the American War of Independence. His attention to detail and general reliability were particularly appreciated by the astronomers and officers dealing with observations on land where valuable instruments and stores had to be brought ashore, protected and

[1] Laborde file in AN.M. C7 154.

accounted for. La Pérouse had been given discretion to promote any two men to the rank of *lieutenant de frégate* and he handed one of these two warrants to Laprise-Mouton on 1 May 1786. This rank was equated to that of *sous-lieutenant de vaisseau* following the reorganisation of the navy in 1786.[1]

Jean-Guillaume Law de Lauriston was born at Chandernagor, French India, on 8 September 1766, one of the six sons of Jean Law de Lauriston, a governor of the French settlements in India who had been instrumental in organising and financing the 1769–1770 expedition of the *St Jean-Baptiste* to the Pacific under Jean-François de Surville.[2] Jean-Guillaume returned to France with his family in 1776 and sailed as a cadet volunteer based on Toulon before joining the *gardes de la marine* at Brest on 1 June 1782. He was appointed to the *Solitaire* on 18 August, bound for the North American theatre of war; the *Solitaire* was taken on 6 December by HMS *Ruby* and HMS *Polyphemus* and Law de Lauriston spent some time as a prisoner, returning to Brest in February 1783. He served in the *Téméraire* from 8 March to 14 May, in the *Guyane* from 31 May 1783 to 13 March 1784 and in the *Séduisant* from 15 May 1784 until the end of the year. He was then granted three months' recuperative leave and returned to Brest in May to help get the *Astrolabe* ready for the voyage to the Pacific. He received a grant of 500 *livres* for this work and was formally appointed to the *Astrolabe* from 11 July. He was promoted to *lieutenant de vaisseau* on 1 May 1786.

Law de Lauriston was a wealthy, well-connected young officer who had his own library, consisting of the narratives of the voyages of Byron, Wallis, Carteret and Cook, but he was also serious and hardworking, and appreciated by his superiors. He had served under Clonard in the *Guyane*, sailing to Riga, and had received high praise from his captain. Fleuriot de Langle commented in a letter to Fleurieu written from Macao on 18 January 1787 that he displayed great ability and talent for astronomical observations. In fact the loss of the La Borde brothers at Lituya Bay had put great pressure on De Langle who soon decided to hand over all the astronomical observations to Law de Lauriston.

[1] La Pérouse to Minister, letter of 25 September 1787, Petropavlovsk.

[2] On Law's family and for further sources, see John Dunmore, *The Expedition of the* St Jean Baptiste, pp. 15–8.

Pierre Le Gobien joined the *gardes de la marine* at Brest on 1 June 1782 and within a fortnight sailed in the *Terspichore* where he remained until 18 March of the following year, then transferred to the *Téméraire* where he met Law de Lauriston. The *Téméraire* was decommissioned at Brest on 14 May 1783, whereupon Le Gobien joined the *Nécéssaire*. On 11 August 1784, after only a brief period of leave, he sailed for India in the *Subtile* under La Croix de Castries, the nephew of the Minister of Marine. The *Subtile* joined Bruny d'Entrecasteaux's *Résolution* and sailed with him to Macao where he hoped to join up with La Pérouse's ships. He missed them, however, and D'Entrecasteaux sent the *Subtile* to the Philippines for which the expedition had sailed. In view of La Pérouse's losses at Lituya Bay, on the Northwest Coast of America, Le Gobien, among others, was transferred to his expedition and he joined the *Astrolabe* on 9 April 1787. He was promoted to *lieutenant de vaisseau* second class from 5 March 1788, but the news did not reach him before the expedition sailed from Botany Bay.[1]

Henri-Marie-Anne-Jean-Baptiste Mel de Saint-Céran, the son of a government official, was born at Montauban, not far from La Pérouse's native Albi. He joined the navy as a *garde de la marine* in Toulon in July 1781 and almost immediately went to sea in the corvette *Badine*. He then served successively in the *Bien-Aimé* (1782), the *Eveillé* (1783), the *Etoile* and the *Médée*, being discharged from the latter at the end of 1784 and given three months' leave on grounds of ill-health. On 11 July 1785 he was appointed to the *Boussole* as a *garde*, but was promoted to *enseigne* on 1 July 1786. However, he had been discharged at Manila on 16 April on account of his health. After a period of recovery he embarked in the *Calypso* in 1789 and *Thétis* in 1790; when the latter was at Mahé, a French settlement in India, he remained ashore, it is assumed once more on health grounds.

Pierre-Armand-Léopold Guirald de Montarnal was born on 15 October 1765 at Senergues, near Aurillac in Auvergne. His family was related to the Rességuiers; he was therefore connected with La Pérouse through the navigator's mother. He joined the *gardes de la marine* at Brest in July 1781, sailing at once in the *Robuste* then, at the end of the year, in the *Tourterelle*. A year later, in November

[4] AN.M. C7 176.

1782, he joined the *Diadème* and in January 1783 the *Sceptre*, serving for a few weeks under La Pérouse. The war, however, was ending and the ship was in the process of being decommissioned. Montarnal spent from May to October 1783 in the *Tiercelet* and most of 1784 in the *Nymphe*. Discharged at Brest on 31 January 1785, he enjoyed a brief period ashore before his formal appointment to the *Boussole* on 11 July. He appears on the muster rolls as a *garde*, but provision had been made to promote him to *enseigne*. He was drowned at Lituya Bay, Northwest Coast of America on 13 July 1786.[1]

Anne-Georges-Augustin, Chevalier de Monty (the spelling Monti is also found), was born on 21 September 1753 in a well-connected family. He joined the navy as a *garde de la marine* at Brest on 22 March 1770. He first went to sea in the frigate *Aurore* in May 1772 as part of the squadron commanded by D'Orvilliers. He became a *garde du pavillon* in 1773 and from 1775 to 1778 served successively in the *Zéphyr*, in the *Zodiaque*, once more in the *Zéphyr*, and in the *Dédaigneuse* which captured the English frigate *Active* on 1 September 1778.

On 20 December 1778, Monty joined La Motte-Picquet's *Saint-Esprit* until March the folllowing year when he followed La Motte-Picquet on to the *Annibal* for the expedition to Martinique. It was at this point that his destiny and La Pérouse's crossed, for Ternay had been planning an expedition to the Indian Ocean on which La Pérouse was also to go; however, in January it was learned that Pondicherry, a crucial French base for the Indian Ocean operations, had fallen, while St Lucia in the West Indies had also been lost. It became more urgent to reinforce the French West Indies than to plan attacks on British possessions in India – the war, after all, centered on the rebellious American colonies. La Pérouse in the *Amazone* and Monty in the *Annibal* both sailed to the West Indies. Monty then took part in a series of battles, off Grenada and Savannah, between December 1779 and March 1780. In May 1781 he transferred to the *Indien,* then the *Bretagne* and finally the *Protecteur* in which he sailed to the port of Rochefort where he was discharged in February 1783.

He had been promoted to *lieutenant d'infanterie* in 1778, *lieutenant*

[1] AN.M. C7 137.

de vaisseau first class in May 1781 and *capitaine de fusiliers* in 1782. His final posting was to the *Vénus* in which he served from February to September 1784. He was made a knight of the Order of St Louis on 24 October 1784. He was appointed Fleuriot de Langle's senior officer in March 1785 and went at once to Brest to supervise the preparations. His qualities as a sailor and an organiser had been long recognised by La Pérouse and De Langle, but he was also a gifted astronomer and had won the astronomy prize in his final year at the cadet school.

He was promised the rank of *capitaine de vaisseau* if his services on the La Pérouse expedition came up to expectations. The promotion was granted, effective from 14 April 1788, but by that time he had sailed from Botany Bay as La Pérouse's first officer, having transferred to the *Boussole* after the Tutuila massacre of 11 December 1787. He therefore never knew that he had finally reached that higher grade.[1]

Ferdinand-Marc-Antoine Bernier de Pierrevert, was born at Pierrevert in Provence; his mother was Euphorie de Suffen Saint-Tropez, sister of the famous admiral Pierre-André Suffren Saint-Tropez, a hero of the Seven Years War and the American War of Independence. Several of his relatives were in also naval officers, one of them, Antoine-Melchior, commanding the *Bellone*, being killed in action in India in 1782. Ferdinand joined the *gardes de la marine* at Toulon on 17 February 1778. He served in the *Fantasque* under his uncle and took part in various actions in Grenada and at Savannah. On 1 January 1780 he transferred to the *Solitaire,* was again involved in a series of action, including in Chesapeake Bay. He remained in America until 1782 when he returned to Toulon and was granted a lengthy period of leave to serve in Malta with the Knights of St John of Jerusalem. He had risen to the grade of *enseigne de vaisseau* in 1780 and of *brigadier des gardes* in 1782. He was back in Toulon in February 1785 and asked to be allowed to travel to Brest where he arrived on 8 June; he was then appointed to the *Boussole*. He was promoted to *lieutenant de vaisseau* on 1 July 1786, but was drowned a few days later at Lituya Bay, in Alaska.[2]

[1] There are various references to Monty in AN.M. C1; his personal file is held in AN.M. under ref. C7 219.

[2] AN.M. C7 27.

II. The Surgeons

*La Pérouse had hoped to take with him surgeons who were permanently attached to the navy and who had been trained in the naval medical schools, but their numbers were never adequate for wartime needs. During the American War of Independence, the port of Brest was to send out 708 vessels and had to cope with a series of epidemics (dysentery, typhus, and typhoid) and face the pressures on medical services brought about by the hostilities and the greatly increased activity of the port itself. There were only 91 naval surgeons on the permanent staff at Brest when war broke out; another 57 were based on Rochefort. The balance had to be made up by mobilising surgeons through the *levée* system; even this was insufficient for the navy's needs. When the war ended, a few – a couple of dozen, in fact – were transferred to the permanent staff; the rest were sent back to their home towns or left to fend for themselves. The permanent surgeons were in a privileged position which enabled them to choose easier appointments than La Pérouse could offer, or simply to insist on a well-earned period of leave. However, La Pérouse was able to select the best of the *levée* men for his ships.

Jean Guillou. Not a great deal is known about this man who was probably a young doctor from Brittany. He was conscripted after the American War of Independence broke out and is known to have been serving in the naval storeship *Forte* from 3 May to 14 December 1784. He must have had a successful record prior to this, because he was highly regarded among the local naval medical authorities and was selected by them and approved by La Pérouse and Fleuriot de Langle to join the *Astrolabe* as assistant surgeon. He went on board on 17 July 1785. Fleuriot de Langle expressed his appreciation of his skill and dedication on several occasions, pointing out also that he carried out botanical research when opportunities arose of going ashore.

Simon-Pierre Lavaux (or Lavau) was called up at the beginning of the American War of Independence and joined the frigate *Licorne* on 5 April 1777 as second surgeon. He remained with this ship until the end of June, then worked in Brest hospitals during the severe epidemics of 1778. In 1779 he worked as second surgeon in the *Neptune,* commanded by the Comte d'Hector who was to play a major role in the preparations for the La Pérouse expedition; the *Neptune* formed part of Admiral D'Orvilliers' fleet which was badly affected by epidemics of dysentery and typhus during a 104-day voyage and lost a thousand dead. He was then transferred to the *Aigrette* whose surgeon was ill and one of whose assistants died in the epidemic; the ship has to return to port because there were too few men left to work her.

Lavaux next served in the *Scipion*, then in the *Nymphe*, 26 guns, which fought off HMS *Bienfaisant*, 64 guns, on 19 July 1780. However, on 2 August, the *Nymphe* came up against HMS *Flora* off Ushant and her luck ran out. Her captain was killed and the French ship taken; out of a complement of 290 officers and men, 60 were killed and 80 wounded; Lavaux was also taken prisoner and sent to Falmouth where he tended th French wounded. Freed at the end of the end, Lavaux joined the *Héros* as senior surgeon.

The *Héros* was the flagship of Suffren Saint-Tropez who was sailing for India. He was to remain in the Indian Ocean for three years, taking a leading part in a campaign which cost over 6000 lives, 2300 in battle and the rest from sickness. The *Héros* was involved in this campaign and its aftermath until March 1784, and not surprisingly Lavaux, totally exhausted, tried to obtain a shore appointment, either at Pondicherry or in the Ile de France. He was unsuccessful in this, but Suffren wrote him a glowing testimonial on 18 August 1784: 'Mr Lavau has carried out his duties with distinction. One is fortunate indeed to have such capable men working under one. An appointment cannot be made to reward him adequately, but until an opportunity arises of using his talents, I formally request for him a pension of 600 *livres*.'[1] Technical difficulties prevented his being taken onto the permanent medical staff at Brest, to say nothing of the pressures being exerted by other naval captains on behalf of deserving surgeons during the months which followed the end of the American War of Independence, but Suffren wrote again on his behalf on 25 February 1785, concluding: 'If all the other medical officers had been like him, the fleet would have lost infinitely fewer men.' The pension Suffren had asked for was approved and Lavaux's name was sent to the Minister of Marine, Castries, with recommendations from the senior surgeon Billard and the naval chaplain Fr Camille de Rohan. On 13 April,

[1] AN.M. 3JJ 384.

Lavaux received his warrant as a naval surgeon and instructed to stand by for a new appointment. He formally joined the *Astrolabe* on 17 July 1785.

Like his colleague on the *Boussole*, Lavaux was granted the status of naturalist. He was also promised a pension on his return to Brest. Fleuriot de Langle wrote on a number of occasions to the Minister expressing his appreciation of Lavaux's skill and character, for example from Macao on 18 January 1787: 'I have not lost a single man and have not even anyone sick. I have nothing but praise for Mr Lavaux, my senior surgeon, and Mr Guillou, my second surgeon. Their foresight has greatly contributed to the crew's good health. Happily they have had so far a good deal of leisure. They use this leisure during our calls to increase their knowledge of botany and natural history and to collect items for the royal collection.' La Pérouse echoed De Langle's praise and reported the day before the expedition left Petropavlovsk: 'Mr de Langle and I required Mr Lavaux, who has a particular gift for speaking and understanding foreign languages, to give new evidence of his skill....He succeeded with the utmost patience and after great difficulties to draw up a Gotchy and a Bitchy vocabulary', these being tribes met along the Siberian and Sakhalin coasts.

Lavaux accompanied Fleuriot de Langle to the fatal watering place at Tutuila in the Samoan Islands on 11 December 1787. He sustained a severe head wound and had to be trepanned by his colleague Rollin. How fit he was to continue his duties in the *Astrolabe* is not clear, but his name appears on the list of those who sailed from Botany Bay on 10 March 1788, so it can be assumed that he recovered sufficiently to continue on board for the final stage of the voyage. An alternative would have been for La Pérouse to leave him at Port Jackson and have him repatriated by one of the English vessels, but the French were bound for the Ile de France and that is where Lavaux had once hoped to settle. Had fate not been so much against the expedition, his wish might have been realised.

Jacques-Joseph Le Cor (also commonly found as Le Corre)was born in 1759. In 1771 – that is, at the age of 12 – he was a temporary cadet and endeavouring to enter the Brest medical school; admission was through a competitive entrance examination, a standard French procedure, with the students listed in accordance with their marks and the required number of entrants selected from the highest scorer downward. Le Cor was not successful and tried again each year until 1776 when he was admitted as a student with an allowance of 240 *livres* a year plus his meals. The profession may have had a certain status and the surgeons were not badly paid, but promotion to the higher grades was not easy and death took a heavy toll: out of the 33 hopefuls aged between 10 and 24 who were competing for a place with him, only a few of whom could hope to be accepted until the American War of Independence at last provided some unexpected opportunities, four would die and only three ever reach the rank of senior surgeon – or four, if one includes Le Cor who was promoted posthumously.

Le Cor soon went to sea: in the frigate *Zéphyr* in 1776–77, in the *Boudeuse* in 1777–78, and in the *Henry* in December 1778. He served as a temporary assistant surgeon until he passed the examinations for the grade of assistant surgeon second class in 1779, whereupon he sailed in the cutter *Folkstone* as acting senior surgeon. He was then aged 20.

From 1780 to 1782, he worked as surgeon in the *Ménage*, but when hostilities came to an end he found life more difficult. He seems to have got into financial difficulties, leaving a debt of 800 *livres* due to a goldsmith acting no doubt as a private banker, as was frequently the case with goldsmiths. He was however highly regarded by senior members of the medical corps at Brest and by his teachers. They had no hesitation in agreeing to his request to sail with La Pérouse. He joined the *Boussole* on 17 July 1785 as second surgeon.

Claude-Nicolas Rollin was born at Neufchâteau in Lorraine in 1752 but probably educated at the Paris medical school. He was conscripted as an assistant surgeon for the *Sibylle* on 12 April 1778 and subsequently transferred to the *Ville-de-Paris*. He was soon faced with a vast number of casualties to treat: he was present at the battle off Ushant of 27 July 1778 and in the following year, from June to September, took part in the disastrous combined Spanish and French naval operations off Spain. After a campaign lasting 104 days the *Ville-de-Paris* had lost 61 dead, including two of the nine surgeons, and 560 men had been wounded; returning to Brest in

[1] AN.M. C7:171.

September 1779, the Guichen Squadron of which Rollin's ship was part landed over 8000 sick – and an epidemic spread through Brest, affecting nearly 35000 people and causing 4420 deaths. Rollin avoided being affected by sailing right away in the *Bretagne*, under Du Chaffault.

From January 1780 to March 1781 he worked as senior surgeon in the frigate *Gentille* which sailed to Newport, Rhode Island, to join Ternay's forces. La Pérouse was then in charge of the *Amazone* and the two men met, probably around September-October 1780 before La Pérouse sailed back to Brest. Rollin took part in the Battle of Cape Henry in February 1781, during which HMS *Romulus*, 44 guns, was captured; Rollin transferred to this ship which the following month was in action again at Cape Henry, this time against HMS *London*, 98 guns. Back in Newport, Rollin once more met La Pérouse who had returned from Brest in the *Astrée*. Rollin was still serving in the *Romulus*, which one day under a new name, the *Résolution*, would sail to Macao under D'Entrecasteaux in the hope of meeting the La Pérouse expedition in eastern waters. Rollin remained with the *Romulus* until 19 June 1783, taking part in various operations off the American coast, including the Chesapeake campaign.

He was back in Brest in November 1783 and formally demobilised on 1 January 1784. He could only hope now that he might be successful in getting a position as one of the navy's permanent surgeons. He obtained two valuable certificates, testimonials of his ability and hard work during the American war: one from Billard, the chief surgeon of the port of Brest and one from a senior teacher-demonstrator at the Brest school of surgery. He then travelled to Nancy where he obtained a doctorate in medicine. His services had been recognised and he was listed among those who could be granted at least an honorary position. A specific appointment was not yet forthcoming.

The expedition to the Pacific was by now being planned and La Pérouse put forward Rollin's name. He had stressed to Fleurieu that 'a man of real talent' would be needed for such a long voyage and his proposal seems to have met with no opposition. On 4 June 1785, Rollin's appointment was formalised in a letter from Castries, the Minister of Marine, to Langristin, the commissioner-general at Brest: 'I have been given excellent reports on Mr Rollin, auxiliary surgeon, who sailed in the King's ships throughout the war and distinguished himself by his talents and his behaviour. Mr de la Peyrouse who was in a position to know him and appreciate him in North America has asked me to let him sail with him, and I have been pleased to agree. These various considerations have led me to obtain for Mr Rollin one of the positions of ordinary surgeon currently unfilled at Brest and to have sent to him the warrant I shall forward to you as soon as the Admiral has signed it. You will accordingly add him to the lists at the salary of 1200 *livres* a year starting from the first of this month, and arrange for his appointment as senior surgeon of the storeship the *Boussole*.'[1] Rollin was granted 800 *livres* as an outfitting and equipment allowance and left for Brest at the end of June 1785. He was also promised a pension at the conclusion of the voyage if the mortality rate on the *Boussole* did not during the voyage exceed three per cent. A separate advice of the Minister's decision was dispatched to La Pérouse who was then in Paris.

Rollin's status was enhanced by his being included among the expedition's scientists as a botanist and naturalist. La Pérouse's confidence in him was fully justified; the mortality rate was well below the three per cent figure; when Collignon was wounded at Castries Bay, La Pérouse credited Rollin with saving his arm, and when his colleague Lavaux was badly wounded at Tutuila Bay, Rollin trepanned him. He wrote detailed reports on the natives of Chile, Easter Island, Alaska, California, Tartary and Sakhalin, and in this respect can be regarded among the forerunners of anthropological science.[2]

III. Scientists and Artists

Gérault-Sébastien Bernizet was born at Pézenas, in southern France. Not a great deal is known about him before his appointment on 28 May 1785 as surveyor and assistant to Monneron. He joined the *Boussole* in July and received a salary of 1200 *livres* a year payable, after the first year, to his father in Pézenas: this suggests that he was fairly young and unmarried.

[1] AN.M. C2 108, No. 4.

[2] 'Dissertation sur les habitants des îles de Pâque et de Mowée' (AN.M. 3JJ 387, No. 9); 'Mémoire phisiologique et pathologique sur les Américains' (AN.M. 3JJ 387, 111:7); 'Dissertation sur les habitans de l'île de Choka, et sur les Tartares orientaux' (AN.M. 3JJ 387, 111:8).

Jean-Nicolas Collignon was born in Metz, eastern France, in 1761. He was selected by André Thouin, from the Paris botanical garden, to look after the plants and seeds taken by the expedition, plant and sow as appropriate in places the ships called at, collect new plants from these countries and tend them, and keep a journal. He belonged to a family that had worked as gardeners 'from father to son', as Thouin pointed out. Thouin issued detailed instructions to guide him and Collignon considered himself to be working primarily for him. This loyalty led to an early clash with the botanist Lamartinière who sought to use him as his assistant even as the expedition was being organised in June 1785. La Pérouse saw the danger inherent in such a situation, and avoided it by appointing the botanist to the *Astrolabe* and taking Collignon on board his own *Boussole*. Collignon received 50 *livres* per month and had been granted 600 *livres* prior to his departure to outfit himself for the voyage and obtain the material he required. He was untiring in his endeavours and followed Thouin's instructions to the letter. He was injured in an accident with a firearm off the coast of Korea and partly lost the use of one hand. He did not send instalments of his journal back to Thouin from the various ports of call, so that his notes were lost in the wreck, but he wrote regularly to Thouin and his letters provide some useful information.[1]

Joseph Lepaute Dagelet (the name sometimes appears as D'Agelet, but this is probably a mistaken ennoblement, not unusual at the time) was born at Thonne-la-Long, in the Meuse, eastern France, on 25 November 1751. The Lepaute family was well-known among clock and instrument makers. The young man went to Paris in 1768 to stay with his uncles who were acquainted with the famous astronomer Lalande. Joseph studied under Lalande and showed great aptitude for astronomy. When Lalande was invited to recommend someone for the La Pérouse expedition, he selected Dagelet who had already sailed to southern waters with Kerguelen in 1773–74, had carried out a number of observations and even brought back several rare botanical specimens; furthermore he had

[1] The naturalist Buffon kept in close touch with Thouin and advised him on the botanical work that needed to be done and even in more mundane matters such as Collignon's status on the expedition. Documents and correspondence on this aspect of the voyage are held at the Muséum d'Histoire Naturelle library, Paris, under MSS 882, 1928, 1978 and 1985.

kept clear of the disputes which had plagued that expedition. Dagelet became the youngest member of the Académie Royale des Sciences. When the La Pérouse voyage was being planned, Dagelet was working at the Ecole Militaire and a request had to be made to the Minister of War for him to be transferred to the navy.

Dagelet was not eager to go. His aged parents depended on him for financial help, he had agreed to marry his cousin Henriette Lepaute, and his experiences with Kerguelen had not endeared him to lengthy voyages of exploration. The Minister of Marine, Castries, agreed to pay his parents a pension of 750 *livres* if some misfortune should befall the young man during the voyage. Dagelet anyhow felt that he could not really refuse the appointment. He appears to have been an amiable and serious-minded man whom La Pérouse often praised and who got on well with those who sailed with him in the *Boussole*. His appointment was that of senior astronomer at the not inconsiderable salary of 3000 *livres*; his connections made it relatively easy for him to obtain quality instruments for his work, and he was given the services of Pierre Guéry as his assistant.[1]

Gaspard Duché de Vancy was born in 1756, a grandson of Joseph-François Duché de Vancy (1668–1704), a dramatist and poet of some reputation.[2] He studied under the famous artist Joseph-Marie Vien (1716–1809), one of the founders of neo-classicism and the teacher of Louis David. Gaspard Duché de Vancy, however, spent his early years as an artist at Court, drawing more in the style of Watteau and Fragonard than following the formalised historical compositions which his teacher was working on; he also travelled in the provinces in search of experience and, one suspects, commissions, because although reasonably well connected he seems to have had very little money. He went to Italy and produced several views of Rome and Naples, and in 1784 crossed to London, five of his works being exhibited at the Royal Academy.

Marie-Antoinette is known to have been fond of the young artist and may have helped him to be taken on for the La Pérouse expedition. Vien wrote a letter of recommendation to Fleurieu

[1] G.L. Lepaute, *Notice sur la familly Lepaute*, Paris, 1869, p. 17.

[2] Not a great deal was known about Gaspard Duché de Vancy's background prior to a contribution by Madeleine Pinault, from the Musée du Louvre, whose 'Duché de Vancy, dessinateur de l'expédition de La Pérouse' appeared in *Colloque Lapérouse Albi 1985*, pp. 213–23; this contains a number of interesting anecdotes and a useful short bibliography.

which probably clinched the affair and Gaspard was appointed to the *Boussole* as a 'drawer of figures and landscapes' at a salary of 1500 *livres*; he received an advance of one year's pay before leaving Paris. La Pérouse liked him and praised his talent on several occasions, and also recommended that something be done to ensure his future after the expedition returned to France. A number of his sketches were lost in the wreck, but fortunately those he had completed and was satisfied with were sent to France from various ports of call. Duché de Vancy is listed on the muster roll among those who sailed from Botany Bay in March 1788, but the existence of a drawing at the Musée des Beaux-Arts at Bensançon, attributed to him but clearly made in the early nineteenth century, led some authorities to wonder whether he had left the *Boussole* and perhaps after spending some years abroad during the French Revolution had made his way back to France; this seems however too unlikely to be credible.

Dufresne is something of a mystery. He was well connected and his brother Bertrand, who is far better known, was a counsellor of state and controller general of finance for the ministry of marine and the colonies. He was appointed to the expedition at a late stage, with little enthusiasm on the part of La Pérouse who warned Dufresne's protector, the Minister of Finance Calonne, that the lists were closed and that Dufresne would have to be paid by his ministry; he also pointed out that life on board ship was notable for cramped conditions and a lack of comfort.[1] Nevertheless, Dufresne joined the *Astrolabe* as a supernumerary naturalist on 18 June. His knowledge of natural history appears to have been adequate without being outstanding, although little is known about his studies or his activities in the field of science, but he had the good sense to stay in the background. The circumstances of his appointment – which may have caused some to wonder whether he was not there as some kind of ministerial agent to keep an eye on how things were being run – forced him to remain a loner and he was far from happy on the voyage. As early as 12 February 1786, at Concepción, he asked to be released, saying, 'if you deny me the favour I am seeking I shall consider myself a prisoner on board and compelled

[1] Letter from La Pérouse to Calonne, undated, AN.M. 3JJ 386, 267.

to view the days that will elapse before I can land as moments of the deepest sadness.'[1]

He nevertheless made himself most helpful in negotiations between the natives of Alaska and the French and later in the Gulf of Tartary, and La Pérouse began to appreciate his services and found a useful compromise when the expedition reached Macao: selling the furs the French had obtained on the Northwest Coast proved to be difficult and slow, and he put Dufresne in charge of the negotiations; this saved him time and the French got a better bargain than would have been the case otherwise. Dufresne could therefore be left at Macao without either side losing face. He went ashore on 1 February 1787 and shortly after sailed back to France in the *Maréchal-de-Ségur* taking with him a selection of the best furs for Queen Marie-Antoinette and a detailed report on furs and the fur trade.

Pierre Guéry was born at Aunay-en-Beauce, of a modest family. He was an armourer and clockmaker by profession, who had developed skills in repairing and perhaps making scientific instruments. His appointment as 'second armourer, mechanic and watchmaker' involved him mostly in helping the astronomer Dagelet; it was a good opening for someone of his background, well paid at 60 *livres* per month, plus 400 *livres* paid to him at Paris for his outfit and other requirements, but his letters to his wife, Anne-Louise, who was working as a servant and whom possibly he had only recently married, reveal a lonely and rather unhappy young man.[2]

Jean-Honoré-Robert de Paul, Chevalier de Lamanon (sometimes written La Manon) was born on 6 December 1752 at Salon-de-Provence, southern France, the younger of the two sons of a minor nobleman who had determined that the elder would enter the navy and the other the church. Soon after their father's death, the two brothers forsook these careers and went travelling through Europe and began to study natural history, physics and other sciences – in many respects, they were typical eighteenth-century *philosophes*. They returned to Salon in 1780, the elder brother managing the family estate and taking part in local affairs, while Robert wrote scientific papers and resumed his travels. In Paris he founded the

[1] Letter to La Pérouse. AN.M. B4:319.
[2] Four of these are held at AN.M. B4:319.

Musée de Paris, published further papers, including one in the *Journal de Physique* which was run by the Abbé Mongez with whom he would one day sail in the *Boussole*, and went home once more to Salon to work on a major work, the *Nouvelle Théorie de la Terre*, which he did not complete.

In April 1785, his friend the mathematician and *philosophe* Condorcet wrote to him about plans that were being made for a major expedition to the Pacific Ocean; although he had recently been elected mayor of Salon and his mother pleaded with him not to leave, he went to Paris and persuaded the influential Duc de la Rochefoucauld to urge Fleurieu to accept him for the position of naturalist.[1] He succeeded but argued over the amount he should be paid, claiming that it should equal to what Dagelet was to receive; Fleurieu tactfully suggested that it was infra dig for a gentleman to be paid an annual salary and proposed a single grant of 12,000 *livres* for the voyage, a quarter of which would be paid on appointment – since this was equal to the 3000 *livres* Dagelet was to receive, the compromise was a neat one; it furthermore pleased Lamanon's mother, since technically her son was not being taken on as part of the staff and could leave the expedition and come home from any port of call. He joined the *Boussole* as a physicist, meteorologist, mineralogist and botanist.

Lamanon was not an easy man to deal with, and a number of clashes arose between him and La Pérouse. Partly this was due to the problem any captain faces when he has scientists on board who want to spend as much time as possible working ashore. In part also, the strains were caused by a fundamental difference of opinion between the philosopher and the realist; La Pérouse had little time for the liberal views of the scientists and *encyclopédistes* who believed that man was innately good and that institutional structures had a corrupting influence; Lamanon, on the other hand, defended the Rousseauist view that man in a primitive state retained his natural goodness, even when La Pérouse drew his attention to the wretched state of the natives they met. When Lamanon was killed in Samoa on 11 December 1787, La Pérouse commented, with a mixture of despair and irritation: 'I am a thousand times more angry with the philosophers who praise the savages than with the savages themselves.' But Lamanon's depth of knowledge, insatiable

[1] Letter of 25 April 1785, AN.M. 2JJ 103.

curiosity and boundless energy cannot be questioned. He was 'without doubt one of the most interesting figures among the expedition's scientists.'[1]

Joseph-Hughes de Boissieu de Lamartinière (at times written La Martinière) was born on 26 January 1758 at Saint-Marcellin in the Dauphiné region of France, the ninth child of a doctor and local councillor. The name of Lamartinière is one which, as in the case of La Pérouse, was added to his family name when he left home for further studies; he qualified as a doctor at the Montpellier medical school, but found traditional medicine too restricted by hidebound attitudes for his enquiring mind. He began to specialise in botany and moved to Paris where he continued his studies under the notable botanists Antoine de Jussieu and André Thouin. When La Pérouse approached the Comte de Buffon for names of suitable naturalists on 1 May 1785, the latter suggested Lamartinière and another young botanist Du Bosc d'Antic; the latter decided not to go on the expedition, and Fleurieu announced Lamartinière's appointment on 21 May.[2] He was paid 2400 *livres* a year.

Lamartinière was energetic and indeed impatient to start work: as soon as he arrived at Brest he began scouring the countryside for signs of any unusual vegetation; he was sardonic about the plant and flower artist Prévost the elder's absent-mindedness and lethargy; he wanted to organise things in his own way and take over Collignon as his assistant. La Pérouse avoided clashes by appointing Lamartinière to the *Astrolabe* and Collignon to his own *Boussole*. It was only the first of a series of tense situations which La Pérouse had to deal with – his problems in this respect were encountered by most other leaders of such expeditions, but it can be said that La Pérouse had fewer of them to trouble him than the average naval commander.[3]

Louis Monge, born at Beaune, was the younger brother of Gaspard Monge who was soon to acquire fame as a mathematician and

[1] Gaziello, *L'Expédition de Lapérouse 1785–1788*, p. 146.

[2] The interesting and somewhat romantic background to Lamartinière's selection is described by Bruno Guirimand, in 'Lamartinière, Bosc d'Antic et Madame Rolland', *Colloque Lapérouse Albi 1785*, pp. 359–63.

[3] See the article by H. Cordier, 'Deux Compagnons de Lapérouse [Lamartinière and Clonard]' in *Bulletin de la Section de Géographie*, XXXI, 1916, pp. 54–82, reissued as an offprint.

Minister of Marine. Louis was equally talented, rapidly gaining a reputation as an astronomer and, like Dagelet, a professor of mathematics at the Ecole Militaire in Paris, but his health was very indifferent. La Pérouse requested his release from the Maréchal de Ségur, Minister for War, so that Monge could join him on his expedition as astronomer sailing in the *Astrolabe*. Monge was enthusiastic enough, but his health could not stand the strain of the voyage and the discomforts of life on board ship; he became so unwell during the first couple of weeks that La Pérouse and De Langle had little difficulty in persuading him to leave the expedition at Tenerife and await an opportunity to sail home.

Jean-André Mongez (sometimes found as Mongès) was born in 1751, the younger brother of Antoine Mongez, a prominent archeologist, member of the Académie des Sciences and eventually political activist. Jean-André was a canon regular attached to the church of Sainte Geneviève in Paris, but in effect a savant, specialising in ornithology, entomology and chemistry and a member of a number of learned societies, including the Société d'Histoire Naturelle and the regional academies of Rouen, Dijon and Lyons. In addition he was the editor of the *Journal de Physique*, at the time also known as the *Observations sur la physique, sur l'histoire naturelle et sur les arts*, a title that more accurately reflects the wide range of interest it covered. He was taken on the *Boussole* as chaplain and physicist, being paid 600 *livres* a year in each capacity. On 17 June 1785, prior to his taking up his position, he was appointed a corresponding member of the royal botanical gardens – the Jardin et Cabinet du Roi – which was headed by the celebrated naturalist Buffon. The warrant was issued as 'an honour which Bro. Mongez deserves as much for his attitude and his devotion to duty as for the depth of his knowledge in all branches of natural history [which will enable him] to carry out during the course of the voyage the research outlined to him by the Comte de Buffon and send him back the various items he will have been able to collect.'[1]

Paul Mérault de Monneron was born on 29 February 1748, the son of Antoine de Monneron, a lawyer and salt tax inspector of Annonay in the Vivarais region and of Barbe Catherine Arnaud who was related

[1] AN. O 1:128, Secretariate for the Royal Household, 1785, f. 164–5; and AJ xv 510, item 372.

to the great Dupleix, governor-general of French India. He was one of their twenty children, several of whom attained considerable prominence. One of his brothers, Charles, entered the service of the French India Company and became a member of the *Conseil Supérieur* of Pondicherry; another, Pierre-Antoine, sailed with Surville on the *Saint Jean-Baptiste* expedition of 1769–70; four of them, including Pierre, eventually became deputies to the National Assembly.[1]

Paul de Monneron was educated at the Mézières school of engineering and qualified as a military engineer in 1770, serving at Briançon and Saint-Omer in France before going to Guadeloupe at the request of its governor, the Comte d'Arbaud, who expressed his complete satisfaction with his energy and ability. This led to Monneron, who held the rank of captain in the corps of engineers, being 'lent to the navy' in May 1782 by the Minister for War, the Marshal de Ségur, for the raid into Hudson Bay. Monneron joined the *Sceptre* under La Pérouse at Santo Domingo. He displayed great skill during the landings and in the attacks on Forts York and Prince of Wales and became a close friend of La Pérouse who sought his services at an early stage for the Pacific voyage. La Pérouse told Fleurieu that Monneron was eager to travel to new parts of the world and would have liked to stay in Hudson Bay to study the Eskimo population.

Monneron shared in the planning of the expedition, going to London in April 1785 to obtain up-to-date information on the treatment and prevention of scurvy, and to obtain certain scientific instruments unavailable in France. He gained the friendship of the artist John Webber, who had sailed in the *Resolution* on James Cook's third voyage, and he also became acquainted with Sir Joseph Banks who showed himself kindly disposed and helpful towards the French undertaking.[2] Monneron was formally appointed as *ingénieur en chef* on 28 May and joined the *Boussole*. He planned to leave the expedition at the Ile de France when the ships were on their way home and make his way to India where his family had important commercial connections.

[1] On the Monneron family, see John Dunmore, *The Expedition of the St Jean-Baptiste to the Pacific 1769–1770*, London, 1981, pp. 8–9, which lists several studies on them and the world of trade and finance in France and French India.

[2] Monneron's role and the early preparations for the La Pérouse expedition have been studied in considerable detail by Catherine Gaziello and form the major part of her invaluable *L'Expédition de Lapérouse 1785–1788*.

Guillaume Prévost joined the *Astrolabe* as botanical artist at the salary of 1200 *livres* and was at least an acquaintance, if not a friend, of the botanist Lamartinière. He seems to have been a strange man, enthusiastic at first, then withdrawn and morose: 'very absent-minded', commented Lamartinière.[1] He found that he was expected to help with drawings of insects, birds and fishes, but refused, keeping to plants and flowers which were his speciality. Lamartinière in despair drew some of the animals himself although, as he wrote to Fleurieu, 'I have never used a pencil in my life, but Mr Prévôt having continually refused to drawn any insects, fishes or birds...I have been forced to imagine that I could draw.'[2]

His nephew Jean-Louis-Robert, son of a well-known painter of flowers and similar still lives, joined the *Boussole*. It would appear that the father had been appointed to the expedition, but decided not to go. Jean-Louis-Robert, known as 'Prévost the Younger' or 'Prévost the Nephew', was quite young and as eager as his uncle was sulky, and he was kept busy drawing natural history specimens collected by the naturalists. Like his uncle, he was paid at the rate of 1200 *livres* a year, a considerable sum for one so young.

Claude-François-Joseph Receveur was born on 25 April 1757 in a farming family of Noël-Cerneux, not far from the Swiss border. One of his brothers was also a priest, the other became mayor of his village; a cousin of his taught theology at Besançon and another relative was the well-known Fr Parrenin, a Jesuit missionary who died in Pekin in 1741. After a brief period of army service, Joseph Receveur entered the Franciscan order, then joined the Paris Friars Minor as Brother Laurent. He began to devote himself to natural history and read a number of paper to the Académie des Sciences. Between 1776 and 1780 he undertook a number of scientific tasks for the naval service which earned him a bonus of 1500 *livres*.[3]

Fr Receveur was appointed to the *Astrolabe* in July 1785 as chaplain and botanist at the rate of 50 *livres* per month in each capacity, but received one year's pay in advance in Paris for his outfit and

[1] In a letter to the King's Gardener André Thouin. Bibliothèque du Muséum d'Histoire Naturelle, MS 1928:2/30.

[2] AN. AJxv 511:416/ 2.

[3] The major source on Fr Receveur is A. Gauthier, Le Père Receveur, aumonier de l'expédition La Pérouse à bord de l'*Astrolabe*', *Courrier des Messageries Maritimes*, 40, May-June 1974, pp. 24–34. His file is held at AN.M. ref. C7 270. An active Père Receveur Commemoration Committee now exists in Australia.

equipment. Energetic and uncomplaining, Fr Receveur was a popular member of the expedition who earned the praises of both captains during the voyage. He was wounded at Tutuila, Samoan Islands, in the attack of 11 December 1787 and is generally believed to have died of his wounds in New South Wales, becoming the first Frenchman to be buried on Australian soil. The precise cause of his death, however, remains open to argument.[1]

Jean-Baptiste Barthélémy de Lesseps was born at Sète on the Mediterranean on 27 January 1766 in a family of diplomats – his father was then French consul-general at Hamburg and soon after moved to the same position at St Petersburg, and his uncle was the king's representative in the Austrian Netherlands. Barthélémy's own nephew would one day acquire world fame as the builder of the Suez Canal and the originator of the Panama Canal. He had just arrived from Moscow with despatches when he was appointed to the expedition as 'Russian interpreter'. La Pérouse and Fleurieu had originally planned to invite a Russian naval officer to join the expedition to ensure there were no difficulties when the French called in Kamchatka and were sailing in waters where Russia had major interests, but they realised that this would make their plans too public at an early stage and they endeavoured instead to find a former employee of a Russian family or of the Russian embassy in Paris. Their discreet enquiries, even involving the head of the police, Jean Le Noir, were unsuccessful, so the Minister of Marine, Castries, suggested the young De Lesseps who spoke fluent Russian. He was given the status of vice-consul with a salary of 1500 *livres* a year and joined the *Astrolabe*.[2]

He was a pleasant and popular shipboard companion, who tried to make himself useful although he had little knowledge of ships or natural history. He left the expedition at Petropavlovsk on 29 September 1787 with a copy of La Pérouse's journal, with letters and reports, and a letter addressed to the Minister in which the expedition's leader praised Lesseps for all the help he had given him.[3] The journey across Siberia and Europe was a real epic, faced as the young man was with primitive roads and tracks, the enormous

[1] On his state of health prior to his death at Botany Bay and the circumstances surrounding it, see Appendix, pp. 564–9.

[2] AN.M. 3JJ 389, 22, and Archives de Brest 1A 47:14.

[3] Letter of 27 September 1787 from Kamchatka.

distance, the harsh climate, and a half-civilised and badly policed empire, but he succeeded, arriving at Versailles on 17 October 1788; we owe him the survival of many of the expedition's most important documents. He was presented to the king by La Luzerne, Secretary of State for the Navy, and the narrative of his travels was ordered to be published at the public expense – it appeared in 1790 and was promptly translated into English, German, Italian, Dutch and Swedish. When the D'Entrecasteaux expedition was being prepared to look for the lost ships, De Lesseps wrote a lengthy and detailed report to assist the searchers.[1]

De Lesseps resumed his diplomatic career. In 1794 he was embassy secretary at Constantinople, but was interned when Napoleon invaded Egypt. In 1802 he was sent to St Petersburg, then to Moscow where the Maréchal de Lauriston, a cousin of Guillaume Law de Lauriston who had been lost with the *Astrolabe*, was ambassador. War and the French army's retreat from Moscow forced his return to France. He subsequently was posted to Lisbon. When Patrick Dillon brought back to Paris the first relics of the expedition which he had found at Vanikoro, De Lesseps, by then an old man, tearfully identified them.

THE SHIPS

The expedition was planned at a time when France believed that England was contemplating her own expedition to the Alaska coast. It was therefore important to plan quickly and in secrecy an approach to a major voyage of exploration which was bound to create problems for those officials involved in the preparations who were not let into the secret. Thus, the ships were selected and work on refitting them begun without the port commander at Rochefort, where these activities were proceeding, being told of their purpose.

The Minister of Marine, the Maréchal de Castries, issued the first instructions[2] without even telling La Pérouse that he had done so.

[1] AN.M BB4 992. Lesseps' personal files are held at SHM (Personnel) and at the Archives du Ministère des Affaires Etrangères (Personnel:45). See also Hélène Richard, *Le Voyage de Dentrecasteaux à la recherche de Lapérouse*, Paris, 1986, p. 50.

[2] AN.M, 3JJ 386, No. 2, p. 94.

This was soon put right, and La Pérouse went to Rochefort, returning on several occasions to check on progress, but still unable to tell the port commander anything, a situation which he found very embarrassing because the commander, Latouche-Tréville, was a friend of his and the captain of the *Hermione* which had sailed under his orders in America, taking part in the engagement of 21 July 1781 off Cape Breton. It was more than merely embarrassing: it impeded the free and open discussion of the modifications which La Pérouse wanted carried out on the two ships allocated to him for his voyage.

What La Pérouse did not want was the kind of ship used by Kerguelen in 1773–74 – the *Rolland*, of 900 tons – which had proved totally inadequate for coastal surveys. Castries and Fleurieu both shared this view, and James Cook had proved, years before, that beauty and and imposing appearance were far less important than manoeuvrability and space below deck. On 6 March 1785, the Minister selected the *Portefaix*, a storeship or *flute* of 450 tons, and a few days later the *Utile*, a transport vessel or *gabare*, of 350 tons.[1] The *gabare* was well adapted for the loading and transport of bulky goods, having no 'tween-decks; this was a drawback in a long voyage where cargo was not being carried, so work began on restructuring the *Utile* to provide cabins and storerooms. It was also necessary to protect the hull against worms in warmer seas and ice in northern latitudes, so plans were made to strengthen it and to have it studded, in preference to copper-sheating it, as La Pérouse worried that the copper sheets might be ripped off by ice floes. Studding involved nailing the entire area exposed to the sea with flat-headed tightly positioned nails. The quantity of nails required was not easily obtainable at Rochefort, especially as secrecy was being maintained and time was pressing. The officials involved found it hard to understand what the whole purpose of the work really was, and some of the nails were either too long or too short.

It soon became clear that the strengthening and restructuring of the *Utile* would add considerably to the weight and so reduce the *Utile*'s draught that she threatened to become unmanageable. Sketch plans showed that if a 'tween-deck was to be constructed to accommodate officers and men, portholes would have to be situated close to the ceiling and even then they would be no more than

[1] Archives de la Marine, Rochefort 1 A:59, 89 and 92.

a foot above the waterline. No lights at all would be acceptable for a short voyage – to America, for instance – but La Pérouse who knew what was being contemplated realised that life below decks would soon become dangerously unhealthy if air could not circulate, especially in the tropics. The port officials looked helpless in front of a problem they could not understand, and were relieved when the *Utile* was abandoned. The *Portefaix* sailed from Rochefort so it could be re-equipped in Brest, where naval stores and facilities were far more extensive, while the search for a new second ship was set in motion.

A decision was made to look for a vessel comparable to the *Portefaix*. The choice fell on the *Autruche*, a storeship of 450 tons built in 1781, which had recently sailed to St Pierre and Miquelon near Newfoundland, and was about to sail for the Baltic.[1] She was in fact very similar to the *Portefaix*, and work on both ships could proceed much more expeditiously because much of the work that needed to be done was a mere matter of duplication. Time was beginning to press, for the secrecy insisted upon at Rochefort had resulted in too much time being wasted, and the abandonment of the *Utile* had compounded the problem. Work began on the *Autruche* in Brest on 21 April; by the time the *Portefaix* joined her, on 13 May, she was fully studded and only repairs and outfitting were needed. Secrecy anyhow was no longer necessary, although details of the proposed campaign were not made widely known.

The Comte d'Hector appointed Morel d'Escures, who had already been selected for the voyage, to supervise work on the *Portefaix*. The Rochefort engineer, Pennevert, who arrived with her, now realised the importance of the proposed expedition, and although it had been thought that he could be appointed to join the staff of one of the two ships, it was soon apparent that some of the work he had carried out needed doing again: what might have adequate for a crossing of the Atlantic or a voyage to the Indian Ocean would not do for a three to four-year circumnavigation. Pennevert was sent back and Hector ordered much of the work to be done again. However, although he had written to the Maréchal de Castries about the difficulties he was encountering, he soon wrote again to reassure the Minister that work was progressing

[1] Letter from port commander the Comte d'Hector to Minister, 6 April 1785, AN.M. 296 AP, 8.

well: 'Have no worries, My Lord, about what is being done to advance work on [the *Portefaix*] to the stage already reached with the *Autruche*. I am conscious of the care and attention these two ships require; I am seeing to this work with even more care than if I was going to command the expedition myself.'[1]

The galleys were to cause the most problems. English-made cooking stoves were provided for each ship, but the requirements of French cooks were not the same as those of Royal Navy cooks. Bread is an important item of French diet, and French bread requires a special approach. In spite of alterations made by a skilled Paris artisan, the loaves that came out were either burnt or undercooked. Furthermore, scientists on the expedition would have their own needs, for experiments or preserving activities of various kinds. Hector realised that there was insufficient time to modify the stoves and test them properly. Another requirement was a distilling machine to supply drinking water from sea water. Space and the risk of fire, as well as an inordinate consumption of firewood, were problems which needed to be dealt with urgently.

A distilling machine had been invented by the Frenchman Poissonnier in 1763 which was widely used in the French navy.[2] Langle suggested to Hector that they endeavour to combine it with a French traditional galley stove. Cautiously, Hector kept the Minister informed, in case the experiment ended in disaster and caused a fire: 'Mr de Langle is constructing a galley on board the *Autruche*, with which a cucurbit will be combined. I am waiting for it to be completed to compare its effectiveness with that of the English stove... The galley will not be set up on the *Portefaix* until Your Lorship has made a decision.'[3]

As it turned out, Langle's arrangements turned out to be a complete success. The cooking structure took up less space than the complicated English stove; it could be combined with the Poissonnier distilling machine, saving firewood. Castries authorised the installation of a similar stove and distilling machine on the *Portefaix*.

[1] Comte d'Hector to Minister 16 May 1785, Archives de Brest 1 A 165:473. The problems encountered by the unfortunate Pennevert as a result of insufficient informative and the need for secrecy are outlined in Gaziello, *L'Expédition de Lapérouse 1785–1788*, pp 96–101.

[2] Pierre-Isaac Poissonnier, chief naval surgeon. La Pérouse had sailed in the *Six-Corps* in which this cucurbit had been tested and he had been impressed by it. Archives de Brest 1 A 46:361 and 1 A 165:515.

[3] Letter of 30 May, Archives de la Marine, Brest, 1E 215.

Tests carried out on 17 June removed all doubts about the Langle scheme, and the English stoves were sent on to Le Havre to be modified at leisure and installed on other ships if they proved satisfactory.

Langle was particularly concerned about the quality of drinking water on his ship. He did not share the old traditional view that water taken on board at the port of departure, however old, was better than fresh water found on some distant shore. La Pérouse was a traditionalist who backed his opinion by pointing out that no one on board the ships had fallen ill as a result of drinking water taken on board many months earlier. His view was that sediment fell to the bottom, leaving the water quite pure. Langle, who was of a more scientific bent, was interested in chemical reactions and the benefits of distillation. Both men were to argue once more over drinking water when they were at Tutuila, in the Samoas, and Langle, determined to get fresh water from a small watercourse ashore, paid with his life for what La Pérouse considered pig-headedness.[1]

Another of Langle's concerns was a workable windmill to provide the flour needed daily for the crews. Flour perished quickly in the hold and it was soon attacked by rats; and when the French called at ports run by Europeans, they expected to buy mostly wheat and other grain, and not much flour. Grinding wheat was a slow and cumbersome task, difficult to carry out at all when the weather was bad. Langle saw to the installation of windmills on the poop-deck of each ship. A spare was taken as well, which La Pérouse gave to the Spanish missionaries at Monterey.

New names had to be found for the two ships. They were no longer storeships carrying supplies to and from French ports, but royal units which were to show the flag in many parts of the world. *Portefaix* – which means 'load carrier' or 'stevedore' – may have been suitable when the ship was first commissioned, but it would hardly do for one of the King's ships. *Autruche* – or 'ostrich' – was scarcely more dignified. New names were chosen: the *Portefaix* was to become the *Astrolabe*, and the *Autruche* the *Boussole*. Then, for a reason that remains obscure, and may be no more than a clerk's original error, the names were reversed in a note dated 26 June. The *Boussole* as we know it is the former *Portefaix*, and the *Astrolable* the

[1] See letter from La Pérouse to Fleurieu, 7 February 1787, Botany Bay.

former *Autruche*. This is of no particular importance, except when one reads documents made out before 26 June. The change becomes apparent in the sketches prepared for the decorations planned for the two ships. The wooden sculpture designed for the *Boussole* shows the French crest with three fleurs-de-lis flanked by two cherubs busying themselves with navigational instruments – but the sketch is labelled as being for the *Astrolabe*.[1] A similar reversal occurs in the more simple design proposed for the second ship: the *Astrolabe* had merely the French crest, and again this is shown as a requirement for the other vessel. The carvings are correctly labelled in the 1797 Milet-Mureau edition of the Voyage. The sculptures were made at Brest in pine and lime-tree wood, and cost 332 *livres* 15 *sols*.

Boats were required for a variety of purposes, such as raising or setting anchors, inshore exploration, going ashore or upriver. Particular care was needed for a voyage of exploration in little known areas. The Minister had two pilot boats ordered, of the kind used by pilots at Bordeaux in the Gironde estuary. New ones were obtained and sent to Rochefort, where one was placed aboard the *Portefaix* and the other despatched to Brest with a crew of five men under the orders of a river pilot. The Comte d'Hector was impressed by it, until he realised how heavy it was; it simply could not be hoisted on board with the other small craft he was assembling. Fourteen small boats were finally built or purchased for the expedition, although it seems that La Pérouse took only ten.[2] Each of the ships took a longboat, a smaller ship's boat, a 'Biscay boat' and a yawl, plus a number of small boats of various types, including a Biscay boat, to be assembled later on the voyage.

The Biscay boats had space for two masts, the prow and stern were pointed and raised; one of the masts was set in straight, the other sloped. They were reputed to be highly manoeuvrable, used by fishermen and others along the Atlantic coast, and adaptable in a number of situations. As it turned out, they proved disastrous: as Catherine Gaziello points out, it was the Biscay boats which were wrecked at Lituya Bay, being impossible to control once they

[1] AN. M. B4:319.

[2] This is indicated in a letter from Lesseps to D'entrecasteaux when the search for the lost expedition was being mounted: '[it seemed to M. Hector that] in surch an undertaking it was better to have more than to be short of what was necessary'. Archives de la Marine, Brest, 1A 165:447.

became swamped, whereas the small standard ship's boat, even though similarly swamped by the swirling water near the pass, struggled through.[1]

La Pérouse also took what he called a 'Bermuda boat', a decked craft of 18 tons, to be assembled on the voyage when the need arose. He had seen such boats on his expedition to Hudson Bay, small sloops with a large triangular sail and standing bowsprit, which were fast and manoeuvrable, and particularly useful in an emergency when it might be necessary to send out for assistance. The design was not known at Brest, and La Pérouse had to sit down with Langle to jog each other's memory and draw what they wanted.[2] Fortunately, they were advised by a skilled designer, Guignace, and a boatbuilder, Forfait, and together they got their Bermuda sloop made, each piece being numbered and stored for easy reassembling when required.

The French were naturally anxious to take with them the most up-to-date navigational instruments available. There was in this field a clear, but not unfriendly rivalry between Great Britain and France, the two main naval and sea trading powers of the time. La Pérouse and Fleurieu were in a difficult situation, insofar as they wanted to organise an expedition which could favourably be compared with what James Cook had achieved, without formally asking the English authorities for their advice – for otherwise it could become apparent that French successes, when they came, were due, at least in part, to their rivals' knowhow.

This is not to say that French scientists were less competent or not as active as their British counterparts: what mattered was to gain the benefit of the latest knowledge gained by English sailors.

Paul Monneron, who spoke good English, was chosen to travel to London to seek additional information at first hand about James Cook's last voyage and especially about the latest antiscorbutics. Cook had been successful in keeping at bay the dread scourge of scurvy, and it was a sensible humanitarian motive that sent Monneron off to England in early April 1785 to find out what he could about the great navigator's methods from someone who had sailed with him. There were a number of conflicting theories about scurvy, the true cause of which, an insufficiency of vitamin C, was not

[1] Gaziello, *L'Expédition de Lapérouse 1785–1788*, p. 109, n.155.
[2] Ibid., p. 110, n.158.

finally determined until the early twentieth century. Monneron's mission to London, although unofficial and not publicised, was in every way laudable – and a valuable by-product would be information about the best scientific instruments to take, how to deal with the various native peoples encountered, and the trade goods these preferred. As we shall see, although the British government kept aloof, Monneron was made welcome in London and received a great deal of assistance.

To begin with, he contacted, not a naval officer, but John Webber (1750–1793), the portrait and landscape painter who had sailed with James Cook on his last voyage. Monneron easily befriended him, gaining his confidence and his support by asking him to paint his portrait. No artist, in the competitive world of late eighteenth century portrait painters, could resist such a commission. On 11 April he wrote his first and most detailed report to La Pérouse. 'I think what should be taken is what the English call malt: it is an oat flour used in the process of brewing beer. The *weetwort* mentioned by Clerke (or beer malt) was made on board as the need arose.'[1]

In fact, James Cook's success in preserving good health among his crews was more the result of common sense, attention to detail, the experience of a lifetime spent at sea and good luck than deductive scientific reasoning. As J.C. Beaglehole comments, 'If he had read Lind's *Treatise of the Scurvy*, of which the second edition, published in 1762, would have been close enough to his hand, he would have embraced every opportunity to accumulate lemons. He never mentions lemons, or Lind; and among the antiscorbutic substances experimentally placed in his ships by the Admiralty, it is no wonder that he thought meanly of lemons and oranges from which the unsuspected vitamins had been assiduously boiled out; he preferred even the wort, 'the inspissated juice of malt', which certainly was no cure.... Cook could carry out no chemical analysis, but his experience was enough.'[2] Although he paid little attention to the fruit itself, he did have with him small quantities of

[1] Monneron's letters and reports are held at the Archives Nationales, Marine, Dépôt du Service central hydrographique, 2JJ 102 (Fleurieu documents) and 3JJ 388 (Scientific papers relating to La Pérouse). Monneron's stay in London is extensively described in Gaziello, op.cit., with a number of his letters to La Pérouse reprinted in her Appendix VI.

[2] J.C. Beaglehole, *The Life of Captain James Cook*, London, 1974, pp. 703–4.

lemon juice supplied by the Admiralty, but this was but one of the items supplied to him, and he paid no particular attention to it.

Nevertheless, James Cook had achieved results beyond anyone's expectations. A sailor's life was a cheap commodity in the eighteenth century, and few captains would feel too much concern about those who fell victim to scurvy or some other disease and had to be, in John Masefield's colourful term, 'dumped overboard' – but, human feelings aside, no captain can manage a ship when most of his crew are sick or dying. Scurvy was a nightmare on a long voyage, the 'plague of the open sea', and once it exceeded the expected norm, disaster followed. That norm, for the merchantment of the French India Company on a two-year return voyage to the East, was 20%.[1] When a larger proportion than this fell victim to scurvy, as is clearly shown in Surville's voyage to the Pacific in 1769–70 the consequences for the voyage as a whole could be catastrophic. Surville's *St Jean-Baptiste* was forced to veer south towards New Zealand because 62 men had died in the less than four months since his emergence into the Pacific, north of the Philippines; in many respects, the change of plan was a blessing and it enabled, not just some exploration to be carried out, but many of the sick to recover; but scuvy soon reappered and he was forced to abort his plans and make for South America, where he lost his life and the ship was impounded by the Spaniards; by then a hundred men had died of scurvy and related fevers out of a total complement of 177 men: the percentage was 56.5%, nearly three times what shipowners estimated for a two-year voyage to eastern seas – and Surville's campaign had not lasted one year.

Earlier, Louis de Bougainville, with the *Boudeuse* and the *Etoile*, had been more fortunate, partly because he was lucky enough to land on a number of Pacific islands, some of which he discovered, and obtain fresh food. But the last stage of his voyage was a nightmare, with the men trying to eat rats and old goastkin bottles, and when he put in at Mauritius he sent almost 80 men to the shore hospital. A number recovered, so that overall his losses scarcely reached five per cent of the total complement, but still no

[1] See Claude Chaligné's grim picture of the India trade in *Histoire des services de santé de la compagnie des Indes orientales de 1663 à 1793*, Paris, 1961.

one could find out why scurvy struck some expeditions more severely than others.[1]

The situation had been no better on the British side or indeed on the Portuguese or the Dutch side. Once fleets and merchant vessels could venture into more distant seas, the problems worsened. Ports of call along the route were not useful merely to refit ships or refresh crews: they could also provide fresh food. As far back as 1502, the Portuguese authorities had settled at St Helena to establish vegetable gardens for their sailors; the Cape of Good Hope, settled by the Dutch in 1652, was an invaluable source of fresh fruit and vegetables; Mauritius, or the Ile de France, as Bougainville discovered, was equally valuable.

But could scurvy be prevented or cured, when fresh food was unobtainable? Secret remedies and elixirs were sold, without anyone being quite sure whether they were effective or why. Monneron visited a number of apothecaries around Fleet Street and bought some flasks of 'portable broths' which he carefully wrapped up and sent to La Pérouse: Webber believed them to be highly effective against scurvy, as were some tablets Monneron purchased on his advice.

Uncertainty about the causes of scurvy and consequently about preventive measures had focussed extraordinary attention on James Cook's achievements in maintaining his crews in remarkably good health. This led La Pérouse to overlook the importance of citrus fruit which, as Beaglehole pointed out, Cook did not appreciate as he was in all probability unaware of James Lind's *Treatise of the Scurvy*. La Pérouse did have a copy of Lind's book in his ship's library, because Monneron bought one in London and brought it back with him, and he also had on board Poissonnier des Perrières's *Traité des maladies des gens de mer*, of 1767, an influential work in which the use of oranges and lemons was strongly recommended. These books had no discernible influence on La Pérouse who concentrated his efforts on emulating Cook, rather than on studying recent medical theories on the causes and possible prevention of the disease.

[1] Taillemitte, *Bougainville*, I, 41. Health and sickness on board naval ships in the eighteenth century have been studied in recent years by Adrien Carré in France (e.g. 'Hygiène navale et fièvre des vaisseaux au XVIIIe siècle' in *Revue du corps de santé des armées*, (June 1964); 'Essai de synthèse des maladies de gens de mer au XVIIIe siècle', in *Compte-rendu du 91e Congrès national des Sociétés savantes*, Rennes, 1966, I, pp. 11–29) and by Sir James Watt in Britain.

What La Pérouse did was to develop a careful programme of hygiene and medical inspections, for which he required the co-operation of all his officers and scientists. The former were expected to ensure that the ships, especially below decks, were kept clean at all times, and to see to the personal cleanliness of all the men. To achieve this, the crews were divided into small groups, one officer being responsible for each squad. The surgeons were required to report at frequent intervals on the general health of the men, while the botanists were sent in search of fresh fruit and vegetables at every place of call, paying particular attention to anything that might have some antiscorbutic properties.

It was of course essential to ensure that the men were physically fit before the ships ever sailed. They were carefully selected: those of the *Astrolabe* were handpicked by Langle himself, and a number of them came from his own district of Brittany, so that in many case he knew their background and their moral background as well; La Pérouse was too busy to deal with the recruitment himself, so the task was delegated to Clonard, with strict instructions to accept only those who he was satisfied were in good health and would prove an asset on the voyage. It would seem, however, that less care was taken over the servants, one of whom was found to be affected by tuberculosis which finished him off as the expedition struggled along the fogbound Northwest Coast.

La Pérouse was determined to ensure that the food supplied to him was in a good condition and sufficient for his needs. Dishonest contractors were a constant problem in the major ports where ships set out on lengthy voyages – for once they had sailed away, they would not be back for many months, or in some cases for years, and sharp practices could not be traced back to the suppliers. The naval authorities laid down precise requirements, which all contractors had to meet, but the captains themselves had to ensure that the quality of what they accepted was adequate, and that the food was properly stored. Regular inspections of the supplies stowed down in the hold were essential to avoid wastage and to prevent the food going bad.

At first, since the voyage was expected to last up to four years, the Comte d'Hector and La Pérouse decided to provide the ships with enough food for that length of time. Hector's calculations soon showed that there would not be enough room in the two vessels for such quantities. La Pérouse settled for a three-year supply: the balance could be bought at various ports of call.[1] This gave a total of 240 tons of dry food, grain, biscuit and so on, for each ship, plus 180,000 litres of wine, and enough water for five months on the basis of three litres per man per day. Live animals were also supplied: 30 sheep, 40 pigs, 5 head of cattle, 400 heads of poultry, and the fodder, grain, water, etc, needed to keep them alive for as long as possible. The care taken over these purchase paid dividends, for there was practically no wastage during the first twelve months; after that, the ship's biscuit, always difficult to protect from worms and rats, began to deteriorate. Butter, heavily salted, came from St Malo; sauerkraut, which kept well and had been much used by James Cook, was brought in quantity and personally checked by Hector. Other items which Monneron had recommended as antiscorbutics were supplied under his supervision and with the personal advice of the specialist Poissonnier.[2]

Clothing for the sailors had to be provided for every type of climate. The voyage of Kerguelen to the South Indian Ocean in 1772–4 and La Pérouse's own expedition to Hudson Bay in 1782 had highlighted the need to ensure that the sailors were supplied with warm clothing once the ships reached high latitudes, in part to preserve their health, in part to ensure that they could work the ships satisfactorily in adverse conditions. The sailors' own stock of clothing was inspected before the ships sailed, and additional items were provided when, as was so often the case, it was found that the men had insufficient or worn-out spare shirts and trousers: part of the cost of these additional supplies was deducted from their pay. Woollen socks, woollen caps, heavy flannel vests and spare lengths of heavy cloths were taken on board, to be issued when the need arose. These measures proved their worth when the expedition sailed to Alaska and later to Siberia and Kamchatka.[3]

Monneron's time in England had confirmed all that La Pérouse had read and learned from his own experience. There were no secret remedies to discover, and one hears little more about the broths and anti-scurvy cures Monneron had bought in England. The expedition would in fact contribute little to the understanding of scurvy, but confirm that hygiene was of primordial importance

[1] AN. M. 3JJ 386, 3:5.

[2] Monneron's role in seeking out antiscobutic products and having them sent to Brest is detailed in Gaziello, *L'Expédition de Lapérouse 1785–1788*, pp. 188–9.

[3] Dunmore and Brossard, *Le Voyage de Lapérouse 1785–1788*, 1985, I, p. 49.

in combating any kind of illness on board ship; La Pérouse was to report to Fleurieu from Botany Bay: 'my theory on scurvy can therefore be boiled down to these few aphorisms, which do not come down from Hippocrates: any kind of food suitable for man and able to make up for daily losses, outside air introduced as often as possible in the 'tween-decks and the hold; the damp caused by fog countered by fumigations and even by braziers; cleanliness and the frequent inspection of the sailors' clothing; regular exercise, adequate sleep without encouraging laziness.'[1] His common sense dominated all his conclusions. The old sailors' tales that scurvy resulted from too long an exposure to 'sea air' and thus needed to be prevented or cured by walks ashore, he rejected as baseless: the real trouble was the stench below decks; worm-eaten biscuit and rotting meat could only weaken the sailors' constitution, whereas fresh food, of whatever kind, was bound to be beneficial; wine, coffee, spruce beer, malt, all these were worth having only because they kept well, but 'all the spirits of cochlearia and all the remedies that are kept in bottles are mere short-term palliatives'.[2]

Monneron's voyage to London, however, had a broader purpose than checking on the latest medical developments: he was to obtain all the information he could on advances that might have been made in the science of navigation. Both James Cook and La Pérouse lived at a time of important developments, especially in dealing with the problem of determining longitudes – for without knowing the precise longitude of a ship or a headland, navigation and exploration were doomed to be plagued by guesswork and inaccuracies. By the 1770s and 1780s new instruments, new methods of calculating distances, new astronomical tables and all kinds of related scientific advances were coming to the aid of those who ventured into distant seas.

This does not mean that the old methods had been superseded. The measurement of lunar distances, the calculation of the angular distance between the moon and the sun or one of the fixed stars was still beset with problems. It can be noted that during the voyage there were gaps of ten to twenty days during which observations were not possible, and the distance travelled by the ships and their

[1] Letter of 7 February 1788.
[2] Ibid.

position were still worked out by dead reckoning combined with results obtained from the marine chronometers.

The speed of the ships had been calculated by the *loch*, a triangular piece of wood thrown overboard, to which was attached a rope divided into measured sections and rolled onto a wheel; the length unrolled within a specified time gave an indication of the speed of the vessel. Strictly the knots were to be placed at intervals equal to 1/120 of a mile. Timing was estimated, in the absence of watches, by means of a sand-glass which was intended to equal 1/120 of an hour. The Ministry of Marine had set the knot distance at 47 feet 7 inches, but pilots had their own ideas and the sand-glasses, or alternative methods adopted by some sailors such as counting aloud or reciting set phrases, compounded the inaccuracy of the method. If dead reckoning was to be of any use, it needed to be balanced by the observations of officers and scientists, careful observations and calculations whenever conditions allowed. Once marine chronometers became available – and they were still scarce and costly in the last decades of the eighteenth century, dead reckoning dropped out of use. As a first stage, it ceased to be mentioned when qualified officers or, better still, scientists, were able to make accurate astronomical observations; but numerous were the pilots, helmsmen and sailors who still placed their trust in the old methods, watching drifting pieces of wood or seaweed to estimate the speed of a current, observing the flight of birds to guess at a ship's distance from land or arguing over the changing colour of the sea or the significance of a change in a cloud formation.

However impressive the advances that had been made in drawing up tables by which navigators could more accurately estimate their longitudes by calculating lunar distances, advances due to the skill of such men as Tobias Mayer and Nevil Maskelyne,[1] the difficulty was still knowing what the time was at the basic point of reference, which was either the Paris Observatory or Greenwich Observatory, in order to work out the difference and consequently the distance between a ship's position and the reference point. Water clocks or clocks with pendulums were of no use on board

[1] Johann Tobias Mayer (1723–62) was a German astronomer, superintendent of the Göttingen observatory, the author of lunar and solar tables published from 1752 in Germany and forwarded to the English government in 1755. Nevil Maskelyne (1732–1811) was the author of the *British Mariner's Guide* (1763) and the Astronomer Royal from 1765; he began publishing his *Nautical Almanac* in 1766.

a moving vessel. Huygens[1] was one of the first to develop, in 1656 and 1664, watches which could resist the violent motion of a ship of wide variations in temperatures and climate, but their accuracy was still inadequate for long voyages and above all voyages of exploration.

Rewards were offered to encourage instrument makers and watchmakers to work on the problem. Again, Franco-English rivalry is evident, the Board of Longitude in England and the Minister of Marine Rouillé[2] in France both offering financial incentives. John Harrison completed his fourth timepiece in 1759, which after five years of exhaustive trials was officially recognised as the answer to the problems navigators had been facing for so long. James Cook was able to sail with one, a copy made by Larcum Kendall, a famous instrument maker. In France, Pierre Le Roy made two chronometers which were specially tested in the *Aurore* in 1768. Of greater importance was Ferdinand Berthoud, a Swiss watchmaker who settled in Paris and became official watchmaker to the King and the Ministry of Marine. He developed a total of 73 timekeepers of various types which were tested on several voyages, including that of the *Isis* led by Fleurieu.

All these developments occurred in the 1760–1780 period. The problem remained cost and scarcity. Only a few captains could afford or obtain a modern chronometer. Thus in 1790, Etienne Marchand, setting out for a voyage to the Pacific and a circumnavigation, sailed without a chronometer – and did so fairly successfully.[3] As far as La Pérouse was concerned, it was important for him to obtain the most up-to-date instruments available in England as well as in France, and to this end Monneron was requested to obtain the latest and the best available in London. He visited George Adams, one of the leading instrument makers of his day, and bought some azimuth compasses; from Jesse Ramsden, he obtained two theodolites, four steering compasses, two night telescopes, four thermometers and two sextants; at Troughton's in Fleet Street he found another

[1] Christiaan Huygens (1629–95), Dutch astronomer, devised the telescope that bears his name and wrote *Horologium Oscillatorium* (1763) on oscillation and its relation to the length of a pendulum.

[2] Antoine-Louis Rouillé (1689–1761), Minister of Foreign Affairs.

[3] John Dunmore, *French Explorers in the Pacific*, 1965–69, I, p. 346. Fleurieu, *Voyage autour du monde pendant les années 1790, 1791 et 1792 par Etienne Marchand*, Paris, 1798, I, pp. 39–40.

sextant and a pantograph; from Nairne and Blunt he got two barometers. In all he spent over £4000.[1] But what assumed greater important, symbolic as well as real, was the help he received from Sir Joseph Banks.

However much Monneron may have tried to disguise the true purpose of his stay in London – going so far as to invent a Spanish shipowner, Don Inigo Alvarez, on whose behalf he claimed to be making enquiries concerning a possible commercial voyage through the South Seas – it did not take long for Banks to discover that Monneron was there on behalf of La Pérouse. Banks' rejection of national boundaries or national rivalries when it came to scientific research was one of his most admirable traits: if the French were planning to send an expedition to the Pacific, and especially if their aim was to complete the work which James Cook had had to leave unfinished, they should be assisted. La Pérouse, furthermore, was highly regarded in London as a result of his humane treatment of Samuel Hearne and his men during the Hudson Bay raid. When he learned that Monneron was having difficulty in finding satisfactory dipping needles, Banks prevailed on the Board of Longitudes to lend him the two which Cook and Clerke had used during their last voyage; they were both the work of Edward Nairne, and were forwarded to France in a specially made locked box.[2]

The French however were satisfied that no new advances had been made in respect of the timepieces. La Pérouse took with him one small English chronometer, but no reason was found to give any particular preference to English timekeepers. Ferdinand Berthoud's proved very satisfactory, La Pérouse reporting after eighteen months of navigation that he had formed the opinion that 'this artist' had reached the highest standard possible. Lunar distances, corrected when the ships put into a port where longitudes could be checked, produced when combined with Berthoud's timekeepers quite satisfactory results, with errors seldom exceeding 20′ or 25′.

Monneron's final duty in London was to obtain information about the kind of gifts the French should take for the islanders they might meet. Here again, Monneron had recourse to the fictional

[1] See on this Gaziello, *L'Expédition de Lapérouse 1785–1788*, pp. 153–4. She also gives details on the instruments purchased by the various scientists for their own use on the voyage.

[2] AN.M. B4:318.

Inigo Alvarez who, he claimed, had asked him to find out 'in the greatest detail possible the kind of trade goods the English take with them when sailing through those seas...for instance the size of the axes, if it is desirable to have small, medium and large ones. It would also be useful if you could obtain some information on the quality of these instruments, and even get some some samples that might enlighten me.'[1] Not all that La Pérouse took with him was the result of John Webber's suggestions, or of other gossip Monneron collected, for it forms a strange and sometimes incongruous cargo, but judging from Monneron's correspondence he took a great deal of care in ensuring that the French would have with them a wide selection of items which, according to his English informants, the Pacific islanders would appreciate. Perhaps this is one of the oddest aspects of the role the English played in the preparation of the voyage.[2]

THE INSTRUCTIONS

The text which follows includes the final proposal drawn up for King Louis XVI and approved by him; however, the king made a number of marginal comments in his own handwriting; these are reproduced here as footnotes. This is followed by the official instructions issued to La Pérouse in five sections. To these instructions were appended various documents, such as a list of the officers, scientists and other passengers, notes on geography, table of latitudes and longitudes, memoirs from the Académie Royale des Sciences and from the Société Royale de Médecine, memoir for the gardener, list of books to be taken on board, summary list of scientific instruments, etc. Some of these are reproduced elsewhere in this edition or referred to in the Introduction. In all, the royal copy consists of xxx + 282 pages. It is bound in leather with the royal arms in gold blocking. It is currently held at the Bibliothèque Mazarine, Paris, under reference No. 1546.

[1] Ibid., p. 300, quoting a letter from Monneron to La Pérouse, dated London, 11 April 1785, in AN.M, 2JJ 102, no. 9.

[2] The list is held with Louis XVI's copy of the Instructions at the Bibliothèque Mazarine, ref. 1546. Items listed range from axes to bells and dragoon's helmets.

Plan, Instructions, Memoirs & other items relative to the Voyage of discovery ordered by the King under the command of Mr de La Pérouse Captain of His Majesty's Ships commanding his frigates the *Boussole* and the *Astrolabe* despatched from the Port of Brest in 1785

Plan for a Campaign of Discovery of 15 February 1785

Captain Cook's voyages have made Europe aware of vast countries, scattered islands and groups of islands, some discovered in olden times by the first navigators who entered the Great South Sea, but forgotten since the time of their first discovery; and others whose existence was not known.

But although this voyager, famous for all time, has greatly increased our geographical knowledge; although the globe he travelled through in every direction where seas of ice did not halt his progress, is known well enough for us to be sure that no continent exists where Europeans have not landed; we still lack a full knowledge of the earth and particularly of the Northwest coast of America, of the coast of Asia which faces it, and of islands that must lie scattered in the seas separating these two continents. The position of several islands shown to lie in the southern ocean between Africa and America, whose existence is known only from reports made by the navigators who discovered them, has not yet even been determined; and in eastern seas several areas are still only roughly sketched out. Consequently a great deal remains to be done by a nation that is prepared to undertake the completion of the description of the globe. The Portuguese, the Spanish and the Dutch in earlier times, and the English in the present century, have opened up new routes to navigation; and everything seems to invite the French who share the empire of the seas with them, to perfect a work of which, until now, they have only done a small share.

The advantages that can result from a voyage of discoveries, in the favourable atmosphere of a time of peace, both for the progress and extension of national trade and for the perfecting of geography, have led me to give sympathetic consideration to the proposals that have been submitted to me for such an enterprise. The plan presented to me had as its main object the establishment of a fur trade based on the Northwest Coast of America with the furs being shipped to China where their sale is both guaranteed and lucrative. Indeed, judging from the accounts of Captain Cook's last voyage, a cargo worth 90 to 100 thousand *livres tournois*, in woollen cloth and items of iron and copper, could be sufficient to buy in America 2500 sea-otter skins which would produce more than 600 thousand *livres* in China; to which should be added the profit to be made on the goods from Asia that could be obtained there in exchange for this merchandise, to be taken to Europe and sold there.

The plan of this campaign can be presented from two points of view.

In the first case, Your Majesty's ships would carry a cargo of assorted goods to buy the furs on the American coast; and after the benefits that can derive for France from the double set of transactions, in America and China, had been confirmed in this manner, Your Majesty's subjects would be invited to follow this new branch of commerce, either by private transactions, which would be allowed for this purpose, or by the India Company which could include it in its privilege. On the other hand, one could have this commerce initiated and attempted by a ship belonging to private individuals, operating under the protection of Your Majesty's ships; and I have already received offers from a company whose speculations are being directed towards this object. However, this latter approach would face a difficulty, in that it would be necessary to waive, for this expedition, the privilege held by the India Company, and to allow the return to France of goods from China in the particular vessel which had obtained these goods in exchange for the furs bought on the Northwest Coast of America. It cannot be overlooked that vessels sailing in accordance with the India Company's privilege, who might have made up their cargoes in China at the usual prices and in the usual form, would suffer a severe disadvantage when selling them in Europe if they were competing with the former: because by delivering Chinese goods at prices considerably below those of direct traders it would still be sure of much higher returns than those the India Company's operations produce under the most favourable circumstances.

But the commercial enterprise which is only a subsidiary consideration in the proposal for a campaign of discovery will be the subject of a separate memorandum. I shall deal in this one only with matters related to parts of the globe to be surveyed by Your Majesty's ships; and I shall merely indicate broadly the connection there may be in respect of navigation between the commercial undertaking and the voyage of discovery.

I have therefore the honour to propose to Your Majesty the provision of two of his storeships, one of 500 to 600 tons, the other of 300, which it is believed are the most appropriate vessels, in view of their structure, for a voyage of discovery. They will be equipped with everything necessary or useful for a campaign due to last three years; and nothing will be overlooked that might contribute to the complete success of the enterprise, and to the preservation of the crews in such a lengthy navigation through unfrequented seas.

From my calculations, the cost of this expedition will not exceed 637 thousand *livres*, spread over three years; and this sum includes payments by way of salary or living expenses payable in respect of seven scientists or artists, such as astronomers, botanists, mineralogists, surveyors and draughstmen who will be employed on this expedition so that Your Majesty may obtain all the benefits one can expect from it.

I shall accordingly restrict myself to a summary of the discoveries to be made; I shall fix the main periods of the campaign; and to indicate the links there could be between a commercial undertaking and the main purpose of the expedition, I shall assume that the two warships will be joined by a merchant vessel operating under the former's protection, that will see to the purchase of furs on the Nortwest Coast of America, and will be entrusted with the task of taking them to China, and the subsequent series of operations required to bring the proceeds back from China to Europe.

The two storeships will be sent from France around the middle of May.[a,1] They will be able to call at the Cape Verde Islands to obtain wood and water. Leaving these islands, they will set a course that will enable them to cross the Line in a longitude appropriate for the time of year. The two ships will separate after crossing the Line, to increase the chances of making discoveries, survey the

[a] Good.

[1] Alphabetic footnotes indicate marginal comments by Louis XVI.

Southern Ocean in a minimum of time, determine the position of some known islands and verify the existence of some others.[a]

The first ship will seek the islands of Gough, Diego Alvarès and Tristan da Cunha and will go up as far as the so-called Cape Circumcision which Captain Lozier Bouvet discovered in 1739.[b] She will then sail west to seek Sandwich Land and the island which Cook called Georgia which, to all indications, is likely to be the one discovered in 1675 by the Frenchman Antoine La Roche and rediscovered in 1756 by Duclos Guyot of St Malo.[c] La Roche also discovered some 200 leagues to the north of it another island which he named Isle Grande and which has not been sighted by any navigator since. The location of all these islands in the southern Ocean makes their determination a matter of considerable interest. If they can offer good havens, if one finds water and wood there, they can serve as ports of call for ships on their way to the South Sea; and they would be preferable to the Cape Verde Islands which, being too near the port of departure, offer resources at a time when ships are not yet in a pressing need. The island of Grande, in particular, which La Roche reported as being large and attractive, with a good port on the east coast, with abundant timber, water and fish, and uninhabited, would become a point of major importance if hopes of lucrative returns were to lead French shipowners to engage in whale hunting in this part of the ocean where it was already known that this cetacean is plentiful even before the activity and energy of the American Republicans confirmed it by bringing part to the ports of the northern part of that continent the product of whales they had caught last year in the Magellanic Seas.[d]

The second storeship will seek and visit the islands that lie closer to the coast of southern America, such as the islands of Trinity and Martin Vas, of Ascençaon, the above-mentioned Isle Grande, and Pepys Island.[e] The latter was discovered in 1683 by Cowlei, an Englishman, in 47 degrees of southern latitude. This navigator

[a] This separation must not occur: it is too dangerous in unknown seas.

[b] Good for this clause.

[c] The island of Georgia and Isle Grande are the most important features of this region, on account of the whale fisheries; I do not know whether the search for the above-mentioned small islands and Cape Circumcision should not be put off until the return voyage.

[d] Pointless.

[e] Trinity Island could be visited on the way to Isle Grande, to ascertain whether the English have completely evacuated it.

declares that it has water, timber, birds, fish and a port able to take a thousand ships. The existence of this island is however still doubtful, because since it was first discovered it has not been sighted. The same storeship will look for the Funnell Islands along the parallel and 6 degrees east of the meridian of the Malouine or Falkland Islands, and will then go back to sail along the coast of Patagonia to visit its ports.

The merchant vessel could follow this second ship's course which will be shorter than that of the first storeship: or if, in order to save costs, the owners thought it advisable to send her later she could be given a sealed packet containing information about the first rendezvous of the King's storeships.[a]

As the Strait of Magellan is adequately known following the voyage of Mr de Bougainville and those of the English, the ships will not endeavour to enter this pass, which would lengthen their navigation to no purpose. The first storeship will then make for Staten Land in order to round Cape Horn: the second one will pass by the Strait of Le Maire or off Staten Land: and the joint rendezvous will be the harbour of Christmas Sound (Christmas Port) situated on the western coast of Tierra del Fuego and at the entrance to the Great South Sea.[b]

It is estimated that the second storeship could reach this harbour towards the middle of October, and the first one towards the middle of November. It is then that the merchant vessel should also arrive in order to continue her voyage under the protection of His Majesty's storeships.[c]

The three vessels will see to their requirements and their repairs in the harbour of Christmas Sound, and will continue on their way to the South Sea.

There does not seem to be much research needed in the southern part of this sea: Captain Cook sailed as far as the 73rd degree of latitude; he criss-crossed in every direction this vaste expanse of ocean situated between New Zealand and the coasts of Patagonia and Chile without coming upon any island or indication of land. One could simply go as far as the 64th degree, avoiding the spaces where Cook has sailed, in order to verify the existence of a land, a

[a] At Christmas Bay.

[b] Agreed for the rendezvous in case of separation.

[c] It ought not to be reached until December; Cape Horn is too difficult to round earlier.

port and some islands visited by Drack in 1577, which have not been found.

A search remains to be carried out in the southern part of the South Sea between the tropics, on one side, for islands associated with the coast of America, such as the islands of St Felix and St Ambrosio, discovered in 1579 by Sarmiento in latitude 25 degrees, the islands of the Tripods in approximately 18 degrees, the Gallapagos Islands and others further west known to the Spanish but whose position is not known by other Europeans, and in succession the islands situated between America and the Sandwich Islands, namely Passion, Socorro, Nublada, Maso and Los Mayos, and Noca-Partida, known only through the map appended to Anson's voyage, on which these islands are shown on the basis of a manuscript Spanish chart which this English admiral took from the Manila galleon he captured in the South Sea.[a]

This survey can be carried out by the first storeship, while the second one, bearing further west as she leaves the harbour of Christmas Sound, will go to seek in the 38 deg. of latitude approximately 550 leagues west of Chile, the high land which a Spanish brigantine, bound for the island of Chiloé from Callao, discovered in 1714, coasted along for an entire day and believed to be inhabited because, during the night, they saw fires lit on land. This second ship will similarly seek in the 32 degrees of latitude, approximately 900 leagues from the continent, islands said to have been discovered by the Spanish in 1773 and which, in accordance with their policy, they did not want to make known to other nations for fear that in time of war these islands might provide refuges for warships and privateers wanting to disrupt their coastal trade.[b] The second storeship could then put in at Mendoça's Marquesas Islands, from where she could sail for the Sandwich Islands which will be set as the second place of rendezvous for the three vessels.[c]

[a] All these may be sought if they do not disrupt the voyage and at the Captain's discretion, together with those proposed for the second storeship.

[b] The separation of the storeships could occur in this sea, as it is much calmer. One of the storeships could haul along the coast of Chile and Peru, looking for the above-mentioned islands. The second could follow the plan suggested in this clause, by visiting Easter Island to check whether human beings are dying out as stated by Captain Cook; and, by crossing the Line at some point other than where Captain Cook crossed it, one might possibly discover some new islands on the way to the Sandwich Islands.

[c] Endorsed as the second rendezvous.

It is assumed that they will be able to reach these latter during March 1786.

The captains will obtain provisions and will see to the curing of meats in accordance with the new method successfully adopted by Captain Cook. They will dock and repair their vessels, and will assemble and fit out a Bermudian boat that will have been taken on unassembled and will get it manned by officers and men from their crews.

They will leave the Sandwich Islands when these operations are complete and will set sail for the Northwest Coast of America, arranging their timetables so that they arrive in sight of that coast during the month of May.

They will survey it with the utmost care from Cape Mendoçin to the environs of the Northern Strait.

If a merchant vessel has joined the King's ships, the expedition's commander will take particular care to assist her in her fur dealings; and he will assess the most suitable point of the Coast where one could establish, on the return journey, a small settlement which would need to be protected from any hostility or insult on the part of the natives of the country, should a second voyage to this Coast be envisaged. In that case, the commanding officer of that factory would be given the Bermudian boat and men in sufficient number to protect the outpost.

It will be noted that Captain Cook, having been hampered by winds, was unable to examine this Coast between the 45th and the 50th parallels (where he found King George's Entrance), and between the 50th and the 55th; and that it is in this gap that one can assume would be found the Entrance discovered in 1603 by Juan de Fuca, and the one of Martin d'Aguilar, which might possibly communicate with Hudson Bay through lakes and rivers.[a]

After the ships have visited these coasts by going up to the Northern Strait[b] and back, and the merchant vessel has completed her trading in furs, the latter will sail with her cargo to Canton: and the King's ships will once more go the the Sandwich Islands where they could arrive at the end of October. Along this route, one will look for the island of Pasaros, the other for the islands of Santa-Maria and La Gorda shown on the above-mentioned the Manila galleon chart.

[a] This is the area that must be more carefully explored.
[b] Or at least up to the tip of the Alaskan peninsula.

If supplies of furs had been plentiful and there was some hope of establishing a regular trade, the cargo ship could return to this coast the following year, by sailing direct from Canton where she would have obtained new trade goods, and would take on the furs that would have been bought during the winter through the trading post established there and which could be relieved in the second year. But if it was felt that the first voyage was sufficient, the King's ships would take the Bermudian boat with them.

Whatever decision had been made in this respect, the two storeships, after the repairs had been carried out, the crews refreshed and supplies obtained in the Sandwich Islands, could set sail before the beginning of 1787.

The second storeship will make for the West-North-West and North-West to explore the sea comprised between these islands and Japan, which was not investigated by ships under Captain Cook's command. She will seek in particular islands discovered prior to 1610 by a Spanish vessel sailing from Manila to New Spain. They are believed to lie in 37½ degrees of northern latitude, approximately 28 degrees east of Japan. The Spanish vessel's captain reported that one of these islands is high, extensive, inhabited by white, civilised people and rich in gold and silver. This report led the King of Spain in 1610 or 1611 to send a ship from Acapulco to take possession of this island, but this enterprise, badly run, was a failure; and there is no indication that this project of discovery has been renewed since.[a]

After looking for this island, the storeship will make for the north in order to arrive at the beginning of May in the port of Awatskha, on the southern coast of the Kamtschatka peninsula, where she will be able to see to her needs.

She will be in a position to sail again around the middle of June.

At this stage a most interesting part of the voyage of discovery will begin. The Kuril Islands will need to be carefully explored and more particularly the southernmost islands which, not being under Russian domination, although inhabited, could offer facilities for a sound establishment should France find enough commercial advantages to warrant a trade in furs being developed by the new route

[a] The time of the second departure from the Sandwich Islands, the period when a visit to the seas around Japan is proposed, is winter, and seas are very rough in latitudes as high as those north of Japan.

which seems to be open.[a] We still have only the most confused notions about all the land and islands situated north-east of Japan. There is between that kingdom and the continent of Asia a long channel which has not been investigated. One can also attempt to land in ports situated on the north-east and east coast of Japan, to ascertain whether the Japanese are as unwelcoming in that area as the Dutch report them to be at Nangasaki.[b] It is known that Japan is a big buyer of furs. This would be an additional outlet for those one might obtain subsequently on the Northwest Coast of America, and possibly a means of opening up with that kingdom a bartering trade, either direct or through the inhabitants of the southern Kuril Islands, who in view of their proximity to Japan must have contacts with those parts of the coast that are nearest to the Kurils. All this part of the globe is generally so little known that it would be an important service to geography and in all likelihood to commerce if one could bring back to Europe precise details on it.

It is assumed that the work this would require can keep the second storeship occupied until September or October 1787, at which time she would put into Canton in order to carry out repairs and obtain food supplies, and from there go to Batavia, which would be the second rendezvous for the two storeships.

While the second one would be visiting, as has been said, the waters off Japan, the other would be carrying out researches of equal significance. Like the second one, it would sail from the Sandwich Islands at the beginning of 1787 and would set out to seek the island of St Peter and then St Bartholomew, the Pescadores Islands, Esteran and the Swimmers, and from there go to Queen Charlotte Islands where she could obtain water, wood and some fish.[c] She could then continue with the important discoveries started in this area in 1769 by Mr de Surville, which Capn Cook did not sight. The French navigator only discovered parts of the coast, but everything tends to show that they belong to the famous Solomon Islands discovered long ago by Quiros, which may be,

[a] Agreed for this clause and the preceding one, if it is possible to sail in those seas at this period, with the proviso that the storeships must not separate after their first departure from the Sandwich Islands.

[b] This clause is of importance if it is possible to develop a fur trade in N.W. America.

[c] The two storeship would make this journey together if they were unable at this point to go into the Sea of Japan.

out of all the islands in this region, those which are most worthwhile investigating, because it is not likely that everything Quiros told the King of Spain concerning the wealth and fertility of these islands is no more than the figment of a feverish imagination.

When the exploration of these islands has been completed, the first storeship will make for the south-eastern point of New Guinea, and will sail along the entire eastern part of that great island's south coast, of which only the western part is known. She will then pass through Endeavour Strait: and if the vessel's condition and the supplies permit, she will enter the Gulf of Carpentaria, discovered in early times by Carpentaire, a Dutchman, who gave it his name, and from where, it is known, the first navigators of that nation who landed there brought back items that promised a lucrative trade, but the mystery with which the Dutch East Indies Company surrounds all its operations has not allowed other Europeans to gain a better knowledge of that part of New Holland.[a]

The first storeship will end its operations in these waters by going to Batavia where she will find the second storeship.

After obtaining food and refreshments for their return voyage to Europe, both will sail for the Ile de France where they will take on what they require to complete their navigation back to France.

During their crossing, they will endeavour to sight the islands of Denia and Marseeven, situated approximately 6 degrees south of the Land of Hotentots; the islands of Ascension, Saxemburg, Ferdinand de Noronha, St Matthew, and St Paul, and the shoals which are suspected to lie in this area following reports made by the captains of the vessels *Vaillant* and *Silhouette* in 1754 and 1761.

The general plan of this interesting expedition has merely been outlined here; but if Your Majesty agrees that it should be undertaken, detailed Instructions will be drawn up in which all the sections of the proposal will be further developed. A careful assessment is required to decide more precisely the islands where the vessels will be able to obtain food supplies, and to fix with greater

[a] If the condition of the ships and their provisions allowed it, instead of going through Endeavour Strait, they could go south, explore the west coast of New Caledonia of which Captn Cook only saw the eastern side, and thence could go to refresh and repair in Queen Charlotte Sound in New Zealand where there are reasons to believe the English are planning some establishment. After repairs, the ships would sail west to make a landfall on Van Diemen Point in New Holland, sail along the entire south-west coast of this great island which remains unknown today, and then sail for Batavia or directly to the Isle de France.

precision and safety the various periods of the campaign. It could even be possible, if the proposed objective of trade on the North-west Coast of America was abandoned, to change the route of Your Majesty's ships, and to reserve this exploration of the Coast for the second year of navigation. In either case, the points to be discovered would not be changed, but the order of their exploration could be altered. Furthermore, the detailed proposal will have appended an hydrographic map in which will be gathered, in the same presentation, the early discoveries, those that have been confirmed by this century's navigators, the new discoveries we owe to the voyages of Captain Cook and the ships under his command, and to those of Messrs de Bougainville, de Kerguelen, Surville, Marion and other Frenchmen, and what remains to be done to complete the knowledge and the description of the terrestrial globe.

PRELIMINARY NOTE

In drawing up a plan of navigation for the voyage of discovery whose command has been entrusted to Mr de la Pérouse, care has been taken to choose for His Majesty's ships routes which in the various seas have not been followed by any of the navigators who have preceded him, in order to increase the number of discoveries and, through this campaign, to enable the great work of the complete description of the terrestrial globe to make considerable progress.

It has however been necessary to list as places of call islands that are already known, and where one can be confident Mr de la Pérouse will be able to obtain provisions, by the process of barter for which a quantity of goods of all kinds has been selected in a range likely to appeal to the islanders with whom he will be dealing. But while places of call that are already frequented have been proposed to the French commander, care has been taken to bring him there by routes that have not yet been followed; and among the number of goods provided one has not forgotten to include a number that are not yet known in the islands where he is likely to land, so that the local natives will easily realise that the nation bringing them is new to them and one which had not yet visited them.

Various methods of calculations have been adopted to estimate the duration of the various crossings. Along ordinary routes and in open seas, it has been assumed that the ships could, with the trade winds, cover 30 leagues in 24 hours; in areas where caution requires one to heave to for part of the night, only 25 leagues have been estimated for the same period of time: and only 20 leagues when the ships are carrying out exploratory work; and in this last case a certain number of days have been added for the time lost exploring and examining a coastline. It is on these bases that some broad estimate of the durations of crossings has been made; but all these calculations are relative to the circumstances in which the ships might find themselves, to events occuring during their navigation and unforeseen accidents.

The total duration of the voyage will inevitably exceed four years. It would have been impossible to carry out in a lesser space of time all the aims His Majesty has outlined, both in the notes He has written in His own hand in the margin of the first memoir and in the summary He has made of the same objectives. The known dates of the monsoons, which differ north and the south of the Equator, are factors which have to be taken into account when planning the route, and which seriously impede navigation in the seas adjacent to the archipelago and mainland of Asia, because it is necessary to enter each region only at a determined time when the winds are favourable. Taking the monsoons into account has required very considerable work in order to adjust the routes without thereby adding overmuch to the length of the campaign, and to ensure in particular that each crossing did not exceed the limits imposed by the need to carry enough wood and water for the requirements of the respective crews, taking due note of the capacity of each ship. Furthermore, His Majesty's ships are supplied with ammunition of every kind, in quantities that are more than adequate for four years of navigation, to which will be added the fortuitous resources which accounts of modern navigators have indicated and which Mr de la Pérouse's prudence and energy will enable him to obtain on his various calls. Captain Cook's last voyage lasted four years, two months and twenty-two days; and his ships were not as well provided as those of His Majesty will be.

If, as the expedition commander's zeal and skill allow us to expect, all the objectives listed in the proposal are carried out, Mr de la Pérouse's voyage will leave to navigators wishing to attempt further explorations, merely the merit of giving us fuller details on a few parts of the globe.

It is now necessary to outline the procedure adopted for the preparation of the hydrographic charts to be handed over to the ships' commanders after His Majesty has approved them.

A first map of the Southern Ocean has been drawn up, on which the tracks of the navigators on their voyages of discovery have been drawn based on their journals; and those still to be made or checked are then shown. This map has been drawn up from the best French, Spanish, English and Dutch charts, and in accordance with the astronomical observations by which the position of the main features of continents and islands were determined.

The extent of the Great Ocean, commonly called South Sea or Pacific Sea, has required it to be split into three bands or zones; of which the first contains the Great Southern Ocean, or the space contained between the Antarctic Polar Circle and the Tropic of Capricorn; the second the Great Equatorial Ocean, or the space contained between the two tropics; and the third, the Great Northern Ocean, or the seas contained between the Tropic of Cancer and the Arctic Polar Circle.

In order to draw up this map, extracts were taken from the journals of all the navigators of the present century and of earlier times who have sailed in the Great Ocean: the detailed charts they made were consulted, and have been incorporated by means of reductions into the general map: on it were traced the routes of all the navigators, ancient and modern, to compare recent discoveries with those made in previous centuries and to prove, in some cases, that they were the same.

This general map of the Great Ocean is the result of all that navigators and geographers have produced to this day. The detail of the various items researched and those set in motion will not be outlined here; such a list would require a volume of its own. It will be sufficient to join to the Royal Memoir to serve as instructions for Mr de la Pérouse instructive notes on several parts which require greater detail; and a collection of thirty-seven other maps or original charts of less frequented seas will be added to the two general maps of the Southern Ocean and the Great Ocean.

N.B. – On the general maps accompanying this memoir the routes of the old Spanish navigators are shown in yellow, those of the Dutch in green; those of the French in blue; those of the English in various colours, namely, Byron's in orange, Wallis's in bistre, Carteret's in purple, and Captain Cook's three voyages in red, identified as follows:

1st Voyage .... o——o——o——o
2nd Voyage .... oo——oo——oo——oo
3rd Voyage .... ooo——ooo——ooo——ooo

Mr de la Pérouse's projected navigation is indicated by a heavy black wavy line ~~~~ and by dots only, for those routes that remain undecided on account of the freedom given him to favour one route over another, depending on his circumstances.

MEMOIR

from the King
to serve as special instructions for Mr de la Pérouse,
Post-Captain, commanding His Majesty's frigates
Boussole and Astrolabe

His Majesty, having had his frigates, the *Boussole*, commanded by Mr de la Pérouse, and the *Astrolabe*, by the Vt de Langle, both post-captains, commissioned in the port of Brest, to be used on a voyage of discovery, will make known to Mr de la Pérouse, to whom He has entrusted the overall command of these two vessels, the tasks to be carried out during the important expedition which He has placed under his leadership.

The various objectives which His Majesty has in mind in ordering this voyage have required the separation of the present Instructions into several sections, in order to explain more clearly to Mr de la Pérouse His Majesty's particular intentions in respect of each of the objectives he will have to deal with

The 1st part will contain his itinerary or plan of navigation, following the order of discoveries to be made or perfected; and to it will be appended a collection of geographical and historical notes which may help to guide him in the various researches he is to carry out.

The 2nd part will deal with aims related to politics and trade.

The 3rd will outline operations relative to astronomy, geography, navigation, physics and the sundry branches of natural history; and it will indicate the functions of the astronomers, physicists, naturalists, scientists and artists employed in the expedition.

The 4th will outline to Mr de la Pérouse the attitude he must adopt towards the uncivilised peoples and natives of the various countries which he will come upon or explore.

The 5th part, finally, will indicate the precautions he is to take to preserve the health of his crews.

FIRST PART

Plan of the Voyage or Proposed Navigational Routes

1785 Year

Mr de la Pérouse will sail from Brest roadsteads as soon as all his preparations are made.

Beginning of August

He will put in at Funchal, Madeira; and at La Praya in the island of St Yago. He will obtain some barrels of wine at the first of these ports and will complete laying in wood and water at the latter where he will also be able to obtain some refreshments. He will bear in mind, however, that his stay at La Praya should be as brief as possible because the climate is very unhealthy there during the season when he will be calling.

He will cross the Line in 29 or 30 degrees of western longitude, Paris meridian; and if the winds allow, he will endeavour to reach Penedo de San Pedro and determine its position.

Beginning of September.

He will seek the island of Trinity, anchor there, where he will be able to obtain wood and water, and will carry out a specific objective indicated in his instructions.

Leaving this island, he will sail for the latitude of La Roche's Isle Grande, in 35 degrees of western longitude, will follow the parallels of 44 to 45 degrees as far as the 50th degree of longitude, and will give up his search for this island if he does not come across it by the time he reaches this meridian. If he prefers to tackle it from the west, he will still restrict his search to the area situated between the above-mentioned meridians.

1st October

He will then make for the Land of La Roche, named Georgia Island by Cook, in 54 degrees south. He will approach it by its north-west point; and he will explore in particular the south coast which has not yet been investigated.

25 October

From there he will seek Sandwich Land, in 57¼ degrees south; he will note that Captain Cook was able to examine only a few features of this land's west coast, and that its extent to the east and south is not known. He will pay particular attention to the east coast, to then sail along it towards the south and round it in this area, if the ice does not present an insurmountable obstacle to his research in the season when he will be surveying it.

10 November

When he has ascertained the extent of this land to the east and south, he will set sail for Staten Land, round Cape Horn, and anchor in Christmas Sound (or Christmas Bay) on the south-west coast of Tierra del Fuego, where he will obtain wood and water. But should he find it too difficult to sail west, on account of the winds that usually prevail in this region and the currents that sometimes run strongly east, he would make for the coast of Brazil in a latitude appropriate to his circumstances, would follow this coast with variable winds or land breezes, and could even call at the Malouine Islands which offer different types of resources. He would then pass through Le Maire's Strait or round the eastern point of Staten Land, in order to make for Christmas Sound which, in every case, is to be the lst rendezvous for His Majesty's ships in case of separation.

15 December

Leaving Christmas Sound, he will set a course that will enable him to cross the meridian of 85 degrees west in latitude 57 degrees south; and he will follow this parallel as far as the 95th degree of longitude, in order to seek the land and port of Drack.

He will then cross the meridian of 105 deg. at the 38th parallel which he will keep to until the 115 deg. of longitude, to try and identify a land said to have been discovered by the Spanish in 1714 in 38 degrees of latitude between the 108th and 110th meridians.

After this search, he will go to the latitude of 27 degrees 5 minutes on the meridian of 108 deg. west, to seek along this parallel Easter Island situated in 112° 8′ of longitude. He will anchor there in order to carry out the specific objective listed in the second part of the present instructions.

From this island, he will made for the latitude of 32 degrees on the meridian of 120 degrees west; and will keep to the said parallel as far as 135 deg. of longitude, to seek a land sighted by the Spanish in 1773.

1786 Year

At this point, 135 degrees of longitude and 32 of latitude, the two frigates will separate. The first will go up to the middle parallel between 16 and 17 degrees and will remain on it from the 135th to the 150th meridian west of Paris, from where she will sail for the island of Otaiti. The space between 16 and 17 degrees of latitude not having been explored over an expanse of 25 degrees of longitude by any of the modern navigators, and all the area around these parallels being sprinkled with low islands, it is likely that the ship following the route outlined above will find new islands which may be inhabited, as is the case, with most of the low islands in these waters.

At the same time, the second frigate, leaving from the same point of 32 degrees of latitude and 135 of longitude, will sail north up to 25 degrees 12 minutes, and will endeavour to settle on this parallel from the 131st or 132nd meridian. There she will seek the island of Pitcain, discovered in 1767 by Carteret and situated in 25 deg. 12′ of latitude. This island's longitude is still uncertain because that navigator had no way of determining it through observations. It is most desirable for this longitude to be accurately determined, because once its position is satisfactorily known it would be used to correct, step by step, those of the other islands or lands discovered by Carteret.

Leaving Pitcairn Island, the second vessel will sail west and then north-west, to seek in turn the islands of Incarnation, St Jean-Baptiste, St Elmo, Cuatro Coronados, St Michael and the Conversion of St Paul, discovered by Quiros in 1616, which are believed to lie to the south-east of Otaiti, and which have not been sighted or even sought by navigators in this century. The second vessel will reach by this route the 150th meridian west and the 19th degree of latitude from where she will go to Otaiti.

End of April

It is assumed that the two ships will be able to arrive there during the last days of April.

This island will be the second rendezvous for the King's ships in case of separation.

The two frigates will firstly anchor in the Bay of Oheitepoha, situated at the north-east point of the island named Tiarraboo or Otaiti-Ete, which is to windward of Matavai Bay, situated at the northern point or Point Venus; and they will then put in at the latter in order to have, through these two calls, greater possibilities of obtaining the refreshments they will require.

1st June

Mr de la Pérouse will leave Otaiti after a stay of one month. He will be able to visit, on the way, the islands of Huaheine, Ulietea, Bolabola and others of the Society Islands, to obtain further supplies of food, provide these islands with European articles useful to their inhabitants, and sow seed, plant trees, vegetables &c which could in time offer new resources to European navigators crossing this ocean.

Leaving the Society Islands, he will sail north-west, to reach the latitude of the island of St Bernard of Quiros, around 11 degrees. He will only carry out this search from the 158th to the 162nd meridian; and from latitude 11 degrees he will proceed to the north-west up to the fifth parallel south and the meridian of 166 to 167 degrees. He will then set course for the south-west to cross, in that direction, the area of sea situated north of the Friendly archipelago, where it is likely he will find, according to reports made by the natives of these islands, a large number of other places not yet visited by Europeans and which must be inhabited. It would be desirable for him to rediscover Quiros' Island of the Beautiful People, which he must look for between the parallels of 11 and 11½ degrees, from the 169th degree of longitude up to the 171st; and in turn the Navigators Islands of Bougainville, from where he would go on to the Friendly Islands to obtain refreshments.

15 July

Leaving the Friendly Islands, he will make for the latitude of the Isle of Pines, situated at the south-east point of New Caledonia; and after sighting he will haul along the south-west coast which has not yet been visited; and he will check wether this land consists of a single island or of several.

If after examining the south-west coast of New Caledonia, he can reach the Queen Charlotte Islands, he will try to find Mendana's Santa Cruz Island and determine how far it extends to the south.

But if the winds are unfavourable for such a route, he will make a landfall on the Islands of Delivrance, at the eastern point of the Land of the Arsacides discovered in 1769 by Surville. He will follow its southern coastline which this navigator, nor any other, did not see; and he will verify whether, as is likely, these lands represent a group of islands which he will endeavour to outline. It can be assumed that they are peopled on the south coast, as is, as we know, the north coast: he may be able to obtain some refreshments there.

He will similarly endeavour to examine an island situated north-west of the Land of the Arsacides, whose eastern coast was sighed by Mr de Bougainville in 1768. But he will carry out this search only to the extent that he will feel confident of reaching after that, without difficulty, Cape Delivrance, at the south-eastern point of the Louisiade. And before reaching this cape, he will survey, if he can, the eastern coast of this land.

From Cape Delivrance, he will set his course so as to pass through Endeavour Strait, and he will endeavour to verify, during this passage, whether the land of the Louisiade is continguous with New Guinea; and he will survey all this part of the coast, from Cape Delivrance up to the island of St Bartholomew to the east-north-east of Cape Walsh, which is very imperfectly known at present.

It would be very desirable for him to visit the Gulf of Carpentaria; but he should note that the north-west monsoon, south of the Line, begins around 15 November, and that the range of this monsoon is not so fixed that it cannot at times reach beyond the 10th degee of southern latitude. It is therefore important to exercise the utmost diligence in this investigation, and to be careful to combine route and speed so as to cross the meridian of the south-west point of Timor before 20 November.

If, against all expectations, he had not been able to obtain refreshments, water and wood on the lands he had visited since the time of his departure from the Friendly Islands, from where it has been assumed he would have sailed around 15 July, he would put in at Prince Island, at the entrance to Sunda Strait, near the western point of the island of Java.

15 and 20 November

On leaving Prince Island or, if he had not been forced to put in there, emerging from the channel north of New Holland, he will set a course so as to make his landfall on the west coast of this land; and he will begin this survey as high, towards the Equator, as the winds will allow. He will sail along the west coast, and will pay particular attention to the south coast, most of which has never been explored; and he will end at the southern land of Van Diemen, in Adventure Bay or Frederick Henry Bay.

From there he will go to Cook Strait, at will put in at Queen

Charlotte Sound, situated in this strait between the two islands that form New Zealand. This port will be the third rendezvous for the frigates in case of separation.

He will repair his vessels, and will obtain refreshments, water and wood.

1787 Year
1st March

It is assumed that he will be able to sail from this harbour during the first days of March 1787.

Emerging from Cook Strait or New Zealand Strait, he will go to the parallels of 41 to 42 degrees and will remain on them until he reaches the 130th meridian west. Upon arriving at this longitude he will sail north to the winds and latitude of Mendoça's Marquesas Islands. He will put in, in order to see to the requirements of his ships, at the port of Mendana's Madre de Dios, on the western coast of the island of Sta Catarina (Cook's Port Resolution). This port will be the fourth rendezvous for the ships in case of separation.

It is asumed that this crossing may take two months, and that he will be in a position to set sail around the 15th of May.

If on his departure from Mendoca's Marquesas Islands the winds were favourable enough for him to follow a northerly route, he could explore some of the islands east of the Sandwich group. He would then go to the latter islands where he could take on additional provisions, but not stay there.

15 May

He will sail, as soon as he can, for the American coast; and for this will go north as far as the 30th degree, in order to get away from the trade winds and be able to come upon the said coast in 36 degrees 20 minutes at Punta de Pinos, south of the port of Monterey, identifiable by means of the mountains (or Sierra) of Sta Lucia.

It is probable that he could reach this coast around the 10th or 15th of July.

15 July

He will concentrate on exploring areas that were not seen by Captain Cook, and about which the accounts of Russian and Spanish navigators provide no information. He will investigate with the greatest care whether, in parts that are not yet known, there might not exist some river, or some narrow gulf, that communicate with some part of Hudson Bay by way of the interior lakes.

He will carry out his investigations as far as Behring Bay and Mount St Elias; and he wil visit Port Bucareli and Port Los Remedios, discovered by the Spanish in 1775.

As Prince William Sound and Cook River have been adequately explored, he will not attempt to visit them; and from Mount St Elias he will set sail for the Shumagin Islands near the Alaskan peninsula.

He will then visit the Aleutian archipelago, and in turn the two groups of islands west of it, whose true position and number are not known, and which form, with the coasts of Asia and America, the great basin of the Northern Gulf.

After completing this exploration, he will put in at the port of Awatskha, or St Peter and St Paul, at the south-eastern extremity of the Kamtschatka peninsula. He will endeavour to reach it around the 15th or 20th of September. And this port will be the fifth rendezvous in case of separation.

There he will diligently see to his vessels' requirements, and will obtain the necessary information to ensure he can obtain provisions when he returns in 1788.

He will combine his operations so as to allow him to sail during the first ten days of October.

10 October

He will coast and explore all the Kuril Islands, the north-east, east and south coast of Japan; and depending on whether, as the season avances and he reaches lower latitudes, the winds will be more or less favourable and the seas more or less calm, he will extend his investigations to the islands east and south of Japan, and to the islands of Lokeyo, as far as Formosa.

After concluding this exploration, he will put in at Macao and Canton (or Manila, depending on circumstances). This port will be the sixth rendezvous in case of separation.

31 December

It is assumed that he would arrive there towards the end of 1787.

1788 Year

He will have his ships repaired and restocked and will await in port the return of the south-west monsoon, which usually settles in at the beginning of March. He will, however, be able to delay his departure until 1 April if his crews need a longer rest and if, from information obtained, he considers that his navigation towards the north would be too strenuous earlier than this.

1 April

Whatever the length of his stay, he will, upon leaving this port, set a course to pass through the strait which separates the island of Formosa from the coast of China, or between that island and those that lie east of it. He will cautiously explore the west coast of Korea and the Gulf of Hoan Hay, without venturing too far into it, also ensuring that he remains in a position to round without difficulty the south coast of Korea with south-west and southerly winds. He will then examine the eastern coasts of this peninsula, of Tartary, where there is a pearl fishery, and of Japan on the opposite side. Europeans have absolutely no knowledge of any of these coastlines.

He will pass through the Strait of Tessoi, and will visit the land known as Yeso, and the land called Staten Land by the Dutch and Nadezda by the Russians, about which we have only the vaguest notions derived from a few old accounts which the Dutch East Indies Company allowed to get abroad but whose accuracy has not been checked.

He will complete the survey of those Kuril Islands which he might have been unable to visit in the previous November when he sailed from Awatska to Macao. He will pass between some of these islands, as close as he can manage to the southern point of Kamtschatka; and he will put into the port of Awatska, the seventh rendezvous in case of separation.

1 August

After repairing and provisioning his ships, he will set sail during the first days of August.

He will seek the latitude of 37 degrees ½ north on the meridian of 180 degrees. He will sail west to seek a land or island said to have been discovered, before 1610, by the Spanish. He will continue this search as far as the 165th degree of eastern longitude.

He will then go south-south-west and south-west to find the archipelago situated in this direction to the north-east of the Islands of Thieves or Marianas.

He will be able to call at the island of Tinian; but he will adjust the length of his stay and his subsequent route with the north-east monsoon which only begins in October north of the Line; so that when leaving Tinian, he can haul along and survey the new Carolines situated south-west of the island of Guahan, one of the Marianas, and east of Mindanao, one of the Philippines. He will carry out this exploration as far as the islands of St Andrew.

15 November

He will then put in at the island of Mindanao, in the port situated on the south coast of the island behind Sirangam Island.

1 December

After a fortnight's stay, during which he will lay in refreshments, he will make for the Moluccas, and will be able to call at Ternate to obtain further supplies.

Since the north-west monsoon, then blowing south of the Line, would not allow him to pass through Sunda Strait; he will take advantage of variable winds found near the Equator to pass between Ceram and Bouro, or between Bouro and Bouton; and he will endeavour to come out between some of the islands to the east or west of Timor.

As he will by then have passed parallel of 10 degrees south, it is likely that he will find himself free of the north-west monsoon, and that he will easily progress west with easterly and south-easterly winds, and reach the Ile de France which shall be the ships' eighth rendezvous in case of separation.

1789 Year

1 February

He will stay at the Ile de France only as long as is absolutely necessary to prepare for the return journey to Europe, and will take advantage of the last days of summer for the navigation still facing him in the seas south of the Cape of Good Hope.

15 or 20 February

Leaving the Ile de France, he will make for the parallel between 54 and 55 degrees south in order to seek Cape Circumcision, discovered in 1739 by Lozier Bouvet. He will reach this latitude in 15 degrees of eastern latitude, and will follow the parallel of 54 to 55 degrees as far as the Paris meridian, or longitude zero. Once arrived there, he will give up searching for this land.

If he then felt that his ships were not adequately supplied with water and food for the return to Europe, he would put in at the Cape of Good Hope to get them in a condition appropriate for continuing their navigation; and this port would be the vessels' 9th rendezvous in case of separation.

Whatever his decision in this matter, he will endeavour to find, on his way back to Europe, the islands of Gough, Alvarès, Tristan d'Acunha, Saxemburg and Dos Picos; and if he finds them he will determine their position which is still uncertain.

July or August

He will return to Brest where it is likely that he will be able to arrive in July or August 1789.

Although Mr de la Pérouse's route is laid down in the present instructions, and the periods of his calls and durations of his stays are indicated herein; His Majesty did not intend that he should be compelled to adhere in all respects to this programme. All the calculations herein contained as a rough estimate are subject to the development of his campaign and to unforeseeable accidents. All this could lead to greater or lesser changes to the plan of his operations; and the purpose of the present instructions is merely to advise Mr de la Pérouse of the discoveries still to be made or clarified in the various parts of the globe, and of the route which appears appropriate to follow in order to carry out these investigations, combining his different crossings and the dates of his various calls with the seasons and the winds prevailing or recurring in each region. His Majesty, therefore, taking into account Mr de la Pérouse's experience and wisdom, authorises him to make such changes as will seem to him to be necessary in situations that have not been foreseen, keeping as close as possible, however, to the plan which has been outlined, and furthermore keeping to the requirements of the other sections of the present instructions.

SECOND PART
Aims relating to politics and trade

His Majesty has outlined for Mr de la Pérouse, in the first part of these instructions, the route he should follow for the explorations he is to carry out in the greater part of the globe: He will now indicate in this section the various objectives related to politics and trade which require his particular attention on his various calls, so that the expedition which His Majesty has ordered, contributing to the improvement of geographical knowledge and extending the area of navigation, may also in other respects carry out His intentions in respect of the interests of His crown and the advancement of His subjects.

1. The stays Mr de la Pérouse is to make at Madeira and St Yago will not be long enough for him to obtain a precise knowledge of the condition of these Portuguese colonies; but he will overlook

nothing that might give him some information on the forces with the Portuguese Crown maintains there, on trade carried out by the English and other nations, and on important matters which it might be interesting to know.

2. He will ascertain whether the English have completely evacuated the island of Trinity; whether the Portuguese have settled there, and what kind of settlement the latter may have set up there since the evacuation.

3. Should he succeed in rediscovering Roche's Ile Grande, he will ascertain whether it offers some convenient and safe harbour where wood and water might be obtained; what facilities it may offer for a settlement in case the whale fisheries should attract French shipowners into the southern Atlantic Ocean; whether some part of it can be fortified to advantage and be defended by a small force, in other words a post which would be appropriate for an establishment situated so far from the assistance and protection of the mother country.

4. He will examine the island of Georgia to the same ends. But it is probable that this island, situated in a higher latitude, will offer fewer facilities than can be expected from Ile Grande's location, and that the ice that encumbers the sea for part of the year in the neighbourhood of Georgia would present serious obstacles to ordinary navigation and would dissuade fishermen from making this island a place of retreat and rendezvous.

5. The islands of the Great Equatorial Ocean will present few opportunities for observations related to politics and trade: their distance would seem likely to discourage European nations from establishing any settlements on them; and Spain alone could be interested in occupying islands which, situated roughly mid-way between her American and Asiatic possessions, would offer points of call and refreshment for her trading vessels crossing the Great Ocean. Whatever the correctness of this comment, Mr de la Pérouse will devote his main attention to the study of the climate and different products of the various islands of this ocean where he effects a landing; to discovering the practices and customs of the countries' natives, their religious practices, their form of government, their manner of waging war, their weapons, their seagoing craft, the distinctive character of each group, what they may have in common with other native peoples and with civilised nations, and especially what characterises each one.

In those islands where Europeans have already landed, he will endeavour to find out whether the natives made a distinction between the different nations that visited them; and he will try to identify the opinion they may have formed of each one in particular. He will assess the use they have made of the various goods, metals, tools, cloth and other objects Europeans brought them. He will enquire whether the cattle and other live animals and birds Captain Cook left on some of these islands have multiplied; which types of European seeds and vegetables have done best; what method the islanders used to cultivate them, and the use to which they have put the outcome. Finally, he will in all places verify the reports made by navigators who have published accounts of these islands, and he will endeavour in particular to find out what may have escaped his predecessors' attention.

During his call at Easter Island, he will confirm whether human beings are dying out, as Captain Cook's observations and opinion seem to indicate.

When he goes past the island of Ulieta, he will endeavour to become acquainted with Omaï, the islander whom the English captain brought back there during his third voyage; he will find out from him how he was treated by his compatriots after the English left, and what use he made, for the good, well-being and improvement of his country, of what he must have learned during his stay in Europe.

6. If, during the travels and explorations Mr de la Pérouse will be making in the Great Equatorial Ocean and the continental coasts, he met on the seas some vessel belonging to another power, he would act towards its commanding officer with all the courtesies and consideration established and agreed between civilised and friendly nations; and should he meet one, in some harbour belonging to a people considered savage, he would work with the captain of the foreign vessel so as to avoid any dispute or altercation between the crews of the two nations who might find themselves ashore at the same time, and to give each other assistance in the event of either being attacked by the islanders or savages.

7. During his visit to New Caledonia, Queen Charlotte Islands, the Land of the Arsacides and that of the Louisiade, he will carefully assess which of the products of these countries, which are located in the torrid zone and in the same latitudes as Peru, can offer new opportunities for trade; and setting aside the reports, no doubt

exaggerated, made by the old Spanish navigators on the fertility and wealth of some of the islands they discovered in this part of the world, he will merely note that comparisons based on geographical aspects and on the knowledge provided by modern voyages lead to the possibility that the land discovered by Surville in 1769 may be the islands discovered in 1567 by Mendana and known since that time under the name of islands of Solomon as a consequence of the riches which, rightly or wrongly, people subsequently attributed to them.

He will examine with the same care the northern and western coastlines of New Holland, and especially that part of these coasts which, being situated in the torrid zone, may also possess products associated with countries located in the same latitudes.

8. He will not have to carry out the same investigations in the islands of New Zealand, which the English navigators' accounts have made known in great detail; but during his stay in Queen Charlotte Strait, he will find out whether England has established or plans to establish some settlement in these islands: and should he discover that one has been established, he will endeavour to go there to obtain a direct knowledge of the condition, strength and purpose of this settlement.

9. If, while exploring the Northwest Coast of America, he should on some points of this coast come upon forts or factories belonging to His Catholic Majesty, he will take good care to avoid anything that might cause umbrage to the commanders or heads of these settlements; but he will stress to them the links of blood and friendship that unite the two sovereign so closely, in order to obtain in this manner all the assistance and refreshments he might need and which the country can supply.

It appears that Spain intends to extend her claims as far as Puerto de Los Remedios, near the fiftieth degree of latitude; but nothing indicates that when she had it explored in 1775 any settlement was established there, or at Puerto Bucareli situated some two degree further south. As far as can be ascertained from reports from that country reaching France, active possession by Spain does not extend beyond the ports of San Diego and Monterey, where she has erected small forts guarded by detachments sent from California and New Mexico. Mr de la Pérouse will endeavour to discover the condition, strength and purpose of these settlements, and to confirm that they are the only ones Spain has established on this coast.

He will similarly ascertain the latitude at which one can begin to buy furs, the quantities the Americans can provide, which goods and items would be most appropriate to buy furs with, what facilities there might be for an establishment along this coast should this new branch of commerce offer enough advantages to French traders to lead them to engage in it in the hope of exchanging the furs in China where they can be sold easily and profitably. He will similarly endeavour to find out which types of fur can be purchased, and whether otter furs, which are the most valuable in Asia where the demand is great, are the most common types in America. He will take care to bring back to France samples of all the various furs he can obtain; and since he will have occasion, later in his voyage, to put into China and possibly Japan, he will ascertain which type of furs is easier and more profitable to sell in each of these empires; and what benefits France can expect from this new branch of commerce. Finally, he will endeavour during his stay on the American coasts to discover whether the settlements in Hudson Bay and the forts and factories in the interior and on the lakes, or some province of the United States, have opened up, by the intermediary of nomadic natives, some form of communication, some trade or barter, with the peoples of the Northwest Coast.

10. It is probable that when he visits the Aleutian Islands and the other groups situated further south of the Great Northern Basin, he will come upon some Russian establishment or factory.

He will endeavour to ascertain their constitution, strength, purpose; the extent of Russian navigation in these waters; which vessels and men they use; how far their trade extends; whether some of these islands recognise Russian domination or whether they are all independent; and finally whether the Russians have not progressed, gradually, onto the American continent.

He will use his stay in the port of Awatska to widen the knowledge which may be obtained in this respect and at the same time, if possible, increase our knowledge of the Kuril Islands, the land of Yeso and the Japanese empire.

11. He will explore the Kuril Islands and the land of Yeso, cautiously and with circumspection, both in respect of his navigation in a sea which is not known to Europeans and is reputed to be stormy, and in the relations he may establish with the inhabitants of these islands and lands, whose character and customs must be close

to those of the Japanese who may have brought some into subjection and be in contact with the rest.

He will see from the geographical and historical notes appended to the present instructions that Russian domination extends only over a few of the Kuril Islands, the closest to Kamtschatka; he will ascertain whether, among the southern and independent islands, there may not be one where, in the eventuality of a fur trade opening up for France, it may be possible to set up an establishment or factory that could be protected from any outrage on the part of the islanders.

12. In respect of Japan, he will endeavour to sight and explore the north-east coast and the east coast and to land at one of her ports to verify whether the Japanese do in fact raise insurmountable obstacles to any commercial transaction or barter by Europeans; and whether through the appeal of furs, which are known to be most attractive to them, one might not be able to persuade ports on the east or north-east coast to allow vessels to bring some in, and in exchange supply tea, silks and similar other products of their soil and manufactures. The prohibitory laws of this empire, which every account reports to be very strict, may not be observed on the north-east and east coasts with the same severity as at Nangasaki and on the south coast which is too close to the capital for any chance of their being relaxed.

13. When Mr de la Pérouse reaches Macao, he will take the necessary steps to spend the winter at Kanton. He will, to this end, contact Mr Vieillard, His Majesty's consul in China, and will ask him to make the appropriate approaches to the Chinese government.

He will take advantage of his stay in that port to ascertain precisely and in detail the current state of each country's trade; and he will examine this important issue in all the aspects it might be useful to know.

He will obtain all the information he will consider useful for his subsequent navigation in the seas north of China, on the coasts of Korea and eastern Tartary, and to all the lands and islands remaining to be explored by him in this region.

He will not forget to obtain, if possible, a Chinese and Japanese interpreter, and a Russian interpreter, for his second call at Awatska. He will settle with them for the time he will have to retain their services on the vessels; and on his return will leave them at Mendaão or at the Moluccas.

14. He should be warned that Japanese bandits are often very numerous in the seas between Japan, Korea and Tartary: the weakness of their vessels requires him to take no other precautions than to be on his guard at night, in order to avoid being surprised by them: but it might be useful to try to catch up with one of them, and persuade him by gifts and the promise of a reward, to pilot His Majesty's ships during the exploration of Yeso, part of which is believed to be under Japanese domination, in the Strait of Tesso which the Japanese must know, and in the exploration of the Kuril Islands which they are in a position to visit. The same pilot could also be useful to visit some harbour on the west coast of Japan, should circumstances not have allowed him to land on some points of the east or north-east coast. But whatever use Mr de la Pérouse makes of the said pilot, he will only follow his advice and indications with the utmost caution.

It is also appropriate for him to engage, if he can, the services of fishermen from the Kuril Islands, to act as guides in those islands that lie close to Kamtschatka.

Mr de la Pérouse will thus try to complete, by sailing north, the exploration of the islands he might not have been able to visit when he sailed from Awatska to Macao, and to make up on the west coast of Japan for what he might not have been able to do on the east and north-east coasts.

The exploration of the coasts of Korea and Chinese Tartary must be carried out with great prudence and restraint. Mr de la Pérouse is advised that the Chinese government is very quick to take offence. He must consequently avoid flying his flag and make himself known on these coasts, and allow no operation likely to arouse that government's disquiet, because of the possibility that it might affect French vessels coming to trade in Kanton.

15. In the search and exploration Mr de la Pérouse will make among the Caroline Islands, of which only the name is known by most European nations, he will try to ascertain whether the Spanish have set up any establishment there, as they have often planned to do. He will report on their products, as with all the islands he may discover north-east and west-south-west of the Mariana Islands.

16. During his stay at one of these islands, Tinian, he will obtain information on the establishments, strength and trade of the Spanish among the islands of this archipelago and the surrounding area.

He will carry out similar investigations at Mendanao to find out, as far as he can, the political, military and commercial situation of this nation in the Philipine Islands.

17. During his stay in the Moluccas, he will not forget to obtain all the information he can on the situation of the Dutch in these islands. He will in particular assess the advantages which may derive for England's trade from the freedom which that power obtained by its latest peace treaty with Holland to sail and trade throughout the seas of Asia; and he will endeavour to find out the use England has made of this freedom, and whether as a result she has already succeeded in opening up new branches of commerce in this part of the world.

18. If Mr de la Pérouse puts in at the Cape of Good Hope, he will obtain precise information on the present state of that colony; on the forces which Holland, or the Dutch East Indies Company, maintains there since the outbreak of peace, and on the fortifications, new and old, that defend the town and protect the anchorage.

19. In general, in all the islands and all the ports of the continents, occupied or frequented by Europeans, where he will call, he will, with prudence and to the extent that circumstances and the length of his stays allow, carry out all the investigations required to make him conversant in some detail with the nature and extent of each nation's trade, the land and sea forces each one maintains there, the links based on interest and friendship that may exist between them and the chiefs and natives of the countries where they have settlements, and generally all matters of significance for politics and commerce.

THIRD PART

Operations related to Astronomy, Geography, Navigation, Physics and the various Branches of Natural History

His Majesty having appointed two astronomers to work under the orders of Mr de la Pérouse in the expedition He has entrusted to him, and having supplied the two frigates with all the astronomical and navigational instruments one can use on sea or land; he will see that during the voyage neither of the astronomers overlooks any opportunity of carrying out all the astronomical observations which may seem useful to him.

The most important task for the safety of navigation is to determine accurately the latitudes and longitudes of places where he lands or in sight of which he sails. To this end, he will advise the astronomer working on each frigate to oversee most attentively the performance of the chronometers and to seize every favourable opportunity to check while on land whether they have remained regular during the crossing and to assess by means of observations the daily change that may have occurred, in order to take this movement into account and determine with greater precision the longitude of islands, capes and other noteworthy features which he may have found and surveyed in the period between two verifications.

As often as the condition of the sky shall allow, he will order measurements of the distance between the moon and the sun or the stars to be taken by means of instruments provided for this purpose, in order to calculate the ship's longitude and compare it to the one indicated by the chronometers at the same place and time: and he will take care that such observations are multiplied so that the average result of different operations can give a more precise determination.

When he sails within sight of some island or land where he does not propose to land, he will be careful to remain on the same parallel, as far as possible, at the time when the altitude of the sun or some other planet is to be calculated in order to determine the ship's latitude: and he will settle on this same meridian for the moment when observations are to be made to determine the longitude. In this way he will avoid any error of position and estimate of distance which could adversely affect the accuracy of the determination.

He will require daily observations to be made, weather permitting, of the declination and inclination of the dipping needle.

Immediately upon arriving in a harbour, he will select an appropriate site on which to erect the tents and the observatory, and will set up a guard.

Separately from observations relating to the determination of latitudes and longitudes, for which every known and practicable method will be used, and those needed to assess the declination and inclination of the dipping needle, he will ensure that any celestial phenomenon which may be visible is observed; and on every occasion he will give the astronomers all the help and facilities necessary for the success of their work.

His Majesty has no doubt that the officers and *gardes de la marine* employed on the two frigates will themselves zealously carry out, in conjunction with the astronomers, every observation which may be of some value to navigation; and that the latter, for their part, will be anxious to advise the former of the result of their work and impart the theoretical knowledge which may contribute to perfecting the science of navigation.

Mr de la Pérouse will have a double set of registers kept on each frigate, in which will be recorded each day, both on land and at sea, astronomical observations, those related to the use of the chronometers, and all others, as they are made and before they are the subject of calculations, noting only the known error in the functioning of the instrument being used if this has been found by the usual checks. Each astronomer shall keep one of these two registers, and the other shall remain in the hands of each of the commanding officers. Each astronomer shall in addition maintain a second register in which he will similarly record, day by day, all the observations he makes; and he will note as well, for each operation, all the calculations leading to the final result.

At the end of the voyage, Mr de la Pérouse will hand over the two registers kept by each astronomer after they have certified them to be true and correct and signed them.

2. When Mr de la Pérouse lands in a port about which it may be desirable to have some information related to military matters, he shall have the country examined by the chief engineer who will provide him with a detailed report on everything he has noticed and with plans he may have been in a position to draw.

Mr de la Pérouse shall have accurate charts drawn of all the coasts and islands he visits; and if they have already been explored he will check the accuracy of descriptions and charts provided by other navigators.

To this end, when he sails along coasts and within sight of islands he will have very precise bearings taken by means of the variation compass; and he will bear in mind that the bearings that are the most useful for map-making are those where a cape or other noteworthy feature can be related to another.

He will use the officers from each frigates and the *ingénieur géographe* to survey and draw careful plans of the coasts, bays, ports and anchorages he will be in a position to inspect and explore; and he will append to each plan instructions detailing everything relating to the approach and identification of the coast, the entrance and exit from the ports, the manner of anchoring and mooring and the best place to obtain water, the depths and the quality of the bottom; dangers, rocks and reefs; prevailing winds; breezes, monsoons, their duration and the dates of their changes; in short all the information that can be of use to navigators.

Every chart of a country, coast and harbour shall be drawn in two copies; one shall be handed to each of the commanding officers; and at the end of the voyage Mr de la Pérouse will be given all the charts and related information.

His Majesty leaves it to him to decide when to assemble the decked boats taken on each frigate in parts. He will presumably await his call at Otaiti for this; and these boats can then be used to advantage following the frigates in the exploration of the equatorial archipelago, to explore the coasts, look for bays, harbours and anchorages, and for every operation requiring shallow-draught boats.

3. The physicists and naturalists His Majesty has appointed to make observations in their respective areas during the voyage will be used for physics and natural history, in that branch of knowledge to which each one has given preference.

Accordingly, Mr de la Pérouse will prescribe the research they will have to carry out in all areas, and will hand over to them the appropriate instruments and apparatus. In allocating tasks, he will be careful to avoid duplications, so that each scientist's enthusiasm and knowledge may fully contribute to the overall success of the expedition.

He will make known to them the contents of the memoir the *Académie Royale des Sciences* has forwarded to His Majesty, in which that society indicates the particular observations it would like the physicists and naturalists to make during the voyage. He will request them to contribute, each one in his own field and according to circumstances, to meet the objectives outlined in that memoir.

He will similarly advise the chief surgeons in each frigate of the *Société Royale de Médecine*'s memoir, so that they may both attend to the observations that would meet that society's hopes.

During his navigation and at each port of call, Mr de la Pérouse will have a register kept in which will be daily recorded every observation that relates to the condition of the sky and the sea, to winds, currents, variations in the atmosphere and everything concerned with meteorology.

During his stays in ports, he will have observations made on the characteristics, character, customs and practices, temperament, language, form of government and number of the inhabitants.

He will have studies made of the nature of the soil and products of the various countries, and of everything relating to the globe's physical properties.

He will ensure that natural, terrestrial and marine curiosities are collected from each of the three kingdoms; he will get them classified according to category, and will have drawn up, for each species, a descriptive catalogue indicating where they have been found, and the use to which the local natives put them; and if they are plants, the virtues they attribute to them.

He will similarly see to the collecting and classification of clothes, weapons, ornaments, furniture, tools, musical instruments and all items used by the various people he will visit; and every object shall bear a label and the number corresponding to its catalogue number.

He will require the artists embarked on the two frigates to draw sketches of the land and of all noteworthy sites, portraits of natives in the various countries, their dress, ceremonies, games, buildings, seagoing crafts and of all products of the land and sea in the three kingdoms, drawings of which he may consider useful to understand the descriptions provided by the scientists.

All the drawings made during the voyage, all the boxes containing natural curiosities, as well as the descriptions thereof and the books of observations, will be handed over to Mr de la Pérouse at the conclusion of the voyage; and no scientist or artist shall retain for himself or for anyone else any item of natural history or any other object which Mr de la Pérouse considers worth including in the collection intended for His Majesty.

4. Prior to his return to the port of Brest at the end of the voyage, or before reaching the Cape of Good Hope if he has to call there, Mr de la Pérouse shall collect every journal of the campaign that may have been kept on the two frigates by the officers and *gardes de la marine*, by the astronomers, scientists and artists, pilots and other persons: he shall charge them, on behalf of His Majesty, with

maintaining absolute silence on the aim of the voyage and the discoveries that may have been made, and shall require thereon their word of honour. He shall moreover assure them that their journals and papers will be returned to them as soon as His Majesty shall have given His permission for this to be done.

FOURTH PART
Policy to be followed towards the natives of countries where His Majesty's two frigates might land.

The accounts of all the navigators who preceded Mr de la Pérouse in the seas where he is to sail will have given him indications of the characters and practices of some of the various peoples he will have to deal with, both in the islands of the Great Ocean and on the Northwest coast of America; His Majesty is quite confident that, on the basis of these readings, he will take care to follow the wise behaviour of some of the navigators who have preceded him and avoid the errors of some others.

When he arrives in each country, he will take steps to obtain the friendship of the main chiefs, as much by proofs of his goodwill as by means of gifts; and he will ascertain the resources available there for the needs of his vessels. He will make every honest endeavour to establish links with the country's natives. He will try to find out which European goods or objects they seem to prize the most; and he will make up an assortment of such items as may appeal to them and encourage them to engage in barter.

He has no doubt felt how necessary it is to take every precautions prudence would advise in order to maintain his superiority against the crowd, without being compelled to use force; and however welcome the savages make him, it is important for him to remain on the defensive, because of the danger that his feeling of confidence might encourage them to attempt some surprise attack.

Whatever the circumstances, he shall send no longboat or other boat ashore which is not armed with its guns, supplied with muskets, swords, battle-axes and an adequate quantity of war ammunition, and under the command of an officer whom he will instruct never to lose sight of the boat under his charge and to keep it guarded by several men.

He will not allow any officer or crew to sleep on land for any other reason than official duties; and those persons whose functions may compel them to stay ashore will retire before nightfall in the tents erected to serve as observatory and store. He will set up a guard whose duty shall be to see to the safety of this establishment which shall always include one officer to maintain order among the sailors and soldiers appointed for this work, and prevent by a constant and active watch any attack or venture on the part of the savages.

He will take care to moor His Majesty's frigates so as to be in a position to protect the establishment; and he will advise the officer guarding it of the signals he should give in case of danger.

As soon as these arrangements have been made, he will organise means of obtaining food for his crews and seeing to other requirements; and after making a selection from among the goods, tools and objects of all kinds which have been supplied to the two frigates, he will set up a store for them ashore protected by guards. But since he has been made aware that the islanders of the Great Ocean cannot stop themselves from stealing, he will be careful not to place temptation in their way by presenting too large a selection of goods in the same place, and only to take ashore each day the items that are to be used for barter during the day. He will decide the value of these exchanges and will never allow anyone to exceed the amount he has determined for each item, for fear that if too high a price is accepted at the early stages for foodstuffs he wishes to purchase, the natives would use this to refuse subsequently to sell them at a lower price.

He will establish a single store for both frigates; and to maintain order and prevent any form of abuse he will select one officer to deal with the savages; and he will appoint the petty officers or others who are to operate the store under his supervision. No officer or any other member of his staff or crews will be allowed, under any pretext, to carry out any form of barter, unless Mr de la Pérouse has granted his express permission and fixed the rate of exchange.

If any member of the crews should steal, in order to take it ashore, any item belonging to the vessels, or any goods intended for barter, Mr de la Pérouse shall punish him in accordance with the regulations in force: and he would inflict more severe punishments on any who, being on duty at the store, should abuse his trust and appropriate any item for fraudulent purposes.

He shall instruct all the members of the crews to co-exist in amity with the natives, to try to obtain their friendship by a courteous behaviour and fair dealings; and he shall forbid them, under threat of the severest penalties, ever to use force to take from the inhabitants anything they might refuse to hand over voluntarily.

On every occasion, Mr de la Pérouse shall behave with the utmost gentleness and humanity towards the various peoples he will visit during his voyage.

He will display zeal and consideration in everything that can improve their standard of life, by supplying their country with European vegetables, fruits and other useful trees, teaching them how they should be sown and cultivated; explaining the use to which these gifts can be put, their purpose being to multiply on their soil products that are necessary to people who draw almost all their food from the land.

If imperative circumstances, which caution must lead us to anticipate during such a long campaign, should ever compel Mr de la Pérouse to use the superiority of his weapons over those of uncivilised people, in order to obtain, in spite of their opposition, items needed for his survival, such as food, water or wood, he should only use force with the utmost moderation and should punish most severely any of his men who exceeded his orders. In all other cases, if he cannot obtain the natives' friendship by kindness, he shall endeavour to restrain them by fear and threats, and will have recourse to arms only as a last extremity, only as a means of defence, and in circumstances when any tolerance would inevitably place the ships and the King's subjects in danger. His Majesty would consider it one of the greatest accomplishments of the expedition if it could be concluded without a single man losing his life.

FIFTH PART
On Precautions to be taken to preserve the health of the crews

As Mr de la Pérouse is aware of His Majesty's intentions in respect of the behaviour he should maintain towards the natives people and the care he should take to ensure that, when the French call, far from it proving to be a misfortune for these people, it should on the contrary provide them with advantages they lack, he will undoubtedly feel that particular attention should be devoted to the wellbeing of the crews engaged on the expedition which His Majesty has entrusted to him.

The vessels placed under his orders are supplied with an abundance of all that could be needed to prevent illnesses at sea, or to halt their progress, and to supplement the ordinary and counteract their effect. He will ensure that these various remedies are used as required and moderately; and he will especially see to all the resources which may be available at the various calling places, in order to obtain for his crews refreshments and a healthy sustenance to make up for the long use he will have to make of salted meat.

His Majesty leaves it to Mr de la Pérouse's wisdom to determine the most appropriate method of distributing, on both frigates, the food which is stored in the holds. He will ensure that any part of these supplies which may show signs of going bad, and which such precautions could help to save, is examined and aired during his stays in port.

He will overlook no opportunity of supplying fresh fish to his crews, and to renew his stocks of salt provisions by the means which have been provided for him, and by using the method successfully followed in recent times by navigators sailing in the Great Ocean.

Mr de la Pérouse is aware that one of the most effective precautions one can take to preserve the crews' health is to pay close attention to the maintenance of the cleanliness of the ships and men. To this end he will adopt all known means, such as ventilators, fumigations, perfumes, to renew and purify the air in the hold and the 'tween-decks. Daily, whenever possible, he will have the crews' hammocks and clothing laid out in the open; and so that the sailors and other persons making up the complement do not neglect their personal hygiene, he will divide them into sections to be inspected and supervised by various officers of the two frigates. Each of these shall report weekly to the captain on the conditions of the clothing and the requirements of each section under his supervision; and the spare clothing which His Majesty has ordered to be taken on board shall be distributed to the two ships' crews as and when Mr de la Pérouse requires it to be done and allotted in accordance with his instructions.

Mr de la Pérouse shall establish the strictest rules of discipline among the crews of both frigates and will ensure that these rules are not relaxed in any way. But this strictness, which is appropriate in any of the services, and essential in a campaign of this duration, shall be tempered by the paternal care he owes to those who share in his hardships: and His Majesty, knowing the sentiments that govern his behaviour, is confident that he will constantly strive to obtain for his crews every facility and comfort he will be able to grant them without adversely affecting the interests of the service and the aims of the expedition.

His Majesty could not give Mr de la Pérouse a greatest mark of His confidence in his zeal, ability and wisdom than by entrusting to him one of the most extensive enterprises every undertaken. Some of the navigators who preceded him in the task of discovery have shown him great lessons and great examples; but His Majesty is persuaded that, as eager for glory, as determined to increase human knowledge, and as resolute as his models, he will deserve one day to serve in his turn as an example to those who, driven by the same courage, will want to attain the same renown.

At Versailles, twenty-sixth of June 1785

[*signed*] Louis

[*countersigned*]
Marshall de Castries

[a] Summing up what is proposed in this memoir and the comments I have made, there are two parts: one relating to trade and one to exploration. As for the first of these, two main points, the whale fishery in the southern ocean between South America and Cape of Good Hope, the other is the fur trade in north-west America, to be transported to China and, if possible, Japan. As for the exploration part, the main points are the N.W. coast of America, which fits in with the commercial part; the voyage in the seas around Japan which also fits in with it, but in this respect I believe the season proposed in this memoir is badly chosen; the Solomon Islands and the south-west of New Holland. All the other points must be subordinated to those; and one must limit oneself to what is of most use and what can comfortably be carried out in the three years proposed.

THE VOYAGE

Apart from Dufresne, the scientists had received their orders by 28 May 1785. For the previous week and until mid-June, Monneron's purchases had been arriving from England. Lord Dorset, the British Ambassador in Paris, reported to Lord Camarthen:

> Monsieur de la Pérouse will sail from Brest the latter end of this month with only two ships. The King had formed great expectations from the intended voyage of that able officer, but M. de la Pérouse himself is less sanguine, and even despairs of succeeding in the search of new discoveries, after the attempts that have already been made by Captain Cooke [*sic*].

The end of May came and went, but La Pérouse had not sailed. However Dorset picked up some fascinating rumours which he transmitted to the Foreign Secretary on 9 June:

> I had particularly mentioned the orders [La Pérouse] had received to touch at New Zealand, with a design of examining into the nature of the timber there, which is of an excellent quality for repairing ships, but more particularly for masts. I can now inform your Lordship, from good authority, that 60 criminals, from the prison of Bicêtre, were last Monday conveyed under a strong guard and with great secrecy to Brest where they are to be embarked on board M. de la Pérouse's ships, and it is imagined that they are to be left to take possession of this lately discovered Country.[1]

Two days after the date of this despatch, the Maréchal de Castries gave the scientists a farewell dinner at Versailles.[2] Shortly after, they left for Brest. On the 28th, La Pérouse had a final meeting with Louis XVI. It is the subject of a famous formal painting by Monsiau now in the Versailles collection.[3] On the 30th, Castries took La Pérouse

[1] See O. Browning (ed.), *Despatches from Paris 1784–1790*, 2 vols, London, 1909, p. 58.

[2] Letter from Prévost to Thouin, [?] June 1785. Bibliothèque du Muséum d'Histoire Naturelle MS 1928, 2, 38:1.

[3] Musée de Versailles. The painting dates from 1817, by which time Louis XVI's brother had ascended the throne as Louis XVIII. This fulfilled a wish expressed by Louis XVI, see L.E. Le Brun, *Souvenirs de Madame Louise-Elisabeth Vigée-Lebrun*, Paris, 1835–7, I, p. 12, and II, p. 63, quoted in Gaziello, *L'Expédition de Lapérouse 1785–1788*, p. 75.

to the Trianon Palace to meet Marie-Antoinette, and the next day Jean-François left for Brest. There was no time for any farewells to his wife, Eléonore.

De Langle was waiting for him for a few final decisions. Should barter goods be left behind, or food? There was not room for everything. La Pérouse chose to leave 100 sacks of flour and some crates of biscuit, because he could always buy food with the trade goods.[1] Chaos and crowding were inevitable when a ship was on the point of sailing. For the scientists, this new world was well-nigh unbelievable. Not only were the ships crammed below, but the decks looked like a farmyard: there were five cows tied around the mainmast, 30 sheep in the longboat, 20 pigs along the gangways, 200 hens in cages along the poop deck. Perishable food was secured in every corner – potatoes, beans, fruit, salads, cabbages. Fish hung down from the shrouds, slowly drying in nets. The cabins were small and cramped, and the presence of the savants ensured that normal accommodation would be even more restricted. The main council room in each ship had been partitioned into small cabins; one or two areas separated by lengths of sailcloth were designated studies.

Thus in the *Astrolabe*, Langle had a cabin on the poop deck, Flassan, Boutervilliers, Law and Lesseps shared the council room, Monti had a cabin on one side of it, Blondelas on the other, Vaujuas and Marchainville had a cupboard-like cabin near them, while D'Aigremont, La Martinière, Prévost and Dufresne were given a partitioned space christened for the occasion Chambres des Savants. There would be only minor changes possible to this arrangement for the next two-and-a-half years.

On 11 July 1785 the two ships, with their total complement of 225 men, were hauled by boats our into the stream. But the winds were unfavourable: a week went by, then another. The Count d'Hector sent a spare storeship to anchor between the two frigates; it served as a dormitory for the men, reducing the overcrowding while they waited for the wind to change.[2] Finally, on 1 August

[1] La Pérouse to Minister, 5 July 1785. 'I...am convinced that after a period of two years, having passed through Endeavour Strait, I will find at Timor or at Princes Island the rice I would need and that by then my flour will have completely gone bad.' AN.M. C7 165, 7.

[2] Hector to Minister, 25 July 1785. 'Concerned that [the men] might develop some sickness, I sent the storeship *Saumon* to anchor between the two frigates.' Archives de Brest, 1A 165:568.

1785, to shouts of 'Long Live the King', the *Boussole* and the *Astrolabe* sailed out into the Atlantic.

Nothing of note happened on the run south to Madeira, La Pérouse reported, which meant nothing untoward, no blustering gales, no angry squalls. There was still congestion on deck and below; the settling into the unfamiliar world of the sea for some, the establishment of a routine for all. They eyed each other as polite strangers, officers who shared memories of past campaigns, scientists for whom the vessels were merely means by which they could set up experiments and seek new specimens. By their very functions scientists and sailors were at odds; there would be clashes at times, inevitably, but the real wonder of it all is how few these were.

The first occurred not at Madeira, but at Tenerife where Lamanon, anxious to climb the Peak and carry out his observations, had to be told that the expedition could not pay for the number of mules he had ordered. The incident revealed to all a split between the two men which La Pérouse outlined in a letter to Fleurieu, refering to him as ignorant in everything outside his own specialty, a hothead with a streak of meanness in him. The two men kept clear of each other, and the strain abated somewhat in due course.[1]

But excursions ashore were a form of release for the scientists cooped up on board with no real work to do. Lamartinière wrote to Thouin that on landing in Madeira his first feeling was a mad desire to run up the mountains.[2] The days must had seemed long between the morning meal, at 9 a.m., when cold meat or soup was served with whatever vegetables were available, and 4 p.m. when the main meal was laid out, consisting of soup, meat, bread, wine and coffee. There were private stores, but they had to be eked out for a voyage of such indeterminate length. And it was not easy to read or work in narrow cabins occupied by two or three men.

Thus Madeira on 13 August and Tenerife on the 19th were memorable ports of call for them. Crossing to South America was a different matter – six weeks before any land was sighted, and even so it was only the small island of Trinity where the Governor was so frightened of possible designs on his wretched island that he offered no assistance and prevented the naturalists from examining

[1] La Pérouse unburdened himself of his problems in a private letter to Fleurieu of 28 August 1785, AN. M. 3JJ 386 2–19.

[2] Letter of 9 January 1787 from Macao. AN. M. AJxv, 111, 416:1.

the flora. It was not until 6 November that the two vessels anchored off the island of Santa Catarina, Brazil.

After a brief stay, La Pérouse set out for Cape Horn. In this region of fogs and storms, the two ships could easily become separated. He told de Langle that, should this happen, they would meet in Le Maire's Strait, and failing that, in Tahiti. At this point, therefore, La Pérouse still intended to follow his original instructions – across the southern Pacific, practically following the tracks of Bougainville as far as the New Hebrides and on to Australia. But there was to be no separation. By Christmas the ships were sailing together with a good south-westerly breeze and the southern summer was beginning. In blue skies and calm sea, the officers were even able to lower boats and go shooting for birds. Albatross and petrel, served with a piquant sauce, provided a nice change of diet.

By mid-January La Pérouse was sailing south between the coast of South America and the Falkland Islands. A week later he was within sight of the Strait of Magellan, and making speedily for Le Maire's. There was no problem, apart from occasional fog. He veered south-west towards the Horn, rounding it with far more ease than he had dared to hope. It made him a little disdainful of its dangers, blaming fear of the Cape on 'an old prejudice that should disappear.'[1]

And now came the change of plan. He had been given discretion and he used it drastically. Instead of sailing west into the South Pacific, he would go north. It was only early February and he realised that he could easily reach the Northwest Coast in time to spend the summer months surveying its innumerable islands and inlets.

Thus he sailed north, along the coast of Chile to the port of Concepción. It was the main town of the southern strip of this long, meandering country squeezed out between the Pacific Ocean and the Andes. It was a strange, closed world, held back by the Spanish policy of exclusiveness which banned all foreign shipping and controlled every facet of its trade. The women's garments belonged to a bygone age – 'made with that old gold or silver cloth we used to manufacture in Lyons'. The manners were redolent of ancient Spain; the district, where barely ten thousand people resided,

[1] La Pérouse blamed the Horn's bad reputation on George Anson's report on his 1740 voyage. See Journal, Chapter II.

was filled with convents and monasteries, but there was more superstition about than devotion.

Nothing illustrates more dramatically the remoteness and enforced isolation of Concepción than the fact that La Pérouse could not find it where his charts showed it to be. More than 30 years earlier, an earthquake had so devastated the town that it was decided to rebuild it on a new site eight miles away, but no one in Paris, neither Fleurieu nor his colleagues at the Dépot des Cartes et Plans had been able to inform La Perouse about it.

It mattered little, for pilots came out to assist him, bringing messages of welcome from the Governor. The Spanish government had passed on news of the French expedition to their South American possessions, and the ships were expected. Fruit, vegetables and fresh meat were brought out in small boats. The Spaniards could not withhold their astonishment: not one of La Pérouse's men was ill, an unheard of situation for vessels arriving from Europe.

The stay lasted three weeks – from 24 February to 17 March 1786 – and it left the most pleasant memories on all sides. For the people of Concepción, it was a welcome relief from crushing boredom; for the French it was a respite from the long months spent at sea. There was a series of receptions, balls and dinners. La Pérouse was able to meet the military commander of the district, 'Monsieur Higuins', who hastened back from one of his endless campaigns against the restive Araucanian Indians. He was Ambrosio O'Higgins, soon to become Governor of Chile, and the father of Bernardo O'Higgins, 'The Liberator'.[1]

Concepción looked charming and tempting. Two men deserted, whom La Pérouse did not bother to get back. He did not want any reluctant sailors with him. But he hung on to Dufresne. The unfortunate man was bored, and no one, including himself, seemed too sure why he had joined the expedition; but he did know about trade and the fur market, so that a deal was struck between the two men – Dufresne would report on the fur trade, buy furs from the natives of the Northwest Coast and sell them in China. After that, he would be put ashore to find his own way back to France.

The humanitarian aims of the expedition cannot be overlooked.

[1] Monneron wrote a brief report on the colony, entitled 'Chily', dated 30 March 1786. AN. M. 3JJ 386, 111:22.

The exploration of little-known areas, hydrographical research, natural history, cartography, ethnography, the assessment of the political balance in the Pacific, the potential for trade, all these had their place in the plan, but there was another aspect:

'Of all the benefits which the King's generosity can bestow on the inhabitants of newly discovered countries, plants that can help feed mankind are without doubt those which will bring them the most lasting benefits and can best increase their happiness.'[1]

This was no mere platitude. The ships were packed with seeds, grains, plants, potatoes; and there were still live animals aboard. The inhabitants of Chile had a surplus of crops. The expedition loaded more grains, fruits, fresh meat for its own use. But Concepción hardly qualified as newly discovered, or its inhabitants in need of European skills, since the settlement dated back to the early sixteenth century.

So La Pérouse, instead of making north for Valparaiso or Monterey, sailed west to Easter Island. It enabled him to play his part in eliminating from the charts the land of Davis, a mythical island which many navigators and geographers had speculated about.

He stayed less than a day at Easter island, leaving behind a considerable quantity of useful gifts – goats, sheep, pigs, seeds of orange trees, lemon trees, maize, 'and generally of every species that can succeed in their island'. The French did more – they travelled inland and Collignon sowed cabbages, carrots, pumpkins, maize and beet in soil he considered appropriate, planting small trees in other places. Was all this owed to the personal generosity of the King? So ran the fiction, because it was traditional to do everything in the King's name. It may well have been Louis XVI's wish but this was the age of the *philosophes* and above all of the Noble Savage. For the first time, the two ships had anchored among a primitive people. And Jean-Jacques Rousseau had speculated, in writings which had become enormously popular, that if civilised Europe contained so much that was corrupt and oppressive, civilisation itself and not man was the corrupting factor; consequently primitive man, still unaffected by the social and economic evils of civilisation, should be happy and indeed noble. It was not his own way of life that European man should bring to the

[1] Dunmore & Brossard, *Le Voyage de Lapérouse 1785–1788*, I, p. 9. See also Gaziello, *L'Expédition de Lapérouse 1785–1788*, pp. 59–65; and 'Instructions', Part IV, above.

natives, but simply new crops that could raise their standards of life without developing greed and ambition.

Jean-Francois was no Rousseauist. He was down-to-earth, clear-eyed; a practical man, a sailor with no time for theories evolved by philosophers, academics or drawing-room geographers. Again and again, he would inveigh against those who pontificated without any first-hand experience. Man was man wherever he lived. Kindness need not be blind.

> La Pérouse had already taken a dim view of the goodness of primitive people when, towards the end of the American War, after destroying some British forts on Hudson Bay, he left food and arms for the defeated enemy lest they fall defenceless into the hands of the Indians.[1]

At Easter Island, he found the islanders such shameless thieves that their sheer impudence made him laugh. He took no punitive action. Indeed, seeing them stealing hats from the sailors, he told his men he would replace their losses, so that they would not get angry and start fights to get their property back.

This view of natives was not born of bitterness but of realism. Why should he be led into a false attitude towards human nature by theories evolved in fashionable salons? He had read all the accounts of voyagers who had sailed before him. Marion du Fresne had been through it all, had believed in that paradise of Rousseau's philosophers, and been killed; Cook had been murdered in Hawaii. What reason could there be for assuming that native people in distant lands were any different from his own men, rogues and drunkards many of them, kept under control only by a stern but paternal discipline, simple, credulous sailors from Brittany or Provence, praying to saints no one else knew much about, or rascals who had fled their homes in search of adventure, quick to wench and quick to brawl?

Although he was a product of the Jesuits, La Pérouse verged on the agnostic, but he was more tempted to believe in original sin than in natural goodness. Above all, he responded to what he saw, laughing with the good humour of the southerner, while shaking his head at human behaviour. The Easter Islanders were not thieves because of their innocence, unaware of any difference between the

[1] McKenna, 'The Noble Savage in the *Voyage* of La Pérouse', *Kentucky Foreign Language Quarterly*, XII, 1, 1965, p. 29.

'thine' and the 'mine'; they were merely bold pickpockets who knew what they were about. 'I esteem them far less because they seemed capable of reflection', he wrote in his journal – but this is merely realism and far from Rousseau's extreme view that 'the state of reflection goes against nature and a man who ponders is a depraved being'. He would be equally clear-eyed and unsentimental on the Northwest Coast; he would be unimpressionable in Kamchatka; and he would note in the Samoan Islands that Lamanon who had remarked 'these men are worth more than us' was killed by the islanders the next day.[1]

La Pérouse's view is not that of a *philosophe* in the Age of Enlightment, nor of a traditionalist. It is pragmatic, closer to the Physiocrats who were at that very moment attempting to reform the economic structure of France, and who were motivated by the belief in 'progress' that was to be the hallmark of the nineteenth-century bourgeois. He had criticised both the policy of Spanish exclusiveness and the number of religious establishments in Chile because they stood in the way of economic progress. In California, he would criticise the missionaries because they were not developing the local Indians quickly enough into active Europeans. He was against religion where it preached inaction; he disliked the monks because they were contemplative, but praised them when they acted like missionaries of progress. One is tempted to point out in this context how firmly he had insisted on his ship's chaplains being useful crew members as well as pious men.

So he took his precautions, landed on Easter Island with armed men, guffawed at the antics of the thieves, dispensed gifts and forgiveness in equal doses, but harboured no illusions. He sailed away during the night. This was all the punishment he wished to inflict. The only illusion he had was that, when they found him gone in the morning, they might regret that their behaviour towards him had driven him away.[2]

Precautions were also needed in the next island group which the two ships called at – the Hawaiian Islands, then known as the Sandwich Islands from the name James Cook had given them. It was here that the famous English navigator had been killed, for

[1] See 'La Pérouse and the Noble Savage', below.

[2] This is La Pérouse's concluding section of his Chapter IV. In the 1797 published version Milet-Mureau qualifies La Pérouse's reserved optimism by writing 'this possibly fanciful notion'.

reasons Europeans could only ascribe to perfidiousness, since only days earlier the islanders had fêted him. So on 30 May 1786, when La Pérouse landed on Maui, he did so under the protection of 40 armed soldiers. He need not have worried. The reception the islanders gave him was as friendly as anyone could wish. They brought him pigs; he gave them axes, lengths of iron, and some of the commemorative medals that had been specially struck for the expedition. Here he found barter, not theft:

> My imagination was attracted by the thought of comparing them to the Indians of Easter Island. . .every advantage was on the side of those men of the Sandwich Islands, even though I was wholly prejudiced against them on account of the death of Captain Cook. It is more natural for navigators to regret so great a man than to examine coolly whether some incautious action on his part might not have, in some way, forced the inhabitants of Oahu to resort to justified self-defence.[1]

As far as he knew, no other Europeans had landed on Maui. Strictly, he could have laid claim to the island in the name of Louis XVI, but he considered such a practice ridiculous and immoral. What right have Europeans, he wrote, to lands their inhabitants have worked with the sweat of their brow and which for centuries have been the burial place of their ancestors? The real task of explorers was to complete the survey of the globe, not add to the possessions of their own rulers.

After 48 hours, sailing along the west coast of the islands, La Pérouse passed through Kauai Channel, north of Oahu, towards the more austere Alaska coast.

* * *

By 6 June, the weather was becoming colder, the sky whiteish and dull. Soon fog appeared, damp and clinging. The sailors' clothes were cold and wet, 'with never a ray of sunshine to dry them'. The surgeon suggested adding quinquina to the morning grog, but it had to be done secretly, 'otherwise the men would certainly have refused to drink it'. Whales 'of the largest species', loons and ducks showed that land was not far. On the 23rd, at 4 a.m., the fog parted

[1] Reflexions of May 1786, Chapter VI.

and suddenly a long chain of snow-covered mountains stretched out ahead. The expedition had reached Mt St Elias.

It was here that Vitus Bering had sailed in 1741. What he had seen at the height of the northern summer was what La Pérouse now saw in the same season: 'a sterile treeless land ... a black plateau, as though burnt out by some fire, devoid of any greenery, a striking contrast with the whiteness of the snow we could make out through the clouds'. But this was the world of the sea otter, the Alaskan seal, the blue and the Arctic foxes – it was the heart of the fur trade. Bering had died miserably on his way home, the coastline barely charted, but enough of his crew had returned to Kamchatka with tales of a dense population of fur-bearing animals for the fur rush to begin. Although until 1775 only Russians sailed the Alaskan coast, the numbers of the fur animals and indeed of the Aleut Islanders dropped dramatically. but there was still a great deal of money to be made. The Spaniards, anxious to preserve their claims to the entire Pacific seaboard, sent Juan Pérez in 1774 to the Queen Charlotte Islands. In 1775 Juan Francisco Bodega reached the site of modern Sitka in southern Alaska.[1] All this was claimed for Spain, but in 1778 James Cook staked a claim for England and charted the coastline by means off a running survey to latitude 65°N.

In 1778 the Russians formed a trading company under Gregor Shelikov and the first European settlement was planted, not on the continent, but on Kokiak Island, strategically situated in the western part of the Gulf of Alaska.[2] Now the French had come, with Dufresne assiduously writing notes for a report on the fur trade and France's chances of joining the bonanza. For La Pérouse, hydrography was more important. Although Cook had surveyed the coastline there were innumerable inlets and bays in this deeply indented coast, many of them still very imperfectly known. There was also the tantalising possibility of a North-West Passage, from the Atlantic to the Pacific, the northern pendant to Magellan's Strait in the south. People had sought it in vain from the Atlantic side: it might be possible to discover it from the Pacific coast.

The two ships sailed slowly in thick, intermittent fog, down the coast. On the 26th, La Pérouse sent three boats to reconnoitre a bay

[1] Dunmore, *Who's Who*, pp. 192–3, 31–2. W. Cook, *Flood Tide of Empire: Spain and the Pacific Northwest 1543–1819*, New Haven, 1973.

[2] Chévigny, *Russian America*, New York, 1965; R.V. Marakova, *Russians in the Pacific 1743–1749*, Kingston, Ont., 1975.

which might be a useful inlet. It led nowhere, but as Monti had led the survey La Pérouse gave it his name. It was in all probability Yakutat Bay, no mean bay, but no passage to the interior either. The fog closed in. To ensure he could chart the coast without a break, he tacked out to sea, then back again. It was slow, bone-chilling work off a coast that remained bleak and inhospitable.

By 1 July 1786 the ships were just west of Mount Fairweather. Time and again, the boats were lowered to examine the coast. Along it there were now men waving and canoes manoeuvring between the rocks. The next day a bay appeared, shown on no chart and, La Pérouse assumed, never before sighted. It was wide, its waters still and calm. 'If the French government had any plans for a trading post in this part of the American coast, no nation could claim any right to oppose it'. He called it Port des Français. It is now known as Lituya Bay.

Excellent though it proved as an anchorage, entering it was difficult. The wind changed, there were rocks not far below the surface. 'Never in the thirty years that I have spent at sea have I seen two ships so near destruction'.

The danger once behind him, La Pérouse settled in for a stay of almost a month. A camp was set up on a small island, and the scientists began their observations, while the men collected firewood and fresh water and La Pérouse organised the exploration of the tortuous inlet. The bay appeared to be closed by great glaciers, five of them, grinding their way slowly from steep bare mountains, the silence broken only by the cries of lonely wild birds and occasional fall of enormous blocks of ice; but at the back of this bay he hoped to find channels by which he might enter 'into the interior of America . . . it might lead to some great river running between two mountains, and [this] might have its source in one of the great lakes of northern Canada'.[1]

But there was no way through. The fiords were closed off by waterfalls, ice, or sheer rock faces. And if this was summer, how dismal a place would Lituya Bay be in winter? Could anyone really contemplate a settlement in such a spot, even with the rewards to be gained from the fur trade? The natives were unprepossessing, willing to trade fish and furs for clothing, nails and implements,

[1] Extracts from Chapter VII of La Pérouse's journal. On the search for a north-west passage, see 'Instructions' for 15 July 1787, although these assumed that La Pérouse would be sailing north up the coast from Monterey.

but even more willing to steal. Law and d'Arbaud, on duty at the observatory, were robbed of a musket, their spare clothes and a notebook in which the astronomical observations had been entered. 'I am willing,' wrote La Pérouse, 'to admit that it is impossible for a society to exist without some virtues, but I am forced to state that I did not have the wisdom to notice any.' As for the women, he dismissed them as 'repulsive.'

Nevertheless, and without much faith in the transaction, he agreed to buy the island from the man he took to be the local chief, but without the 'Eskimo interpreter' which Monneron had hoped to recruit in London it was not easy to communicate. It is unlikely in any case that an interpreter could have been found who understood the particular language of these people. For their part, the Tlingit people had taken the French at first for the servants of Yehlh, their bird creator, who had returned to earth in the form of a raven. It was only after an elderly warrior had ventured on board the vessels that they realised these were men in some gigantic form of canoe, and not ghostly spirits. From that moment, the French became fair game for thieves – strangers towards whom no hospitality was due.[1]

While La Pérouse was readying the ships for departure, Monneron and Bernizet completed their charting of the bay. Then disaster struck – 'more cruel than sickness and the thousand other happenings of the longest voyages.' D'Escures had been sent to sound the bay, so that Monneron could show the various depths on his chart. La Pérouse had cautioned him not to venture too close to the rocks near the pass which had proved so dangerous when the expedition had first entered the bay. Apart from that, they could go hunting ashore and picnic. 'It was as much an outing as it was useful.' But d'Escures went too close, the tide was racing madly, and first his boat then the *Astrolabe*'s pinnace were carried away and capsised. It was all over in less than ten minutes.

Six officers and 15 men were drowned, including d'Escures, Pierrevert, La Pérouse's young cousin Montarnal, Flassan and both the Labordes. There were no bodies washed ashore, merely the implacable sea breaking on the black rocks. La Pérouse erected a small cairn on the island, which he named Cenotaph Island, placing

[1] See G.T. Emmons, 'Native Account of the Meeting between La Pérouse and the Tlingit', *American Anthropologist*, 1911, pp. 294–8.

underneath a bottle with a message setting out the tragedy and giving the names of the dead. Lamanon composed the message:

At the entrance to this port twenty-one brave sailors perished.
Whoever you are, mix your tears with ours

The tragedy affected La Pérouse for a long time. The blame lay with d'Escures, he had no doubt of that, but as if he felt the need to justify his own actions beyond argument he copied at length the instruction he had given him in writing, including the warnings about the pass, and indeed the admonishment he gave d'Escures after his second-in-command 'asked me if I took him for a child.' A man of 33, who had already commanded warships! he added. What more could he have done?

The death of the two Laborde brothers was particularly tragic. On 3 May 1787 Lord Dorset reported the tragedy to London:

> Two sons of Mons. de la Borde [formerly the Court Banker] were unfortunately drowned on this occasion, to the great grief of their family who are inconsolable at the loss of two very promising young men.[1]

Tragedy was to continue to pursue the family: their father would be guillotined in 1794.[2]

Unfavourable winds, the hope that some survivors might yet be found, and the need to make a number of changes on board the ships kept the expedition of Port des Français until 30 July. The deaths eased the pressure on space; it was melancholy work, but the belongings of the dead men had to be moved, some to be stored, some to be auctioned, and their cabins altered to provide greater comfort for the living. And there were promotions: d'Arbaud to *enseigne*, and Broudou to *lieutenant de frégate*.[3]

La Pérouse by now realised how impossible was the task he had been set. The innumerable inlets of the coast would require months of painstaking exploration if the riddle of North-West Passage was

[1] Browning, *Despatches*, 1909 p. 188.

[2] Jean-Joseph de Laborde, court banker, bibliophile and patron of the arts, had close links with the aristocracy (his daughter married the Comte de Noailles); what made him a target of the revolutionaries during the Terror was as much his involvement with government finances as his links with the court. The great chemist Lavoisier was guillotined for the same reason. See Y. Durand, *Les Fermiers Généraux au XVIIIe siècle*, Paris, 1971, especially pp. 186–7, 512, 536–7.

[3] La Pérouse to the Minister, letter of 19 September 1786 from Monterey.

ever to be solved, but he had to keep his sense of proportion. His voyage was one of general Pacific exploration. He had been delayed for three weeks in Lituya Bay, and less than three months had been allowed to survey the entire coastline, largely because he wanted to devote the following summer months to exploring the colder regions of the Asiatic coast.

The result was an extraordinary period of activity, for which everyone on board was mobilised, charting, surveying, checking, sacrificing only the time-consuming reconnaissance of minor bays and inlets. In effect, he was compelled to drop the search for the North-West Passage. He was coming to the belief that it was a chimera, a theory evolved with no backing evidence by those who believed that somehow the world had to be symmetrical and that a southern strait must be balanced by a northern passage.

On 4 August 1786, the fog cleared to reveal Cross Sound, marking the beginning of the Alexander Archipelago. If the sea was fair, the winds were contrary. In 24 hours the French covered less than 10 leagues. The coast was wooded, the snow-covered ranges had fallen away to the north or lay hidden behind the persistent low cloud. 'Here, I am convinced, we could find twenty different harbours.' The fog, swirling in each evening, parted reluctantly when the sun rose again. Sitka Sound opened out, then the protean inlets of Baranof Island with so many headlands and hills 'that it is enough to change one's position a little to change their appearance.'

Christian Sound, a vast opening, marked the beginning of the end of the archipelago and the many islands that lie offshore from Prince of Wales Island like retainers protecting their master. The westerly breeze was more favourable, but currents drove the ships towards the open sea. The Spanish charts were of little help. 'Maurelle's Bucarelli harbour is in this part; I have found nothing in his map or in his account that could enlighten me.'[1]

By the 9th La Pérouse was crossing Dixon Entrance towards Queen Charlotte Islands. A strong north-westerly breeze helped, but the fog closed in. By the evening, although than a league from the coast they could hardly see it. There was a brief glimpse of land on the 10th, but the wind increased to a fresh gale and the ships

[1] Francisco Antonio Maurelle (1754–1820) had been on the Pacific coast since the early 1770s. He sailed from San Blas to the Alexander Archipelago in March 1775, Dunmore, *Who's Who*, pp. 176–7.

veered away. On the 11th, not far from Cape Knox on Graham Island, the fog was so thick that the *Astrolabe* could not be seen from the *Boussole* even though shouted orders could be heard. Four days went by, frustrating and filled with danger, for the winds had dropped. On the 17th the fog cleared and careful observations were possible. The French were in latitude 53′ 12′, within sight of Moresby Island, a lonely world of deep inlets and tall dark trees, filled with the cries of seabirds.

Suddenly, 'the coast of America' seemed to end.' It was the southern tip of the Queen Charlotte Islands to which La Pérouse gave the name of the man who had done so much to help with the preparations in Brest, the Comte d'Hector; today, Cap Hector has assumed the name of Cape St James. Fleurieu, whose name went to grace the northern point of Vancouver Island has fared no better.

Thus, the expedition was passing Queen Charlotte Sound and starting its survey of the west coast of Vancouver Island. It was a matter of completing Cook's work. Ideas about discovering the North-West Passage had gone. So La Pérouse avoided Queen Charlotte Sound and, later, Juan de Fuca Strait; this decision lost him the opportunity of making his mark on the hydrography of the region, but it saved him from becoming bottled up in the narrowing straits behind Vancouver Island, and from the disappointment of having to turn back from one of the inlets of the coast; Vancouver Island is far too large a land mass for someone sailing past it not to assume that it forms part of the continent itself.[1]

Clearer weather would have helped, but fogs remained his persistent companions. August was running out, an early autumn was pursuing him all the way down the coast. He had difficulty even in identifying points visited by the Spaniards – which was not surprising since so many of the reports were vague and the old charts fanciful. Even James Cook's Nootka Sound was hard to find: on 25 August, 'a very thick fog, rising up at about five in the afternoon

[1] The complexity of the task is shown by the length of time George Vancouver spent on exploring the Northwest Coast – from April 1792 to December 1794, allowing for wintering in the Hawaiian Islands. It is 'a coast so remarkably complicated that Vancouver's systematic and painstaking survey ranks with the most distinguished work of the kind ever done', J.C. Beaglehole, *The Exploration of the Pacific*, 3rd ed., London, 1966, p. 322. On Vancouver, see W. Kaye Lamb (ed.) *The Voyage of George Vancouver 1791–1795*, London, 1984. La Pérouse's instructions did not allow him the time he would have needed for anything approaching a detailed survey.

hid the land altogether.' It lasted five days, making a sighting of Juan de Fuca Strait impossible. And now the coastline changed. There were few bays, but violent coastal currents. This was Oregon. There was work to be done from 47° to 45° north, since Cook had not charted this coast in detail, but fogs, currents and calms hampered the French survey. It was slow, dangerous, irritating work.

The first half of September was spent on this. The scientists welcomed the fog, which gave them a chance to rest, the sailors found it increasingly exhausting, as the two ships had to change course, alter sails, and manoeuvre close together. The decks were constantly wet, the rigging ever cold and clammy. Each headland was like another prayer for deliverance along a string of beads: Cape Flattery, Cape Lookout, Cape Blanco, Cape Mendocino, Point Arena, Point Reyes, and at last the wide expanse of Monterey Bay.[1]

On 15 September 1786, the *Boussole* and the *Astrolabe* dropped anchor, two cablelengths from land. The Spaniards sent pilots on board, and the fort of Monterey fired its gun salute in welcome.

Monterey was a mere 15 years old when La Pérouse arrived. The bay had been discovered in 1602 by Sebastian Vizcaino who overpraised it, so that when the Spaniards decided to establish a settlement there in 1770 they had difficulty in even recognising it and they overlooked the far superior harbour of San Francisco, a mere 40 miles further north.

At first, the Spaniards found conditions so harsh that they contemplated abandoning the place altogether – a familiar pattern in the story of colonisation. An overland route from Mexico to California was essential. The trail was blazed in 1773 from Sonora, thus linking Monterey with the rest of Spanish America. There were still miserable establishments, poorly kept, unprosperous. The San Carlos mission at Monterey soon moved to the Carmel River further south. Recruiting settlers was more difficult than finding Franciscans willing to run the missions; most of those who came were soldiers, glad enough to marry and farm a small strip of land in this fertile district. Apart from the squabbles of petty officials,

[1] The arrival at Monterey and the stay in California take up Chapters X and XI of La Pérouse's narrative. Spanish administrators in Chile, Peru, Mexico and Manila had been forewarned of his arrival and instructed to assist him by a circular letter from José de Galvez de la Sonora, Minister for the Indies, dated 19 May 1785, AN. M. 3JJ 386, 4, and AN. M. 3JJ 388, 111/2:8

the religious festivals and the occasional Indian raid, Alta California slumbered quietly in pastoral simplicity.

The arrival of the French ships was a welcome break in the sleepy routine of Monterey. News had already travelled from Concepción that they were likely to come and should be received as guests of the King. Here were the first foreign vessels to enter the bay, the first Frenchmen to visit Spanish California, men of education and talent, and moreover men who brought news of the distant north coast where, before long, Spain would clash with Russia and Britain. The Governor – of the two Californias, as his grandiose title put it – was a pioneering figure in his own right. Pedro Fagés[1] had left Sonora as a mere lieutenant in charge of a couple of dozen soldiers back in 1769; he had served under Gálvez and Portolá, and worked tirelessly and efficiently to build up the settlement. La Pérouse reported in his journal:

> His government covers an area more than eight hundred leagues in circumference; but his real subordinates are two hundred and ninety-two cavalrymen who have to supply garrisons for five small forts and squads of five or six men to each of the twenty-five missions established in the old and the new California. Such small means are enough to contain approximately fifty thousand Indians who roam this vast part of America, of whom about ten thousand have embraced Christianity.

The viceroy in Mexico usually gave him a free hand, although occasionally forced to arbitrate between his secular representative and the spiritual power of the missionaries, currently represented by Fermin Francisco de Lasuen, another great figure of early California. On the whole, they co-existed satisfactorily. Lasuen was in the process of transforming the economy of the country. Mission industries were being set up to diversify the agriculturally-based mission stations. Artisans were being brought from Mexico, the Indians were being taught carpentry, house building and a wide range of new trades. It was the organisation and aims of the missions which most impressed La Pérouse. These were no obscurantist priests living on tithes and benefices, but pioneers developing for their flock a new social and economic structure. The enterprise

[1] Pedro de Fagés's account of the years he spent in Alta California has been translated by H.I. Priestley, *A Historical, Political and Natural Description of California*, Berkeley, 1937. La Pérouse's quoted comments are from his Chapter X.

was based on paternalism, but to a Galaup this was a sound and sensible basis for a society, far better than the romantic sentimentality of the Noble Savage supporters.

Consequently, much of la Pérouse's journal of his 10–day stay consists of detailed comments on the administration of the missions. They provide an invaluable outsider's report on the early days of California, punctuated by notes of appreciation for the kindness shown to him by the people, who pressed gifts on him, sent supplies of all kinds on board and had to be forced to accept anything in return.

Life was organised communally, with food cooked centrally and distributed to each family, and with the tribal structure and customs retained to the extent that this was compatible with Christianity. It was, in its way, a strangely medieval world, as with serfs attached to a monastery, but without the abbot having the temporal power of a feudal lord. The missionaries had so far succeeded in keeping its lay equivalent – the Governor of Monterey – at bay, but their theocracy, which had arrested time in a world of its own, could not forever resist the growth of secularism. Eventually, the very prosperity and fertility of California would overwhelm it.[1]

La Pérouse's no-nonsense approach to native peoples saved him from viewing the Indians romantically; it made him equally clear-eyed about the Spanish. Here was a land of 'inexpressible fertility' in which progress was held back by an economic and political structure that belonged to another age. There was no trade, no enterprise, no ambition. The missionaries impeded the Indian's intellectual development: the Spanish policy of exclusiveness isolated California from the rest of the world and even from other Spanish territories.

There were signs that this would not last. The key was the fur trade which had already attracted Spanish attention:

> We found at Monterey a Spanish official named Vincent Vassadre y Vega; he had brought instructions for the Governor to gather all the otter skins of his four 'presidios' and ten missions . . . M. Fages assured me he could supply ten thousand of them; and as he knew the country he added that if the China trade involved a turnover of

[1] 'La Pérouse's social philosophy, while not necessarily incompatible with the faith of a Christian, nevertheless stands apart from it', R. Pomeau, 'Lapérouse Philosophe' in *Approches des Lumières*, Paris, 1974, p. 362.

thirty thousand skins, two or three establishments north of San Francisco would soon provide them.

La Pérouse's arrival confirmed Spain's fears that other European nations were beginning to take more than a passing interest in the fur trade. Cook was being followed by La Pérouse, just as Dixon would follow the French, and over the entire Northwest Coast loomed the threat of a Russian advance. The Spanish would shortly send Martínez in the *Princesa* and Haro in the *San Carlos* to check on all these reports – and the stage would then be set for the Nootka crisis which almost led to a major war.[1]

On 23 September 1786, the French sailed from Monterey Bay, assisted by Martínez's sailors. 'I can only inadequately express my gratitude', wrote Jean-François. It was not only Martinez and other naval officers, but Fagés, Lasuen and his missionaries, the soldiers even 'who had rendered a thousand services'. In return, Collignon had planted potatoes and other seeds, but California was a real paradise – 'the gardens of the Governor and the missions were filled with an infinity of vegetables' – and the ships were laden with supplies in preparation for the voyage across the Pacific to China.

La Pérouse had obtained an old Spanish chart of the central Pacific. It did not seem to be very different from one he had found in Anson's *Voyage*.; not a great deal had been discovered in 150 years. La Pérouse's first task was to look for the island of Nuestra Señora de la Gorta: its existence was doubtful and he eliminated it finally from the map. On the other hand, he discovered an island far to the north-west of Hawaii, which he named Necker Island in honour of the famous Minister of Finance who had recently attempted – and failed – to reform France's chaotic tax system. The island was as austere as his opponents accused Necker's policy of being: 'it is really only a rock about a thousand yards long . . . there

[1] In March 1789, Manuel Antonio de Florez, Viceroy of Peru, despatched two ships to Nootka Sound (El Puerto do San Lorenzo) to ensure that Spanish sovereignty was recognised. A fort was erected at Nootka. Captain Colnett in the *Argonaut* appeared shortly after; his ship was captured as were two other vessels which appeared shortly after. The British however were in no mood to give up the Northwest Coast and the incident led the two nations to the brink of war. France, in the throes of the Revolution, was in no position and indeed in no mood to assist the Spaniards who eventually had to abandon their claims. The events have been dealt with in W.R. Manning, *The Nootka Sound Controversy*, New York, 1966; see also W. Kaye Lamb, *The Voyage of George Vancouver*, I, pp. 20–26.

is no tree visible ... the rock is bare ... the sides were steep, like a well, and the sea broke wildly everywhere'.

It was a danger later navigators needed to be aware of. How little known these seas were was shown a few evenings later. It was the finest night and the calmest seas the French had seen since they had left Monterey: this made the dangers ahead all the more vicious, since the waves scarcely broke over the rocks that waited silently ahead. When the lookout sighted them they were a mere 350 yards away. The ships veered just in time. By then the depth had fallen to nine fathoms. The frigates sailed to the south, no more than a couple of hundred yards away. It had been so sudden, so eerie, that La Pérouse began to wonder whether it had not been a mere illusion.

Too many navigators have left a mirage on the charts. He needed to be sure. He sailed back in the morning and there it was – a rocky islet surrounded by reefs and sandbanks 'like a circle of diamonds surrounding a medallion'. He named it French Frigates Shoals, a name it has retained.[1]

His route now took him towards the Mariana islands. Asunción Island, in the north of the group, was reached on 14 December 1786. It was a bitter disappointment. 'A horrible place', it was little more than a black cone surrounded by a little land, on which fortunately a few coconut trees did manage to grow. The French obtained about a hundred nuts, although with some difficulty; but they were suffering from the strain of a long voyage which often causes sailors to over-estimate, or in this case under-estimate, an eventual landfall. Thus Tahiti had looked like a paradise associated with all the lyrical legends of Ancient Greece when Bougainville reached in 1768 – and so Tahiti had received extravagant praise as the abode of virtues and home of the Noble Savage.[2] La Pérouse, after nearly three months, hoped for some landfall on an equally attractive tropical island. All they had seen so far, apart from the endless sea, was Necker Island and French Frigate Shoals. Now Asunción Island appeared to complete a bleak trio, with little to offer to passing navigators.

[1] La Pérouse reported this to the Minister of Marine in his letter of 3 January 1787, sent from Macao.

[2] See on this H. Jacquier, 'Le Mirage et l'exotisme tahitiens dans la littérature', *Bulletin de la Société des études océaniennes*, VII, 1944–5, pp. 3–7, 50–76, 91–114, and Taillemitte, *Bougainville*, especially the 'Post-scriptum sur l'isle de la Nouvelle-Cythère ou Tayti', II, pp. 506–10.

The strain of the long crossing was beginning to show. The sailors and their officers had their daily routine to occupy them: the scientists had very little to do. Once they had written their reports, sorted their specimens, checked over their meagre library, little remained to be done during the long hot days and the equally long hot nights. The astronomers at least could work with the officers, but the naturalists were plainly bored. Lamanon, ever proud and rebellious to shipboard discipline, clashed with La Pérouse and others and became the leader of a cabal. When the *Boussole* and the *Astrolabe* reached Macao on 1 January 1787, La Pérouse naturally stayed on board, but the scientists took quarters ashore – without consulting him. Not surprisingly, he did not invite them to the few receptions held on board or on land. Lamanon, Lamartinière, Monges and Father Receveur wrote him a letter of complaint, to which he replied that he could not ask them since he did not know where they were living. They pointed out, with some justification, that it would not have been difficult for him to enquire if he had really bothered to make the effort. Angered by his insolence, La Pérouse had them brought to the ships and kept under arrest for 24 hours. They had to learn who was in charge and what naval discipline meant.

Letters went off to Paris, each side putting its case to the Minister. La Pérouse unburdened himself in a letter to Fleurieu: 'I must admit that these Lamanons and Monges have tired me of all these learned makers of systems.' Dagelet he could stand, but these others, 'above all Lamanon', were 'devilish fellows who try my patience beyond endurance.'[1] Dagelet, the mild hardworking astronomer, had written a letter to his cousin Sully-Lepaute on arrival in Macao which gave in simple terms the background of the quarrel: 'We have just completed a voyage of over a hundred days, it has seemed like a thousand to everyone, and like most on board I needed a landfall. But everything is over. I will settle on land amongst the Chinese and there I hope to get back to normal in a few days.'[2] Wisely, the Minister had the letters filed away and the argument, which was months old by the time the correspondence reached him, was forgotten.

[1] AN. M. 3JJ 389, 151, 156.

[2] Letter of 1 January 1787, written on board, quoted in G. Lepaute, 'Notice Biographique sur Le PauteDagelet', *Bulletin de la Société de Géographie 1888*, p. 296.

Macao was a world apart, a strange, irrational toehold on the great inimical land of China, surviving on sufferance, the target of contempt and fear. Not a Portuguse colony, but still a Chinese possession leased to Portugal, it was less a gateway to Canton that a foreign settlement tolerated by China to contain the foreigners and limit their influence. Beyond Macao, China remained a dangerous closed world, eternal and enigmatic.

It was above all a source of great wealth. There were 41 foreign ships at anchor, including 29 flying the English flag, five the Dutch, but only two from France. It illustrated with vivid accuracy the relative positions of the European powers in Canton.

One of the French ships was the *Marquis-de-Castries* newly arrived from Manila, part of a small force commanded by Bruny d'Entrecasteaux and intended to protect French traders in Eastern waters. It was no easy task, with constant vexations by Chinese administrators and the haughty jealousy of the English India Company. In fact, D'Entrecastreaux was to be surprisingly effective in countering this combined opposition. In another context, his link with la Pérouse was a sad one: when the expedition disappeared, d'Entrecastreaux was to be sent on a long and, unhappily, fruitless search.

However pleasant it was to meet French officers again, La Pérouse and all on board were disappointed by the absence of letters from home. The ship that was expected to bring them from the Ile de France had been held up. It was little consolation to hear general news about the situation in Europe 'which was absolutely the same as when we had left it.' The Portuguese Governor tried to make La Pérouse as welcome as he could: he had been in Goa 12 years earlier when Jean-François was in command of the *Seine* and there he had married. Now Doña Maria entertained him surrounded by her children. 'Nowhere in the world could anyone find a more delightful picture: the most beautiful of children surrounded the loveliest of mothers.' Jean-François' thoughts would have gone back to Eléonore. The lack of mail meant there was no letter from her. She had thought herself pregnant for a while, but it had been a false alarm. Would she have a second chance?

His mind turned to other problems. The furs had to be sold, but prices had plummeted since the days of Gore and King. Furs that would have fetched 100 piastres in 1780 now fetched less than 15. The best were set aside to be forwarded to Queen Marie-

Antoinette. Dufresne, who was to be left behind, much to his relief, would take them back to France, but, as it turned out, his help was needed in another direction. La Pérouse had contracted to sell a thousand furs to a Portuguese dealer. The prices, an average of nine and a half piastres, was low enough, but the cash was not forthcoming and the time of sailing was approaching. Chinese merchants were brought in, but knowing the position the French were in, made an offer that was even lower. There was nothing for it but to store the furs and let Dufresne continue the negotiations. The French Vice-Consul, Philippe Vieillard, did his best to help. It was little enough, for the consulate was hardly influential, but it helped save the French from being cheated.[1]

The stay in Macao proved to be a mixed bag. It might be fine for the scientists who wanted a break from the strains of shipboard life, but it was fraught with danger for the men for whom the town had little to offer but taverns and brothels. Macao, with an overwhelmingly Chinese population, was surrounded by a wall beyond which no foreigner could go. The teeming world of China was not a place a Frenchman could venture in: if he got into a scrape, he could not be helped; if he were robbed or beaten, there would be little chance of redress.

On 5 February 1787, the *Boussole* and the *Astrolabe* sailed out, taking six Chinese sailors aboard each frigate to make up for the losses sustained in Lituya Bay.

★ ★ ★

At best the French were non-committal about their stay in Macao. It was a new experience, different from anything they had encountered previously, but they could hardly have left with regrets or looked back with nostalgia. Macao was a claustrophobic world. There had been a chance to rest during those four weeks, some pleasant interludes, a few receptions, but no strolls in a pleasant countryside, no excursions along a quiet seashore.

Instead, there had been vexations and arguments both among themselves and with the town's traders. Even the climate had not smiled on them: 'most of us had a temperature and heavy colds

[1] Sundry correspondence on this episode is held in AN. M. 3JJ, 386, 60–8. Dufresne's report on the fur trade is at AN. M. B4 318. See also, Gaziello, *L'Expédition de Lapérouse 1785–1788*, pp. 210–12.

which disappeared when we reached the more pleasant climate of Luzon.'

This was three weeks later, on 28 February 1787, when the two ships dropped anchor in Cavite, the port of Manila Bay. The Spanish authorities were a little surprised that the French should prefer the dull neighbourhood of Cavite to the colour and social life of Manila where the population was close to 40,000. News of the expedition had been received from Spain months earlier and the Governor was eager to welcome La Pérouse, but Cavite was where the shipyards were situated and the ships could be repaired easily and more cheaply.

There were opportunities for visits to Manila, in spite of a mediocre road and the great heat. The Spaniards very sensibly disappeared for a lengthy midday siesta, but the French found it hard to accustom themselves to the practice. However early they left the ships in the morning La Pérouse could hardly find all the time he needed to appraise the state of the colony and pass his usual down-to-earth judgement on its administration and prospects. The beauty of the scenery, the blue expanse of Manila Bay, the colourfulness of its busy streets, the exotic blend of races, might enthuse the romantics among his officers: his own objectiveness was never impaired.

For one thing, the Philippines were not a colony in the true sense of the word, a place like California where colonists were encouraged to settle. Luzon was more a feudal dependency of the King of Spain who had divided most of it into large estates, a number of them allocated to religious orders. Consequently the Philippines were 'still like the landed estates of great noblemen that remain fallow but could make a fortune for several families.'

Manila was excellently situated to become a great trading centre. That it was not, was due to a number of reasons. Basic was the Spanish policy of exclusiveness which protected their American possessions at the expense of the Philippines. The Edict of 1593 had banned direct trade between the Philippines and Spain; goods, in theory at least, had to be shipped to Europe by way of Spanish America, an absurdly uneconomic procedure. Gold and other precious goods could be sent by only one ship a year – the famous Manila Galleon which even then was limited to a cargo value of three quarters of a million *pesos*. Contraband and false invoices helped to swell this total – the *San José* in 1784 had taken almost three million *pesos*' worth – but the policy still throttled the economy of the Philippines.

In addition, Spain lacked the foothold in China which Macao represented for Portugal, and consequently the geographical advantage which Manila possessed could not be exploited. Indeed the reverse occurred: junks from China came each June for the Manila Fair, bringing silks, tea, jade and porcelain. To benefit from this, Spain would have needed a strong merchant navy and Manila the right to send ships by the Cape of Good Hope route. Instead, trading was limited to luxury goods in sufficient quantities to fill the Manila Galleon, and the great opportunities offered by the eastern trade fell to the English, the Dutch and the French.[1]

The Governor who welcomed La Pérouse was Don Brasco y Vargas, an enlightened man who had been struggling since 1778 to change Madrid's centuries-old policy. He was on the verge of success. A Company of the Philippines had at last been set up, to trade in competition with the monopolistic annual galleon, and in 1789, Madrid would finally decide to turn Manila into a free port. It could have become the emporium of the East had this move been made earlier. As it was, although Manila's trade boomed – there would be 50 trading vessels in Manila by 1795 – it was too late. The influence of Great Britain would soon become overwhelming.

The climate had its drawbacks, particularly at the beginning of the hot season, which normally lasts from April to July. The French spent March and early April in Manila Bay, and they found what often happens at this time of year: the temperature rising into the nineties. The colds and fevers were replaced by stomach cramps. In the case of Lamanon and d'Aigremont, these developed into dysentery. Local remedies were of little avail. The stifling heat made the narrow cabins unbearable. On 25 March, d'Aigremont died.[2] Apart from a servant who had died of tuberculosis during the crossing to Easter Island, this was the first case of death by illness the expedition had recorded.

[1] The stay in the Phillipines and La Pérouse's comments take up Chapters XIII and XIV of his narrative. His 'Rapport sur Manille', dated 10 September 1787 from Petropavlovsk is at AN. M. 3JJ 386, 111:69, and 387, 111:10.

[2] Dysentery contracted at Macao was made worse by the easy availability of fresh fruit and other foodstuffs obtained at Manila. In the case of D'Aigremont, La Pérouse blames him for attempting to cure himself with brandy and hot spices. Journal, March 1787, AN. M. 3JJ 387, 295–6.

In the meantime, Bruny d'Entrecasteaux himself reached Canton on his flag-showing mission, found La Pérouse gone and sent the frigate *Subtile* to bring him news and an offer of help. The news was stale – over 10 months – but the help was welcome. La Pérouse took one officer and four men for each of his ships. Pierre Le Gobien, an officer in his early twenties, joined the *Astrolabe*; Pierre-Louis Guillet de la Villeneuve, a couple of years older, joined the *Boussole;* but young Mel de Saint-Céran's health was giving concern, and rather than risk a second death in Manila Bay, La Pérouse sent him home. The *Boussole* had gained Gabriel de Bellegarde, a young man from the storeship *Maréchal-de-Castries,* while in Macao, so numbers were adequately balanced. Nothing, however, could be done to compensate for the losses sustained in North America.

★ ★ ★

Although the Spaniards warned La Pérouse that the north-east monsoon would continue for another month, he decided to take a chance and sail for Formosa (as Taiwan was then known) and Japan on 9 April 1787. To begin with, luck favoured him. Within a few days he had sailed up the coast of Luzon to Cape Bojador. Then the monsoon blew so steadily that it seemed determined to show how wrong the French had been and how right the Spanish. Formosa was not sighted until the 21st. The winds remained implacable.

Hoping that the north-easterly might be less strong and regular in Formosa Strait, the French sailed up along the west coast of the island. It was a dangerous decision. Formosa had rebelled against her Chinese overlords and a Chinese fleet was somewhere to the north, landing troops to put down the rebellion. La Pérouse thought it wiser to stay some distance from the coast of China which was closed to all foreigners.[1] This meant sailing past the

[1] In his 'Mémoire sur Formose' of 10 September 1787, La Pérouse outlines a proposal for a French occupation of Formosa, possibly in association with Spanish forces based on Manila: 'I venture to declare that two frigates, four corvettes, five or six armed longboats, with vessels suitable for the transport of four thousand men, with artillery and all the necessary supplies, would be enough for such an expedition to succeed; which a wise man would not risk with fewer means, although possibly twelve or fifteen hundred men might seem to be adequate for those enterprising men who, having nothing to lose, play their war games, in times of peace or war, without giving thought to the degree of humiliation which a great power would

Pescadores Islands which were only roughly shown on his charts. Almost everything went wrong. The winds did not abate – the weather was 'frightful' – the boats had to be lowered to take soundings along the little-known Penghu Channel, and the Chinese fleet lay straight ahead. Uncharted rocks appeared, seemingly closing the channel. The sea was so wild it was not possible to tell whether the waves were breaking against rocks or were merely whipped up by the gale. 'Never in my life have I seen heavier seas.' La Pérouse turned back. He would have to sail up the east coast of Formosa.

By the time he reached that conclusion it was May. He might as well have stayed in Manila waiting for the monsoon to change. But all had not been wasted. The astronomers had been able to survey part of the coast and clarify some points on the rough charts. And now the winds generously turned to speed them on their way north.

Passing through the Sakishima group, La Perouse entered the East China Sea, sailing almost due north until 21 May when he sighted Cheju-do which guards the entrance to Korea Strait and thus to the Sea of Japan. No other expedition had ventured into these little known waters and none was welcome. Korea was a land forbidden to foreigners: anyone shipwrecked on this coast could expect to spend the rest of his life as a slave. The Japanese, on the eastern side, were scarcely more welcoming: foreigners were likely to face death or imprisonment, unless the head of the Dutch trading post at Nagasaki, itself kept under strict control, could intervene.

La Pérouse preferred to sail close to the Korean coast which offered better opportunities for hydrographic work. No boats came near, even though the ships were within two leagues of the shore, but the French were shadowed by two small vessels that hugged the coast behind them. 'It is more than likely that we have aroused concern on the coast of Korea because, during the afternoon, we saw fires lit on every headland.'

---

suffer if it failed against people whose courage, weapons and military skill are very much inferior, but in my opinion far above the contemptuous attitude Europeans adopt towards them.... If this expedition were to be undertaken together with the Spanish, the Manila base would greatly help its success.... the first years [of occupation] would be very costly [but] one would certainly be able to land in the ports of Fokien on the other side of the Formosa Channel....' AN. M. 3JJ, 386, 111:72, and 387, 111:11.

Finding the coast beginning to trend north and west, La Pérouse veered east towards Japan. It was 27 May. A small island hove into sight which was not shown on any of the charts. He named it Dagelet Island 'after our astronomer who saw it first.' It is modern Ullung-do, a distant possession of South Korea. He sent Boutin in a boat to seek an anchorage, but the few inhabitants there were fled into the hills.

It was important to fix the position of some feature of the coast of Japan so as to have some reference point for further hydrographic work, but the French were plagued by recurring fog. Closeness to the shore spelt danger not merely because of rocks and islands not shown on the charts, but also because of the presence of other vessels. On 2 June, two Japanese ships were in sight, one so close that they could hail her – but since neither side could understand the other's language the encounter was more comic than useful.

On 4 June, the French saw seven ships; on the 5th they saw ten. Then they sighted Cape Noto, the prominent headland of central Honshu. Ten days spent fixing its longitude and latitude with great care enabled them to assess with final accuracy the width of the Sea of Japan and, by using Captain King's position for the eastern coast, the width of Honshu. Although bothered by the fog, La Pérouse was able to get close enough to the coast of Japan to see 'the trees, the rivers, the landslips' and a little further on houses and 'a kind of castle'.

As for landing, that was out of the question. After early missionary successes, Christianity had been banned by a series of edicts issued between 1633 and 1636, enforced with great brutality. Japan had closed its doors against the world. Even trade with China was cut back drastically - by the time La Pérouse reached Japanese territorial waters no more than ten junks a year entered a major port such as Nagasaki. A few trading vessels were sent out from Japan to Manila, Cochinchina or Siam, but under such strict control that in practice no Japanese were allowed out of the country. And if any subject of the Empire took it into his head to escape, he could expect death or slavery in the nearest accessible country, Korea: further north the cold bare lands of Sakhalin and the Kurile

[1] La Pérouse's narrative, Chapter XV, a lengthy section which Milet-Mureau considered necessary to split into three.

Islands constituted an inhospitable and uneasy no man's land between Japan and Russia. The Dutch, being Protestants and traders rather than missionaries, had been allowed a small foothold through Deshima, in Nagasaki. It was no more than a hatchway through the cultural wall that defended Japan from the influences and the ambitions of the outside world. Through it passed small quantities of cloth, spices, sugar, ivory, in exchange for Japanese porcelain, silks, laquer boxes, copper and camphor. Any deviation from this strictly regulated pattern could mean death.[1]

The French veered back to the Asian continent. 'Our landfall was precisely the point that separated Korea from the Tartary of the Manchus'. This is where present-day Vladivostok is situated. Tartary held a host of romantic and less romantic associations for eighteenth century westerners. It was the end of the enormous Eurosian landmass which begins on the Atlantic with the Breton peninsula and dies away in the mysterious Sea of Japan. Little was known about it, so that imagination had free reign. The name raised visions of a world of darkness – for was not not Tartary the lowest hell of antiquity, Tartarus, far below Hades itself? What was known of its people was unflattering – the naturalist Buffon made allowance for the harshness of the climate 'uninhabitable for any other nation', and Voltaire wrote them off as 'rough, stupid and brutal'.[2] Missionaries had sent back reports usually based on vague rumours; infrequent Russian travellers brought back information that was a little more reliable, and essentially it remained a mysterious land, ill-traced on the maps, unappealing to the imagination.

[1] La Pérouse's instructions required him to check whether the Japanese were still utterly opposed to contacts with foreigners outside the Nagasaki enclave, and whether their rigid rules of exclusion might be less firmly enforced on the east and noth-east coast, especially if foreign vessels came with offers of furs. See Instructions relating to commercial and political aims, item 12.

[2] Voltaire has gained some notoriety for his contempt for distant countries and potential colonies, in particular for his dismissal of French Canada as 'a few acres of snow', but his main targets as a philosopher and reformist were political corruption and social ossification in Europe. La Pérouse, like many others in his day, was influenced by Voltaire and some of his works were available on board (cf. De Lesseps, AN. M., BB4:992), but his opinions on native peoples was more balanced and based on first-hand knowledge. This led him to reject Jean-Jacques Rousseau's ideas on primitive man, but at the same time making allowance for Voltaire's sometimes tongue-in-cheek attacks on colonial settlements. See Gaziello, *L'Expédition de Lapérouse 1785–1788*, pp. 221–34; Dunmore, *Pacific Explorer*, pp. 191–2, 253–4.

Entering Tartary opened up for the expedition an illusion of suitably theatrical dimensions. The vessels sailed towards the land:

> We could see the mountains, the gullies, in a word all the details of the terrain and we could not imagine where we could have entered a strait which could only be that of Tessoy which we had already rejected; in such a situation I thought that I should hug the wind and steer S.S.E. for the northern point of Yesso Island; but soon these hills and gullies disappeared; the most extraordinary fogbank I have ever seen had caused this error; we saw it dissolve; its shapes, its shades rose up into the clouds and we fortunately had enough daylight left to ensure that no doubt remained about the non-existence of this fantastic land. I sailed all night over the sea space it seemed to have occupied and at daybreak nothing could be seen.[1]

The fog swirled in like a curtain, then parted to reveal a steep coastline on which no landing was possible. The scientists were impatient to go ashore and the officers to complete their survey. 'This was the only part of the globe that has escaped the attention of the tireless Captain Cook'. They had to wait until 23 June, when they dropped anchor in a small bay which Jean-Frencois named Ternay Bay after his great mentor and friend. One can still find Ternei Bay on most modern maps.

There were animals about – deer and bears – but no inhabitants. At least none were alive: a tomb on the edge of a brook contained two bodies, wrapped in bear skins and wearing small skull caps, surrounded by small artifacts, a few tools and a bag of rice to see them on their journey to the other world.

Four days later, the two ships sailed north, hugging the coast, but still seeing no inhabitants. On 4 July, a bay was explored and named, ephemerally, Suffren Bay. The Sea of Japan was being left behind. They were sailing into the Tartar Strait. On the starboard side, the coast of Sakhalin was moving closer. La Pérouse edged towards it and on the 12th he dropped anchor in a bay which he named after De Langle but which is probably modern Tomari. And at last he met the natives.

A sketch by Duché de Vancy recorded this meeting, on 13 July 1787. From it, a famous engraving was made, quite faithful to the original, with only a slight overlay of romantic exoticism and the inevitable addition of artistic balance and perspective. In both, La

[1] Journal, Chapter XV, June 1787.

Pérouse is shown with the middle three buttons of his uniform undone and the lower ones struggling to hold in his paunch. The long months of arduous navigation had done nothing to reduce his weight. The poverty of the natives was transformed by the engraver who embellished their clothing and gave several bystanders the appearance of Romans in a classical tragedy.[1] But La Pérouse's pleasure at the meeting cannot be exaggerated. Poor though they might be, they were not thieves and had to be pressured into accepting gifts. Their leaders, venerable elders with long white beards like Chinese sages, told them how they traded with the mainland and with other tribes who lived further north on their own island – for an island it was, with a navigable strait into the Sea of Okhotsk.

This was important news from the point of view of geography, but what mattered was whether the pass was navigable, since shallow straits would endanger the frigates. As it eventually turned out, the old man had underestimated the draught of the heavy French ships. La Pérouse decided to proceed with caution. It was the anniversary, to the very day, of the Lituya Bay tragedy and no one on board could have failed to remember that on 13 July 1786, in a treacherous pass, 21 of their number had perished.

The expedition slowly sailed north until 19 July when it dropped anchor in a bay close to modern Uglegorsk. La Pérouse called it D'Estaing Bay. Once again, the natives confirmed that Sakhalin was an island. They themselves were from the mainland, having crossed over for fish. Sakhalin appeared to be less and less populated as the French proceeded north, but fish were astonishingly plentiful. Clonard, sent to survey a small rivermouth, came back with 1,200 salmon 'although his men had neither nets nor lines' – they had simply killed them with sticks.

* * *

On the 23rd, another bay appeared, and now La Jonquière, La Pérouse's protector and friend, could be given his memorial on the charts. There were a few huts scattered about, but no inhabitants.

[1] The transformation of original sketches and drawings into pictures or engravings rearranged according to the Romantic style has been detailed at length in Bernard Smith, *European Vision and the South Pacific*, Oxford, 1960; 2nd ed. Sydney, 1984.

The coast was becoming more sandy, the depths were gradually dropping with each sounding, and Jean-François began to worry that the strait that lay ahead might be no more than a jumble of sandbanks and shallows. For every league that he sailed north, the depth dropped by three feet. Three more days went by. The shores on both sides, when not obscured by fog, looked barren and uninhabited. There was no current to indicate the existence of a central channel. He lowered two boats, with Boutin and Vaujuas, and sent them to sound ahead of the ships and to the side as well, for a sudden gust of wind could drive either frigate onto a sandbank. The crew had fallen silent. There was only the low whistle of the wind, now rising through the rigging, and the screams of sea birds.

Vaujuas returned at midnight. He had gone one league ahead, into the strait, and had not found more than six fathoms anywhere. There is in fact a navigable channel, as the Russian Nevelskoi was to discover in 1849, but Vaujuas missed it.[1]

The weather was worsening. It took four hours to raise the anchor; the capstan had broken and three men had been wounded. The frigates turned back south, towards the Tartary coast. When the fog cleared, they discovered a bay 'which seemed very deep and offered a commodious and safe anchorage'. It was the evening of 28 July 1787. La Pérouse named the bay after the Marquis de Castries. It is still known as De-Kastri Bay today.

Anxious to reach Kamchatka before the end of the short summer, La Pérouse cut his stay in Castries Bay to five days. The anchorage was safe, the inhabitants courteous and generous, the surroundings attractive – at least to the scientists. Lamanon who had been in poor health for some time could not be kept on board.[2] He joined Monges and Receveur on their walks along the shore and into deep gullies in search of plants. The officers went hunting.

[1] Sketches showing sounding taken along the coast make it clear that the French accepted that Sakhalin was an island. Whether the channel was navigable for ships was a question which time and weather did not allow them to resolve. See Dunmore & Brossard, *Le Voyage de Lapérouse 1785–1788*, II, p. 320.

[2] Letter from Lamanon to an unnamed friend, 29 September 1787, Petropavlovsk, admitting that he is finding the voyage 'somewhat drawn out'. AN. M. 3JJ 389, 170. La Pérouse in turn was a little terse about him in a letter to Fleurieu written on 25 September: 'The Chevalier de Lamanon is sending you...two memoirs for the Marquis de Condorcet. You can decide...whether they can be sent on without inconvenience, but he sets great value on them and believes that one sails around the world in order to add up the spines of a sea urchin.' AN. M. 3JJ 389, 141.

Collignon, the gardener, went around sowing seeds, as his instructions required him to do. Although this was midsummer it was still cold. He was caught in a sudden freezing shower and tried to light a fire with gunpowder. It blew up in his hands, breaking his thumb. Rollin's ministrations saved him from losing his arm, but the surgeon had other worries: several of the men had reported swellings of the gums and legs. Scurvy was making its appearance. It was time to leave.

The expedition sailed back the way it had come, hugging the coast of Sakhalin to find the southern straits that would lead into the open sea. Strong gales blowing up from the south did nothing to help. It took a week to reach Langle Bay which they had left on 14 July. Two days later, a gap appeared, but it was merely a channel between the coast and an uncharted island. It was Monneron's turn to gain immortality: La Pérouse named the discovery Monneron Island and it appears as Ostrov Moneron on the present-day charts. Soon came better news: the appearance of a cape that heralded the southern extremity of Sakhalin.

This Cape Crillon, like the other geographical features named by La Pérouse, has retained its name, somewhat Russianized as Mys Kriljon. The strait that opened the way to the Sea of Okhotsk and enabled the expedition to make for Kamchatka without delay remains La Pérouse Strait to this day.

It marked the end of weeks of slow and dangerous navigation, but also of an invaluable survey of unknown waters. It was one of the most rewarding parts of the entire voyage. The east coast of Sakhalin and the chain of the Kuril Islands they had now reached were better known, the Dutchman Martin de Vries in the *Kastricum* having sailed in this area in 1643, as did King in the *Resolution* in 1784. There was still much that was uncertain, points that should be clarified, positions to be calculated with greater precision, observations to be made, but the tension and excitement of sailing into the unknown had gone. The Kurils stretch away like a set of links binding Japan to the Kamchatka peninsula. La Pérouse passed through it between the central islands of Urup and Simusir – through what is known as Boussole Strait – back into the Pacific and along the eastern coast. 'I believe this channel to be the finest of all those that can be found among the Kurils.' It was the kind of praise that reflects a sailor's relief at nearing a long-hoped-for haven. The date was 30 August 1787.

On 6 September, the expedition anchored at Petropavlovsk in Avacha Bay, the main town of Kamchatka, and indeed at that time the only one.

Kamchatka was the edge of Asia and had only recently become the furthest end of the Russian Empire. The empty wastes of Siberia had grown to include the Kamchatkan peninsula which in 1760 were placed under the control of the military governor of Okhotsk, 700 miles to the west across the sea. There was little to govern; there were no roads, few tracks, scattered inhabitants surviving on fishing and hunting. Only Petropavlosk, with a hundred or so people, had any value: it was strategically situated in the northern Pacific and although icebound for several months of the years was at the time the only port Russia could use in the east. The Russian view of Kamchatka, at least from the impression their hosts were anxious to give him, was rosier than La Pérouse's own:

> Since the winter is generally milder in Kamchatka than at Petersburg or in several provinces of the Russian empire, the Russians talk of it as we do of Provence, but the snow that surrounded us as early as the twentieth of September, the white frost covering the ground every morning at the same period, and the greenery that was as faded as in the month of January around Paris, all this told us that the winter was of a harshness the people of southern Europe could not support.[1]

The people, however, were hospitable. They saw few visitors, they knew La Pérouse was due to call, and they granted him every facility. There were hunting and fishing expeditions and even what passed for a grand ball in this lost outpost where Russian formality merged oddly with local customs. There were pilgrimages to tombs: that of Delisle de la Croyère, a French scientist who had travelled across Siberia to Kamchatka, joined Bering's expedition of 1741 and, worn out by his travels, died in Avatcha, and that of Charles Clerke, commander of the *Resolution* on James Cook's third voyage, who had died just before his ship droped anchor in Kamchatka on 22 August 1779.

One great disappointment on arrival at Petropavlosk had been the absence of mail from France. The Minister knew the expedition was bound for Kamchatka, and indeed had arrived a little earlier than expected. Already in Macao the French had suffered a similar

[1] Chapter XVIII of La Pérouse's narrative is entirely devoted to the call made at Avatscha Bay.

blow. It was now more than two years since they had sailed from Brest; being seemingly forgotten and cut off from all news added greatly to the hardships they had to endure.

Bitterness was short-lived. A courier arrived with the mail packets from Okhotsk. With an unbeatable sense of drama, he burst in during the ball, just as the Kamchatkan ladies in a sweaty swoon concluded their dances. The ball ended, the dancers being dismissed with glasses of brandy. There were letters from families and despatches from Versailles. There was no bad news for anyone, but several were to receive promotions. La Pérouse was promoted to the rank of *chef d'escadre* – commodore – and Clonard to post-captain.[1] All the guns of the port fired a salute to celebrate the goods news. It was a long and memorable night.

Among the despatches was an important letter from the Minister of Marine. The English were apparently planning a settlement in New South Wales. La Pérouse was asked to discover the extent of these plans. There was no better way for France to obtain a first-hand report; the political aims of the voyage, never paramount, never obtrusive, were always to be borne in mind.[2]

On 21 September, La Pérouse had written to Castries that he would continue his voyage by sailing to Guam, then down to the Solomons and across to New Zealand. This was consistent with the original plan which, although it envisaged la Pérouse as sailing west from Tahiti, laid down a route which would have taken him to the Solomons, the New Hebrides, New Caledonia and to Queen Charlotte Sound in New Zealand.

A change of route was now forced on him. He advised Castries on the 28th that he would make for Botany Bay at once. He would avoid the dangerous waters around the Solomons and New Hebrides and sail instead almost due south to the Samoa group and sweep back west to Botany Bay. All being well, he should be there within three months.[3]

[1] See La Pérouse's letter of thanks to the Minister, dated from Petropavlovsk, 28 September 1787. The promotion was operative from 2 November 1786.

[2] French expectations of an English settlementwere originally centred on Queen Charlotte Sound in New Zealand where James Cook had refitted his ships and rested his crews on several occasions. This seemed a more logical base from which to establish British influence over the South Pacific. See section No. 8 of the political and commercial aims in the Instructions issued to La Pérouse.

[3] La Pérouse to Minister, Petropavlovsk, 28 September 1787; La Pérouse to Fleurieu, Petropavlovsk, 28 September 1787.

Preparations for a prompt departure began. There had never been any intention to remain in Petropavlosk for more than a few weeks. The brief summer was ending. Early flurries of snow gave warning of that to anyone who might have been lulled into overconfidence by the Russians' boast that a Kamchatkan winter could equal one in southern France. But there was one important matter to be arranged: the despatch of reports and journals to Paris. La Pérouse had been cautious in what he had sent home from Monterey: the Spanish were not always dependable and communication with the rest of the Spanish world was slow and irregular. The presence of French officers in Manila and Macao had made things easier there, but Petropavlosk was a lonely port, soon to be further isolated by snow and ice. No ship would call for months. The only route for the expedition's mail was overland to Moscow – and for this La Pérouse called on young Lesseps who spoke Russian, knew the people, and held the rank of vice-consul.

De Lesseps's voyage across Asia and Europe is an epic in itself. Eastern Siberia was little known, even to the Russians; there were few roads, few river crossings, a mere sprinkling of inhabitants; distances were immense and he was expected to travel during the winter months when snow obliterated the tracks, made rivers hazardous to cross, and the bitter cold killed off both men and animals. The spring would not make matters any easier, since the thaw rendered roads impassable and the break-up of the ice swept away bridges.

The two frigates sailed from Avatcha Bay on 30 September 1787. Lesseps left a week later. His plan was to cross the peninsula to the west shore and either sail to Okhotsk or follow the coast which ran north and south in a thousand-mile arc. Merely crossing the peninsula to Bolsheretsk, less than a hundred miles as the crow flies, took a fortnight and involved building a raft to cross the Bolchaiareka River. Bolsheretsk was a dismal place, with fewer than 300 inhabitants. Lesseps stayed there until late January while a caravan of 35 sleighs was assembled. It snowed most days. The tracks to the next village were obscured by snow or blocked by drifts – and he was still travelling north. In March he was following the shores of the northernmost bays of the Sea of Okhotsk. The grey skies merged with the grey horizon, hiding the coastal ranges. It was an alien silent world, save when a sudden blizzard screamed down from the unseen mountains. At the end of April he reached Yamsk, a desolate outpost in a frozen inlet, but at least there was a road of sorts to speed him down to Okhotsk itself which he reached on 8 May.

Eager to leave, he made his way inland along the route to Yakutsk, 800 miles away, but his six sleighs, essential in winter, were useless in the thaw. Spring had turned the tracks into quagmires in which the sleighs bogged down. He dragged them back to Okhotsk, bought what horses the township could spare him, 'frightful, half-starved beasts', and on 6 June left again for Yakutsk. After that, it was a matter of sailing on the Lena River, not downstream unhappily, because, easier though this would have been, the Lena flows north towards the mysterious frozen expanse of the Laptev Sea. He sailed upstream in a primitive riverboat towards Lensk and Kirensk, mere huddles of log houses, tiny lonely military posts scattered in the empty wilderness of central Siberia. At Kirensk, his boats broke up among the rapids. He completed the journey to Irkutsk on horseback. It was time to turn north-west, in a carriage this time, bumping over the hardback ruts of the road to Krasnoyarsk, and then west, clear of the great marshlands, towards the north-south wall of the Urals. He was hurt in an accident after leaving Kazan but he pressed on, driven by the need to avoid the early onset of a second winter. It was September by the time he crossed the Volga, but he was now approaching Novgorod and St Petersburg where he arrived on 22 September 1788. He had been nearly a year on the way and although he did not know it – nor did anyone else – La Pérouse and his friends had long since been shipwrecked.[1]

Meanwhile, La Pérouse had sailed from Kamchatka, first looking for land reported to have been seen by the Spaniards somewhere along the parallel of 37° 30′ north. The crew were told to keep a look-out, and the first man to see land would have it named after him and was promised a golden *louis* in addition. There were flights of birds around 14 October, ducks or cormorants, useful signs of land, but nothing was seen of the island 'rich in gold' which now La

[1] Lesseps to the Comte de Luzerne at Versailles, dated 31 October 1788, AN. M. 3JJ, 386, 87, 12 pp. Personal file of De Lesseps in Archives du Ministère des Affaires Etrangères, 'Personnel', v. 45. J.B. de Lesseps, *Journal historique du voyage de M. de Lesseps, consul de France, employé dans l'expédition de M. le Comte de La Pérouse*, 2 vols, Paris, 1790; English translation, London, 1790; German translation, Riga and Leipzig, 1790; Dutch translation, Utrecht, 1791.

Pérouse finally erased from the charts. The search cost one young sailor's life; he fell from the yards and disappeared in the waves, drowned or killed by the fall.[1]

The cold of the northern autumn gave way to the heat of the tropics as the ships sailed south, an abrupt change affecting the health of the crews and their morale. La Pérouse ordered frequent rations of coffee to restore waning energy. Kamchatka had provided very little in the way of fresh supplies, and everyone, the officers included, subsisted on tough dried meat and ship's biscuits. On 6 November, eight bonitos were caught, providing a welcome feast for all on board, but even so they had to be shared between 200 people.

The route was almost due south. The expedition crossed the Line on 21 November 1787 for the third time, in empty seas and growing despondency. Finally, on 6 December the lookout sighted the first of the Samoan islands, the easternmost Tau, then Tutuila. At last here, among islands which Louis de Bougainville had called the Navigators, the French could find the supplies and refreshments his men so badly needed. He could see numbers of coconut trees, villages set among the greenery on the hill slopes, and islanders manoeuvring canoes with the skill that Bougainville had so admired.

The appearance of the Samoans concerned La Pérouse from the start, although Langle found them pleasant enough. They were robust – heavier and stronger-looking than most of the French sailors – and they looked wild and unruly. La Pérouse had a market set up on shore, with a protecting line of soldiers, and brisk, if tumultuous, bartering began. The climate was pleasant, the soil seemed fertile and there was an abundance of fruit and fish. He noted, however, the presence of scars on the bodies of the islanders, indicating 'that they were often at war or quarrelling among themselves'. Nature, he wrote, had provided these as warnings that Man in a state of near savagery and of anarchy was more harmful than the fiercest of beasts. These were not the words of a follower of Rousseau, but La Pérouse trusted only his own eyes. There were minor incidents, such an attack on one of the sailors and an attempted theft of a sword, but these were only to be expected. There would be no trouble as long as reasonable precautions were taken.

[8] Gilles Henry, from the *Astrolabe*, killed on 15 October 1787.

He was therefore worried when Langle insisted on going into a small bay to get fresh drinking water. There was enough water on board, but Langle wanted fresh water, while La Pérouse considered that what he had in the barrels was of a good enough quality for the rest of the crossing to Botany Bay. It was apparently (for we have only La Pérouse's own account of it) a fairly heated discussion at the end of which La Pérouse gave way.[1]

So, on the morning on 11 December 1787, Langle led a group of 60 men to the shore of a 'charming village' he had seen earlier. The tide was out and the shoreline looked less attractive as the boats neared it. It was also more difficult to land and to roll the barrels ashore. Worse still, the boats were out of sight of the two frigates. By the time the barrels had been filled over a thousand had gathered along the shore. The tide had still not turned; the longboats, now heavily laden, would not float. Langle realised that he would have to wait. He was vulnerable, stranded on this lonely beach in boats encumbered by heavy barrels. Suddenly, with a great roar, the Samoans attacked.

By the time the boats struggled back to the *Astrolabe* and the *Boussole* it was after five – and some of the boats had not made it. Langle was dead, as were Lamanon and ten of the men. Many others were wounded: Boutin had five head wounds, Colinet's arm was broken, Fr Receveur had almost lost an eye.

Once the wounded were cared for, the crews readied for reprisals. The ships were still surrounded by canoes trading their fruit and their poultry, but La Pérouse realised that this very fact proved their innocence. He would not allow the innocent to be punished in place of the guilty. All that he permitted his men to do was to fire one blank shot to warn the canoes away and to prevent others from joining them. And when the next day the canoes returned, not to trade this time, but to shout challenges and yell their scorn, he ordered but one shot more to disperse them. The Samoans fled, saved by La Pérouse's sense of justice and Louis XVI's insistence that no indigenous people be harmed except in cases of self-defence.[2]

[1] La Pérouse to Fleurieu, 7 February 1788, Botany Bay; Journal, Chapter XIX; AN.M. 3JJ 387, 40; AN. M. 3JJ 389, 164.

[2] As well as La Pérouse's journal and his letter to Fleurieu of 7 February 1788, there is a letter on the tragedy from Dagelet to Condorcet (Bibliothèque de l'Institut, MS 867:4), one from Collignon to Thouin (Bibliothèque du Muséum d'Histoire Naturelle, MS 1928:2, 22) and one from Lauriston to his parents, SHM, MS 378).

The two frigates sailed from Massacre Bay, Tutuila, on 14 December. Whatever illusions La Pérouse might have harboured had vanished. His anger was directed more towards the philosophers who praised the simplicity of primitive man in order to condemn the evils of contemporary European civilisation. 'Lamanon whom they massacred was saying the day before that these men are worth more than us.'[1]

As had happened after the Lituya Bay disaster, shipboard life had to be reorganised. The dead men's belongings had to be sorted, to be sent eventually to their families, or auctioned among the crews. Monti took over command of the *Astrolabe* by virtue of his position as first officer; Clonard who was senior to him would take over when it was convenient to transfer him from the *Boussole*. Young Lauriston became responsible for astronomical observations.[2] Others, the wounded, were compelled to do less, and their tasks had to be allocated to others. It was depressing work. A pall fell over the ships as they sailed west to the other islands of the Samoan group – Upolu and Savai'i – but the sailors who had laughed and catcalled at the girls and waved at the men, now remained silent. When canoes came out to the ships, offering coconuts, pigs and poultry, and asking for cloth or beads, La Pérouse reduced canvas but he made no attempt to land anywhere and any signs of challenge or warlike attitudes were met by the display of firearms.

In this mood, the French sailed on to two islands that lay close together, one very high, the other flat. They were Tafahi and Niuatoputapu, which the Dutchman Schouten had called Traitors Island. This name, given by Schouten after a sudden, unprovoked attack, confirmed the French in their own attitude, but in fact the islanders were quite friendly and more honest in their dealings than the Samoans had been. Nevertheless, contacts were limited and carefully supervised. Barter was carried out by means of baskets lowered overboard. The French did not land and the islanders were not allowed onto the ships.

A storm blew up, causing the French to leave hurriedly and the canoes to flee back to the shore. 'The night was frightful.' Heavy rain poured down, rapidly finding its way below decks. A clammy

[1] Letter written from Botany Bay, dated 7 February 1788.

[2] However he had effectively been in charge for almost a year. La Pérouse to Fleurieu, 7 February 1788, Botany Bay, AN.M. 3JJ 389, 165. The tables of longitude and latitude are held in AN.M. 3JJ 387:105, 1–6.

damp filled all the cabins; clothes and bedding were soaked and uncomfortable; the wind seemed merely to bring more hot humid air into the rolling, creaking ships. The depressing rains lasted more than a week. On 27 December, the *Boussole* and the *Astrolabe* reached the Vavau group in the northern Tongas, which the Spaniard Francisco Maurelle had visited in 1781, but whose position he had not determined accurately. Bernizet and Dagelet worked to correct this error, which they found to be in the region of six degrees of longitude.

The appearance of scurvy among the crews further depressed La Pérouse. He ordered regular issues of brandy and water for the men and the killing of small pigs bought in Tutuila. These measures helped, and the swellings in legs and gums which worried the surgeons disappeared. What mattered now was reaching Botany Bay. The bad weather, the need to sail cautiously through the Tongas, the small amount of food they had managed to buy from the few islanders they allowed near the ships, determined the French to get away as soon as they could. On the first day of 1788, La Pérouse ordered the expedition to sail west by south-west direct for Australia.[1]

It was a route no one had yet followed. There was little to be found on the way, except Pylstart Island, or Ata, already seen by Abel Tasman nearly 150 years, a lonely island south of the main Tonga group. Even so, La Pérouse would not have gone near it had not the winds driven him towards the south. It gave him the minor satisfaction of correcting the position James Cook had assigned to it on the charts – the Englishman had placed it four miles too far south.

But now the winds dropped, the skies cleared and the expedition found itself becalmed. It remained three days in view of this bare rocky island, scarcely a mile across. A welcome gale blew up on 6 January, driving the French south-west, through heavy seas admittedly, but this was the kind of progress they had prayed for. On the

[1] Although La Pérouse could boast that he reached Botany Bay without a single case of sickness on board either vessel, he did not hide the fact that the long voyage had taken its toll. 'You will take me for a centenarian when I return... I have no teeth and no hair left, and it will not be long before I become senile,' he wrote to his friend Le Coulteux in Paris (BN, NAF, 393, 114). There is no reason to believe that others had not been similarly affected. Admiral de Brossard hints at a 'crypto-scurvy' spreading through the ships during the final leg from Tutuila to Botany Bay, Dunmore & Brossard, *Le Voyage de Lapérouse 1785–1788*, I, p. 166.

13th they were in sight of Norfolk Island. There was little hope of getting supplies since the island was believed to be uninhabited, but La Pérouse took pity on the bored naturalists 'who, since our departure from Kamchatka, have had very few occasions to consign any observations to their journals.' He sent Clonard to look for a landing place, but everywhere the sea was breaking angrily at the foot of steep cliffs. It was not worth risking any lives for. The expedition sailed on and the scientists went back to their books and their endless card games.

A few days later, they could still make 'their little bets', but in a geographical context. There was something to speculate about: a multitude of seabirds surrounding the ships. How close were they to land? Were the vessels near some rocks or a shore? Would they see some other part of Australia before Botany Bay? There were no answers, for the birds soon vanished. Then, on 23 January 1788, the French gathered on deck. They could see a low coastline some 20 or 30 miles away. On the 24th they tacked to round Cape Solander and reach the shelter of Botany Bay.

When they did, they beheld a sight they had not seen since Manila: British ships at anchor. Captain Phillip's fleet had arrived with convicts, soldiers and administrators to set up the penal settlement that was soon to develop into a thriving colony. This was what La Pérouse had been told to investigate, forsaking his original plans of exploration in the central and south-west Pacific. As it was, the English were already preparing to leave for Port Jackson, a few miles to the north, leaving the French in possession of the bay. The *Boussole* and *Astrolabe* remained there for over six weeks, then, on 10 March 1788, they weighed anchor. The sailors of Captain Phillip's fleet saw them sail past, going north, not far from the coast. They were the last white men ever to see them.

LA PÉROUSE AT BOTANY BAY

Most of what we know about the time spent by the two frigates at Botany Bay – and that is not a great deal – is derived from reports and comments by British officers. These were busy enough with setting up a penal colony and a base of sorts in New South Wales after a long and difficult voyage out from England. The French arrived just as Captain Phillip's ships were getting ready to transfer from Botany Bay to Port Jackson, a few miles to the north. They were short of supplies, and likely to face a near-famine in months to come; their sails and ropes were worn; the convicts, not surprisingly, were looking out for an opportunity to escape or overwhelm their guards. Nevertheless, the unexpected appearance of two French ships off the Australian coast aroused enough interest to warrant being recorded, and a number of visits were made to the French ships and vice-versa during the period of their stay.

According to his custom, La Pérouse would have despatched his own detailed report on the British settlement from his next major port of call, which in all likelihood would have been Mauritius. Sending a report back to France from a host country through its own mail service was something he always avoided doing.[1] As a result, we lack his views on the nascent settlement of Sydney Town and a valuable outsider's view of New South Wales's first beginnings. What he wrote in his journal and in his letters to Fleurieu and to the Minister of Marine is useful, because it gives us a broad overview of his stay in Botany Bay and a fairly clear indication of his future plans, but it is of little use to historians of early Australia.

Several books were published from 1789 by officers of the first Fleet, and some of them were promptly translated into French. The first of these was Watkin Tench's *A Narrative of the Expedition to Botany Bay, with an Account of New South Wales* (1789), published in France in 1789 as *Voyage à la Baie Botanique avec une description du nouveau pays de Galles Méridional... & quelques détails relatifs à M. de la Peyrouse* [sic] *pendant son séjour à la Baie Botanique.* Tench was in charge of a detachment of soldiers who sailed in the *Charlotte*, he was a man of some education, quite fluent in French, and Captain Phillip relied on him as his interpreter. His *Narrative* was very

[1] This policy was made clear in an early letter to the Minister of Marine: 'As my despatches have to travel overland in America and go through the city of Mexico, I do not dare to send you on this occasion details of our campaigns, nor to forward the charts we have drawn or the numerous and precise observations we have recorded . . . We have made some important discoveries; but details cannot be given in code, and they will reach you from China by means of a French ship.' La Pérouse to the Minister, Monterey, 19 September 1786. See AN.M 386, III:2, No. 42 and AN.M. 387, III:5–11 containing sundry reports by La Pérouse and others, usually with a covering letter.

popular, and there were a number of other editions and translations.[1]

Naturally enough, he was busy with settling in at Port Jackson where, once the ships had tied up, his soldiers were responsible for guarding the convicts being landed in a country where there were no buildings and no camps. What he writes, however, is as informative as any other record we have on sighting the French ships, the stay in the bay and the departure:

> Judge of my surprize on learning from a serjeant, who ran down almost breathless to the cabin where I was dressing, that a ship was seen off the harbour's mouth. At first I only laughed, but knowing the man who spoke to me to be of great veracity, and hearing him repeat his information, I flew upon deck; upon which I had hardly set my foot, when the cry of 'Another sail' struck on my astonished ears. Confounded by a thousand ideas which arose in my mind in an instant, I sprang upon the barricade and plainly descried two ships of considerable size standing in for the mouth of the Bay. By this time the alarm had become general, and everyone appeared lost in conjecture. Now they were Dutchmen sent to dispossess us, and the moment after storeships from England, with supplies for the settlement... It was by Governor Phillip that this mystery was at last unravelled, and the cause of the alarm pronounced to be two French ships., which, it was now recollected, were on a voyage of discovery in the southern hemisphere. Thus our doubts were cleared up, and our apprehensions banished; it was, however, judged expedient to postpone our removal to Port Jackson, until a complete confirmation of our conjectures could be procured.[2]

A similar, though briefer, report is given by John White, in his *Journal of a Voyage to New South Wales* (London, 1790): 'While these preparations [for the move to Port Jackson] were being made, every person was surprised to see, in this part of the world, two large ships plying hard in the offing to get into the bay. It was seen, in the evening, that they had French colours flying; but the wind blowing pretty strong out of the bay, they were unable to get in.'[3]

[1] The 1789 *Voyage* which was published by Letellier in Paris was matched in the same year by *Relation d'une expédition à la Baie Botanique* published by Knapen fils. The Letellier *Voyage* then appeared in 1790 as *Voyages dans le pays des Hottentots...et dans la Nouvelle Hollande....accompagnés de détails précieux relatifs à M. de la Peyrouse*. A *Voyages à la Baie botanique* appeared in 1791 in Paris, Brussels, Liège, the Hague and Leyden. A German translation was published in 1789 in Frankfurt and Hamburg.

[2] *Narrative*, pp. 49–50.

[3] *Journal*, p. 119.

Convicts, realising that the ships were not British and likely to leave soon, naturally endeavoured to find an asylum on board. La Pérouse, however, had no wish to take on men who were probably unsavoury characters and to antagonise the British authorities at the same time; to reassure Phillip, he gave his word that he would turn away any escaped prisoners who came up to his frigates. He was soon put to the test:

> The convicts, during this interval, were employed in cutting wood for fences, and to collect provender for the cattle and sheep, as the soil produced very indifferent pasture, although it was in the middle of the New Hollanders' summer. An aversion to labour, however, induced some of the new settlers to project an escape for Europe, on board the French ships; these efforts were, however, in a measure frustrated; the officers of the French ships would not hearken to any proposals except those made by the fair; for it was discovered two days after Mons. La Perieux [sic] had sailed that two women were missing.[1]

It is hardly likely that La Pérouse would have agreed to women being granted asylum, and no solid evidence exists that any of the convicts succeeded in stowing away on either vessel. It is far more probable that convicts who escaped from Port Jackson and failed to return tried to make their way to some other port which they imagined existed along the coast – some believed they might reach China – and were either killed by aborigines or died of exhaustion. The only exception was thought to be a Frenchman named Paris, as John White reports:

> Many of the convicts who had been missing had been at Botany Bay. They had offered themselves to the French navigators on any terms, but not one of them had been received. This refusal obliged them to return . . . As the French commodore had given his honour that he would not admit any of them on board, it cannot be thought that he would take them. The convict [one man reported missing], it is true, was a Frenchman named Peter Paris, and it is possible that on that account, he might have been concealed through pity by his countrymen, and carried off without the knowledge of the commanding officer.[2]

[5] Report in *The Gentleman's Magazine*, London, March 1789, p. 274.

[6] White, *Journal of a Voyage*, p. 125–6. The possibility was first mentioned by E. Blosseville in *Histoire des colonisations pénales dans l'Angleterre et l'Australie*, Paris,

That convicts appeared around the French ships within a matter of days is confirmed by other writers, such as Watkin Tench whose job it was to keep watch over the prisoners: 'In spite, however, of all our precautions, they soon found the road to Botany Bay, in visits to the French, who would gladly have dispensed with their company.'[1] There were other visits, far more welcome, by British officers, sometimes on the very day that their French counterparts were on their way to Port Jackson:

> 8th [February]. A party of the gentlemen of the garrison set out by land to pay a visit to the French at Botany Bay; from whom they met with the most hospitable, polite and friendly reception and treatment.... At the same time as the party from hence were gone, Captain Clonnard [sic] came round in a boat, on a visit of ceremony to Monsieur de la Peyrouse to the Governor. He brought with him some dispatches, which he requested might be forwarded to the French Ambassador at the court of London, by the first transport that sailed to England. The captain stayed all night, and returned the next morning.[2]

John Hunter, captain of the *Sirius*, was another visitor: 'I determined to visit Monsieur de la Pérouse before he should depart; I accordingly with a few other officers sailed round to Botany Bay in the *Sirius*'s longboat. We staid two days on board the *Bussole*, and were most hospitably and politely entertained, and very much pressed to pass a longer time with them.'[3] Hunter also quotes from Lieutenant King's Journal:

> On the 1st of February at daylight in the morning, Lieutenant Dawes, of the Marines, and myself, left Sydney-Cove in a cutter in order to proceed to Botany Bay and visit Monsieur de la Peyrouse, on the part of Governor Phillip, and to offer him any assistance he might stand in need of... We arrived on board the *Boussole* at ten o'clock in the morning, and were received with the greatest attention

1831, p. 134, and taken up by Anny P.L. Stuer, *The French in Australia*, Canberra, 1982, p. 41. However, this man is listed as Peter Parris, sentenced at Exeter on 17 March 1783, and there is no reliable evidence that he was French, other than the French appearance of his name – but the patronymic Parris is quite common in England, with its many variants: Perry-Parry-Parish.

[1] Op. cit., p.62.

[2] White, *Journal*, pp. 125–6.

[3] J. Hunter, *Historical Journal of the Transactions at Port Jackson & Norfolk Island*, London, 1793, p. 76.

> and politeness by Monsieur Peyrouse, and the few officers he had... The wind coming on, I accepted Monsieur Peyrouse's invitation to pass the day with him, and to return to Port Jackson the following morning.... After dinner, I attended M. Peyrouse and his officers on shore where I found him quite established; he had thrown round his tents a stockade, which was guarded by two small guns, and in which they were setting up two long-boats which he had in frame. An observatory tent was also on shore, in which were an astronomical clock, a quadrant and other instruments under the care of Monsieur D'agelet, Astronomer, and a member of the Academy of Science at Paris.... In the evening, I returned to the *Boussole*, and was shown all the drawings they had made during this voyage; and at five o'clock the next morning I set out on my return to Port Jackson.[1]

This account is of particular value, because it gives a clear insight into the activities of the French at the time and the fairly substantial shore establishment. There was in fact little time to spare for socialising: La Pérouse was anxious to set out as quickly as possible on the final stage of his voyage, and the English were busy establishing their settlement, preventing the convicts from escaping and protecting themselves from attacks by aborigines.[2] Phillip himself confirms this:

> M. de la Peyrouse during his stay there had set up two long boats, the frames of which he had brought with him from Europe. There had not been much intercourse between the French and the English during this interval: both being too busily employed to waste their time in parties of pleasure. Captain Clonard had waited on Governor Phillip with the letters that were to be forwarded to the French ambassaor; and a few of the English officers had gone over by land about the same time to pay a visit to Botany Bay; both parties were of course received with politeness and hospitality. Some few of the convicts contrived to abscond, and endeavoured to get admitted into the French ships, but were, with great propriety, rejected.[3]

A couple of letters to friends in French give some insight into the daily circumstances of the French during their stay. Dagelet wrote

[1] Ibid., pp. 289–92.

[2] Watkin Tench reports that two men were killed and others attacked and badly wounded while working ashore at Port Jackson (*Narrative*, pp. 85–6).

[3] Arthur Phillip, *The Voyage of Governor Phillip to Botany Bay, with an Account of the Establishment of the Colonies of Port Jackson and Norfolk Island* (first edition, London, 1789; subsequent reprints London and Dublin, 1790), pp. 99–100.

to Condorcet: 'Please excuse this untidy letter; I am blinded by the bites of the [sand]flies I am overwhelmend by in my wretched observatory',[1] while La Pérouse mentions the stockade he had built in a letter to Fleurieu: '...to ensure the safety of our longboats which are already very advanced and will be usable by the end of the month. These precautions were necessary against the Indians of New Holland who, although very weak and not numerous, are like all savages very mischevous and would burn down our boats if they had the means to do so.'[2]

Both Phillip and Tench mention the death of Fr Receveur. Tench merely states that he 'died, and was buried on the north shore.' Phillip, on the other hand, adds: 'His death was occasioned by wounds which he had received in the unfortunate encounter at the Navigators Islands.'[3] However, as Phillip says, there was little intercourse between Port Jackson and Botany Bay, and his comment may be the result of hearsay or of his own officers' speculation. Receveur died on 17 February, by which time the exchange of visits seems to have been over.

The English saw the expedition leave on 10 March and recorded both the departure and the route taken by the frigates. 'They sailed the 10th of March,' wrote Phillip, 'I believe, to return to the Northward.'[4]

The two frigates' probable route may be inferred from the outline of his proposed itinerary which La Pérouse sent to Paris, in accordance with which he would have sailed from Botany Bay past Port Jackson, going north-east and making for Tonga. On board, the naturalists were working on the numerous items they no doubt collected along the shores of Botany Bay, the artists completing the drawings and sketches they had made, while La Pérouse and his close associates were compiling the 'Report on New South Wales' and related documents which, on the basis of what they had done in California and Manila, we can assume they also wrote on the Australian settlement and probably the aborigines. Monneron, as

[1] Dagelet to Condorcet, Bibliothèque de l'Institut de France, MS 867 No. 4.

[2] La Pérouse to Fleurieu, 7 February 178, AN. M., 3JJ 389–22 (16), 3.

[3] See Tench, *Narrative*, p. 98, and Phillip, *Voyage*, p. 100.

[4] 'The First Despatch to Australia.' Phillip to Lord Sydney, Sydney Cove, 15 May 1788, *Historical Records of Australia*, I, p. 17. O. Rutter, *The First Fleet: The Record of the Foundation of Australia from its Conception to the Settlement at Sydney Cove*, Sydney, 1937, p. 136.

he had done at other European settlements, would have been drawing up a report on the new colony's military forces and sketchy defences. All these, unfortunately, were lost in the shipwreck at Vanikoro.

LA PÉROUSE AND THE NOBLE SAVAGE

La Pérouse's comments on the indigenous people he met in the Pacific Islands and along the Pacific rim gain in significance if they are set in the context of western European thought in the eighteenth century.

In the days of what has been called the Age of Enlightenment, philosophers were preoccupied with social and political theories which reflected both internal and external concerns. The French influence was, if not paramount, at least of major importance. The *Philosophes* were driven by the social and political problems which France and a number of her neighbours were facing, to seek a theory that would explain social evolution and historical processes and, using this as their basis, to formulate a new, more rational political structure. As Frenchmen, they were all to some extent influenced by René Descartes, whom they saw as having laid down the foundations for all logical reasoning, but who stressed the importance of self-analysis and the interiorisation of experience. Although they were eager to find a practical solution to the very real problems they could identify around them, they were essentially theorists. Bougainville and La Pérouse were scornful about closet geographers who elaborated theories about the shape of the world in their studies without having ever travelled: La Pérouse was to be equally scornful of closet philosophers or closet proto-anthropologists who had never encountered a primitive people in their own environment.

The situation in which the French found themselves as the eighteenth century drew towards its close was a fairly parlous one. France, once a great European power with a glittering court, the envy of the civilised world, was struggling to maintain her position vis-à-vis the rising stars of England and of smaller nations such as the Dutch and the Prussians. The French treasury was empty, corruption was all too evident, the court of Louis XV had ended its days in depravity and profligacy, that of Louis XVI seemed indecisive and incompetent. Self-analysis led inevitably to an examination of the world beyond France's frontiers and a painful process of comparison. If France's glory was waning, if her people were poor and suffering, why were Holland and England wealthy, or at least so much better able to cope with temporary setbacks? Was there a process of evolution in history which caused some nations, like the Spanish, to attain a state of power and greatness and then, like a flower past its time, to fade into impotence and decay? Could the process be analysed and, hopefully, arrested?

Jean-Jacques Rousseau in his *Discourse on Inequality* saw the rot setting in as soon as man began to evolve from his first rural and family-based condition to that of employer and exploiter: Rousseau was standing at the edge of an emergent capitalist Europe and not liking what he saw. 'Progress' seemed inevitably to lead to inequality, corruption and misery. Conversely, logical reasoning suggested, an absence of this pernicious progress should mean happiness:

> As long as men were content with their rustic huts, as long as they confined themselves to sewing their garments of skin with thorns or fish bones . . . in a word, as long as they applied themselves solely to work that one person could accomplish alone . . . they lived as free, healthy, good and happy men.[1]

Rousseau became identified with the theory of the 'Noble Savage' – in its primary sense of *salvaticus*, an inhabitant of the forest, natural man, innately good, but corrupted by civilisation or progress. The theory was not new, for the Golden Age, the original Garden of Eden, the summer-filled bucolic world, is a recurrent myth in human thought. The yearning for such a state was already expressing itself at the time in terms of the pastorale and, at the highest level of society, in Marie-Antoinette's rustic but clean-scrubbed hamlet at the Petit Trianon in Versailles. Rousseau expressed it in a form that caught the imagination of the French just when philosophers and the general public were becoming preoccupied with the place of man in society and the validity and the structure of existing political systems.

[1] Jean-Jacques Rousseau, *A Discourse on Inequality* (trans. M. Cranston), Harmondsworth, 1984, p. 115.

Sharing his contemporaries' passion for surveys and classification and presenting his views in logical terms, he showed man evolving through a series of stages, beginning with the true *sauvage* roaming through the forest in search of food, going on to embryonic forms of society brought about by an increase in population and the need to survive through co-operation, until dependence on farming and early manufactured artefacts – the tyranny of 'iron and wheat' – led gradually to the division of labour and the ownership of private property, with the consequence that laws had to be established to protect the owners and defend their property, and thus regulate a society that would rapidly become corrupted by greed, selfishness and the exploitation of the less fortunate.

This concept of a primitive Golden Age, which ran counter to the Church's doctrine on original sin, was only revived after the Reformation and the discovery of America which brought Europeans into contact with a number of 'primitive' societies. Missionaries such as the Jesuits and the Franciscans were sympathetic in their judgments if paternalistic in their attitude, and they produced accounts which seemed to provide a factual base for theories on the essential goodness of Natural Man.

Later observers produced a different picture. 'The things they discovered gave the *philosophes* a *frisson* of rather alarmed pleasure, for the habits of the unspoiled savage were less reconciliable with the traditional ideas of virtuous Natural Man than had been supposed.'[1] However, the Pacific Ocean still remained, inadequately explored until the later eighteenth century, holding the promise of islands and peoples as yet undiscovered, living in isolation, unaffected by Western civilisation, where Rousseau's ideas might be tested anew. For the French especially, from Bougainville and his companions onward, Rousseauism – often simplified into a basic and ill-digested form – was an important theory which they could not fail to take into account when they reported on the new societies they encountered.[2]

The most starry-eyed supporters of the Noble Savage theories were the naturalists, who were friends and associates of many *philosophes*, and the younger officers, in other words, those who

[1] Cobban, *Rousseau and the Modern State*, London, 1934; 2nd ed., 1964, p. 147.

[2] For a brief survey of the background and some implications of this, see John Dunmore, 'Rousseau's Noble Savage: A New Zealand Case History', in *Captain James Cook: Image and Impact*, ed. Walter Veit, Melbourne, 1979, II, pp. 160–72.

had had little or no previous contact with native populations. Other were more realistic, among them La Pérouse. But even in France, among closet philosophers, Rousseau had his challengers. However uneasy they might have been about the political condition of France, rural poverty, the wealth and the inherited privileges of the aristocracy and the inabilitiy of her administrators to cope with the country's financial and social problems, many philosophers could not see that Rousseau's ideas had any practical application, or that a rejection of civilisation and a return to a pastoral or sylvan existence would lead to universal happiness. Voltaire, who was essentially a reformist aiming to cure the French malaise, favoured political reform, some kind of constitutional monarchy and freedom of expression. The life of a savage, however depicted, held no appeal for him. Buffon, the author of the massive *Histoire naturelle*, could not accept that technological progress was either reversible or that it was desirable to reverse it. And navigators like Bougainville, who came up against the reality of 'natural societies in the unspoilt Pacific, soon lost any illusions they had:

> Truly when one sees these savages [the inhabitants of Tierra del Fuego], however much one would like to act like a philosopher, one could not prefer man in this state of nature to that of civilised.[1]

He had found them almost naked, huddled in tiny huts, eating raw or semi-cooked shellfish, their teeth rotten, their appearance wretched beyond description. Savage in the primary meaning of the word they might be, noble in their behaviour towards each other they could well be, but enviable they were not.

His spirits rose somewhat when he reached Tahiti where the climate was so much better. Rousseau might have been closer to the mark had he added that the Noble Savage, to achieve the desired level of primeval happiness, needed to live in a warm climate and in fertile surroundings. Bougainville, however, soon discovered the flaws: the class structure, the rigid and oppressive rules of a society constricted by ancient myths and traditions, buttressed by privilege and birthright. What seemed to be unrestricted sexual freedom and adequate food in a pleasant environment certainly looked appealing, but what the *philosophes* were really seeking, especially the non-Rousseauists among them, was a

[1] Taillemitte, *Bougainville*, I, p. 285.

social structure and a form of government that was not based on birth or brute force, where poverty could be banished or palliated, where men and women could live at peace and promote the arts and the sciences in an atmosphere of individual freedom. They saw this as the desirable next stage in the evolution of European life, not as a return to a mystical pastoral past. Tahiti was a delight after the hard months at sea, but it was no blueprint for a new Europe.

Bougainville and La Pérouse, well-travelled, more down-to-earth than naturalists like Philibert Commerson, who proclaimed himself the *adorator perpetuus* of Tahiti,[1] or Lamanon – that 'worthy follower of Jean-Jacques Rousseau'[2] – men who had never been out of Europe before, were practical men of action who shared the views of the French political reformists.

What La Pérouse writes about the indigenous people he met is therefore devoid of any philosophical preconceptions. He describes what he sees, without any artifice, although he remains conscious that his readers, and indeed those around him in his ship, would be aware of Rousseau's writings, whose influence was so widespread. 'The entire world of intellectuals shook under the romantic breath of Rousseau' as one commentator has written.[3] La Pérouse in fact owned a bust of Rousseau, as well as one of Voltaire.[4]

La Pérouse's harshest comments about indigenous people are found, not unexpectedly, after the attack the French sustained in Samoa and the death of his close friend De Langle. Until then, his views had been devoid of sentimentality, severe at times but usually fairly good-humoured. He was somewhat patronising in his comments on the Easter Islanders and their propensity for theft, but there was no sign of anger. They stole, skilfully and repeatedly,

[1] BN, NAF 9407, 146–7. He wrote of Tahiti that he had found there 'the state of natural man, born essentially good, free from all preconceptions, and following, without suspicion and without remorse, the gentle impulse of an instinct that is always sure because it has not yet degenerated into reason.' His report, 'Post-scriptum sur l'isle de la Nouvelle-Cythère ou Tayti' is reprinted in Taillemitte, *Bougainville*, II, pp. 506–7.

[2] The label used by Catherine Gaziello to describe both him and his brother, Gaziello, *L'Expédition de Lapérouse 1785–1788*, p. 146. For Lamanon's shipboard library, which contains Rousseau *Discourse on Inequality*, see ibid., p. 294.

[3] S. Morau-Rendu, *L'Idée de la bonté naturelle chez Jean-Jacques Rousseau*, Paris, 1929, p. 315.

[4] J. d'Estampes, 'Catalogue descriptif et méthodique de l'exposition . . . du centenaire de la mort de Lapérouse', in *Bulletin de la Société de Géographie 1888*, reprinted as 30 pp. booklet, Paris, 1888.

from their French visitors. La Pérouse took steps to avoid any clash between them and his sailors who could be held responsible for property they lost ashore; he offered to replace what was stolen from them. He left a little earlier than planned, without farewells and at night, in the somewhat naive expectation that this might cause the islanders to rue their thievish behaviour and feel some remorse for their actions.

He was neither unfriendly nor unsympathetic towards the Indians of the Northwest Coast or the various groups he met along the bleak shores of Tartary and Sakhalin, but he saw nothing to be envied in their simple but harsh existence. The Californian Indians he befriended through the Spanish missionaries, whose work he praised while expressing some regret about their paternalistic and near-theocratic administration which he felt held them back from 'progress'. In this, as in many of his comments, he shows his links with the Physiocrats who believed that increasing the productivity of the soil was the key to prosperity, and who advocated *laisser faire* and free trade. This becomes more evident in the chapter on the Philippines, a country with a fertile climate and a vast potential for greater agricultural production, which had been held back for centuries by monopolistic and restrictive practices as well as a land-owning system imported from feudal Spain. His criticisms of the Chinese administration arose from the same underlying philosophy: without freedom, mankind cannot progress; commerce must be freed, the exchange of goods must not be hampered, traditional practices stifle entreprise, an oppressive government instils fear and paralyses the human spirit and all hopes of innovation.

La Pérouse sailed to the Samoas with few illusions about indigenous people, but also no greater preconception than that a form of free government – not a semi-feudalistic form of rule by chieftains – was the key to the advancement of mankind. The islands were fertile, but the 'progress' which Physiocrats would hope for was held back by a 'feudal government' which maintained local rivalries and led to internecine warfare. The resultant anarchy ravaged the country just as it had done in medieval Europe. The French *philosophes* and their allies in other European countries were engaged on the struggle to wipe out the last vestiges of feudalism; this would be a prolonged and costly battle, and men like La Pérouse and the scientists on board his ships were hardly likely to defend the feudal structures so evident in the South Seas.

Far from endorsing the views of the Rousseauists, La Pérouse was moved to write that 'man when almost savage and in a state of anarchy is a more evil being than the wolves and tigers of the forests'. Obviously, he had shed much of his earlier tolerance. This we can put down at least in part to weariness and indifferent health, for only a few weeks later he was to write to a friend in France that he had aged so much that, balding and toothless, he would hardly be recognised by his family and acquaintances.[1] He found the natives turbulent and quarrelsome from the moment he reached their shores and was in no mood to judge them with any sympathy.

The murder of his friend De Langle and others who so rashly exposed themselves to danger confirmed his views. Nevertheless, he took no reprisals, ordering his men away from their guns and telling them to lay down their muskets. He had no way of identifying the guilty and he was not prepared to see the innocent punished. But he was reinforced in his opinion that one should not trust men living in semi-primitive conditions, however paradisiac their surroundings might seem, and there can be little doubt that he regarded the aborigines of New South Wales and in due course the islanders of Vanikoro in the same light.

The Tutuila tragedy cannot be explained with any certainty. The participants are long gone, and what we have is La Pérouse's account and verdict on the incident, but not the Samoans'. The earliest enquiries that could be made on the spot were by European missionaries, much later, whose presence inspired awe and fear in their respondents.[2] De Langle's error in going ashore at low tide, out of sight of the frigates, provided the opportunity and was a primary cause of the disaster. The French, a number of whom were sick brought ashore for a breath of 'land air', were in a weak position; they were not guests towards whom the Samoans could feel any responsibility; they were rich in tempting, mysterious,

[1] Letter of 7 February 1788 to Lecoulteux de la Noraye, in BN NAF 9424: 'You will take me for a centenarian; I have neither teeth nor hair, and I believe I shall soon be entering my dotage...warn my wife that she will take me for my grandfather.'

[2] Prior to the arrival of missionaries and traders, the Tutuila episode had inevitably led to adverse reporting and picturing of the Samoans and other Pacific Islanders, especially in romanticised or sensationalised accounts, poems and plays. The bleak picture gradually improved as Europeans began to frequent the islands and settle among the people. See on this Jocelyn Linnekin, 'Ignoble Savages and Other European Visions: the La Pérouse affair in Samoan history', *Journal of Pacific History*, 26:1, 1991, pp. 3–26.

alien goods, and on a number of occasions, unable to distinguish one chief from another or indeed from commoners, the French had caused resentment by making gifts to some and not to others. The Samoan social structure was furthermore far more complex than the Europeans realised: the chiefs or *matai* were not hereditary leaders, but elected heads of extended families; status mattered – indeed, it could be said to rule Samoan society – but there was no way the French, with practically no knowledge of the language, could discern its subtleties. Where they believed they were making friends, they were in fact causing friction. Where they thought they were meeting natives they had come across on a previous occasion, they were probably favouring outsiders whom the local villagers resented.[1] A number of elements played their part in the tragedy: the warlike atmosphere of Samoa, the visitors' lack of knowledge of the situation, De Langle's rashness, French weariness after a long and strenuous voyage, the Samoans' dislike and fear of the strange aliens, sheer cupidity and crowd hysteria. Premeditation can probably be excluded – canoes were trading peacefully around the frigates throughout the incident, and the islanders did not think of attacking until they realised the French were at a serious disadvantage.

This tragedy and others like it, such as the murder of Marion du Fresne in New Zealand in 1772 and of James Cook in Hawaii in 1779, helped to undermine the concept of the Noble Savage, at least until recent times. Its effect on La Pérouse and the whole expedition was quite evident. It lowered morale to such an extent that it never really recovered. It made the French suspicious and prepared to fear the worst whenever they next encountered native people, leading them, for instance, to erect a palisade around their boat-building yard in Botany Bay. It may have made it impossible for them even to attempt to establish friendly links with the aborigines of the bay – who, admittedly, would have found it difficult to distinguish between Captain Phillip's English settlers and soldiers and La Pérouse's sailors and scientists. And it may well have contributed to the final tragedy at Vanikoro.

[1] French ships have called at Tutuila on a number of occasions and a monument was erected at Massacre Bay in 1883 and again in 1937. The officers of the *Fabert*, calling in 1887, were told that the attackers were actually outsiders, from the island of Upolu, where the bodies of the slain were taken back as trophies. See Fleuriot de Langle, *La Tragique Expédition de Lapérouse et Langle*, Paris, 1954, p. 196. However, this may have been no more than a ploy by the villagers to shift the blame to others.

THE SEARCH FOR LA PÉROUSE

The *Boussole* and the *Astrolabe* should have reached the Ile de France (Mauritius) in December 1788. A stay to refit the ships and rest the crews could then have been expected, but news of their arrival at the Indian Ocean outpost should have reached France by April 1789. The expedition itself would then in all probability have arrived at Brest in June or July of that year.[1]

When no news came and the weeks went by, anxiety began to spread among the members of the various families and the naval authorities in Paris. Louis XVI himself was concerned and enquired on a number of occasions, right up to the time of his execution, whether there was any news of the expedition. Scientists who had assisted during the period of planning were equally anxious about the fate of the two ships and of their colleagues and friends.

It was a time of great unrest and upheaval in France. While La Pérouse was away, the king had been compelled to call together the Estates-General, the nearest equivalent the French had to a parliamentary body, which had not met since 1614; this move set in motion a flurry of political activity that soon became uncontrollable, leading to civil disorder and riots, including the capture by the Paris mob of the Bastille, a fortress and prison which symbolised the despotic power of the Bourbon monarchy, on 14 July 1789. Nevertheless, the government still had time to spare for La Pérouse, especially as the Comte de Fleurieu, who had played an important role in the planning of the voyage, was appointed Minister of Marine in 24 October 1790, a post he was to hold for over six months.

[1] The disappearance of the two frigates and the story of the discovery of the wrecks in the island of Vanikoro have been detailed by Admiral Maurice de Brossard who was personally involved in the search for relics in 1964. His first account was given in his *Rendez-vous avec Lapérouse à Vanikoro*, Paris, 1964, pp. 93–270; the story was retold in his *Lapérouse: des combats à la découverte*, Paris, 1978, pp. 565–608 and further brought up to date and summarised in his chapter 'Disparition et recherche de l'expédition' in Dunmore & Brossard, *Le Voyage de Lapérouse 1785–1788*, I, pp. 185–207. See also J. Dunmore, *Pacific Explorer: The Life of Jean-François de la Pérouse 1741–1788*, pp. 282–98. A detailed study of the early moves for a search for La Pérouse, leading to the D'Entrecasteaux expedition, will be found in Hélène Richard, *Le Voyage de D'Entrecasteaux à la recherche de Lapérouse*, Paris, 1986.

In fact, Fleurieu did not wait until his new appointment before requesting that a search be mounted and asking for Louis XVI's assistance. Basing himself on a letter he had received from La Pérouse, dated Botany Bay 7 February 1788, and information sent on by Captain Phillip that the two frigates had sailed from the bay on 10 March 1788, making for the north or north-east, he drew up a report in April 1790 in which he suggested that an accident might have occurred in the area extending from Tonga in the east to the Louisiades archipelago in the west, although he did not exclude the possibility of the expedition having come to grief somewhere along the northern or north-western coast of Australia.[1] It was a truly enormous stretch of little known and unfrequented seas. One of the few European ships sailing in these waters might come upon something, but what was really needed was an expedition that would retrace La Pérouse's proposed route from Botany Bay to Tonga and thence to New Caledonia, New Guinea and the Ile de France. What Fleurieu hoped was that, whatever disaster had befallen the *Boussole* and the *Astrolabe*, there might still be some survivors attempting to make their way back to Botany Bay or struggling on to one of the Dutch settlements.[2]

As a first step, requests were made to London and to Madrid to assist with the search. The British were sending vessels to their new colony in New South Wales, and from there to various islands and to China for supplies. The Spaniards had just despatched an expedition from Cadiz which had already left in July 1789 and was due to sail to Alaska, the Philippines, Macao and Australia. This was the expedition of the *Descubierta* and the *Atrevida*, led by Alessandro Malaspina and José Bustamente, that was making its way to Montevideo, the Falkland Islands, Cape Horn and the South American coast.[3] However, it did not leave Acapulco for the Northwest Coast until May 1791 and was not to reach the South West Pacific until the beginning of 1793.

Pressure mounted during 1790 for a properly organised expedition to search for La Pérouse and other possible survivors. The

[1] Brossard, 1978, pp. 565–6.

[2] A report that La Pérouse had actually reached Batavia in 1789 appeared in the *Moniteur* of 2 February 1790. It seemingly originated from Captain Berkley [Barkley] who told Sir Joseph Banks who in turn advised the Académie des Sciences. Richard, 1986, pp. 21–2. On Charles William Barkley, see Dunmore, *Who's Who*, pp. 12–13.

[3] Brossard, 1978, pp. 566–7; Richard, 1986, p. 24.

Académie des Sciences put forward the name of Louis de Bougainville who had already sailed on a major voyage of exploration and made important discoveries in the very area through which La Pérouse had declared his intention to sail.[1] Bougainville was in command of naval units in the port of Brest, which might have made it possible for him to organise in the minimum of time an expedition to the Pacific, but he was battling against the revolutionary mood then sweeping through France and endeavouring to cope with demands to democratise the navy and with cases of rank insubordination. Furthermore, the likely cost of a search expedition – in excess of 600,000 *livres* – was a matter of concern to an administration facing national bankruptcy. Nothing was done for several months and this particular project lapsed.

Active in the margin was Jean-Joseph de Laborde whose two sons had been drowned at Lituya Bay on the Northwest Coast. He had read a paper to the Académie des Sciences in April 1790 on the discoveries made in the Solomon Islands by Jean-Marie de Surville,[2] and had followed this with a proposal for a privately financed rescue voyage. Himself a man of considerable means, he opened a subscription list in the hope that ordinary citizens might contribute to the costs of an eventual expedition. The response was apparently inadequate, for the scheme lapsed, but his lobbying continued. There were others, better placed than he in the world of science, who were determined to press for an expedition to the South-West Pacific. The La Pérouse undertaking, after all, had been no mere aristocrat's whim, but a scientific voyage in keeping with the mood of the Age of Enlightenment, staffed by scientists, colleagues and friends of the men who were not only ushering in a new era of knowledge but who were playing an active role in the new egalitarian society now dawning. On a less idealistic level, some felt bitterly disappointed that the wreck of the two ships had in all probability resulted in the destruction of the numerous natural history specimens, drawings and descriptions which the expedition's scientists were bringing back with them, and it is interesting to note that when the D'Entrecasteaux expedition was being planned, the learned societies drew up new lists of suggestions and

[1] Brossard, 1978, p. 567.

[2] BN, NAF 9425, published in *Mémoire sur la prétendue découverte faite en 1789 par des Anglois d'un continent qui n'est autre chose que la Terre des Arsacides...*, Paris, 1790.

recommendations for scientific work in parts of the Pacific which La Pérouse had clearly not intended to make for when he left Botany Bay, and which it would be therefore pointless for ships looking for survivors to include in their itinerary.[1]

The Société d'Histoire Naturelle, formerly the Société Linéenne, took over the role of pressure group from the Académie des Sciences. It met on a number of occasions since its change of name in August 1790, and at a meeting in January 1791 discussed petitioning the National Assembly. As a mere scientific organisation, it could not do so itself, so it prevailed on a deputy to present it on its behalf. This was done on 22 January, received with enthusiasm and at once referred to the Comité d'Agriculture et de Commerce for a report. The committee chairman was François-Pascal Delattre, Member for Abbeville and an outspoken advocate of free trade with all France's overseas possessions. Delattre wasted no time. His report was presented on 9 February; it urged that immediate steps be taken to organise a rescue expedition.

The proposal was debated with all the fervour and colourful eloquence typical of the revolutionary period: 'May they return to our shores,' concluded the report, 'even though they die of joy as they kiss this free land.'[2] Delattre's proposal was agreed to. The problem was the cost. The economic troubles that had been the immediate cause of the Revolution remained and were in fact worsening day by day. Delattre estimated the outlay at 400,000 *livres* plus 200,000 *livres* for each of the two years the expedition was expected to be away. As an interim measure, the Assembly passed a decree on 15 February, promising 10,000 *livres* and a life pension to anyone discovering traces of the lost frigates. The day before, Fleurieu had made their loss official by ordering the navy to close the expedition's account as at 31 December 1788, this being the latest date by which La Pérouse had said he would reach the Ile de France. Action promptly followed: on 25 February the Assembly approved a total budget of one million *livres* for a rescue

[1] 'Observations générales de la Société d'Histoire Naturelle sur le voyage à entreprendre pour aller à la recherche de M. de la Peyrouse', Bibliothèque du Muséum d'Histoire Natuelle, MS 46:1, reprinted as Annexe IV in Richard, 1986, pp. 297–300.

[2] F.P. Delattre, *Rapport sur la recherche à faire de M. de la Pérouse, fait à l'Assemblée Nationale*, reprinted in the *Procès-verbal de l'Assemblée Nationale*, vol. 17, 6 February 1791.

expedition. Once this expenditure was approved, Fleurieu could set the machinery in motion. This he did with impressive speed – it was to be ready to sail by September. Louis XVI ratified the Assembly's action when he signed, on 7 April, the 'Loi relative à la découverte des deux frégates françaises *La Boussole* et *L'Astrolabe*'.

Eléonore de la Pérouse, meanwhile, was active in Paris on her own behalf. She had little money and like the wives of those who had sailed with her husband, she was faced with Fleurieu's decision that the expedition's accounts would be closed as at the end of 1788, for this meant that the men's pay would be stopped at that date. The men's wives petitioned the navy and Fleurieu was successful in getting the Assembly to examine their plight.[1] They were helped and Eléonore was promised 40.000 *livres* – but there was more sympathy for the sailors' wives than for her. The treasury was empty and the ponderous administrative machinery was slowing down day by day. Payment was postponed time and again, but eventually a compromise was worked out when it was agreed to publish an account of the voyage: she would get whatever proceeds would come from it.[2]

Others came to the fore. As a result of the Assembly's offer of financial grants to anyone discovering traces of the lost expedition, four merchants from Lorient came forward with a proposal of their own. They sought a permit to send a ship to Kamchatka where they would buy furs, take them down to China and search for La Pérouse on the way there and back. They had even selected a vessel, the 300–ton *Flavie*, to be commanded by Magon de Villaumont. It was clear that they were more interested in trade than in looking for the lost frigates, and their request was laid aside.[3]

A second proposal came forward from Aristide-Aubert Dupetit-Thouars, who had been inspired by Laborde and had written to Fleurieu as early as January 1791.[4] Dupetit-Thouars, an experienced and well connected naval officer, proposed to sail in a brig, more manoeuvrable among small islands than a larger vessel and requiring a smaller crew and consequently less in the way of supplies. His plan was to raise private finance, as Laborde had tried to

[1] AN. M. B4:319.

[2] Eléonore's appeals spread over several years. Her letters are at AN. M. c7 165, 72, 73, 74, 76, 79, 82, 84.

[3] BN, NAF 9425, 319.

[4] AN. M. BB4 :992. Dupetit-Thouars file.

do, sail to Australia and New Guinea in the area which La Pérouse intended to visit on the final stage of his voyage, and then go to Alaska where he would purchase enough furs to pay for the expedition's costs and, hopefully, refund the subscribers. The appeal of the fur trade was once again evident, as a practical way of financing his undertaking and appealing to the more hesitant potential subscribers. An interesting detail in his proposal was a call at the Cape Verde Islands to obtain lemons as a way of keeping scurvy at bay – in this, Dupetit-Thouars showed that he was more a disciple of Lind[1] than a follower of James Cook.

Dupetit-Thouars' problem was that the National Assembly was in the process of authorising a major search expedition which would sail under the command of Bruny d'Entrecasteaux. Dupetit-Thouars then offered his services in that connection, but for reasons that are not clear, his request was declined. Undeterred, he proceeded with his original plan, launching an appeal for funds for a separate voyage under his own command, putting forward, tactfully, that two expeditions would be better than one.

Louis XVI headed the subscription list, but money did not come in as readily as he had hoped. Dupetit-Thouars made a new approach to the Minister of Marine, suggesting that his own expedition might be combined with D'Entrecasteaux – thereby defeating his own arguments that two expeditions would have a better chance of success than a single one. His proposal was rejected, but an appeal for finance which he made to the Assembly in late 1791 was more successful. He was in fact dealing with a new parliamentary body, the old National Assembly having been dissolved and replaced on 1 October by the Legislative Assembly; since members of the National Assembly had declared themselves ineligible for re-election, handing over the task of making laws to a largely brand-new body, he was able to interest a number of members who had no preconceptions about the whole undertaking. They voted him a sum of 10,000 *livres* and their endorsement for an expedition combining trade with a search for La Pérouse.[2] This grant, however, was still not enough, and D'Entrecasteaux's expedition had already sailed. Dupetit-Thouars' impressive tenacity did not allow him to weaken. He mortgaged his property and his

[1] James Lind (1716–94), author of a *Treatise of the Scurvy* (1753).
[2] Rapport and 'Projet de décret' published in the *Moniteur*, 22, 24 December 1791.

relatives', and obtained from the Assembly an advance of two years of his pay as a lieutenant. With this he bought the *Diligent* at Rouen, equipped it and sailed on 22 August 1792.

Doomed he was to fail. Even so, his failure came through a gesture of romantic generosity. At Sao Nicolau, Cape Verde, he found some 40 marooned Portuguese sailors whom he took on board. The crowded ship was struck by an epidemic, so that by the time he reached Fernando de Noronha off the coast of Brazil nearly a third of his men had died and all were in poor shape. The French moreover were not welcome. The Revolutionary Wars had begun in Europe, the French monarchy had been abolished, Louis XVI and Marie-Antoinette were in prison, facing charges of treason and soon to be guillotined. The situation was a challenge to established authority everywhere. Dupetit-Thouars was arrested and his ship seized; he was then sent to Lisbon and held until the intervention of the French government enabled him to be freed, sell his ship, pay off his remaining crew and eventually make his way back to France. In time he was given a new command, but was killed in action at the Battle of the Nile on 1 August 1798. Four years later, the government saved his family from penury by repaying the debts he had incurred to finance his illfated expedition.

The D'Entrecasteaux Expedition

The choice of a suitable leader for the official search expedition was one of Fleurieu's last actions before he ended his relatively brief term as Minister of Marine on 15 May 1791. He had time to recommend Bruny d'Entrecasteaux to the king who gave his approval on 22 May;[1] the new Minister of Marine, Antoine Théve-nard, notified D'Entrecasteaux a few days later.

Joseph-Antoine Bruny d'Entrecasteaux was born at Aix-en-Provence[2] on 8 November 1737. He joined the *Gardes de la Marine* at Toulon in 1754 and served in the West Indies and the Mediterranean. He then took part in a number of hydrographic expeditions: in 1764 under Lieutenant de Chabert, in 1765 under Larache

[1] Approval note signed by Louis XVI, AN. M. BB4:992.

[2] This is the general view because he was baptised at Aix, and it was normal to baptise children as soon as possible after their birth. However, there is an equally strong tradition that he was born in the family castle of Entrecasteaux, near Draguignan.

and in the French expedition to Corsica in 1769. Promoted to *lieutenant de vaisseau* in 1770, he sailed to the Levant and served under Admiral de Suffren in the *Alcmène*. He obtained his first command, the *Aurore*, in 1777, was promoted to *capitaine de vaisseau* in 1779 and took part in various engagements until the end of 1782. In December 1783, Fleurieu appointed him Assistant Director of Ports and Arsenals. As Fleurieu's close collaborator he helped with the planning of the La Pérouse expedition. At this point, his career was blighted by a particularly brutal murder committed by his nephew, and he returned to active service, sailing to the East as commander of the *Résolution*. With the *Subtile*, he was sent to China to protect French trading interests, and for this he tried a new route, sailing against the monsoon by way of the Dutch East Indies and the Philippines. This near-impossible feat was carried out without loss and impressed both the Chinese and his superiors back in France: in his letter of appointment, Thévenard wrote:

> His Majesty, in entrusting to your care such an important mission, remembered that, in your campaign of 1785 and 1786 on the coasts of China and Cochinchina, you displayed outstanding qualities and that sailing against the monsoon you faced the dangers inherent in a perilous navigation tracing a new route through unknown seas.[1]

He was appointed Governor-General of the Ile de France and the Ile Bourbon in 1787, a post he kept until the end of 1789 when he returned to France, taking over command of the *Patriote*. His appointment to lead the search expedition brought him back into close contact with Fleurieu who had begun to draw up his instructions. He was being entrusted with a double mission, to search for La Pérouse and any possible survivors of the expedition by retracing the route he had planned for the final stage of his voyage, and to carry out a heavy programme of scientific and hydrographic research, taking with him a number of scientists who were to collect botanical, zoological and other specimens.

He was given two storeships, fairly similar to La Pérouse's own *Boussole* and *Astrolabe*, the *Truite* and the *Durance* which were renamed the *Recherche* and the *Espérance* and re-equipped as frigates. D'entrecasteaux was to command the *Recherche*, while the second vessel would be led by Jean-Michel Huon de Kermadec, whom he

[1] SHM, Vincennes, CC7:53.

knew, for he had sailed with him in the *Résolution*, and whom he hastened to appoint. As his own first officer, he was given Alexandre d'Hesmivy d'Auribeau who was only 31 and whose health was not good; he had however an excellent reputation as a sailor. Most of D'Entrecasteaux's officers in fact were young: Rossel, on the *Recherche*, was only 26, the same age as Trobriand on the *Espérance*. Kermadec at least was 43 but, like D'Auribeau, his health was not really good enough for a long and strenuous voyage.

D'Entrecasteaux carried with him the seeds of the Revolution. Leaving the troubled shores of France did not mean escaping the virus of unrest and challenges. Some of his officers, such as D'Auribeau, Rossel and De Boynes, belonged to the nobility; others belonged to lesser families, were *volontaires* of middle-class descent, or endorsed the new ideals of the Revolution. However, it was among the scientists that one finds strong followers of the revolutionary movement, in particular the botanist Jacques-Julien Houtou de la Billardière who was to prove a particular thorn in the royalists' flesh. Taking scientists on board always presented problems, for not only were they unaccustomed to naval discipline, they also suffered from the discomforts of shipboard life and the lengthy period at sea when they were unable to engage in botanical or other research.

Brest, where the ships were prepared for the voyage, was a hotbed of rumours and republican activity. The king's flight from Paris in June, followed by his arrest at Varennes, and the constitution of September 1791 which sought to turn France into a constitutional monarchy, all of which followed the abolition of the privileges of the aristocracy, gave rise to heated arguments at every level of society and to the growth of new political groupings in the port.[1]

The expedition sailed on 29 September 1791, making first for Tenerife and then for Capetown. There, on 18 January, D'Entrecasteaux received a report from the Ile de France which caused him to alter his plans. Two French captains, Magon d'Espinay and Préaudet, had met Captain John Hunter, the former commander of the *Sirius* which had sailed with the First Fleet to New South Wales, and was now on his way home in the *Waaksamheyd*, who told them that he had seen natives wearing European uniforms on one of the Admiralty Islands, and that the uniforms seemed to be French.

[1] The expedition was the subject of a detailed study by Hélène Richard, *Le Voyage de D'Entrecasteaux à la recherche de Lapérouse*, Paris, 1986.

Hunter had added that La Pérouse had told him, while at Botany Bay, that he intended to sail in this area.

There was no clear reason why La Pérouse should have deviated from his original plan and made for the north of New Guinea instead of the Gulf of Carpentaria, and it was even stranger that he should have told Hunter this at the same time as he was writing to his superiors in Paris to inform them that he was planning to explore northern and north-western Australia. Odder still, Hunter who was at the Cape when D'Entrecasteaux arrived made no attempt to contact the French and sailed home within a few hours of their arrival. Nevertheless, D'Entrecasteaux felt that he could not ignore the information which the governor of the Ile de France had taken the trouble to send him, and he accordingly sailed for the Admiralty Islands by way of the Moluccas, hoping to reach Sunda Strait before the south-east monsoon. Heavy seas and contrary winds held him back, his frigates made little progress and much of the food on board had become uneatable. On 6 March he gave up and veered south-east towards the south of the Australian continent. He reached Tasmania in April, carried out some important hydrographic operations which took him a month, and made for New Caledonia, reaching the Isle of Pines of 16 June. He was retracing La Pérouse's route. On 17 July he was in New Ireland and went on to the Admiralties.

The French found no sign of any wrecks, although the reef was littered with bleached tree trunks which, from a distance, might give the impression of wreckage, but 'to hold on to the belief that these were the remains of ships it would have been necessary to admit that an entire fleet had been shipwrecked.'[1] As far as the islanders were concerned, far from wearing anything that could be mistaken for French uniforms, they went practically naked. D'Entrecasteaux went on his way and made his way towards western Australia, Cape Leeuwin and once more Tasmania where he remained between 21 January and 21 February 1793. He then went to Tonga, arriving on 23 March and leaving on 9 April, but he obtained no information of any value about the missing French ships:

> One can consequently consider it as certain that Mr de la Pérouse never called at this latter island [Tonga Tabu] nor at Anamuka. If the

[1] E.P.E. de Rossel, *Voyage de Dentrecasteaux envoyé à la recherche de La Pérouse*, Paris, 1808, I, pp. 132–3.

Boussole and the *Astrolabe* are among the ships that were sighted near Vavau the conclusion is that Mr de la Pérouse sailed from that island without any mishap. It cannot be surmised that he put in at any of the other islands of this archipelago and left without leaving any trace of his passage, as one finds numerous traces of Cook, who came here many years before Mr de la Pérouse, and of Bligh's visit which took place only one year after the period when Mr de la Pérouse could have been here.'[1]

It was evident from the enquiries made by the French that the missing frigates had not been seen when they sailed along the western islands of the Haapai group, and that they had not returned later. D'Entrecasteaux's next stop was in New Caledonia, at Balade on 18 April. It was a fruitful call for his scientists, but it produced no new information about La Pérouse. By now the expedition's leaders were in very poor health. Huon de Kermadec died on 6 May, and D'Entrecasteaux spent most of the time in his cabin. On 13 May, having sailed along the long line of breakers along the northern reefs, he made for the Santa Cruz Islands.

On the 16th at 6 a.m. a land was sighted from the *Recherche*, which appeared to be divided in two and form two islands; its middle bore East 1° North. At the same time, but less distinctly, they saw a more extensive land which lay from North 7° East to North 20° West. We estimated that this was Mendaña's Santa Cruz Island and the other two were the islands Carteret calls Lord Edgecumbe's Island and Ourry. Another island was sighted shortly afterwards bearing East 32° South. All these islands belong to the group Carteret called Queen Charlotte Islands. . . . The island we sighted bearing East 32° South had not been seen by Carteret. We called it Recherche Island. We saw it as such a distance that we were unable to show it with any accuracy on our charts; we nevertheless determined its latitude and longitude, and it must be within a few minutes of 11° 40′ of [southern] latitude and 164° 12′ of longitude, Paris meridian. . . . The winds were so slight and the sea so rough that we could not approach Santa Cruz all day.'[2]

[1] Rossel, 1808, pp. 302–3.
[2] Rossel, 1808, p. 368. Recherche Island was Vanikoro, probably sighted by Lorenzo Barreto in the sixteenth century, but first reported by Carteret. See Andrew Sharp, *The Discovery of the Pacific Islands*, Oxford, 1960, pp. 52–3, 110. Seen by Edward Edwards in the *Pandora* on 13 August 1791 it was then named Pitt Island. Edwards went close enough to see smoke rising on the shore, but he made no attempt to investigate or come any nearer. See Dunmore, *Who's Who*, pp. 13–14, 95–6.

The expedition had reached the place where La Pérouse's ships had been wrecked, but it sailed on. The French were in no condition to explore new discoveries. Scurvy and dysentery had affected half the crews. On 20 July D'Entrecasteaux died. Since Huon de Kermadec had predeceased him, overall command fell to D'Auribeau who was himself so unwell that Rossel had to take over for a time. He led a depressed and squabbling expedition towards the East Indies, where he hoped the Dutch would assist him. What none of the French knew was that France and Holland were at war, that their homeland was now a republic, their former king tried and executed.

The first Dutch officials they met, when they called at Caieli, in Buru, were friendly and helpful. The two ships struggled on to Surabaya where they arrived on 19 October 1793. They got no further. The Dutch authorities gave only humanitarian assistance: as far as the expedition was concerned, it was on its own. Political arguments divided the leaders and disaffected the crews, in addition to which the French were faced with financial problems. The remainder of the cargo was sold, but as it consisted largely of baubles for island trade, it did not fetch a great deal. Borrowing from the Dutch became increasingly difficult. In February 1794, D'Auribeau, whose sympathies lay with the royalists, decided to thrown in his lot with the *émigrés*; those who harboured republican views were arrested, some being sent to Batavia, others interned inland in Java. In March 1795 all the surviving members of the expedition were given permission to make their way back to France if they wished, but not in their own ships, for the *Recherche* and the *Espérance* were kept as security for the debts they had incurred. D'Auribeau had died in August 1794, Rossel was captured on the way home and the documents and natural history specimens he had with him were sent to England – they were to reach France in due course as the result of an intervention by Sir Joseph Banks.

The disintegration of D'Entrecasteaux's expedition, due almost entirely to the political situation back in Europe, has overshadowed its real achievements. Admittedly, it failed to find any trace of La Pérouse's ships, although it is believed that a few survivors may still have been alive on Vanikoro at the time the *Recherche* and the *Espérance* sailed past; but the true value of the voyage is found in the heavy volumes of Rossel and the botanist La Billardière, with their essays on natives, plants and currents, in the delicate charts of the cartographer Beautemps-Beaupré, and above all on maps of Australia and the south-west Pacific where many of the explorers' names remain today as tributes to their courage and their determination. It was a natural consequence of the search that D'Entrecasteaux should complete La Pérouse's mission by exploring in detail the area where the frigates had been lost and whence he had been unable to send reports.

The mystery of La Pérouse's disappearance remained; France, engaged on the mightiest struggle of her history since the Hundred Years War, could spare nothing more for such a forlorn hope. Public interest in the expedition did not, however, wane altogether. The men's wives and dependants were helped by extending the date when their husbands could be paid into 1793, and in some cases small pensions were granted.[1] The account of the voyage was published in 1797, the proceeds intended to assist Eléonore de la Pérouse's own finances, but the financial returns were disappointing and she remained in straightened circumstances until she was granted a pension of 2,400 francs in 1804.[2] However, translations in English, German, Danish, Dutch and Italian were promptly published and sold well. Fiction also took a hand, and the misadventures of La Pérouse soon appeared in poetic form and on the stage.[3]

Peter Dillon

It was obvious that traces of the 1788 expedition would only be found by accident. Navigators such as George Bass, Nicolas Baudin, Matthew Flinders, Louis de Freycinet, Louis Duperrey, all bore in mind the possibility that some clue might be discovered during their travels, but the eventual solution was provided by an Irishman, Peter Dillon, in 1827.

Dillon had sailed among the Pacific Islands for many years. In 1813, while an officer on board the *Hunter*, he had landed a German, Martin Bushart (or, more probably, Buckhardt) with his

[1] Authority issued by Jean Dalbarade, Minister of the Navy, 3 November 1793, to pay the families until the return of D'Entrecasteaux's expedition. AN. M. C6 956.

[2] Decree signed by Napoleon. AN. M. C7 165:8

[3] August von Kotzebue's *La Peyrouse: Ein Schauspiel in zwei Aufzügen* was written in 1797. John Fawcett's *La Pérouse, or the Desolate Island* was produced at the Theatre Royal, Covent Garden, in 1801. Both plays were very popular. La Pérouse and his disappearance have been the subject of other plays, of poems (the first written in 1794), ballets, and novels (from 1797 down to the present day). See 'Achievements', below.

Fijian wife and 'a lascar or East Indian sailor' on tiny Tikopia Island in the Santa Cruz group, just south-east of D'Entrecasteaux's Recherche Island. He heard nothing more from them until 1826 when he returned to the island in his own *St Patrick* on his way from Chile to India. All three were alive, but the lascar was seen offering for sale the silver guard of a sword of European manufacture. Dillon questioned the man who answered that it had been obtained from the neighbouring island which he had visited six years earlier:

> The natives then informed him that those things which he had seen, with the sword guard, had been brought in their canoes from a distant island, which they called Malicolo, and that two ships, such as the *Hunter* was, had been wrecked there, when the old men now in Tucopia [*sic*] were boys, and that there yet remained at Mannicolo [*sic*] large quantities of the wrecks. The lascar confirmed this report and said he had been there about six years back, and that he had seen and conversed with two old men who belonged to the ships.... I immediately came to the conclusion that the two ships wrecked must be those under the command of the far-famed and lamented Count de la Pérouse, as no other two European ships were lost or missing at so remote a period[1]

Dillon sailed without delay for the island, which was Vanikoro, but contrary winds and the poor condition of his ship prevented him from landing, and he thought it wiser to sail for Calcutta, where he at once informed the British authorities of his discovery. The sword guard was identified as being of French origin. Subsequent investigations showed it to have been manufactured in 1777 or 1778 by François-Maximilien Fouasse, of Rue de la Pelleterie, Paris; it is now in the Musée de la Marine in Paris.

The British were sufficiently impressed to agree to an expedition leaving without delay for Vanikoro; Dillon's *St Patrick* not being considered equal to the journey, another ship, named the *Research*, was provided. Dillon sailed on 27 January 1827. With him went Eugène Chaigneau, representing the French government, and a somewhat eccentric surgeon, Dr Tytler, who challenged Dillon's command and whom the Irishman managed to leave behind at Hobart, Tasmania. There, Dillon left a message for Dumont

[1] Dillon, *Narrative and Successful Result of a Voyage in the South Seas performed by order of the Government of British India to ascertain the actual fate of La Pérouse's expedition*, London, 1829, I, pp. 33–4.

d'Urville, who was leading an expedition to the Pacific and who would also be looking for traces of the La Pérouse expedition. Dillon went on to New Zealand and to Tonga, where he obtained new information which indicated that La Pérouse had visited the archipelago. From Tongatapu, Dillon sailed to Rotuma and to Tikopia, where he arrived on 5 September; he purchased more European relics – four bells, two small church bells, half a brass globe – made further enquiries about the two ships and proceeded to Vanikoro, the scene of the disaster.

Vanikoro is an unattractive and unhealthy place. Malaria is still endemic there, and in Dillon's day there were few prophylactics or palliatives. The natives were also clearly on their guard. Nevertheless, Dillon's first officer, Russel, completed a circuit of the island, drawing up an adequate chart, and Dillon was able to purchase a quantity of important items of European origin, most of which had come from a place on the reef which the islanders showed him, 'in front of the village of Paiou'. On the western bank of a river in the same area, he found a space along the shore, some 720 feet wide and 420 feet deep, which had been cleared of trees, and where the natives told him Europeans had built a camp and constructed a makeshift boat. This tied in with what a Tikopian had told him a few days earlier:

> He had been at Mannicolo for about five years.... From the natives he learned that the two ships alluded to in this narrative ran on shore in the night on reefs some considerable distance from the land. The one which got on shore near to Whannow was totally lost, and such of the crew as escaped to land were murdered by the islanders. Their skulls were offered to the deity in a temple where they remained many years, and were seen by many Tucopians. The narrator did not see the skulls himself but believed they were now mouldered away. The ship which had been wrecked at Paiow, after being on the reef, was driven into a good situation. The crew of these ships consisted of several hundred men. The ship stranded at Paiow was broken up to build a two-masted ship. The people, while employed building the two-masted ship, had a fence built round her of wooden palisading, within which they lived. There were several of the islanders friendly disposed towards them: others were very hostile, and kept up a continual war with the shipwrecked people. When the new vessel was built, all but two men embarked in her, and sailed away for their native country, after which they never returned.[6]

[1] Dillon, 1829, II, p. 120.

Dillon[1] endeavoured to obtain more details from the people of Vanikoro, with moderate success, and Dumont d'Urville who arrived some time later gathered additional information. It was clear that the two ships had been wrecked in a wild storm that had destroyed huts and uprooted trees. The islanders were split between some who regarded them as men coming from a strange country, and those who saw them as evil spirits. The two men left behind were referred to as *mara*, meaning spirits; one had died some four years earlier – one assumes, around the year 1823 – the other came under the protection of a local chief who was defeated in a tribal war and forced to flee to another island.

After approximately a month at Vanikoro, Dillon sailed for Santa Cruz, where he thought the defeated chief might have fled, but no one had heard of him. Sickness by now was ravaging his crew. He therefore made for New Zealand, arriving at the Bay of Islands on 5 November 1827, returned to India and made his way to London and to France. He was received by King Charles X who bestowed on him the knighthood of the *Légion d'Honneur* and made sure he received the 10,000 francs which the National Assembly had promised back in 1791 to anyone who brought back news of La Pérouse; he received in addition a pension of 4,000 francs.

The relics he brought back were placed on display at the Musée Dauphin in the Louvre, which was eventually to become the Musée de la Marine. They were examined by the ageing De Lesseps who was able to identify several of the items as coming from the *Boussole* and the *Astrolabe*.

Dumont d'Urville

Jules-Sébastien-César Dumont d'Urville sailed from France on 25 April 1826 in the same ship in which he had previously completed a circumnavigation under Duperrey, the *Coquille*, which was renamed the *Astrolabe*. It was to be a long voyage of exploration and scientific research, but the Minister of Marine had added: 'Your voyage will have added interest if you succeed in discovering traces

[1] On Dillon, see J.W. Davidson, *Peter Dillon of Vanikoro: Chevalier of the South Seas*, Melbourne, 1975.

of La Pérouse and his unfortunate companions.'[1] Once Dillon's reports became known, it became important to let Dumont d'Urville know. Dillon himself left a message for him at Hobart, but by then D'Urville had already sailed to the Tongan archipelago where he arrived on 20 April 1827 and stayed a month.

At Tongatapu he learned that D'Entrecasteaux had been wrongly advised and that the evidence pointed to the fact that La Pérouse had visited the islands, not admittedly going to Tongatapu, but to Nomuka. The late Tu'i Tonga's granddaughter told him of a tradition that two ships had anchored at Nomuka before D'Entrecasteaux's visit, that they flew a white flag and after some ten days had sailed westwards. This however gave him no direct clue about La Pérouse's ultimate fate, and he continued on his way. As he sailed towards Fiji and New Guinea, he was in fact following fairly closely La Pérouse's actual route, but nothing drew him to Vanikoro. It was only after he had sailed around Australia and put in at Hobart that he found out about Dillon's voyage. By then it was December 1827. He sailed as soon as he could for Tikopia and Vanikoro where he arrived on 1 February 1828. Dillon had left four months earlier.

Dumont d'Urville at first anchored, as Dillon had done, on the eastern side of Vanikoro, near the island of Tevai, then moved to Manevai, nearer the shore. He remained at Vanikoro until 17 March. To begin with, the islanders were reluctant to talk to the French, to admit that there had ever been a wreck on their island or even that Dillon had recently called. Gradually, D'Urville was able to get them to sell a few items, and in time show him a site near the reef east of Paiou where a vessel had once been wrecked. This enabled the French to bring up an anchor, several guns, some lead and porcelain. These with the various objects he had bought on land satisfied him that this was indeed the place where the two ships had been lost.

The island as before took its toll on the visitors. By the time the French were ready to sail, only some fifteen men were fit enough to work the ship. D'Urville himself was laid low by a fever, but he had erected a monument with a simple inscription: 'To the memory of La Pérouse and his companions. The *Astrolabe*. 14 March 1828'.

[1] Comte de Chabrol to Dumont d'Urville, April 1826, in Dumont d'Urville, *Voyage de l'Astrolabe*, Paris, 1832–4, I, p. liii. The full title of this edition gives emphasis to this part of his instructions: *Voyage de découvertes autour du monde et à la recherche de La Pérouse…sur la corvette l'Astrolabe pendant les années 1826–1829*.

To save it from the islanders' destructive cupidity, the monument was put together without nails.

D'Urville sailed on 17 March. On 2 June Tromelin arrived in the *Bayonnaise*. He obtained a few more French items from the islanders, added a medal to the monument to mark his passage and went on his way.

The mystery of La Pérouse's disappearance was now solved: the two frigates had been wrecked on Vanikoro during what was probably a cyclone. What was still uncertain was whether both vessels had struck at the same place or not: did one get into trouble, whereupon the other had manoeuvred without success to come to her rescue, or had both struggled helplessly in the darkness? Dumont d'Urville had been shown a site that was a good mile north-west of the one Dillon had been told about. Dillon's charts showed two separate locations, one close to Paiou, the other near Tannema. There were also reports of a wreck near Vanu, a village on the Northwest Coast. According to D'Urville, what he had brought back had belonged to the *Astrolabe* – where then was the *Boussole*? The answer depended on further investigations at the various sites, but Vanikoro is an isolated island, seldom visited now and even less in the nineteenth century. Dumont d'Urville called again on 6 November 1838 during his second great voyage with the *Zêlée* and the *Astrolabe*, but he found nothing of particular interest.[1]

It was 1883 before another attempt was made to survey the various sites. The Governor of New Caledonia, Pallu de la Barrière, sent the *Bruat* to Vanikoro. Three 900–pound anchors were brought up and sent to France; they are in Albi at the foot of the La Pérouse monument. It became a regular practice for small French naval units to call at Vanikoro, but no systematic programme of investigation was developed until 1958 when the French Resident in the New Hebrides, Pierre Anthonioz, went himself on a diving expedition and found another anchor. By now, diving techniques had made considerable progress; the cumbersome equipment which made it so difficult and expensive to look for remains of a ship along a submerged reef had been superseded by diving suits with a self-contained supply of oxygen, giving the diver greatly

[1] The riddle of Vanikoro was the subject of M. de Brossard's *Rendez-vous avec Lapérouse à Vanikoro*, Paris, 1964, updated in his section 'Disparition et Recherche de Lapérouse' in Dunmore & Brossard, *Le Voyage de Lapérouse 1785–1788*, I, pp. 185–207, particularly in the final sections.

increatly mobility and freedom of movement. Anthonioz's amateur expedition gave rise to a large-scale official expedition in June 1959.

Reece Discombe

Reece Discombe, a New Zealand resident in Vanuatu, had a wide experience of diving and recovery expeditions in the south-west Pacific. In addition, he spoke fluent beach-la-mar, the simplified *lingua franca* of the islands, and therefore could communicate with the islanders and gain their confidence. With various helpers and members of the local Kauri Timber Company, he was able to bring up in 1959 a wealth of relics, including three guns, six anchors, bronze pulleys, cannon balls, nails, lead and pewter ingots. His talks with the natives proved less rewarding – he was given three different sites for the wrecks. He returned in 1962, 1963 and 1964. On this last occasion, he found so many items on the sea floor and along the reef that the French authorities at once authorised a new expedition with the naval patrol boat *Dunkerquoise*.

The Dunkerquoise brought up a ship's bell, two swivel guns and various smaller items before a cyclone forced her to curtail her stay, but this gave the French the chance of observing the effects of the storm on the reef and the lagoon, and to visualise the difficulties La Pérouse would have faced in 1788. Particularly interesting was a strong current running across the lagoon towards Tanema, the place along the shore where Dillon had been told the islanders saw bodies washed up and survivors struggling ashore. The *Dunkerquoise* returned twice to Vanikoro, in June and in December 1964 when further items were raised, including parts of pumps, swivel guns, pieces of lead, broken plates and some 'green stones' which were eventually to prove that La Pérouse had indeed been to New Caledonia. What could not be brought to the surface was carefully recorded, and later voyages, some organised by the Solomons Association, were able to salvage them.

The Fate of the Expedition

For a number of years, people were satisfied with knowing that the expedition had come to grief at Vanikoro. Whether the remains of both frigates had been found near each other or whether one had been lost further north was difficult to assess. Dumont d'Urville was confident that he had found relics from the *Astrolabe*, and the name of Astrolabe Reef was given to the site he had worked on. The accounts given over a period of years by the natives added confusion to the picture and made an acceptable reconstruction of the events even more difficult. It was not after the Discombe expeditions that a satisfactory analysis could be made, and even this required a careful collation of all the material which had been collected over the years. This was achieved by François Bellec, Director of the Naval Museums, who published his results in 1983.[1]

This confirmed that the two ships had been wrecked on the same reef in front of Paiou, relatively close together. Over the years, storms and currents had, to some extent, mingled some of the débris and carried others some distance away, thus laying the foundation for confusion and arguments. But it was now possible to reconstruct the final stage of the La Pérouse expedition.

The *Boussole* and the *Astrolabe* had weighed anchor from Botany Bay on 10 March 1788, sailing as far as one can ascertain east-north-east for the Tongan archipelago and put in at Nomuka. After a brief stay, the ships sailed probably due west along a route which had not yet been explored and in that case reached Tanna and the Loyalty Islands; they then sailed around the north-eastern extremity of New Caledonia to the south coast,[2] sailed past the Isle of Pines and may have put in at or near Numbo Bay just north of present-day Noumea.[3] Continuing along the south coast, La Pérouse would have reached the northern reef and veered north-

[1] 'Le Naufrage de l'Expédition Lapérouse: une nouvelle analyse d'un dossier mal connu', *Neptunia*, 149, 150, 152 (1983). See also his *La Généreuse et Tragique Expédition de Lapérouse*, Rennes, 1985, pp. 253–66.

[2] Evidence for the almost direct route to the Loyalty Islands and thence to the north-east of New Caledonia rests on the 'green stones' found by Reece Discombe in 1964. Analysed, they proved to be diabase with traces of pumpelliyte fairly common in this region; in addition, Jules Garnier, who discovered the rich nickel deposits of New Caledonia, reported having seen a chief carrying a sword which he identified as being of French manufacture and dating from the eighteenth century. 'Traces du Passage de La Pérouse à la Nouvelle-Calédonie', *Bulletin de la Société de Géographie*, November 1869, pp. 407–13, reprinted as an offprint.

[3] The likelihood of this was outlined by François Bellec in *Neptunia*, 152 (1983) and is based on the discovery of a graphometer manufactured in 1781 currently in the Musée de la Marine, Paris.

east towards the Santa Cruz group where he met his fate. He would consequently have been the first European to sight the Loyalty Islands, a possibility confirmed by D'Entrecasteaux who reported having seen islanders from Uvea who held up a varnished plank which appeared to be of European origin.

Island traditions, however contradictory in respect of the sites of the shipwreck, point to an attempt by the French to build a boat and leave Vanikoro. This implies survivors. A number of men undoubtedly managed to make their way ashore, probably on different points of the west coast. Some were killed, being seen as evil spirits associated with the cyclone, but others managed to stay together and establish some sort of camp, in all probability in the Paiou area. Parts of the ships, stores and other items presumably got washed ashore and were salvaged. Sickness, however, took its toll, and if forty or fifty men survived the wreck and the native raids their number would have been reduced by fevers; even so, the material they disposed of to construct the makeshift boat was only sufficient for a small craft and when the French were ready to leave, so tradition has it, two were left behind, possibly on the grounds of inadequate space, possibly because they were ill. If sickness was the reason, they recovered, for islanders reported that two men lived on Vanikoro for another 30 years – in which case they must have done so under the protection of local chiefs. The reason why they stayed may well have been some friendly links they had established with islanders, which may have made them decide to try their luck and stay behind.

La Pérouse may have been one of those who survived the wreck and sailed away in the makeshift craft: Captain Bénier of the *Bruat* which called at Vanikoro in 1883 was told that the men who left in the small boat were led by someone called 'Pilo', a name that could be taken for a native version of La Pérouse.[1] But nearly a century had elapsed, and the name could well be that of another French, such as Jean Guillou, surgeon on board the *Astrolabe*.

The craft may not even have got out of the lagoon, with natives waiting to attack it at the pass. If it did, it had nothing but difficult choices to make: going to New South Wales, with the dangers of the great Barrier Reef, to the Dutch East Indies, which meant a

[1] P. Fleuriot de Langle, *La Tragique Expédition de Lapérouse et Langle*, Paris, 1954, pp. 226–8.

slow and tortuous navigation south of New Guinea, to the Philippines or Guam, a voyage of 2,500 miles. There is no clue, save one and a tenuous one at that: in 1840 the French corvette *Danaïde*, visiting Ponape in the eastern Carolines, was told that 50 years earlier a small boat with white men aboard had landed nearby, all the men being killed by the natives.[1] The mystery will never be solved.

If the two men mentioned as being left behind survived the departure of the makeshift boat, there is a final touch of tragedy: 'We are left to meditate on the sad disappointment of the survivors who probably did not see D'Entrecasteaux's ships, but surely saw on 13 August 1791 Captain Edwards's *Pandora* sailing along the reef on the south side of Vanikoro.'[2]

After all the hardships of the long voyage, the shipwreck in a cyclone in uncharted seas, the struggle to survive in a harsh and unhealthy environment, they had to see their only hope of rescue disappear into the horizon.

THE ACHIEVEMENTS

What can be said about an expedition which was lost with all its original documents, reports, daily logs, and the bulk of its naturalists' drawings and collections? Did the mystery of the lost frigates overshadow its achievements? To a considerable extent, La Pérouse's greatest misfortune was the amount of speculation that went on about the fate of his ships: a Romantic age seized upon the tragedy, wrote plays, poetry and novels about it, and what had been accomplished was eclipsed.

It has been said that the death of James Cook was one of the great dramatic points in Pacific history.[3] Another of these great dramas was the disappearance of La Pérouse and his two ships with their complements of men, prominent officers and leading scientists, into nothingness. Cook's third voyage suffered from the commander's

[1] G. Froment-Guiyesse, *La Pérouse*, Paris, 1954, p. 154n.
[2] Dunmore & Brossard, *Le Voyage de Lapérouse 1785–1788*, I, p. 207.
[3] J. C. Beaglehole, *The Life of Captain James Cook*, London, 1974, p. 698.

death in a similar way; the events in Hawaii captured the attention of educated Europe and turned people's minds away from what had been achieved during that voyage. The parallel between Cook and La Pérouse is worth drawing. France had hoped for someone who could stand close to the man they called 'the incomparable Cook', and in la Pérouse they found their hopes realised, even in the tragic end that befell them both. Thus, one can say of La Pérouse, as did Beaglehole of Cook, that:

> He was profoundly competent in his calling as a seaman. He was absolutely professional in his trade as an explorer. He had, in large part, the sceptical mind: he did not like taking on trust. He was therefore the great dispeller of illusion. He did have imagination, but it was a controlled imagination that could think out a great voyage in terms of what was possible for his own competence. He could think, he could plan, he could reason; he liked to be able to plan clearly for a specific objective. But he liked to be elastic: there was always in his mind, as he planned, the possibility of something more, the parenthesis or addendum; there was also the sense of proportion that made him, more than once refuse to waste time looking for what he was not sure to find.[1]

Cook's death, of course, was only one incident on a voyage which did not end with his death. However shocked his officers and men may have been, whatever other losses the expedition sustained, the work he had done and others with him was not lost. In the case of La Pérouse, the vast collections of plants, animals and mineralogical specimens – with a few exceptions – were destroyed; the collective experiences of a voyage that had lasted almost three years, covered thousands of miles, an entire human dimension – all that was lost.

But at every port of call where the French felt that onward transmission was feasible and safe, they posted back their letters, reports and journals to government officials and friends. These documents lie today in the National Archives in Paris, housed in the former home of the Rohan-Soubise family, a town residence of elegant classical proportions. The most precious of all is La Pérouse's own journal – not his captain's log, admittedly, which vanished with his ship, but his detailed personal narrative, irrational syntax and erratic spelling included.

[1] Ibid.

The expedition swept from the maps a number of islands which had troubled geographers and sailors alike. It produced a careful survey of the complex Northwest Coast of America and the mysterious coasts of distant Tartary. The frigates criss-crossed the Pacific in a breathtaking pattern, verifying latitudes and longitudes, adding their own discoveries – Necker Island, French Frigate Shoals, and in the Samoan group Savaii, Manono and Apolima – thereby tidying up the map of this vast ocean which was still only emerging from centuries of conjectures and speculation.

The *mémoires* sent back included lengthy reports on Chile, on the fur trade, on American Indians, the people of Easter Island and of Tartary, on California, Formosa and Manila, taking up over 200 pages of manuscript, plus tables of longitudes and latitudes, bearings and hydrographic informations, observations on currents, water temperature and climatic conditions. And there were enough charts and drawings to enable Milet-Mureau to add engravings to his account of the voyage. They enshrine, with the journals, the letters and the scraps of notes and jottings, a world of endeavours, hardships and devotion to the cause of knowledge.

They reflect the dual nature of the expedition. It was a voyage of exploration, but also one of scientific research. The presence of naturalists on board added immeasurably to the value of the undertaking, but it led to a number of clashes. A sailor is a man of the sea and the coast. La Pérouse and Langle wanted to solve the mysteries of unfrequented seas and unexplored coastlines; as officers in their country's navy, they were interested in ports they visited, their defences and their potential; as men of the Age of Enlightenment, they were interested in the human communities they came upon. The naturalists, on the other hand, were eager to spend as long as possible on land, collecting items of flora and fauna, as well as geological specimens, and to add whatever new treasures of natural history the shore and the immediate hinterland might have to offer them. Conflict was difficult to avoid: James Cook, whose fame rests on his hydrographic achievements, found Joseph Banks, the botanist, the scion of the English gentry, the landlubber, a difficult man to deal with, and there was no Banks on the second voyage; and the two Forsters drove him beyond the edge of irritation.

La Pérouse faced the same dichotomy. His naturalists were hard to control; they were not seamen, they had little understanding of naval discipline and the problems of navigation; some were all too conscious that they carried with them the hopes and the influence of powerful learned societies. The strain began to show as soon as the expedition reached the Canaries. Lamanon wanted to climb the Peak of Tenerife. This would waste time on an island that was already well known, and who would meet the cost of his excursion? Lamanon thought the expedition, with its scientific aims, should bear the cost. It was his first opportunity to carry out the research for which he had agreed to sail. La Pérouse who knew how much there was to do, and how much it would all cost, turned him down. Poor Lamanon, a kind man who sent bean seeds to his friends because the crops had failed and the local peasants were starving, had to knuckle under. At times a figure of fun, he knew little about the sea, and he dutifully turned his spy-glass towards the horizon when the young sailors told him the tropics were coming into sight.

But as the days went by, he with his friends began to get used to the ship's routine. La Pérouse did his best to avoid anything more serious than an occasional argument. Only the older Prévost remained surly throughout the voyage because he considered he was not given enough room to do his work, and could not draw properly on a rolling ship. Monge never got used to the sea and had to be left behind. Dufresne, whose role on board was never clear, had to be found things to do and gladly left the expedition in Macao.[1]

The Tenerife incident is not as petty as it seems. For La Pérouse, the peak was a known landmark and that was enough for him. But for the scientists, it still retained its mystery. Its height had not been accurately determined, and the best method of calculating such heights was a subject of current debate among mathematicians and in learned assemblies. Its very presence among this sprinkling of islands off the African coast was equally puzzling in an age when the formation of mountain ranges was the subject of conflicting theories. Lamanon's letter to the Minister of Marine of 26 August

[1] The splits between seamen and scientists was becoming a major factor as France began increasingly to organise scientific voyages of exploration. 'The problem reappears during the D'Entrecasteaux voyage to burst out into the open during Baudin's and to lead to a clear change of policy with Freycinet: from the voyage of the *Uranie* [1817–20] maritime exploration became the exclusive reserve of seamen who, as the need arises, act as astronomers, anthropologists, botanists, etc.' Gaziello, *L'Expédition de Lapérouse 1785–1788*, p. 198.

1785 gives us a glimpse of the scientists' eagerness to seize every opportunity to work ashore and solve problems.[1] It shows how much they must have achieved during the voyage, how many notes, articles, analyses, drawings and sketches they must have worked on, and how much was lost at Vanikoro.

La Pérouse was equally impatient to begin his work. Before he entered the Pacific, he had to decide whether La Roche's Isle Grande existed or not. There was a growing body of opinion which tended to dismiss it as fiction, but La Pérouse had to be satisfied, because erasing an island from the charts is a serious matter, bringing with it a heavy responsibility: if there was such an island, even though the position generally assigned to it was wrong, and a ship were to be lost on it, the blame would fall on his shoulders. So he spent three weeks on a search before he gave up, convinced that this part of the South Atlantic Ocean was empty.

The next port of call was Concepción in Chile. Both scientists and sailors found much to do. It could be claimed that the town and its surroundings should have been known to Europeans and that there was little more to be discovered – but the maps provided by the Ministry of Marine reveal how little was known, since they showed the town located on a site which had been abandoned 35 years earlier. Anything the French could send back was of use: changes taking place in the administration, the port's defences, the people in charge of them, daily life, relations between officials from Spain and the settlers, unruly Indians and the real extent of Spanish influence, the power of the Church, and a mass of hydrographic and geographic information. Rollin, Monneron, La Martinière for their part wrote reports and notes to be sent back to France and to bear witness to their energy and their sense of duty.

La Pérouse then made for Easter Island. It enabled him to confirm that there was no sign of the fabled Davis Land; it did not warrant more than a careful look-out, for by then too much evidence had accumulated to prove it did not exist. He had already analysed reports of Drake's mysterious land, somewhere west and south-west of Cape Horn, and satisfied himself that it did not exist either and was nothing more than some sighting of Tierra del Fuego. Easter Island, isolated and mysterious, was more promising, for he was only the fourth European navigator to call there.

[4] AN. M. 3JJ 386, 111:1, No. 16.

James Cook's observations were shrewd and accurate, and there was not a great deal La Pérouse could add to the Englishman's comments. But the notes and reports written as a result of this brief stay provide yet more evidence of the energy of the scientists and the sailors. Bernizet measured the statues; De Langle went exploring with the naturalists, and Lamanon, La Martinière and Receveur collected numerous specimens which, once the ships set sail, they began to analyse and describe; young Prévost drew plants and animals from life or from their sketches, but his uncle, grumbling as ever, remained aloof.

Hawaii – the Sandwich Islands as they were ephemerally known – had only been visited by James Cook before La Pérouse sighted them. Tragically, Cook lost his life there, but he had spent a total of six weeks among the islands. What could La Pérouse hope to find when he had to follow such a meticulous hydrographer and such a careful observer? There were a few places his predecessor had not visited, such as the channel between Maui and Kaloohawe, and Molokini Island. His reward will be a bay that bears his name on the south-west coast of Maui. He did not, however, spend much time on exploration and, to the despair of his naturalists, he did not let them go searching for specimens ashore.

The real unknown was the Northwest Coast of America, about which rumours abounded: the possible existence of a North-West Passage to the Atlantic, the wealth that might derive from a seemingly inexhaustible trade in furs, inland waterways and uncharted islands. Commercially and strategically, the coast could be of considerable value to France and it warranted the closest examination.

What the expedition discovered was carefully scrutinised in Paris and Versailles. Originally, French officials, Claret de Fleurieu in particular, had envisaged an expedition to the Northwest Coast to investigate the possibilities offered by the fur trade; exploration was a secondary consideration.[1] The reports made by La Pérouse and Dufresne and De Lesseps' verbal comments made it clear that the coast was dangerous and that buying furs was not as simple as some imagined; furthermore the Chinese market was fraught with difficulties and merchants could waste time and money coping with some of the vexatious measures adopted by the Chinese. Even

[5] Details at AN. M. 3JJ 389, 29. See Gaziello, *L'Expédition de Lapérouse 1785–1788*, pp. 49–51.

more important was the complex political situation, with Spanish claims being put forward – something which La Pérouse's stay at Monterey made him appreciate fully – Russian encroachments and British plans. He purchased Cenotaph Island in Lituya Bay without much faith in the value or the validity of the transaction: that was as near as he got to laying any foundation for a possible French base on the coast. The French government and French traders were saved from making futile plans and wasting money on voyages to the Northwest Coast; the only Frenchman who ventured on such an expedition, Etienne Marchand in 1791, enthused by comments made to him by Portlock, found fur prices had risen to uneconomic heights and, when he got to Canton, discovered that the Chinese had put a ban on further imports.[1]

La Pérouse's sound judgment and his refusal to allow himself to be carried away from popular notions, especially those of the *philosophes* back in France, are reflected in his reports and his correspondence. Had the great storm of the Revolution not swept through the French administrative and political structure, planners and strategists in Paris and Versailles would have found his comments invaluable at a time when the story of the Pacific was beginning to move from the stage of exploration to that of colonial expansion. But the curtain had not yet fallen on exploration, and La Pérouse was able to contribute a great deal to the map of the Northwest Coast. Between the fogbound capes and bays, new names could be added: the La Croyère Islands, the Kérouarts, Cape Hector, Cape Buache, Cape Fleurieu, the Sartines Islands, the Neckers – names which did not always survive, because other navigators were soon to follow him. Port des Français might have been kept as a memorial to those who lost their lives in its turbulent and icy waters, but the native name of Lituya Bay has replaced it.

The Californian visit was one of the most important La Pérouse was able to make on the American continent. It was here, behind the cool fog which for so long hid the bay from him, that the wave of the Spanish *conquista* had finally died, lacking the strength to reach the great bay of San Francisco, less than a hundred miles to the north, which would have offered Spain such a valuable seaport.

[1] E. Marchand, *Découvertes des Iles de la Révolution*, Marseilles, 1792, but more especially C. de Fleurieu, *Voyage autour du monde pendant les années 1790, 1791 et 1792 par Etienne Marchand*, Paris, 1798–1800.

The French were the first non-Spanish Europeans to put into Monterey Bay, about which very little was known. Their reports are invaluable because the Mission at Carmel, the Spanish outpost at Monterey and the Indians themselves were soon to be destroyed. The Franciscan Fathers were unable to save the Indians from pressures coming from Spain and later from the United States, and they themselves were almost eliminated. Much of what we know about the Indian population comes from the writings of La Pérouse and his colleagues, and probably much more was lost in the shipwreck.

La Pérouse despatched to Versailles a detailed report on the extent of Spanish defence forces and their potential for further advances; he added details on Spanish claims to the Northwest Coast and the plans they were making to counter Russian and British incursions; and he added his views on the prospects for the development of Californian agriculture and trade if Madrid's policy towards these distant dominions was modified to allow more local independence. The naturalists sent on their own reports, Rollin writing on ethnography and medicine, La Martinière on insects he came upon, Collignon reporting to Thouin on various plants which he felt could be of value to France's economy. Monneron wrote on what he saw as California's future, but there was no way he could guess at the eventual development of the United States or at the presence of the gold which would transform the region during the mid-nineteenth century rush.

The French looked at Spanish California as outsiders. They found a strange world, where there was more goodwill than many of them had expected, but which, as men of the Enlightenment, they saw as backward and held back by outdated traditions. The Church was still the dominant power; it meant well and it protected the Indians from the worst forms of exploitation, but at the same time it kept them under a severe form of control, assisted in this by the State, which La Pérouse equated with a form of medieval serfdom. He felt a great deal of admiration for the self-sacrificing lives of the Franciscan missionaries who had travelled so far away from home and their own civilisation to work for the Indians, but to his practical mind he saw them as holding the natives in an alien time-warp with little prospect of improving their material status.[1]

[1] See his report in AN. M. 3JJ 387.

There was little new to discover in Monterey apart from reporting on the Spanish settlement. Once he left and sailed across the Pacific, there were possibility of making new discoveries. He added Necker Island and French Frigate Shoal and La Pérouse to the map. He avoided as much as he could routes followed by previous navigators, and particularly the tracks of James Cook, knowing that wherever the Englishman had been the seas had been carefully surveyed.

In China, there were no discoveries to be made either, but he could report on the problems traders encountered in the Far East and the lack of an adequate French presence. The obstacles he had to surmount to dispose of the furs bought on the Northwest Coast enabled him to flesh out the report he would send back to France on the future prospects of the fur trade which so many viewed in an optimistic light.

The stay in Manila gave the French another view of Spain's colonial structure and strengthened their belief that reforms and freer trade were essential if Spanish territories were ever to prosper. La Pérouse drew up a comprehensive report on the administration, on unrest among the local population, on moves to do away with the trading monopolies, and on the quality of the soil which, if only the peasants were encouraged to produce more, would richly reward the enterprising. As for Manila itself, it could, if trade were freed up, grow in importance until it challenged the dominant position of the Dutch settlements.

The periods spent in Spanish California, at Macao and in the Philipines enabled La Pérouse to compare three countries ruled by different forms of despotism. In California, the missionary fathers were endeavouring to set up a colonialist theocracy which, however, stifled social and economic progress; in China, oppression and corruption were the dominant aspects of a regime which he found detestable; in the Phillipines, commercial monopolies and a feudal approach to land ownership paralysed commercial endeavours in an otherwise extremely fertile country. His reactions are clearly those of a *philosophe*. His views echo those of Montesquieu on the evils of despotism, and time and time he expresses his support for an end to commercial exclusivism and the policies of the Physiocrats. Where religion presents an obstacle to the rise of a new society and advances in agriculture and manufacturing, he condemns it. In this again he shows himself as a true man of the Enlightenment.

From Manila the expedition made for largely unknown waters. The French sailed close to Formosa at a time when the island was in open rebellion against China; this was a perilous undertaking in itself and the situation precluded any close survey of the coastline, but La Pérouse sat down to write his report on Formosa which, added to his report on Manila, summarised his impressions on these eastern seas.[1] Practical and realistic as ever, he did not urge French intervention, even though some expansionists favoured fishing in these troubled waters. He hinted that it might be possible, but he restrained himself to a few comments on prospects for trade, fully aware that any French establishment would have to be backed by a garrison and adequate naval support. His aversion for colonial adventures was rooted in experience, for in his lifetime he had seen France lose Canada and India, and England lose her American colonies.

The next stage of the voyage, from Formosa to Petropavlosk, is the most important in respect of exploration. Most of the coast was unknown, shown on charts by uncertain lines or dots, blanks spaces about which nothing certain was known, the subject of travellers' tales and vague rumours. The coastlines marked the frontiers of forbidden worlds: China, Japan and Korea. Even shipwrecked mariners could expect little mercy if a sudden storm drove their vessel ashore. Tartary was a no man's land where one could attempt to land and communicate with the local inhabitants, but only because the writ of the Chinese and Japanese rulers had not reached that far to close these distant frontiers to foreigners. There was therefore much the French could discover, from Dagelet Island to the Kurils, and the names they left behind have not yet been erased by history. Ternay, Suffren, Langle, Castries, Monneron, Crillon, La Pérouse Strait, all these may still be found on today's maps, in modified spelling maybe, but as a lasting tribute to the expedition. The problem of the island of Segalien, or Sakhalin, was not entirely resolved, because the narrows that separate it from Asia were too dangerous and meandered too much. La Pérouse tended towards the belief that a pass existed, but that it was too shallow for vessels such as his. Rough shipboard sketches show the way through, but without any indications of depths. The coastlines,

[1] AN. M. 3JJ 386, 111:72 and 387, 111:11, 'Rapport sur Formose'; AN. M. 3JJ 386, 111:69 and AN. M. 3JJ 387, 111:10, 'Mémoire sur Manille'.

however, both along the Asian shore and along Sakhalin, finally emerged from obscurity.

Young De Lesseps's epic journey across Siberia and eastern Europe brought a great deal of information back to France. It was a sensation, and his narrative became a much-translated bestseller. He brought with him further chapters of La Pérouse's journal, his reports on his achievements in the East, reports by scientists, and a number of letters. Thanks to him, we have, among other documents, Rollin's report on the people of Tartary and the neighbouring islands and Lamanon's lengthy dissertation on *terebratulae.*[1]

Meanwhile the expedition was sailing towards the fabulous islands of Rica de Oro and Rica de Plata. La Pérouse made a special effort to check that they did not exist anywhere in the vast northern Pacific. Eliminating them finally from the map was a signal service to navigators, now that the attention of the European powers had turned to the Northwest Coast of America and a possible regular trade in furs with the East, leading to more ships attempting to sail across the northern Pacific.

The original plan, to sail to New Zealand, had been amended by instructions received from Paris. From the point of view of new discoveries, this was fortunate, because New Zealand had been adequately charted by James Cook and had already been visited by the Frenchmen Surville and Marion du Fresne. Going instead to Botany Bay to report on the penal settlement England was setting up would provide useful first-hand information for officials in Versailles, and it took La Pérouse along a different route, towards unknown islands. The price, admittedly, was the tragedy at Tutuila, a worse one even than at Lituya Bay, but the islands of Savaii, Manono and Apolima were added to the map. In addition, the imperfectly known Samoas were more clearly perceived and the charts were corrected.

La Pérouse reached Botany Bay four days after the British First Fleet. Had it not been for the affray at Tutuila, he would have got there ahead of it, and history could have recorded the pleasant scene of the French welcoming the British to New South Wales – such minor scenes are what most people remember about history! It was

[1] Rollin, 'Dissertation sur les habitants de l'ïle de Choka et sur les Tartares orientaux...', AN. M. 3JJ 387, 111:8; Lamanon, 'Mémoire sur les térébratules...', AN. M. 3JJ 386, 111:4–2.

not to be, but the arrival of La Pérouse's two ships was undeniably a surprise for the English and their convicts. His stay is Sydney is commemorated by the district which now bears his name, a museum and the tomb of Father Receveur – to whom fell the doubtful honour of being the first Frenchman to die in New South Wales.

After Australia, we enter an area of speculation. There can be little doubt that La Pérouse went to New Caledonia, but no report came forward of anything he may have discovered there. There is a total blank until 1827–28 when Dillon and Dumont d'Urville proved that the expedition had been wrecked on Vanikoro. But the first search for La Pérouse itself gave rise to numerous discoveries: the Kermadec Islands with Esperance Rock and Raoul Island, Beautemps-Beaupré Island in the Loyalties, the islands of Renard, Misima, Deboyne and Bonvouloir in the Louisiades, the Dentrecasteaux Islands, the Trobriands. The large volumes of Rossel's account of D'Entrecasteaux's voyage, La Billardière's two-volume narrative, the naturalists' reports and Beautemps-Beaupré's delicate charts, all these followed on from the La Pérouse expedition.[1] The French government sent out the D'Entrecasteaux expedition specifically to search for the lost *Boussole* and *Astrolabe*, and in any assessment of the achievements of the La Pérouse expedition we must include the scientific and hydrographic results of the voyage of the *Espérance* and the *Recheche*.

As we have pointed out, the disappearance of La Pérouse attracted so much attention that it tended to obscure the importance of the voyage itself and all its achievements, but one should not be too surprised by this. The Pacific Ocean had long attracted the attention of writers and artists. Writers of utopias had seized upon it as a locale for their ideal societies; exoticism, fashionable throughout the eighteenth century, associated with theories of the Noble Savage and of primitive societies uncorrupted by western civilisation, had given rise to much speculation and to much fanciful writing. The disappearance of two large ships, with their popular

[1] E.P.E de Rossel (ed.), *Voyage de Dentrecasteaux envoyé à la recherche de La Pérouse*, Paris, 1808; J.J.H. de la Billardière, *Relation du voyage à la recherche de La Pérouse*, Paris, 1799; C.F. Beautemps-Beaupré, *Atlas du voyage de Bruny-Dentrecasteaux*, Paris, 1807. Translations of Labillardière's account appeared in English, London, 1800, German, Weimar, 1800; Hamburg, 1801; Vienna, 1804, with a description in Latin of plants collected during the voyage, J.J.H. de Labillardière, *Novae Hollandiae Plantarum Specimen*, Paris, 1804.

officers and well-known scientists, was bound to capture the popular imagination. A mystery unsolved holds far greater fascination for the great mass of readers and will cause more ink to flow than any scientific achievements or coastal explorations. It offered scope for fictional accounts of sightings and rescues on distant Pacific shores and for new utopian fantasies or political tracts, as in the case of the anonymous *Fragments du dernier voyage de La Pérouse* and *Découvertes dans les mers du Sud: nouvelles de M. de la Peyrouse jusqu'en 1794.*[1]

It presented opportunities also for theatre managers. Kotzebue's *La Peyrouse: Ein Schauspiel* was written in 1797, promptly published and translated into Dutch, English, French and Italian. Pantomimes and pantomimical dramas with the Lapérouse expedition as their theme made their appearance at much the same time. John Fawcett's *Pérouse or the Desolate Island*, probably the most successful, was presented at the Theatre Royal, Covent Garden, in February 1801; other performances soon followed in the provinces, including one in Swansea in 1809 with Edmund Kean. In France, Hapdé's *Lapeyrouse ou le voyageur autour du monde* was performed in 1810. Melodramas on the La Pérouse theme were well received in various countries until the 1860s. Playtexts were published and sold well. In Italy, a ballet in three acts was presented in Naples in 1822. Poets joined in, writing verses in praise of the expedition, which unfortunately were seldom memorable. Somewhat fictionalised biographies and narratives of the voyage were soon written – the first in the English language being *The Life of the Celebrated Navigator La Pérouse* of 1800 – and they have continued to appear down the years; La Pérouse's sad love affair with Eléonore Broudou was the subject of Gérard Peru's *Le Mariage de Lapérouse* of 1947.[2]

While the voyage and the disappearance spawned a literature of its own, which kept the name of La Pérouse well in the public eye for over two centuries, the real achievements of his expedition have become better known and it has achieved the status of a major undertaking in Pacific exploration, well able to stand comparison with the achievements of James Cook.

[1] Published in Quimper, Brittany, in 1797, reprinted in facsimile edition with an English translation and notes in 1985 (J. Dunmore (ed.) *Fragmens du dernier voyage*..., 2 v., Canberra, 1785); *Découvertes* was also an anonymous work, published in Paris, probably in 1798.

[2] See J. Dunmore, 'The Literature of Lapérouse' in Ian F. McLaren, *Lapérouse in the Pacific...An Annotated Bibliography*, Melbourne, 1993, pp. ix–xi.

THE JOURNAL OF JEAN-FRANÇOIS DE GALAUP DE LA PÉROUSE

PREFACE

I could have entrusted the writing of my journal to a man of letters. It would have been in a purer style and sprinkled with reflections which would never have occurred to me; but that would have meant presenting oneself behind a mask, and one's natural features, whatever they might be, seemed preferable. I have on several occasions regretted, on reading accounts of Captain Cook's last two voyages, that he had borrowed another man's pen for his first narrative.[1] His descriptions of the customs, practices and art of various peoples left nothing to be desired, and the details of his navigation have always provided me with the enlightenment which I was seeking in order to guide my own: such advantages no editor can retain, and often the word which he sacrifices in order to create a more harmonious sentence is the one which a navigator would have preferred to all the rest.

Anyhow one cannot be attracted by such works without, at times, wishing to be in the traveller's shoes, but at each line one meets only his shadow; and the actor who takes his place, although no doubt more elegant and more stylish, is an imperfect substitute. His various chapters were not written as the voyage proceeded; the outline of his navigation is evenly presented, although inevitably, being so vast and covering both hemispheres, it had undergone a thousand changes. His reflections lack the variations that arise out of the slightest events. In the end the man of letters shoulders aside the voyager, so to speak, and should he have his own preconceptions he will select from the journal only those facts which are likely to justify them. It was to avoid this danger that I refused all outside assistance. What might have made my narrative more

[1] John Hawkesworth (c.1715–73) was given the task of preparing an account of James Cook's first voyage which, with other narratives, appeared in 1773 under the title *An Account of the Voyages undertaken...for making Discoveries in the Southern Hemisphere*. The liberties taken with the original texts resulted in a number of complaints, although in fairness to him it must be admitted than he had been asked to provide a work which would appeal to the general reader.

interesting will appear in another work, by M. de Lamanon: quadrupeds, fishes, insects, these have been, each in turn, the subject of his meditations – his desire to see everything, to combine everything, to describe everything had no bounds other than those imposed by Nature herself; clouds, air, soil, stones, minerals, all these were brought into this naturalist's vast programme. Fathers Mongez and Receveur were his collaborators and his disciples; they rightly deserve the gratitude of students of physics and natural history, as do both Prevôts, the uncle and the nephew, who painted everything that related to that discipline. Mr de la Martinière has enriched botanical science with a wealth of new plants; those who read the description of a newly discovered plant often admire only the scholarship of the person who has classified it: they hardly spare a thought for the great hardships, the risks even, incurred by the one who filched it, so to speak, from Nature, who climbed mountains which were almost inaccessible and whose sanctuary was violated through his enthusiasm alone. However, in this account, we shall mention only those common plants we found in the forests or along the shore, and which protected our crews from scurvy, as well as providing us, after our lengthy crossings, with a pleasant and healthy sustenance.

Among my helpers let me mention the Vicomte de Langle, whose advice so often guided my navigation; Mr de Clonard, my first officer; Mr Rollin, our senior surgeon, whose care preserved our health; Mr Dagelet, from the Academy of Sciences, who carried out the most precise observations of all the noteworthy features of the different islands and coasts we sailed along; Mr de Monneron who assessed the military and political importance of various places; Mr Bernizet who drew up the charts; Mr Duché, whose lifelike and elegant drawings depicted objects better than our descriptions could; and finally all the officers of both ships, who risked their lives a hundred times in boats, large and small, to ensure the safe navigation of our frigates, guiding them through shoals and rocks.[1]

[1] In two marginal notes, La Pérouse mentions that Rollin wrote several memoirs for the Royal Society of Medicine and that Dagelet was preparing various memoirs on astronomy for the Academy of Sciences.

CHAPTER I

Reason for commissioning the two frigates. Period in Brest roadstead. Crossing from Brest to Madeira & to Tenerife. Stay in both these islands. Visit to the Peak. Crossing of the Line. Arrival at Trinidade; unsuccessful search for the island of Ascencaön. Stay at the island of Sta Catarina, on the coast of Brazil.

AUGUST 1785

The former spirit of discovery seemed to have vanished entirely. The voyage of Ellis[1] to Hudson's Bay in 1747 had not fulfilled the hopes of the subscribers who had met the cost of this undertaking; they had not even had the satisfaction of advancing the solution of the important question of a northwest passage into the Western Ocean.

Captain Bouvet[2] in 1739 thought he had sighted land in 54°S. It appears likely today that it was only an icefield, and this error set back the progress of geography; the makers of systems who, deep in the recesses of their studies, trace the shape of the continents and islands of the earth, had concluded that this so-called Cape Circumcision was the northern point of the southern lands, the existence of which, they claimed, seemed proved as being necessary to preserve the equilibrium of the globe.

[1] Henry Ellis (1721–1806) joined in 1746 an expedition in search of a northern passage into the Pacific Ocean by way of Hudson Bay. His *A Voyage to Hudson's Bay, by the Dobbs Valley and California in the years 1746 and 1747 for Discovering a North-West Passage* was published in 1748. Appointed governor of Georgia in 1758 and of Nova Scotia in 1761, he died at Naples in 1806.

[2] Jean-Baptiste-Charles Bouvet de Lozier (1706–88) sailed from Lorient on 19 July 1738 with the *Aigle* and the *Marie* and made for the southern Atlantic. On 1 January 1739 he sighted a snow and ice-covered land to the east-north-east which he believed belonged to the southern continent; he named it Cape Circumcision. In 1808, Captain Lindsay of the *Swan* identified the so-called cape as an island to which he gave Bouvet's name. Today, Bouvetøya is a Norwegian possession.

These two voyages, understandably, discouraged the private individuals who, actuated only by simple curiosity, were sacrificing considerable sums for a question which, for many years, had ceased to be of interest to the various European maritime powers.

Finally, in 1764, the King of England, George III, issued instructions for a new expedition which was placed under the command of Commodore Byron;[1] the accounts of this voyage and of those who followed Byron, Wallis, Carteret and Cook, are available to everyone.

In November 1766, Mr de Bougainville[2] sailed from Nantes with the frigate *La Boudeuse* and the storeship *Etoile*; he followed more or less the same route as the English navigators, discovered several islands, and his *Voyage*, interestingly written, played a significant part in giving the French the taste for discoveries which had been reborn with such strength in England.

In 1771 Mr de Kerguelen[3] was sent on a voyage to the southern

[1] John Byron (1723–86) sailed from Plymouth on 3 July 1764 with the *Dolphin* and the *Tamar*. He sailed across the Pacific, by way of the Tuamotus and put in at Tinian. Appointed governor of Newfoundland in 1769, he was promoted to rear admiral in 1778. Commanding a squadron off Grenada in 1779, he was defeated by the fleet of Admiral D'Estaing of which the *Amazone*, commanded by La Pérouse, was part. The others mentioned are Samuel Wallis (1728–95) who sailed in August 1766 with the *Dolphin* and the *Swallow*, and discovered Tahiti and several other Pacific islands; Philip Carteret (?–1796), who had sailed with Byron and left with Wallis, having been given command of the *Swallow*; he became separated from Wallis but made a number of discoveries during his voyage; and James Cook. Accounts of all four voyages (including James Cook's first voyage) were written by John Hawkesworth and published in three volumes in 1773 (see note 1 above). A French translation appeared in 1774 in four volumes, the work of J.B.A. Suard, under the title *Relation des voyages entrepris par ordre de S.M. Britannique actuellement régnante pour faire des découvertes dans l'hémisphère méridional et successivement exécutés par le commodore Byron, le capitaine Carteret, le capitaine Wallis et le capitaine Cook*.

[2] Louis-Antoine de Bougainville (1729–1811), commanding the *Boudeuse*, sailed from Brest on 15 December 1766 for the Falkland Islands and Montevideo where he was joined by the *Etoile*. Leaving Rio on 14 November 1767, he sailed for the Strait of Magellan, Tahiti and the western Pacific where he made a number of discoveries. The account of his voyage, published in 1771, was an instant success, being reprinted in two volumes in 1772, the year when the first English edition also appeared.

[3] Yves-Joseph de Kerguelen-Tremarec (1734–97) sailed in search of a southern continent on 1 May 1771, going firstly to the Ile de France (Mauritius) where he obtained two ships, the *Fortune* and the *Gros-Ventre*, then as far south as the forty-ninth parallel where he discovered a land which he enthusiastically described as 'populated and cultivated'. Returning to France, he was given the *Rolland* and the *Oiseau* with enough supplies and men to found a colony. Sailing from France on 26 March 1773, he reached the newly discovered land on 14 December, but found it snow-covered, fog-bound and uninhabited. After sailing somewhat aimlessly in rain

continent, whose existence at the time was not even questioned by geographers. He came upon an island in October of that year; bad weather prevented him from completing this discovery; filled with the ideas of all the savants of Europe, he never doubted that he had sighted a headland of the southern lands. His anxiety to make his discovery known did not allow him to delay his return for a moment: he was received in Europe like a new Christopher Columbus. A warship and a frigate were immediately got ready in order to pursue this important discovery: the choice of ships was so extraordinary that of itself it shows how enthusiasm excludes reflection. Mr de Kerguelen was instructed to chart the so-called continent he had sighted; the lack of success of this second voyage is well known; but even Captain Cook, the leader among navigators, could not have succeeded in such an undertaking, with a ship of 64 guns, a frigate of 32, and 700 men; perhaps, I should add, he would not have accepted such a command and would have ensured that other ideas prevailed.

Finally, Mr de Kerguelen returned to France, no wiser than on his first voyage; people lost interest in discoveries, the late king had passed away during that voyage, the war of 1778 turned minds towards quite different projects; but no one forgot that our enemies' *Discovery* and *Resolution* were still at sea and that Captain Cook was the friend and the light of every European nation.[1]

The major aim of the 1778 war was to ensure that peace reigned at sea. This wish was met by the Peace of 1783. The same spirit of justice which had led nations to take up arms so that the flags of the weakest of countries were as respected as those of France and England, turned in peacetime to what could contribute to the greatest wellbeing of all peoples. The sciences, by improving manners, have perhaps contributed more to the happiness of society

---

and fog for about a month, he went back to France where he was court-martialled, partly for having wasted so much public money through his exaggerated claims, but mostly for neglecting his instructions to sail home by way of the Pacific and for unsatisfactory conduct on board his ship. He was sentenced to six years imprisonment, and served four. The land he discovered is Kerguelen Island, in the southern Indian Ocean.

[1] Cook's ships were covered by an international agreement. The French Minister of Marine, Sartines, had issued an order stating: 'The King's wish is that should there be a final break between France and England Captain Cook should be treated as if he was in command of ships belonging to friendly or neutral countries'. (AN.M, B4–313, 315.)

than good legislation. The voyages of the various English navigators, in extending the range of our knowledge, have properly merited universal admiration. More than anyone, the King appreciated the excellence, the talents and the great character of Captain Cook; but in such a vast field there will still remain, for centuries, new knowledge to acquire, coastlines to survey, plants, trees, fishes to describe, volcanic minerals to examine, peoples to study and perhaps to make happier! For indeed, a new farinaceous plant, a new fruit, are inestimable benefits for the inhabitants of the islands of the South Seas.

These various thoughts led the King to accept a proposal for a circumnavigation which was submitted to him by the Maréchal de Castries.[1] With his own hand, he drew up a large part of the instructions which have been given to me; he desired that scientists of every description should be assigned to this expedition: Mr Dagelet, from the Academy of Sciences, and Mr Mongez, both teachers of mathematics at the military school, were taken on as astronomers, the former on the *Boussole*, the latter on the *Astrolabe*; Mr de la Manon, from the Royal Academy of Turin, corresponding member of the Academy of Sciences, was entrusted with that part of the natural history of the earth and its atmosphere which is known by scientists under the name of geology.[2]

The abbé Mongez, canon regular of St Genevieve, editor of the Paris *Journal de Phisique*,[3] was to study and analyse minerals and contribute to the advancement of the various areas of physics; Mr de Jussieux[4] singled out Mr de la Martinière, a doctor from the Montpellier medical school, for botanical work; he was given as assistant a gardener from the Royal Gardens, Mr Collignon, to cultivate and preserve the sundry types of plants and seeds which

[1] Charles, Marquis de Castries (1727–1801), served in the army for some twenty years before joining the administrative service as governor of the Lyons region. He was Minister of Marine from 1780 to 1787; after the outbreak of the Revolution he left France and died in exile in Germany.

[2] The term geology was relatively recent, having been first used around 1755.

[3] The *Journal de Physique* was originally known as *Observations sur la physique, sur l'histoire naturelle et sur les arts* but the nature of most of its contents and the clumsiness of this title led to the abbreviated form being used; the title was formally changed in 1794.

[4] The Jussieu family was prominent in the botanical sciences throughout the eighteenth century. The particular member referred to here is Antoine-Laurent Jussieu (1748–1836), professor of botany at the Paris Muséum d'Histoire Naturelle from 1770 to 1826.

we might have the opportunity to bring back to Europe; this gardener was selected by Mr Thouïn.[1] Messrs Prevôst, uncle and nephew, were appointed to paint all matters relating to natural history; Mr du Fresne, an able naturalist and knowledgeable in all the various items held in the natural history collections of Paris, was placed at our disposal by the Controller-General. And Mr Duché de Vancy was ordered to embark in order to paint costumes and landscapes and in general everything which often cannnot be described. The kingdom's learned societies were eager in this context to give evidence of their zeal and their keenness for the advancement of the sciences and the arts: the Royal Academy of Sciences, the Royal Society of Medicine each sent a memorial to the Maréchal de Castries on the most important observations which we should carry out during this campaign.

The abbé Theissiér[2] from the Royal Academy of Sciences proposed a method to prevent drinking water from going bad. Mr du Fournis,[3] an architect, added his comments on trees and on the study of sea levels. Mr le Drû[4] in his paper suggested that we carry out a number of magnetic observations in different latitudes and longitudes; he sent us a dipping needle he had made, which he asked us to compare in accuracy with the two dipping needles lent to us by the directors of the London Board of Longitude. At this point I must express my gratitude to Sir Banks[5] who, having discovered that Mr de Moneron could not find a dipping needle in London, kindly lent us those which had been used by the famous Captain Cook: I received these instruments with a religious feeling of respect towards the memory of that great man.

Mr de Moneron, a captain in the Royal Engineers, who had gone with me on my expedition to Hudson's Bay, was taken on as chief

[1] André Thouin (1747–1824) was the King's Gardener, professor at the Muséum d'Histoire Naturelle, and the author of numerous papers on botany and agriculture.

[2] Alexandre-Henri Tessier (1741–1837), agronomist, naturalist and doctor, was a member of the Academy of Sciences and of the Medical Society.

[3] This is probably Léon Dufourny (1754–1818) who worked in Italy between 1784 and 1794 and was appointed in 1803 professor at the Paris school of architecture.

[4] Nicholas-Philippe Ledru (1731–1807), Royal Physicist, was well known for his popularisation of scientific subjects; one of his interests was marine cartography.

[5] Sir Joseph Banks (1743–1820) had become a major figure in scientific circles not merely in England but throughout Europe. He was to assist a number of foreign scientists and played an important role as a mediator during the Revolutionary and Napoleonic wars. See on international co-operation during this period Gavin de Beer's *The Sciences Were Never at War*, London, 1960.

engineer. His friendship for me as much as his interest in voyages led him to seek that position; he was required to survey various places and draw the plans. Mr Bernizet, a physical geographer, was assigned to assist him in this work.

And finally Mr de Fleurieu,[1] knight, a former captain of the king's ships, the director of ports and arsenals, personally drew the charts which were to serve us during the voyage. To them he added a complete volume consisting of the most erudite of notes, and of an analysis of the various voyagers from Christopher Columbus to our own times; I owe him a public acknowledgement for all the information I received from him and for the marks of friendship which he so often showed towards me.

The Maréchal de Castries, Minister of Marine, who had suggested me to the King for this command, had issued most precise instructions to the ports that everything which could contribute to our expedition's success should be made available to us. The Count d'Hector,[2] lieutenant general, commander of the navy at Brest, met this request with the zeal and the energy which he had displayed during the recent war, and although in charge of the largest French port he supervised in detail my ships' commissioning as if he himself was to command them. I had been allowed to choose my own officers; I selected Mr de L'angle, post-captain, commanding officer of the *Astrée* during my expedition to Hudson's Bay, who had shown on that occasion the greatest evidence of talent and character. A hundred officers offered their services, to Mr de L'angle and to me, for this voyage; all those we selected were men of outstanding knowledge; the list of these companions of mine is appended to my journal. Finally, on 26 June I received my instructions in Paris: I had the honour of taking my leave of the King on the 28th and to receive his verbal orders on the principal aspects of

[1] Charles-Pierre de Claret, Count de Fleurieu, (1738–1810) played a crucial part in planning the voyage. As Director of Ports and Arsenals, a position he was appointed to in 1776, he had been involved in naval planning during the American War of Independence. A protector and friend of La Pérouse, he was to draw up the instructions given to D'Entrecasteaux when he was sent in search of La Pérouse's lost ships. Pressure of work led him to decline an offer, in 1791, to write the official account of the voyage of the *Boussole* and *Astrolabe*.

[2] The Count d'Hector (1722–1808) had had along career in the navy. He was appointed director-general of the port and arsenal of Brest in 1779 and head of the naval forces there since 1781. He had chaired the court-martial which had investigated the Kerguelen expedition in 1775 (see note 7 above). He was related to de Langle who had married his niece in 1783.

my campaign. The Maréchal de Castries presented me to the Queen on the 30th of the same month, at the Trianon, and I left for Brest on 1 July, arriving on the 4th.

I found the preparations well advanced; the loading of various items had been suspended until I arrived because it was necessary to choose between some articles that were useful for bartering with natives, and food supplies, which I would have liked to take on, for several years: I gave the preference to barter goods, thinking that they would enable us to obtain fresh food whereas by then the supplies we had on board would have become quite tainted.

In addition, we had on board a small decked vessel, of about 20 tons, two Biscay longboats,[1] a main mast, a main piece for the rudder, a capstan; in short, all my frigate contained was incredible. My first officer, Mr de Clonard, who was in charge of the stowing had carried out his task with the wisdom and zeal he has shown ever since he joined the service.

The *Astrolabe* had taken on exactly the same items. We were in the roadstead on the 11th, so cluttered that it was impossible to operate the capstan, but we were leaving during the good season and hoped to reach Madeira without encountering any bad weather. The Count d'Hector ordered that we should anchor in the roadstead with anchors from the port, so that we would have only to let go of our cables when the winds allowed us to sail.

We held the review on the 12th. On the same day the timekeepers were brought on board each ship; our marine chronometers had been under observation on board for a fortnight. Messrs D'Agelet and Monges had arrived at Brest before me, as had the other savants and artists, and before the arrival of the two astronomers the Viscount L'angle and the chevalier d'Escures had checked the operations of the chronometers, but the timekeepers they used for comparison purposes were so poor that the work had to be done again.

On the evening of 13 July, Mr Dagelet handed me the following note: 'On our arrival we found at Brest an astronomical observatory in the gardens of the administration, where Messrs de Langle and d'Escures were carrying out observations to check the accuracy

[1] Known as the *barca longa*, it was widely used along the south-west coast of France and the northern coasts of Spain and Portugal; its shape made it easily manoeuvrable in rough seas.

of the marine timekeepers; but as the instruments belonging to the Brest Academy, particularly the pendulum regulators, they had been using were in a very poor condition they concluded after a few days that they should compare all the timekeepers with No. 25 which was in the observatory. When our instruments were set up on shore I verified the accuracy of my timepiece by means of the sun and lunar readings, and comparing each day timepieces Nos 18 and 19 with information signalled from the ships I established the following table of their accuracy:

Day of the month	No. 18. Loss on Paris mean time	No. 19. Loss on Paris mean time
18 June	36.48″.8‴	27.51.0
30 ditto	37. 7.1	27.47.7
1 July	37.19.0	27.45.0
2 ditto	37.31.0	27.44.2
3 ditto	37.39.5	27.45.4
4 ditto	37.51.8	27.44.0
5 ditto	38. 5.0	27.42.0
6 ditto	.. .. ..	27.42.1
7 ditto	38.36.7	27.42.1
8 ditto	38.49.3	.. .. ..
9 ditto	39. 3.0	27.48.8
10 ditto	39.13.6	27.42.5
11 ditto	39.27...	stopped
12 ditto	.. .. ..	0.36.6
13 ditto		0.36.4

The westerlies held us back in the roadstead until the first of August. There was fog as well as rain; I was afraid that the dampness might affect the health of our crews; however, we sent ashore only one man, suffering from a fever, in the space of 19 days; but we discovered six sailors and a soldier affected by a venereal disease, which had escaped the notice of our surgeons when they carried out their inspection.

The stay in the Brest roadstead was not wasted for Messrs de la Manon and Mongez. They carried out several experiments and observations which will be recorded in the physics and natural history volumes to be printed following this narrative.

I sailed from Brest on 1st August. My crossing to Madeira was uneventful; we dropped anchor there on the 13th. The winds were constantly favorable: this was a real necessity for our ships which being overladen in the fore section were hard to handle. During this brief crossing, on fine nights, Mr de Lamanon regularly observed luminous points in the water, which in my opinion are the result of the dissolution of marine elements. If they had been insects they would not be so widespread, from the Pole to the Equator, and they would favour certain climates.

We had not even dropped anchor at Madeira when Mr Johnston, an English merchant, despatched to my ship a boat laden with fruit. Several letters had been sent to him from London recommending us to him, letters which surprised me greatly as I was unacquainted with the people who had written them. We would not have found a more helpful or more friendly welcome among our own families and among our oldest friends than the one we received from Mr Johnston: after calling on the Governor and the father-in-law of the French Consul we dined at his home and made arrangements to lunch at the country home of the English Consul where a delightful reception was arranged. We had been invited to spend the day there, but we had to spare part of it for Mr Montero[1], chargé d'affaires at the French consulate in the absence of the consul who was in Paris. We decided therefore to lunch at the former's home and dine at the latter's. Nothing could be more charming than the site selected by Mr Murai[2] three miles away in the mountains above Funchal. It happened to be the date when the island's greatest feast is celebrated; the ceremonies were held in the church of Nostra Señora d'el Monte, situated approximately 100 *toises*[3] above the country residence to which we had been invited. This church is to Madeira what the Holy House of Loreto is to Italy. Practically all the island's inhabitants, in their best clothes, were standing along the roadside or in groups under nearby trees, or by the side of the streams which come down from the moutain. The English Consul

[1] Montero, the French consul's father-in-law, was probably Pedro Jorge Monteiro who arrived from Brasil in 1763 with his wife Maria Thereza de Gusmao, and who was director of the tobacco monopoly. The English trader was probably William Johnston, a partner of Francis Newton, founder of Cossart, Gordon & Co. Ltd which still trades in the islands. (Information kindly supplied by R.F. Blandy, honorary British consul in Funchal.)

[2] Charles Murray was appointed British consul in 1771, a position he retained until 1802.

[3] A *toise* was an French unit of measurement equal to six feet or one fathom.

had opened his estate to all these people, which gave this spot, delightful in itself, a sense of festivity which words cannot describe....

Mr Murray is a man of taste and of the most noble countenance. He has spent a thousand *écus*[1] on this hillside; he followed Nature throughout without constraining her, and like a sculptor who visualises the shape of a Roman or an Athenian hero in a block of marble, he saw in the steep slope of this mountain a park which could be as appealing as those one finds around Paris or London: in truth, such enchantment can only be found in Madeira. At the foot of the mountain, as one leaves the town, one comes upon all the trees of America; the banana tree, the *jamberosa*,[2] the lemon tree, these offer a new spectacle every two hundred *toises* ; within 3/4 of an hour one comes across as great a change of climate as if one had journeyed from Antibes to Dunkirk. The white and red grapes we saw lining the path as we left the town were only good for verjuice at Mr Murray's, but we enjoyed the shade of the tallest of trees; chestnuts trees with their fruit, and apple trees replaced the American ones I mentioned; waterfalls and lawns replaced the scorched soil of the foothills. Mr Murray had three charming nieces staying with him, who were about to sail for Jamaica; fresh-complexioned and pretty, like the spot where we met them, they contrasted with the yellowed and sunburnt women of Madeira: one could have sworn they had never set foot in Funchal. Generally speaking, Portuguese women in Madeira are very dark, although I met at the English consul's Madame de Souza, the wife of the colony's administrator, who was a very handsome woman; but she was a native of Pernambuco in Brazil. Mrs Murray is a woman of some 35 years of age who has some charming children; she played the harpsichord and made us welcome in her home in a most dignified manner; we enjoyed the greatest freedom: those to whom music did not appeal could stroll in the gardens. A luncheon consisting of fruit was served at one o'clock, and at 3 we went sadly down the hill to dine at Mr Montero's, which we would have found a more attractive prospect had we not had to leave Mr Murray's estate where the best society of the island had gathered. Tables were already set under

[1] The *écu* was a silver coin bearing the royal coat of arms on one side; its silver content and value varied through the centuries.

[2] What La Pérouse calls a *jamberosa* is the *jambosa* or *jambo*, commonly known as the rose-apple.

marquees when we were getting on our horses, although the way is so steep that I walked most of it, feeling that I was not thereby compromising a sailor's honour. At 4 o'clock, very tired, I arrived at the residence of our consul's father-in-law; almost all my companions had ridden down, all but two or three who, no better horsemen than I was, had followed my example.

Had it not been for the pressing circumstances in which we found ourselves, it would have been pleasant indeed to linger awhile in Madeira where we were so well received, but we were unable to carry out the purpose of our visit, as the English have caused the price of wine to rise to an excessive figure: we could not have bought a barrel of four hogsheads for less than thirteen or fourteen hundred francs, whereas the same quantity cost only 600 francs at Tenerife. Accordingly, I gave instructions to get ready to sail on the next day, August 16th. The sea breeze did not stop until 6 p.m. and we set sail at once, but before we left Mr Johnston sent by way of gift a prodigious quantity of fruits of all description, a hundred bottles of Malmsey wine, half a barrel of rum, and some candied lemons; not for one minute during my stay at Madeira did I lack some attention on his part.

Our crossing to Tenerife took only 3 days; we dropped anchor there on the 19th at 3 p.m. I sighted the islet of Salvages[1] on the morning of the 18th and sailed along its east coast at a distance of about ½ league. It is quite safe and although I did not have the opportunity of taking soundings I am convinced there is a depth of 100 fathoms up to a cablelength from shore. This island is completely scorched; it has not a single tree; it seems to be made up of layers of lava and other volcanic matter. We took several readings to determine its position.

The various observations of Messrs Fleurieux, Verdun and Borda[2] leave nothing to be desired in respect of Madeira, the

[1] The Selvagens group is situated some 150 miles south of Madeira. Three in number and uninhabited, they are not quite as bleak as La Pérouse describes them: they provide enough sustenance for small herds of goats.

[2] Jean-Charles de Borda (1733–99), mathematician and astronomer, had begun his career in the army; he was later appointed to Brest and placed in charge of naval installations. In 1771 he sailed with the navy's astronomer, Alexandre Guy Pingré, and his friend Verdun de la Crenne, to test the chronometers made by Leroy and Berthoud. Between 1774 and 1776 he sailed to the Azores, the Canaries and Africa on surveying expeditions, and in 1778 published with Pingré and Verdun *Voyage fait par ordre du Roi en diverses parties de l'Europe et de l'Amérique…*

Salvages and Tenerife; and accordingly our observations had no other object than the verification of our chronometers which had been well enough checked through Mr Dagelet's observations in Brest to allow us to depend for a few days on the longitudes they gave us. The arrival at Madeira was very useful to assess the degree of accuracy we could expect from them. The longitude calculated within sight of land, checked against that of the town of Funchal, showed a difference of only three minutes from that determined by Mr de Borda. Our brief stay in that island did not allow us to set up an observatory. Messrs Dagelet, d'Escures and Boutin simply took a few bearings from the anchorage, which I did not get charted because it is published in various Voyages. On the 18th of August we took a few bearings of the Salvages island, of which I append an accurate chart. I think that I can give its longitude as $18^{d}13'$ and its latitude as $30^{d}\ 8'\ 15''$, Paris meridian. As soon as I arrived at Tenerife, I had an observatory set up on shore; we took our instruments there on 22nd August and checked our timekeepers by readings of the sun or of stars, in order to verify as promptly as we could the functioning of the two frigates' chronometers: the detailed workings will appear in the volume containing the tables; but our observations showed that No. 19 had lost only 18″ since 13th July, the final day of our observations in Brest; our small timepieces No 29 and No 25 had lost, the former one minute 0″ 7 tenths, and the other a mere 28″; thus, in a space of 43 days, the greatest error was only a quarter of a degree of longitude. After several days of observations and of continuous comparisons we again established the daily progress of these timekeepers. Mr Dagelet found that No 19 gained $2''\frac{55}{100}$ in 24 hrs, No 29 $3''\frac{6}{10}$ and No 25 $0''\frac{8}{10}$ From this, this astronomer drew up a table of their apparent movement, correcting it for the variations caused by the temperature as measured by the thermometer and the swings of the pendulum. Mr Dagelet had some doubts about the manner in which the table of the variations of No. 19 should be drawn up in view of the lack of details on the experiments carried out in Paris; he warns that it would be very useful for users of chronometers to carry out more experiments and that there should be fewer calculations in the interpolations needed to obtain the results, especially when pendulum swings come into the corrections, which requires a set of double tables and leaves some uncertainty on the way the ordinates of the curve should vary. He tested the pendulum on 27, 28 and 29

August and noted the number of oscillations, within a determined time, to assess the strength of the gravitation of bodies at different latitudes; several observations were made of the latitude and the longitude of Santa Cruz of Tenerife, which we believe we can set at 18^d 36′ 30″ of longitude and 28^d 27′ 30″ of latitude;[1] we concluded our work with experiments on the compasses but found such divergences that we will list them only to show how little the dipping needle has reached the level of perfection required to deserve the trust of navigators; however, we assume that the amount of iron present in the soil of the island of Tenerife has played a significant role in the enormous variations we noted: these various results will appear in the previously-mentioned volume of tables.

On the morning of 30 August I set sail with a fairly fresh N.N.E. breeze. We had taken on board each vessel 60 pipes[2] of wine, an operation which had required us to empty half our holds to get out the empty barrels: this task took us ten days. In fact, the slowness of the suppliers held us up: this wine came from *L'orotava*,[3] a small town situated on the other side of the island.

I have already explained how our astronomers had spent their time; our naturalists also wanted to put their stay in Santa Cruz roadstead to good use: they set out for the Peak with several officers from both ships. Mr de la Martiniere went botanising along the road and found several unusual plants; Mr de la Manon measured the height of the peak with his barometer which went down to 18 inches 4 twelths 3/10. The reading taken at Santa Cruz at the same time gave 28 inches 3 twelths. The thermometer which showed 24^d 3/10 at Santa Cruz remained constant at 9 degrees at the top of the peak. I leave it to each reader to estimate the height of the peak as he prefers – this method is so much open to argument that I prefer the data to the results.[4] Mr de Moneron, Captain in the

[1] Santa Cruz lies in 28°27′ and 16°14′W (of Greenwich, or 18°34′ of Paris). The position given by Lapérouse is therefore quite adequate.

[2] The size of a pipe differed from region to region; the Malaga pipe was equivalent to 396 litres. It can be estimated that La Pérouse took 24,000 litres on board.

[3] La Orotava is situated on the north-west coast of Tenerife, about 4 miles from Puerto de Santa Cruz. However, transport would have been by boat around the coast and would have taken quite some time.

[4] There are two peaks at the centre of Tenerife, *El Piton*, the 'true' peak, 3,711 m. high, and Chahorra, 3,103 m. high. There are other peaks close by as well, and the Peak of Tenerife, *El Pico de Teide*, actually covers two-thirds of the island. Disagreement over its height was, not surprisingly, fairly common among early visitors.

Engineer Corps, also went up the peak, intending to survey it from sea level, the only method which had not been tried so far. He is experienced in this type of work, so that local difficulties should not have stopped him unless they were truly insurmountable. Mr de Moneron found that the obstacles were much less than he had imagined: he could see the sea from every stopping point, and a horizon of 40 leagues gave him a level and a 3rd point additional to his two sighting points, so that within a day he had completed all the difficult travel and had reached a kind of plain which was still high above sea level but easy of access. He was rejoicing that the completion of his task was in sight when he was faced by problems with his guides which he was unable to overcome: their mules had had nothing to drink for 72 hours and neither pleas nor money could persuade the muleteers to stay any longer. So Mr de Moneron was forced to leave unchecked a work which he considered finished, and which had cost him great hardships and a considerable sum of money, as he had been forced to hire 7 mules and 8 men to carry his baggage and help him in his work; in order not to waste entirely the fruit of his endeavours, he recorded the main points. One day might now be sufficient to complete this survey which could provide a more accurate result than any of those recognised so far by various travellers.

Marshall the Marquis of Branciforte,[1] Governor-General of all the Canaries, displayed the utmost courtesy towards us during our stay in the roadstead. We celebrated the feast of St Louis[2] at his residence, to the sound of all the guns in town and on our vessels, and I gave a double ration of food and wine to our crews so that they could share in the festivities.

We were able to sail only at 3 p.m. on the 30th of August: we were even more laden with goods than when we left Brest; but each day would reduce their quantity. Apart from wood and water, we would need for nothing until we reached the islands of the South Sea: I planned to obtain these two items at Trinidade, because I had decided not to call at the Cape Verde islands which are very unhealthy at

[1] Miguel de la Grue Talamanca de Branciforte had been governor since 1784. He became viceroy of New Spain in 1794.

[2] The feast of St Louis, one of the French kings, was logically enough France's national feast day under the Old Regime, and was celebrated on 25 August. When Milet-Mureau published the first official account of the voyage, during the French Revolution, he naturally omitted this passage.

this time of year, and our crews' health is the most precious item – it was in order to preserve it that I ordered the decks cleared daily from 8 a.m. to sunset and disinfected; but to ensure that everyone had enough time for sleeping I divided the crew into 3 watches, so that 8 hours of rest would follow 4 hours on duty. As I had on board only the number of men that was strictly necessary for our work, this arrangement could only be maintained when the sea was smooth, and I was compelled to revert to the old practice when I was sailing in stormy seas. Nothing noteworthy occurred until we reached the Line. The trade winds left us around 14^d N. and stayed W. to S.W. as far as the Line: they forced me to keep to the African coast which I followed at about 60 Ls.

We crossed the Line on 29 September at 18$^{d.}$ I would have liked, in accordance with my instructions, to cross it much further W, but fortunately the winds constantly bore us towards the E and without this I could not have sighted Trinidade, because we found S.E. winds at the Equator and they kept with me as far as 20^d 25′ S., so that I always steered close to the wind and was able to reach the latitude of Trinidade only some 25 Ls to the E. Had I reached the island of Pennedo de St Pedro[1] I would have found it difficult to round the eastern point of Brazil.

According to my reckoning, I passed over the shoals where the vessel *Prince* was believed to have touched bottom in 1747. We had no indication of land apart from a few birds known as frigates[2] which followed us in fairly large numbers from 8^d of latitude N to 3^d of latitude S. At the same time our ships were surrounded by tunny fish,[3] but we caught very few of them because they were so large that they broke all our lines; those we caught weighed about 60 pounds.

I must warn here that seamen who fear to come across calms at the Equator are mistaken: we had not a single day without winds and rain on only one occasion – admittedly, it was abundant enough to allow me to fill 25 barrels.

[1] Pennedo de San Pedro appeared in some charts as a danger in approximately 0°55′N and 29°W of Paris.

[2] The frigate bird, with its distinctive forked tail, is found in many oceans. In the areas then being crossed by the expedition, one can find the *Frigata magnificens* and the *Frigata minor* (especially the *F. minor Nicolli* common near Brazil), the *Frigata ariel*, and especially the *F. ariel Trinitatis*.

[3] These were probably the *Thynnus atlanticus*, common in the western ocean.

Fear of becoming carried too far E. into the Gulf of Guinea is equally groundless. One meets S.E. winds very early; they bear one only too rapidly towards the W., and had I known this I would have run free with the S.W. winds which I found constant N. of the Line which I could have crossed at 10^d thus being able to sail off the wind along the parallel of Trinidade. A few days after leaving Tenerife we lost those clear skies common in the temperate zones: a dull white, halfway between haze and cloudiness, became dominant; the horizon did not extend to 3 Ls; but after sunset the mist cleared and the nights were always very fine.

On 11th October we took a number of lunar readings to determine our longitude and check the operation of our timekeepers. We found, taking the median of ten sets of readings carried out with quadrants and sextants, that our longitude was 25^d 15′; at 3 p.m. our No. 19 timepiece gave 25^d 47′. We repeated the same kind of observations on the 12th at around 4 p.m.; the average result gave a longitude of 26^d 21′ with No. 19 giving at the same time 26^d 33′. Averaging these sets of results we found that the longitude obtained by No. 19 is 27′ further W. than the one obtained by the altitudes. This assumption guided us in determining the longitude of the Martin Vaz islands and of Trinidade. We also calculated the latitudes with the greatest care, not only by precise observations of the sun but by taking numerous readings close to the parallel which were adjusted to true noon through other observations. The greatest margin of error resulting from this method should not exceed 20″.

At 10 a.m. on 16 October, we sighted the Martin Vaz islands bearing N.W. distant 5 Ls. They should have been W. but the currents had taken us 13′ S. during the night, and unfortunately the winds which had blown steadily from the S.E. until then veered N.W. which forced me to tack several times to approach the islands which I sailed past at a distance of approximately 1½ Ls. After determining their position and taking bearings so as to lay down their relative position on the chart I sailed starboard tack close to the wind towards the island of Trinidade which is about 9 Ls W.¼S.W. from Martin Vaz. These Martin Vaz islands are, properly speaking, no more than rocks; the largest has a circumference of about ¼ L; it is bare rock with no topsoil. There are 3 small islands, very close to each other: from a distance they look like 5 headlands. At sunset I sighted Trinidade[1] bearing W.8^{d}N. The winds were still N.N.W. I spent the night on short tacks keeping E.S.E. of the island until dawn when I made for the shore, hoping to find the sea calmer within its shelter. At 10 a.m. I was only 2½ leagues from the S.E. point which bore from me N.N.W., and I saw at the back of the cove which was formed by this headland a Portuguese flag in the middle of a small fort surrounded by 5 or 6 wooden houses. The sight of this ensign aroused my curiosity; I decided to despatch a boat ashore to find out when the English had ceded and evacuated the island, because I could already see that I would find at Trinidade neither the water nor the wood which I needed; we could see only a few trees on the heights and the waves broke everywhere with such fury that we could not expect our boats to land easily – I accordingly decided to keep tacking during that day so as to find at daybreak enough wind to reach the anchorage or at least to send my boat ashore. I hailed the *Astrolabe* to let her know my plans and added that we would not tack in any particular order: our meeting point at sunrise was to be the cove where the Portuguese post was situated. I told Mr de L'angle that the one who would be closer would send his boat ashore to find out what supplies we could expect from this place. The next day, the 18th October at 5 a.m. the *Astrolabe* being only ½ L from the land sent its Biscay boat under Lt de Vaujuas. Mr de la Martinière and Father Receveur, an indefatigable naturalist, accompanied this officer; they landed between two rocks at the back of the cove, but the waves were so high that they would certainly have perished without the assistance given by the Portuguese who pulled the boat onto the beach to protect it from the angry sea; everything was saved except a grapnel which was lost. Mr de Vaujuas counted approximately 200 men, of whom only 15 wore a uniform, the others being in shirtsleeves. The commander of this outpost (it is not a settlement since there is no agriculture) told him that the

[1] Trindade is situated in 20°30′32″S. and 29°50′W. of Greenwich, i.e. almost due west of Martin Vaz. In 1777 the Spanish fleet called at Trinidade for a fortnight and left a small garrison on the island. It reverted to the Portuguese, at least nominally, when this garrison left, being attacked by ships commanded by a Scotsman, MacDouall, who was in the service of Portugal. Theoretically, Trinidade had a strategic value which was of interest to the Portuguese and consequently to her enemies; the governor of Brazil finally decided to establish a military establishment on it, but maintaining it was costly and its anchorage was too poor to attract the main powers.

governor of Rio de Janeiro[1] had taken possession of the island of Trinidade about a year ago; he did not know, or claimed not to know, that the English had recently occupied it, but nothing that was told Mr de Vaujuas can be relied on: the commander thought it was his sad duty to disguise the truth on every issue: he claimed that his garrison consisted of 400 men and that his fort held 20 guns – we are convinced that not a single gun was mounted near the establishment. This officer was so fearful that we might notice the dismal condition of his administration that he would not allow Mr de la Martinière and Father Receveur to leave the edge of the shore to go botanising, and after showing Mr de Vaujuas every external sign of kindness and courtesy urged him to re-embark, telling him that the island produced nothing, that food supplies were sent out from Rio de Janeiro every 6 months, and that there was hardly enough wood and water for his garrison, and even then these two items had to be brought some considerable distance down from the hills. His detachment helped to launch our boat back to sea. I too had sent my boat ashore at daybreak, commanded by Lt de Boutin, accompanied by Mr de la Manon and Mr de Moneron; but I had instructed Mr Boutin not to land if the *Astrolabe*'s boat had arrived before him: in that case he was to take soundings in the bay and chart it as best he could within the minimum time – consequently Mr Boutin went up only to within a rifleshot of the shore; all his soundings gave him a rocky bottom mixed with a little sand; Mr de Monneron drew the fort as easily as if he had been on the beach, and Mr de la Manon was able to see that the rocks were only basalt or molten material coming from extinct volcanoes; Father Receveur confirmed this opinion, bringing back a few stones, all of which were of volcanic origin, as well as some sand which was mixed with broken shells and coral. From reports made by Messrs de Vaujuas and Boutin, it was clear that we would not find at Trinidade the wood and water we needed; I decided to make for the island of Santa Catarina on the coast of Brazil: it was the old calling place for French ships on their way to the South Sea. Frésier[2] and

[1] Brazil's governor had transferred his headquarters to Rio de Janeiro in 1763; in 1772, following the abolition of the state of Maranhao, Rio became the colony's administrative centre. There were two *subalternas* administered from Rio: Santa Catarina and Rio Grande de San Pedro.

[2] Amédée-François Frézier (1682–1773) had served in the infantry before transferring to the corps of engineers. He was sent to Chile and Peru to strengthen the

Admiral Anson[1] had no trouble in obtaining what they required there. As I did not want to waste a single day I gave the preference to Santa Catarina over Rio de Janeiro where the various formalities would have taken up more time than was necessary to obtain our water and wood; but as I sailed towards the island of Santa Catarina I decided to verify the existence of the island of Ascencaön which Mr D'aprèz[2] places 100 leagues to the W. of Trinidade and only 15′ further S. According to the journal of Mr Ponsel de la haye, captain of the frigate *Renomée*, I felt certain that various navigators, including Mr Frézier, a very enlightened man, believed that they had landed at Ascencaon whereas they had really been to Trinidade: in spite of Mr Ponsel de la haye's authority, I believed that this point should be cleared up. The two days we spent S. of the island of Trinidade enabled us to take bearings from which Mr Benizet drew a plan of the S. part of the island; it differs very slightly from that of Dr Halley[3] which was given me by Mr de Fleurieux; the enclosed drawing by Mr Duché de Vancy is such a striking likeness that it would be enough to ensure that no navigators coming upon the S. part of Trinidade would be mistaken. This island is little more than a sterile rock; one only finds any greenery and a few shrubs in some very narrow gorges among the hills; it is in one of these valleys in the S.E. of the island, which is no more than 300 *toises* wide, that the Portuguese have placed their establishment.

Nature had certainly never intended that this rock should be inhabited; it would hardly feed a hundred young kid; but the

---

colonies' defences and wrote a valuable *Relation du Voyage de la Mer du Sud aux côtes du Chily et du Pérou fait pendant les annees 1712, 1713, 1714*, Paris, 1716.

[1] George Anson (1697–1762) sailed from England in 1740 with six ships, intending to raid Spanish possessions in America. By the time he reached the Pacific in 1741, only three of his vessels remained; he nevertheless attacked Paita, in Peru, and captured the Manila galleon in 1743. *A Voyage round the World in the years MDCCXL I, II, III, IV* appeared in 1748.

[2] Jean-Baptiste Nicolas Denis d'Après de Mannevillette (1707–80), astronomer and hydrographer, sailed on a number occasions to the East and to Africa, mostly in the service of the French India Company. He headed the French company's chart and map library at Lorient from 1762 to 1780. His great *Neptune Oriental*, published in 1745 and reissued in an updated version in 1775, appeared in an English version in 1782 as *The East India Pilot*.

[3] Edmund Halley (1656–1742) had sailed in the *Paramour Pink* in 1698 to carry out astronomical and hydrographic work in the Atlantic, published in his *General Chart* of 1701. He became Astronomer Royal in 1720 following the death of John Flamsteed.

Portuguese were afraid that some European power might have used it for unauthorised trade with Brazil – that is the only reason, undoubtedly, for their anxiety to occupy an island where, in every other respect, everything presents them with a heavy burden.

Latitude of the main islet of the Martinvaz islands ... 20^{d} 30′ 35″
Longitude ditto, per readings .... 30^{d} 30′ ....
Latitude of the S.E. point of the island of Trinidade 20^{d} 31′ ....
Longitude ditto, per readings .... 30^{d} 57′ ....

On 18 October at midday, I sailed W. for Ascencaön, until the evening of the 24th when I decided to abandon this search. I had by then covered 115 Ls on a W. route and the weather was clear enough to see 10 Ls ahead; accordingly, having followed the parallel of 20^{d} 32′ and being able to see for at least 20′ N. and S., having hove to each night after the first 60 Ls and covered the area which was in sight at sunset, I can declare that the island of Ascencaön does not exist anywhere up to approximately 7^{d} of western longitude from the island of Trinidade and between the latitudes of 20^{d} 10′ and 20^{d} 50′, as I was able to see this entire area. On 25 October we were assailed by a fierce storm; at 8 p.m. we were at the centre of a circle of fire; lightning lit up every corner of the horizon; St Elmo's fire[1] appeared at the point of the lightning conductor, but this phenomenon was not limited to us: the *Astrolabe* which did not have a lightning rod had St Elmo's fire at the top of her masts. From that day we had constant bad weather until we reached the island of Santa Catarina. The coast of Brittany is less fogbound in winter than is this part of the Brazilian coast in spring. I dropped anchor on 6 November between the island of Santa Catarina and the mainland, in 7 fathoms, muddy bottom. The middle of the island of Alvaredo bore N.E., Flamingo Island S¼SE and Gal Island N.

It is very remarkable that after 96 days of navigation we had not a single sick. The changes of climate, the rain, the fog, nothing had affected the health of our crews; but the quality of our food supplies was excellent, we had cleared all decks daily, the crew had been

[1] Saint Elmo's Fire is a luminous electric discharge which appears on mastheads during storms. Sailors in the Mediterranean considered this discharge to be a visible sign of the protection of their patron saint, St Ermo or St Elmo, the popular name of the Dominican St Peter Gonzalez.

divided into three watches in accordance with Captain Cook's practice, and my officers and I had taken the greatest care to ensure their spirits were high: each evening, weather permitting, they danced from 8 to 10 p.m.

CHAPTER II

Description of Santa Catarina island. Observations & Events during our stay. Departure from Santa Catarina. Arrival at Concepción.

The island of Santa Catarina extends from 27^d 19′ 10″ to 27^d 49′ of latitude E. to W. Its width is only 2 leagues. A channel separates it from the mainland, which is only 200 *toises* across at its narrowest. Nuestra Señora del Destero,[1] the capital of this district, where the Governor resides, is situated by these narrows. It contains at the most 3000 residents and 400 houses. Its appearance is very pleasant. Mr Duché de Vancy made the enclosed drawing. In 1712, according to Frezièr's account, this island was a refuge for vagabonds who fled there from various parts of Brazil; they were only nominally Portuguese subjects and recognised no one's authority: the country is so fertile that they could survive without any help from neighbouring settlements and they had so little in the way of money that nothing they had could attract the greed of the Governor General of Brazil and tempt him to submit them. The vessels that called here gave them in exchange for provisions only clothes and shirts, of which they were in great need. It was only in 1740 that the Court of Lisbon established a regular administrative structure in the island of Santa Catarina and the nearby mainland. This administration extends 60 Ls N. to S., from the San Francisco River to the Rio Grande in the south.[2] It has a population of 20,000 people and I saw so many children among these families that I believe it will soon be

[1] More correctly Nossa Senhora do Desterro, the settlement dates from 1678. Its modern name is Florianopólis.

[2] The administrative area of Santa Catarina is situated between the provinces of Sao Paulo and Rio Grande de Sao Pedro. Jose Silva Pais was appointed governor in 1739 with instructions to establish an orderly settlement and protect it against pirates and foreign raiders. The administrative structure was reorganised several times between 1739 and 1750. See on this C.R. Boxer, *The Golden Age of Brazil 1695–1750*, Los Angeles, 1962, pp. 251–3.

infinitely greater. The soil is extremely fertile, and produces all kinds of fruits, vegetables and grain crops. It is covered in evergreen trees, but they are so intertwined with brambles and lianas that one cannot cross these forests without cutting a path through them with axes: in addition one needs to watch out for snakes whose bite is deadly. All the houses, on the mainland as well as on the island, are built along the shore. The trees surrounding them give out a delightful scent, consisting in large part of orange trees and of aromatic trees and shrubs. In spite of these advantages, the country is very poor and extremely lacking in manufactured goods, so that the peasants go almost naked or covered in rags: their soil which is very suitable for growing sugar cane cannot be developed on account of the lack of slaves which they are too poor to buy. Whaling is very successful, but it is a monopoly of a Lisbon company[1] which has three shore stations along the coast, catching about 400 whales a year, sending the oil as well as the spermaceti to Lisbon by way of Rio de Janeiro. The local people are merely spectators of this activity which brings them no gain, and unless the government comes to their assistance and grants them charters or other forms of encouragement which might lead to trade, one of the finest places on the earth will continue to languish and will be of no benefit whatever to its mother country.

The anchorage at Santa Catarina is very easy; one finds bottom, mud, at 70 fathoms 18 Ls off shore and this depth decreases gradually until one reaches 4 cablelengths from the shore where one finds 4 fathoms. The normal pass is found between the island of Alvaredo and the northern point of Santa Catarina; there is also a pass between the islands of Gal and Alvaredo, but one has to know it, and my boats were so busy during our stay that I was unable to take soundings. The best anchorage is found half a league from the island where the fortress is built, in six fathoms, muddy bottom, the citadel bearing S.3^{d}W., the fort on the large headland S.60^{d}E.; one is then between several watercourses, on the mainland as well

[1] La Pérouse was an opponent of trade monopolies, being in this respect in sympathy with the French reformers of his day. British and American whalers were by then encroaching on the Lisbon traders' monopoly, and already, in 1773, the whaler Lothrop from Rhode Island had received permission to hunt in these waters. The monopoly ended in 1801 when no applicants came forward. See D. Alden, 'Yankee Sperm Whalers in Brazilian Waters and the Decline of the Portuguese Whale Fisher (1773–1801)', *The Americas*, XX (January 1964), pp. 267–88.

as on the island, and depending on the wind one can choose between several coves to effect a landing: this point is very important as it is difficult to manoeuvre longboats through the channel which, up to the narrows leading to the town, is two leagues wide: the sea is choppy, the currents are very strong and the waves always break on the side opposed to the wind; the tides are very irregular, running N. and S. from the two passes up to the narrows; it rises only by 3 feet.

It seemed that our arrival had caused a great deal of concern on land; the various forts fired several warning shots, which led me to drop anchor early on and send a boat ashore with an officer to explain that our intentions were quite peaceful and make known our needs in water, wood and supplies. Lt de Pierrevert, whom I despatched on this errand, found that the small garrison at the citadel was under arms; it consisted of 40 soldiers under the command of a Capt who promptly sent a message to the town for the Governor, Don Francisco de Baros, a brigadier in the infantry. The latter had read of our expedition in the Lisbon Gazette,[1] and a bronze medal which I sent him left him with no doubts about the purpose of our call. Most precise and clear instructions were issued to supply us with what we needed, at a fair price, and an officer was appointed to each frigate to assist us. We sent them to buy supplies from the inhabitants with the commissary clerks.

On 9 November, I moved closer to the fortress from which I was at a small distance. I went on the same day with Mr de L'angle and several officers to pay a visit to the commander of that post, who gave us an 11-gun salute; my ship returned it. The next day I sent my boat, commanded by Lt Boutin, to Nostra Señora del Destero to express my thanks to the Governor for the generous manner in which all our needs had been met. Messrs de Monneron, de la Manon and Father Mongèz went with this officer, as did Messrs de la Borde Marchainville and Father Receveur who had been sent by Mr de L'angle for the same purpose; they were all received with the utmost politeness and cordiality. Don Francisco Baros, Governor of this district, is aged about 70; he speaks perfect French and is knowledgeable on almost all the sciences connected with our voyage. Our people dined with him. He told them during dinner

[1] The *Gazeta de Lisboa* was published between 1778 and 1820. Among other items, it reported the arrivals and departures of ships and of leading personalities.

that the island of Ascencaön did not exist, but that nevertheless, following Mr d'aprèz's account, the Governor General of Brazil had sent a ship the previous year to cover all the locations previously assigned to that island, and that, as the Capt of the ship had found nothing, it had been erased from Portuguese charts to prevent perpetuating an old error. He added, in respect of the island of Trinidade, that it had always been part of His Most Faithful Majesty's possessions and that the English had evacuated it at the first request made by the Queen of Portugal, the Minister of the King of England having added, moreover, that his country had never authorised such a settlement which was nothing but a private venture. The boats of the *Astrolabe* and the *Boussole* were back at 11 the next morning. They told me that a visit by the colony's chief of staff, Don Antonio de Gama, was expected very shortly, but he only arrived on the 13th, and he brought me a most courteous letter from his superior. The season was so advanced that I had no time to lose; our crews were in the best of health, and I flattered myself when I arrived that we could sail within five or six days after taking on our stores, but the S. winds and the currents were so violent that communication with the land was often cut, which delayed my departure.

I had chosen Santa Catarina in preference to Rio de Janeiro because the formalities required in a large town always result in wasted time. This call offered other advantages; food supplies of all kinds are plentiful, a large ox costs 8 piastres, a 150-lb pig 4, two turkeys 1 piastre. One has only to throw a net to haul it in filled with fish. We bought 500 oranges delivered on board for 1 *écu*; vegetables were also available at a very modest price. And finally, to add to the description of this place an indication of the hospitable nature of its good inhabitants, let me describe how, my boat having capsized in the cove where I was having wood cut, the locals who helped to save it insisted on our sailors having their own beds, themselves lying down on mats in the middle of the room which was the setting for this hospitable behaviour, and a few days later brought back to the ship the boat's sails, mast, grapnel and flag, objects which would have been very precious to them and most useful for their canoes. Their manners are gentle; they are good, polite, helpful, but superstitious and jealous of their wives who never appear in public.

Out hunting, officers shot several different brilliantly coloured birds, including a roller[1] of a very fine blue colour, which has not been described by Mr de Buffon[2] but which is very common in this country.

Not anticipating the problems that kept us for twelve days in this anchorage, we did not send our chronometers ashore, expecting that we would spend no more than 5 or 6 days here. This caused us little regret because the sky was almost always cloudy. We therefore determined the longitude of this island only by lunar readings.

According to our observations, the most E. and N. point of Santa Catarina Island can be fixed at 49^{d} 49′ west of Paris, latitude 27^{d} 19′.

On the evening of the 16th, everything being on board, I sent my despatches to the Governor who had kindly agreed to have them sent on to Lisbon; they were addressed to our Consul General there, Mr de St Marc. Everyone was allowed to write to his family or friends. We were hopeful of sailing on the morrow, but the N. winds which would have been so helpful had we been out at sea held us back in the cove until 19 November. I set sail at daybreak. Calms forced me to drop anchor for a few hours and we were clear of all the islands only at nightfall.

We had bought enough oxen, pigs and poultry at Santa Catarina to feed the crews at sea for over a month, and we had added orange and lemon trees to our collection of trees which, since our departure from Brest, had survived perfectly in the boxes made in Paris under the care and supervision of Mr Thouïn. Our gardener had also obtained supplies of seeds of oranges, lemons, cotton, maize and of rice and generally speaking of all the comestibles which, according to the accounts of English navigators, the inhabitants of the S. Sea lack and which can contribute to their happiness, and are more suitable for their climate and their way of life than the vegetables of France of which we were also bringing an immense quantity.

On the day of our departure I handed over to the *Astrolabe* some new signals, much more comprehensive than those we had used

[1] Roller is a common name applied to the *Coracias* sp. because of the manner in which the birds tumbles or rolls in flight. Most are brightly coloured, predominantly blue.

[2] George-Louis Leclerc de Buffon (1707–88) was the leading French naturalist of his day, keeper of the Paris botanical gardens, and author-editor of the monumental *Histoire naturelle* which was published in 44 volumes between 1749 and 1804.

until then; we were going to sail through stormy seas and in fog, circumstances which required fresh precautions. We agreed with Mr de L'angle that our first place of rendezvous in the event of our becoming separated would be the port of Good Success in the Strait of Le Maire,[1] assuming that we had not passed it by 1st January; the second would be Venus Point on the island of *Otaiti*.[2] In addition, I advised him that I would restrict my work in the Atlantic sea to a search for the island of La Roche[3] as I had insufficient time left to seek a passage S. of the land of Sandwich.[4] I greatly regretted that I could not begin my campaign by the E., but I did not dare to change so radically the plan adopted in France, because I could not have then received anywhere the letters I was told to expect from the Minister which could have given me instructions of great importance.

The weather was very fine until the 28th when we encountered a violent squall from the E.; this was the first since we had left France, and I was pleased to find that, although our vessels were not good sailers, they behaved very well in bad weather and could cope with the heavy seas we would have to meet. At the time I was in 35 degrees 24′ of latitude and 43^{d} 40′ of longitude. I was steering E.S.E. because, in my search for Isle Grande, I intended to place myself 10^{d} E. of the position allocated to it in the various charts. I recognised that I would have a great deal of trouble to reach that

[1] Strait of Le Maire separates Staten Island (the Isla de los Estados) from Tierra del Fuego. It was discovered by Jacob Le Maire and Willem Schouten in 1616. During his first voyage to the Pacific, in January 1769, James Cook anchored in the Bay of Good Success (Bahia Buen Suceso) which is on the western side of southern Tierra del Fuego in cold and boisterous weather and lost two negro slaves.

[2] Point Venus provides another link with James Cook: it is the site of the observatory set up by Cook on the northern coast of Tahiti in 1769.

[3] Antoine de la Roche was an English merchant of French parentage who, on his way back from Chile in 1675 discovered South Georgia and, sailing north-north-east, came upon an island he named Isle Grande. This latter discovery was reported by Francisco de Leixas y Lovera in his *Descripción geografica, y Derretero de la region austral magellanica*, Madrid, 1690, and included in the works of Charles de Brosses (*Histoire des navigations aux terres australes*, Paris, 1756) and James Burney (*A Chronological History of the Discoveries in the South Sea or Pacific Ocean*, London, 1803–7). It is now generally accepted that La Roche had been driven east by winds and currents and had merely come upon a headland of South Georgia.

[4] This is not to be confused with the Sandwich Islands, or Hawaiian group. The South Sandwich islands lie to the east of South Georgia. It is obvious that, had he sailed into Antarctic waters, La Pérouse would have been considerably delayed and in fact would have been able to add little to the information brought back by James Cook in 1775.

longitude, but anyhow I would have to sail a considerable distance W. to get to the Strait of Le Maire and all the distance I covered in that direction along the parallel of Isle Grande would bring me closer to the Patagon coast where I needed to take soundings before rounding Cape Horn. Furthermore, as I believed that the latitude of Isle Grande was not known with any certainty I would be more likely to come upon it if I tacked between 44 and 45^{d} of latitude than if I sailed in a straight line along 44^{d} 30′ as I could have done sailing from W. to E., since the W. winds are almost as constant in these latitudes as the E. winds are in the tropics.

It will soon become apparent that I gained nothing from my plans and that after 40 days of fruitless searching, during which I encountered 5 squalls, I was forced to set sail for my next destination.

On 7 December I was on 44^{d} 38′, claimed to be the latitude of Isle Grande, and in 34^{d} of longitude, Paris meridian, according to readings taken the previous day. We saw a great deal of seaweed and for several days we had been surrounded by birds, but of the albatross and petrel types who never go near land, except at the breeding season.[1]

Nevertheless these weak indications of land kept up our hopes and consoled us for the frightful seas through which we were travelling, but I was concerned by the thought that I still had 35^{d} to cover to reach the Strait of Le Maire where I was anxious to arrive before the end of January.

I tacked between 44 and 45^{d} of latitude until 24 December. I covered 15^{d} of longitude along this parallel, and on 27 December I gave up my search quite convinced that the island of La Roche does not exist, and that the kelp and petrels do not provide evidence of nearby land since I saw weeds and birds until I reached the Patagon coast. The map, on which my route is indicated, will show better than these comments the route I followed. I am convinced that navigators who will come after me will be no luckier than we were, but one should undertake this search only when one is steering E. to go to the Indian Sea; it then involves no greater hardship and takes no longer to cover 30^{d} along this parallel than on any other, and if one has not found any land at least one has come nearer one's

[1] Petrels are common in these waters. The albatrosses could be the royal albatross (*Diomedea epophora*) or the great albatross (*Diomedea exulans*).

destination. I am quite certain that the Isle Grande is like Pepys Island[1] an imaginary land that has never existed. La Roche's account which claims that he saw great trees lacks any plausibility: it is quite certain that one can find nothing more than shrubs in 45[d] on an island situated in the middle of the southern ocean since one does not find a single large tree on the island of *Tristan d'Acugna*[2] which is situated in a latitude far more suitable for vegetation and in every respect in circumstances similar to those of the so-called island of La Roche.[3]

On 25 December the winds veered S.W. and remained thus for several days. They forced me to sail W.N.O. and to leave the parallel I had been following for 20 days. As I had by then passed the position assigned to the island of La Roche on all the charts and the season was very advanced I decided to follow only the route which would get me W., as I was very anxious not to have to round Cape Horn in the bad season, but the weather was more favorable than I dared hope; the gusts came to an end with the month of December and January was almost as fine as July on the coasts of Europe: the winds ranged only from N.W. to S.W. but we could unfurl all our sails and wind changes were so clearly indicated by the state of the sky that we had no doubt about when they would change and could alter course to get the best advantage – as soon as the horizon became hazy and the sky cloudy the S.W.

[1] Pepys Island was reputed to have been discovered by Ambrose Cowley in January 1684 in 47°40′S and fairly close to the mainland. It was so named by William Hacke, who reported this discovery in his *A Collection of Original Voyages*, London, 1699, in honour of Samuel Pepys, former Secretary of the Admiralty. It is probably part of the northern Falklands group.

[2] Tristan da Cunha, discovered by a Portuguese in 1506, remained uninhabited until the beginning of the nineteenth century when it was annexed by Britain. Its earlier reputation as a bleak, treeless rocky island was however undeserved: it can support a population of a few hundred farmers and fishermen.

[3] At the bottom of the page, La Pérouse added the following afterthought: 'I know that South Georgia referred to in that navigator's journal has been rediscovered, but I greatly doubt that he is entitled to the honour of being regarded as its first discoverer; according to his journal there is a channel 10 leagues wide between Bird Island and Georgia, whereas this channel is really only one league wide, an error that is rather too gross for any seaman of the slightest experience if he is talking of the same spot; it is however on the basis of such a strained argumentation that Isle Grande has been located between 35 and 50° of longitude, Paris meridian.' South Georgia was 'rediscovered' by James Cook who took possession of it in January 1775. It had probably been sighted once before, by the Spanish merchant ship *Léon* in 1756. See on this island, Robert Headland, *The Island of South Georgia*, Cambridge, 1984.

winds veered W. Two hours later they came from the N.W. Conversely as soon as the weather cleared we knew the winds would soon come back to S.W. by W. I do not think that in 66 days of navigation the winds came from N. or S. by E. for longer than 18 hours.

We had a few days of calm with the sea smooth, during which the officers of the two frigates went hunting in the boats and shot a considerable number of the birds which surrounded us almost constantly. These expeditions, usually fruitful, provided fresh food for our crews, and on several occasions we shot a fairly large quantity of these birds in order to give out a share to everyone. The sailors preferred them to salt meat and I believe they played an important part in preserving their health.

We only killed during these operations some large and small albatrosses and 4 types of petrels. These birds, skinned and served with a piquant sauce, were almost as good as the scoter ducks eaten in Europe during Lent. They were so accurately described by the naturalists who accompanied Captain Cook[1] that I think it sufficient to provide drawings of them so that ornithologists can be sure that we met the same species as Messrs Banks, Solander and Forster[2] who described them so well.

On 14 January we at last came within sounding depth of the Patagon coast, in 47° 50′ of latitude and 64° 37′ of longitude according to our latest readings. We never missed an opportunity of taking readings when the weather was favorable, and the officers of the frigate were so experienced and were of such assistance to Mr D'agelet that I do not think our longitude could be out by more than half a degree.

[1] The scoter is more often referred to as tough and uneatable. However, the European scoter, *Oidemia nigra* and *Oidemia fusca*, was eaten along the northern Atlantic coast and was recognised by church authorities as a fish for the purpose of Lenten and Friday abstinence from meat.

[2] Sir Joseph Banks and Daniel Solander sailed as naturalists on Cook's first voyage. Banks notably described birds encountered during the circumnavigation in his journal eventually published in 1962. Johann Reinhold Forster and his son George sailed in the *Resolution* on the second voyage; the former published his *Observations made during a Voyage round the World* in 1778, but his son had written his own narrative in 1777. It is interesting, in view of La Pérouse's wording, to note that the first account published in French of Cook's first voyage was entitled *Supplément au Voyage de Bougainville, ou Journal d'un voyage autour du monde, fait par MM Banks et Solander*, Paris, 1772; it was based on the account reputedly written by James Magra. It is known that La Pérouse had a French edition of Hawkesworth's account of Cook's first voyage on board, but which other editions of the voyages he had cannot be determined with certainty.

On the 21st we sighted Cape Fair Weather, or the northern headland of the Gallegos River on the Patagon coast;[1] we were about 3 leagues from land in 41 fathoms, bottom small gravel or small clayish pebbles the size of peas. Our longitude, observed at midday, checked against the chart of Captain Cook's second voyage, showed only a difference E. of 15′. We sailed along the Patagon coast at a distance of 3 to 5 leagues.

On the 22nd we sighted at midday the Cape of Virgins bearing 4 Ls to the W. It is a low land with no greenery. The sketch supplied by the editor of Admiral Anson's Voyage seemed to be quite accurate, and it is correctly located on the map of Cook's second voyage.[2]

All our soundings from the Cape of Virgins gave us mud or pebbles mixed with mud, which one usually finds near river-mouths; but on Tierra del Fuego we almost always got a rocky bottom and only 24 to 30 fathoms although we were 3 leagues from land, which led me to believe that this coast is not as safe as that of the Patagons.

Captain Cook's chart gives with the utmost precision the latitude and longitude of the various capes of this land.

The coastline between these capes has been drawn from good bearings, but full attention could not be given to details, which are so important for safe navigation. Captain Cook and all the other navigators can answer only for the routes they followed and the soundings they took, and it is possible that, when the sea was calm, they passed near banks or reefs where the waves were not breaking, and so this navigation requires much more care than in our European countries.

I have gone into these details to stress the degree of trust which one can have in those types of charts, the best there are no doubt, made while sailing through vast spaces, and it was impossible for ancient navigators before the discovery of methods of observing distances to attain such precision; it is now such that I can put as much faith, within 20′, in the accuracy of the points we verified as I can in the accuracy of longitudes calculated in London or Paris.

[1] Rio Gallegos, some 60 miles north of the Strait of Magellan.

[2] Cabo Virgenes is the northern headland at the entrance of the Strait of Magellan which at this point presents a wide opening and two large bays, Posesión and Lomas. Anson in 1740 described it as a flat headland situated in latitude 52°21′S and longitude 71°44′W; the latitude is reasonably correct, but the longitude is 3° out. See *A Voyage round the World*... ed. G. Williams, Oxford, 1974, p. 80.

On the 25th at 2 o'clock I sighted Cape San Diego bearing S. 1 L. It forms the western point of the strait of Le Maire. I had coasted along the shore at that distance since the morning and I had followed on Captain Cook's chart the bay where Mr Banks landed to look for plants while the *Resolution* waited for him under sail.[1]

The weather was so favourable that I could not display the same courtesy towards our naturalists. At 3 o'clock I entered the strait, having turned Cape San Diego at ¾ of a league, where there are breakers which extend, I believe, for only a mile, but having seen the sea breaking much further out I steered S.E. to avoid them; I soon realised that this was caused by the currents and that the San Diego reefs were quite some distance away.

As there was a good N. breeze, I was able to approach Tierra del Fuego; I coasted along it half a mile off shore and found the weather so favourable, and the season being so advanced, that I decided to give up the call at Good Success Bay and proceed without delay to round Cape Horn. I felt that I could not take on needed supplies in less than 10 or 12 days, this being the time I took at Santa Catarina because in these wide bays where the seas break heavily on the shore the boats cannot operate for half the time; and if in addition S. winds were to prevent me from leaving Good Success Bay once I was ready the good season would have passed and I would have risked damage and weariness for our crews which would have been very prejudicial to my voyage.[2]

These factors led me to decide to make for the island of Juan Fernandez[3] which is on my way and where I would find water and wood, with much better supplies than the penguins of the Strait. I did not have a single sick at the time; I still had 80 barrels of water and Tierra del Fuego has been so often visited and described that I could not flatter myself that I would find anything new to say about it.

[1] La Pérouse is mistaken here: Banks sailed in the *Endeavour*.

[2] The Bay of Good Success, about half-way through the strait on the Tierra del Fuego side, is a commodious bay with a good anchorage, where James Cook spent five days from 15 January 1769. It proved unfortunate, however, for Sir Joseph Banks and his small party who went botanising ashore and were overtaken by a freezing wind and snow. Two black servants lost their lives. Cook, *Journals*, I, 80.

[3] Juan Fernandez, roughly in the latitude of Valparaiso and some 500 miles from South America, consists of two main islands, Mas-a-tierra and Mas-a-fuera. They were a frequent place of call for ships sailing into the Pacific or along the American coast.

During our passage of the Strait of Lemaire the natives, as is their custom, lit great fires along the shore in order to get us to anchor: there was one on the northern point of Valentin Bay. Like Captain Cook I was convinced that one can drop anchor in any of these bays, where I can find wood and water but less game no doubt than in Port Christmas[1] on account of the natives who spend a good part of the year there.

Throughout our navigation through the Strait at a half league from the shore we were surrounded by whales; it is evident that they are never disturbed – our ships did not frighten them, they were swimming majestically half a pistol shot from the frigates; they will be the sovereigns of these seas until such time as whalers come to make the same war against them as in Spitzbergen or Greenland. I doubt that there is a better place for this type of fishing anywhere in the world. Ships would anchor in safe bays, with at hand water, wood, some antiscorbutic plants and seabirds; without going a league, their boats could take all the whales they want to fill their hold. The only inconvenience is the length of the voyage which requires about five months of navigation for each crossing, and I believe one can stay in these waters only in December, January and February.

We were not able to make any observations on the currents in this strait; we entered it at 3 p.m., the moon being in its 24th day, and they bore us rapidly to the S. until 5 o'clock when the tide turned, but as there was a fresh gale blowing from the N. we easily sailed against it.

The horizon was so hazy in the E. that we had no glimpse of Staten Island which however was less than five leagues away, this being the total width of the strait. We sailed along Tierra del Fuego close enough to see the natives with our spyglasses; they were tending huge fires, this being their only way of expressing their wish to see ships putting in.

We had prepared the various gifts we intended giving them, which perhaps will be handed out five or six miles from these parts.

Another, more powerful motive had led me to give up a stay in Good Success Bay. I had been formulating a new plan for quite

[1] Valentin Bay is situated east of Good Success. It was the number of fires lit along the shore and inland which led Magellan to give Tierra del Fuego its distinctive name. Port Christmas is Christmas Sound, so named by James Cook on Christmas Day 1774.

some time, on which I could not reach a decision until we had rounded Cape Horn.

This plan was to go this year to the N.W. coast of America. I knew that if I had not been instructed to do so, it was because it was feared that I might not have time to carry out such a lengthy navigation before winter, as such a project offered a great many advantages, the first being to follow a new track and cross parallels along which it was possible to come upon undiscovered islands; the second was to visit more expeditiously all the places I had been instructed to, by spending two years in the northern hemisphere and two years in the southern hemisphere, returning to France after four years of navigation with at least three spent under sail. Since my instructions clearly stated that I was authorised to carry out the King's orders in the manner which I considered best for the success of my campaign, I was waiting, before definitely adopting this new plan, to know only the date when I would at last have entered the South Sea.

I rounded Cape Horn with much greater ease than I would ever have dreamt; I am now convinced that this navigation is no different from what it is in high latitudes, and that its difficulty is based on an old prejudice which the Voyage of Admiral Anson has played a large part in preserving among seamen, but which ought to disappear.[1]

On 9 February I was athwart the Strait of Magellan, in the South Sea, sailing for the island of Juan Fernandez. According to my reckoning I had sailed over the so-called Land of Drake, but I wasted little time searching for it because I had no doubt that it did not exist. Ever since my departure from Europe I had thought of little else but the routes of the old navigators; their journals are so badly written that one needs, so to speak, to guess what they were, and geographers who are not sailors are generally so ignorant that they have been unable to cast the light of reasonable criticism on journals that were in great need of it; they consequently drew islands that did not exist which, like phantoms, have vanished before the new navigators.

[1] Anson's opinion of Cape Horn was based on his truly awful experiences in this area. Wild gales, torrential rain, snow flurries and rough seas were his lot, and his expedition suffered not only material damage but deaths and injuries among his men as well. Admittedly, he was sailing in March-April when the westerlies are particularly fierce, whereas La Pérouse was sailing in January, in the southern summer.

Admiral Drake, emerging from the Strait of Magellan in 1578,[1] was assailed after sailing for five days in the great western ocean by violent gales which lasted almost a month. It is difficult to follow his various routes, but finally he had sight of an island in 57^d of latitude S. He put in and saw a great many birds. Sailing then N. for 20 leagues he found more islands, inhabited by natives who had canoes; trees and antiscorbutic plants grew on these islands: how could one fail to identify from this account Tierra del Fuego itself where Drake landed and in all likelihood the island of Diego Ramirez situated more or less in the latitude of the so-called island of Drake? Tierra del Fuego was not known at the time. It was only in 1616 that Le Maire and Schouten found the strait which bears their name and always persuaded that there was, in the S. hemisphere as in the N. hemisphere, land extending to the neighbourhood of the pole, they thought that the S. part of America was intersected by channels and that like Magellan they had found a second strait. These erroneous notions were likely to mislead Admiral Drake who was borne 12 to 15^d East of his reckoning, as has happened in the same waters to a hundred other sailors; and this possibility becomes a certainty when one thinks that a ship from his squadron which veered N. while his leader was sailing S. entered this very Strait of Magellan from which he had just come out, clear proof that he had made very little progress W. and that Admiral Drake had not left the longitude of America. One may add that it is inconceivable that an island at a considerable distance from the mainland and in 57^d of latitude could be covered in trees while the Malouine Islands[2] which are in 53^d have no ligneous plants, that

[1] Francis Drake's expedition took place in 1577–80. Carried south by a storm after leaving the strait, he came upon inhabited islands which he named after Queen Elizabeth. The Elizabethides appeared henceforth on a number of charts, as well as a Drake Land situated south of the strait and extending towards the far south. Drake himself did not believe that South America extended into a land mass towards the pole, and claimed he had reached the southernmost extremity of the world; this argument was resolved when Schouten and Le Maire rounded a southerly cape which they named after the town of Hoorn in Holland, but a Drake's Land survived on many charts, usually stretching into the southern Pacific.

[2] The French did not refer to the Falkland Islands by their English name, but as the Iles Malouines, or islands of St Malo from the many French navigators and merchants from that port who had contributed to its discovery or used it as a landfall. French interest in establishing a colony on the deserted islands dates from the early eighteenth century and culminated in the settlement established by Louis de Bougainville in 1764. The Spanish form of the name, Malvinas, is currently used in Argentina.

there is not a single inhabitant on these islands, not even on Staten Island which is only separated by a channel of 5 leagues from the mainland, and finally the description Drake gives of the natives and their canoes, the trees and plants, is so applicable to the Pecherets[1] and generally to all we know of Tierra del Fuego that I wonder how Drake's island can still subsist on today's charts.

The W.S.W. winds were so favourable to go N. that I wasted no time on this pointless search and continued on my way towards the island of Juan Fernandez, but having examined the food supplies I had on board I saw that we had very little bread and flour left as I as well as Mr de L'angle had been forced to leave 100 quarters at Brest owing to lack of space; in addition worms had attacked the biscuits: they did not render them uneatable, but they had reduced the quantity by about a fifth. These various factors made me decide to choose Concepción instead of Juan Fernandez. I knew that this part of Chile was rich in grain, which is cheaper there than anywhere in Europe, and that I would find quantities of other foodstuffs at a most reasonable price. I therefore altered my route a little more to the E.

On the evening of the 22nd I sighted the island of Mocha which is about 50 leagues to the S. of Concepción. Fear of being carried N. by the currents had made me veer towards land, but I believe this is unnecessary, and that it is enough to place oneself on the latitude of the island of Santa Maria[2] which one should keep in sight at a distance of approximately 3 leagues because there are rocks below the surface that extend well out to sea off the N.E. point of this island.

[1] Pécherets, sometimes thought to be a derivation from the French word for fishermen, comes from Bougainville's account; he gave them this name because this was a word often used by the Fuegans who came alongside his ship. See L.A. de Bougainville, *Voyage autour du monde par la frégate du Roi*, La Boudeuse, Paris, 1771, I, p. 276. However, it is unlikely the natives were referring to themselves or their territory: it is more probable that it was a term indicative of peaceful intentions or, according to Robert Fitzroy, *The Narrative of the Surveying Voyages of H.M. Ships* Adventure *and* Beagle, London, 1839, II, p. 358, a request for gifts.

[2] Isla Mocha was Francis Drake's first place of call after his misfortunes in the Strait of Magellan. He was made welcome by the inhabitants who were mostly escaped prisoners or refugees from the mainland, but when some of his own men tried to land on Chilean soil they were routed and Drake sailed away. The Isla Santa Maria, further north, lies at the entrance of the Golfo de Arauco. The Biobio River rises in the Andes and has its mouth in the gulf. Talcahuano has acquired some importance today; it was a struggling fishing village in La Pérouse's day.

After rounding the island, one can range along the coast. All the dangers are then above water and close to the shore. At the same time one comes into sight of the mamelons of Biobio, two hillocks whose name explains their shape; one steers a little N. of them towards the headland of Talcahuano which forms the entrance to the Bay of Concepción which extends 3 leagues E. to W., similarly N. to S., but this entrance is reduced by the island of Quiriquine, situated in the middle, creating two entrances: the eastern one is the safest and the only one in use; it is about one league wide; the western one between Quiriquine and Talcahuano Point is barely a quarter of a league wide; it is infested with rocks and should be navigated only with a good pilot.

One finds bottom along the coast from Santa Maria Island to the entrance of the bay of Concepción. At 3 leagues from shore the sound gave 70 fathoms, black ooze, and once we were inside the bay 30 fathoms E. and W. of the northern point of the island of Quiriquine; the depth gradually decreases until two musquet shots from shore when it reaches 7 fathoms. There is excellent anchorage in this bay, but one is sheltered from the N. winds only in front of the village of Talcahuano.

We turned the point of Quiriquine Island at two p.m., but the S. winds which had been so favorable to us until then became contrary. We tacked variously while taking good care to continue sounding: with our glasses we sought the town of Concepción which, from Fraisier's plan,[1] we knew should have been at the back of the bay in the S.E. but we could see nothing.

At five p.m. pilots came alongside who told us that this town had been destroyed by an earthquake in 1751 and existed no longer, a new town having been built 3 leagues from the sea on the banks of the Biobio River.[2] We also learnt from these pilots that we were expected at Concepción and that the letters of the Spanish Ambassador had preceded us. We continued tacking to reach the back of

[1] The reference is to Amédée François Frézier, author of the *Relation du Voyage...aux Côtes du Chily et du Pérou*, Paris, 1716. It was published in England in 1717 under the title *A Voyage to the South Sea and along the coast of Chili and Peru in the years 1712, 1713 and 1714* with a preface by Edmund Halley.

[2] The old town of Concepción, founded on the present site of the town of Penco in 1550, suffered a bad earthquake in 1730; it was rebuilt but was destroyed by another earthquake followed by a tidal wave in 1751; the governor, Don Ortiz de Rozas, then decided to rebuild it on its present site. This was done in 1754, and it is interesting that, thirty years later, the French were unaware of its correct location.

the bay and dropped anchor at 9 p.m. in nine fathoms approximately a league to the N.E. of the Talcahuano anchorage where we were to go in the morning. Towards ten o'clock that evening Mr de Postigo, a frigate captain in the Spanish navy, came aboard, having been sent by the commander of Concepción; he slept on board and left at daybreak to report back, having indicated to the pilot the anchorage we should select, and before riding back he sent us fresh meat, fruits and vegetables in greater quantities than we needed for our crews whose good health seemed to surprise him. Possibly no vessel had ever before rounded Cape Horn and reached Chile without having any sick, but there was not one on either of our ships.

At 7 a.m. we weighed anchor and, towed by our boats, we anchored at eleven o'clock on 24 February in Talcahuano cove in 7 fathoms, black ooze. The middle of the village of Talcahuano bearing S. 21^{d}, Fort St Augustine S., Fort Galves near our watercourse N.W. 3^{d} W.

We had been taking readings since our arrival on the coast of Chile. Our longitudes differed very little from those of Don Georges Juan[1] made on this same coast, but as we consider modern methods to be far superior to those in use in 1744 we will situate the N. point of Santa Maria island in latitude 37^{d} 1′ and longitude 75^{d} 55′ 45″ west of Paris, the middle of Talcahuano village in latitude 36^{d} 42′ 21″ and long^{e} 75^{d} 20′, in accordance with the observations made by Mr Dagelet in our tent observatory set up on the shore; the appended plan was drawn by Don Georges Juan, it is so accurate that we only had to verify it, but Mr Bernizet, engineer geographer, has added part of the course of the Biobio River in order to show where the new town has been built and the track that leads to it.

[1] Jorge Juan y Santacilla (1713–73) was sent to America with Antonio de Ulloa and a group of French scientists in 1734. He spent eleven years in South America, then collaborated with Ulloa in the compilation of the *Relación histórica del viaje a la America meridional*, 5 vols, Madrid, 1748, and of reports which were eventually published in London in 1826 as *Noticias secretas de America*. He also wrote a number of nautical and scientific works.

CHAPTER III

Description of Concepción. Manners and customs of the inhabitants. Departure from Talcahuano. Arrival at Easter Island.

The Bay of Concepción is one of the most convenient one could find anywhere in the world. The sea is calm, there are practically no currents, although the tide rises 6 feet 3 inches. It is high at 1.45 on days when the moon is new or full. This bay is only open to N. winds which blow solely in the winter season of this region, that is from the end of May until October; this is the rainy season, the rains falling throughout this monsoon season – for one can use such a term for these winds which are constant and followed by S. winds that last for the rest of the year and bring the finest of weather. The only anchorage where one is sheltered from these northerly winds in winter is in front of Talcahuano on the S.W. coast. This anyhow is today the sole Spanish settlement in the bay, the old town of Concepción having been destroyed by an earthquake in 1751; it was built at the mouth of the San Pedro River to the E. of Talcahuano. Its ruins are still visible but they will not last as long as those of Palmyra, as buildings in this country are made of mud or bricks cooked in the sun; roofs are in cannelated bricks like those of several southern provinces of France.[1]

After the destruction of this town, which was swallowed up by the sea rather than toppled by the earth's tremors, the residents dispersed and camped on the neighbouring heights; it was only in 1763 that they chose a new location a quarter of a league from the Biobio River and 3 leagues from the old town of Concepción and the village of Talcahuano. They built a new town: the bishop's seat,

[1] The Mediterranean or Spanish tile was in common use in southern France, dating back to Roman days. The adobe brick was introduced to Chile from Mexico, but the heavy and prolonged rains of the southern region made it an unsuitable building material. Early French travellers have commented on the poor condition of many buildings in Chile.

the cathedral, the religious houses were transferred to it; it covers a wide area because the houses have only one storey in order to better resist earthquakes which occur almost every year. This new town has about ten thousand inhabitants; it is the residence of the bishop and of the military governor of this diocese which, to the north, joins that of Sant Iago, capital of Chile, where the Governor General resides; it is bounded on the east by the Cordillera and stretches to the south as far as the Strait of Magellan, but its real frontier is the Biobio River a quarter of a league away;[1] all the country south of the said river belongs to the Indians, with the exception of the island of Chiloé and of a small district around *Baldivia*. One cannot call these people subjects of the King of Spain with whom they are always at war. Consequently the functions of the military governor are of the greatest importance: this officer is in command of the regular forces and of the militia, which gives him considerable authority over all the citizens who, in civil matters, are ruled by a corregidor; he is in addition in sole charge of the defence of the country, compelled to fight or to negotiate unceasingly. A new administrative system is about to replace the old. It will not be very different from the structure of our colonies; authority will be divided between the military and the civil commander, but it should be noted that there is no appeal body in the Spanish colonies: those whom the King endows with his authority are also the civil judges, helped by a few legal assessors. One feels that since justice is not meted out by judges of equal status, the leader's opinion will always be supported by those of inferior rank, and so justice is in the hands of one person whom one must assume to have no prejudices and to be both dispassionate and blessed with great wisdom if such a system is to have no drawbacks.[2]

No place in the world is more fertile than this part of Chile.

[1] The date given by La Pérouse is incorrect: Concepción was rebuilt from 1754. It has suffered badly from earthquakes since, the next serious disaster struck it in 1835, just as Charles Darwin on the *Beagle* expedition was reaching it. The carnage and destruction made a strong impression on him; see Burkhardt and Smith, *The Correspondence of Charles Darwin 1821–1882*, Cambridge, 1985–91, I, p. 419; R. Keynes, *Charles Darwin's* Beagle *Diary*, Cambridge, 1988, pp. 286–93.

[2] There were several tribunals in Chile at the time – for commerce, mining and religious affairs – but only the *audiencia*, the court dealing with criminal and civil cases, had real significance and power. In addition to its presiding judge, there were four assistant judges, the *oidores*, and two counsels, the *fiscales*.

Wheat yields 60 for one, the vine produces equally abundantly, the countryside is covered with immense herds which multiply, without any attention, beyond anything one can say – the only labour required is to erect fences around each one's property and leave in these enclosures cattle, horses, mules and sheep. Commonly a large ox costs eight piastres, a sheep three quarters of a piastre[1] but there are no buyers and the inhabitants' practice is to kill a large number of bullocks, the leather and tallow being kept. These two items are sent to Lima. They also smoke-dry some of the meat for the crews of the small coastal vessels of the South Sea.

No disease is peculiar to this country, but there is one which is carefully preserved and which I dare not name; those fortunate enough to avoid it live to a fairly advanced age:[2] there are several centenarians in Concepción.

In spite of so many advantages, this colony is far from having made the progress one would expect from its situation which is so favorable for increasing its population, but the government's influence ceaselessly counterbalances the benefits of the climate. The restrictive policy is in force throughout Chile. This realm whose products, if they reached their maximum, could supply half Europe, whose wool would be enough for all the manufacturers of France and England, whose meat if salted would produce an enormous income, this country has no trade: four or five small vessels bring annually from Lima sugar and tobacco, with a few items of European manufacture which the wretched inhabitants can obtain only at second or third hand after they have been subjected to enormous customs charges in Cadiz and Lima and finally when they enter Chile; in exchange they can only offer wheat (the price of which is so low that the farmer sees no reason to clear any more land), tallow, leather, and a few planks of timber, so that the balance of trade is always against Chile which cannot, with its gold and these few exports pay for the sugar, the Paraguayan tea,[3] the

[1] La Pérouse commonly uses the term 'piastre', whereas the currency of Chile was the peso and the invoices he received for his purchases were made out in pesos.

[2] Behind this convoluted paragraph hides no doubt a reference to venereal diseases. However, a more widespread and deadly disease at the time was smallpox.

[3] The *yerba maté* (*Ilex paraguayensis*) is a tea with tonic properties greatly prized in South America. Maté was exported to Chile by the Cape Horn route and through Buenos Aires across the Andes by the Mendoza trail.

tobacco, material, linen, cambric and the various smallwares required for daily life.[1]

From the very summary description which I have given, it is evident that if the Court of Spain does not change its system, if free trade is not allowed, if the various duties levied on imported goods are not eased, and if one fails to realise that a very small duty on a very large consumption is more profitable for the Treasury than a heavy tax which destroys this very consumption, the kingdom of Chile will never reach the degree of growth which it should expect from its geographical situation.[2]

Unfortunately, this country produces a little gold. Nearly all the rivers are gold-bearing; by washing the soil the inhabitant can earn, so they say, half a piastre a day. But since food is very abundant, he has no real need which might encourage him to work. Having no contact with outsiders, he knows nothing of our arts or our wealth, and there is nothing he can feel a desire for which would overcome his inertia. The land stays fallow; the most active among them are those who devote a few hours to sluicing the river sand, which saves them having to learn a trade. And so the homes of the richest inhabitants lack furniture, and all the workers of Concepción are foreigners.

The women's dress consists of a pleated skirt made of the old silver or gold material which used to be made in Leon, but these skirts, which are reserved for special occasions, can be transmitted like diamonds in a family and pass from grandmothers to granddaughters. However these adornments are within the reach of quite a small number of citizens and one must remember that most of them have nothing to wear.

[1] Monopolist and exclusive policies, which La Pérouse disliked (see note below), were not entirely at fault. In fact, Madrid had attempted to allow greater freedom by its 1778 decree on trade between Spain and its colonies. Admittedly, change was very slow and a number of powerful traders clung to their own charters and monopolies. Trade was hampered by poor transport, the Araucanian wars, the relatively small population of Chile, but also by a number of taxes such as the ecclesiastical tithe, the *almojarifazgo*, a 5% tax on all imports, and the *alcabala*, or local toll of between 2 and 6% on all goods and products.

[2] France was the scene of a prolonged economic debate during much of La Pérouse's lifetime. He was a supporter of the physiocrats and an admirer of the economist and financier Jacques Necker; all these saw in agriculture and various levels of free trade the solution to the problems of France and other European countries whose commerce was being stifled by rigid and outdated systems of taxation and trade controls.

Idleness, more than credulity or superstition, has filled this kingdom with convents for girls and monasteries for men. The latter enjoy a far greater freedom than in any other country, and the misfortune of having nothing to do, of belonging to no family, of being bachelors without being set apart from the world, and living in retirement in their cells. These various circumstances have turned them, as can be expected, into the worst characters in America. Their impudence cannot be described. I have seen some staying at a ball until midnight, admittedly set apart from good society and placed among the menservants. No one was better than these friars at providing information to our young officers in respect of places they should have known about only to preach against them.

The common people of Concepción are great thieves, and women of that same class very complaisant; it is a degenerate race with an admixture of Indians; but the upper class, the true Spanish, are extremely polite and helpful. I would be failing in my duty if I did not describe them in accordance with their character which I will endeavour to make known by narrating our own story.

I had hardly dropped anchor in front of the village of Talcahuano when a dragoon brought me a letter from Mr Quexada, the temporary commander, telling me that we would be received like their own compatriots, adding with the utmost courtesy that his sovereign's instructions were on this occasion wholly in accordance with his own feelings and those of the people of Concepción. This letter was followed up with all kinds of refreshments which everyone had hastened to give; we could not consume so much and scarcely knew where to store them.

Compelled to give my first attention to repairing the ship and sending our timekeepers ashore with our quadrants, I could not go at once to express our gratitude to the commander. I was eagerly waiting for the chance of fulfilling this duty when he anticipated me, and came on board with the chief officers of the colony. I returned this visit the next day, accompanied by Mr de Langle and several officers and passengers. We were preceded by a detachment of dragoons of which the commander had sent half a company to camp at Talcahuano – it had been placed under our command, together with their horses. Mr Quexada and Mr Sabatero, a major in the artillery and the local commander, came to meet us a league down from Concepción. We all went to Mr Sabatero's where we were served an excellent dinner, and at night a great ball was held to which all the leading ladies of the town were invited.

The dress worn by these ladies has been painted by M. Duché de Vancy. It is very different from what our eyes were used to: a pleated skirt which reveals half the leg and is affixed well below the belt, stockings with red, blue and white stripes, shoes so stubby that the toes are folded over giving the impression of an almost rounded foot – that is the dress of Chile.[1] Their hair is unpowdered; behind, it is divided into small plaits falling down to their shoulders. Their bodice is usually made of some silver or gold cloth, covered with two mantillas, one of muslin, the other (which is worn over it) of wool of different colours, yellow, blue or pink. These woollen mantillas are worn over the ladies' heads when they are in the street and it is cold, but in their apartments they normally wear it over their knees, and there is a kind of muslin mantilla game in which it is continually adjusted, at which the ladies of Concepción display much grace. In general they are handsome women and so courteous and friendly that there certainly is no port in Europe where foreign navigators could be welcomed with such affectionate and charming manners.

The ball came to an end at around midnight. As the homes of the commander and of Mr Sabatero did not have room for all the French officers and passengers, the residents eagerly offered us beds, and we were thus dispersed in the various districts of the town.

Before dinner we had paid visits to the leading citizens and to the Bishop, a man of intellect and an excellent conversationalist; and one whose charity is of a type often found among Spanish bishops. He is a Peruvian creole.[2] He has never been to Europe and owes his advancement only to his virtues. He told us of the regret Mr Higuins,[3] the commander in chief, would feel at being held back by

[1] The short skirt was known as the *faldellin* below which peeped out the underskirt, the *justán*, which was decorated with lace. The Bishop of Santiago, Manuel de Alday y Axpe, was reputed for his fulminations against such immodest dress.

[2] Creole, from the Spanish *criollo*, meant a person born in the colonial territory. It did not imply in French usage that the person concerned was of mixed European and Indian or African blood.

[3] Ambrosio O'Higgins was born at Ballinary, Co. Sligo, probably in 1720. Sent to Spain to be educated by one of his uncles who was a Catholic, he turned to trade rather than religion and sailed to Peru as the representative of a firm of Cadiz merchants. He established useful connections with the colonial administration, and

his campaign against the Indians on the frontier during our brief stay in his territory; the good everyone spoke about this soldier, the general esteem in which he was held, made me regret that circumstances were keeping him away. A message had been sent to him; his reply came while we were still in town: it announced his impending return – he had just concluded a glorious peace which was certainly very necessary for his people whose distant homes were exposed to the ravages of these savages who massacre men and children and carry women off into captivity.

The Indians of Chile are no longer those Americans of old in whom European weapons struck terror. The multiplication of horses which have spread into the immense wastes of America, that of the cattle and sheep which is also very considerable, have transformed these people into real Arabs, comparable in every respect with those who live in the deserts of Arabia. Always on horseback, a journey of two hundred leagues is nothing to them. They travel with their herds and feed on their flesh and milk, and sometimes on their blood;[1] they dress themselves in their skins of which they also make helmets, breast plates and shields. The introduction of these two animals has thus had the most marked influence on the way of life of all the people who live between Santiago and the Strait of Magellan. They follow almost none of their ancient practices, no longer live on the same fruits, no longer wear the same clothes and bear a greater resemblance to the Tartars or the people who live along the shores of the Red Sea than with their ancestors of two centuries ago.[2]

---

after a visit back to Spain settled in Chile. He displayed great military and diplomatic skills in the wars against the Araucanian Indians. He was promoted to brigadier in 1783 and had been appointed commander of the Concepción district shortly before La Pérouse's arrival. He later became Governor of Chile and, in 1796, Viceroy of Peru. He died at Lima in 1801. His son Bernardo (1778–1842) acquired even greater fame as the leader of the independence movement.

[1] Marginal note by La Pérouse: 'I have been assured that they sometimes bleed their cattle and their horses and drink their blood.'

[2] The Araucanian Indians consisted of a number of different tribes with fluctuating alliances. They waged a relentless struggle in defence of their tribal domains, going to war against the Spanish invaders as early as 1561, and not finally submitting until 1818. The Biobio River had been fixed as the frontier between them and the new settlers in 1612, but intermittent warfare continued long after that. The 'glorious peace' signed by O'Higgins during La Pérouse's visit was merely one more of the many truce agreements which gave the Araucanians and the Spanish some respite from the struggle. O'Higgins's immediate need was for a breathing spell in which to reorganise his administration.

It is not hard to understand how fearful these people must seem to the Spanish. How can one follow them on such long journeys? How can one prevent gatherings which bring together people spread over four hundred leagues and can turn into armies of thirty thousand men?

Mr Higuins has succeeded in attracting the goodwill of these natives, and has given the most signal services to the sovereign he has adopted, for he was born in Ireland in one of those families that were persecuted for their faith and their old attachment to the House of Stuart. I cannot fail to pay tribute to that loyal soldier, whose personality is so strong that, like the Indians, I gave him all my trust after an hour's conversation. His return took place soon after his letter arrived: I had hardly learnt of its contents when he arrived at Talcahuano, and once again I was forestalled, for a cavalry commandant is more at ease on horseback than a French navigator, and Mr Higuins who is in charge of the country's defences is as accustomed to it as I am to the sea.[1] His courtesy exceeded that of Mr Quexada, if that is possible; his politeness was so genuine, so friendly towards all the French that words cannot express our gratitude. We decided to offer a general reception before we sailed, as indeed we owed it to all the residents, and to invite all the ladies of Concepción. A vast tent was erected along the sea shore; there we entertained at dinner a hundred and fifty people, both men and women, who had been good enough to undertake the 3-league journey to respond to our invitation. This dinner was followed by a ball, a fireworks display, and finally a paper balloon large enough to provide a spectacle.[2]

The next day, that same tent was used for a great dinner for the crews of both frigates. We ate at the same table, Mr de Langle and I, and every officer down to the least of the sailors in accordance

[1] As he did on the occasion of his stay at Madeira, La Pérouse does not hesitate to admit that he was no horseman. The reference to the Stuart allegiance underlies the links between the old Irish families and both Spain and France following the defeat of James II who had made his last stand in Ireland. Irish Catholic families who had not emigrated after 1689 and the coming of the penal laws nearly all had relatives abroad who assisted them in various ways.

[2] This may not be the first appearance of the aerial balloon in Chile, but it is certainly one of the earliest. The invention of the Montgolfier brothers dates from April 1783, and Parisians were able to witness the first ascension of a balloon in August of that year. At first animals were sent up, but this was soon followed by human passengers. La Pérouse was in Paris during much of this time.

with their rank on board. Our plates were wooden bowls. We drank a barrel of wine to the King's health and to the good success of our expedition. All the sailors displayed mirth and jollity: they were leaving in better health and a thousand times happier than on the day we sailed from Brest.

In turn, the commander-in-chief wanted to offer a reception. We all went to Concepción, with the exception of the duty officers. Like Mr Quexada, Mr Higuins came to meet us a league from town and led our cavalcade to his residence where a table was laid for a hundred guests. All the officers and residents of any standing had been invited, together with several ladies. The healths of the kings of France and Spain were toasted to the accompaniment of gun salutes. Each course was marked by a Franciscan improviser reciting Spanish verses celebrating the unity which reigned between the two branches of the House of Bourbon and their respective subjects. There followed a great ball during the night where all the ladies came dressed in their finest attire. Masked officers danced a very fine ballet. Nowhere in the world could one find a more charming entertainement; it was given by a man who was loved throughout the country and for foreigners who had the reputation of belonging to the nation the most reputed for its gallantry towards the ladies.

But these social pleasures and this great welcome did not make me lose sight of my main purpose. I had announced on my arrival that I would sail on 15 March, and that if before that date our ship was repaired, and our food supplies, water and wood loaded on board, everyone would have the opportunity of going ashore. Nothing was more likely to get the work done more quickly than such a promise of which the outcome caused me as much unease as it pleased the sailors, because wine is easily available in Chile, every house is a tavern and the common women of Chile are almost as free with their favours as those of Tahiti.[1] There was however no unruliness and our surgeon did not advise me that this concession had any untoward consequences.

[1] Although La Pérouse never went to Tahiti, the island's reputation was widely known following the voyages of Wallis, Bougainville and Cook. The voyage of Bougainville in particular helped to publicise the charms of the island women, and some of his companions rose to hyperbolic heights, notably the naturalist Commerson. (See his 'Post-scriptum sur l'isle de la Nouvelle-Cythère ou Tayti' in E. Taillemite, *Bougainville et ses compagnons authour du monde 1766–9*, Paris, 1977, II, pp. 506–10.)

During our stay at Talcahuano Mr D'agelet regularly made comparisons to check the working of his timepieces. We were very satisfied since our departure from France of No. 19 which Mr D'agelet found in Chile had lost only 3″½ on Paris average time which shows a difference of only half a second on its daily movement in Brest and of one second from what had been observed at Tenerife.

The small timekeepers Nos 25 and 29 varied sufficiently for us to lose confidence in them. On the 15th at daybreak, I gave the signal to weigh anchor, but the winds settled at N. They had been regularly S.S.W. to S.W. during our stay in this anchorage; the breeze rose normally at 10 a.m. and dropped at the same time in the evening, dropping earlier if it had begun at an earlier time and vice-versa, lasting until midnight if it had started at midday, so that there was about 12 hours of winds and as long with none: this rule prevailed without fail until the 15th when after a total calm and a burning sun they settled N. A strong gale blew from this quarter, accompanied by heavy rain during the night of the 15th to 16th, but on the 17th at around midday a light S.W. breeze came up with which I sailed. It was quite weak and took us only a couple of leagues out of the bay where we remained in a dead calm but with the sea still very rough from the last effects of the northerly. Throughout the night we were surrounded by whales – they swam so close to our frigates that they threw water on board as they blew. It should be noted that not one has ever been harpooned by a resident of Chile; nature has accumulated so many benefits in that kingdom that it will be several centuries before this branch of industry is developed.

On the 19th the S. winds allowed me to leave the coast. I set a course for the E. of the island of Juan Fernandez which I did not sight because, as its position was determined by Feuillée[1] at Concepción, it is not possible that there should be an error of 10′ in longitude.

On the 23rd I was in latitude 30ᵈ 29′ and longitude 85ᵈ 51′

[1] Louis Feuillet (1660–1732), also found as Feuillée, took religious orders but devoted himself to scientific work and travel, including a voyage to South America in 1707–11. He is the author of *Journal des observations physiques, mathématiques et botaniques faites sur les côtes orientales de l'Amérique méridionale et dans les Indes occidentales*, 3 vols, Paris, 1714–25, as well as a treatise on the medicinal plants of Peru and Chile.

according to our timekeeper No. 19 which since our departure from Concepción had kept such good time with the No. 18 of Mr de L'angle that the results given by these two did not vary by two minutes up to the moment of our arrival at Easter Island. This was not the case in the cold climate of Cape Horn: it would seem that the table of temperatures given to Mr Dagelet by Mr Berthoud in Paris was not exact and that the difference was great enough to cause No. 18 to record an error in longitude of more than one degree from the Strait of Lemaire until our arrival on the Chilean coast.

On the 24th the winds settled in the easterly quarter. They did not vary by 5^{d} until we were about a hundred and twenty leagues from Easter Island.

On 3 April in latitude 27^{d} 5′ and longitude 107 we had winds blowing from the N.E. to the N.W. We also saw some birds, the only ones we encountered, since we passed the island of Juan Fernandez because I do not take into account one or two brown gulls[1] which had been briefly sighted during our six hundred league crossing. These winds are the surest indication of land, but physicists may have some difficulty in explaining how the effect of a small island in the middle of an immense sea can extend as far as 100 leagues; furthermore it is not enough for a navigator to presume that he is that distance from an island if nothing tells him at which point of the compass he can find it. The direction of the birds' flight after sunset has never told me anything, and I am quite convinced that what determines their movements in the air is the attraction of some prey: I have seen at nightfall sea birds flying towards ten different compass points, and I believe that even the most enthusiastic augurs would not have dared to draw any conclusion from this.

On 4 April I was only 60 leagues from Easter Island. There were no birds to be seen, and the winds were N.N.W. In all likelihood, had I not known the precise position of the island, I would have altered course in the belief that I had sailed beyond it. These reflections are made on the spot, and I am forced to admit that islands are discovered only by chance and that very often plans which seemed very wise have led navigators away from them.

[1] The term La Pérouse used is the now obsolete *taille-vent* or *goéland brun*, the lesser black-backed gull.

On 8 April at 2 p.m. I saw Easter Island[1] bearing from me W. 5^{d} S. distant 12 leagues. The sea was very rough, the winds N. They had not been steady for four days, shifting from N. to S. by W. I do not believe that the proximity of a small island was the cause of these changes, and it is likely that the trade winds are not constant at this time of year in 27$^{d.}$ The headland in view was the E. point. I was on the exact spot where Captain Davis had come upon an sandy island and twelve leagues further on a land lying W. which Captain Cook and Mr Dalrimple believed was Easter Island rediscovered in 1722 by Roggewin, but these two sailors, although very well informed, did not sufficiently analyse what Waffer reported: he says (page 300 of the Rouen edition) that Captain Davis, leaving from the Galapagos with the intention of returning to Europe by way of Cape Horn and of putting in only at Juan Fernandez, felt a terrible blow in 12^{d} of southern latitude and thought he had struck a rock; he had constantly kept to a southerly route and believed himself to be 120 leagues from the American continent; he later learnt that there had been an earthquake in Lima at the same moment. Having overcome his fear, he kept on S. to S.¼S.E. and S.E. until he reached 27^{d} 20′ and reports that at 2 a.m. a sound like a sea breaking on the shore was heard from ahead of the vessel; he hove to until morning and saw a small sandy island with no rocks around it; he came up to within a quarter mile of it and saw further off, 12 leagues to the W., a large land which was taken for a group of islands on account of breaks along it. Davis did not survey it and continued on his way to Juan Fernandez, but Waffer states that this small sandy island is 500 Ls from Copiago and 600 from the Galapagos. It has not been sufficiently pointed out that this result is impossible: if Davis, being in 12^{d} of southern latitude and 150 Ls from the American coast, sailed S.S.E. as Waffer states, and obviously this buccaneer sailed with the E. winds which are very frequent in those waters, and taking into account his intention to going to Juan Fernandez island, there can be no doubt, as the Abbé

[1] Discovered on Easter Sunday 1722 by Jacob Roggeveen, the island is situated in 27°07′S and 109°22′E. Its Polynesian name is Rapa-nui or Great Rapa, but the name is of fairly recent origin; Te Pito-te-henua is another local name, meaning the world's navel, or the world's end, again a name of doubtful antiquity. The island is a Chilean possession, its Spanish name being Isla de Pascua. The point first seen by La Pérouse was on the north-eastern side of the island and is now called Cabo O'Higgins.

CONCEPCIÓN BAY

1. Chart of Concepción Bay, by Bernizet, 1785, showing the Talcahuano anchorage in the south-west and, further south, the settlement of Mocha and the Biobio River. AN 6 JJ1:24.

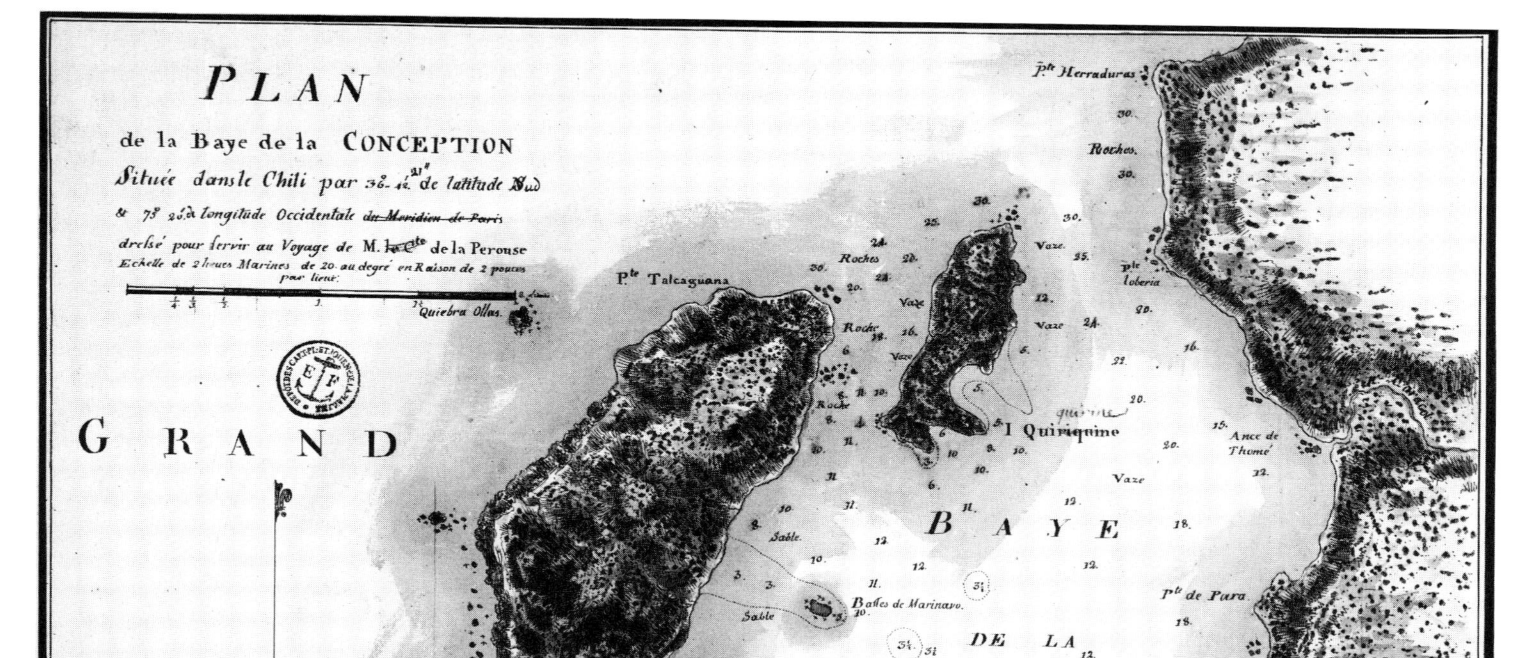
PLAN
de la Baye de la CONCEPTION
Située dans le Chili par 36.d 42.' 21" de latitude Sud
& 73.d 20.' longitude Occidentale du Meridien de Paris
dressé pour servir au Voyage de M. le Cte de la Perouse
Echelle de 2 lieues Marines de 20. au degré en Raison de 2 pouces par lieue.
Quiebra Ollas.
GRAND
Pte Talcaguana
Pte Herraduras
Roches.
Pte Loberia
Roches
Roche
I Quiriquine
Anse de Thomé
Vaze
BAYE
DE LA
CONCEPTION
Basses de Marinavo.
Sable
Mouillage
Talcaguana
Pte de Para

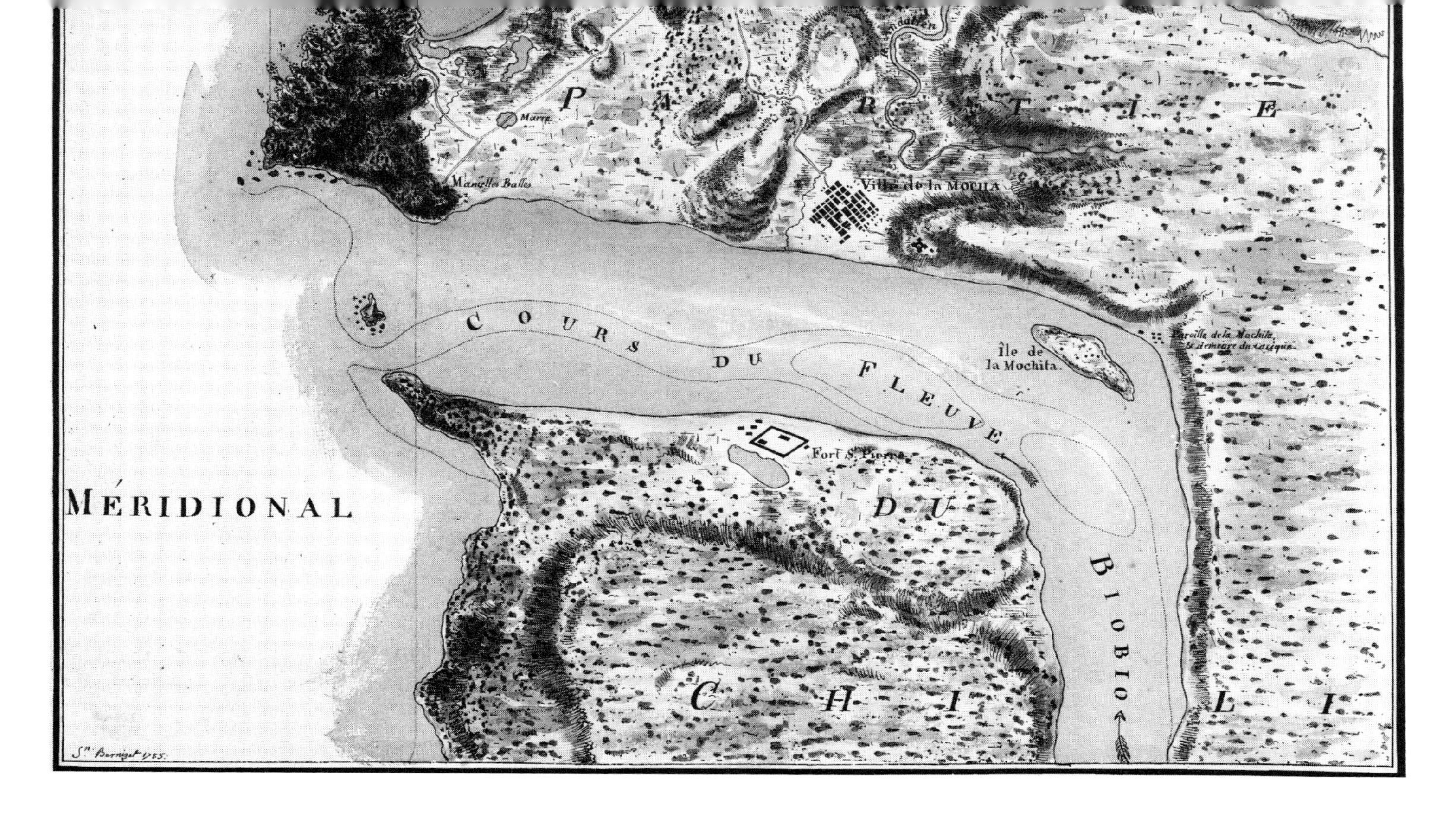
P A R T I E
MÉRIDIONAL
D U
C H I L I
Marre
Ville de la MOCHA
Île de
la Mochita
Fort S. Pierre
COURS DU FLEUVE
BIOBIO
Sn. Bernizet 1785.

2. French officers and natives at Easter Island, 'drawn from life by Duché de Vancy, 9 April 1786'.

Pingré has already indicated, that Dampierre's calculations were wrong and that Davis Land, instead of being 500 Ls from Copiago, is only 200 leagues. It is therefore likely that Davis's two islands are those of San Ambrosio and San Felix, a little further N. than Copiago; but the buccaneers' pilots were not fussy and worked out their latitudes roughly to the nearest 30 or 40′. I would have spared my readers this little geography lesson if I had not had to oppose the views of two men deservedly famous; I must say however that Captain Cook was still unsure and says that if he had had time he would have solved the problem by sailing E. of Easter Island. As I covered 300 Ls along this parallel and saw no sandy island I think that no doubt should now remain and the question seems to me to be finally settled.[1]

I sailed along the coast of Easter Island at a distance of 3 leagues during the night of 8 to 9 April. The sky was clear and in less than 3 hours the winds had veered from N. to S.E. At daybreak I made for Cook's Bay – that is the one where one is best sheltered from the N. to S. by E. winds.[2] It is only open to the W. winds and I had hopes that they would not blow for several days. At 11 a.m. I was only a league from this anchorage; the *Astrolabe* had already dropped anchor. I anchored quite close to that frigate, but the undertow was so strong that our anchors did not hold and we were forced to raise them and tack a couple of times to regain the anchorage.

This setback in no way lessened the natives' enthusiasm. They

[1] Davis Land, or David Land, has its origins in the 1687 voyage of the buccaneer Edward Davis who was sailing in the *Batchelor's Delight* from the Galapagos to Tierra del Fuego when he encountered a shady island behind which he had a glimpse of a higher land. This episode was referred to by William Dampier who, either from his own conclusion or from what Davis had told him, added 'This might probably be the Coast of Terra Australis Incognita.' *A New Voyage round the World*, London, 1697, p. 352. But Dampier had not sailed with Davis; Lionel Wafer, who had, provided the information that Davis had intended to put in at Juan Fernandez, which would have required a different route from the one Dampier had built his assumptions on. See L. Wafer, *A New Voyage and Description of the Isthmus of America*, ed. L.E. Elliot-Joyce, Oxford, 1934, p. 125. The Abbé Pingré in his *Mémoire sur les découvertes faites dans la Mer du Sud avant les derniers voyages des Anglois et des François* (Paris, 1778) commented that people like Davis 'were better at piracy than at determining the positions of the places where they found themselves.' (p. 69). The conclusion that the islands in question were San Ambrosio and San Felix is now generally accepted.

[2] James Cook put in at Hangaroa Bay on 14 March 1774 on the west side of Easter Island. The main town is situated here. The name of Bahia La Pérouse has been given to an open bay on the northern coast. It was formerly known as Spanish Bay.

swam behind us up a league offshore, and climbed aboard with a cheerfulness and a feeling of security which gave me the most favourable opinion of their character. A more suspicious people might have feared, when we set sail, to see itself torn from its relatives and carried away far from home, but the thought of such perfidy did not even seem to occur to them. They went about in our midst, naked and with no weapons, a mere string around the waist with a bunch of herbs to hide their natural parts.[1]

Mr Hodgés, the painter who had accompanied Captain Cook on his second voyage,[2] has very inaquately reproduced their features. Generally speaking they are pleasing, but they vary a great deal, and do not have, like those of Malays, Chinese or Chileans, a character of its own.

I made them various gifts. They preferred pieces of printed cloth, half an ell in size, to nails, knives or beads, but they greatly prized the hats of which we had too few to give to more than a very few. At 8 p.m. I took my leave of my new guests, making them understand by signs that I would be going ashore at dawn. They returned to their canoes, dancing, and jumped into the sea when within two musket shots from the shore over which the sea was breaking strongly; they had taken the precaution of making small parcels with my gifts, and each one had placed his on his head to protect it from the water.

[1] A grim fate lay in way for future generations of islanders who themselves had had a tragically turbulent history. In the 1860s, Peruvian ships raided the island and carried away a thousand of them to work in guano mines; only a few survived; raids and attacks continued into the 1870s when a half-insane French adventurer took over the island; by 1872 when he was killed the population was down to 111 natives.

[2] William Hodges (1744–97) had studied under Joseph Wright whose theories on the effect of light clashed with the current classical tradition. Hodges's drawings and paintings made during the voyage of the *Resolution* reflect the various trends of his day and the growing strength of the Romantic movement. See on this artist Anthony Murray-Oliver, *Oil Paintings by William Hodges R.A.*, Wellington, 1959.

CHAPTER IV

Description of Easter Island. What happened to us there. Manners and customs of the inhabitants.

Cook's Bay, Easter Island, of which I append a map, is situated in 27^{d} 11′ of southern latitude and 111^{d} 55′ 30″ west of Paris.[1] It is the only anchorage that is sheltered from the prevailing S.E. and E. winds. One would run great risks with a W. wind, but it never blows from that quarter unless it has veered E. to N.E. and then N and after that W. One has time to weigh anchor and it is enough to be a quarter of a league away in order to be safe. This bay is easy to find: after rounding the two rocks that lie at the S. point of the island, one should sail along the coast a mile from land, and soon one sees a small sandy cove which is the surest landmark; when this cove bears E. ¼ S.E. and the two rocks I mentioned are hidden by the point one can drop anchor in 20 fathoms, sandy bottom, a quarter of a league from land. If one is further off, the depth is 35 to 40 fathoms and it increases so rapidly that the anchor does not hold – that is what happened to us: we were forced to raise it and return to the anchorage, thus wasting 6 hours. Landing is equally easy, at the foot of one of those statues which I will mention in greater detail later.[2]

At dawn I made all the necessary arrangements for our landing. I flattered myself that I would have friends ashore, having showered gifts on all those who came aboard the previous day, but I had pored too much over the accounts of various travellers not to know that these natives are big children who are so excited by the sight of our belongings that they cannot stop themselves trying to get hold of them. Accordingly I felt that they should be controlled by fear,

[1] Easter Island lies in latitude 27°07′S and longitude 109°42′W of Greenwich or 111°42′W of Paris. Hangaroa Bay lies in 27°09′S and 111°46′W of Paris.

[2] There are in reality three small islets or rocks off the southern point: Motunui, Motuiti and Motu Kaokao. The small cove that leads to Hangaroa is Hangapiho.

and I ordered quite a display for our landing which was carried out with four boats and 12 armed soldiers. Mr de Langle and I were followed by all the passengers and officers, except those needed on board the two frigates. Including the crews of our rowing boats, there were 70 of us.

There were four or five hundred natives[1] waiting for us along the shore. They were unarmed; some wore pieces of white or yellow cloth, but most were naked. Several were tatooed, with their faces painted with some red colour. Their shouts and their features expressed joy. They came forward to help us to come ashore.

The island in this area is about 20 feet above sea level. The mountains are 7 or 800 *toises* inland, and the land slopes gently down from the foothills to the sea. This space is covered with greens which I think are suitable for cattle; this type of vegetation, interspersed with large stones which appear to be merely resting on it, seems to me to be identical with the one found in the Isle de France and called pumpkins[2] because most are the size of that fruit; and these stones which we found so troublesome when we were walking along are a blessing of Nature because they keep the soil fresh and damp and make up in part for the beneficial shade of trees which these islanders have been unwise enough to cut down, no doubt in times long past,[3] causing the land to be burnt by the sun and has reduced them to a situation where they have neither gullies nor streams nor sources. They did not realise that on small islands lost in the middle of an immense ocean only the freshness of a tree-covered land can hold and condense the clouds, thereby maintaining a constant rainfall over the hills, which then spreads down in streams and sources over different areas. Islands deprived of such benefits are doomed to a horrible drought which gradually destroys plants and shrubs, and renders them uninhabitable. Mr de Langle

[1] La Pérouse regularly uses the term 'Indian' for the islanders, but their association with the American continent and South American Indians is contested; they are overwhelmingly Polynesians.

[2] La Pérouse is referring to pumpkins grown in the Isle de France or Mauritius. The genus *Cucurbita* includes the gourd and the squash as well as other species. The troublesome presence of large stones is commented upon by a number of travellers.

[3] The soil of Easter Island is very porous and exposed to salt air. Polynesian immigrants who probably brought coconuts with them found an island which in all likelihood had few trees and was not suitable for the coconut. The theory of early inhabitants being the cause of an ecological disaster is not sustainable, but undeniably human settlement worsened a bad situation.

and I had no doubts that these people owe their unfortunate condition to the carelessness of their ancestors, and it is likely that the other islands of the S. Sea only have water on account of having inaccessible mountains where it was impossible to cut down trees owing to the difficulty of transporting them down to the shore. Thus Nature has been kinder to these other islands only by seeming to be meaner, since it reserved for itself areas they could not reach. A long period spent in the Isle de France, which has so many similarities with Easter Island, has taught me that trees never grow again unless they are sheltered from the sea breezes by other trees or stone walls. And it is that knowledge which led me to the theory that the inhabitants of this devastated island have less cause to complain about their volcanoes, which have been dead for a long time, than about their own imprudence; but since Man is a being who, above all others, can adapt to every situation, these people seemed to me to be less unfortunate than they did to Captain Cook and Mr Forster.[1] They had reached this island after a long and painful voyage, short of everything, sick of the scurvy, and they found no water, no wood, no pigs; a few hens with some bananas and potatoes are a very meager comfort in such circumstances; and their accounts reflect their situation. Ours was immeasurably better; our crews were in the best of health. We had obtained in Chile all we would need for several months, and all we wanted from these people was the opportunity of doing them some good: we were bringing them goats, ewes, pigs; we had seeds for orange and lemon trees, cotton and maize and broadly of everything that was likely to succeed in this island.

Our first care after landing was to make an enclosure with armed soldiers in a circle; we told the inhabitants to leave this space clear; we put up a tent there, and I had all the gifts brought ashore which I intended to offer them, as well as sundry animals; but as I had given express orders that no shot should be fired, adding that natives who might prove too troublesome should not even be

[1] Cook and Forster were not unfair in their comments. The islanders were, as with La Pérouse, inveterate thieves, but the English appreciated how tempted they were, living on an isolated island so lacking in natural resources. See Cook, *Journals*, II, pp. 350–9. Johann Reinhold Forster (1729–98) was on board with his son Johann George Adam Forster (1754–94); he wrote *Observations made during a Voyage round the World*, London, 1778; he had gone ashore with Richard Pickersgill on 15 March, Cook remaining on board as he was unwell. Their report decided him to sail without delay, the island having nothing to offer.

driven away with rifle butts, the soldiers were soon exposed to the greed of these islanders, whose number had grown – there were at least 800 of them. Among them were at least 150 women; many of them had pleasant features, and they offered their favours to anyone willing to give them a present; the natives were urging us to accept them, some of them showing us by example the kind of pleasure we could expect: it was separated from the spectators by a simple cloth of native manufacture, and while these women were teasing us, our hats were being snatched from our heads and our handkerchiefs from our pockets. They all seemed to be accomplices in these thefts for no sooner were they carried out than, like a flock of birds, they all fled at the same moment; but seeing that we did not use our muskets they came back within a few minutes to renew their caresses and wait for the opportunity of committing another theft. These tricks went on throughout the morning, but as we were to leave during the night we had no interest in educating them. Instead we enjoyed ourselves watching all the efforts the islanders made to rob us, and in order to remove any pretext for some act of violence which might have a tragic outcome I told the soldiers and the sailors that I would replace hats that might be stolen from them.[1] These natives were unarmed; 3 or 4 at the most, in such a crowd, had a kind of club[2] made of wood and hardly dangerous; some appeared to possess some authority over the rest – I took them to be chiefs and gave them medals which I tied around their necks with a chain; but I soon noticed that they were in fact the worst thieves, although they gave the impression of trying to chase those who stole our handkerchiefs, but with no intention of catching them.

We had only 8 or 9 hours to spend on the island, and we did not want to waste this time. I handed over the protection of our tent and our belongings to Mr d'Escures, my senior lieutenant, placing

[1] Hat thefts are reported by Roggeveen, Gonzalez and Cook. A. Métraux comments: 'The ancient Easter Islanders were fascinated by headgear, and to satisfy this passion they risked the reprisals of Europeans whose hats they stole. This fascination sometimes took on comic forms. Eyraud reports in one of his letters that there was nothing they could not turn into a hat. Calabash, half a melon, a bird's remains, everything seemed acceptable. A native was even seen proudly wearing two buckets, one fitted into the other.' *L'Ile de Pâques*, Paris, 1941, new edn 1980, p. 63. See also Métraux's *Ethnology of Easter Island* (Bernice P. Bishop Museum, Honolulu, 1940).

[2] Cook also mentions these clubs, called paoa.

him in command of this important post and of all the soldiers and sailors who had gone ashore. We then split into two groups; the first, under Mr de Langle, was to go as far as possible into the interior of the island, to sow seeds in every place that appeared suitable for them, to study the soil, the plants, any cultivation, the population, the monuments and, in general, anything of interest among these quite extraordinary people. Those who felt themselves strong enough to cover a good distance went with him: he was accompanied by Messrs Dagelet, de la Manon, de la Martiniere, Father Receveur, the abbé Mongèz, Mr Duché, Mr Du Fresne, and the gardener. The others, including myself, were satisfied with visiting the monuments, platforms, houses and plantations within a league of our establishment. Mr Hodges's drawings of the statues is a very imperfect rendering of what we have seen,[1] and Mr Forster's conclusions, who believes them to be the work of a much larger population than exists today, do not strike me as any better; these shapeless busts, the largest of those we measured being only 14 feet 6 inches high, 7 feet 6 inches across the shoulders, 3 feet thick at the stomach, 6 feet wide and 5 feet thick at the base, could well be the work of the present population which, without exaggeration, I would estimate at two thousand. The number of women struck me as being fairly close to that of the men because the number of children I saw was similar to any other country's, and although out of the 1200 people who gathered around the bay on our arrival there were at the most 300 women, I concluded that islanders from this extremity of the island had come to see our vessels, and that the women, either because they were

[1] Hodges's paintings and drawings were altered, with greater elements of romanticism, by the engravers who provided the plates for editions of Cook's voyages. His *The Monuments of Easter Island*, an oil painting now in the Greenwich Maritime Museum, is essentially 'an essay in the depiction of light and weather.... The statues are blocked in broadly with an eye mainly to the visual patterns they help to establish against the sky.', Bernard Smith, *European Vision and the South Pacific*, 2nd edn, Sydney, 1984, pp. 71–2. La Pérouse is right in some of his comments, as the statues depicted by Hodges look strangely elongated. George Forster's conclusions were that the monuments are 'so disproportionate to the present strength of this nation, it is most reasonable to look upon them as the remains of better times', *A Voyage round the World*, London, 1777, I, pp. 593–4. Easter Island's past, with its statues, its form of writing and its legends, remains a mystery; the possibility of an American Indian influence has been put forward by Thor Heyerdahl in *American Indians in the Pacific* (London, 1952), *The Art of Easter Island* (London, 1976), and *The Archeology of Easter Island*, Santa Fé, 1961.

more delicate or were busy with their household tasks or their children, had stayed at home, so that we saw only those who live near the bay. Mr de Langle's account confirms this view: he came across numerous women and children in the interior of the island, and we all went into those caves where Mr Forster and some of Captain Cook's officers thought at first that the women might be hidden. They are underground houses, of the type I shall describe shortly, where we found small bundles of firewood, the largest pieces of which were no more than 5 feet long and no thicker than an ordinary leg. One cannot however deny that the inhabitants had hidden their women when Captain Cook visited them in 1772 but I cannot guess why, and possibly we owe to his noble behaviour towards these people the trust they showed us, which enabled us to better estimate their numbers.

All the monuments which remain today, and which Mr Duché has very accurately drawn, seem very old. They are located on *moraÿs*[1] because one finds numerous bones nearby. One cannot doubt that the government of the island, which has become more democratic, has so levelled the conditions of life that there is no chief left powerful enough to ensure that a large number of men will preserve his memory by erecting a statue to him. Instead of these *colossi*, they put up stone cairns, with the top stone whitewashed. These cenotaphs which can be made by one man in an hour are put up along the seashore, and a native showed us by lying down that the stones covered, or were near, a grave. Then, raising his hands to the sky, he obviously endeavoured to indicate that they believed in an after-life: I had great reservations about this, and I must admit that I thought they had no such belief, but having seen this done on several occasions, and Mr de Langle who had travelled in the interior of the island having told me the same thing, I have no more doubts about it, and I think it is a view generally shared by our officers and passengers. However, we found no sign of any religious practices, because I do not believe anyone should take the statues for idols, although they seemed to show some veneration towards them, just as we display for tombs. These colossal busts, whose dimensions I have already given and which reveal little

[1] The term *morai* or *marae* was mainly an open space in front of a meeting house; it acquired in time a more sacred character, but it was not reserved exclusively for funeral ceremonies. In Easter Island the sacred platform on which the statues stood was called an *ahu*; it was frequently, but not inevitably part of a *marae*.

EASTER ISLAND

3. Easter Island, unsigned (by Bernizet?). Actual size 40 cm × 70 cm. AN 6 JJ1:26B.

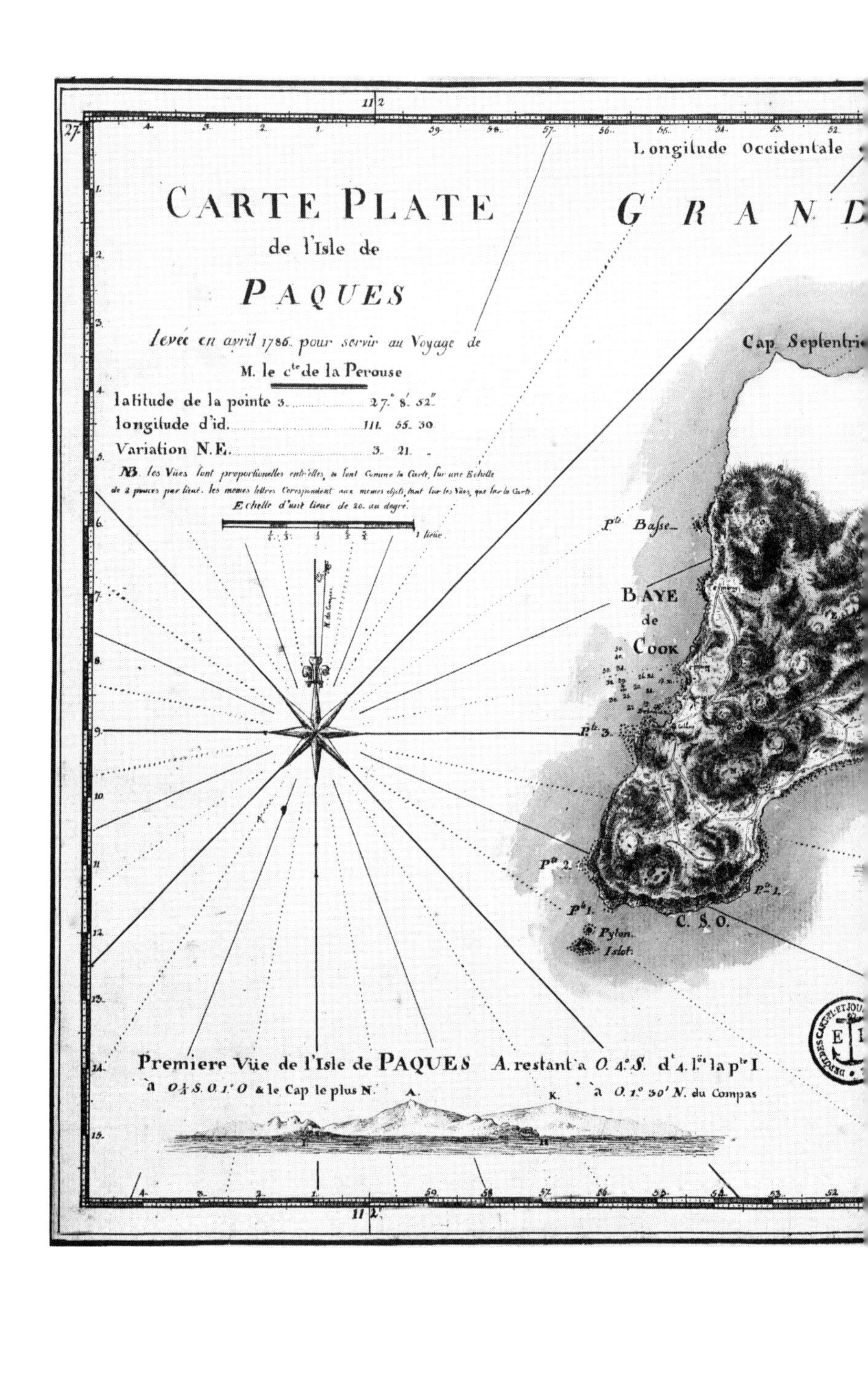

CARTE PLATE
de l'Isle de
PAQUES
levée en avril 1786. pour servir au Voyage de
M. le c^te de la Perouse
latitude de la pointe 3. 27.° 8.' 52."
longitude d'id. 111. 55. 30
Variation N.E. 3. 21.
NB. les Vües sont proportionelles entr'elles, et sont Comme la Carte, sur une Echelle
de 2 pouces par lieue. les memes lettres Corespondent aux memes objets, tant sur les Vües, que sur la Carte.
Echelle d'une lieue de 20. au degré.
1 lieue.
Longitude Occidentale
G R A N D
Cap Septentri
P^te Basse
BAYE
de
COOK
P^te 3.
P^te 2.
P^te 1.
P^te 1.
C. S. O.
Pylon.
Islot.
Premiere Vüe de l'Isle de PAQUES A. restant a O. 4.° S. d^t 4. l^es la p^te I.
a O¼ S. O. 1.° O & le Cap le plus N.
a O. 1.° 30' N. du Compas
A.
K.
112.

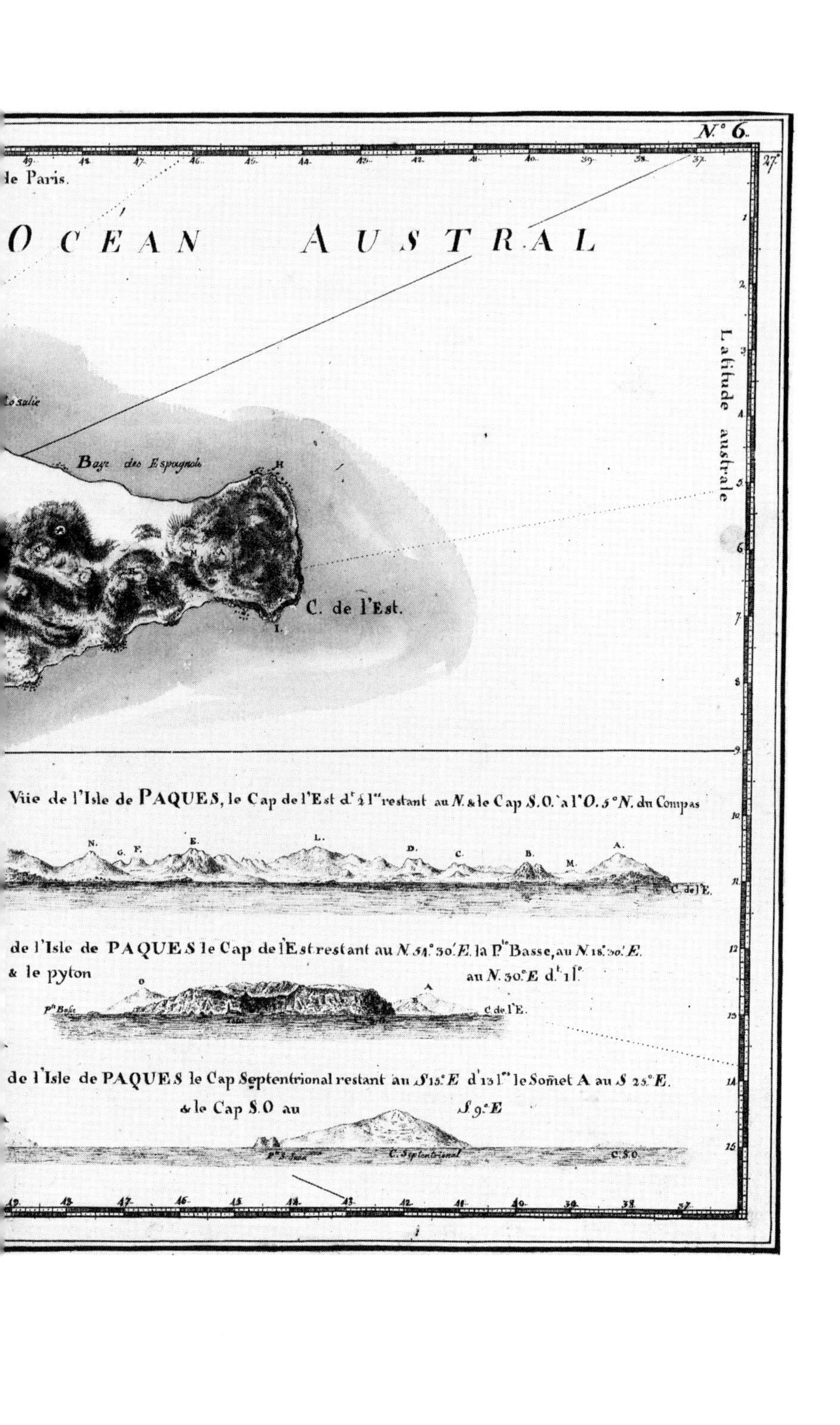

N.° 6.
de Paris.
OCEAN AUSTRAL
Latitude australe
Baye des Espagnols
C. de l'Est.
Vüe de l'Isle de PAQUES, le Cap de l'Est d.t à 1.l restant au N. & le Cap S.O. à l'O. 5° N. du Compas
C. de l'E.
de l'Isle de PAQUES le Cap de l'Est restant au N. 54° 30' E. la P.te Basse, au N. 18° 30' E.
& le pyton au N. 30° E d.t 1 l.e
C. de l'E.
de l'Isle de PAQUES le Cap Septentrional restant au S. 15° E d.t 13 l.es le Somet A au S 25° E.
& le Cap S.O au S 9° E
C. Septentrional
C. S.O.

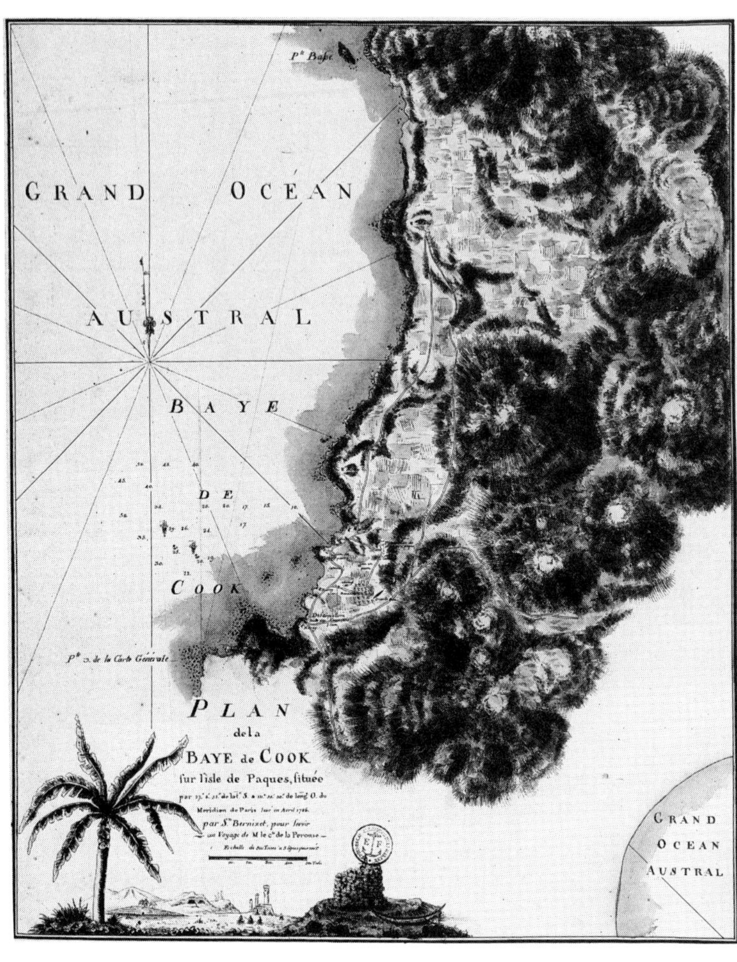

4. Cook Bay, Easter Island, by Bernizet. The French are shown to have landed and set up a tent in the south of the cultivated low land near a 'morai'. Actual size 66 cm × 50 cm. AN 6 JJ1:28C.

talent for sculpture on the part of these islanders, are of volcanic origin, known among naturalists as *lapillo*;[1] it is so soft and light a stone that some of Captain Cook's officers thought it might be a manufactured stone made up of some mortar which hardened in air. He explained how one could raise a fairly considerable weight without any fulcrum, but we are certain that it is a volcanic stone, very light, and that one can, with levers 5 or 5 feet in length and slipping stones underneath, as Captain Cook explains very clearly, raise a much greater weight, and that a hundred men would be enough for such a task. There would not be space around it for a greater number. And so the magic disappears,[2] the lapillo stone, which is not artificial, can be given back to Nature, and one concludes that, if there are no new monuments on the island, it is because equality reigns and it is not worth being the king of a people who go about naked, feeding on sweet potatoes[3] and yams, and conversely these natives, who do not go to war since they have no neighbours, have no need of a chief with wide authority.

I can only hazard guesses about these people's customs, whose language I could not understand and whom I saw for only a day, but I had the experience of earlier travellers whose accounts I knew by heart, and I could add my own reflections.[4]

Hardly a tenth of their land is under cultivation, and I am sure that 3 days of labour are enough to provide a year's subsistence for each of them. The ease with which they can provide for their necessities led me to believe that the fruits of the earth are held in common, all the more so because I am fairly certain that their houses are, at least within a district. I measured one situated close to

[1] Lapillo is a general term for a light stone of volcanic origin. The statues were made of trachyte, a stone rich in feldspar. James Cook's comments on what he called the 'grey stone' were based on reports made to him by Pickersgill and others, as he himself was not able to travel far on the island.

[2] Cook and Lapérouse's conclusions on the method of erecting the statues are generally accepted today and agree with recent investigations. However, for many years, visitors to the islands were told by the inhabitants that the statues had been put up by ancestors with magical powers.

[3] La Pérouse normally uses the word *patate*, which is a slang word for 'potato'. However, he is referring to the Polynesian kumara, the *Ipomoea batatas*, and his use of 'patate' is quite appropriate. The yam, found on most Pacific islands, is the *Dioscorea*; the variety he found on Easter Island is probably *Dioscorea alata*.

[4] There had been three expeditions to Easter Island before La Pérouse's, details of which we included in his Instructions: Jacob Roggeveen in 1722, Felipe Gonzalez in 1770 – who took possession of it in the name of the Spanish king and named it Isla de San Carlo – and James Cook in 1774.

our establishment; it was 310 feet long, 10 feet wide, and 10 feet high in the middle section; it had the shape of an upturned canoe. One could enter only through two doorways 2 feet in height, and by sliding on hands and knees. This house can hold over 200 people – it is not a chief's house, as there is no furniture and he would not know what to do with such space. It constitutes a real village, with 2 or 3 other small houses at a short distance. There is probably a chief per district whose function is to look after the crops, whom Captain Cook thought was the owner, but if that famous navigator had some trouble in obtaining a substantial quantity of potatoes and yams, it was less on account of a shortage than of the need to get a general agreement on their sale.[1]

As for the women, I dare not state whether they are held in common in the district, and the children belong to the state; it is certain that no native seemed to have a husband's authority over any of them, and if they belong to individuals then they are very prodigal with them. Some houses are situated underground, as I have indicated, but others are made of reeds, which proves that there are marshes in the centre of the island; these reeds are very artistically arranged and provide a perfect shelter from the rain. The building is set over a slab of freestone about 18 inches thick;[2] at intervals holes have been dug into which poles are placed to form the framework, which are bent back into an arch; reed mats fill the spaces between these poles.

One cannot question the identity of these people with those of other South Sea islands, as Captain Cook pointed out. The same language, the same features; their cloth is similarly made with the bark of the mulberry[3] but it is very scarce because drought has destroyed these trees; those who survived are only 3 feet high; they are even forced to surround them with stone walls to protect them from the wind – one must add that these trees never exceed the height of these walls.

[1] The population was indeed divided into tribes and subtribes. As was the case throughout Polynesia, land was not individually owned but held in common by a subtribe; it was not under the protection of a chief, but of a *tapu* following an official pronouncement or ceremony. Cook, like many others, thought of land tenure in European terms, with a flavouring of feudal rule, a view which caused and continues to cause a wide range of problems with settlers and administrators.

[2] Marginal note by La Pérouse: 'These stones are not sandstone but solid lava.'

[3] The fairly simple dress of the Easter Islanders was made of the leaves and young stalks of the *Broussonetia papyrifera*.

I have no doubt that in other times their products were the same as those of the Society Islands. The fruit trees will have perished on account of the drought, like the pigs and the dogs for whom water is an absolute necessity; but man, who can drink whale oil in Hudson Strait, can get used to anything, and I have seen these natives drinking sea water like the albatrosses of Cape Horn.[1] We were in the rainy season; there was a little brackish water in holes by the shore, and they offered it to us in gourds, but it repelled even the thirstiest; and I do not flatter myself with the thought that the pigs I gave them will multiply, but I do hope the goats and ewes, who drink but a little and like salt, will succeed.[2]

At 1 p.m. I returned to the tent, intending to go back on board so that my first lieutenant, Mr de Clonard, could in turn go ashore. I found almost everyone hatless and with no handkerchiefs; our gentleness had emboldened the thieves, and I was treated no differently from the others: an islander who had helped me down from a platform took away my hat as soon as he had rendered me that service, and he fled as fast as he could, followed as usual by all the others; I did not have him chased, and I did not want to claim the exclusive right to be protected from the sun since almost no one else now had a hat. I continued my examination of the platform; it is the monument which gave me the highest opinion of the skill these people used to possess in the art of building – the pompous term of 'architecture' is inappropriate here. They do not seem to have ever known about cement, but they excelled at cutting and shaping stones which were placed and fitted together in accordance with all the rules of the art.

I collected samples of these stones, which are a type of lava of different densities. The lightest, which consequently is the first to disintegrate, forms the facing on the land side; the covering which

[1] It is possible that La Pérouse saw some islanders rinsing their mouths in sea-water, but he also saw them drinking close to the shore from water found in hollows among the rocks. This was probably rainwater or water seeping through the cliffs, as the porous nature of the soil allows rain to soak through quickly and form small underground streams that come out near the shore. This water is usually brackish and unappealing, but it is not, as he thought, as salty as seawater.

[2] There is no real evidence that the animals La Pérouse left behind were used for breeding; they are believed to have been eaten soon after his departure. The lack of water made cattle or pig farming very hazardous. It was not until the end of the nineteenth century that the firm of Williamson & Balfour succeeded in establishing sheep farming, which now represents the main source of income of the island.

faces the sea is made of an infinitely more compact lava so that it will last longer, but I know of no instrument or material these islanders have which would be hard enough to cut this latter stone; possibly a longer stay on the island would have enlightened me.[1] At 2 p.m. I returned to the ship and Mr de Clonard went ashore. Soon two officers from the *Astrolabe* came to advise me that the natives had committed a new theft which had led to a fairly serious clash: divers had cut the cablet of the *Astrolabe*'s boat beneath the waterline and carried away its grapnel; this was only noticed when the thieves were some distance inland. As we needed the grapnel two officers with several soldiers gave chase but they were met with a hail of stones. A blank musket shot fired into the air had no effect – they were finally forced to fire with bird shot, with no doubt a few pellets hitting one of these natives because the stoning came to an end and our officers were able to return quietly to our tent; but it was impossible to catch up with the thieves who must have been surprised at being unable to exhaust our patience.

They soon came back to our establishment and started again to offer their women, and we were as good friends as we had been when we first met. Finally at 6 p.m. everything was back on board – the boats came back to the ships and I gave the signal to get ready to weigh anchor. Before we did Mr de Langle gave me an account of his travels into the interior of the island, which I will describe in the next chapter. He had sown seeds throughout and given the islanders every indication of kindness. I must nevertheless complete their portrait by recording that a kind of chief to whom Mr de Langle was giving a couple of goats, a male and a female, was taking them with one hand and stealing his handkerchief with the other.

It is certain that these people have different ideas about theft than we do; they clearly feel no shame about it, but they know quite well that they are committing an unfair action and immediately take flight to avoid the punishment which we would have meted out in proportion to the crime if we had had to stay on the island for any length of time, because our extreme gentleness would have had an unfortunate outcome in the end and a few blows with a rope would have made these islanders more amenable.

[1] Tuff, as this volcanic stone is called, hardens in the air, especially in salt air; the side facing the sea was consequently harder than the protected side. This property may be the reason why Pickersgill and others wondered whether the islanders had used a form of mortar when building their structures.

No one who has read the accounts of the most recent travellers could take the South Sea natives for savages; on the contrary they have made great advances towards civilisation and I believe that they are as corrupted as they can be, given their circumstances.[1] My opinion on this is not based on their various thefts, but on the way they went about it; the cheekiest scoundrels in Europe are less hypocritical than these islanders; all their displays of friendship were a pretence and their features did not display a single feeling that was genuine. The native one needed to be the most wary about was the one to whom a gift had just been made and who seemed to be the most anxious to do anything for you.

They displayed a brutal behaviour towards girls of 13 or 14 to drag them towards us in the hope of receiving payment for them; the repugnance displayed by these young native girls was evidence that the laws of the land were being violated in their case. No Frenchman took advantage of the barbarous power that was being offered to them, and if there were a few moments of tenderness they were reciprocal. The women were even the first to display such feelings.

I have found here all the arts of the Society Islands, but with far fewer means of practising them because of the lack of raw materials. The canoes have the same shape, but they are made only with very narrow pieces of timber 4 or 5 feet long, and at most they can take four men; I saw only 3 in that part of the island, and I would not be surprised if soon, because of the lack of timber, there were none left. Anyhow they have learnt to do without them, and swim so well that in the heaviest of seas they can go out for 2 leagues and on their return, for the pleasure of it, they look for the part of the shore where the waves break more fiercely.

There seemed to me to be little fishing available around the coast and I believed that almost all their food comes from the vegetable kingdom – they eat sweet potatoes, yams, bananas, sugar canes and a small seaweed which grows among rocks along the shore and is

[1] This passage contains more than a touch of irony. Its background is the theory of the Noble Savage and the corrupting influence which civilisation was believed to have had on natural man. Jean-Jacques Rousseau (1712–78) in particular had been advancing theories along such lines. La Pérouse, however, was highly sceptical about the claim that civilisation and the corruption of natural man progress at the same rate; his opinion will be strengthened and more angrily expressed after the episode of the Tutuila massacre in the Samoan group.

similar to the raisin – like weed found near the tropics in the Atlantic;[1] one cannot count as a source of food the few hens found on the island which are very scarce.

Our travellers found no land birds, and seabirds are not common.

Their fields are cultivated with a great deal of intelligence: they pull up weeds, pile them up, burn them and use the ashes to fertilise the soil. Banana trees are set in straight lines. They also cultivate the *solanum* or morel[2] but I do not know for what purpose. If I knew they had heat-resistant containers I could believe that they eat them like spinach as in Madagascar or the Isle de France, but they have no other means of cooking their food than the method practised in the Society Island, of digging a hole in the ground and covering their sweet potatoes or yams with burning-hot stones and coal mixed with soil, so that everything they eat is cooked as in an oven.[3]

The care they took to measure my ship showed me that they did not look upon our skills in the way unreasoning beings might. They examined our cables, our anchors, our compass, our steering wheel, and came back the next day with a string to check the measurements, which gave me to think that they had discussed it on land and that some doubts remained. It lowered them in my esteem that they could reflect in this way – I left them a subject for thought which maybe they will not discuss, and it is that we made no use of our strength against them, although they were not unaware of our power since the mere act of taking aim with a musket made them run away; but on the contrary we only landed on their island to do good to them; we showered gifts on them, we patted all those who were weak, especially children still at their mother's breast; we sowed all kinds of useful seeds in their fields; we left pigs, goats and ewes in their settlements, where in all likelihood they will multiply; we asked for nothing in return, and yet they threw stones at us and robbed us of everything they could carry

[1] This would have been some variety of *Fucus*, probably the *Fucus vesiculosus*.

[2] The name Solanum applies to a wide variety of plants, including the potato and the aubergine. The reference here may be to the *Solanaceae aculeatissimum* or the *S. nodiflorum* which are found in the Marquesas and the Hawaiian group and may have been brought to Easter Island in early migrations.

[3] The umu which involves digging a ditch or a hole in which a fire is lit to heat the stones on which the food, covered up with leaves and soil, is to cook, is widespread throughout Polynesia. It makes up, as La Pérouse points out, for the lack of cooking utensils that are fire-resistant.

away. As I have said it would have been unwise, in other circumstances, to behave with such softness, but I was determined to sail during the night, and I flattered myself with the thought that when they no longer saw us at dawn they would ascribe our prompt departure to the understandable displeasure we should have felt at their behaviour, and that possibly this thought might make them better people. Whatever foundation there might be to such idle speculation, it will not greatly concern navigators, as this island offers almost no resources for vessels and is only 25 to 30 days from the Society Islands.[1]

[1] The distance from Easter Island to Tahiti is roughly 4,000 km or 2,500 miles. Roggeveen took over a month to reach the Tuamotus and six weeks to arrive at the Society Islands. Bougainville covered the equivalent distance Easter Island to Tahiti in five weeks. La Pérouse's editor, Milet-Mureau, changed this sentence, somewhat oddly, into 'being at a short distance from the Society Islands'.

CHAPTER V

Travels into the interior of the island by the Viscount de Langle. New observations on the customs of these people, the quality of the soil, their crops, arts, &c

I left at 8 a.m. accompanied by Messrs Dagelet, de la Manon, de la Martiniere, Father Receveur, the abbé Mongèz, Mr Duché, Mr Dufrêsne and the gardener. We firstly went 2 Ls E. towards the interior of the island; it was very arduous walking through hills covered with volcanic stones, but I soon noticed the presence of paths allowing easy access between the huts; we took advantage of these and visited several plantations of yams and sweet potatoes. The soil consisted of a thick loam which the gardener judged suitable to grow our seeds; he sowed cabbage, carrot, beet, maize and pumpkin seed, and we endeavoured to explain to the islanders that these seeds would produce fruit and roots they could eat; they understood us perfectly, and from that moment showed us the best places where they wanted to see our new crops. To these leguminous plants we added seeds of orange and lemon trees and cotton, indicating to them that these were trees and that what we had previously sown were plants.

We saw no other shrubs than the paper mulberry and the mimosa.[1] There were also fairly extensive fields of solanum which these people seemed to be cultivating in soil exhausted by yams and sweet potatoes. We went on our way towards the mountains which, although relatively high, all end in easy slopes and are covered with grass.[2] We saw no gullies or torrents. After travelling some 2 Ls E. we turned back S. towards the S.E. coast along which

[1] Not only La Pérouse but Forster uses the term mimosa; the shrub is the *Toromiro* (*Sophora toromiro*).

[2] Easter Island is a roughly triangular island with an extinct volcano at each corner, Mt Terevaka rises to 1,969 ft (600 m). Grass grows well inland and today supports a substantial sheep population.

we had sailed on the previous day and on which I saw with my glass a large number of monuments. Several were toppled over; it would seem that these people do not bother to restore them. Others were standing, with their platforms half-ruined. The largest I measured was 16 feet ten inches high, including the topknot which measures 3 feet one inch, and is made of a very light porous lava; its width across the shoulders was 6 ft 7 inches and its thickness at the base 2 feet 7 inches.

Having then noticed a small group of huts, I directed my steps towards this kind of village; one of the houses was 330 feet long and shaped like an upturned canoe; very close to it we saw the foundations of others which had disappeared, they consist of cut lava stones with holes about 2 inches in diameter. This part of the island seemed better cultivated and more populated than the area of Cook Bay; it has also more monuments and platforms. I saw on the different stones that make up these platforms rough drawings of skeletons and I noticed the presence of holes blocked up with stones, leading, I thought, into caves containing the bodies of the dead. A native explained by eloquent sign language that this is where they were buried and that later they went up into the heavens.[1] Along the shore we came upon several small stone cairns, similar to the way cannon balls are stored in artillery grounds, and saw human bones nearby and near the statues, all of which faced out to sea. During the morning we went up to 7 different platforms on which there were statues, standing or fallen, and they differed only in their sizes. Time had caused greater or smaller ravages according to their age, but we found near the last one a kind of human figure made of reeds, 10 feet tall; it was covered with a white cloth of local manufacture; the head was of natural size, the body slim, the legs fairly in proportion; a kind of string bag was hung around its neck, covered with a white cloth; it seemed to me to contain some grasses, and next to this bag was the representation of a child two feet in length whose arms were stretched out as on a

[1] The numerous underground caves have been used over the centuries by Easter Islanders to seek refuge, hide their women and children and sacred possessions. They have been described by a number of anthropologists, including Thor Heyerdahl – see his *Aku Aku: Paskeöyas Hemmelighet*, Oslo, 1957, English transl. London, 1958. Those near the platforms, which de Langle mentions, were used to bury the bodies of chiefs and their relatives following a drying-out period on the platforms. The stone cairns, however, when not near an *ahu*, were probably warnings to passers-by that a field was *tapu*.

cross, with legs dangling. This figure could not have been there for many years, and it is possibly the kind of statues which are now put up for the chiefs. Next to this same platform, one could see two parapets that might have formed an enclosure 384 feet long and 324 feet wide. I do not know whether it was a water reservoir or the start of a fortress built against enemies, but it seemed to me that this construction had never been finished.

Continuing on our way at sunset, we met about 20 children walking under the direction of a few women, who seemed to be going towards the houses I have already mentioned.

At the end of the S. point of the island, we saw the crater of an old volcano, whose size, depth and evenness aroused my admiration as it did that of my companions. It is shaped like a truncated cone; its upper lip, which is the wider, seemed to be two thirds of a league in circumference; one can estimate the size of the lower lip by assuming that the wall of the cone makes a 30° angle with the vertical. This lower lip forms a perfect circle; the bottom is marshy; one can see several ponds of soft water, the surface seeming to be above sea level; I estimate that the depth of this crater is at least 800 feet.[1]

Fr Receveur who climbed down told me that this marsh is edged with the finest banana and mulberry plantations. It appears, as I had observed when I was sailing along the coast, that a large landslide had occurred on the seaward side which caused a great breach in the crater; this breach is equal in height to a third of the crater and in width to a tenth of its upper circumference. The grass along the sides of the cone, the marshy area inside it and the fertile nature of the nearby land make it clear that the volcano has been long extinct. I saw at the bottom of the crater the only birds I have come across on the island; they were sea swallows.[2] Nightfall forced me to go back towards the ships. Close to a house I saw a large number of children who fled when I approached; it seemed possible that this house was where the children of this district lived; they were too much of the same age to belong to the two women who seemed to

[1] De Langle had walked roughly to the centre of the island, then turned south to Vinapu Cove; he then reached the crater of Rano Kao, 1,345 ft high (410 m.), which covers some 250 acres and contains a lake with trees and shrubs along its edges.

[2] The sea swallow or tern belongs to the *Sterninae* sub-family of gulls. The sea swallow is, strictly, the *Sterna hirundo*, the common tern, which nests on the ground.

be in charge of them. There was a hole near the house where yams and sweet potatoes were being cooked in the manner of the Society Islands.

Back in the tent, I gave to 3 different inhabitants, the 3 types of animals we had set aside for them. I chose those which seemed most likely to breed.

These islanders are hospitable. They gave us sweet potatoes and sugar cane on several occasions, but never missed a chance to rob us when they thought it safe to do so.

A tenth of the island at most is under cultivation. Cleared plots are shaped like a long square, very regular and with no fencing. The rest of the island up to the top of the mountains is covered with a very rough grass. This was the damp season, and I found the soil damp up to one foot down. A few holes in the hills also contained some fresh water, but I saw nowhere any form of running water. The soil struck me as being of a good quality and I have no doubt that it would be fertile if it could be watered. I saw no implement which these people might use to cultivate their fields; I believe that, after clearing it, they make holes in the earth with wooden stakes and thus plant their sweet potatoes and yams. We came across on a very few occasions some mimosa shrubs with stalks never exceeding 3 inches in diameter. My guess as to the way these people are governed is that they form but one nation, divided into a number of districts equivalent to that of the *moraÿs* because I noticed that the hamlets were built close to these cemeteries. I believe the crops to be the common property of the inhabitants of a district, and since the men offer, without any delicacy, their women to strangers, I am not far from thinking that they do not belong to any particular man[1] and that when the children are weaned they hand them over to other women whose task it is, in each district, to see to their physical education. I met twice as many men as women, and I do not know whether they are less numerous on this island or whether, less venturesome than the men, they stayed at home. My

[1] This type of observation is common among early travellers to the Pacific. Polynesian society was far more complex than they could imagine, and it was ascertained eventually that the girls and women available to sailors belonged to a lower class or were still unmarried and consequently under Polynesian customs allowed greater sexual freedom. It should not be overlooked either that goods available on European ships were greatly tempting for islanders who had limited resources and no manufactured goods, and little to offer in exchange to the visitors whose interest in women was all too obvious.

estimate of the total population is 2 thousand people, and I do not think it is dropping, because several new houses were being built, but I also believe that when the island was wooded this nation was considerably larger. It would be desirable for these islanders to devote their energy to the building of water tanks; they would thus make up for one of the greatest misfortunes they have to face and would perhaps live longer, for I did not see a single man who appeared older than 65 – if it is possible to estimate the age of a people one knows so slightly and whose way of life is so different from ours.

CHAPTER VI

Departure from Easter Island. Northerly route through an area which had never yet been crossed by any navigator. Astronomical observations. Signs of some island between 10^d and fifteen of latitude S. Turtles, birds of all types sighted daily in these waters. The two frigates sail abreast in order to cover a larger area. We have no sighting of Nublada or of Roca Partida, but the birds and turtles provide us with evidence of the existence of one of these two islands. Birds and turtles disappear completely in 16^d. All indications of land cease although we were nearing the groups situated on Spanish charts in the same latitude as the Sandwich Islands: a valid reason for believing that these islands are the same as the group further West which Captain Cook thought he had discovered. I travel 500 Ls along this parallel to turn this opinion into evidence. Arrival at the Sandwich islands; I travel through a channel which the English were not in a position to investigate. Anchorage in the bay of Kerriporepo, island of Mowee: meeting with the local natives; their customs, their character; our barter trade with them. Departure. Passage between the island of Morotoi and Woahoo. The same shoal of fish that provided food for us from Easter Island followed us until we dropped anchor, but disappeared when we stopped sailing.

Sailing from Cook Bay, Easter Island, on the evening of the 10th, I set a northerly course, coasting along this island in the moonlight at 1 L. off shore. We only lost sight of it at 2 p.m. the next day when we were 20 Ls away. Until the 17th the winds blew steadily from the S.E. to E.S.E. The weather was very clear, and it did not change or become cloudy until they veered to E.N.E. They remained in that quarter from the 17th to the 20th, and we began to catch *bonito* which followed our frigates until the Sandwich Islands and supplied a complete daily ration for the crews for six weeks; this good food kept us in the best of health and, after 10 months of navigation during which we spent only 25 days at anchor, we did not have a single case of sickness in our two vessels. We were sailing through unknown waters. Our course was roughly the same as Captain Cook's of 1777 when he sailed from the Society Islands to the N.W. coast of America, but we were some 800 Ls further E.[1] I held the hope that I might make some discovery on a crossing of 2000 Ls; I kept sailors aloft throughout, and a reward was promised to whomever would sight land first. In order to cover a larger area, our frigates sailed abreast together during the day, leaving a gap of 3 to 4 leagues between them.

During this crossing, as on all other occasions, Mr Dagelet never missed an opportunity to make observations. They agreed so well with Mr Berthoud's chronometers that the difference never exceeded 10 to 15 minutes – they backed each other up. Mr de Langle obtained results that were equally satisfactory, and daily we could tell the direction of the currents from the difference between our dead reckoning and our observed longitude; they were bearing us W. until the 1^d of southern latitude at a rate of about 3 Ls a day, and then reversed E. at the same speed until the 7^d N. when they resumed their W. direction, and when we arrived at the Sandwich islands, our longitude differed approximately 5^d from our observed latitude, and if, like the navigators of old, we had had no means of observation, we would have situated the Sandwich islands 5^d too far E; it is the direction of these currents, which was not carefully estimated in early times, that caused the errors found on Spanish charts; for it is noteworthy that all the islands of Quiros, Mendana and other navigators of that nation have recently been found, but always placed too close to the coast of America on their charts.[2] I

[1] In December 1777, on his third voyage, James Cook sailed from Bora Bora, on a NNE course. He discovered Christmas Island on Christmas Eve and sailed on to discover the Hawaiian group, which he named the Sandwich Islands after John Montagu, fourth Earl of Sandwich and First Lord of the Admiralty, a name which gradually fell into disuse.

[2] The three sets of currents encountered were the Pacific South Equatorial Current, which bears west, the South Equatorial Countercurrent, which bears east, and the North Equatorial Current, which bears west. They made estimates of the distance travelled difficult for sailors using the ancient methods of loch measurement. The longitudes reported by early Spanish navigators on their voyages of discovery – Alvaro de Mendaña's discovery of the Solomon Islands in 1567–8, and the subsequent voyages of Mendaña and Quiros in 1595 and of Quiros in 1605 – almost inevitably resulted in an underestimate of the distances separating their newly-found territories from their ports of departure in South America. The other navigators La Pérouse refers to include Magellan, Saavedra, Villalobos and Legaspi. He had been given

ought even to add that if the pilots had not endured a little loss of pride when we found a daily gap between their reckoning and our observations, we would probably have had an 8 or 10^d error on our arrival, and consequently would have placed, in less enlightened times, the Sandwich Islands 10^d too far E.

These thoughts left me with severe doubts about the existence of the group of islands the Spanish call the Mesa, Las Mojas, La Disgraciada; it appears on the chart which Admiral Anson captured on board of the Spanish galleon, and which the editor of his journal had engraved, in exactly the latitude of the Sandwich Islands, and 16 or 17^d further E.[1] My daily differences in longitude led me to believe that these islands were absolutely identical, but what finally convinced me was the name Mesa, which means a table, given by the Spanish to the island of *Owhyhee* [Hawaii]; and I had read in Captain King's description of this particular island that, after rounding the eastern point of this island, one found a mountain called *Mouna-Roa* which is visible for a long time.[2] It is, he says, flattened at the top and forms what sailors call a plateau – the English term is even more expressive, for Captain King called it 'table-land'.

---

detailed updated summaries of what was known at the time on the various islands they had encountered.

[1] The reference is to the 'Chart showing the Track of the *Centurion*' printed in Richard Walter's *A Voyage round the World in the Years MDCCXL, I, II, IV by George Anson*, London, 1748, which had appeared in a French translation, *Voyage autour du monde fait dans les années 1740 à 1744*, a year later. It shows in approximately 20°N and 142°W a group of three islands, Los Mojos, which Anson had not sighted but which appeared on a Spanish chart he had obtained. However, on other Spanish charts, the word *Mira* is found, giving rise to speculation that *mesa* which, as La Pérouse correctly states, is Spanish for 'table' is nothing more than a copyist's error and that we have here a mere warning to sailors, *Mira como vas* ('Watch how you go'). Los Mojos, or Los Majos, might be a deformation of Los Mauges, a name found on a map by the Dutch geographer Ortelius (reproduced in E.W. Dalhgren, *The Discovery of the Hawaiian Islands*, Uppsala, 1917) and could refer to the Maug Islands, three in number, discovered by Magellan in latitude 20°N but in a quite different longitude. A discussion of these various problems will be found in A. Sharp, *The Discovery of the Pacific Islands*, Oxford, 1960, pp 67–8.

[2] The identification of La Mesa with the mountain of Mauna Loa loses validity if one does not accept that the Spanish names refer to the Hawaiian Islands. Whether Spanish navigators discovered the group has been a subject of argument for many years; see for a more recent discussion, O.H.K. Spate, *The Spanish Lake*, Canberra, 1979, pp. 108–9, and for different viewpoints, Thor Heyerdahl's *Early Man and the Ocean*, London, 1978, and Robert Langdon, *The Lost Caravel*, Sydney, 1975.

Although the season was very advanced and I had no time to lose in order to reach the coasts of America, I promptly took the decision to follow a route that would change my opinion into evidence: if I was wrong the outcome would be the discovery of a second group of islands which had been forgotten by the Spanish for maybe over a century, and determining its position and its precise distance from the Sandwich Islands. Those who know me will not harbour the thought that I was guided in this research by a desire to take away from Captain Cook the honour of this discovery – full of admiration and respect for the memory of this great man, I shall always regard him as the first among navigators and the one who determined the precise situation of these islands, who surveyed their coastline, made known the customs, habits and religion of the inhabitants, and paid with his blood for all we know of these people: he is the real Christopher Columbus of this country, of the coast of Alaska and of almost all the islands of the South Sea; chance can lead the most ignorant of men to discover some islands, but only men of his calibre leave nothing further to be known about the countries they have seen. Seamen, philosophers, physicists, each one finds in his work what is his particular interest. Everyone perhaps, but certainly every navigator, owes him a tribute of praise, so how could I refuse mine just as I was arriving among the islands where he so tragically ended his career?

On 7 May in latitude 8^{d} N. we saw numerous birds of the petrel variety, with frigates and tropic birds.[1] The two latter seldom go far from land, so it is said. We also see a number of turtles[2] passing alongside. The *Astrolabe* caught two which Mr de Langle shared with us and which were excellent. The birds and turtles followed us until we were in 14^{d}, and I have little doubt that we passed close to some island, presumably uninhabited as in the middle of these seas

[1] There is seldom enough information in La Pérouse's journal to allow for a precise indication of the birds he saw. Various petrels are found in these waters, notably the Hawaiian petrel, *Pterodroma phaepygia* and the *P. alba*, as well as the stormy petrel, *Hadrobates pelagicus*, and various members of the *Oceanitidae* family. The same comment applies to the frigate birds, which one could identify as the more localised *Fregata minor ridwayi*, and to the tropic birds which, here, could be the *Phaeton rubricauda* and especially the *P. rubricauda rothschildi*.

[2] There are five species of large turtles in Pacific waters: the largest is the *Dermochelis coriacea*; the *Eretmochelis imbricata* has been used in fine examples of Oceanic art; the *Chelonia mydas* would be prized by gourmets and may be the variety which was so appreciated by the French on this occasion.

a rock would serve more as a haunt for these birds than a cultivated land – we were at the time quite close to Roca Partida and Nublada.[1] I set a course that would bring me more or less within sight of Roca Partida, if its longitude was well determined, but I did not want to sail along its latitude, as I could not spare a single day on this search, in view of my other plans; I knew quite well that this would mean I would not be likely to come upon it, and I felt little surprised when I saw no sign of it; when we passed its latitude the birds vanished, and until we reached the Sandwich Islands we never saw more than 2 or 3 of them a day over a distance of close on 500 Ls.

On 15 May I was in latitude N. 19^{d} 17′ and longitude W. of Paris 132^{d}, that is to say in the same latitude as the island group on the Spanish charts as well as that of the Sandwich Islands, but 100 Ls further E. than the former and 460 Ls E. of the others. Wishing to render an important service to geography by deleting from the charts these pointless names which apply to non-existent islands and merely serve to perpetuate errors that are harmful to navigation, I decided to continue my route as far as the Sandwich Islands so that no doubt might remain; I even planned to pass through the channel separating the islands of *Owhyhee* and *Mowee* [Maui] which the English were not able to explore,[2] and I proposed to land on *Mowhee*, purchase food supplies and leave without wasting an instant. I knew that if I followed this programme only in part and covered only 200 leagues along this route there would still be some doubters left, and I did not want the slightest challenge to be raised to my conclusions.

On 18 May I was in 20^{d} of latitude and 139^{d} of longitude, precisely where the Spanish island of Disgraciada was said to be, and I had no indication of any land.

[1] Notes prepared for La Pérouse told him that Roca Partida and La Nublada had been discovered by Juan Gaetan in 1542, the evidence for this coming from Ramusio's *Raccolte de navigatione e viaggi*, Venice, 1550–9. Gaetan (Gaytan, Gaytano) had sailed with Ruy Lopez de Villalobos who had passed by the Revilla Gigedos group off the Mexican coast. (*Who's Who*, p. 113.) The *Histoire des navigations aux terres australes* of Charles de Brosses (Paris, 1756) included a map by Robert de Vaugondy which showed the two Spanish islands, but placed at some distance from each other. They had featured on maps by Abraham Ortelius in the sixteenth century, but La Nublada was shown as Annublada. Roca Partida is nowadays the name of the westernmost island of the Revilla Gigedos.

[2] La Pérouse uses, with occasional variations, Cook's spellings of Owhyhee and Mowee. The pass in question is Alenuihaha between these two islands.

On the 20th I had sailed through the middle of the entire Las Mojas group and I had never seen the slightest indication of any land close by. I continued to sail W. along the parallel of 20^{d} to 21^{d}. Finally, on the morning of the 28th, I sighted the mountains of *Owhyhee* which were covered with snow[1] and not long after those of *Mowee*, a little lower than the former. I let out more sail to approach, but I was still 7 or 8 Ls from land at nightfall. I spent the night tacking, waiting for daylight to enter the channel formed by these two islands and seek an anchorage to leeward of *Mowee*, near the island of Morikine.[2] The longitudes we observed were so much in agreement with those of Captain Cook that having adjusted our bearings with those of the English chart we had only a difference of 10′, being more E.

At 8 a.m. I saw *Mowhee* point bearing W. 15^{d} N. To the W. 22^{d} NN I could see an islet which the English were not in a position to notice and which does not appear on their chart[3] which, for this area, is very inadequate whereas everything they drew from their own observations deserves the highest praise. The island of *Mowhee* looked delightful; I coasted along it one L. offshore. The coast trends SW ¼W. We could see waterfalls tumbling down the mountainside into the sea, after providing water for the natives' homes; these are so numerous that one might mistake an area of 3 or 4 Ls for a single village; but all the huts were along the seashore and the mountains are so close that it seemed to me that the space available for habitations was less than half a league in depth. One needs to be a sailor and be reduced as we were, in these hot climates, to a bottle of water a day to understand our feelings: the trees crowning the mountains, the greenery, the banana trees we could see around the houses, all this gave rise to a feeling of inexpressible delight; but the waves were breaking wildly against the rocks and, like new Tantaluses,

[1] The Hawaiian Islands have a semi-tropical climate, and snow is found only on the highest peaks. La Pérouse sighted the top of Mauna Kea (4,205 m), the 'white mountain', and since he uses the plural probably also saw Mauna Loa (4,169 m) which is occasionally snow-covered. He later had a view of Heleakala (3,055 m) on Maui, which can also be snow-covered.

[2] This is Cook's Morokinne, the small island of Molokini, between Maui and Kahoolawe at the northern end of Alalakeiki Channel.

[3] It should be borne in mind that La Pérouse uses the Paris longitude and that when he compares his readings with those of Cook's charts, he has to adjust his calculations to take into account the English use of the Greenwich longitude. There are three tiny islets, uninhabited rocks, which could qualify for La Pérouse's islet at this point. Two are shown on the French chart, but neither is named.

we were reduced to yearning, devouring with our eyes what was beyond our reach.

The winds had strengthened and we were sailing at 2 Ls an hour. I wanted to complete the survey of all this part of the coastline before nightfall as far as Morokine where I hoped to find an anchorage that was sheltered from the trade winds; this plan, forced on me by the overriding circumstances in which we were placed, did not allow me to shorten sail so as to wait for some 150 canoes coming to us from the shore, laden with fruit and pigs which the natives intended to barter for pieces of iron.

Nearly all these canoes came up to one or the other frigate, but our speed was such that they filled with water once alongside us; the natives were forced to let go of the rope we had thrown down to them – they jumped into the water and swam after their pigs, and bringing them back in their arms they then lifted their canoes over their shoulders, emptied the water and happily clambered back in, endeavouring to row back to the position they had forsaken near our frigates and which others had at once taken over until the same misfortune befell them; I saw over 40 canoes swamped in this manner, so that although our trading with these good people was greatly welcomed by both parties we were unable to obtain more than 15 pigs and a little fruit, and possibly missed the chance of buying another 300.

The canoes were equipped with an outrigger. Each one carried 3 to 5 men. The length of the average canoe was possibly 24 feet, with one foot in width and much the same in depth.[1] I weighed one of this size which did not exceed fifty pounds. It is with such frail craft that the inhabitants of these islands undertake journeys of 60 Ls, crossing channels where the sea can be very rough, 20 leagues wide like those of the island of *Atooi* and that of *Woahoo*[2] but they are such good swimmers that only seals could be fairly compared with them.

[1] La Pérouse's measurements are correct. David Samwell, surgeon on Cook's third voyage, reported them as being 'generally five to 7 or 8 yards long' and Cook himself states that in general they are 24 feet long. It is possible, of course, that La Pérouse was merely using Cook's measurements. See Cook, *Journals*, III, pp. 282, 1183.

[2] The islands are Kauai and Oahu, separated by the Kauai Channel which is some 75 miles wide. The name Atooi is found on Cook's charts, spelled at times Atowai. The difference in spelling is due to the pronunciation of the letter k as a t, so that, as David Samwell had pointed out, 'Atowai' becomes 'Akowai at Ouwaihee'. See Cook, *Journals*, III, p. 1231.

As we sailed, the mountains receded towards the interior of the island which displayed itself to us in the shape of a relatively vast amphitheatre, but yellow-green. We saw no more waterfalls, the trees were fairly sparsely planted along the plain, and the villages, consisting only of 10 or 12 huts, were quite distant from each other. Every moment made us regret the country we were leaving behind, and we only found shelter when we were faced with a frightful shore, where the lava had once run down as waterfalls do today in the other part of the island.

After sailing S.W ¼ up to the S.W. point of the island of *Mowee*[1] I veered W. and then S.W. to reach the anchorage which the *Astrolabe* had already selected in 23 fathoms, very hard grey sandy bottom, ⅓ of a league from land; we were sheltered from the sea breeze by a large headland topped by clouds whence came from time to time some fierce gusts of winds. The wind veered constantly so that we dragged on our anchors, and – as if this bay was not bad enough – we had to cope with currents which prevented us from veering head on to the wind except during the strong gusts, and made the sea so rough that our boats had great difficulty in working; nevertheless I sent one immediately to take soundings around the ships; the officer reported that the bottom was the same up to the shore, diminishing gradually to 7 fathoms within 2 cablelengths from land; but when we weighed anchor I noticed that the cable was badly damaged and that there were a great many rocks about which may have been covered by a very thin layer of sand.

Natives from villages in this part of the island hastened to come up to the ships in their canoes, bringing goods to barter, such as pigs, sweet potatoes, bananas, arum roots (which the natives call taro)[2] with some cloth and other curiosities forming part of their attire. I was prepared to allow them to come aboard only after the frigate was at anchor and the sails furled: I told them this was *taboo* and this word, which I knew from the English narrative, had all the effect I was hoping; Mr de Langle who had not taken the same

[1] This marks the entrance to present-day La Perouse Bay where the mountain ridges come down to the sea from Haleakala, to which the large headland referred to also belongs. North of the bay is the small village of Makena.

[2] La Pérouse uses the colourful term *pied de veau*, just as English has 'cuckoo-pint', 'lords-and-ladies' and 'wake-robin' to describe the *Arum maculatum*. The taro plant is a member of the same *Araceae* family, the *Colocasia antiquorum*.

precaution found the deck of his frigate disrupted by a crowd of these natives, but they were so docile that it was quite easy to persuade them to return to their canoes. I had not expected such a gentle and considerate people: when I allowed them to come up on board my frigate, they did not make a single move without our permission – they seemed always concerned not to incur our displeasure: they were most meticulous in their bartering; our old metal hoops appealed greatly to them, and they were very skilful in their attempts to obtain them; they never sold a quantity of cloth or several pigs as one lot, fully aware that they would get a better deal by agreeing on a price for each item.

This familiarity with trade, this knowledge of iron which, from their own evidence, they did not get from the English, are new proofs of the intercourse which these people had with the Spanish in early times.[1] That nation, a century ago, had very good reasons

[1] La Pérouse added a long marginal note:

'It seems certain to me that these islands were first discovered by Gaëtan in 1542. This navigator left from the port of Navidad on the west coast of Mexico in 20^d^. He sailed W. and after 100 Ls along this point of the compass (consequently without changing latitude) he sighted a group of islands inhabited by natives who were almost naked: these islands were defended by reefs, they had coconuts and other fruit, but neither gold nor silver. He named them Los Reyes, presumably on account of the day on which he made this discovery, and he named Jardines the island he found 20 Ls further west. It would have been impossible, from this account, for geographers not to place Gaëtan's discoveries exactly where Captain Cook has since found the Sandwich Islands, but the author of the Spanish journal adds that they are situated between the 9th and 11th degree of latitude, instead of saying between the 19th and the 21st as every sailor should deduce from Gaëtan's route. Is the omission of this half-score a slip of the pen, or a political move by the Spanish court who, a century ago, had a real interest in concealing the position of all this ocean's islands? I am inclined to think it is a slip of the pen, because it would have been clumsy to publish that Gaëtan, having sailed from 20° of latitude, followed a direct W. course; if one had intended to mislead readers about the latitude, it would not have been difficult to have him sail in a different direction. Whatever the truth may be, everything agrees, but for the half-score which should be added to Gaëtan's latitude: the same distance from the coast of Mexico, the same people, the same types of fruit, the coral, the same area from N. to S. The position of the Sandwich Islands being approximately between the 19th and 21st degrees, just as Gaëtan's are between the 9th and the 11th, this new proof, added to all those one has already read, seems to me to turn this geographical question into unchallengeable evidence. I could add that there is no island group between the 9th and the 11th degrees – it is the normal route of the Manila galleon.

The argument over the prior discovery of the Hawaiian group by Spanish navigators nevertheless comes up against the fact that other Spanish navigators were never

to conceal the existence of these islands because the western seas of America were infested by pirates who would have found food supplies among these islanders, but who on the contrary were forced to sail W. towards the Indian seas or return to the Atlantic sea by way of Cape Horn. When Spanish voyages to the west were reduced to the single Manila galleon, I believe that this ship, which carried great riches, was compelled by its owners to follow a route that lessened their risks and consequently the cost of insurance (if it was insured), and so possibly that nation gradually lost even the recollection of the existence of these islands which only appear on their old charts, according to which the cartographer of Cook's 3rd voyage included them on his but, as I have already pointed out, 15° too far E.[1] It was so late by the time our sails were furled that I had to put off until the morrow the landing I was intending to make on this island where nothing could cause me to tarry, except a convenient watering place – but we could already see that this part of the coast was deficient in watercourses, as the slope of the mountains kept the rainfall on the weather side. It is possible that just a few days' work on the mountain peaks would be enough to make

---

given any knowledge of it: even though the islands might have provided a base for pirates, and although the Manila galleon kept to its pre-determined route, the presence of islands not too far away, where their ships could find a refuge in a sudden storm would have been of considerable value to the Spanish. Nor would they have resisted the temptation to attempt a settlement on the islands, considering their efforts to found colonies in the south-western Pacific, among the Solomons or on Espiritu Santo. Reports of Gaetan's discoveries furthermore suggest that the islands were relatively low-lying and small, whereas no discoverer could have failed to be impressed by the mountain peaks of the Hawaiian islands. On the other hand, there are tantalising hints of early contacts between the Spanish and the Hawaiians. See, among other studies, E.W. Dahlgren's 'Were the Hawaiian islands visited by the Spaniards before their discovery by Captain Cook in 1778?' *Kungl. Svenska Vet. Handl.*, 57, No.4 (1916), pp. 1–220; J.F.G. Stokes, 'Hawaii's Discovery by Spaniards: Theories Traced and Refuted', *Papers of the Hawaiian Historical Society*, 20 (1939), pp. 38–113; Cook, *Journals*, III, pp. cxvi–cxvii; and note in particular Dahlgren's careful wording: '...visited by the Spaniards...discovery by Captain Cook.'

[1] The charts were drawn by Henry Roberts (1747?–96) who had sailed on Cook's second voyage before joining the *Resolution* as master's mate. Lt Gore referred to him as an assistant hydrographer. William Bligh, however, complained in a letter to James Burney of 26 July 1791 that the charts of the Sandwich Islands were his own work and not Roberts's who merely prettified them, Cook, *Journals*, III, p. 1565. However, Bligh's difficult character is now well-known, and Roberts was certainly the author of a number of charts as well as the General Chart published in the official *A Voyage to the Pacific Ocean in the years 1776...1780*, London, 1784, a copy of which was in La Pérouse's shipboard library together with its French translation of 1785.

such a precious commodity available to all the island, but these natives have not yet reached such a degree of civilisation; it is nevertheless very advanced in certain respects. The English narratives have made their form of government known, and the high degree of discipline which reigns among these islanders proves the existence of an accepted system of authority running from the king to the least of the chiefs and bears on the lower class. My imagination compared them to the inhabitants of Easter Island whose arts are at least as advanced; the monuments put up by them show even a greater intelligence, their cloth is better made and their houses better built, but their government is so democratic that, as no one has the right to put an end to unruliness, they behave like children, admit of no authority and, although I do not see them as bad, all too frequently licence brings about harmful – often fatal-consequences. Comparing the two people, I favoured the inhabitants of the Sandwich Islands, even though, on account of the death of Captain Cook, I was prejudiced against them. It is more natural for navigators to feel regret at the loss of so great a man than to assess coolly whether some imprudent action on his part did not, in some way, compel the inhabitants of *Owhyhee* to have recourse to a justified defence.

Apart from a few squalls which lasted less than 2 minutes, the night was very calm. At daybreak, the *Astrolabe*'s longboat was lowered with Messrs de Vaujuas, Boutin and Bernizet. They had instructions to take soundings in a very deep bay which bore N.W. from us where I suspected the anchorage might be better than ours; but, although convenient, it was not much better than the one we were in, from what these three officers reported, and generally speaking this part of *Mowee* offers navigators neither water nor wood and, providing only very poor sheltering areas must very seldom be frequented.

At 8 a.m., four boats were ready to go ashore from the two frigates; the first two had 20 armed soldiers under the command of Lieutenant de Pierrevert. Mr de Langle and I, together with all the passengers and the officers who were not kept on board through their duties, went in the other two. All this array did not frighten off the canoes who came alongside our ships at dawn. The natives continued to trade, did not follow us to land and kept the confident air which their faces had never lost. Some hundred and twenty people, men and women, were waiting for us on the shore. The soldiers landed first with their officer who laid out a space we wanted to reserve for ourselves; they had their bayonets fixed and carried out their manoeuvres with the same precision as if they had been in the presence of the enemy. These rather frightening activities made no impression on the inhabitants; the women indicated by the most explicit signs that there were no limits to the kindness they were willing to show us; the men were waiting most respectfully until they could guess what the purpose of our visit might be, so that they might meet our wishes.[1] Two natives who seemed to hold some sway over the others came forward, and made a fairly long speech of which I did not understand one word; they each offered me a pig, which I accepted, giving them in return some medals, axes and pieces of iron which were for them gifts of inestimable value. My generosity made the greatest impression: the women displayed even greater signs of friendship, but they were not very attractive; their features lacked any delicacy, and their costume revealed among most of them indications of the ravages caused by venereal diseases. Since none had come aboard from the canoes, I thought that they laid on Europeans the blame for the illnesses of which they bore traces, but I soon realised that, if such was their belief, we were forgiven. I will here hazard my theories, which would have no weight were it not that they are shared by Mr Rollin, my surgeon, a man of considerable wisdom. Both of us are convinced that modern navigators are not guilty of the crime for which they take the blame in their narratives. Mr Rollin saw ill-effects which, in Europe, would have needed twelve or fifteen years to reach such a stage; he examined children aged seven or eight who could only owe their disease to the womb that bore them; but one reads in the English accounts that Captain Cook, who on his first visit only called at *Attoï* and *Oneeheow*, found on his return from the N. nine months later that almost all the inhabitants of Mowee who came up to his vessel in their canoes were affected by this

[1] The welcome and respect accorded to James Cook when he first landed are well known. La Pérouse was not received by men who prostrated themselves before him, but there is no doubt that he was being treated as a personage of high rank. The district visited by La Pérouse became depopulated and M. M. Dondo, writing in 1958, reported that all he could find were traces of ancient habitations and that he could only just make out the outline of the former villages. M. M. Dondo, *La Pérouse in Maui*, Hawaii, 1959, p. 54.

sickness.[1] Since *Mowee* is 60 Ls to windward of *Attooy* it seems to me that this progress would have been very rapid. Being anyhow convinced that these islanders had been in contact with the Spanish in earlier times, I think that it is only too likely that they have been in the same situation as other people for a long time. It is furthermore still unproven that Nature, which everywhere dispenses both good and evil, did not distribute this disease much more widely, and that its genealogy is not merely due to an inflexibility of reasoning.[2]

I felt that I owed this discussion to modern navigators. The whole of Europe, misled by their own accounts, would have reproached them for ever for a crime which the leaders of expeditions thought they had failed to prevent; it would have been said, with justification, that iron, plants, trees and animals were a feeble compensation for such evils.

But all these truths might have had only a ghost to fight. So the only reproach one has to make to these leaders of expeditions is that they took insufficient precautions and that these did not achieve their aims, and although a new disease might not have resulted from their carelessness, it is not proved either that the presence of Europeans did not lead to a greater activity on the part of this poison, and that the consequences of this disease are not more frightening today.

[1] James Cook discovered the islands on 18 January 1778, landing on Kauai. He returned on 26 November, some tenth months later, landing this time on Maui, later going on to Hawaii.

[2] La Pérouse's editor, Milet-Mureau, adds the comment that Bougainville was convinced that Pacific islanders travelled among the various islands, with the implication that diseases could easily be carried from one group to another. The question of which navigator was responsible for the introduction of venereal diseases into the various islands has exercised many minds both in the past and today; the simplistic assumption has usually been that they did not exist before the arrival of the first Europeans and almost all the navigators – including James Cook in the Hawaiian group – took whatever precautions they could to prevent infected sailors from going ashore; almost inevitably, these proved ineffective. According to Edward Riou, of the *Discovery*, Cook's precautions failed to protect the Hawaiians who blamed the English for introducing this plague to their homeland, Cook, *Journals*, III, pp. 474–7. The French, however, encountered no suspicion or blame, which either suggests that the Hawaiians did not blame Cook, or that they recognised La Pérouse as belonging to a different nation or tribe. Another factor, often overlooked, is the similarity between the effects of yaws (*Spirochaeta pallidula*), which is endemic in the Pacific, and those of syphillis (*Spirochaeta pallida*), both producing ugly-looking ulcers which a ship's surgeon of the time would have had difficulty in identifying correctly.

After visiting the village, I ordered 6 soldiers, led by a sergeant, to accompany us. I left the others on the shore under the leadership of Mr de Pierrevert. Their task was to guard our boats, from which no sailor had landed.

Although the French are the first to have stepped onto the island of *Mowee* in recent times, I did not take possession of it in the King's name. This European practice is too utterly ridiculous, and philosophers must reflect with some sadness that, because one has muskets and canons, one looks upon 60 000 inhabitants as worth nothing, ignoring their rights over a land where for centuries their ancestors have been buried, which they have watered with their sweat, and whose fruits they pick to bring them as offerings to the so-called new landlords. It is fortunate for these people that they have been discovered in an age when religion is no longer a pretext for violence and greed. Modern navigators have no other purpose when they describe the customs of newly discovered people than to complete the story of mankind. Their navigation must round off our knowledge of the globe, and the enlightenment which they try to spread has no other aim than to increase the happiness of the islanders they meet, as they add to their means of subsistence by introducing in the different islands bulls, cows, goats, ewes, rams, etc. They have also planted trees and sowed seeds from every country, and brought iron tools which should enable their skills to make very rapid progress. We would have felt ourselves well rewarded for the great hardships this campaign has caused us if we had succeeded in eradicating the practice of human sacrifices that is common among most of the South Sea islanders; yet, in spite of the opinion of Mr Anderson and of Captain Cook, I believe with Captain King that such a good, gentle and welcoming people is not a nation of cannibals.[1] A fearsome religion is perhaps not incompatible with gentleness of manners, and since Captain King says in his narrative that the priests of *Owhyhee* were their best friends, I must conclude that, as gentleness and humanity have made progress among that class of society, which has charge of human

[1] William Anderson (1748?–78) was surgeon on board the *Resolution*; he has left an account of the voyage in which he gives a fairly lengthy commentary on human sacrifices, based on an episode in the Society Islands. He died on 3 August 1778 before the discovery of Hawaii. James King who served as lieutenant in the *Resolution* and the *Discovery* wrote the third volume of *A Voyage to the Pacific Ocean in the years 1776...1780*.

HAWAIIAN ISLANDS

5. Part of the Hawaiian Islands, showing the track of the frigates along the south coast of Maui, by Blondela. Notes indicate that the latitudes were checked with the sextant and the longitudes determined by lunar observations and with the chronometer No. 18. AN 6 JJ1:28A.

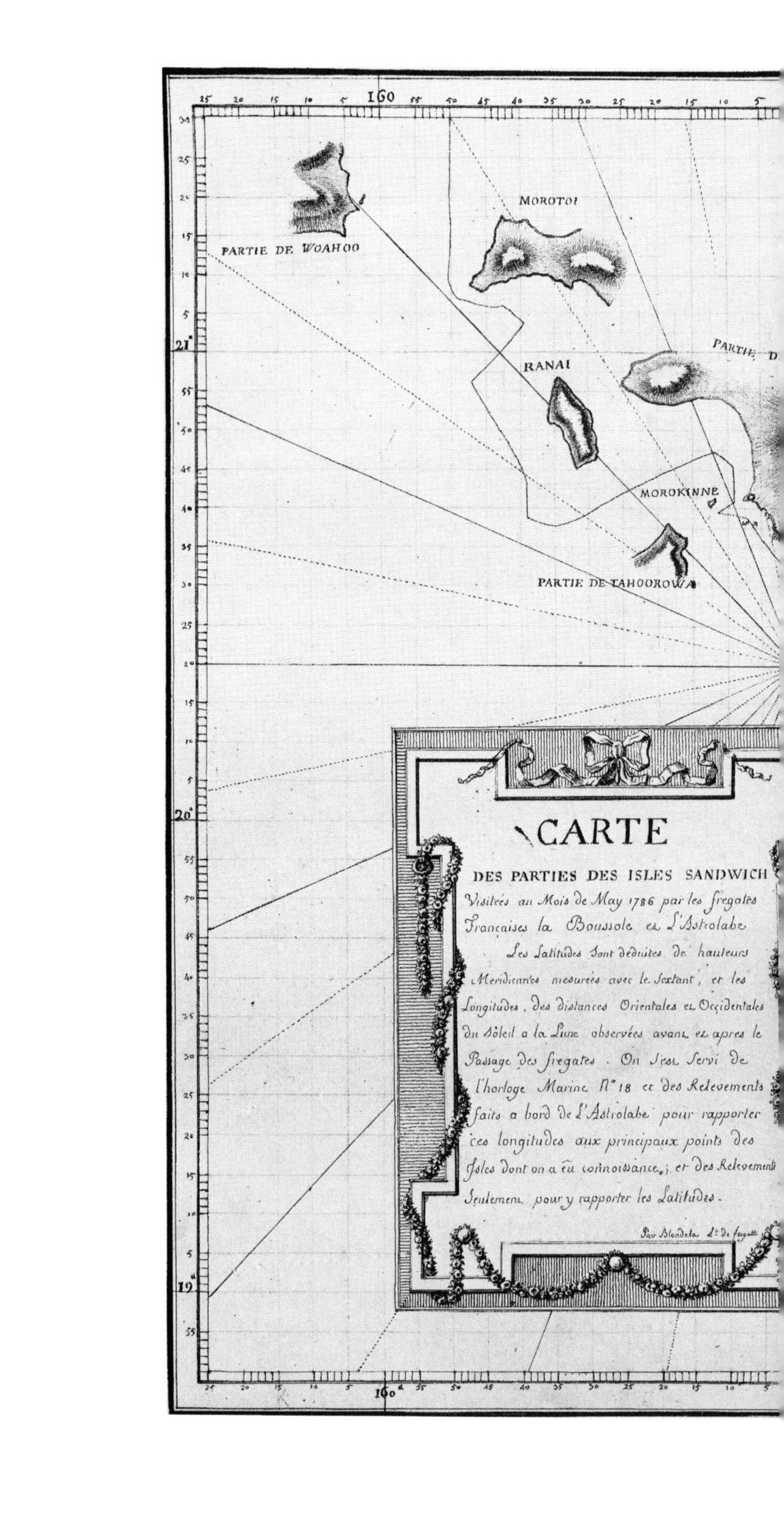
PARTIE DE WOAHOO
MOROTOI
RANAI
MOROKINNE
PARTIE DE TAHOOROWA
CARTE
DES PARTIES DES ISLES SANDWICH
Visitées au Mois de May 1786 par les fregates
Françaises la Boussole et L'Astrolabe
Les Latitudes sont deduites de hauteurs
Meridiennes mesurées avec le Sextant, et les
Longitudes, des distances Orientales et Occidentales
du Soleil a la Lune observées avant et apres le
Passage des fregates. On s'est servi de
l'horloge Marine N° 18 et des Relevements
faits a bord de L'Astrolabe pour rapporter
ces longitudes aux principaux points des
Isles dont on a eu connoissance; et des Relevements
seulement pour y rapporter les Latitudes.
Par Blondela Lt. de fregatte

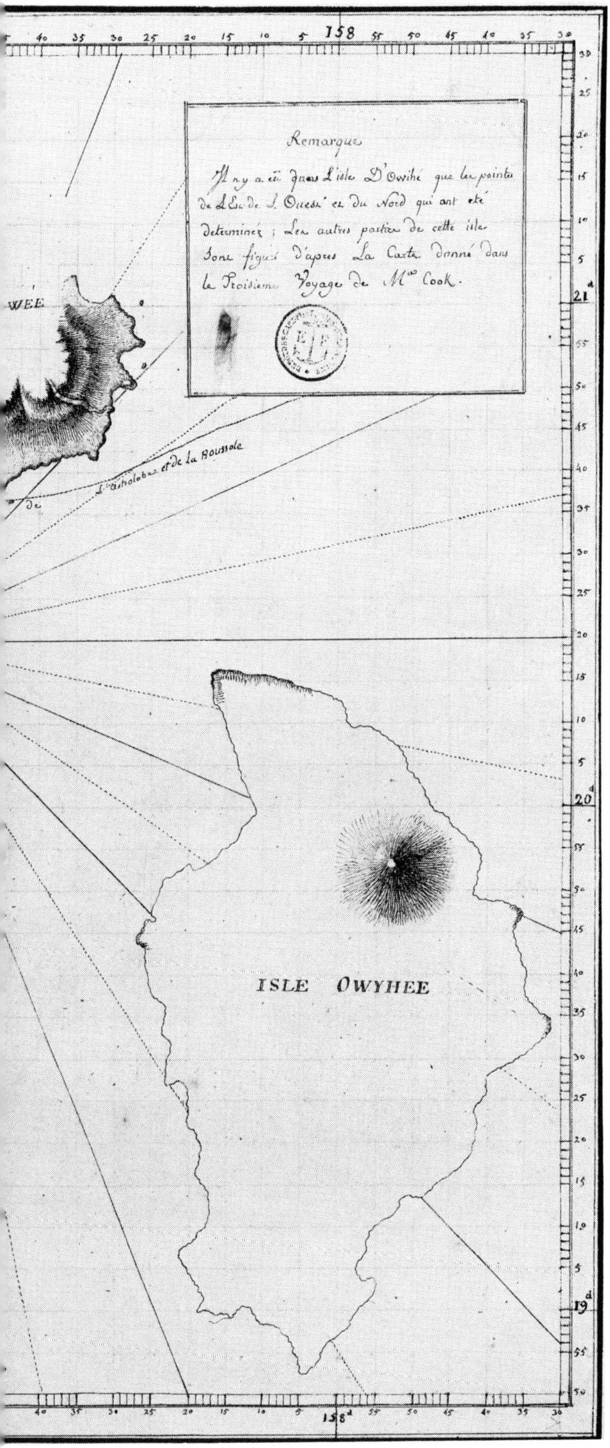

158

Remarque

Il n'y a eu dans l'isle D'Owihé que les pointes de L'Est de L'Ouest et du Nord qui ont été determinez ; Les autres parties de cette isle sont figurés d'apres La Carte donné dans le Troisieme Voyage de Mr Cook.

WEE

L'Astrolabe et de la Boussole

de

21d

20d

ISLE OWYHEE

19d

158d

6. Promerops, California, by J. R. Prévost the younger. SHM 352:15.

sacrifices and presumably profits from their victims, the remainder of the inhabitants must be even less ferocious, and I have no doubt that cannibalism has come to an end among these islanders, although in all probability quite recently.

The soil of the island we visited consists of debris of lava and other volcanic matter; the inhabitants drink only a brackish water obtained in shallow wells that yield no more than half a barrel of water a day. On our walk we came upon four small villages of 10 to 12 houses; they are built and roofed with straw and ressemble those of our poorest peasants, the roofs are coupled, the door is usually situated at the gable end, it is only 3 ½ feet in height and one has to bend to enter – it consists of a small screen which anyhow can open.[1] Their furnishings are merely mats which, like our carpets, make a very clean floor on which these natives sleep. Their only kitchen utensils are gourds of a large size to which they give the desired shape when they are still green; they varnish them and paint various designs on them in black. I saw some which had been glued together, making vases of a substantial size – apparently this glue is damp-resistant and it would have been interesting to discover what it is made with.[2] Their cloth, which they possess in abundance, is made, as is the case with all these people, with the *Morus papiraceûs* – one knows it is a kind of paper,[3] but it seemed to be more roughly made although painted with a wider range of designs. When I came back, I was again addressed by women waiting for me under some trees who offered me several lengths of cloth which I accepted, paying them with axes and nails.

The reader should not expect to find here details on people who

[1] A watercolour by John Webber, 'An Island View in Atooi', now in the British Museum, which was the basis of an engraving in the published narrative of Cook's third voyage, confirms La Pérouse's description. William Ellis's 'A View of Karakacooah Bay, O'whyhee', gives a similar impression. See on these Anthony Murray-Oliver's *Captain Cook's Hawaii as seen by his Artists*, Wellington, 1975.

[2] James Cook had already noted the importance in Hawaiian domestic life of the gourds in which the women made *poi*, a taro-based gruel: 'A few gourds and wooden bowls, make up this whole catalogue of of household utensils.', Cook, *Journals*, III, p. 283. The *kukui* (*Aleurites mulccana*) produces a gum from which the Hawaiians made a varnish which they coloured by mixing in charcoal.

[3] The Hawaiian *kapa* is made from the bark of the *Brossonetia papyrifera*. Its local name is *wauke*. Cook had also bought large quantities of this cloth. A partial list will be found in Adrienne L. Kaepler's *Artificial Curiosities*, Honolulu, 1978; various details and descriptions had appeared in *A Catalogue of the Different Specimens of Cloth Collected in the Three Voyages of Captain Cook to the Southern Hemisphere*, London, 1787.

have become so well known from accounts written by the English. They spent 4 months in these islands, whereas we stayed only a few hours. They had the added advantage of knowing the local language. We must therefore limit ourselves to telling our own story.

We re-embarked at 11 o'clock in very good order, with no confusion, and without having the slightest complaint to make against anyone. We arrived on board at midday; Mr de Clonard had entertained a chief from whom he had bought a fine helmet of red feathers with a cloak,[1] and had also obtained over a hundred pigs, some bananas, sweet potatoes, taro, a great deal of cloth, some mats, an outrigger canoe and sundry other small items of feathers and shells. When we reached our vessels, they were dragging their anchors, and there was a strong E.S.E. gale. We were drifting towards the island of *Morokine* which however was still some distance away, giving time to Mr de Langle and I to haul up our boats. I gave the signal to weigh anchor, but before this could be done I had to let out some canvas to drag it until we were past *Morokine* so that we were drifting only in the channel: if the anchor had caught on some rock and the bottom was not hard enough to enable it to slip over it I would have been forced to cut the cable.

We did not finally raise our anchor until 5 p.m. It was too late to set a course between the island of *Ranai* and the W. of *Mowee*; this was a new channel which I wanted to survey, but it was unwise to attempt it at night.[2] We had unsteady winds until 8 o'clock, which meant we made hardly half a league. Finally the wind settled N.E. I set a W. course, passing at an equal distance between the N.W. point of *Tahoorowa*[3] and the S.W. point of the island of *Ranai*. At dawn I set sail for the S.W. point of *Morotoi* island and coasted along it at a distance of ¾ of a league and emerged, like the English, through the channel which separates the island of *Woahoo* from *Morotoi* which did not seem to me to be inhabited in this part,

[1] These helmets, called *mahiole*, were made with the valuable feathers of the *iiwi* (*Vestiaria coccines* Forster) and the *apapane* (*Himatione sanguinea* Gmelin). Yellow feathers were rarer and of greater value. There were local differences in style with a symbolic significance which is now largely unknown. See on these P. Buck, *Arts and Crafts of Hawaii*, Honolulu, 1957.

[2] The island of Lanai is situated west of Maui and separated by it by Auau Channel.

[3] La Pérouse is following Cook's spellings as well as his route. Tahoorawa is Kahoolawe, just as Morotoi is Molokai which is separated from Oahu by Kaiwi Channel.

although the English accounts state that it is populated in others. It is remarkable that in these islands, the more fertile and healthy regions and consequently the most populated are always to windward. Our islands of Guadeloupe, Martinique, etc, are so like this new group that everything struck me as almost the same, at least in respect of navigation.

Messrs Dagelet and Bernizet took, with the greatest care, the bearings of the part of *Mowee* we sailed along, as well as of the island of *Morokine*. The English, who never came any closer than 10′, could not have given any precise details on them. The latter drew a very good chart to which Mr Dagelet added astronomical readings which are as reliable as those of Captain Cook, and which for the convenience of readers feature in the tables they will find at the end of each volume; they indicate our daily route and our precise position in latitude and longitude, both observed and by dead reckoning.

On 1 June at 6 p.m. we were away from all the islands. We had spent less than 48 hours on this survey, and a fortnight at most to clear up a question of geography which seemed to me of great importance since it removes from the maps five or six non-existent islands. But the fish which had followed us from the neighbourhood of Easter Island up to the anchorage disappeared – since we now had to sail N. we would not have kept them with us for long. A matter worth recording is that the same shoal travelled 1500 Ls with our frigates, that several bonitos which had been wounded by our small harpoons bore the scars on their backs, a form of identification we could not mistake, and thus we recognised every day the same fish we had seen the day before. I have no doubt that if we had not put in at the Sandwich Islands they would have followed us for another two or three hundred leagues, until we reached a temperature they could not have withstood.

CHAPTER VII

Departure from the Sandwich Islands. The trade winds cease at the 30th degree of latitude. Thick fog succeeds them. Birds and seaweed announce the approach of the coast of America. We sight Mt St Elias. We sail along the coast 3 or 4 leagues from the shore. Discovery and survey of Monty Bay by our boats. Our reasons for seeking a better anchorage. We send our boats to examine a very large and wide river. They struggle in vain to enter it and find a sandbank at water level where the currents have made two openings and where the waves break as on the bar at Bayonne. This river being more or less where Captain Cook named Behering Bay, I have kept its name of Behering River. We continue coasting 2 or 3 leagues from shore and find the entrance to a deep bay. We send officers to examine it; they bring back a favourable report. Reasons for our decision to put in there. Risks we run upon entering. Description of this bay which I have named French Bay. Practices and customs of the inhabitants. Our barter with them. In a few days we lay in all the supplies of water and wood we require and, just as we were going to leave, we suffer the greatest misfortune. Narrative of this event. We return to our first anchorage in the W. bay near the entrance, and finally set sail on 31 July, 19 days after the shipwreck of our two boats.

The E. winds continued until we reached latitude 30°. I set a course for the N. The weather was fine and the fresh food we had obtained during our brief call at the Sandwich Islands ensured for three weeks a supply of good and healthy food for the crews of both frigates. However, we were unable to keep our pigs alive for want of food and water; I was forced to have them salted in accordance with Captain Cook's method, but as these pigs were very small, most of them weighing less than 20 pounds, the meat could not be left too long to the action of the salt which would have quickly spoilt and destroyed its substance, and we had to eat it before our other supplies.

On 6 June, in 30^{d} of latitude, the winds veered S.E. The sky became a dull white. Everything indicated that we had left the trade wind area, and I was afraid that we would soon be regretting the fine weather which had kept us in good health and which had enabled us, almost every day, to take lunar readings or at least to check our chronometers.

The fears I harboured about the possibility of fog were soon realised. It appeared on 9 June in 34^{d} of latitude and there was no break in it until the 14th of the same month in $41^{d.}$ My first impression was that these seas were beset with thicker fogs than those which separate Europe from America: I would have been quite mistaken if I had kept to this view, and the fogs of Acadia, Newfoundland and Hudson's Bay[1] undeniably outclass these by their thickness and their persistence. But it was extremely damp, and fog or rain had affected all the sailors' clothing; there was never a ray of sunshine which might have dried it out, and I had had a sad experience during my campaign in Hudson's Bay which led me to suspect that damp cold may be the most active cause of scurvy.[2] As yet no one was affected, but we all no doubt were susceptible to the disease after such a long period at sea. I gave instructions to set buckets of live charcoal under the fo'c'sle and the 'tween-deck where the men slept. I gave out a pair of boots to each sailor and soldier, and the vests and cloth trousers which had been packed up by my orders when we came out of the Cape Horn seas were returned to them.

My surgeon who shared all this work with Mr de Clonard also suggested to me that we should mix a small infusion of *cinchona* to

[1] Acadia, part of what is now New Brunswick and Nova Scotia, was originally a French colony which dated back to the early seventeenth century. It was lost to England in 1713 by the Treaty of Utrecht. In 1755 several thousand French Acadians were deported, an action which caused strong reactions in France and led to an attempt by Louis de Bougainville to settle some of them on the Falkland Islands. La Pérouse became familiar with this part of Canada and with conditions in Hudson Bay during the American War of Independence.

[2] It is interesting to note how even a senior and experience officer such as La Pérouse could theorise on the effects of climate on the incidence of scurvy. The steps he took to protect his men from scurvy were inspired more by James Cook's example than by the views of French naval surgeons. As becomes apparent a little later, he was also concerned that his sailors' innate conservatism might lead them to reject unusual dietary precautions; Cook had to resort to threats and punishments, but La Pérouse turned to subterfuge to make his men drink a little quinine with their grog.

the lunchtime grog.[1] Without altering the taste of the drink, it could have a very salutary effect. I had to order that this mixture should be prepared in secret; without this secrecy the sailors would certainly have refused to drink their grog, but as no one noticed there were no complaints about this novelty which would have met with serious opposition if it had been submitted to everyone's comments.

These various precautions were most successful, but they were not our only concerns during such a long crossing: my carpenter constructed from Mr de Langle's plans a wheat grinding mill which proved of great value.

The supervisors of our food supplies, persuaded that dried grain kept better than flour or biscuit, had suggested that we take on board a very large quantity of it, which we had added to in Chile. We had been provided with millstones 24 inches in diameter and 4½ thick; 4 men were to operate them. We were assured that the Bailli de Suffren[2] had had no other to supply the bread needed by his squadron; there was thus no reason to doubt that they would be quite adequate for crews as small as ours, but when we came to use them the baker found that the grain was merely broken up and not milled, and a full day's labour by 4 men relieved every half hour had produced only 25 pounds of this mediocre flour: as our wheat made up almost half of our means of sustenance we would have been greatly troubled had it not been for Mr de Langle's ingenuity who, with the help of a sailor named Robin[3] who once had been a miller's assistant, thought of adapting the principle of the windmill to our little millstones; he tried at first with some success to use sails which the wind turned, but he soon replaced them with a crank; in this way we obtained as good a flour as from ordinary mills and we could grind two quintals daily.

[1] The grog served by the French navy consisted of one part of brandy to two of water, whereas the British navy usually served rum. La Pérouse comments in a marginal note that grog was 'much safer for crews than neat brandy.'

[2] Pierre-André de Suffren, Marquis of Saint-Tropez (1729–88), French admiral, took part in numerous naval engagements from 1743 until his death in December 1788 when he was about to take command of a fleet in Brest. He gained great renown for his daring and bold strategy, in particular in the Indian Ocean in 1782–3. He had served in the Mediterranean to protect the ships and outposts of the Order of Malta and was given the rank of Bailli of the order in recognition of his services.

[3] The man in question is Laurent Robin who was to be killed in the Samoa group in December 1787.

On the 14th, the winds having veered W.S.W., the sky cleared, usually when the winds were just a few degrees N. of W., the sun then appeared along the horizon; when from W. to S.W., the sky was overcast with a little rain; when from S.W. to S.E. and as far as E., the horizon was hazy with a great deal of damp which reached into our cabins and penetrated throughout the ship. Thus a simple glance at the wind table will always indicate the state of the sky to our readers. This observation is of value for later navigators, and readers who will be kindhearted enough to combine the pleasure they may gain from reading about this campaign with some thought for those who underwent these hardships may perhaps see with interest navigators, after a year at sea, struggling at the ends of the earth against fog, bad weather and scurvy along an unknown coast, which once upon a time was the setting for geographical tales that are too readily accepted by modern geographers.[1]

This part of America as far as Mount St Elias in 60^{d} was only glimpsed by Captain Cook, except for the port of Nootka where he

[1] La Pérouse added a footnote to his manuscript: 'These tales are the voyage of Admiral Fuentes and the pretended navigations of the Chinese and the Japanese on this coast'. His reference is to the voyage of Admiral Bartolomeo de Fonte, who as 'Admiral of New Spain and Peru and Prince of Chile' was reputed to have sailed from Callao in 1640 with four ships and, having penetrated into a deep North American inlet, met a certain Captain Shapley who was on his way out, having sailed from Boston and followed a series of lakes and rivers. The story appeared in the *Monthly Miscellany or Memoirs for the Curious*, London, 1708, and was subsequently used by Arthur Dodds in his *Account of the Countries adjoining to Hudson's Bay*, London, 1744. Dodds and others treated the voyage as factual and the French geographer Joseph-Nicolas Delisle, who learned about it during a stay in St Petersburg, included it in a memoir he presented to the French Academy of Sciences in 1750; collaborating with the cartographer Philippe Buache, he published a number of maps on this little known area, including a *Carte générale des découvertes de l'amiral de Fonte* (1752). To make matters worse, a certain Juan de Fuca, a Greek working for the Spanish authorities, reported on a voyage made to the Northwest Coast in 1592 when a passage leading into the interior of North America was supposedly discovered. Geographers' belief that a northern passage between the Atlantic and the Pacific oceans existed, equivalent to the Strait of Magellan in the south, helped the tales to become widely accepted as fact, in spite of denials by the Spanish, including Andres Burriel's early *Noticia de la California*, vol. III, Madrid, 1575. The Spanish, however, were believed to be eager to conceal the existence of the North-West Passage in order to keep other nations away from it. As for voyages by Chinese navigators, they were less likely to have occurred than some by Japanese sailors; both Chinese and Japanese rulers forbade overseas travels by their subjects, although Chinese sea trade was authorised towards the south. However, the 'Black Current' or Kuroshio from Japan to Alaska may have brought about accidental drift voyages by Japanese fishermen; see on this F. Kakubayashi, 'Japanese Drift Records and the Sharp Hypothesis', *Journal of the Polynesian Society*, 90, 4 (1981), pp. 514–24.

put in.[1] From Mount St Elias to the point of Alaska as far as Icy Cape, this famous sailor followed the coast with all the determination and courage of which all Europe knows he was capable; consequently, the exploration of that part of America which lies between Mount St Elias and the port of Monterey is a work of great importance for navigation and commerce; but it would require several years, and we do not hide the fact that, as we could only spare two or three months, on account of the time of year, and because of the vast programme of our expedition, we will leave a lot of detailed work to be done by later navigators: several centuries may pass before all the bays and ports of this part of America are thoroughly known; but the real trending of the coast, the latitude and the longitude of the more important features, ensure that our work will have a value that no sailor can overlook.

The winds were constantly favourable from the time we left the Sandwich Islands until we sighted Mount St Elias. As we progressed N. and approached America, we saw seaweed passing alongside, of a type that was quite new to us. A ball the size of an orange topped a hollow stem of 40 to 50 feet in length; this weed was like the stem of an onion plant which has gone to seed (but very much larger).[2] The largest of whales, the loons and the ducks also indicated the approach of land. Finally we saw it on the 23rd at 4 a.m. The fog, clearing, allowed us to see all of a sudden a long snow-covered mountain range – we could have seen it 30 leagues earlier if the weather had been clear: we identified Bhering's Mount St Elias, its peak visible above the clouds.[3]

The sight of land, which ordinarily makes such a pleasing impression after such a long navigation, did not have that effect on us.

[1] James Cook, coming from Hawaii, reached the American coast in bad weather near Cape Foulweather, in latitude 44°55′ N. He then proceeded north and northwest, whereas La Pérouse soon followed a southerly route.

[2] The weed in question was probably the *Pelagophycus* or *porra* for which the Spanish looked for as their galleon approached the continent. The broad description given to their pilots was of a seaweed with a very long stem ending in a yellow or reddish onion shape. See on this W. L. Schurz, *The Manila Galleon*, New York, 1939.

[3] Vitus Bering, a Dane in the service of Russia sailed on two major voyages of exploration from Kamchatka. On the second of these, he sailed in June 1741 with the *St Peter* and the *St Paul* which was commanded by Aleksei Chirikov. Separated from the latter, Bering sailed on to Alaska, sighting a range of mountain on 16 July; he named the highest Mt St Elias, the 20th of July being that saint's day. See *Who's Who*, pp. 24–6, 56–8.

The eye rested painfully upon all this snow covering a sterile and treeless land. The mountains seemed to be a little distance from the sea which was edged by a rocky plateau a hundred and fifty or two hundred *toises* in height, black as though it had been burned by a fire, lacking trees and greenery of any kind, which contrasted strikingly with the whiteness of the snow we could discern above the clouds; it formed the base of a long mountain range that seemed to stretch out for 15 Ls from E. to W.[1] At first we thought we were close to it; the crest of these mountains seemed to be above our heads and the snow gives out a light which deceives eyes that are not used to it, but as we advanced we saw in front of the plateau a lowlying land covered with trees which we took for islands behind which it was likely that we would find a shelter for our vessels as well as wood and water. I was planning to explore these so-called islands from quite close with the easterlies that blow along the coast, but they veered S. The sky became quite black in that part of the horizon; I thought it wiser to await a more favourable occasion and sail close to the wind along the coast. We had observed $59^{d}\ 21'$ at midday. Our chronometers gave a longitude of $143^{d}\ 23'$. A thick fog covered the land during the 25th, but on the 26th the weather was fine; the coast became visible at 2 a.m. with all its indentations; I sailed along it 2 leagues off. The sounding-line gave a depth of 75 fathoms, muddy bottom. I was very anxious to find a harbour and soon had hopes that I had found it.

I have already mentioned a plateau 150 to 200 *toises* in height which formed the base of enormous mountains a few leagues inland. We shortly noticed to the E. a low tree-covered headland which seemed to be attached to the plateau and end some distance from a second mountain range we could see further E. We were all fairly unanimous that that the plateau ended at this low tree-covered point and that it was an island separated from the mountains by a inlet probably running E. and W. as did the coastline, and that we would find a convenient haven for our ships in the supposed channel.

I set course for this headland, sounding repeatedly; the smallest depth was 45 fathoms, muddy bottom. At 2 p.m. the calms forced me to drop anchor; the breeze had been very weak all day, variable

[1] The St Elias Mountains extend from the Wrangel Mountains to the neighbourhood of Mt Fairweather; they are the highest coastal range in the world.

W. to N. At midday we observed 59^{d} 41′ and our chronometers indicated the longitude as 143^{d} 3′. We were 3 Ls S.W. of the headland which I still assumed to be an island. At 10 a.m. I had sent my frigate's longboat under Mr Boutin to examine the channel or bay; Messrs de Monti and de Vaujuas, each in a boat, had gone from the *Astrolabe* for the same purpose, and, at anchor, we were waiting for their return. The sea was very calm, the currents running S.S.W. at half a league an hour, which confirmed my feeling that if the wooded headland was not by a channel it was at least part of a large rivermouth.

The barometer had dropped 6 twelths in 24 hrs. The sky was very black; everything indicated that bad weather was about to replace the flat calm that had forced us to anchor: finally, at 9 p.m. our 3 boats were back, and the 3 officers were unanimous that there was no channel or river, and that the coastline merely curved to the N.E. into a fairly deep semi-circular bay; that the sounding-line indicated that the depth in the bay was 30 fathoms, muddy bottom; but that there was no shelter from the S.S.W. to E.S.E. winds which are the most dangerous. The waves broke strongly on the shore which was littered with driftwood. Mr de Monti had landed with great difficulty and, since he was in charge of this small group of boats, I named the bay Monti Bay.[1] They added that our mistake was due to the wooded headland being joined to much lower land, totally devoid of trees, which created the impression that it went no further. Messrs de Monti, de Vaujuas and Boutin had taken bearings of the various points of this bay, and it is from their measurements that Mr Bernizet drew a chart of it. Their joint report left no doubt on the course we had to follow; I gave the signal to weigh anchor and as the weather seemed so unpromising I took advantage of a light N.W. breeze to sail S.E. and get some 3 or 4 leagues from the coast.

The night was calm but foggy; the winds were constantly changing until eventually they settled E. from which quarter they blew very strongly for 24 hrs.

[1] La Pérouse was then in latitude 59°41′N; close by is Yakutat Bay which is in latitude 59°45′. There can be little doubt that this is Monti Bay. It is not a rivermouth, but, past the 'semi-circle' stretch of the bay itself, it contains several inlets and fjords fed by the snow and ice of the encompassing St Elias Mountains. This bay is still sometimes called Bering Bay, from Cook's identification with the Russian discovery; it was named Almirantazzo by the Spanish and Admiralty Bay by Nathaniel Portlock.

On the 28th the weather improved. We observed 59^d 19′ of latitude and, according to our chronometers, 142^d 41′ of longitude. The coast was very hazy and we could not identify the points we had seen the day before; the winds were still E., but the barometer was rising and everything indicated a change for the better. At 5 p.m. we were only 3 Ls from land with 40 fathoms, muddy bottom, and as the fog had cleared slightly we were able to take bearings which linked up with those of the previous day; the historical narrative of this voyage does not contain all the detail of these bearings, the reader will find the outcome of this work on our charts, and all the data we used have been handed over to the navy's Depot des Plans et Journaux[1] but navigators and serious students of geography will be glad to know that, in order to add greater precision to the views and sketches of the coastline or the more important features, Mr Dagelet took care to verify and correct the bearings taken by compass, by measuring the reciprocal distances of the bluffs, calculating with the sextant the angles they formed between them, and at the same determining the height of the mountains above sea level. This method, without being completely error-proof, is precise enough to enable navigators to judge at what distance they are from the coast by their elevation, and it was by this method that this academician was able to calculate the height of Mount St Elias at 1980 *toises* and its position at 8 leagues inland.[2]

On 29 June we observed 59^d 20′; our chronometers gave a longitude of 142^d 2′. We had made 8 Ls E. in 24 hrs. The S. breeze and the fog continued throught the 29th and the weather did not clear until midday on the 30th. We had only momentary glimpses of the low land from which I was never more than 4 leagues away. According to our reckoning we were only 5 or 6 Ls E. of the bay

[1] French naval captains had been required to keep a detailed journal of their navigation since 1689, and an edict of 25 March 1765 repeated these instructions, specified in greater detail the captain's obligation to check that his officers did the same, and required these journals and associated documents to be handed in, on request, to the port commandant. The captain's journal was automatically to be handed in to the port commandant on his return or to the Minister of Marine if so requested. There were *Dépôts* in Brest, Toulon and Rochefort and a central navy *Dépôt des Cartes et Plans* in Paris for journals and charts of major interest.

[2] Mt St Elias is 5,489 metres (18,008 ft) in height; as the *toise* is equivalent to 1.949 metres, the height given of 1,980 *toises* gives only 3,859 metres, a considerable difference. Furthermore, Mt St Elias is some 50 km from the coast, more than the 8 leagues recorded by Dagelet. It is possible that the French scientist mistook another peak, such as nearby Mt Augusta (4,288 m. or 15,300 ft) for Mt St Elias.

which Captain Cook named Bering Bay.[1] The sounding-line regularly gave 60 to 70 fathoms, mud; our observed latitude was 58ᵈ 55′ and our chronometers gave a longitude of 141ᵈ 48′. I set course for land, all sails out, with a light W.S.W. breeze. We could see to the N. 33° E. a bay which seemed very deep and which at first I took to be Bering Bay. I came to within a league and a half of it: I clearly saw that some very low land was joined to the higher land as at Monti Bay and that there was no bay, but the sea was of a whitish colour, almost fresh water, and everything indicated that we were close to the mouth of a very large river as it changed the colour and the saltiness of the sea two leagues out to sea. I gave the signal to drop anchor in 30 fathoms, muddy bottom, and sent the longboat, commanded by Mr de Clonard, my first officer, with Messrs Monneron and Bernizet. Mr de Langle also despatched his Biscay boat under the command of Messrs de Marchainville and Degremont. The 3 officers were back at midday; they had gone along the coast as close as the breakers had allowed them and had found a sandbank at sea level at the entrance of a large river which flowed into the sea by two fairly wide openings, but each one had its own bar similar to the one of the river at Bayonne[2] on which the waves broke so violently that our canoes could not approach. Mr de Clonard spent 5 or 6 hrs looking in vain for an entrance; he saw some smoke, which indicates that the country is inhabited, and from the ship we could see that the sea was calm away from the

[1] George Vancouver held the view that Cook had definitely identified Yakutat Bay with Bering Bay, *A Voyage to the North Pacific Ocean and round the World* (London, 1798), III, pp. 208–9: 'The part of the coast off which we had thus been cruising since the preceding Thursday appeared from its latitude, and relative situation with these two very conspicuous mountains, to be that part where Captain Cook supposed that Beering had anchored....But in this neighbourhood no such bay or island exists.' Later Vancouver came to Yakutat Bay and concluded 'it is hardly probable that Beering could have anchored any where else....This bay then, since no other exists within the limits in question, must be the same which Captain Cook meant to distinguish by the name of Beering's Bay.' (W. Kaye Lamb's edition in *The Voyage of George Vancouver 1791–1795*, London, 1984, IV, pp. 1315, 1321. Bering's Bay may well have in fact been Controller Bay. The difficulty is that this coast is frequently fogbound and dangerous and precise surveying is difficult from offshore. Dry Bay in 59°08′ is a more likely identification for what La Pérouse calls Cook's Bering Bay.

[2] Bayonne is a major port in southwest France, situated at the confluence of the Adour and its tributary, the Nive. The port consists of an outer harbour, or roadstead, and the port proper, which is the rivermouth of the Adour; it is obstructed by a shifting bar and is tidal, but it is nevertheless a busy port, although one which calls for careful navigation on the part of shipmasters.

sandbank, and a basin several leagues in width and two leagues in depth. Therefore it is possible, when the sea is calm, for ships, or at least for boats, to enter this gulf; but as the current is quite fierce and the sea can become very rough over these bars from one moment to the next, the mere appearance of this place should be sufficient to keep navigators away, and if this is the bay where Bhering landed it is more likely that his boat crew were lost through the fury of the sea rather than through the barbarity of the Indians.[1] I have kept the name of Bhering River for this river, and it seems to me that the bay of that name which Captain Cook suspected rather than saw (since he passed 10 or 12 leagues from it) does not exist.

On lst July at midday I sailed with a light S.W. breeze coasting along the shore at a distance of two or three leagues. When anchored we had observed 59^{d} 7′ of latitude and 141^{d} 17′ of longitude, according to our chronometers. The rivermouth then bore from me N. 17^{d} E. and Cape Fairweather E. 5^{d} S. We sailed along the coast with a light W. breeze 2 or 3 leagues offshore and close enough to see with the spyglass any men who might have been walking along the shore, but I saw breakers everywhere which would have made it impossible to land.

On the 2nd at midday I sighted Mount Fairweather bearing N. 6^{d} E.; we observed 58^{d} 36′ of latitude; our longitude according to our timepieces was 140^{d} 31′ and our distance from land 2 Ls. At 2 p.m. we sighed a bight a little E. of Cape Fairweather, which seemed to us to be a very fine bay; I set course to get within one league of it and sent the yawl with Mr de Pierrevert to go with Mr Bernizet to examine it.[2]

[1] La Pérouse corrects this in a marginal note: 'This reflection is an error, because it was Captain Ticvicot and not Cap. Bering who lost his men.' Vitus Bering and Aleksei Chirikov sailed from Avatscha, Kamchatka, with two ships in June 1741. They soon became separated, Bering eventually dying on the island which now bears his name. Chirikov sighted the northwest coast of America on 15 July near Cape Addington, then sailed north towards what are now Baranof and Chichagof islands; on 18 July he entered Lisianski Inlet and sent two boats ashore on northern Chichagof, neither of which returned. This episode did not therefore occur near the area where La Pérouse was when he penned these comments, but almost 100 miles further south. See F. A. Golder, *Russian Expansion on the Pacific: 1641–1850*, Glendale, 1914, New York, 1971, and his *Bering's Voyages*, New York, 1922–55, R. H. Fisher, *Bering's Voyage: Whither and Why*, Seattle, 1977, G. V. Barratt, *Russia in Pacific Waters 1715–1825*, Vancouver, 1981.

[2] Cape Fairweather, with Mount Fairweather (4,663 m., 15,300 ft) inland behind it, marks the end of the St Elias Mountains. It lies in 58°54′N and 139°52′W of Paris. Roughly 15 miles south is Lituya Bay which is La Pérouse's *Port* (or *Baye*) *des Français*, a deep, narrow inlet penetrating into the mainland towards the Fairweather Range.

The *Astrolabe* sent out two boats for the same purpose, commanded by Messrs de Flassan and Bouterviliers. From the ship we could discern a large rocky ledge behind which the sea was quite calm; this ledge seemed to extend 300 or 400 *toises* from E. to W. and ended about two cablelengths from the headland, leaving a fairly wide opening, so that Nature seemed to have created at the end of America a harbour like Toulon[1] but more extensive and suitable, with a depth of some 3 or 4 leagues. Messrs de Flassan and Boutervilliers gave a most favourable report: they had gone in and out of the pass several times finding a depth of 7 to 8 fathoms and of 5 fathoms when they came to within a ship's length of one or other of the extremities; they added that there was a depth of 10 to 12 fathoms inside the bay with good holding ground. Following their report I decided to make for the pass. Our boats were taking depths and had instructions to place themselves each of them at one of the extremities when we got closer to the headlands so that the vessels had only to pass between them.

We soon had sight of natives making friendly signs to us, laying out and waving white coats and various types of furs; several canoeloads of them were fishing in the bay, where the sea was calm as in a basin whereas it was breaking angrily on the rocks, but it was quite calm in the pass, which was further proof that there was a considerable depth.

At 7 p.m. we came up to the entrance. There was little wind and the tide was ebbing so fast that we could not counter it. The *Astrolabe* was driven away fairly fast and I was compelled to drop anchor in order to avoid being carried by a current about whose direction I was unsure, but when I was satisfied that it was going out to sea I weighed anchor and joined the *Astrolabe* , quite uncertain about what I should do on the morrow. The fierce current, which our officers had not mentioned, had made me very doubtful about this harbour; I knew that there are always problems going in and out of narrow passes when the tide flows strongly, and compelled to explore the American coast during the good weather I felt that a forced stay in this bay which I would be able to leave only

[1] Toulon is the major French naval base on the Mediterranean. The bay, which opens to the east, has two divisions, the *Grande Rade* and the *Petite Rade*, the latter providing a fine anchorage for a large fleet and leading to various basins and dockyards. The bay is sheltered on the north and west by high hills, closed to the south by a peninsula and protected on the eastern side by a huge breakwater.

when favourable circumstances came together would adversely affect the outcome of my expedition. Nevertheless I kept on tacking during the night, and at dawn I called out my thoughts to Mr de Langle, but the report from his two officers was so favourable – they had taken soundings in the pass and inside the bay, and pointed out that they had rowed several times successfully against that current which had seemed so strong to us, so that Mr de Langle was convinced that this place of call was highly suitable and his reasons seemed to be so sensible that I was soon persuaded.

This harbour had never been seen by any navigator – it was 60 leagues N.W. of Puerto de los Remedios, which is the limit of the Spanish navigations 200 leagues from Nootka and at about the same distance from Williams Sound; thus if the French government had any plans for a trading post along this part of the American coast, no other nation could raise the slightest objection.[1] Furthermore, the peace we found inside this bay was very appealing to us, as we had to re-arrange almost entirely our cargo in order to get out 6 guns which had been placed at the bottom of the hold in Brest, as without them it would have been unwise to sail into the China Seas which are infested with pirates.[2]

We set sail at 6 a.m. to reach the entrance as the flood-tide ended; the *Astrolabe* went ahead of my frigate, and as on the previous day we had placed a boat at each point.

The winds were blowing from W. to W.S.W.; the entrance opened out N. and S.; so everything looked favourable, but at 7 a.m. while we were in the pass the winds veered to W.N.W. and N.W.¼ W. so that we had to shiver the sails and even hoist some more sail. Fortunately the tide bore our frigates into the bay, making us pass within half a pistol shot of the E. point rocks. I dropped anchor inside the bay in 3½ fathoms, rocky bottom, within a stone's throw of the shore.

[1] La Pérouse can be credited with the discovery of Lituya Bay and a careful survey of the nearby coastline, but a number of Spanish expeditions had been sent to the Northwest Coast in recent years, of which La Pérouse was not aware. Bruno de Hezeta in the *Santiago* and Francisco de Bodega in the *Sonora* had sailed from the port of San Blas to the islands of Chichagof and Kruzof in 1775 and named Puerto de los Remedios an inlet between them. Other expeditions sailed in 1774 and 1779 and more would soon follow, the intention being to assert Spanish rights over the coast in the face of growing activity by Russian and British traders, giving rise to the international dispute known as the Nootka Incident.

[2] La Pérouse at this point adds a marginal note: 'We were due to arrive in China in the first days of February.'

The *Astrolabe* had found herself in similar circumstances and like the *Boussole* had anchored in the same depth and same ground. In the 30 years I have been sailing I have never seen two ships so close to destruction, and this happening at the end of the world would have greatly increased our misfortune; but there was now no danger, the longboats were quickly lowered, we laid out grapnels and small anchors and, before the tide had dropped to any extent we were at anchor in 6 fathoms. However, we touched bottom a few times but so slightly that no damage was done to the vessel. Our situation would have had no inconvenience had we not been anchored over a rocky bottom that extended for several cablelengths around us, which was quite contrary to what Messrs de Flassan and de Boutervilliers had reported – this was not the time to pass comments: we had to leave this bad anchorage, but the speed of the current was a serious obstacle;[1] its fierceness forced us to lower a bower anchor, and I was constantly afraid of seeing the cable cut and of being dragged towards the shore. Our concern increased further when the winds freshened from W.N.W.; the frigate was pressed against the land, the stern quite close to the rocks; towing away was out of the question. I had the topgallants lowered and awaited the end of this bad weather which would not have presented any danger if we had been anchored over a better ground.

I lost no time in getting soundings of the bay. Soon Mr Boutin reported that he had found an excellent sandy plateau 4 cablelengths to the W. of our anchorage where we would be in 10 fathoms; but further on towards the N. there was no ground at 60 fathoms except at half a cablelength from the shore where one obtained 30 fathoms muddy bottom. He also told me that the N.W. wind did not reach the interior of the bay and that he had found a dead calm.

Mr Descures had been sent at the same time to explore the back of the bay on which he gave a most favourable report; he had gone round an island near which we could anchor in 25 fathoms, muddy bottom; no spot was more suitable for our observatory; pieces of wood were strewn along the shore and cascades of the purest water tumbled from the mountain tops down to the sea. Curiosity had

[1] These violent currents will be the cause of the disaster of 13 July. Lituya Bay has a bad reputation; the natives were aware of the danger and modern instructions to navigators warn of the tide causing dangerous rips in a south-west wind and that the neap tide lasts only 10 to 20 minutes. *South-East Alaska Pilot*, London, 1945, p. 405.

led him to the end of the bay, two leagues beyond the island – it was full of blocks of ice, and he saw the openings of two great channels. Anxious to let me know of his discoveries he had not surveyed them further, and upon his return, our imaginations led us to think that we might possibly penetrate into the interior of America by one of these channels. At 4 p.m. as the wind had dropped we were towed over Mr Boutin's sandy plateau, and the *Astrolabe* was able to weigh anchor and reach the island anchorage. I joined that frigate the next day, helped by a light E.S.E. breeze and our boats and longboats.

During our enforced stay at the entrance of the bay we had been constantly surrounded by native canoes. They offered us, in exchange for iron, fish, skins of otters and other animals as well as sundry small items from their clothing. To our great astonishment they seemed to be accustomed to trade and were as skilful in their deals as the ablest buyers in Europe. Out of all our goods they really wanted only iron; they also took a few beads but more to conclude a deal than as a basis for barter; later we got them to accept plates and pewter pots, but these articles enjoyed only a passing favour, and iron prevailed above everything. They knew about this metal, each one having a dagger made of it hanging around his neck; the shape of this instrument was like the Indians' *cry*[1] but not in respect of the handle which was a simple continuation of the blade, rounded off and with no edge; this weapon was contained in a case of tanned skin and appeared to be their most prized belonging. While we were carefully examining these daggers, they explained by gestures that they used them only against bears and other forest animals; a few were also made of red copper, and they did not appear to prefer them to the others; this latter metal is fairly common among them; they use it more particularly for necklaces, bracelets and various other ornaments; they also decorate the tip of their arrows with it.[2]

[1] The natives were able to trade skins and fish for knives along the coast with occasional Russian, Spanish or English vessels, but the main source of supply of this prized item was through trade with other tribes living in the interior. La Pérouse is referring here to the Malay *creese* or *kris*, a dagger with a sharp, wavy blade.

[2] Copper is abundant in northwest America, as local names indicate: Copper Mountain, Copper River, Copper Centre. John Meares came across pieces of ore weighing up to a pound and learned that they were obtained through barter with northern tribes. See *Voyages made... from China to the North-West Coast of America* (London, 1790), p. 247. The ore was processed by heating until it was sufficiently

The great question among us was to know where these two metals came from. It was possible to assume that copper was found in this part of America, and that the Indians could make it into blades or lingots; but iron may not exist in its natural state anywhere in Nature or at least it is so rare than most mineralogists have never seen it. We could not accept that these people had the skill to turn iron ore into metal. We had seen on the day we arrived some bead necklaces and a few items of yellow copper which, as is known, is a compound of copper and zinc. Thus everything led us to believe that the metals we had seen came either from the Russians, or employees of the Hudson Company or American traders who travel into the interior of America, or finally from the Spanish; but I shall explain later that it is more likely these metals come from Russians. We have brought back many samples of this iron; it is soft and as easy to cut as lead, and it may not be impossible for mineralogists to determine its country of origin.

Gold is in no greater demand in Europe than iron is in this part of America, which is further proof of the scarcity of this metal, of which to tell the truth everyone owns a small quantity, but the desire for this form of riches is no easier to satisfy among these natives than the thirst for gold is in our continent. On the day we arrived we received a visit from the chief of the main village; before clambering aboard he appeared to be praying to the sun, and then gave us a long speech which was ended by some fairly pleasant songs that bore quite some resemblance to our religious plain chant; the Indians from his canoe accompanied him and repeated the same tune in chorus. He then came on board with a large number of his followers and they danced for an hour, singing at the same time excellently in tune. I gave several presents to this chief, which made him greatly troublesome because he spent every day some five or six hours on board and I was forced to make him further frequent gifts if I did not want to see him leave in a state of displeasure and often uttering threats (which was not very dangerous).

As soon as we had settled behind the island nearly all the bay's

---

malleable to fashion into knives or ornaments. G.T. Edmonds, 'Copper Neck Rings of Southern Alaska', *American Anthropologist*, 10 (1908), pp. 644–9. Iron was scarce, obtained through barter and sharpened with stones. See E. Gunther, *Indian Life on the North-West Coast of America*, Chicago, 1972, Appendix 2.

natives came up. The news of our arrival no doubt spread rapidly through the neighbourhood; we saw several foreign canoes arriving, loaded with otter skins which we bartered for axes, adzes, and iron bars; the Indians gave us their salmons for old hoops, but they soon became more difficult and we could obtain that fish only with nails or small iron objects. I think that there is no country where the sea otter is more common than in this part of America and I would not be surprised if a trading post with a trading range of a mere 40 or 50 leagues would collect ten thousand skins in a year. Mr de la Manon will give a description of that amphibious animal from information supplied by Mr Rollain, senior surgeon on my fregate, a man of great learning who personally skinned, dissected and stuffed the only one we are bringing back to France. Unfortunately it was at the most 4 or 5 months old and weighed only eight and a half pounds. The *Astrolabe* had caught one which had presumably escaped from the natives because it was badly wounded; that otter seemed fully grown – it weighed at least 70 pounds. Mr de Langle had it skinned in order to get it stuffed, but as this was at the time of the crisis we faced when we entered the bay this work was not properly done and neither the head nor the jaw was kept.

The sea otter is an amphibious animal, better known through the beauty of its fur than from anyone's precise description. The Indians of Port des Français call it *skeeter*, the Russians name it *Colry Morsky* and call the female *Maska*; some naturalists have mentioned it under the name of *Sarikovienne*, but the description of the *Sarikovienne* provided by Mr de Buffon is not in the least appropriate for this animal which is like neither the Canadian otter nor the European one.[1]

As soon as we reached our second anchorage, we set up the observatory on the island (which I have named Cenotaph Island,

[1] The sea otter (*Enhydra lutris*) has almost disappeared, a victim of human greed for its beautiful fur. At the time of La Pérouse's voyage, it could be found from northern Alaska to California, in the Aleutian Islands, on the coast of Kamchatka and even in northern Japan. Its destruction began in Kamchatka and the Aleutians as the Russian fur traders, the *promyshlenniki*, advanced towards the American continent. The reference in the text is to George-Louis Leclerc de Buffon, the French naturalist and author of the monumental *Histoire naturelle*, who uses the word 'saricovienne' in his article on quadrupeds, but in connection with the beaver or *Castoridae* family. In Siberia the sea otter was known as *morskie bobry* and in Alaska as *morskie kalanie* (which La Pérouse inverts as 'Colry morsky'). The local Tlingit people called it *yuxch*; the term 'skeeter' has not been identified as a Tlingit word.

after the sad monument we erected to the memory of our friends). We also put up tents for our sailmakers and our blacksmiths, and there we deposited the barrels from our cargo which we entirely restowed. Since all the Indians' villages were on the mainland, we felt confident that we would be safe on our island, but we soon had evidence to the contrary; we had already discovered that the natives were great thieves, but we did not suspect their untiring energy and their determination to carry out the longest and most difficult plans. They soon taught us to know them better; they spent every night watching for the appropriate occasion to rob us, but we had good lookouts on our vessels and they seldom defeated our vigilance; I had moreover established the law of Sparta: he who was robbed was punished, and if we did not applaud the thief, at least we did not complain, so as to avoid incidents which might have had fatal consequences.[1] I did not close my eyes to the fact that this extreme mildness made them insolent; I had however endeavoured to convince them of the superiority of our weapons: we had fired a cannon loaded with ball in front of them, to show that they could be reached from a distance, and a musket fired in the presence of a large number of these Indians had gone through several breastplates similar to one they had sold us after making us understand by gestures that it was proof against arrows and daggers.[2] Our hunters who were skilled men shot birds over their heads, and I am quite sure they did not think that they were frightening us, but their behaviour showed me that they had little doubt that our patience was inexhaustible, and soon they forced me to give up the camp I had set up on the island. At night they would land on the sea side,

[1] The reference is to Xenophon's *The Spartan Constitution*, X, in which he states that, whereas other states were content to punish a wrongdoer, Lycurgus tended to inflict punishment on those who were neglectful and were robbed, defrauded or kidnapped, thereby affecting the state through the weakening of one of its citizens.

[2] The French were not the only victims of such thefts. Cook had already complained and fired small shot on at least one occasion at a thief, such deterrent being unavoidable 'or these Rogues wou'd have rifled the Ship', but this was at Nootka, further south. Cook, *Journals*, III, p. 1329. Because of their fishing expeditions along the coast where Russian traders operated and where Cook had already been, the Tlingit of Lituya Bay would not have been unfamiliar with muskets, and the demonstration provided by the French was probably no more than an interesting spectacle. Their breastplates or body shields were made of branches over which layers of tanned skins, mostly moose skins, were stretched. Four are on display at the Museo Naval of Madrid. Two brought back by Cook's expedition are in the British Museum, but they were not obtained from Tlingit Indians.

cross a wood of thickets we could not enter even in daytime, and crawling snakelike on their stomachs, without disturbing a single leaf, they managed to steal something in spite of our sentries. Finally they succeeded in entering by night the tent in which Messrs Law de Lauriston and d'Arbaud, who were on duty at the observatory, were sleeping, and stole a silver chased musket and these two officers' clothing; a twelve men squad did not notice them and the two officers did not wake up; this final theft would not have worried us unduly had we not also lost the original notebook in which we had recorded all our astronomical data since our arrival in Port des Français.

These problems did not prevent our boats and longboats from gathering wood and obtaining water; all our officers were constantly on duty in charge of various squads of workers which we had to send ashore; their presence and discipline held the natives in check, and while we were hastening preparations for our departure Messrs de Monneron and Bernizet were surveying the bay in a well-armed boat; I was unable to allocate them any naval officers as they were all busy, but I had arranged for the latter to check all the bearings and to take soundings before we sailed; we planned then to set aside 24 hours for a bear hunt, having seen traces of these animals in the mountains, and anxious to start on account of the time of year I wanted to leave without wasting a moment.

We had already been to the end of the bay which is perhaps the most extraordinary place on earth. Imagine a vast basin, whose depth in the centre is impossible to estimate, edged by great, steep, snow-covered mountains; not a single blade of grass can be seen on this immense rocky mass which Nature has condemned to perpetual sterility.[1] I have never seen a single breath of wind disturb the surface of this water which is affected only by the enormous blocks of ice that fall quite frequently from five different glaciers, making as they drop a sound that echoes far into the mountains. The air is so clear and the silence so deep that the voice of one man can be heard half a league away, as can the sound of birds which have laid their eggs in the hollows formed by the rocks. This is the

[1] Lituya Bay is dominated by three peaks which commemorate the La Pérouse expedition: Mt Crillon named by La Pérouse after Félix-François-Dorothée de Berton, comte de Crillon – 'my friend' – Mt Lapérouse and Mt Dagelet, both these names having been bestowed following the Western Union expedition to the area in 1871.

channel by which we planned to enter into the heart of America; we thought that it might lead to a great river running between the mountains, which had its source in one of the great lakes in northern Canada.[1] Such was our dream, and now here is the reality: we left in the two longboats of the *Boussole* and the *Astrolabe*: Messrs de Monty, de Marchainville, de Boutervilliers, Fr Receveur, with Mr de Langle, while I was followed by Messrs Dagelet, Boutin, St Cèran, Duché and Prêvost. We entered the W. channel. It was wise to avoid going along the mountain edge on account of the falling stones and blocks of ice, and finally we reached, having covered no more than a league and a half, a cul-de-sac closed off by two immense glaciers.

In order to penetrate into that inlet, we were compelled to push aside the ice blocks which covered the sea; the water was so deep that half a cable's length from shore I found no depth at 120 fathoms. Mr de Langle, Mr de Monty, Mr Dagelet and several other officers wanted to climb the glacier: they covered two leagues after frightful efforts, forced to risk their lives jumping across crevasses of great depth. All they saw was snow and ice which presumably continue as far as the top of Mount Fairweather.

My boat stayed by the shore during this time. A block of ice falling into the water more than 400 *toises* away caused such a disturbance that it was overturned and carried a fair distance onto the edge of the glacier. This mishap was quickly put right and we all went back to the ships, having completed in a few hours our voyage into the interior of America. I had sent Messrs de Moneron and Bernizet to visit the E. inlet; it ended as this one did against two glaciers. These two channels were drawn and are shown on the map of the bay.

The day after this excursion the chief came aboard, with a larger suite and better adorned than usual, and after much singing and dancing he offered to sell me the island on which our observatory was situated, reserving himself the right, no doubt, together with the other Indians, the right to rob us there.[2] It was unlikely that this

[1] These comments relate to the North-West Passage in which La Pérouse had little faith.

[2] The following words were crossed out by La Pérouse: 'as much as they could'. His reservations about the validity of such a sale were fully justified; neither party spoke the other's language and the chief's title to the island was more than tenuous since his people did not actually live in the bay, but merely came there during the

PORT DES FRANÇAIS

7. Chart of Port des Français, Northwest Coast of America. Unsigned. July 1786. AN 6 JJ1:30.

BASSIN DU O.
Grand Fond
LE PORT
Île du Cœnotaphe.
LA RADE
LA PASSE
GRAND OCÉAN SEPTENTRIO

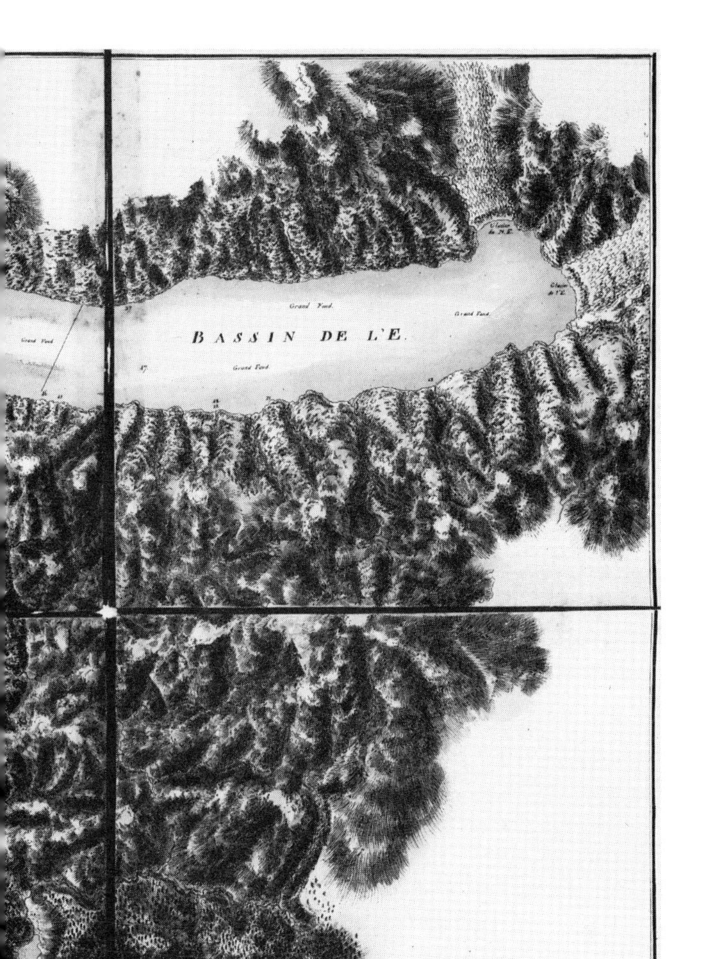

PLAN
DU
PORT DES FRANCAIS

Situé sur la Côte du N.O. de l'Amerique Septentrionale, par 58° 37' de latitude, & 140° 5' de longitude Occidentale du Meridien de Paris, levé en juillet 1786 pour servir au Voyage de M. le Cte de la Perouse.

Echelle de Mille Toises en Raison de cinq lignes pour cent toises

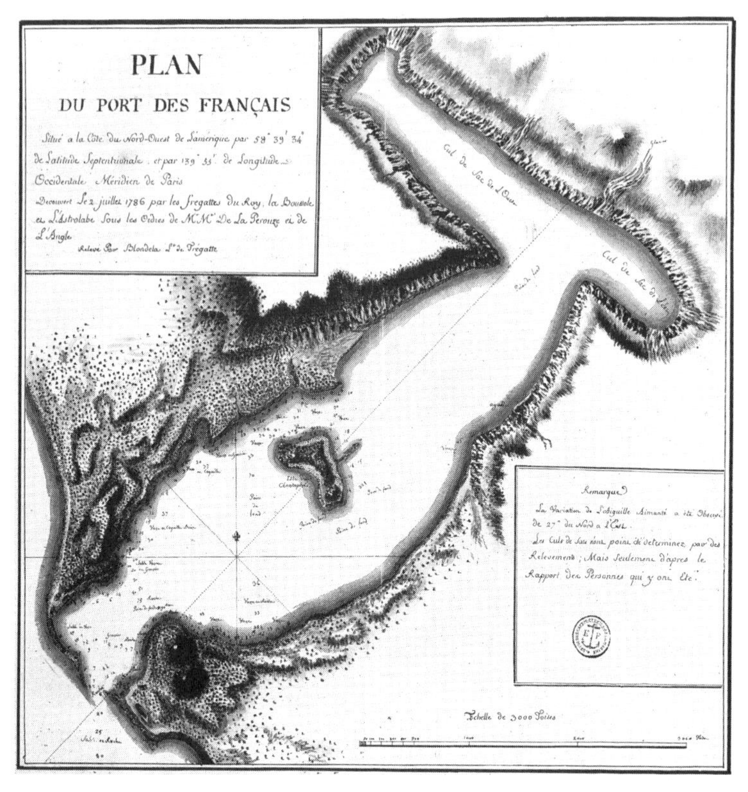

8. Detailed chart of the anchorage in Port des Français, Northwest Coast, by Blondela. 'The dead ends [named the Western Basin and the Eastern Basin respectively in the main chart] have not been laid down by means of bearings but only from reports made by people who went there.' Actual size 51 cm × 51 cm. AN 6 JJ1:31B.

chief owned any of the land; the system under which these people live is so democratic that the country probably belongs to the whole group; however, as numerous natives were witnesses to this transaction, I was entitled to conclude that they were giving their support to it, and I accepted the chief's offer, convinced anyhow that this contract of sale could be disallowed by many tribunals if ever these people challenged it, because we have no proof that the witnesses represented anyone or that the chief was the real owner; nevertheless, I gave him several ells of red cloth, some axes, adzes, iron bars and nails; I also gave presents to all his followers. Having thus concluded and settled the deal, I took possession of the island with the usual formalities – I had a bottle buried under a rock, in which was an advice that possession was taken, and I placed nearby one of the bronze medals struck before our departure from France.

Meanwhile our main task, the purpose of our stay, had been accomplished; our guns were in place, our cargo restowed and we had taken on as much water and wood as when we sailed from Chile. There is no harbour in the whole world as convenient for the speedy completion of work that is often so difficult in other countries: waterfalls (as I have already stated) coming down from the mountain tops drop the clearest water straight into barrels held in the longboats, drift wood lies around along the shore which borders a sea as placid as a lake. The chart drawn up by Messrs de Monneron and Bernizet was completed, as was the calculation by Mr Blondelas of a base point which had been used by Mr de Langle and Mr D'Agelet and most of our officers to calculate trigonometrically the height of the mountains. Our only regrets concerned Mr Dagelet's notebook, but this misfortune was almost compensated for by the various notes we had found. In a word we considered ourselves to be the happiest of navigators, having arrived at such a great distance from Europe without a single case of sickness or one man affected by scurvy.

But at this point the greatest misfortune, the most unforeseeable, was waiting for us. It is with the greatest sorrow that I will describe

---

summer season. It is probable that the Tlingit were suggesting that the French could erect their own camp on the island and return in later years. The long struggle they waged against the Russians and their opposition to Russian fortified settlements makes it unlikely that they would have ever recognised any French claim to the island.

a disaster a thousand times more cruel than sickness or than any other event in the longest sea journeys. I have set myself the duty of writing this account, and I do not hesitate to admit that the regret I have felt over this event has been a hundred times accompanied by tears, and that time has still not succeeded in lessening my sorrow; every object, every moment brings back to mind the loss we have sustained in circumstances where we felt that we had so little to fear.

I have already stated that the soundings were to be recorded by the officers on the plan drawn by Messrs de Moneron and Bernizet; consequently the Biscay boat of the *Astrolabe*, to be commanded by Mr de Marchainville, was ordered to be ready for the following morning, and I had mine prepared together with the small boat which I placed under the orders of Mr Boutin. Mr Descures, my first lieutenant, a Knight of St Louis, was in charge of the *Boussole*'s Biscay boat and of the small expedition. As his zeal had seemed to me to be a little excessive at times, I felt it necessary to give him his instructions in writing; these were so detailed in respect of the caution he was to exercise, that he asked me 'if I took him for a child', adding that he had already commanded the King's ships; I explained in a friendly manner the purpose of my instructions, saying that Mr de Langle and I had taken soundings in the pass two days earlier, and that I had felt the officer commanding the 2nd boat which was with us had gone too close to the point which he had even scraped; I added that youthful officers believe that it is stylish to climb on the parapet of a trench during a siege and that this same attitude leads them to beard breakers and rocks when in a boat, but such thoughtless daring could have the most deadly consequences in a campaign such as ours when these kinds of dangers present themselves at every moment. After this conversation, I handed him the following instructions, which I also read out to Mr Boutin; they will indicate better than any description the mission entrusted to Mr Descures and the precautions I took.

Written instructions given by Mr de la Pérouse to Mr Descures

Before indicating to Mr Descures the purpose of his mission, I warn him that he is expressly forbidden to expose the boats to any danger and to go near the pass if the sea is breaking over it. He will leave at 6 a.m. with the other two boats commanded by Messrs de Marchainville and Boutin, and will take soundings from the pass up to the small cove E. of the two hillocks; he will record the depths on the plan I have given him or he will make a sketch plan from which they can be taken; if the sea is not breaking over the pass but is somewhat rough he will, seeing that this task is not urgent, put off the taking of depths to another occasion, bearing in mind that when tasks of this kind are carried out in difficult conditions they are always badly done. It is likely that the best time to approach the pass is when the tide is slack at around half past eight.[1] *If circumstances favour it, he will endeavour to measure its width by means of a log line, and will place the three boats in parallel lines, sounding in this order ≡ i.e. along its width or from E. to W. He will then take soundings from N. to S., but it is unlikely that he will be able to carry out this second operation during the same tide, as the current will have become too strong. While waiting for the slack water, or if the sea is rough, Mr Descures will take soundings in the interior of the bay, especially in the cove behind the two hillocks where I think there should be an excellent anchorage; he will also endeavour to determine on the plan the limits of the rocky and the sandy bottoms, so that the safe ground can be known; I think that when the channel south of the island is hidden by the point near the hillocks one is above a good sandy ground; Mr Descures will check whether my theory is correct; but I repeat once again that I beg him to act with the utmost caution.*

Should these instructions leave me with any feeling of anxiety? They were given to a man of 33, a Knight of St Louis, who had commanded some of the King's ships. So many reasons to feel confident! Since many of my readers will be seamen and will know the roadsteads of Port Louis and Lorient, let them visualise two frigates at anchor behind the island of St Michael sending their boats to take soundings in the Port Louis roadstead, with express orders not to go near the Citadel if the sea is at all rough. That was exactly our situation, with this difference, that the sea is calmer in the Port des Français on the coast of America than it is in the Port Louis roads.[2]

[1] La Pérouse adds the marginal note: 'and at 7.15 he was drowned'.

[2] Lorient (originally L'Orient) was founded by the French India Company in the seventeenth century on the estuary of the Scorff River. On the opposite shore is the old town of Port-Louis, defended by ramparts and a citadel which juts out into the roadstead. Port-Louis and its harbour, on the Blavet, was in use well before the Middle Ages. 'One day in June 1706 there were 550 sails in the harbour.' H.F. Buffet, *La Ville et la Citadelle du Port-Louis* (Rennes, 1962), p.109. The eighteenth

Our boats left as ordered at 6 a.m. It was as much a pleasure trip as a working expedition: they were to hunt and to lunch under trees. With Mr Descures I sent Mr de Pierrevert and Mr de Montarnal, the only relative I had in the navy,[1] whom I loved like a son; never had a young officer given me such expectations, and as for the Chevalier de Pierrevert he had already acquired what I expected very soon from the former.

Our seven best soldiers made up the crew of this Biscay boat on which my master pilot had also gone to take the soundings; Mr Boutin was seconded in his small boat by Mr Mouton, Frigate Lieutenant. I knew that the *Astrolabe*'s boat was commanded by Mr de Marchainville, but I did not know whether there were other officers as well.

At 10 a.m. I saw my little boat coming back. Somewhat surprised as I was not expecting it so soon, I asked Mr Boutin before he had a chance to come on board whether there was something new; I feared at first an attack by the natives; Mr Boutin's appearance was not reassuring: the greatest sadness showed on his face. He soon told me of the awful disaster he had just witnessed and from which he had escaped only because his firm character had enabled him to see what resources he still had in such a great peril. Carried (by following his commanding officer) towards the breakers leading to the pass while the tide was flowing out at 3 or 4 leagues an hour, he decided to present the stern of his boat to the waves so that, pushed by them and abandoning himself to them, they would not swamp his boat, but nevertheless he was likely to be carried out to sea by the tide. Soon he saw the breakers in front of him and found himself in the open sea: more concerned about the safety of his comrades than his own, he rowed along the edge of the breakers in the hope of saving some; he even went back among them, but the tide continued to drive him out. In the end he climbed on Mr Mouton's shoulders in order to scan a wider scene: it was all in vain, everything had sunk out of sight!...

---

century saw the beginning of the decline of Port-Louis, which ceased to be a naval base in 1769 and to have a branch of the Admiralty in 1784, and the total dominance of Lorient, but in the days when La Pérouse was writing the area would have been very familiar to most sailors.

[1] La Pérouse refers here to a blood relative, as he also had with him on the expedition his brother-in-law Frédéric Broudou – although strictly Broudou had joined as a *volontaire* and could not be regarded as officially in the French navy until La Pérouse promoted him later to *lieutenant de frégate*.

And Mr Boutin returned at slack water, the sea having calmed. This officer has retained some hope for the *Astrolabe*'s Biscay boat, having seen only ours disappear below the waves. At the time Mr de Marchainville was a quarter of a league away from the danger, that is to say in waters as tranquil as those of the most sheltered harbour; but that young officer, driven by a sense of nobility which undoubtedly was marked by carelessness, since any assistance is out of the question in such circumstances, but having too upright a character, too great a courage, to allow himself such a thought at a time when his friends were in such extreme danger, he sped to their aid, threw himself among those same breakers and, a victim of his noble character and of the disobedience of his commander's to the strictest instructions, perished as he had done.

Soon Mr de Langle came on board, as distressed by sorrow as I was, and told me in tears that the misfortune was far worse than I thought. He had, since our departure from France, made a strict rule never to send the two brothers to carry out the same duties together, and he had given way on this one occasion to the wish they had expressed to go strolling and hunting together – as this was how we both had looked at the expedition of our boats which we considered to be as little endangered as if they had gone out in the Brest roadsteads on a fine day.

The natives in their canoes came at that very moment to tell us of this sad event. The gestures of these rough men indicated that they had seen the loss of the two boats and that any help would have been in vain. We filled their arms with presents and tried to get them to understand that all our riches would belong to the one who could save a single man.

Nothing was more likely to arouse their feeling of humanity, They ran along the seashore and spread out on both sides of the bay. I had already despatched my longboat, commanded by Mr de Clonard, towards the E., this being the more likely area where anyone who (against all appearances) might have had the good fortune to escape would have come ashore. Mr de Langle went to the W. shore so that no area might remain unsearched, and I stayed on board in charge of the two vessels, with the necessary crews, to ensure that we would be safe from the natives against whom caution dictated we should always be on our guard. Almost all the officers and several other people had followed Messrs de Langle and Clonard; they covered 3 leagues along the seashore, where not the slightest debris had been washed up. However I had retained a little hope: the mind cannot accustom itself easily to the transformation of a pleasant situation to such deep sorrow; but the return of our boats and longboats destroyed this illusion and completed my utter dejection which the strongest words cannot only imperfectly describe. I will record here Mr Boutin's own account; he was a friend of Mr Descures, and we do not share the same views on that officer's lack of caution.

Mr Boutin's Account

On 13 July at 5.50 a.m. I left the *Boussole* in the small boat; my orders were to follow Mr Descures who commanded our Biscay boat, and Mr de Marchainville was to join us, in charge of the *Astrolabe*'s Biscay boat. The orders which Mr Descures had received in writing from Mr de la Pérouse and of which I had been advised, required him to use these three boats to take soundings in the bay and record the depths (in accordance with the bearings) on the chart he had been given, to take soundings in the pass if the sea was calm and even to measure its width, but he was expressly forbidden to expose to the slightest danger the boats placed under his command and to go near the pass if the seas were breaking or even if there was any swell. After passing the W. point of the island near which we were anchored, I saw that the seas were breaking right across the pass and that it would be impossible to approach. At the time Mr Descures was ahead of me, oars raised, and seemed to be waiting for me, but when I had come within a musket shot he went on, and since his boat was much faster than mine he repeated this manoeuvre several times so that I was never able to catch him up. At 7.15, having continued to make for the pass we were only two cablelengths away;[1] our Biscay boat changed course and I followed in its wake; we steered to get back into the bay, leaving the pass behind us, and my boat [was] behind the Biscay boat within hailing distance; I could see the *Astrolabe*'s boat a quarter of a league away inside the bay; Mr Descures then hailed me, saying with a laugh, 'I think that the best

[1] Marginal note by La Pérouse. '& I had expressly forbidden going near that pass if it was breaking'.

thing we can do is to go and have lunch, as the seas are breaking horribly in the pass'. I replied that this was quite evident and that I imagined our work would be restricted to determining the limits of the sandy bay on the port side as one enters. Mr de Pierrevert who was with Mr Descures was about to reply, but having glanced towards the E. he saw that we were being carried by the tide; I saw it too and immediately both boats rowed energetically towards the north in order to get away from the pass which was still 100 *toises* away, and I did not think we were exposed to the slightest danger since by gaining a mere 20 *toises* we still had the option of beaching our boats on the shore. After rowing for more than a minute without being able to progress against the current I tried in vain to reach the E. coast. Our Biscay boat, ahead of me, also attempted without success to reach the W. coast. We were thus forced to veer N. to avoid being carried athwart the breakers: the first waves were breaking a short distance from my boat; I thought it advisable to lower the grapnel but it did not hold; fortunately the cablet was not fixed to any of the thwarts – it slid completely into the sea and freed us from a weight that could have been fatal. All at once I found myself among the biggest waves which almost swamped my boat; it fortunately did not sink and responded to the tiller so that I could always present the stern to the waves, which gave me the greatest hope that we might escape from this peril.

Our Biscay boat had moved away from me while I was lowering the grapnel and found itself just a few minutes later among the breakers – I had lost sight of it when the first waves came upon me; but in one of the moments when I was being lifted by the swell I saw it again half submerged some 30 or 40 *toises* ahead; it was athwart; I saw neither men nor oars; my only hope had been that it would make headway against the current, but I was only too convinced that it would perish if it was carried away because, in order to escape, one needed a heavier boat which could answer to the tiller in such a situation to avoid capsizing; unfortunately it had neither of these qualities. I was still among the breakers, looking in all directions, and I saw behind me that the waves formed a bar across my horizon and that the breakers seemed to continue well to the W. I finally realised that if only I could just make 50 *toises* to the E. I would find less dangerous waters; I made every effort to succeed, struggling to starboard between each wave, and at 7.25 I was out of danger, having only a strong swell and a few small waves caused by the W.N.W. breeze to contend with.

After bailing the water out of my boat I sought ways of rescuing my unfortunate comrades, but I had lost all hope.

From the moment I had seen our Biscay boat submerged among the breakers I had always struggled E. and had got away only after several minutes. It was impossible for the shipwrecked men to get away from the direction of such a fierce current as they found themselves in, and they must have been dragged away by the tide which flowed out to sea until 8.45. And anyhow, how could even the best swimmer resist for more than a few moments to the fierceness of those waves? However, as I could carry out a reasonable search only in the area where the current was running, I set course to the South, alongside the breakers on my starboard side, changing course continually towards some seals or bunches of seaweed which, from time to time, had raised my hopes. Since the sea was very rough, my range of vision, when I was atop a wave, extended a fair distance and I would have been able to sight an oar or some débris more than 200 *toises* away.

Soon I began to look towards the E. point of the entrance. I noticed some men making signals with their cloaks; they were natives (as I have since discovered), but at the time I took them for the crew of the *Astrolabe*'s boat, and I imagined that they were waiting for the slack tide to come to our rescue: I had no inkling that our unhappy friends had fallen victim to their noble rashness.

At 8.45,[1] as the tide had turned, the sea was no longer breaking but there was merely a strong swell. I felt that I should continue my search among this swell, following the direction the ebbing tide had taken; I was equally unlucky in that second search. Before nine o'clock, seeing the tide flowing in from the S.W., and having neither food, grapnel nor

[1] Marginal note by La Pérouse: '& it was the time I had indicated in my order to approach the pass safely because in every case the current would have run into the bay'.

sails, with my crew wet and cold, afraid that I might be unable to re-enter the bay when the tide was in full force, seeing it already running strongly to the N.E., which prevented me from making for the S. where I should have continued my search had the tide allowed it, I returned into the bay, steering North.

Already the pass was almost closed to me at the E. point. The sea was still breaking on the two points, but it was calm in the middle. I finally managed to reach that entrance, going along the portside point on which were the Americans who had signalled to me and whom I had taken at first to be French; their gestures indicated to me that they had seen two boats capsize, and not seeing the *Astrolabe*'s boat I was only too certain of the fate which had befallen Mr de Marchainville whom I knew too well to feel that he would have given a second thought to the futility of the risk he was going to run. However, as one is always inclined to delude oneself, I still entertained the faint hope that I would find him on board our ships where it was possible that he had gone for help: the first words I spoke on reaching our vessels were 'Have you any news of Mr de Marchainville?' The 'No' was for me a confirmation that he was lost.

After all these details, I feel I should explain the reasons for Mr Descures' actions; it is not possible that he ever thought of entering the pass – he only wanted to get close to it,[1] and he thought he was keeping at a distance which was more than adequate for safety; it was this distance that he estimated incorrectly, as I did, as did the 18 people who were in our two boats. I cannot say how easy such a mistake was or why it was not possible to estimate the strength of the current – one might suspect that I am defending my own actions because, I repeat, I believed the distance to be more than adequate and even the coastline which was moving North so rapidly merely caused me to feel surprised. Without wishing to list all the reasons that contributed to make us feel so fatally confident, I must say that on the day we entered the bay our boats took soundings in every direction for more than two hours without sensing any current; it is true that when our frigate

[1] Marginal note by La Pérouse: '& my instructions forbade him to approach'.

were entering they were driven back by the ebb tide, but the wind was so slight that at the same moment our boats were making easy progress against the tide; finally on 11 July our two commanding officers went themselves with several officers to take soundings in the pass; they went out with the ebb and returned with the flood, noticing nothing which might have led them to suspect there existed the slightest danger, especially with well crewed boats. So one must conclude that on 13 July the violence of the current was due to special circumstances, such as an unusual quantity of melting snow or strong winds which had not reached the bay but no doubt had affected the open sea.

Mr de Marchainville was a quarter of a league on the bay side of the pass when I was dragged towards it; I did not see him after that (and I feel only too well that I shall never see him again!). But all those who knew him are aware of what his noble and brave character will have led him to do: it is probable that he saw our two boats among the breakers; unable to understand how we could have been carried towards them, he suspected that a cable had snapped or that oars had been lost, and immediately rowed to our rescue up to the edge of the first breakers; seeing us struggling among the waves, he obeyed only the dictates of his courage and tried to get through the breakers in order to help us or die with us. Undoubtedly this death is a glorious one, but how cruel for the one who has escaped and has lost all hope of ever seeing those who went with him or the heroes who were coming to his rescue!

I could not in my narrative have omitted any essential element or changed any of the facts; Mr Mouton, frigate lieutenant, who was second-in-command of my boat, is in a position to point to any errors if (what I do not believe) my memory has misled me. His firmness, that of the coxswain and of the four men, greatly contributed to our salvation; my orders were carried out among the breakers with the same precision as if the circumstances had been perfectly normal.

(Signed) Boutin

All we had left to do was to leave promptly a country which had proved so tragic for us, had we not owed it to the families of our unfortunate friends to stay some little time; too rapid a departure would have left some concerns, some doubt, in Europe. It might not have been realised that the current does not extend more than a league out beyond the pass and that the boats and the victims could not have failed to be carried out that far; and so if, against all likelihood (on account of the wildness of the sea), someone had succeeded in reaching the shore he could only have done so in the environs of the bay. Consequently I decided to wait for several days, but I left the anchorage of the island and moved to the sandy shelf near the entrance on the W. coast. I spent five days to cover this distance which is only of one league, and during this time we were assailed by a sudden E. gale which would have placed us in dire straits had we not been anchored in good muddy ground where fortunately our anchors did not drag, for we were less than a cable's length from land. In the end, contrary winds kept us there longer than I had intended and we only set sail on 30 July, nineteen days after the event I have described with a heavy heart, the memory of which will for ever fill me with sadness. Prior to our departure, we erected on the island in the middle of the bay a monument to the memory of our unfortunate companions; Mr de la Manon drew up the following notice which he buried in a bottle at the foot of this cenotaph:

> At the entrance to this port, twenty-one sailors perished.
> Whoever you may be, add your tears to ours.
>
> On 4 July 1786, the frigates *Boussole* and *Astrolabe*, having left Brest on 1 August 1785, arrived in this harbour. Thanks to the care of Mr de la Pérouse, head of the expedition, of Mr de Langle, captain of the 2nd frigate, of Messrs de Clonard and de Monty, first officers of the two vessels, and of the other officers and surgeons, none of the illnesses that result from long navigations had affected the crews. Mr de la Pérouse was congratulating himself, as we all did, that we had sailed from one end of the world to the other, through all kinds of dangers, having encountered peoples who are reputed to be barbarous, without losing a single man or shedding one drop of blood. On 13 July 3 boats left at 5 a.m. to add the depths to the chart of the bay that had been drawn up; they were commanded by Mr Descures, Lt, Kt of St Louis. Mr de la Pérouse had given written orders expressly forbidding him to

get close to the current, but at a time when he thought he was still some distance away he found himself caught in it. The brothers De la Borde and Mr de Flassan who were in the second boat were unafraid of the risks of the danger they ran in speeding to the rescue of their comrades, but alas they suffered the same fate! The 3rd boat was commanded by Mr Boutin, Lt. This officer, courageously struggling against the breakers, made valiant but fruitless efforts over several hours to rescue his friends, and owed his survival only to the better quality of his boat, to his wise prudence and to that of Mr Laprise Mouton, Lt, his 2nd, and to the energy and prompt obedience of his little crew consisting of Jean Marie, boatsman, L'Hostis, Le Bars, Corentin Jers & Monens, all four sailors. The Indians seemed to share our sorrow. It was great indeed; moved by this misfortune but not discouraged, we are leaving on 30 July to continue our voyage.
Names of the officers, soldiers & sailors who were shipwrecked on the thirteenth of July at seven fifteen a.m.:

Boussole

Officers

Messrs Descures, de Pierrevert, de Montarnal

Crew

Lemaitre 1st pilot, Lieutaud corp^{al}, and Prieur, Freichaud Barin, Bolet, Fleury, Chaud. All 7 soldiers, the eldest was not 33.

Astrolabe

Officers

Messrs de la Borde Marchainville, de la Borde Bouterviliers, brothers, and de Flassan

Crew

Saulas, corp^{al}, & G^{on} Philiby, Julien Pons, and Pierre Rabier; all 4 soldiers; Homonondrieu, Goulven Terreau & Guillaume Duquesne, all 3 topmen, in the prime of life.'[1]

[1] The names of those lost are: from the *Boussole*, Jean-Baptiste Le Maistre, Pierre Liétot or Lieutot, Pierre Prieur, Jean-Pierre Fraichot, Michel Berrin, Jean Bollay or Bolet, Georges Fleury, Marius Chaub; from the *Astrolabe*, Léonard Soulas, Pierre Philiby, Julien Le Penn, Pierre Rabier, Jean-Hamon Andrieux, Goulven Tarreau, Guillaume Duquène. The Russians found no trace of the French monument when they visited the bay a few years later.

Our stay at the entrance to the bay provided us with a great deal of information on the customs and various practices of the natives, which we would have been unable to obtain in the other anchorage; our vessels were at anchor close to their villages, we visited them several times a day, and daily we had some cause for complaint although our behaviour towards them never changed and we never stopped giving them proof of our mildness and indeed of our goodwill.

On 22 July they brought us débris of our wrecked boats which the waves had pushed towards the E. coast quite close to the bay. Messrs de Clonard, de Moneron and de Monty left at once to cover several leagues towards the E. They were accompanied by the same natives who had brought us these débris, on whom we had showered gifts, and who had told us by gestures that they had buried one of our unfortunate comrades on the shore where the waves had washed him up.

Our officers travelled for 3 leagues over stones along an awful path; every half hour the guides insisted on a new payment or else refused to follow them; finally they entered the woods and fled, and our officers realised, too late, that it was a fraud to obtain more presents.[1] During this expedition they saw immense forests of pine trees of an impressive size; they measured some of 5 feet in diametre which seemed to be more than 140 feet high.[2]

The account they gave us of the natives' tricks did not surprise us; their skill in thieving and roguery is as advanced as that of foxes which are, so they say, the craftiest of all animals.[3] Messrs de

[1] Since neither spoke the other's language and could only communicate in sign language, this interpretation is open to doubt. It is not even certain that the burial, or death, was that of a Frenchman as four of their own canoes had been recently wrecked at the entrance to the bay and one of their leaders drowned. In 1886, G.T. Emmons obtained an account of these events, with the appearance of La Pérouse's two ships occurring only a few days later, from a chief of the Aukqwan tribe of the Tlingit people. From him he also learned of the *Kah-Lituya*, or guardian of the bay, who shakes the surface of the water to prevent canoes from entering. See G.T. Emmons, 'An Account of the Meeting between La Pérouse and the Tlingit', *American Anthropologist*, 13 (1911), pp. 294–8.

[2] There are extensive coniferous forests both along the coast and inland. The reference here may be to the *Abies lasiocarpa* or *Abies grandis* which frequently reach the height mentioned.

[3] The reference to the craftiness of the fox is drawn less from the views of contemporary naturalists than from the traditional tales, probably of Graeco-Roman origin, which produced the *Roman de Renart* in the twelfth century and were widely known in Europe; the wily fox was often used by the writers as a symbol of wit and cunning defeating brute force.

Langle and de la Manon, with several officers and naturalists, had gone on an expedition in the W. two days earlier with the aim of carrying out a similar search, which proved as fruitless as the other, but they came upon an Indian village at the edge of a small river which was entirely barred off by stakes for catching salmon. We had long suspected that this fish came from that part of the coast, but we were not sure; this discovery was of some importance in satisfying our curiosity. Mr Duché de Vancy made a drawing of this type of fishing that will explain better than any description that the salmon, swimming upriver, comes up to these stakes; being unable to get past them, it tries to return to the sea and finds on its way some baskets in the angles of this route; it enters and cannot turn back because they are very narrow and closed at the end; it is caught and in such quantity that the crews of both our vessels were supplied in abundance during our stay and each frigate salted two barrel loads of them.[1]

Our travellers also came upon a moray[2] which proved to us that the Indians customarily cremate bodies and keep the heads: they found one, wrapped in several layers of skin: this monument, drawn by Mr Duche, consists of four fairly strong posts over which is placed a small box of wooden planks containing the ashes in boxes; they opened one of these boxes, unwrapped the skins containing the head, and scrupulously returned everything to its proper place.[3] They added numerous gifts, items of iron and beads

[1] What the French had found was a temporary fishing trap, as the Tlingit did not live permanently in Lituya Bay where they merely erected summer encampments. The salmon swims upriver to spawn and is caught more usually on the way in as a number die off after spawning. Salmon were so numerous that a Tlingit village could easily catch a year's supply in a few weeks. The arrivals and departures from the bay indicate the transient nature of the Tlingit's residence. Milet-Mureau, the editor of the 1797 account of the voyage, added in a marginal note: 'This drawing has not reached us'.

[2] La Pérouse added a marginal note: 'I have kept the term Moray with, better than tomb, indicates exposition, whereas tomb denotes below ground'.

[3] The Tlingit feared drowning at sea because the customary cremation reported by La Pérouse could not be carried out, in which case the soul could not find the rest which the destruction of the body allowed. Other travellers have reported on the Tlingit's funeral practices: Alessandro Malaspina saw a particularly fine tomb at Port Mulgrave, a drawing of which is in the Bauza Collection at the Madrid Museo Naval; the Vancouver expedition came upon a highly ornate one; the Russian Lisianski who destroyed a large number of them in the village of Sitka in 1804 also commented that the posts were painted and decorated. The simplicity of the Lituya Bay stakes therefore seems to point to a less important or provisional exposition platform, unless the death was a recent one and it had not yet been decorated.

– the natives were witnesses of this scene; they displayed some anxiety, but did not fail quickly to remove the gifts our travellers had left, and other interested people, making a similar visit the next day, found only the ashes and the head: they added new riches which met the same fate as those of the previous day, and I am sure the Indians would have liked several such visits daily. But if they allowed us to approach their tombs, albeit with a little reluctance, it was different with their huts: they agreed to let us come near only after removing their women who are perhaps the most repugnant beings in the world.

Daily we [could] see new canoes entering the bay and daily whole villages went out, leaving their place to others; these Indians seemed to be very afraid of the pass over which they never ventured except at slack water, whether ebb or flow; we could clearly see with the glass that when they were between the two points, the chief or at least the chief Indian would raise his arms towards the sun and seem to be addressing prayers to it, while the others were paddling as hard as they could. It was when we asked for some clarification on this practice that we learned that seven very large canoes had been wrecked in the pass not long before. An eighth had escaped; the Indians who had been saved from this disaster dedicated it to their god or to the memory of their companions: we saw it next to a moray (similar to the 1st one I described) which contained the ashes of some of the victims.

This canoe was not like those of the local people which are made out of a hollowed treet trunk raised on each side by a plank attached to the bottom of the canoe; this one had a frame and strakes like our boats, and this well-made structure was sheathed in sealskins; and this was so well sewn that the best workmen in Europe would find it hard to copy it.[1] The sheath I have mentioned, which we measured most carefully, was placed in the moray next to the funeral caskets, and the frame of the canoe, raised on chocks, stood bare next to this monument.

It would have been most interesting to take this sheath to Europe; we were its unchallenged masters, this part of the bay

[1] La Pérouse is correct is concluding that different groups came to Lituya Bay. The canoe he describes may have belonged to the Chugach people further north; see E. Gunther, *Indian Life on the North West Coast of North America*, Chicago, 1972, p. 140. According to G.T. Emmons' informant, it may have come from Icy Strait, to the south, (1911), p. 297.

being uninhabited, no Indian could raise any obstacle; furthermore I am quite convinced that the shipwrecked men were strangers, and I will explain my theory in the next chapter; but respecting the sanctity of the final resting place of the dead is a universal convention and I wished to keep to it. Finally on 30 July at 4 p.m. we weighed anchor with a very weak W. breeze which dropped only when we were 3 leagues from shore. The horizon was so clear that we could see Mt St Elias bearing N.W. adjusted, distant at least 40 leagues.

At eight p.m. the bay entrance bore North 3 leagues, and the sounding-line gave 90 fathoms, ooze.

CHAPTER VIII

Description of Port des Français. Its latitude, its longitude, advantages & inconvenients of this port; its vegetable and mineral products, birds, fishes, shells, quadrupeds; customs & practices of the Indians, their crafts, their weapons, their clothing, their tendency to thieving; strong probability that the Russians alone communicate indirectly with these people; their music, their dances, their passion for gambling. Discussion on their language.

The bay, or rather the port, which I have named Port des Français, is according to our observations and those of Mr Dagelet situated in latitude 58° 37′ and longitude 139° 50′ Paris meridian.[1] The magnetic variation gives a declination of 28° East and an inclination of 74°. The chart I have appended will show its extent and layout better than any description. The sea rises 7½ feet at the new and the full moon; the tide is full at one o'clock. The sea breeze or possibly other causes act so powerfully on the current in the pass that I have seen the tide ebb like the fastest river, and in other circumstances, although at the same phases of the moon, a boat can row up it. I have measured the high-watermark of certain tides at 15 feet above sea level, and it is probable that these tides are those that occur during the bad months of the year. When the S. winds are strong, then the pass can be unmanageable, and whatever the weather it is difficult to enter because of the current; going out can also require a conjunction of circumstances which can delay a ship's departure for several weeks; one can only leave at high tide; the W. to N.W. breeze often rises only at around eleven o'clock, which does not allow one to take advantage of the morning tide; finally the easterlies which are unfavourable seem to me to be more frequent than the westerlies, and the height of the surrounding mountains never

[1] The actual latitude of Lituya Bay is 58°52′N and its latitude 139°55′W of Paris (147°35′W of Greenwich).

allows the land breeze or the N. winds to enter the bay. As this port has great advantages, I thought it worthwhile outlining in detail these drawbacks, and it seems to me that it would not be suitable for vessels sent out merely to trade in fur in a general way: they have to anchor in a number of bays and make a very short stay in each because the Indians will have sold everything in the first week and any waste of time is very harmful to their interests, but a country that would have plans for a trading post on this coast, like those of the English in Hudson Bay, could not find a better location than this one; a simple battery of four heavy guns placed on the main headland would be enough to defend such a narrow entrance which currents make so difficult; the battery could not be turned and captured from the land side as the sea always breaks furiously on the shore and a landing is impossible. The fort, stores and all the trading buildings would be erected on Cenotaph Island which has a circumference of about one league. It can be cultivated; it has wood and water. Ships which do not have to look around for their cargo but would find it collected at a single point would not be greatly concerned about a delay. A few buoys laid out as guides to navigation inside the bay would make it quite easy and safe – pilots would gain experience who, knowing better than we did the direction and speed of the currents at certain times of the year as well as the tides would oversee the arrival and departure of the vessels. And to conclude, our trade in otter furs was so considerable that I have to assume one could not find a greater quantity anywhere else in America.

The climate along this coast seemed to me to be much milder than at the same latitude in Hudson Bay. We measured pine trees six foot in diameter and 140 feet high, those of the same type at Fort Wales and Fort York being nothing more than small trees just good for jib-booms.[1]

Vegetation grows very vigorously for 3 or 4 months of the year. I would not be surprised to see Russian wheat and a wide range of ordinary plants succeed here. We found an abundance of celery, round-leafed sorrel, lupin, wild pea, milfoil, chicory and mimulus. The crew's cooking pot was filled with them every day and for

[1] Fort Wales and Fort York were two British posts in Hudson Bay, which La Pérouse captured, on 9 and 23 August respectively, during his famous 1782 raid. The climate along the northern Pacific coast of America is much milder than it is in Hudson Bay on account of winds and currents and a regular rainfall.

every meal; we ate them in soups, stews and salads, and these herbs played no small part in keeping us in good health. Amongst these kitchen plants, we came upon almost all those that are found in fields and mountain regions of France: angelica, buttercup, violet, and several kinds of grasses suitable as fodder; we could without any risk have cooked and eaten all those herbs if they had not been mixed in with several hardy hemlock plants we did not experiment with.[1]

The woods were full of strawberries, raspberries and currants. We found red-berried elders, dwarf willows, various types of heath that grow in the shade, balsam poplar, aspen, cottonwood and hornbeam;[2] and finally those superb pine trees with which one could make masts for our largest vessels. None of this vegetation is unknown in Europe; Mr de la Martinière found during his various excursions only three plants which he believes to be new, and one knows that a botanist can make a similar find in the environs of Paris.

The rivers were full of trout and salmon, but in the bay we only caught some halibut, a few of which weighted more than 100 pounds, some small wrasse, a single ray, some caplin and a few flounders.[3] As we preferred salmon and trout to all these fishes, and since the Indians sold us more than we could eat, we did very little fishing and then only with the rod. Our work never left us sufficient time to fish with the drag-seine which requires, to bring ashore, 25 or 30 men pulling together. Mussels are piled up in profusion on that part of the shore which is uncovered at low tide,

[1] The celery is probably the *Apium gravoelens*, the sorrel the *Rumex fenestratus* or *R. triangulivalvis*; there are several types of lupins and peas in the area – the latter may have been the *Lathyrus japonicus*. The milfoil could be either the *Achillea millefolium* or the *A. borealis*, the mimulus the *Mimulus lewisii* or *M. guttatus*. The chicory is the *Cichorium intybus*. Among the angelica one can choose the *Angelica lucida* or the *A. genuflexa*. Likely identifications for the others are *Ranunculus repens* for the buttercup, *Viola palustris* for the violet, and *Cicuta douglasii* for the hemlock.

[2] The strawberry is the *Fragaria chiloensis*, but the *F. glauca* is found near water; the raspberry could be the *Rubus arcticus* or the *R. spectabilis*; the currants belong to the *Ribes* family: *Ribes laxiflorum*, *L. bracteosum*, *R. lacustre*. The elder is the *Sambucus callicarpa* Greene. Willows are common: *Salix scouleriana*, *S. tristis*, *S. sitchensis*. The heath is *Cassiope mertensiana*. The poplars were the *Populus balsamifera* Barr, *P. tremuloides*, *P. trichocarpa hastata*. The hornbeam is the *Carpinus betulus*.

[3] The halibut is the *Hippoglossus stenolepsis* Schmidt, the so-called wrasse is the *Ophidion elongatus* Girard, the ray *Torpedo california* Ayres, the caplin *Mallotus villosus* Müller; the flounders are common and include the *Atherestes stomias* Jordan and the *Platichtys stellatus pallas*.

and the rocks are studded with fairly unusual small barnacles. One can also find in the hollows of these rocks various types of whelks and other periwinkles, and I saw on the beach some fairly large chamas. Mr de la Manon brought back from more than two hundred *toises* above sea level some very large and very well preserved petrifications of the shell known by conchiologists as royal mantles and more commonly called scallops; such is not unknown to naturalists, even at much greater heights, but I believe it will long remain difficult to explain in a way that will satisfy every objection; we found no shell of this type on the beaches, although it is known that they are Nature's treasure chest.

Our hunters saw in the woods some bears, martens and squirrels, and the Indians sold us some skins of brown and black bear, Canadian lynx, ermine, marten, miniver, common squirrel, beaver, marmot or monax and red fox. Mr de la Manon also caught a live water-vole or rat. I saw tanned moose or elk skins and an ibex horn – but the most widespread and valuable skin is that of the sea otter, the only amphibious animal with the wolves and the sea bear.[1] There a few varieties of birds, but they are fairly plentiful; the copses were filled with warblers, nightingales, blackbirds and hazel grouse. We were in the breeding season and their song struck me as being as attractive as in Europe. Above us we could see the white-headed eagle and the largest of crows.[2] We caught and killed a kingfisher and saw a very fine blue jay with a few humming birds; the swallow or swift had its nests in the hollows of the rocks along the shore, as well as the black oyster-catcher, the gull, the red-legged guillemot and the cormorant, the

[1] Bears were very common along the coast, including the Yakutat *Ursus nortoni* and the black *Ursus americanus*. The marten is *Marthes americana actuosa*. Squirrels are plentiful, especially the *Sciurus hudsonicus petulans*. The lynx is the *Lynx canadensis*, the ermine the *Mustela erminea alascensis*, the miniver the *Citellus parryi*, the beaver the *Castor canadensis pacificus*, the marmot the *Marmota caligata*, the red fox the *Vulpes alascensis*, the water-vole the *Ondrata zibethicus*, the elk the *Alces gygas* and the ibex the *Oreamnos Kennedy*. The otter is the *Enhydra lutis lutis*, the wolf was probably the *Canis lupus pambasileus*, and the reference to a sea bear probably indicates the presence of the white bear, *Ursus thalarctos maritimus*.

[2] What La Pérouse calls a warbler was probably the *Phylloscopus borealis Kennicotti*; the nightingale is not found is such high latitudes and is no doubt a misidentification; the blackbird is probably the *Euphagus carolinus* Müller and the grouse the *Canachytes canadensis*. The white-headed eagle is the *Haliaeetus leucocephalus* and the large crow the *Corvus corax* which measures up to 60 cm.

only seabirds we saw, together with a few ducks and large and small divers.[1]

But if the flora and fauna of this region approximate what is found elsewhere, its appearance is quite distinct, and I doubt that the deep valleys of the Alps or the Pyrenees present a more fearsome spectacle, which one might perhaps call sublime if it were not situated at one of the ends of the earth and so far from any resource.[2]

The primitive mountains of granite or schist, covered with eternal snows, on which one sees neither tree nor plant, go all the way down to the water and close off like a quay the port I am describing; at the foot of these mountains we found no depth at 160 fathoms a mere ship's length from shore. Their slope is so steep that after the first two or three hundred *toises* the alpine ibex could not climb it, and they are all separated by immense glaciers whose summit is lost to sight and which end at the edge of the sea.

The sides of the harbour are formed by smaller mountains, 800 or 900 *toises* high; these are covered in pine trees and greenery, and one only sees a few patches of snow on their tops;[3] they appeared

[1] The French probably saw the kingfisher *Megaceryle alcyon caurina*, Steller's jay *Cyanocitta Stelleri*, the colibri *Selasphorus rufus* or the rare *Archilochus colubris*. The swallows were probably the *Petrochelidon pyrrhonata* which nests in the hollows of cliffs. The oyster-catcher was the *Haematopus bachmani*. Among gulls of the Alaskan coast one can find the *Larus glaucus* and the *Larus occidentalis*. The red-legged guillemot could be the sea pigeon, *Cepphus columba*, which is not unlike the Atlantic guillemot with which La Pérouse would have been familiar, or the common *Fraternacula corniculata*, both of which have red legs. There are several sub-species of cormorant, including the *Phelacrocorax pelagicus* and the *P. urile*. The wild duck *Anas platyrhynchos* is common in this region and the divers could be the *Gavia arctica pacifica* and the *G. immer*.

[2] In his use of the word 'sublime' (which Milet-Mureau changed for 'pittoresque' in his 1797 edition), La Pérouse reveals the influence of eighteenth-century romantics, especially writers such as Rousseau, who were attracted by grandeur in Nature, steep mountains, precipices, torrents and isolated lakes. Even in English, the term 'sublime' used in connection with nature to describe awe-inspiring vastness or grandeur did not come into use until the eighteenth-century. Milet-Mureau, a more prosaic military man, presumably considered it inappropriately poetical.

[3] La Pérouse actually uses the expression 'a few acres of snow' which would read oddly in this context. Milet-Mureau altered this to one word, 'snow'. La Pérouse shows his acquaintance with Voltaire's sadly famous dismissal of French Canada as *quelques arpents de neige*, a description used in his *Candide*: 'You know that these two nations [England and France] are at war over a few acres of snow in Canada, and that they are spending over this war far more than Canada is worth' (*Candide*, ch. xxiii). The phrase might have roused some echo of pacifism at a time when England and France were once more at war, leading Milet-Murean, who was writing in dangerous time, to amend it.

to be entirely of schist at an early stage of decomposition; they are not entirely inaccessible, but extremely difficult to climb. Messrs de la Manon, de la Martiniere, Mongèz, Father Receveur, Colignon, the most tireless and zealous of naturalists, were unable to reach the summit, but they went up to a reasonable height at the cost of indescribable exertions – no stone, no pebble escaped their vigilance – too good phycisists to ignore the fact that one can find at the bottom of a cascade, at the foot of a mountain, samples of what it is made of, they gathered all they found, which we are bringing back to Europe: ochre, yellow pyrite, a very large and perfectly crystallised almandine, tourmalin in crystal form, granit, schist, hornstone, some very pure quartz, mica, graphite and coal. The ochre and the copper pyrites indicate that these mountains contain iron and copper deposits, but we saw no trace of any other metal.[1]

Nature owed to such a frightful country inhabitants who were as different from civilised people as the site I have just described is from our cultivated plains, as rough and as barbarous as their soil is stony and untilled. They live on this land only to depopulate it; warring against every animal, they feel only contempt for the vegetable products that grow around them. I have seen women and children eating some strawberries and raspberries, but it is no doubt a tasteless meal for these men who live on earth just like the vultures do in the air or wolves and tigers in the forests.

Their crafts are fairly advanced and in this respect their civilisation has made considerable progress, but what tones down man's behaviour and calms ferocity is still in its infancy; their social structure[2] in excluding all forms of subordination means that they

[1] Ochres or coloured sediments indicate the presence of hydrate iron oxide or may be merely an impression created by the presence of copper pyrites. The quartz was more correctly rock-crystal. Hornstone was falling into disuse at the time as a geological term, being too vague and 'applied to many different substances', J. B. M. Bucquet, *Introduction à l'étude des corps naturels tirés du règne mineral*, Paris, 1771, p. 243; the same criticism was being directed at the use of the term schist; geology, like the other sciences, was going through a period of controversy and reform, as shown by H.B. de Saussure's well-known comment: 'Nothing delays the progress of the natural sciences more than these vague terms; they encourage laziness, for once they are used one believes oneself freed from the need for any further research', *Voyages dans les Alpes*, Neuchâtel, 1779–96, I, p. 79.

[2] La Pérouse uses the term 'democracy' which, if so translated, can mislead the modern reader. Milet-Mureau, altered this to 'way of life'. La Pérouse is referring to the apparent absence of local rulers and of a set of formal enforceable laws among the local Tlingit – he had difficulty in identifying chiefs and heads of families among his visitors.

can fearlessly give way to their feelings of vengeance and hatred; irritable and quickly angered, I have seen them time and again dagger in hand set against each other. Exposed to starvation in winter when perhaps a hunt has failed, they live in the greatest abundance in summer, able to catch in less than an hour enough fish for their family; idle for the rest of the day they spend it gambling (which is for them as great a passion as it is for the residents of our great cities).[1] It is one of the main causes of their quarrels. I do not hesitate to state that these people would disappear if to all these vices and all these opportunities for brawls they were to add the misfortune of being introduced to some intoxicating liquor such as brandy, tafia rum, etc.

Philosophers may well protest against this description; they write their books by their fireside: I have been sailing for thirty years. I am a witness of the meannesses and deceit of these people who are presented to us as being so good because they live so close to Nature,[2] but Nature is sublime only as a whole, and it neglects the details. It is impossible to enter a forest when man has not cleared a way into it, to cross plains which although full of greenery are also full of stones and brambles and impenetrable marshes; to live side by side with men who have just stepped out of Nature, because they are barbarous, evil and deceitful. May I be allowed to hold such views, because they have not led me into the belief that I could teach them, at the cost of their own lives, that there is a law of nations that applies to us and to them.

The canoes of these Indians were constantly around our frigates. They spent three or four hours before concluding a barter deal involving a few fishes or two or three otter skins; they took every opportunity to rob us, wrenched off all the iron they could, and in particular looked around for ways of overcoming our vigilance

[1] Gambling was widespread among the Indian people of the Northwest Coast and not only among the Tlingit. Other visitors such as Dixon and Lisianski commented on their addiction and on the simplicity of the game they played. Missionaries later endeavoured, without much success, to curb this passion.

[2] These comments are directed at the supporters of the theory of the Noble Savage and of the corrupting influence of civilisation on the innate goodness of natural man, views which had gained a great deal of support at the time following the writings of Jean-Jacques Rousseau and, among others, the voyage of Louis de Bougainville in 1766–9. This passage, coming relatively early in La Pérouse's journal, makes it clear that he had long held these views and that the attack his expedition later sustained in Samoa, which gave rise to a similar outburst, merely confirmed them.

during the night. I brought the leading men on board my frigate and showered gifts on them – and those very men whom I singled out for such attention never hesitated to steal a nail or an old pair of breeches: when they put on a smiling and gentle look, I was sure that they had stolen something, and very often I pretended not to notice.

I had expressly urged our people to pet the children and heap little gifts on them; the parents were indifferent to this show of kindness which I thought was understood everywhere; the only thought it inspired in them was that by asking for their children to be allowed to come with them when they came up on board they would be able to rob us; and, as part of my education, I had several times the pleasure of seeing the father taking advantage of the moment when we were making a fuss of his child to steal and hide under his skin cloak everything he could lay his hands on.

I pretended to want small items of little value which belonged to Indians on whom I had showered presents; it was a test of their generosity, but it always failed.

I will admit, if one insists, that a society cannot exist without some qualities, but I am forced to say that I lacked the sagacity to discern any. Always quarrelling, indifferent towards their children, tyrants towards their wives who were repeatedly condemned to the heaviest taks, I saw nothing among these people to brighten up this picture. We only went ashore armed and in strength; they were distinctly afraid of our muskets, and a group of eight or ten Europeans was enough to cow a whole village. The senior surgeons of our two frigates were attacked because they were unwise enough to go hunting alone; the Indians tried to take their muskets away, but did not succeed: two men were enough to impress them and make them step back. The same happened to Mr Leseps, the young Russian interpreter, who was fortunately rescued by one of our boats' crews. These tentative acts of hostility seemed so straightforward to them that they did not stop coming on board and never suspected that we might have taken reprisals.

I have given the name of village to 3 or 4 wooden sheds, 25 feet long and 15 to 20 wide, roofed only on the windward side with planks or tree bark; in the middle of this hearth (for I do not know what to call it) was a fire over which some halibut and salmon were hung, drying in the smoke. Eighteen or twenty people lived in each shed: the women and children on one side, the men on the other; it seemed to me that each hut made up a small group which was independent of its neighbour; each one had its canoe and some kind of chief; it went out, left the bay, taking its fish and planks with it without the rest of the village apparently taking the slightest notice.

I think I am right in stating that this port is only occupied during the fine season and that the Indians never spend the winter there; I did not see a single hut that was waterproof, and although the total of Indians in the bay never reached three hundred at any one time we were visited by seven or eight hundred more.

The canoes came and went ceaselessly, each one taking out or bringing back their homes and furnishings which consist of numerous small boxes in which they keep their most precious belongings. These boxes are placed at the entrance of their huts which moreover are dirtier and more smelly than the lair of any known animal; they never take two steps to fulfil a natural need, and for such occasion seek neither shade nor privacy, continuing a conversation they have started as if they did not have a moment to lose, and when it is mealtime they return to their place from which they had not stepped away by a *toise*; the wooden pots in which they cook their fish are never washed – they are used as stewpots, dishes and plates: as those pots cannot be placed over a fire they boil the water by means of red-hot stones which they replace until the food is completely cooked. They also know how to roast them; their method is no different from that of our soldiers in the field. It is probable that we saw only a very small part of this nation which no doubt occupies a fairly considerable part of the coast – they live a nomadic life in summer, looking for food in the various bays like seals, and going inland in winter to hunt beaver and other animals of which they brought us the furs. Although they were always barefoot, their soles were not calloused and they could never walk over stones, which shows that they only travel in canoes or with snowshoes.

Dogs are the only animals with which they have established links. There are usually three or four of them per hut. They are small and like the shepherd dog described by Mr de Buffon. They hardly bark and whistle very much like the Bengal adive, and are so wild that they seem to bear the same relationship to other dogs as their masters do to civilised people.[1]

[1] Dogs played an important part in the life of the Indians. They were used for hunting and transport, as well as a means of protecting villages; they were

The men have the nose and ears pierced and hang various small ornaments. They scar their arms and chest with a very sharp iron instrument which they sharpen by rubbing against their teeth as on a whetstone: their teeth are filed down to the gums, and they use for this operation a rounded sandstone shaped like a tongue.[1] Ochre, soot, graphite, mixed with seal oil, are used to paint their faces and the rest of their bodies with frightful designs. Their hair is worn long, braided and sprinkled, on the occasion of great ceremonies, with the down of seabirds; that is their greatest luxury and it may be reserved for the heads of families. A mere skin or fur covers their shoulders; the rest of their body is completely bare, except for the head which is usually covered with a small straw hat, very artistically plaited; but sometimes they place over their heads two-cornered hats, eagle feathers and also whole heads of bears into which they have inserted a wooden skull-cap. We brought several of these headgears back to Europe;[2] they vary a great deal, but like most of their practices the main purpose seems to be to make them look frightening, possibly in order to inspire greater awe in their enemies.

Some Indians had whole sealskin shirts, and the usual dress of the great chief was a gown of tanned moose hide edged with a fringe of deer hoofs and bird beaks which made a bell-like noise when he danced: this same dress is quite widespread among the natives of Canada and other parts of northern America.

I only saw tattoings on the arms of a few women. These follow a custom which makes them hideous and which I would find it hard to believe if I had not seen it; without exception, they have the

---

sometimes eaten, when starvation threatened. In 1794, Vancouver came across about fifty dogs in a recently abandoned village by Yakutat Bay, *A Voyage of Discovery*, London, 1798, III, p. 230; W. Kaye Lamb ed., *The Voyage of George Vancouver 1791–1795*, London, 1984, IV, p. 1334. La Pérouse describes their bark as similar to that of an adive, a term used at the time for an Asian jackal: jackals have a very distinctive call, unlike the bark of a European dog.

[1] La Pérouse is the only traveller to mention the filing of teeth by means of a tongue-shaped stone. (See E. Gunter, *Indian Life*, p. 144.) His description however is so precise that it is hard to believe he was mistaken. As for the various types of headgear, museums in Europe and America have enough of them in their collections to confirm his description.

[2] La Pérouse wrote this in the expectation that he would return home with these items. Milet-Mureau naturally excised the phrase 'We brought back . . . to Europe' from his 1797 edition.

lower lip split at gum level across the width of the mouth; they wear a wooden saucer which rests against the gums with the split lip serving as an outer edging so that the lower part of their mouths protrudes by two or three inches. Mr Duché Devancy's picture which is of the greatest exactitude will explain better than words this custom, perhaps the most revolting on earth. Young girls have only a needle in the lower lip, and married women are the only ones entitled to the plate; on occasion we urged them to take off this ornament, they did so reluctantly, expressing the same embarrassment as a European woman whose breast is bared; then the lower lip fell over the chin, and the second picture was scarcely better than the first.[1]

These beings, the most repulsive on earth, covered with stinking skins which often were not even tanned, nevertheless aroused some desire among a few individuals, who in truth were very privileged; they first of all expressed reluctance, explaining by gestures that they were risking their lives, but overcome by gifts they insisted on having the sun as their witness and refused to hide in the woods.

One cannot doubt that this heavenly body was these people's god. They were often prayed to it, but I saw no temples or priests or any trace of a religion.[2]

These Indians are approximately of the same height as ourselves; their features are very varied and have no particular trait save the expression in their eyes which is never a gentle one; their skin is generally very brown, because they are constantly exposed to the

[1] This practice was commented upon by James Cook who saw in May 1778 women and girls in Prince William Sound: 'Though the lips of all were not slit, yet all were bored, espicially the women and even the young girls; to these holes and slits they fix pieces of bone of this size [ ] and shape, placed side by side in the inside of the lips; a thread is run through them to keep them together, and some goes quite through the lip.' Cook, *Journals*, III, p. 350. James Colnett made similar comments during his 1787 visit to the Chugach Indians in the *Prince of Wales*, and Spanish navigators found it widespread among the Haida people. Portlock gives additional details: 'In the slit of the lip they have a bone or ivory instrument fitted with holes in them, from which they hang beads as low as the chin. These holes in the lip disfigure them very much, some of them having it as large as the mouth.', *A Voyage round the World*, London, 1789, p. 249.

[2] Most of the early visitors to the Northwest Coast believed the Indians worshipped the sun, but they endowed all nature with spirit life, and paid homage to many forms of spirits. In Port des Français, in addition to the spirit of the glaciers and the warrior spirits at play on their heights, they needed to placate Kah Lituya, 'a monster of the deep who dwells in the ocean caverns near the entrance', Emmons, 'Native Account of a Meeting' (1911), p. 295.

weather, but their children are born as white as ours; they can grow beards, admittedly a little smaller than those of Europeans, but noticeably enough to remove all doubt: it is an error, too easily accepted, to think that the American people are beardless – I have met natives of New England, of Canada, Acadia and Hudson's Bay, and I have found among those various people several bearded individuals; and this made me think that the others customarily pluck their beards out.

They are not stocky; our smallest sailors could have downed the strongest of them in a wrestling match; I saw several with swollen legs, which is very much like scurvy. Their gums however were in good condition; but I doubt that they live to a great age, and I saw only one woman who seemed to be 60: she enjoyed no particular privilege and was like the others required to carry out the tasks that fall upon her sex.

My travels have allowed me to compare different nations, and I venture to state that the Indians of Port des Français are not Eskimos and clearly share a common origin with all the inhabitants of the interior of Canada and the northern parts of America.[1]

Totally different customs and quite distinct features distinguish the Eskimos from other Americans; the former seem to me to be like the people of Greenland, they live along the Labrador coast, Hudson's Strait and a stretch of land right across America as far as the Alaskan peninsula; whether the first home of these people was Greenland or Asia is subject to a great deal of argument: it is an idle topic of discussion which will never be finally settled; it is enough to state that the Eskimos are more hunters than fishermen, prefer oil to blood and possibly to everything else, and very regularly eat raw fish: their canoes are always lined with sealskin and they handle them so skilfully that they hardly differ from the seals and turn over in the water with the same agility as these amphibious animals.

[1] La Pérouse is drawing on his own experience to place the Tlingit within the broader framework of North American Indian ethnology. The distinction he makes with the Eskimos (the Inuit) is correct. The Tlingit formed only one group, estimated at the time to number 10,000 people, roughly equal in size to their neighbours, the Haida people. Both names actually mean 'the people' in their respective languages. Up to 120 tribal groups have been identified as living in the Alaska and British Columbia region, each with its own dialect, but with many similarities in their social structures, religious beliefs and dress. See A. Krause, *The Tlingit Indians*, Seattle, 1956, translated by E. Gunther, and a recent Russian study by C.M. Taksami, *Osnovnye Problemy Etnografi i Historii Niokhov*, Leningrad, 1975.

Their face is square, their eyes and their feet are small, their chest broad, their stature small; none of these features seems to fit the natives of *Baye des Français* who are much taller, thin, not strongly built, clumsy with their canoes which are built with a hollowed-out tree and raised on each side with a plank.[1]

They fish as we do, by erecting barriers across rivers or with a line, but their way of line fishing is rather ingenious. They tie a large seal bladder to each line and let it go in the water; each canoe throws twelve to 15 lines; as the fish is caught, it drags the bladder, the canoe goes after it, and thus two men can supervise twelve or 15 lines and do not have to hold them in their hands.[2]

These Indians have made much greater progress in their crafts than in morals, and their trades are more advanced than those of the South Sea islanders, excepting however agriculture which, by making man more home-loving, ensuring his subsistence and instilling the fear of seeing the land he has tilled being ravaged, is possibly more likely than anything else to soften manners and make him sociable.

The Americans of Port des Français can forge iron, work copper, spin the hair of various animals and sew with this wool a material similar to our tapestries; they mix into this material lengths of sealskin, which makes their coats like the finest silken plush; nowhere are reed hats and baskets more skilfully plaited; they work into them quite attractive designs; they also carve quite adequately all kinds of figures, of men or animals, in wood or stone; they make boxes inlaid with the opercula of shells, quite elegant in shape: they shape serpentine into jewels and polish it like marble.[3]

[1] It is now generally accepted that the Eskimos (Inuit) are of Asiatic origin and were probably the last group to migrate into America by way of Behring Strait. The reference to raw fish is correct – the name applied to them by the Abnaki tribe, from which the term Eskimo is derived, *eskimantsik*, means 'eaters of raw flesh' – but this practice was born of necessity, not choice. La Pérouse's observations are broadly correct.

[2] The relative lack of manoeuvrability of the canoes was the reason why the Tlingit followed a moving bladder: they went after the fish to club them to death lest their struggles cause the canoes to overturn, E. Gunther, *Indian Life*, p. 146.

[3] The observations made by La Pérouse as the first visitor to this lonely part of the world are of considerable importance. Agriculture was not totally alien to the Tlingit who had a few small fields in sheltered places. Iron, on the other hand, was probably obtained by barter with other tribes. The same may well be true of the copper and elaborate clothing seen by La Pérouse: if these items were locally made, they were not plentiful. Wood carving and shell inlay work, however, was widespread along the coast.

Their weapons are the dagger I described earlier, a lance of wood hardened in the fire or of iron, according to the owner's wealth, and finally bows and arrows usually tipped with copper; but the bows are nothing special and much less powerful than those of other peoples.

I found among their jewellery pieces of yellow amber or succin[1] but I do not know whether it is a local product or like iron is an item brought from the old continent by the Russians. I have a strong feeling that this country is the only one which communicates indirectly with these people since it alones brings to European and Asian markets the fur of the otter which has not even been seen by any Canadian trader or employee of the Hudson's Bay [Company].

I have already stated that seven great canoes were wrecked at the entrance to this port. These canoes, of which I append a sketch made after the only one which survived was 34 feet long, 4 wide and six deep; such a size made them suitable for long journeys; they were lined with sealskins, like those of the Eskimos, which gave me and Mr de Langle the impression that Port des Français is a storage area only inhabited during the barter and fishing season; it seemed possible to us that the Eskimos of the *Schamagin* Islands[2] region and of the Alaskan peninsula visited by Captain Cook trade as far as this part of America, bringing iron and other Russian items and returning with otter furs at a profit, since the Russians are so eager to obtain them; the shape of the lost canoes makes this very probable, as does the large quantity of furs we bought, which can be collected here to be sold to these strangers: I am merely putting forward a theory, but it seems to me to explain better than any other the origin of the iron and of other European items.

[1] Succin or amber is a fossil resin exuded from coniferous trees. La Pérouse's speculations on contacts with the Russians were tentative because at the time he was writing little was known about Russian penetration. Based on Irkutsk and Okhotsk, Russian traders had gradually advanced along the Aleutian chain. In 1763 Glotov had reached the island of Kodiak where Shelikov established an outpost in 1783. Thousands of furs began to appear on the Russian and Chinese markets and Russian goods made their appearance along the Northwest Coast. Greater interest in this episode was sparked by the centenary of the acquisition of Alaska by the United States in 1867, and the revival has spread to Russian historians. See H. Chevigny, *Russian America: the Great Alaskan Adventure 1741–1867*, New York, 1965 and J. Gibson, *Imperial Russia in Frontier America*, New York, 1976.

[2] The Shumagin Islands are situated off the south coast of the Alaskan peninsula. James Cook reached them on 18 June 1778.

I have already mentioned the Indians' passion for gambling. What they indulge in, with fierce energy, is a mere game of chance; there are thirty small wooden sticks, each marked differently, like our dice; they hide 7 of them. Each one plays in turn and the one who comes closer to the number marked on the seven hidden sticks wins the agreed stake which is usually a piece of iron or an axe.[1] This game makes them serious and doleful; I have however heard them singing quite often and when the chief came visiting he went around the ship once or twice, singing and holding out his arms crosswise, as a sign of friendship. He then climbed on board and acted out a pantomime which depicted fights, or ambushes or death; the tune which preceded this dance was pleasant and fairly harmonious when sung in chorus. I have had it copied down.[2]

Mr de la Manon is the author of the following dissertation on these people's language of which I shall give only their terms for numbers in order to satisfy those readers who like to compare different idioms.[3]

one	keirrk
two	theirh★
three	neisk
four	taakhoun
five	keitschine
six	kleitouchou
seven	takatouchou
eight	netskatouchou
nine	kouchok
ten	tchinekate
eleven	keirkrha-keirrk
twelve	theirh

[1] The description of this game is fairly accurate; it was widespread along the coast. A number of these sticks are held in the British Museum.

[2] Singing played an important part in Tlingit life and generally had religious implications; certain songs were family-based and were addressed to the family's protective spirits or commemorated an important event. La Pérouse added the following marginal note on group singing: 'Those who have the deepest voices take the tune, a third lower, & the women a third higher than natural singing; some sing on the octave and often pause for two bars at the point where the tune is highest'.

[3] Marginal note: 'Following the Voyage one will find a more extensive vocabulary of the language of the people we visited; it was compiled by Messrs the Abbé Mongèz, de la Manon, Father Receveur, Lavau, Leceps, Monneron, and the first-named was kind enough to write it up.'

thirteen	neisk
fourteen	taakhoun
fifteen	keitschine
sixteen	kleitouchou
seventeen	takatouchou
eighteen	netskatouchou
nineteen	kouchok
twenty	theirha
thirty	neiskrha
forty	taakounrha
fifty	keitschinerha
sixty	kleitouchourha
seventy	takatouchourha
eighty	netskatouchourha
ninety	kouchokrha
one hundred	tchinecaterha★

★to represent the guttural R which these people pronouce even harder than the Germans do the chr we have used rh, as if one was to pronounce *rhabiller* with a strongly rolled r, this being more in accordance with the French language.[1]
★★After each group of ten they begin again with the nouns for the units without repeating the affix for the tenths as we can see from numbers eleven to twenty.

Our letters cannot render the language of these people; they do have certain sounds which are like ours, but several are totally alien to us; they do not use the letters B, F, X, J, D, P, U (the vowel) and in spite of their talent for mimicry never could pronounce the first four of these. The same can be said of the palatalised L and GN; they pronounced the R as if it was doubled and strongly rolled, the *dja*, the *etz*, the *chr* of the people of Provence and the Italians, and the chr of the Germans which they pronounce as harshly as the Swiss of certain cantons They also have an articulated sound which was very difficult to catch; we could not attempt to say it without causing them to laugh: it is partly represented by the letters *khlrl* pronounced as a single syllabe, coming at the same time from the

[1] The phonetic rendering of these Tlingit words is reprinted as set down by the French and was naturally based on their own phonetic system. An English speaker would have written the words down differently, e.g. four might have been tarc'oon, five kaychin, and six claytushu.

throat and the tongue. This syllabe is found in the word *khlrleies* which means hair. Initial consonants are the K, the T, N, S, M. The former are the most frequently used; they have no word which begins with an R and almost all end in *ou*, *oulse*, *oulch* or with a vowel. The rolling of the r, the large number of Ks, and double consonants make this language very harsh; it is less guttural among men than among women who cannot pronounce labials on account of the little wooden round plate, called *katenga*, which they fit into their lower lip.

The harshness of their language is less noticeable when they sing. I have been able to make very few observations on parts of speech on account of the difficulty of communicating abstract concepts by means of gestures.

I did however notice that they have interjections to express feelings of admiration, anger or pleasure. I do not think that they have articles, as I did not find words that recurred frequently and served to link their parts of speech. They are aware of numbers and have words for them, without however distinguishing between singular and plural either by a change in the endings or by articles; I showed them the tooth of a seal – they called it *kaourré*, and gave the same name, unchanged in any way, to several teeth shown together. They have very few collective names. They have not generalised enough their ideas to have any need for words that are a little abstract; they have not particularised them enough to avoid giving the same name to things that are quite different, thus their word *kaaga* means head as well as face, and *alcaou* both chief and friend. I found no similarities between their language and those of the people of Alaska, Norton, or Nootka, nor of the people of Greenland, of the Eskimos, the Mexicans, the *Nadoessis* or the *Chipavas*[1] whose vocabularies I compared; I quoted to them words from these various dialects, but they understood none of them, and yet I varied my pronunciation as much as I could; but although there may not be a concept or a thing which is expressed by the same word by the Indians of Port des Français and by the people I have mentioned, there must be a great similarity of sound between this language and that of King George Sound. In both the K is the

[1] References are to Norton Bay and Nootka Sound in north-west Alaska; the Nadoessis are the Nadouessioux (soon shortened as Sioux), the Chipavas are the Chippewas of the Great Lakes region.

dominant sound, one finds it in almost every word, and the initial consonants and the endings are fairly often the same, and it is not impossible that this tongue may have the same origin as that of the Mexicans, but this origin (if it exists) must go back to very early times, since these dialects have any links only in the basic features of the words and not in their meaning.[1]

I will close this article on these people by saying that we found no trace of cannibalism, but it is such a widespread practice among the natives of America that I do not doubt I would have had to add it to this discussion of their customs if they had been at war and had taken a prisoner.[2]

[1] La Pérouse draws to some extent on the vocabulary recorded by Cook. The surgeon David Samwell who recorded a number of words from the Nootka region in his journal comments on their harsh sound. 'The Language of these Indians is remarkably harsh and guttural, many of their words not to be pronounced by Europeans.', Cook, *Journals*, III, p. 1103. The Indian populations of Mexico also had an Asiatic origin, but their migrations date so far back that one cannot talk of links with the Indians of the northern regions. The Tlingit population has now dropped considerably; their language was studied at the turn of the century, see John Swanton, *Social Conditions, Beliefs and Linguistic beliefs of the Tlingit Indians* (American Bureau of Ethnology, Washington, 1908) and Franz Boas, *Handbook of American Indian Languages*, Washington, 1911.

[2] Cannibalism is reported in the account of John Meares' stay in Nootka Sound. See *Voyages made in the Years 1788 and 1789 from China to the North-West Coast of America*, London, 1790, pp. 255–7. However, the practice seems to have been linked to warfare and only prisoners taken in battle were eaten.

CHAPTER IX

Departure from Port des Français; exploration of the coast of America. The primitive & treeless mountains end at Cross Sound and seem to move into the interior of America. Bay of Islands of Captain Coock. Port of Los Remedios & Bucarelli, of the pilot Morelle; it is not situated on the continent but between some islands which are perhaps 40 leagues away from it: islands of La Croyere. St Carlos Islands. All the coastline we have followed from Cross Sound or at least from Cape Tchirikov consists only of islands as far as Cape Hector: they are at such a distance from the continent that we saw it only to the E. of Cape Fleurieux. Gulf or channel 40 leagues wide and of a depth which circumstances did not allow us to determine, in 51^{d} 57′ of latitude. We could have mistaken it for the entrance to St Lazar channel if the voyage of Admiral de Fuentes was not a fable with no element of truth in it. But it is likely that between the islands I have already mentioned and the continent, there is a small sea 6 or 7^{d} deep to the north like the sea of California. Sartine Islands – wooded headland of Captn Cook on which we verified our timekeepers to ensure the correctness of our readings on this coast. Breaker Point. Small space near Cape Flattery which the fog prevented us from surveying; strong currents near the Round Cape of the Spanish: Necker Islands 1 l. off White Cape. The fog is much thicker and more frequent on this part of the coast than near Mt St Elias and Mt Fairweather. Arrival at Monterey.

AUGUST 1786

The stay I had been forced to make in Port des Français had compelled me to alter my plan of navigation along the Pacific coast; I still had time to coast down it, to determine its trend, but I could not entertain the thought of any other stay and even less of exploring every bay. All my planning had to be subordinated to the absolute necessity of reaching Manila at the [...] of January, and

China during February, so as to be in a position to spend the next summer surveying the coasts of Tartary, Japan, Kamchatka and as far as the Aleutian Islands. I realised with sadness that such a vast programme would only leave enough time to glimpse things and never eradicate uncertainty, but compelled to sail in seas subject to the monsoon I had either to lose a year or reach Monterey between the 10th to the 17th of September, spend only 6 or 7 days there to replace the water and the wood we would have used up, and then cross the Great Ocean as speedily as possible, over a distance of more than 120^{d} of longitude, which as is known is much the same between the tropics as it is along the equator. Justifiably I was afraid that I would not have time to visit the Caroline Islands and those that lie to the north of the Mariana Islands as I had been instructed. The exploration of the Carolines would depend more or less on the circumstances of our crossing which we should expect to be a very long one in view of the poor sailing quality of our vessels; and the geographic situation of these islands which are far to the W. or to leeward did not easily allow me to include them in the subsequent plans of navigation still facing me S. of the Line.

These various considerations led me to fix new rendezvous points with Mr de Langle in case we should become separated; I had previously given him the ports of Los Remedios and Nootka;[1] it was agreed among us that we would now only put in at Monterey, this latter port being preferred because as it was the furthest away we would have more water and wood to replace.

Our misfortunes in Port des Français necessitated cartain changes in staff arrangements. I gave Mr Darbaud, a *garde de la marine* and a highly educated person, a warrant as acting *enseigne*, and I gave a frigate lieutenant's warrant to Mr Broudou, a young volunteer who had given me evidence of his intelligence and his zeal since our departure from France.

Confident that only fame could compensate for the hardships endured in this campaign by the officers and passengers, I decided to sell our furs on behalf of the sailors alone when we reached China, and I issued instructions that Mr Dufrêsne should take on

[1] Juan Francisco Bodega y Quadra, commanding the *Sonora*, and the pilot Francisco Maurelle whom La Pérouse was to meet later, entered a bay in August 1775, which he named Puerto de los Remedios. It was probably Sea Lion Bay (see D. Orth, *Dictionary of Alaskan Place Names*, Washington, 1967, p. 847). Nootka Sound is James Cook's King George's Sound on Vancouver Island.

this task; he carried out these duties with a zeal and an ability which I cannot praise too highly; he supervised the bartering, packing and sale of the various furs; and as I am sure that not a single fur was sold privately this arrangement enabled us to know precisely what the price was in China, whereas had the sailors competed against each other the price would have fluctuated; this was for the best advantage of the sailors who have remained convinced that their interests and their health have been our overriding concern since our departure.

The first days of our new navigation were not lucky ones, and did not satisfy my impatience: we covered only 6 leagues during the first 48 hours; during those two days light breezes varied from N. to S. by E., the weather cloudy but foggy; we were still 3 or 4 leagues offshore and within sight of the low-lying land, but had only occasional glimpses of the high mountains; this was sufficient to link up our bearings and determine with great accuracy the lie of the coast, carefully recording the latitude and longitude of its main features. I would have wished that the winds could have allowed me rapidly to explore this coast as far as to Cape Edgecumbe or Cape Engaño,[1] because it had already been seen by Cap^ne^ Cook who, admittedly, passed at a great distance from it, but his observations were so precise that he could only make very slight errors and, being in as much of a hurry as that famous navigator, I felt that I could not attend to small details any more than he had, that they should be seen to by a special expedition[2] and that this required several seasons. I was most impatient to reach 55^d^ and have a little time to devote to this exploration as far as Nootka where a sudden gale had driven Cap^ne^ Cook some 50 or 60 leagues offshore. It was in this part of America that, according to Mr de Guignes, the Chinese are said to have landed,

[1] Edgecumbe, a headland on the south coast of Kruzof Island at the entrance to Sitka Sound, was sighted by Cook on 2 May 1778 who named it after Admiral George Edgecumbe (1721–95). It was named Cabo del Engaño by Bodega y Quadra.

[2] Marginal note by La Pérouse: 'More compelling reasons still will be outlined in a separate report.' This is a reference to reports requested by the French authorities on possibly trade on the Northwest Coast. Several reports were sent back on this, by La Pérouse and by Dufresne, e.g. La Pérouse's 'Mémoire sur les loutres de mer', AN.M. 3JJ 386, 111:3, but especially the 'Mémoires sur le commerce de pelleteries qu'on pourrait établir à la Côte Nord-Ouest de l'Amérique', AN.M. B4 318, a file on which some official has written: 'This work is very precious'.

and it is also in these same latitudes that Admiral de Fuentes discovered the San Lazaro archipelago.[1]

I had very little faith in Mr de Guignes' conjectures and not much more in the account of the Spanish admiral whose very existence is open to argument; but struck by the remark I have already made that in recent times all the islands and all the countries mentioned in the old Spanish accounts – admittedly surrounded with fabulous circumstances and in very inaccurate latitudes and longitudes – have been rediscovered, I was inclined to believe that some ancient navigator belonging to that industrious nation had sailed into an inlet whose entrance might lie along this part of the coast, and that this single real event might have been the basis for the ridiculous tale of Fuentes and Bernarda.[2] I had no intention of entering such a channel if I found it, because the season was too advanced and I could only have sacrificed my entire plan of voyage to survey it if I had hopes of reaching the sea lying to the E. by crossing America; but being quite sure since Mr Hearn's travels[3] that this passage is a dream I had decided that I would only determine the E. to W. width of the channel and sail a mere 25 or 30 leagues N., depending on the time I could spare, leaving to nations which have possessions

[1] La Pérouse is referring to the imaginary voyage of Bartholomew de Fonte (Fuentes) reported in an English periodical called *The Monthly Miscellany or Memoirs for the Curious* in 1708, which gained wide currency in the early part of the eighteenth century, and to the writings of Joseph de Guignes (1721–1800), in particular his *Histoire générale des Huns, des Turcs, des Mongols et autres Tartares occidentaux avant et depuis Jésus-Christ et jusqu'à présent* 5 vols, Paris, 1756–8 and *Recherches sur les navigations des Chinois à la côte de l'Amérique*, Paris, 1761. Guignes reprinted the claim that in the year 458 the Chinese had established a settlement at 'Fu-Sang' which was identified with the American continent, and that it was situated in approximately 55°N, i.e. on Baranof Island.

[2] Pedro de Bernarda was reputedly the captain of the second ship which Fonte sent to explore a deep rivermouth which led into a large lake; Bernarda then sailed east-north-east through these waters as far as 77°N.

[3] Samuel Hearne (1745–92), an employee of the Hudson's Bay Company, tried on three occasions between 1769 and 1772 to find 'a mountain of copper' mentioned by an Indian chief; he reached the mouth of the Coppermine River in 67°50'N and then returned to Fort Churchill. His travels showed that there were no signs of an east-west passage over a wide area of northern Canada. La Pérouse met Hearne in August 1782 when the Englishman was in charge of Prince of Wales Fort which he captured. 'A fine figure of a man, and well educated', commented La Pérouse who assisted Hearne to return to England. La Pérouse's report on this appeared in the *Gazette de France* of 29 October 1782 and an English account was written by Edward Umfreville and published in London in 1790 under the title *The Present State of Hudson's Bay*. See also G. Williams, 'Remarks on the French Raids on Churchill and York, 1782', *Hudson's Bay Record Miscellany*, XXX (1972), pp. 77–94.

on the American continent, such as the Spanish, the English and the Americans, the task of carrying out a more thorough survey that could be of no importance for the greater aspects of navigation which was the sole purpose of our voyage.

The fog, the rain and the calms did not come to an end until the 4th at midday. We observed 57^{d} 45′ of latitude, 3 leagues from the land which we could not see clearly on account of the fog; it fortunately cleared at 4 o'clock and we were able to recognise without any difficulty Cross Sound[1] which seemed to form two very deep bays where in all likelihood ships would find a good anchorage.

The high snow-covered mountains, with peaks rising to 1300 to 1400 *toises*, come to an end at Cross Sound: along the sea, S.E. of Cross Sound, the land, although still reaching heights of 800 to 900 *toises*, is tree-covered right up to the summits, and the range of primitive mountains seemed to vanish into the interior of America. At sunset the W. point of Cross Sound bore from me N.25^{d}W, distant approximately 5 leagues.[2] At the same time, Mount Fairweather bore from me N.50^{d}W. and Mount Crillon (named after my friend, the Comte de Crillon) N.45^{d}W. This mountain, almost as high as the former, lies N. of Cross Sound, just as Mount Fairweather lies N. of Port des Français; each one is a landmark for its neighbouring port; it would be easy to mistake one for the other when coming from the S. if their latitude did not differ by 15′. Moreover, from all angles, Mount Fairweather seems to be close to two, lower mountains, but Mount Crillon, more isolated, has a peak sloping towards the S. I continued to coast 3 Ls off shore,

[1] Cross Sound was so named by James Cook on 3 May 1778, it being the Feast of the Invention (or discovery) of the Cross. La Pérouse's description is accurate – Cross Sound leads to Glacier Bay and Icy Strait; however, he may be referring to two smaller openings, closer to the sound's entrance: Taylor Bay and Elfin Cove, both of which would be visible from a ship standing off. The high mountains mentioned are the Fairweather Range which ends here, while the lower land is Chichagof Island.

[2] The western point of Cross Sound is Cape Spencer. In the 1797 French account of the voyage, the reference to the Comte de Crillon was omitted – he was imprisoned in 1793, although he had liberal tendencies. Félix-François-Dorothée de Berton, Comte de Crillon, was born in 1748 and served in the Spanish and French armies; a colonel in 1772 and infantry brigadier in 1780, he fought at Minorca, Gibraltar and Jamaica and was raised to the rank of general (*maréchal de camp*). He joined the reformist cause at the Revolution and was appointed lieutenant-general in 1792. Napoleon made him a duke in 1806. He died in 1827. The Paris home he purchased in 1788 is now one of the capital's most exclusive hotels.

with the mountains still very much shrouded in mist; we could only see the low lands at intervals, endeavouring to discern their high points so as not to lose the thread of our bearings.

We were making only very slight progress: our route covered only 10 Ls S.E. in 24 hrs. At daybreak I sighted bearing N. 29^{d} W a cape S. of the entrance to Cross Sound. I called it Cape Cross.[1] Athwart of us lay a multitude of small low islands covered in trees; high hills appeared behind, and we could no longer see the snowy mountains. I went close to the small islands until, from the bridge, I could see the breakers along the coast, and I noticed a number of passes between them which must provide good roadsteads: to this part of the coast Captain Cook gave the name of Bay of Islands.[2] At sunset the entrance to the Port of Los Remedios bore from us E.2^{d}S, Guadelupe Bay E.21^{d}S, and Cape Engaño also E.33^{d}S., but all these capes were ill-defined on account of the mist that surrounded their tops.

I am convinced that one would find 20 different ports over a stretch of coast 25 leagues long from Cross Sound to Cape Engaño, and that 3 months would scarcely suffice to explore this labyrinth. I kept to my original plan when I left Port des Français of determining precisely where these islands began and ended, as well as their trend along the coast and the entrance of the various bays.

On the 6th the weather cleared a little. We were able to check the sun's altitude and compare our chronometers with the real time. Our latitude was 57^{d} 18′ 40″ and our longitude, based on our corrected time observed on Cenotaph Island, 138^{d} 49′ 30″. I have already commented on the high level of accuracy of our Berthoud chronometers. Their daily loss was calculated at 3.6″ at Brest, 3.22″ at Tenerife, 6.55″ at Concepción and 4.8″ at Port des Français, consequently they have lost only 4.542″ a day over a year, and as this retardation is uniform, we must believe that these timekeepers have reached their highest stage of accuracy. The 6th was fairly clear and our bearings were most satisfactory. At 7 pm. we could

[1] La Pérouse should have known that Cook had already used the name Cape Cross, but he was faced with a multitude of islands and capes which, in foggy weather, were not easy to identify from Cook's charts. The cape at the southern entrance to Cross Sound is now known as Cape Bingham, a name bestowed on it by George Vancouver.

[2] La Pérouse was again confused by the number of islands he glimpsed through the fog: Cook's Bay of Islands is further south, by Kruzof Island.

still see Mount Crillon bearing N.66^{d}W., Mount St Hyacinth N.78^{d}E., Cape Engaño E.10^{d}S. It is a low forested land stretching well out to sea, over which rises Mount St Hyacinth which has the shape of a truncated cone, with a rounded summit – its height must be at least 1200 *toises.*[1]

On the morning of the 7th we could see the side of Cape Engaño opposite to the one we sailed along yesterday. Mount St Hyacinth was clearly visible and we saw E. of it a wide bay whose depth was hidden from us by fog[2] but it is so exposed to winds from the S. and the S.E., which are the most dangerous, that sailors should beware of entering it. The land was as high as at the S. of Cross Sound, covered in trees and with a little snow on the tops, which are so pointed and so numerous that a slight change of viewpoint alters their appearance. These peaks are situated some distance inland and form the background; hills nestle up to them, linked to a low and undulating plain ending at the sea; islands like those I have already mentioned spread out in front of this undulating coast; we have recorded only the more noteworthy peaks and shown the others at random to indicate that they are very numerous. Therefore the coast from the N. to the S. of Cape Engaño, for some 10 leagues, is edged with islands; we had passed them all by 10 a.m. The hills were starkly visible and we were able to make out their contours. At 6 p.m. we saw to the N.E. a cape which projected towards the W. and formed with Cape Engaño the S.E. point of a vast opening, a third of which was, as I have already said, filled with small islands. Between the last of these islands and this new cape we sighted two large bays that seemed very deep. I named this latter cape Cape Tchirikov after the famous Russian navigator who landed on this part of America in 1741.[3] To the E. behind the cape one discovers a wide, deep bay which I named Tchirikov Bay. At 7 the same evening I sighted a group of 5 islets separated from the

[1] 'St Hyacinthe' is Bodega's San Jacinto and Cook's Mount Edgecumbe. It is roughly half the height La Pérouse guessed it to be.

[2] This is Sitka Sound, Maurelle's Ensenada del Susto. Cook had sailed past in a sleety shower that soon turned to snow. Sitka's latitude is 57°N; on the 6th, as he sailed south, La Pérouse had recorded his latitude as being 57°18′.

[3] Aleksei Ilich Tchirikov (or Chirikov) (1703–42) sailed from Kamchatka in the *St Paul* in June 1741; a landfall was made in the neighbourhood of Noyes Island, after which he proceeded north past Baranof and Chichagof to the Gulf of Alaska. La Pérouse is referring here to what is now Chatham Strait and the opening which Vancouver was to name Christian Sound. The cape in question would therefore be Cape Ommaney, at the southern end of Baranof Island.

mainland by a channel of four or five leagues, which neither Cap[ne] Cook nor the pilot Morelle mentioned. I named them La Croyere Islands after the French geographer Georges de l'isle de la Croyere who sailed with Cap[ne] Tchirikov and died during the voyage.[1] As night was falling, I set a course to sail wide of them. The W. breeze continued to be favourable throughout the 8th. We observed 55[d] 39′ 31″ of latitude and 137[d] 5′ 23″ according to our chronometers; we could see several wide openings between some large islands that presented themselves to our sight from various angles, and the mainland was so far away we could no longer see it. This new archipelago, quite different from the previous one, begins 4 leagues from Cape Tchirikov and presumably continues as far as Cape Hector. There were strong currents around these islands, and we could feel their effect from 3 Ls away.

The Spanish pilot Morelle's Port Bucarelli is situated in this part of America. I cannot make out his map or the comments intended to explain it, but his volcanoes and his Port Bucarelli are on islands that lie possibly 40 leagues from the mainland, and I must admit that I would hardly be surprised if we had only sailed along islands since we left Cross Sound; because the appearance of the land differs greatly from what it is further N. and I saw the high range of Mount Crillon disappear to the E.[2]

[1] These are the small Hazy Islands, west of Coronation Island, first discovered by Bodega who named them Las Hermanas. Louis (not Georges) de Lisle de la Croyère (c1690–1741) was one of four brothers who all acquired fame in geography, astronomy and history – he added his mother's name, La Croyère, to his father's in order to distinguish himself from them. When his brother Joseph-Nicolas de Lisle was invited to St Petersburg by Catherine I in 1726 he went with him and together they travelled to the northern seas, Lapland and Siberia. He then joined Bering and Tchirikov but died during the 1741 voyage of the *St Paul*. Joseph, who returned to France in 1747, published an account of their travels under the title *Mémoire sur les nouvelles découvertes au nord de la Mer de Sud*, Paris, 1752.

[2] La Pérouse's observations are quite accurate. Prince of Wales Island is surrounded with a multitude of islands on the Pacific side and along Clarence Strait which separates it from the mainland. The Coastal Mountains that now constitutes the frontier between Alaska and British Columbia are snow-covered and would be visible from the open sea only on a very clear day. The 'Bucarelli' in question is Antonio Maria de Bucareli y Ursua, Viceroy of Mexico, who despatched, among others, Hezeta and Bodega on voyages of discovery. Port Bucareli is situated at the north-west of Prince of Wales Island in Sea Otter Sound, close by the island of Heceta (Hezeta). La Pérouse's impatience towards the Spanish navigators is understandable: there are, for instance, no volcanoes in the area; some distant eruption inland might have been visible or it may have been a simple forest fire – either way, the information is of no value to navigators working their way along this deeply indented coastline.

At 7 a.m. on 9 August, still sailing 3 Ls from the shore I sighted the islands of San Carlos;[1] the biggest trends S.E. & N.W. and might have a circumference of two leagues; a long chain links it to some very low islets that project into the channel. I am nevertheless convinced that there is a fairly wide passage, but I was not certain enough to try it out, particularly as it was necessary to sail with the wind and if my guess was wrong it would have been very difficult to round the San Carlos Islands and I would have wasted much precious time; I coasted along the seaward island half a league away and since at midday I was at that distance E. and W. of the S.E. point we determined its latitude with great accuracy as being 54^{d} 48′ and its longitude 136^{d} 19′ west of Paris.

There was a strong W.N.W. breeze. The weather was turning foggy. I crowded on sail to make for the land which was becoming shrouded in mist as we approached it. At 7.30 p.m. we were hardly a league from the coast which I could scarcely make out although I could see the breakers from the bridge. I sighted a large cape bearing E.N.E.; one can see nothing beyond it and we could not estimate how the coast was trending. I decided to alter course and to wait for clearer weather. The fog lifted for only a moment.

At midday on 10 August we observed with our chronometers 54^{d} 20′ of latitude and 135^{d} 20′ 45″ of longitude. I had veered back towards land at 4 a.m. and during that break I saw it a league ½ to the S.E. It looked like an island but the fog lifted for so short a time and over such a small area that we could not make out any details. We did not suspect the presence of land in that point of the compass, which increased our uncertainty over the trend of the coast.[2] During the night we had sailed across powerful currents, the fastest I have ever found at sea, but as our route, by dead reckoning, did not indicate any change, it is probable that they were caused by the tide and thus evened out.

During the night of the 10th to 11th the weather turned very bad. The fog became thicker, there was a fresh gale, and I altered course out to sea until daybreak when we veered back towards land; we went so close to it that, although it was misty, at midday I recognised the same headland as the day before, stretching N.N.E. to S.E.¼ S. which practically ties together all our bearings, leaving

[1] San Carlos Islands are identifiable as the Forrester group, west of Dall Island. It consists really of one large island with a number of rocky islets north and south.

[2] La Pérouse was crossing Dixon Entrance. What he saw the day before was probably Cape Muzon, the southernmost headland of Dall Island.

however an opening of 8 or 9 leagues where we saw no land. I do not know whether the fog hid it from view or if there is some wide bay in this area, which is what I assume in view of the strength of the currents I have already mentioned. If the weather had been clearer, no doubt would have remained as we sailed up to within a league from the coast whose breakers we could see distinctly from the bridge; it trends much more to the S.E. than I imagined from the Spanish pilot who cannot be relied on. At midday we observed 54^{d} 9′ 26″. I continued to sail along the coast, a league away, until 4 p.m. when the fog became so thick that we could no longer see the *Astrolabe* although we were within hailing distance of each other; I veered out to sea. The weather did not clear on the 12th and I stayed 12 Ls from land because I was so uncertain of its trend. The weather was foggy on the 13th and 14th and practically calm. I took advantage of light breezes to make for the shore from which we were still 5 leagues away at 6 p.m.

After leaving the San Carlos Islands we found no depth, even a league from land, with a 120-fathom line.

On the morning of the 15th the weather cleared. We came up to within 2 Ls of the coast. In places it was edged with breakers extending quite some distance out to sea. The wind was E. from which point of the compass we could make out a great bay; the horizon was quite extensive even though the sky was cloudy; we could see the coast for 18 to 20 Ls in each direction. It ran from N.N.E. to S.S.E. and seemed to trend S.S.E. & N.N.W. much further S. than I thought.

At 8 a.m. I had to veer out to sea because a thick fog came up around us; it lasted until 10 o'clock on the 16th when we saw land to the N.E. but not at all clearly. The fog once again forced me to go out towards the open sea. The whole of the 17th was a calm day; the fog cleared at last and I saw the coast 8 leagues away. The lack of wind did not allow me to come near, but we made some excellent astronomical observations; this was the first time since our departure from Port des Français; our latitude was 53^{d} 12′ 40″ and according to our chronometers our longitude was 136^{d} 52′ 57″, and the average of our distances 137^{d} 27′ 58″ or a difference of 37′W. Those of the *Astrolabe* were 15′ E.[1] The W.N.W. breeze

[1] The French had sailed past Dixon Entrance on 10 August and coasted slowly along Graham Island, part of the Queen Charlotte Islands, during the next few days. On the 16th they crossed the narrow channel which separates Graham Island from Moresby Island.

freshened, the weather had remained clear, so I came up to the land and on the 18th at midday I was only a league and a half from it and I saw a bay which was so deep that I could not see its limits. I gave it the name of Bay de la Touche;[1] it is situated in latitude 52^{d} 39′ and longitude 134^{d} 49′. I have no doubt that it offers an excellent anchorage.

A league and a half further E. we saw an inlet where it would also be possible to find a shelter for ships, but this place struck me as much less attractive than Bay de la Touche. Between 55 and 53 degrees the sea was covered with a kind of diving bird of the type Mr de Buffon calls the Kamchatka puffin; it is black, its beak and legs are red and its head has two white streaks that end in tufts like those of the *catakoua*. We sighted a few further S. but they were rare and one could see that they were so to speak travellers: these birds never go further from land than 6 Ls and navigators who come upon them in foggy weather can be fairly certain that they are within that range. We killed two which were stuffed for the King's collection which I believe has never included one, this bird having been known only through Bhering's voyage.[2]

On the evening of the 19th we sighted a cape which seemed to end the coast of America; the horizon was very clear and all we could see beyond was 4 or 5 small islets which I named Kerouart Islands after Mme the Viscountess de Langle and called the cape Cape Hector, a tribute I owed to the commander at Brest who took so much trouble over our preparations.[3] We were held by a dead

[1] A tribute to his friend Louis-René-Madeleine Le Vassor de Latouche-Tréville (1745–1804), who had once hoped to lead an expedition to the Pacific and had corresponded with James Cook. (See J. Forsyth, 'Latouche-Tréville and his Proposal to Explore the South Coast of New Holland', *Mariner's Mirror*, 45:2 (1959), pp. 118–19, and sundry correspondence in BN, NAF 9439.) Latouche-Tréville became a rear-admiral in 1792 and a vice-admiral in 1803. The bay named in his honour is an inlet on the west coast of Moresby Island, probably Inskip Channel or Moore Channel.

[2] This colourful bird, *Lunda cirrhata*, was first described by Georg Wilhem Steller, the naturalist on Bering's voyage of 1741–2. La Pérouse added a marginal note: 'Cap^{n} Cook also met it on the coast of Alaska'. This is correct, Cook mentioning it on 18 June 1778, but the sighting occurred much further north. Captain Clerke in his account uses the more popular name of sea parrot. See Cook, *Journals*, III, pp. 381, 1339. La Pérouse's refers to some of its similarities with a *Catakoua*, a mis-spelling of the French for cockatoo (*cacatoès*).

[3] Cape Hector is Cape Saint James, at the southern end of Moresby Island, in latitude 51°56′N and longitude 131°01′W (133°21′W of Paris). Off this headland are found the islets still known as the Kerouarts, although the name Proctor Islands is now more common; Bodega had sighted them in 1775 and called them Islas de

calm throughout the night 3 or 4 leagues from the shore which we were able to approach at daybreak with a light N.W. breeze; I then had proof that the coast I had been following for 200 leagues ended here and formed what was in all probability the opening of a gulf or very wide channel, as I could not see any land to the E. even though the weather was quite clear. I sailed N. in order to find the other side of the land I had been coasting on the E. I sailed along the Kerouart Islands and Cape Hector a league from shore and crossed some very strong currents; they even forced me to bear away and leave the coast; Cape Hector which lies at the opening of this new channel seemed to be a very interesting feature to determine; its latitude is 51^{d} 57′ 20″ and according to our chronometers its longitude is 133^{d} 35′. Night prevented me from continuing on my N. course and I spent the time tacking. At dawn I resumed my route of the previous day; the weather was very clear; I saw the reverse side of Bay de la Touche which I named Cape Buache[1] and more than 20 leagues of the east coast of the land I had coasted on the W. side during the previous days. Then remembering the shape of the land from Cross Sound, I was inclined to believe that this inlet might resemble the Sea of California and extend, I believe, to the 57^{d} of latitude. Neither the season nor my plans for later allowed me to confirm this, but I wanted at least to determine precisely the E. and W. width of this passage or gulf, as one may wish to call it, and set my course for the N.E. At midday on the 21st I observed 52^{d} 1′ latitude and 133^{d} 7′ 31″ longitude. Cape Hector bore from me S.W. 12 Ls and the sounding-line did not reach bottom. The winds soon veered to the S.E. A thick fog replaced the clear sky which had enabled us to see land 18 or 20 leagues away. A stormy gale blew up; caution did not permit me to continue my route to the N.N.E. I kept to and tacked variously during the night, all the

---

Aves. De Langle's wife was Georgette de Kérouartz, niece of Comte d'Hector. La Pérouse commonly uses his friend's full title of 'Mr the Viscount de Langle' in his text, abbreviated however in the present edition for the sake of simplicity. In the French edition of 1797, the editor, Milet-Mureau, always omits these titles.

[1] La Pérouse's impression of what is known today as the Inside Passage and can be used by ships as far as Juneau beyond 58°N is essentially correct: the Queen Charlotte Islands and Hecate Strait can fairly be compared with Baja California and the Gulf of California. Cape Buache is a headland at the south-western extremity of Moresby Island; La Pérouse named it after Jean-Nicolas Buache de Neuville (1741–1825) who had been working closely with Fleurieu since 1773 and was the author of the geographical notes prepared for the La Pérouse expedition.

topsails reefed. At daybreak, the winds having moderated, although the horizon was still as hazy, I made for the land and saw it through the fog at midday. My estimated latitude was then $52^{d}\ 22'$. The coastline stretched out from the N.¼ N.E. At 4 p.m. the weather cleared again but over a wide area. We could see clearly the American continent with snowy mountains as high at those of Mount Crillon and Mount Fairweather; they were visible at different distances from 8 to 10 Ls inland and behind an infinity of small islands that were no more than 3 leagues away from us. At that moment the sounding-line gave a depth of one hundred fathoms, rocky ground. Before long the fog returned, the weather looked nasty, I veered back out to sea, but fortunately I had taken very good bearings and had checked that the width of this channel or gulf was some 30 leagues W. to E between Cape Hector and Cape Fleurieux,[1] name I had given to the most S.E. island of the new group I had discovered on the eastern side of this channel, and it was behind this group of islands that I sighted the continent whose primitive, treeless and snowy mountains were visible at different distances; and there were peaks that seemed to be more than thirty leagues inland. Since Cross Sound we had seen only hills in comparison and my conjectures about an inlet extending 6 or 7 degrees N. were reinforced. The season did not allow me to throw any more light on this theory. We were already in late August, the fog almost never disappeared, the days were beginning to shorten, but more important than all these reasons my fear of missing the China monsoon made me abandon this search which would have required a sacrifice of at least six weeks on account of the precautions which must be taken during such a navigation that can only be undertaken in June in the longest and finest days of the year. A whole season is scarcely sufficient for such a task which must be undertaken as a special mission. Ours, far more extensive, was satisfied by determining precisely from E. to W. the width of this channel which we have seen or sailed through for a distance of some thirty leagues, as well as establishing for Capes Hector and Fleurieux, the two extremities of its entrance, latitudes and longitudes that deserve to be accepted as being as reliable as those of the best known headlands of

[3] Cape Fleurieu is a headland of Goose Island (La Pérouse actually calls this cape an island) which lies in 51°55′N and 130°45′W of Paris and is situated close to the continent, inside Queen Charlotte Sound. It is but one of a large number of islands along this coast.

the European coast. I was sad to realise that we had made little progress in the 23 days that had elapsed since our departure from *Baye des Français*, and I had not a single day to waste on the way to Monterey. The reader will easily understand that throughout this campaign my mind has always had to range two or three thousand leagues ahead because our routes were dependent on the monsoon in the seas of China and Japan and on the seasons in those of the N.W. of America, of Kamchatka, and the Aleutian Islands. And the complexities were no different in the S. hemisphere since we also had to sail there in high latitudes and cross straits between New Holland and New Guinea that were in all probability subject to the same monsoons as those of the Moluccas and the other islands of that sea.

The fog was very thick during the night. I sailed S.S.W. There was a very fine break at dawn. It did not last long, but at 11 o'clock the sky cleared. We saw Cape Fleurieux bearing N.E.¼ E. and made some excellent observations. Our latitude was 51^{d} 47′ 54″ and our chronometers gave a longitude of 132^{d} 0′ 50″.

We were becalmed all day; the winds came from the N.W. at sunset with the horizon very hazy. I had previously sighted Cape Fleurieux bearing N¼ N.E. Its latitude and longitude as determined by Mr Dagelet are 51^{d} 45′ and 131^{d} 15′ Paris meridian.

I have already mentioned that this cape forms the point of a very high island behind which I no longer saw the mainland which was shrouded in fog. It became even thicker during the night and I often lost sight of the *Astrolabe* whose bell I could hear.

The sky became fine at dawn. Cape Fleurieu bore from me N.18^{d}W. distant 18 Ls. The mainland was then stretching out to the E. The horizon, although not clear, allowed it to be seen for 20 Ls. I sailed E. to approach it, but soon the coastline became fog-bound, and there was a break in the S.S.E. which enabled me to notice a cape in that area.

I altered course in order to avoid getting too far E. running before the wind into a gulf from which I would have a great deal of trouble getting out; I soon realised that this S.S.E. land towards which I was sailing consisted of islands forming different groups stretching from the mainland to the outer islands, on which I saw not a single shrub. I sailed a third of a league away. One could see grass on them and some driftwood along the shore. The latitude and the longitude of the most W. island are 51^{d} 56′ and 131^{d} 38′

Paris meridian. I named these various groups Sartines Islands after a Minister whose name should be dear to every naval officer;[1] it is likely that one would find a passage between them, but it would not be wise to enter it without precautions. Once I had rounded these I made for the mainland, steering E.S.E. It stretched from the N.N.E. to S.E.¼E. The horizon was hazy although quite extensive, we could not see the peaks but we could make out the low lands without difficulty; I tacked throughout the night so as not to go past Cap^{n} Cook's wooded headland which that navigator surveyed[2] and which provided an unbroken run of coast from Mount St Elias to Nootka, enabling me to compare our longitudes with his, erasing any doubt which might have remained on the correctness of all our determinations. At dawn I made for the land, I passed a league and a half from the wooded headland which bore from me N.W.¼N.W. approximately 3 Ls. Its exact latitude is 50^{d} 4′ and its longitude 130^{d} 25′. Cap^{n} Cook who did not come as close to this headland as we did and determined its position only by taking bearings places it on his chart in 50^{d} and 130^{d} 20′ Paris meridian, that is to say 4′ further S. and 5′ further E., but our determination is more reliable because we were much closer to land and our reckoning of the distance was less subject to errors. One should mention here the surprising accuracy of the new methods which within a century will fix the exact location of every point on earth and will do more for geography than all the previous centuries.

On the 25th I continued to sail E. towards the entrance of Nootka which I would have liked to sight before nightfall, although such a sighting would have offered nothing of particular interest after the precise determination of the wooded headland.

[1] These are presumably the Scott Islands, close to the cape of that name, northwestern Vancouver Island. They are in latitude 50°48′, which indicates that the 51°56′ of the journal is a slip of the pen. Antoine-Raymond-Jean-Gualbert-Gabriel de Sartines, Comte d'Alby, (1729–1801) was in charge of the police from 1729 to 1774 at which date he took over the Ministry of Marine; he carried out major reforms throughout the navy and had nine ships of the line built in a single year; he lost this portfolio in 1780 and moved to Spain when the Revolution broke out. Apart from the bare fact that La Pérouse named these islands after him, all references to Sartines were eliminated from Milet-Mureau's account of the voyage. See on Sartines, Jacques Michel, *Du Paris de Louis XV à la marine de Louis XVI: l'oeuvre de M. de Sartines*, Paris, 1983.

[2] Cook's Woody Point was renamed Cape Cook in 1860. It lies in 50°08′N and 130°15′W of Paris. La Pérouse's determination is therefore quite accurate.

Fog which came up very dense at 5 p.m. entirely hid the land and I set course for the Breaker Point 15 Ls S. of Nootka in order to survey the part of the coast that lies between Cape Flattery and this Breaker Point which Cap^{n} Cook was not able to explore. This is a space of approximately 30 leagues.

On the 26th it was still very foggy, squalls came from the N.E. to the S.E. The barometer dropped, but there was no breeze and we were becalmed, the rudder not responding, until the 28th. I had availed myself of a few light airs to get away from the coast which I assumed to lie S.E. We were surrounded by small land birds resting in our rigging; we caught several that are so common in Europe they do not warrant a description; finally on the 28th at 5 p.m. there came a break and we identified Cook's Breaker Point bearing N.[1] The land then extended to the N.E. The break was a brief one, but we were able to take good bearings.

The weather was no clearer on the 29 August, but the barometer was rising and I set course for the land, hoping for a break before nightfall. I was sounding every half hour; we passed over 70 fathoms, sandy bottom and then smooth pebbles at 40 fathoms and, a league further on, 75 fathoms, mud; we had obviously passed over a bank, and it may not be easy to explain how a mound of smoothed stones 150 feet in height and a league in length can be found on a sandy plateau 8 leagues out to sea; one knows that these pebbles only become rounded through rubbing and this heap implies the presence of a current at the bottom of the sea, like a river. At last, as I had hoped, there was a good break in the weather at sunset.

We sighted land from the E.N.E. to the N.W.¼N., bearings that linked up perfectly with those of the previous day. At midday we had observed 48^{d} 37′. According to our chronometers our longitude was 128^{d} 21′ 42″. The last headland we had seen to the S.E. could only be 6 or 7 leagues from Cape Flattery which I would very much like to have seen, but the fog was very dense; on the 30th the seas became wild, the winds ranged from S. to S.W. I veered back towards the open sea and, with a horizon of less than half a league, I set my course parallel along the coast, making for

[1] Cook's Breaker Point had already been named Punta San Estevan by Juan Perez in 1774; this name has been retained as Estevan Point. La Pérouse had now crossed the entrance to Nootka Sound, which was hidden by fog, and passed the entrance to Clayoquot Sound during the night.

the part of America that lies between 47^d and 45^d and represents a gap on Cap^n Cook's chart.[1]

On the 1st at midday I sighted a headland or cape bearing N.N.E. distant about 10 leagues, at 47^d precisely according to our reckoning; the land stretched to the E. I came up within 3 or 4 leagues. It was ill-defined, every feature was shrouded in mist; my latitude observed at midday was 46^d 36′ 21″ and the longitude of our chronometers 127^d 2′ 5″ and from our reckoning 126^d 33′. After sailing 6 Ls E. until the evening my longitude was 126^d 37′ 5″ which proves that this coast trends considerably towards the E. The currents were extraordinarily violent; we were among eddies that did not allow to steer even though the wind was good enough for three knots and we were 5 leagues from land.

I coasted the land during the night having shortened sail towards the S. and a dawn set an E. course to approach the land. We remained in a dead calm 4 Ls from the shore at the mercy of currents which forced us to tack continually, being constantly afraid of striking the *Astrolabe* which was faring no better; we fortunately had a good ground of mud in which to anchor should the currents drive us to the shore; but the sea was quite rough and our cables would have had difficulty in standing fast against the rolling of the ship. The Spaniards' Round Cape bore from us E. 5^d S.; the land then stretched out towards the S.E.[2] At midday our latitude was 45^d 55′ and according to our chronometers our longitude was 126^d 47′ 35″ Paris meridian and according to the distances 126^d 22′. We had at last been able to take these readings the day before and it was the second time since our departure from Port des Français. They differed from the longitude of the chronometers by only 25′ 35″. Such results were a new proof of the excellence of Mr

[1] La Pérouse had crossed the entrance to Juan de Fuca Strait in fog. Cape Flattery is its southern headland. At sunset on the 29th, La Pérouse saw the coast of Vancouver Island from Cape Beale up to Estevan Point. Cook arrived in 44°30′ on 7 February 1778, but the weather forced him towards the open sea – 'a very hard gale, with heavy squals attended with Sleet and snow. There was no choice but to stretch to the Southward to get clear of the coast' – and he did not see land again until he was in 42°45′, approximately, as the weather did not allow very precise observations, and in time, on the 22nd, he returned to the coast in 47°05′, Cook, *Journals*, III, p. 289. This is why La Pérouse talks of a gap in knowledge of the coast between 45° and 47°, but he was not much more fortunate than Cook: on lst September he sighted a cape in approximately 47° which may have been Point Brown at the entrance to Grays Harbour, but fog soon hid it from view.

[2] This is Hezeta's Cabo Redondo, or Tillamook Head in present-day Oregon.

Berthoud's chronometers. This day of calms was one of the most worrying of all those we had spent since we left France; there was not a breath of wind during the night: we sounded every half-hour in order to drop anchor in spite of the heavy seas if we had been drifting towards the land, but we always found 80 fathoms muddy bottom.

At dawn we were at the same distance as on the previous day; we observed as before 45ᵈ 55′. Our bearings were almost the same and, dragged by currents which had reversed we had the impression of having swivelled around a pivot during these 24 hrs.

Finally at 3 o'clock a light breeze came up from the N.N.W. which enabled us to make for the open sea and get away from these currents in which we had been caught for two days; this breeze was pushing along a bank of fog which surrounded us and caused us to lose sight of land. We had no more than 5 or 6 leagues of coast to survey up to the 45ᵈ sighted by Capⁿ Cook, the weather was too favourable, and I was in too great a hurry not to take advantage of this good wind: we crowded on sail and I set course towars the S.¼ S.W. almost parallel to the coast which trends N. & S. The night was very fine; at daybreak we sighted land to the N.¼N.E. The sky was clear in that area, but very hazy further E. We nevertheless sighted the coast in the E.N.E. and as far as E.S.E. but only momentarily. At midday our observed latitude was 44ᵈ 41′ 18″ and our chronometers gave 126ᵈ 56′ 17″ Paris meridian. We were about 8 leagues from the shore which we approached, changing our course slightly E.; at 6 p.m. our distance was four leagues; it stretched from N.E. to E.S.E., very hazy. The night was fine, I coasted the shore which we could discern in the moonlight; at sunrise the fog hid it from us, but it reappeared at midday during a break, from the N.E. to the S.¼S.E. The sounding-line gave 75 fathoms.

Our latitude was 42ᵈ 58′ 46″ and our longitude according to our timekeepers 127ᵈ 5′ 20″. A 2 o'clock we were athwart 9 small islands or rocks approximately 1 L. from Cape Blanc which bore from me N.E.¼E. [I named them Necker Islands.][1]

[1] The expedition was now sailing speedily south. Cape Blanco was passed on the 6th; it was roughly Cook's most southerly sighting along this coast. The sentence between square brackets is crossed out, though still legible, in the MS. The reference is to Jacques Necker (1732–1804), Minister of Finance under Louis XVI and author of a famous *Compte rendu* of 1781 which summarised the parlous state of the country's finances, but led to his dismissal; he was recalled during the early part of the Revolution but had gone back to his native Switzerland by the time the Milet-Mureau

I continued coasting the land, steering S.S.E. three or four leagues off; we could only see the tops of mountains above the clouds; they were tree-covered and we saw no snow on them. At night, the land stretched out as far as the S.E., but our look-outs assured they had seen it as far as S ¼S.E. Unsure how this coast, which had never been explored, was trending, I sailed S.S.W. under shortened sails. At dawn we could still see land from the N. to N ¼N.E. I altered course to S.E. ¼E. to approach it, but at 7 a.m. a thick fog hid it from our sight. We found the sky less clear in this part of America than in the high latitudes, or at least it is during very brief intervals that navigators can see everything which is above their horizon: the land never showed itself once in full; the fog was even thicker on the 7th than on the previous day; however, it did clear at around midday and we sighted mountains tops to the E at a fairly great distance. As our route had taken us S. it is obvious that the land begins to trend E. past 42^{d}. At midday we observed latitude 40^{d} 44′ 50″ and, according to our chronometers our longitude was 127^{d} 17′ 5″.[1] I continued sailing towards the land from which I was only 4 Ls away at nightfall: we then sighted a volcano on a mountain peak bearing E. Its fire was very strong, but soon a heavy fog came up and hid this spectacle from us.[2] We had again to get away from the coast for fear we might meet some headland or island projecting from the mainland. There was a very thick fog: there was a break at around 10 a.m. – we glimpsed the mountain peaks but an impenetrable barrier continued to hide the low lands from us. The weather had considerably worsened, it was blowing up for a gale and the barometer dropped markedly; until nightfall I kept to a S.E. course which as I coasted the shore should also have brought me closer to it, but I had lost sight of it at midday and at dusk the horizon was so hazy that I could have been very close to it without seeing it. As there were signs of an oncoming gale, which had it been from the S.W. could have got me embayed, I decided to veer

edition was being prepared. The islands in question, nine in numbers, are really dangerous rocky islets known as Orford Reef.

[1] La Pérouse was approaching Cape Mendocino, the latitude of which is 40°25′.

[2] A precise identification of this volcano is not easy. East of Cape Mendocino the Lassen Volcanic Park offers a possible answer, and Lassen Peak has a height of 3,187 metres. It is however some 250 km (150 miles) away. A violent eruption is a possibility, more likely, in view of La Pérouse's tone of certainty, than a forest fire somewhere in the Coastal Ranges.

for the open sea with no more than the foresail and the main topsail; the gale blew up but at dawn much less than I had expected; the sky was covered, but the winds moderate. I set an E. course towards the land; the fog soon made me change direction and run more or less parallel to the coast which I assumed was trending S.¼ S.E.. The weather was no clearer on the 10th and 11th. The outcome of these two days of sailing was similarly S.¼S.E. Visibility never exceeded two leagues and was often less than a musket shot. We did however observe a latitude of 36^d 58′ 43″ and our chronometers gave a longitude of 126^d 32′ 5″. The currents or a false dead reckoning had taken us 30′ further south, but we were 16′ N. of Monterey, and I set an E. course direct for the land, although the weather was misty; but visibility extended to two leagues. I tacked throughout the night; the sky was also covered the next day. Nevertheless I continued on my course making for the land; a midday our longitude was 125^d 9′ 35″. I could not see land anywhere; it is true that our horizon was at the most 2 Ls, and at 4 p.m. less than a musket shot. I decided to stand off and on and wait for clearer weather; we must have been quite close to the shore, several land birds were flying around our vessels and we captured a falcon of the gerfalcon species.[1] The fog kept on throughout the night and in the morning until 10 a.m. when we sighted the land, very hazy and quite close. It was impossible to make it out; I came up to within a league, I could clearly see the breakers, the sounding-line gave 25 fathoms, but although I was sure we were in Monterey Bay it was not possible to discern the Spanish settlement in such foggy weather. At nightfall I tacked back towards the sea and at dawn returned to the land in a thick fog which did not clear until midday; I then sailed quite close along the coast and at 3 p.m. we saw Monterey fort and two three-masted vessels in the roadstead. Contrary winds forced us to drop anchor 2 leagues away in 45 fathoms, muddy ground, and the next day we anchored 2 cablelengths from land in 12 fathoms. The commander of these two vessels, Don Esteven Martinez[2] sent us some pilots during the night; the Viceroy

[1] The falcon is question is the *Falco rusticolus*.

[2] Esteban José Martinez Fernández (1742–98) had been second officer of the *Santiago* which sailed to Nootka Sound and probably Juan de Fuca Strait in 1774 under Juan Perez. Currently engaged in supplying Spanish posts along the Mexican and Californian coasts, he was in charge of the *Princesa*, which was being careened at the time of La Pérouse's visit. He was at the centre of the famous Nootka Incident in 1789 which almost led to war between England and Spain. *Who's Who*, pp. 174–5.

of Mexico had advised him and the governor of the Presidio of our expected arrival in this bay.

It is worth noting that, during this long navigation, in the midst of the densest fog, the *Astrolabe* always sailed within hailing distance of my frigate and only went further when I instructed her to in order to investigate the approaches of Monterey.

Before closing this chapter, which will be of interest only to geographers and navigators, I feel that I should put forward my views on the so-called channel of St Lazare of Admiral de Fuentes. I am convinced that this admiral has never existed, and that a navigation into the interior of America by way of lakes and rivers, completed in such a short time, is so absurd that, were it not for the theoretical approach, which is so prejudicial to all the sciences, geographers of any standing would have rejected such an improbable story made up in England, where the Northwest Passage had at the time both supporters and detractors, all defending their particular views with the kind of enthusiasm that was being displayed in France over theological issues a hundred times more ridiculous: Admiral de Fuentes' relation is therefore similar to these pious frauds which reason has since rejected with such contempt and which cannot stand up to arguments; but one can accept as almost a certainty that, from Cross Sound or at least Port de los Remedios, every navigator has coasted past nothing but islands as far as Cape Hector in 52^{d}, and that between the islands and the continent there exists a channel, the width of which E. and W. may vary, though I doubt that it exceeds 50 Ls since it is only 30 at its entrance between Cape Fleurieux and Cape Hector. This channel must be dotted with islands, difficult to navigate, and I am sure that between these islands several passages lead in and out of the ocean; the ports of Los Remedios and Bucarelli of the Spanish are at a considerable distance from the mainland, and if taking possession without following this up with any settlement was not such a ridiculous basis for a claim, theirs in this part of America could be challenged, because it is evident to me that the pilot Morel[1] did not

[1] Francisco Antonio Maurelle (1754–1820) served a pilot of the schooner *Sonora*, commanded by Bodega y Quadra on his 1775 voyage to the Northwest Coast. In 1780–1 he sailed to the Philippines, attempted to return by the southern and central Pacific, and finally got back to America by the traditional northern route; he made a number of discoveries in the Bismarck, Tongan, Fijian and Ellice groups. *Who's Who*, pp. 176–7.

see this continent between 50^d and 57^d 20′. Moreover I am absolutely certain that N. of Cross Sound, at Port des Français, &, we were in America, because the river of Bhering in 59^d 9′, that I wanted explored by our boats which were unable to overcome the currents at the entrance, is so considerable that one can only find one like it in a land extending far into the interior; our frigates anchored at its mouth; the water was whiteish and fresh 3 or 4 leagues from shore; and I believe that this river has a larger flow than that of Bordeaux:[1] so it is possible that the channel between the islands and the continent does not extend further N. than 57^d 30′. I know that geographers can draw lines to the N.E., leave Port des Français and Bhering River in America and extend their channel N. and E. up to the limits of their imagination, but such a work would be an absurdity since it would not be based on facts. It is fairly likely that one could find the mouth of a navigable river on the coast of America that forms the E. boundary of this new channel, because one can hardly claim that the slope of the land sends them all in an E. direction; the Bhering River would be the one exception to such a rule, if it had any followers. It is also probable that there are no bars at the mouth of these theoretical rivers, because as the channel is not very wide it is sheltered by the islands W. of it and one knows that bars are formed by the interaction of the sea and the river currents.[2]

[1] The reference is to the Garonne River and the Gironde estuary.

[2] La Pérouse's editor, Milet-Mureau, added a lengthy comment defending the hypothesis of a North-West Passage, but La Pérouse had not only explored the coast, he had the benefit of personal contact with Samuel Hearne whose travels had disproved the existence of any passage leading to Hudson Bay. See his *A Voyage from Prince of Wales Fort in Hudson's Bay to the Northern Ocean*, London, 1795, p. 303. Russian and English voyages, in particular George Vancouver's, would soon provide further evidence; the *coup-de-grâce* came with Alexander Mackenzie's travels of 1789–92. Milet-Mureau, writing in 1794–6, was fighting a battle which had already been lost.

CHAPTER X

Arrival at Monterey, description of this bay, historical details on the two Californias and their missions; customs and practices of the converted and the independent Indians. Internal administration of the missions; extreme fertility of the Californian soil. Grains, fruits, vegetables of every type, quadrupeds, birds, fishes, shells, &c. Military constitution of these two provinces, the Governor of which resides at Monterey. The missionaries do not recognise his authority: the Viceroy of Mexico is the sole judge of all contentious matters. A new trade in otter furs is about to develop between China and Mexico; a royal monopoly has been established over it; dramatic changes it will inevitably bring about in the Russian trade at Kiakia: the Spanish owe their knowledge of this new branch of industry to the publication of Captain Cook's Voyages.

Monterey Bay, formed by New Year Point to the N. and Cypress Point in the S., is 8 leagues across in this direction and has a depth of about 6 towards the E. where the land is low and sandy;[1] the sea rolls in, with a sound we heard more than a league away, to the foot of sand dunes lining the shore; N. & S. of this bay the land is high and forested; vessels wishing to anchor here should follow the S. coast and after turning Cypress Point, which juts out towards the N., they catch sight of the Presidio[2] and can drop anchor in 10 fathoms behind and a little inland of this point which shelters them from the sea breeze: Spanish vessels planning a long stay at Monterey usually come up to within one or two cablelengths from

[1] Monterey Bay lies broadly between Ano Nuevo Point and Point Pinos near which La Pérouse anchored. Cypress Point, which forms the southern point of Monterey Peninsula, is three miles further south. The Atlas to the *Voyage* shows, on map 34, 'Pine or Cypress Point'. La Pérouse's advice to navigators shows, however, that he was aware of a difference between the two headlands.

[2] The old Presidio, the office of the local governor, was situated on a slope overlooking the anchorage; the Cathedral of San Carlos now occupies part of this site.

shore in 6 fathoms and tie up to an anchor sunk into the sand ashore: they then no longer have to fear the S. winds which are sometimes quite strong, but do not place the ships in any danger since they come from the coast. We found ground everywhere in the bay 4 leagues from land in 60 fathoms, ooze; but the sea is fairly rough and one can only stay a few hours in such an anchorage, waiting for daylight or a break in the fog. The tide is full at the new and full moons, at one thirty; it rises 7 feet and since this bay is very open the current hardly makes itself felt and I have never found it reaching a speed of half a knot. One cannot put into words the number of whales that surrounded us nor their familiarity; they blew constantly, within half a pistol shot of our frigates, and filled the air with a great stench. We were unaware of this effect, but the local inhabitants told us that the water they send up has a very bad smell which is felt at a fair distance, and this phenomenon would presumably not have been a surprise for the fishermen of Greenland or Nantucket.[1]

Fog almost perpetually covers this coast,[2] which makes it fairly difficult to approach; otherwise, there would be few others where this would be easier – not a single underwater rock can be found below the waterline a cablelength from shore where one can drop anchor if the fog is too dense and wait for a break in the weather in order to sight the Spanish settlement situated in the angle formed by the E. and S. coast.

The sea was covered with pelicans 4 or 5 Ls from shore; it appears that this bird never goes out further and navigators who come upon them in fog can be sure that they are at most that distance from land. We saw these birds for the first time in Monterey Bay, and I have since learnt that they are very common on the whole Californian coast; the Spanish call them *alkatros.*[3]

A lieutenant-colonel who resides in Monterey is Governor of both Californias; his realm has a circumference of more than 800 leagues, but his real subjects are 282 cavalrymen who have to serve

[1] Nantucket, in SE Massachusetts, was a base for prosperous whaling operations in the eighteenth century and well into the nineteenth. Whales are now rarely seen in Monterey Bay.

[2] There is some over-emphasis in these comments. Fog rises during the night and usually clears by midday; it is prevalent between May and September only.

[3] The brown pelican (*Pelecanus occidentalis*) is still common in the area. The Spanish word *alcatraz* was loosely used to describe it, but it more correctly refers to gannets, current Spanish having the word *pelícano* for the pelican.

as garrison to five small forts, and supply squads of 4 or 5 men to each of the 25 missions or parishes established in the Old and New California. Such small resources are enough to control and impress some 50,000 Indians roaming in this vast area of America,[1] of whom about 10,000 have embraced Christianity. These Indians are generally small and weak and show no sign of this love of freedom and independence which characterises the people of the N., whose arts and skills they lack; their colour approaches closely that of blacks whose hair is not frizzy – these people's hair grows long and quite strong; they trim it to a length of 4 or 5 inches; several have a beard, others, according to the missionary fathers, have never had one, and it is a question which has not even been resolved in the district.[2] The Governor, who has travelled extensively into the interior and who has lived among these natives for 15 years, assured us that those who are beardless have pulled it out with the shell of a bivalve they use like tweezers: the head of the missions, who has been equally as long in California, maintained the opposite in our presence; it was difficult for travellers to decide between them. Our duty being to report only what we saw, we must say that we saw only half the adults with a beard; in some cases it is quite bushy, and would have been regarded as impressive in Turkey or around Moscow.[3]

These Indians are very skilful with the bow; they killed some tiny birds in our presence; it must be said that their patience as they creep towards them is hard to describe; they hide and, so to speak, snake up to the game, releasing the arrow from a mere 15 paces.

Their skill with large game is even more impressive; we all of us saw an Indian with a deer's head tied over his own, crawling on all fours, pretending to eat grass, and carrying out this pantomime in such a way that our hunters would have shot him from 30 paces if they had not been forewarned. In this way they go up to deer herds within very close range and kill them with their arrows.

[1] Marginal note by La Pérouse: 'They change their place of residence very frequently, depending on the fishing or hunting season.'

[2] La Pérouse added a marginal note: 'We have given our opinion on the beards of Americans in the previous chapter, but we are writing chapters as we proceed, and as we do not have a theoretical structure to fit new facts as we come across them we are not afraid to record them.'

[3] Marginal note: 'The Governor had travelled much more than the missionary, and his opinion would have prevailed in my mind if I had had to choose sides.'

Loreto is the only Presidio of the Old California[1] on the E. coast of this peninsula; it has a garrison of 54 cavalrymen who supply small detachments to the following 15 missions, which are in the care of the Dominican Fathers who succeeded the Jesuits and the Franciscans;[2] the latter have remained in sole charge of the ten missions of New California, The 15 missions dependent on Loreto are: St Vincent, St Dominic, Rosary, St Ferdinand, St Francis de Borgia, St Gertrude, St Ignatius, Guadelupe, St Rosalie, Concepción, St Joseph, St Francis Xavier, Loreto, St Joseph of Cape St Lucar, and All Saints.[3] Approximately four thousand converted Indians, gathered around the 15 above-named parishes, are the only fruit of this long apostolate by the various religious orders that have followed each other in this hard ministry; one can read in Father Venegas' history of California[4] the date when Fort Loreto and the various missions it protects were founded. By comparing their previous state with this year's, it will noticed that the temporal and spiritual progress of these missions is quite slow; there is only a single group of Spanish inhabitants; it is true that the country is unhealthy, and that the province of Sonora, situated on the eastern side of the Gulf of California, just as California is on the western side, appeals much more to Spanish inhabitants who find a fertile soil and rich mines in this country, much more attactive in their eyes than the pearl fisheries of the peninsula which require a certain number of slave divers who are often very difficult to obtain. But

[1] The distinction is between Old California or Baja California and New California or Alta California which corresponds roughly to the modern American state. Loreto is a small town on the Gulf side of Baja California.

[2] Jesuit missions in Mexico go back 1591; they appeared in 1687 in Baja California and on the Gulf of Mexico. The Franciscans began their missionary work around the year 1550. The Jesuits were expelled in 1767 from all Spain's territories, before any missions were established in Alta California. The Dominicans concentrated their attention to Baja California, leaving it to the Franciscans to establish their missions in Alta California. Major studies on these missions include Fr Zephrin Engelhardt's four-volume *The Missions and Missionaries of California*, San Francisco, 1908–15 and José Gabriel Navarro's *Los Franciscanos en la conquista y colonización de America*, Madrid, 1955.

[3] La Pérouse's report on the missions and early California is valuable, although it has been criticised by some apologists as too harsh, but his views are those of an educated eighteenth-century observer who understood the difficult situation facing the missionaries and criticised only a few shortcomings he saw as rectifiable.

[4] Miguel Venegas' *Noticias de la California y su conquista temporal y espiritual* was published in three volumes in Madrid in 1757. It was soon translated into English, French, Dutch and German. A major source for this important work was a manuscript history compiled by Fr Andrés Marcos Burriel.

northern California seems to me to have many more advantages, in spite of its greater distance from Mexico; its first establishment, which is St Diego, dates only from 1769, on the 26th of the month of July.[1] It is the most S. Presidio, just as St Francis is the most N.. This latter was built on 9 October 1776, the Canal of St Barbe in September 1786, and finally Monterey, today the capital and main settlement of the two Californias, on 3 June 1770. It is known that the anchorage of this Presidio was discovered in 1602 by Sebastian Viscaïno[2] commanding a small squadron sent from Acapulco by order of Viscount de Monterey, Viceroy of Mexico: since then, galleons have at times put into this bay on their return from Manila to obtain some refreshments after their lengthy crossing, but it was only in 1770 that the Franciscans set up the first mission there; they have 10 today in which there are five thousand one hundred and forty-three converted Indians; the following four columns will show with the name of the parish, the number of baptised Indians, the date of its foundation and the Presidio from which it depends;[3]

[1] San Diego de Alcala was founded on the 16th, not the 26th of July. It marked the first step in the settlement of Alta California. The viceroy of Mexico despatched three vessels, the *San Carlos*, the *San Antonio*, and the *San José* which was lost at sea, the other two ships losing a high proportion of their crew through scurvy and other diseases. However, two columns were advancing overland led by Gaspar de Portolá and accompanied by the Franciscan Fr Junípero Serra, who was to become one of the great figures of the colonial period, and Fr Juan Crespi who was to sail to the Northwest Coast with Juan Perez in 1774. The various survivors met at San Diego in 1 July, Fr Serra sang the *Te Deum*; the Presidio was erected by Portolá and the mission formally set up on the 16th.

[2] Sebastián Vizcaino (c.1550–c. 1628), more a merchant than a navigator, sailed with three ships from Acapulco on 5 May 1602, reached San Diego on 11 November and Monterey on 15 December; he then went on to approximately Cape Mendocino. He was not the first to discover Monterey Bay: this was the work of Juan Rodriguez Cabrillo who sailed there in 1542 and named Point Pinos; then in 1595 Sebastián Cermeño, returning from Manila, named the bay Bahia de San Pedro; Vizcaino renamed it Monterey Bay in honour of the Conde de Monterey, Viceroy of Mexico. Vizcaino's importance lies in his reports on the bay, 'the best port anyone could desire', which attracted the attention of Spanish officials to Monterey as a suitable port of call for galleons on the Manila run and as a base for the eventual colonisation of Alta California. See on this H.R. Wagner, *Spanish Voyages to the Nortwest Coast of America in the Sixteenth Century*, San Francisco, 1929 and A. del Portillo y Diez Solano, *Descubrimientos y exploraciónes en las costas de California*, Madrid, 1947.

[3] Corrected names and dates are: San Carlos Borromeo, 3 June 1770; San Antonio de Padua, 14 July 1771; San Luis Obispo de Tolosa, 1 September 1772; Santa Clara de Assís, 12 January 1777; San Francisco de Assís, 9 October 1776; San Buenaventura, 31 March 1782; Santa Barbara, 4 December 1771; San Gabriel Arcángel, 8 September 1771; San Juan Capistrano, 30 October 1775 (closed a week later and re-opened on 1 November 1776); San Diego, 16 July 1769.

I must warn here that the Spanish use the general term Presidio for any fort they have, whether in Africa or in America, in the midst of pagan people, which assumes that there are no settlers there but only a garrison living in the citadel. The piety of the King of Spain had maintained these missions until

Name of parish	*Name of the Presidio*	*Date of their foundation*	*Converted Indians*
St Charles	Monterey	3 June 1770	711
St Anthony	ditto	14 July 1771	850
St Louis	ditto	1 Sept. 1772	492
St Clare	St Francis	18 Jan. 1888	475
St Francis	ditto	9 October 1776	250
St Bonaventure	St Barbe	3 March 1782	120
St Barbe	ditto	3 Sept. 1786	–
St Gabriel	ditto	8 Sept. 1771	843
St John Capistrau	St Diego	1 Novem. 1776	544
St Diego	ditto	26 July 1769	858
			5143

now and these Presidios and at great expense, their only purpose being the conversion and civilising of the Indians of these countries, a quite different plan and one much more worthy of praise than his predecessors' or at least that of the greedy men to whom he had delegated his authority; but the reader will soon see that a new branch of commerce may well bring greater advantages to the Spanish nation than the richest mine in Mexico; and that the healthiness of the climate, the fertility of the soil, and finally the abundance of furs of every kind which have a guaranteed market in China, give this part of America incomparable advantages over Old California, whose insalubrity and sterility cannot be balanced by the presence of a few pearls that have to be brought up from the depths of the sea. Prior to Spanish colonisation, the Indians of northern California grew only a little maize and lived almost exclusively on the product of their fishing and hunting; no country has more fish and game of every kind; rabbits, hares and deer[1] were as

[1] The hares and rabbits were the *Lepus californicus* and the *Sylvilagus Bachmani*; the deer the *Cervus elaphus* and the *C. elaphus Nelsoni*.

common as in the royal hunting grounds; otters and seals are as plentiful as in the N., and in winter they kill a very large quantity of bears, foxes, wolves and wild cats.[1] The undergrowth and the plains are full of small grey crested quails that live in groups like those of Europe, but in coveys of three or four hundred. They are plump and taste excellent; the trees provide abodes for the most charming of birds; our ornithologists stuffed several varieties of sparrows, blue jays, tits, spotted woodpeckers, orioles; among birds of prey we saw the white-headed eagle, the great and the small falcon, the goshawk, the sparrow-hawk, the black vulture, the eagle owl and the raven; on the ponds by the sea we found ducks, the grey pelican and the white yellow-crested one, various types of gulls, cormorants, curlews, ringed plovers, small seagulls and herons; and finally we killed and stuffed a *promerops* which most ornithologists thought belonged to the old continent.[2]

The fertility of this land is also beyond words. Vegetables of every description succeed perfectly; we enriched the gardens of the Governor and the missions with differents seeds brought from Paris, which had kept perfectly and will provide them with added benefits.

Crops of maize, barley, peas and wheat can only be compared with those of Chile; our Europeans farmers have no idea of this degree of fertility; the average production of wheat is 70 or 80 to one, extreme cases being sixty and 100. There are very few fruit trees, but the climate is highly suitable for them; it does not differ greatly from that of our southern French provinces, at least it is

[1] The bears included the *Ursus americanus* and the *U. arctos*; foxes were widespread, the *Vulpes macrotis* and the *V. velox* being particularly common; the wolf was the *Canis lupus*, but the term 'wild cat' could be applied to a variety of small felines.

[2] The quail has become California's state bird. La Pérouse is referring to the *Lophortyx californica*. The 'true' blue jay is the *Cyanocitta cristate* which does not normally extend this far west: La Pérouse probably saw the black-headed *Cyanocitta stelleri*. The tits were probably the *Parus atricapillus*; the most common woodpecker in California is the *Melanerpes formicivorus*, unless there was a slip of the pen (*pic* for *pie*) and La Pérouse refers simply to magpies such as the Californian *Pica nuttalli*. The orioles are members of the Icterus family. The white-headed eagle is the *Haliaeetus leucocephalus*, the falcon the *Buteo lagopus*, the goshawk the *Astur atricapillus*, the sparrow-hawk the *Falco sparverius*, the vulture the *Coragyps atratus*, the eagle owl the *Bubo virginianus pacificus* or the smaller *B. v. elachistus*, the raven the *Corvus corax* and the *C. brachyrhynchus*. The yellow crest of the pelican suggests it was the *Pelecanus erythrorhynchus*. The curlew might have been the rare *Numenius borealis* which migrates from Alaska to Patagonia; the plover was the *Charadrius vociferus* and the promerops the *Merops apiaster*.

never any colder but the summer heat is more moderate on account of the constant fogs that make navigation so difficult but give this soil a humidity which is very helpful to its vegetation.

The forests contain pines with edible seed, cypresses, green oaks, the western plane tree and the American *cornythus*;[1] they are sparsely spread out, and a lawn, over which it is very pleasant to stroll, covers the soil of these forests in which one comes across breaks of several leagues forming vast plains full of all kinds of game. The soil, although quite rich, is light and sandy and, I think, owes its fertility to the dampness of the air, because it is very badly watered: the watercourse nearest to the Presidio is about two leagues away – it is a stream that runs near the mission of St Charles[2] and was called Carmel River by the early navigators; this distance, too great from our frigates, did not allow us to get our water there, and we obtained it in ponds situated behind the fort, where the quality was very mediocre, and it would hardly dissolve soap.

The Carmel River, which provides the missionaries and their Indians with a healthy and pleasant drink, could with a little effort irrigate their garden. It is with the happiest satisfaction that I can make known the wise and pious behaviour of their religious who so perfectly serve their sovereign's wishes; I shall not hide what struck me as reprehensible in their internal administration, but I shall proclaim that they are in each case a hundred times better than the rules laid down by their superiors, and that their gentleness and their charity make up for any over-austere or monastical features these may have, especially in the eyes of a traveller who, being more a defender of the rights of man than a theologian, would have wished that the truths of Christianity had been backed by a legislation that would gradually transform into citizens men whose present condition is no different from that of blacks in our colonial settlements that are ruled with gentleness and humanity.

[1] The seeds of the Piñon pine or *Pinus monophylla* are edible and formed an important part of the Californian Indians' diet. The Monterey cypress is the *Cupressus macrocarpa*, the green oak the *Quercus agrifolia* or the *Q. chrysolepsis*, the plane tree the *Platanus californicus* or possibly the *P. racemosa*; the cornythus could have been a filbert, *Corylus californica*, unless it was the western dogwood, *Cornus nuttalli*.

[2] San Carlos mission was moved after a year to its Carmel side in order to be near the small river which flows, not towards Monterey but into Carmel Bay on the other side of the peninsula. There was a tidal creek and estuary near the Presidio, called El Estero, which is today no more than a small pond. See 'El Estero of Monterey', *Noticias del Puerto de Monterey*, xvii (December 1973), pp. 17–20.

I am fully aware of the great difficulties facing such a new programme: I know that these men have a limited range of ideas and even less constancy, that if one ceases to consider them as children they escape from the care of those who have taken the trouble of teaching them; arguments have almost no effect on them: their senses have to be worked upon, and corporal punishment, together with a double ration of rewards, have been the only means so far adopted by their rulers; but would it be impossible for a combination of burning zeal and extreme patience to teach to such a small number of family groups the advantages of a society based on the rights of people? to establish among them a property right, which appeals so universally to mankind, which would lead each one to cultivate his plot in a competitive spirit, or engage in other kinds of activity?

I agree that the progress of this new civilisation would be quite slow, the care needed both tiresome and wearying, the places to which one would have to travel very distant, and the acclaim unheard by the one who would have devoted his life to earn it; and so I do not hesitate to state that ordinary human motivation is not enough for such a ministry, and that only religious zeal with the eternal rewards it promises can justify the sacrifices, the boredom, the fatigues, and the dangers of this kind of life; there only remains for me to wish that the austere, charitable and religious men I met in these missions were a little more philosophically inclined.[1]

I have already freely expressed my opinion of the monks of Chile whose behaviour generally struck me as scandalous.[2] I will with the same respect for truth depict these truly apostolic men who have given up the leisurely life of the cloister to take up a varied burden of fatigues, responsibilities, sollicitude; I will, following my practice, describe our own story side by side with theirs and place before the reader what we saw and learnt during our brief stay in Monterey.

We dropped anchor on the evening of 14 September 2 Ls off shore within sight of the Presidio, and two vessels were at the

[1] This passage should be read in the context of eighteenth-century discussions by the French *philosophes* and others on the social system and desirable political structures.

[2] La Pérouse adds a marginal note: 'One can also meet in Chile some most worthy members of religious orders, but in general they enjoy a freedom which is inappropriate for the vocation they have embraced.'

anchorage; they had fired their guns at intervals of a quarter of an hour in order to show us the anchorage which the fog was likely to hide from us; at 10 p.m. the captain of the frigate *Favorite* came alongside in his longboat and offered to pilot our ships into the port; the frigate *Princesse* had also sent a pilot with her longboat to the *Astrolabe*; we learnt that these two frigates belonged to the King of Spain, and that they were commanded by Don Estevan Martinez, frigate lieutenant from the Department of San Blas in the province of Guadalaxara;[1] the government maintains a small fleet in this port, under the command of the Viceroy of Mexico; it consists of four corvettes of 12 guns and a schooner; their particular function is the provisioning of the Presidios of northern California. They are the very ships that carried out the last two Spanish campaigns to the N.W. coast of America; they are sometimes sent as packetboats to Manila to carry speedily the orders of their Court.

We raised anchor at 10 a.m. and dropped it again within the roadstead at midday; we received a 7-gun salute which we returned, and I sent an officer to the Governor's with the Spanish Minister's letter that had been given to me in France before my departure; it was unsealed and addressed to the Viceroy of Mexico whose authority extends to Monterey although it is eleven hundred leagues overland from his capital.

Mr Fagez,[2] commandant of the fort and of both Californias, had

[1] The *Princesa* and the *Favorita* had sailed under Bodega y Quadra to Alaska in 1779. Martinez was to be sent by the Viceroy of Mexico, Manuel Antonio Flores, in 1788 with the *Princesa* and the *San Carlos* to the Northwest Coast; he returned the following year to re-establish Spanish sovereignty over the coast, but his intervention led to the Nootka Incident which almost resulted in war between Spain and Great Britain. The Department of San Blas referred to in the same paragraph was the *Departemento naval* founded by José de Galvez at the small Pacific coast port of San Blas.

[2] Pedro de Fagés had gone in 1769 with Galvez to establish the settlement at Monterey. He then held the rank of lieutenant and was in charge of 26 Catalan soldiers. When the expedition finally reached Monterey in 1770, only ten or so soldiers were still fit for work. Fagés was named commander of the Presidio and Governor of Alta California. His relations with Fr Serra became strained when Fagés found himself unable to give the missionary all the support he needed for his various establishments. Replaced by Fernando Rivera in 1774, Fagés returned in 1782. His important 1775 report on California has been published in a critical edition by H.I. Priestley as *A Historical, Political and Natural Description of California by Pedro Fagés*, Berkeley, 1937. He made an excellent impression on La Pérouse, but as the Frenchman states, Fagés had fallen out with the Franciscan missionaries: a report on this problem sent to the Viceroy of Mexico in 1785 received an evasive response; by then, his wife, Doña Eulalia de Callis, was suing for divorce and had asked the Mexico *audiencia* to recall him. He left California in 1790.

already received instructions to receive us like ships of his own country, and he carried these out with a grace and a concern which deserve our deepest gratitude;[1] he did not restrict himself to courteous speeches – cattle, vegetables, milk were despatched to our ships in abundance; eagerness to serve us almost disturbed peaceful relations between the commander of the two frigates and the commander of the fort: each wanted the exclusive right of attending to our needs, and when it came to settling our accounts, we were forced to insist on their taking our money; vegetables, milk, poultry, all the work done by the garrison to help us obtain wood and water, were free, and the cattle, sheep and grain were charged at such a low rate that it was evident they were presenting their accounts only because we had been firm in insisting that they did.

Mr Fagez added the utmost courtesy to this generosity; his house was our home, his soldiers were at our orders and we could use any of his horses.[2]

The Fathers of the San Carlos Mission, which is 2 Ls from Monterey, soon arrived at the Presidio. As helpful towards us as the officers of the fort and the two frigates, they urged us to come and dine with them, and promised to give us detailed explanations on the way their missions were administered, on the way of life of the Indians, their arts, their new customs, and generally everything that can be of any interest to travellers; we certainly did not decline these offers which, had we not been forestalled, we would have

[1] Following France's request prior to the despatch of the La Pérouse expedition, the King of Spain had sent instructions to the viceroys of Mexico and Peru and the governors of Chile and the Philippines. From Mexico, Galvez had sent out the following letter, dated 19 May 1785: 'His Most Christian Majesty has advised His Majesty that he has organised a voyage of discovery around the world to perfect and complete those that have been recently carried out, and although it is not that Monarch's intention that this expedition's vessels should call at Spanish possessions in the South Seas, it could happen that an urgent need of food or repairs after some storm or other serious accident might force them to put in at some port on the western coast of the American continent or at islands belonging to the Spanish Crown[...] And our lord the King, desirous of contributing to the success of so useful and so worthy an enterprise, following the ties of blood, and the friendship and mutual understanding prevailing between the two powers, orders me to advise Your Excellency urgently that in each one of the above-mentioned cases you are to give and order to be given (having taken in advance all necessary steps) all the favours and assistance asked for or needed for the French vessels which have a copy of this our order if they do not have the original.' Copy in Archives Nationales, Paris, Marine 3JJ 386 Cn 111:1.

[2] The French editor of the Voyage replaced the word 'horses' with 'subordinates'.

sought ourselves: it was agreed that we would leave in two days' time; Mr Fagez wanted to accompany us and undertook to obtain horses; the journey was over a distance of 2 Leagues – after crossing a small plain full of herds of cattle, and in which there remain only a few trees to provide shelter for these animals against rain or excessive heat, we climbed up some hills and heard the sound of several bells heralding our arrival which had been notified to the religious by a horseman despatched by the governor.

We were welcomed like lords of the parish making their first entrance into their lands; the head of the Mission, wearing his cope and holding his holy water sprinkler, was waiting for us at the church door which was decorated as on the greatest feast days; he led us to the foot of the main altar where he sang the *Te Deum* as an expression of thanks for the success of our voyage.[1]

On our way to the church we had crossed a square in which Indians of both sexes were lined up, their faces displaying no surprise, making it unlikely that we would form any part of their conversations for the rest of the day. The parish church is very clean, although thatched; it is dedicated to St Charles and adorned with quite good paintings, copies of Italian originals: we saw a painting of Hell in which the artist seemed to have borrowed

[1] The French call at Monterey, the first by ships of a foreign power, attracted a great deal of attention. The hospitality shown by the Governor and the Franciscan missionaries was due to the importance of this event, but possibly also to the tension and hence the rivalry between the civil and the religious authorities. A report to the Viceroy by Besadre y Vega dated 20 December 1786 states: 'On 18 September the Count with all the savants and people of the two frigates went to the Mission of San Carlos and was received by Fr Firmin Francisco Lasúen and three other religious wearing the cope with the cross and the candle bearers who led him into the church...A light and simple collation was then served...All these expression of religion and friendship were received by such extraordinary effusions on the part of the French that I cannot describe them...' (Mexico, *Archivo general: Historia: 396*). See also I.B. Richman, *California under Spain and Mexico* (Boston and New York, 1911), pp. 164–5. Duché de Vancy sketched the scene outside the church; La Pérouse gave this to Fr Lasúen, and it is now in the Museo Naval, in Madrid. A painting based on this drawing and attributed to Tomás de Suría was eventually presented to the mission and placed in the church where Frederick William Beechey, of the *Blossom*, saw it and offered to buy it 'for 1000 pesos'. ('Descripción topografica de las missiones, pueblos y presidios del norte de la Nueva-California', *Revista científica y literaria de Mejico*, I (1845), pp. 327–9. A few years later, the French navigator Dupetit-Thouars asked to see this painting, but it had gone, apparently given to one Juan de la Guerra (H.R. Wagner, 'Four Early Sketches of Monterey Scenes, *California Historical Society Quarterly* (Sept. 1936), p. 213). A watercolour in the Museo Naval of Madrid (MS 1723–1) may be a copy or possibly even the original of this picture.

something from Calot's imagination.[1] But since it is imperative to make a strong impression on the minds of these new converts, I am convinced that such a representation has never been more useful in any country, and that it would be impossible for Protestantism, which bans images and nearly all the other ceremonies of our Church, to make any progress among these people; I am not sure that the picture of Heaven, which faces that of Hell, produces as good an effect on them. The quietism it represents, this gentle happiness of the Elect, are very exalted notions for such rough individuals; but it was necessary to place rewards next to punishments, and an essential duty not to misrepresent in any way the kind of delights which religion promises us.

When we came out of church, we passed along the same lines of Indian men and women, who had not left their post during the *Te Deum*; only their children had moved away a little and clustered in groups near the missionaries' house which faces the church with the various stores; the Indian village is on the right, consisting of some 50 huts housing the seven hundred and forty individuals of both sexes (including the children) who make up the Mission of St Carlos or Monterey.

These huts are the most wretched one can find anywhere; they are round, 6 feet in diameter by 4 in height; a few stakes the thickness of an arm stuck into the ground and joined to form a vault at the top make up their frame; eight or ten bundles of straw roughly arranged on these stakes more or less protect the inhabitants from rain or wind, and more than half this hut remains open when the weather is fine; their only precaution is to keep two or three bundles of hay in reserve near their huts.

This architecture, widespread in the two Californias, has never been changed, in spite of the missionaries' endeavours; the Indians say that they like the open air, that it is convenient to be able to set fire to one's house when it becomes infested by too many fleas and to build a new one in a couple of hours; the independent Indians who move around so much, like all hunting people, have another reason as well; this space of 6 feet by 4 in height in enough to house two families.

The colour of these Indians is similar to that of negroes; the

[1] Jacques Callot (1592–1635), prolific French engraver born at Nancy, whose 'The Miseries of War' depict the true horrors of war and especially civil war.

religious' house, their stores, built of brick and mortar, the threshing floor on which they crush the grain, the cattle, the horses, everything brought to mind a homestead in Sto Domingo or any other colony; the men and women are brought together by the sound of the bell, a religious leads them to work, to church and to all their exercises and, we say this in sorrow, the similarity was even greater in that we saw men and women in irons, others were in the stocks[1] and, finally, the sound of whipping could well have reached our ears, this punishment being included, although carried out with little energy.

The replies the religious gave to our various questions left us in no doubt about the system of government of this kind of religious community, for no other word can be used to describe the legislation they have established; they are its temporal as well as its spiritual directors; the produce of the soil is left to their administration; there are 7 hrs of work a day, 2 hrs of prayers and 4 or 5 on Sundays or feast days which are days of complete rest and divine services; corporal punishment is administered to Indians of both sexes who fail in their religious duties, and several sins which in Europe are reserved to divine retribution are punished by being placed in irons or in the stocks. Finally, to complete this comparison with religious communities, once a neophyte has been baptised, it is as though he had made eternal vows; should he escape to return to his parents in the independent villages, he receives three summonses to return, and if he refuses, the missionaries call upon the Governor's authority who sends his soldiers to tear him away from his family and take him to the mission where he is sentenced to receive a certain number of lashes;[2] these

[1] La Pérouse adds in a marginal note: 'These stocks consist in a heavy beam, sawn crosswise, in which a hole has been made large enough to take a leg; a hinge links one of the ends of this beam, which has been cut in half; it is opened at the other side in order to let the prisoner's leg pass through, and it is closed with a padlock; he is forced to lie down in a rather uncomfortable position.'

[2] Fagés disliked having to hunt down escaped Indians. It involved more risks than La Pérouse suspected and hampered his colonising and pacifying efforts. This was why he opposed the missionaries' plans for more rapid expansion. La Pérouse added, by way of marginal note: 'As these people are at war with their neighbours, they can never travel further than 20 or 30 Ls.' Nearby Indians gradually accepted mission life and became known as Mission Indians, but inland tribes and those living north of San Francisco retained their independence until the mid-nineteenth century. The reports sent back by the La Pérouse expedition are particularly valuable because these natives have now vanished. See F.W. Hodge (ed.), 'Mission Indians of California', *Handbook of American Indians North of Mexico*, Washington, 1907, I, pp. 873–4,; and on the San Carlos Mission Indians, A.L. Kroeber, *Handbook of the Indians of California*, Washington, 1925, pp. 462–73.

people lack courage to such an extent that they never resist the 3 or 4 soldiers who so brutally transgress the rights of people, and this practice, against which reason rises in protest, is kept up because some theologians have decided that one could not in conscience administer baptism to men who are so flighty and so inconstant unless the state became, so to speak, their godfather and guaranteed their perseverance.

Mr Fagèz's predecessor (Mr Philipe Neve)[1] who died 4 years ago, commander of the internal provinces of Mexico, a man of great humanity and a Christian *philosophe*, had complained against this practice. He believed that the progress of the faith would be faster, and the Indians' prayers more pleasing to the Supreme Being, if they were not made under compulsion; he would have preferred less monacal constitutions, more civil liberty for the Indians, less despotism in the executive power of the Presidios which can be ruled by men who are barbarous and avaricious, and that it might have been necessary to moderate their powers by appointing a magistrate who would be in a way the Indians' tribune and had sufficient authority to protect them from abuses: this just man had been serving his King since his youth, but he did not have the prejudices common to people of his condition, and knew the drawbacks of a military administration which is not moderated by some intermediary authority; but he must have realised how difficult this conflict between 3 authorities would be difficult to control in a country that was so far away from the Viceroy of Mexico, since the religious who are so pious and, I can say it, so worthy of respect, are already almost openly at odds with the Governor who, for his part, impressed me as a loyal soldier and a good servant of the King.

We wanted to witness the distributions made at each meal, and as all days are alike for these orders of religious, the reader will know the routine of a whole year as we follow the story of one day.

[1] Felipe de Neve, Governor from 1777, is regarded as the founder of Los Angeles (Nuestra Señora de la Reina de los Angeles) in 1781 – or 1786, when the settlers' property rights were formally confirmed. He favoured the *pueblo* or Indian village over the mission settlement, which brought him into conflict with the missionaries. His 1779 *Reglamento* proclaimed the overriding powers of the governor over the colony and all its inhabitants, but his lack of resources made it difficult to carry out his programme, and the Viceroy of Mexico, his superior, needed to pacify religious authorities both in California and back in Spain. Neve did however force the missionaries to allow Indians under their control to elect their representatives.

Like the missionaries, they rise with the sun, go to prayers and Mass which lasts an hour, and meantime they cook some barley flour in 3 great cauldrons set up in the middle of the square, the grain having been roasted before being ground. This kind of porridge the Indians call *atole*,[1] and of which they are very fond, is seasoned with neither butter nor salt, and would taste very insipid to our palates.

Each hut fetches its residents' ration in a bark pot; there is neither confusion nor disorder and when the cauldrons are empty the scrapings are given to those children who have most successfully memorised their catechism.

This meal lasts ¾ of an hour, after which they all go to work; some go ploughing the land with oxen, others dig in the garden; each one, in a word, is employed in the homestead's activities, always supervised by one or two religious.

The women are largely employed in household tasks, looking after their children, and roasting and crushing the grain, a very slow, laborious task because their only method is crushing it on a stone with a roller, more or less as is done with chocolate in Europe. Mr de Langle who witnessed this operation gave his mill to the missionaries, and it would be difficult to render them a greater service; four women will now do the work of a hundred, and there will be time left to spin the wool of their flocks and manufacture some rough cloth; but until now the religious, more concerned with the interests of Heaven than with temporal matters, have been very neglectful of the need to introduce the more common crafts; they are so austere in respect of themselves that they do not have a single room with a fireplace even though the winter is quite severe, and the greatest saints have not led a more edifying life.[2]

[1] *Atole* was traditionally a gruel made with maize, to which milk was added once cattle were introduced.

[2] La Pérouse adds the following marginal note: 'Father Firmin de la Suen, President of the missions of New California, is one of the most estimable and respectable men I have ever met; his gentleness, his charity, his love for the Indians are beyond words. One would need to go back to the apostles to find men who could be compared to him.' Fermín Francisco de Lasúen (1720–1803) first worked as a missionary in Baja California. He arrived in New California in 1773 and took over the general direction of the missions on the death of Fr Junípero Serra in 1783, a position he held for the rest of his life. At the time of La Pérouse's visit, he was still following Fr Serra's policies. Firm and evout, but less fiery than his predecessor, he founded a number of new missions, including Santa Cruz, San José and Santa Barbara.

At midday, bells ring out for dinner. Everyone leaves their work, and as for breakfast they send for their allocation in the same container, but this second gruel is thicker than the first: peas and beans are added to the wheat and maize. The Indians call it *poussole*.[1] They go back to work at 2 o'clock until 4. At 5 evening prayer; it is followed by a new allocation of *atole* similar to the morning's; these 3 distributions suffice for the subsistence of the majority of these Indians, and this highly economical soup could be adopted during our years of scarcity. It would be necessary to add some kind of seasoning. The entire skill in this new cuisine consists in roasting the grain before crushing it; since the Indians have no earthen or metal containers for this operation, they carry it out in baskets made of bark with small burning coals; turning these baskets rapidly and with greal skill they succeed in causing the grain to swell and burst without setting fire to the container which is so combustible, and we can guarantee that the best roasted coffee does not attain the level of torrefaction which these Indians can achieve with their grain; it is distributed to them in the morning, and the slightest dishonesty when returning the flour is punished with the whip, but they risk this fairly rarely. These punishments are ordered by Indians magistrates called *Caciques*; there are 3 in each mission, chosen by the people from those the missionaries allow; but to give a proper idea of this so-called magistrature, we must say that they are like the chiefs of the homes, passive individuals, who carry out the wishes of their superiors, and that their main function is to act as beadles in the church and keep good order there as well as an attitude of prayer. Women are never whipped in the public square, but in an enclosed space, fairly distant, maybe so that their cries do not arouse too much compassion, which might cause the men to rebel; but these latter are exposed to the view of all their fellows so that their punishment can serve as an example; they usually beg for mercy, in which case the executioner reduces the strength of the blows, but the number is always irrevocably determined.

Rewards take the form of small distributions of grain, with

[1] *Pozole* is a soup made with wheat, corn, red beans, peas and a little bacon; recipes differed from place to place. See Edith Webb, *Indian Life at the Old Missions*, Los Angeles, 1952 and Ana B. Packman, *Early Californian Hospitality*, Glendale, 1938. [Details supplied by Mrs Amelia W. Elkington, of Monterey, herself the author of a book of old Californian recipes.]

which they make cakes cooked in embers, and on days of special feasts the ration is of beef; a number eat it raw, especially the fat which is to them as delicious a food as the best butter or the best cheese. They skin all types of animals with the greatest skill, and like ravens utter cries of pleasure when they are fat, and devour with their eyes the parts they are most fond of.

They are often allowed to fish and hunt on their own account, and when they return they most of the time offer the missionaries a gift of fish or game, but they do so strictly in proportion to their needs, taking care to increase it if they know that new guests are visiting their superiors; the women keep a few hens around their huts, giving the eggs to their children; these hens belong to them, as is the case with their clothes and their few other household and hunting articles; it is not known that they have ever robbed each other, even though their doors and locks merely consist of a bundle of straw placed across the entrance when the residents are away.

These customs may appear patriarchal to some of our readers who overlook the fact that there are no belongings in any household that could tempt the cupidity of the neighbouring hut; since their food supplies are assured, their only remaining need is the procreation of other beings as dull as themselves. The men, in order to adopt Christianity, have made greater sacrifices than the women because polygamy was allowed, and it was even their practice to marry all the sisters of a single family; the mission women, on the other hand, enjoy the advantage of receiving the caresses of only one man. I must however admit that I did not understand the unanimous report of the missionaries on this so-called polygamy;[1] how can a savage people accept it, because, as the number of men and women is roughly equal, it imposes a forced continence on several of them? unless faithfulness between spouses is not compulsory as it is in the missions, where the religious take care to lock up one hour after supper the women whose husbands are away as well as all girls over the age of 9; these same women and girls are supervised during the day by matrons; all these precautions are still insufficient, and we have seen men in

[1] Polygamy was widespread, but La Pérouse was not aware that divorce was relatively easy, so that Indian society was not arbitrarily divided into married men and lifelong bachelors. A.M. Gibson, *The American Indian: Prehistory to the Present*, Lexington, 1980, pp. 52–3.

the stocks and women in irons for having outwitted the vigilance of the female Arguses for whom two eyes is not enough.

The converted Indians have retained all their ancient customs that their new religion does not prohibit; same huts, same games, same clothes – the richest of these is an otter skin cloak covering the back down to the groin; the laziest have only a length of cloth supplied by the mission to hide their nakedness and a small rabbit skin coat covering their shoulders down to the waist: it is tied under the chin with a string, the rest of the body is completely naked, as is the head; some however have very skilfully plaited hats.

The women wear a coat of ill-tanned deer skin; the mission women customarily make this into a little corset with sleeves; with a small reed apron and a skirt of deer skin over their loins coming halfway down their legs, this is their only dress. Girls under 9 wear only a simple belt, and the children of the other sex all go naked.

The men and the women's hair is trimmed to a length of 4 or 5 inches. The Indians of the *rancherias*[1] who lack iron instruments carry out this operation with burning brands. Their custom is also to paint their bodies in red or, when they are mourning, in black. The missionaries have banned the former, but have had to allow the other because these people are very attached to their friends; they shed tears when they are reminded of them, even though they lost them a long time ago, and feel offended if one should inadvertently pronounce their names in their presence.[2] Family ties are not as strong as those of friendship; children hardly acknowledge their fathers; they leave his hut when they can see to their own subsistence; but they remain attached longer to their mother who brought them up with an extreme kindness and never beat them, except when they displayed cowardice in their little fights against children of their age.

[1] As La Pérouse says in a marginal note – 'Names of villages of independent Indians' – a *rancheria* was a small village; *rancho* originally meant a hut or a small farmhouse and was later adopted to describe Spanish settlers' farms and in time their cattle stations, the word then being Anglicised into *ranch*. Later, the U.S. administration used the word *rancheria* for Indian reservations.

[2] The missionaries mainly opposed paintings that were associated with old beliefs and magical rites. Mourning and the colour black were acceptable as equating with European practices. Later generations of missionaries allowed traditional Indians festivals, such as those associated with the seasons, which similarly seemed to reflect European or Christian festivals. The Bancroft Library at Berkeley owns a 1806 drawing of a feast day at San José Mission, showing Indians decorated in red, white and black.

Old men no longer able to hunt live as dependents of their villages and are fairly well considered. These independent Indians are very frequently at war, but fear of the Spanish makes them respect the missions, and this may well be one of the reasons for the increase in Christian villages; their weapons are the bow and arrows tipped with a silex that is most artistically fashioned; these bows, made of wood and bull sinews, are very superior to those of Port des Français.

We were assured that they ate neither their prisoners nor enemies killed in combat, with the exception of a few pieces of chiefs or of the bravest men they have defeated and killed on the field of battle; and this is less as a sign of hatred and revenge than as a tribute to their valour, in the belief that this food can increase their courage: as in Canada they tear off the hair of those they have beaten and tear out their eyes which they know how to preserve from corruption and which they keep carefully as tokens of their victory; their custom is to burn the dead and deposit their ashes in *morays*.[1]

They have two games which take up all their leisure time; the first, which they call *takersia*, consists in throwing and rolling a small ring 3 inches in diameter into a space of 10 square *toises*, weeded and surrounded with bundles of brushwood; the two players each hold a stick, the length of an ordinary cane five foot long; they attempt to thread this stick through the ring while it is moving; if they succeed they score two points, and if the ring when it stops rolling simply lays on their stick, they score one. The game is won with 3 points, and it provides them with quite energetic exercise because the ring or the sticks are continually in motion.

The other game, called *toussi*, is quieter; it requires 4 players, two on each side: each one hides in one hand a piece of wood while his partner makes a thousand gestures to attract the attention of the opponents, and it is rather strange for an observer to see them squatting in front of each other in utter silence, watching faces and looking out for the slightest clue that can help them to

[1] Contrary to what is now a general impression, scalping was not a widespread practive among Indians, and unusual among western tribes; it was more common in eastern Canada and on the eastern seaboard of North America. Cremation, however, was current in California. Note that La Pérouse uses the term *moray* here and elsewhere to indicate a space reserved for ceremonies of a religious nature.

guess which hand holds the piece of wood; they win or lose a point according to whether they have guessed correctly or not, and it is the winner's turn to hide the piece of wood; the game is won with 5 points; the usual stake is beads and, among the independent Indians, their wives' favours.[1] The independent Indians have no idea of any god or any after-life, except for some nations in the S. who had some vague notion prior to the arrival of the missionaries; they situated their paradise in the middle of the sea where the elect enjoyed a freshness they never encountered in their burning sands, and they believed Hell to be in the hollows of mountains.[2]

The missionaries, always convinced as a result of their preconceptions or possibly of their own experience that these men's reason is never developed, which justifies their treating them like children, allow only a very small number to become communicants; these are the tribe's geniuses, those who like Descartes and Newton would have brought enlightenment to their century and their fellows by teaching them that 4 and 4 make 8, a calculation beyond the grasp of the vast majority. The mission system is not likely to raise them out of this ignorance: everything is combined towards the rewards of the next life, and the most common crafts, even our village surgery, are ignored; several children die from hernias that the slightest skill could cure, and our surgeons were fortunate enough to help a few of them and teach them to use bandages.

If the Jesuits (it must be agreed) were neither more pious nor more charitable, they were far more skilled, and the immense structure they built up in Paraguay must arouse the gratest admiration; but they will always be reproached for their ambition and perhaps their prejudices which led to this communal system, so inimical to the progress of civilisation, that has been all too servilely

[1] Some of these games were versions of what La Pérouse had encountered on the Northwest Coast. Gambling was widespread among American Indians. The names varied from one tribe to another – there was a multitude of dialects in California. See Gibson, *The American Indian*, p. 81.

[2] Indian religious beliefs varied from region to region, but in general it was linked to their physical environment and strongly marked by animism. Illnesses were caused by an imbalance which affected relations with spirits; magical potions and incantations were then resorted to; tribal myths about their origins and migrations were also important; the after-life was more a happier form of their present way of living than an idealised 'paradise'.

imitated throughout the missions of California.[1] This form of government has become a real theocracy for the Indians who believe that their superiors are in constant direct communication with God whom they cause to come down daily onto the altar. Sheltered by this belief, the Fathers live in the greatest security; their doors are not even closed at night when they are asleep.

And although the history of their mission does have one instance of a murdered religious, it is known that this assassination took place during a riot brought about by an act of carelessness, because homicide is very rare, even among the independent Indians.[2] Even so, murder is only punished by universal contempt; but if a man is killed by several people, he is said to have deserved his fate, since he has brought on himself the ire of so many enemies.

Northern California, the most northerly settlement of which is S. Francisco in latitude 37[d] 58′, has no other boundaries, in the opinion of the Governor of Monterey, than those of America, and our vessels when they went as far as Mt St Elias did not reach its limits. The motives of piety which moved the King of Spain to sacrifice considerable sums for the maintenance of his presidios and of the missions, are today strengthened by powerful reasons of state, which can turn that government's attention towards this precious part of America where sealskins are as common as in the Aleutian Islands and other parts frequented by the Russians.

[1] La Pérouse was writing only a few years after the suppression of the Jesuit Order – Pope Clement XIV's decree, *Dominus ac redemptor noster*, was issued in July 1773 – and the publication of the highly influencial *Histoire philosophique et politique des établissements et du commerce des Européens dans les deux Indes* by the Abbé Raynal in 1770. The transformation of the communal way of life of the Indians into a modern system of independent farmers and traders was far more difficult than La Pérouse and other critics of the Paraguayan and Californian missions imagined. Missions were run rather like small theocracies, as he states, but the missionaries did not exploit their charges and their standard of living was not much better than that of the Indians. Fr Lasúen was about to adopt policies aimed at training the Indians under his care to become more self-supporting, but, as in Paraguay with the Jesuits, time was against him, and demand for land by European settlers was growing. The secularisation laws issued by the Mexican government in 1833 led to the disintegration of the missions, and the Indians lost their protectors. Monterey surrendered to the American John Sloat in 1846; Nueva California was ceded to the United States in 1848 and the gold rush of 1849 brought in thousands of new immigrants. The Indians were rapidly marginalised into inadequate *rancherias*; by 1900 their number had dropped to an estimated 12,000; the former 'Mission Indians', stranded between two cultures, were the most affected, and the San Carlos Indians vanished altogether.

[2] The murder did not occur at San Carlos, but at San Diego. Fr Luis Jayme (1740–75) was killed there on 5 November 1775 during a brief rebellion.

We found at Monterey a representative of the King of Spain named Mr Vincent Vassadre y Vega; he had taken instructions to the Governor of Monterey to gather all the sealskins of his 4 presidios and of the 10 missions, the King reserving that monopoly to himself; Mr Fages assured me that he could supply 10,000 of them annually, and since he knew the country he added that if the China trade involved a turnover of thirty thousand skins two or three settlements to the N. of S. Francisco would soon supply the needs of that country's trade.

One may express some surprise that the Spanish who have such close connections with China by way of Manila, where the anchorage is constantly filled with Chinese boats, have until now overlooked the value of this precious fur. They owe this knowledge to Captain Cook and the publication of his book, from which they will derive the greatest benefits; and so that great man has sailed for all the nations, and his own can claim over the others merely the glory of his undertaking and of having given birth to him.

The [sea] otter is an amphibious animal as common along the whole western seaboard of America, from 28^{d} to 60^{d}, as seals are on the coasts of Labrador and Hudson's Bay.[1] The Indians who are not such sailors as the Eskimos and whose canoes at Monterey are simply made of reed,[2] capture them only on land with snares or else kill them with sticks if they find them away from the shore; they hide behind rocks because this animal is very easy to scare and dives immediately; until this year a seal skin was worth only two hare skins; the Spanish did not suspect that they could be in demand; they had never sent any to Europe, and Mexico was too hot a place for them to suspect that there could be any sale for them.

It seems to me that there will be within a few years very great

[1] La Pérouse is endeavouring to make the distinction between the sea otter ('loutre marine'/*Lutra marina Enhydra lutris*) whose pelt was highly prized, and the common seals ('loup marin'/*Phocidae* family) whose skin was more often used for leather clothing. However, there are many varieties of seals, including the valuable northern fur seal (*Callorhinus ursinus*) of the Bering Sea and Pribilof Islands region which migrates south as far as Baja California. The terminology of his day was imprecise, his own knowledge limited, and interpretations made no easier by the use of the term 'sealskin' to describe the otter fur.

[2] Marginal note: 'Those of the Sta Barbara Channel and San Diego have wooden canoes, rather like those of Mowee [Maui], but without an outrigger.'

changes in the Russian trade at Kiakia[1] which will have great difficulty in facing this competition; the comparison I have made of otter skins at Monterey with those of *Baye des Français* leads me to believe that those of the S. are somewhat inferior; but the difference is so slight that I am not entirely sure, and I doubt that this inferiority could make a difference of 10 per 100 in the sale price. It is practically certain that the new Manila Company will try to capture this trade, and this is the best thing that could happen to the Russians, because it is in the nature of monopolies to bring death or at least sluggishness to everything associated with them, from which they suck out all the life, and only freedom can give trade all the activity it is capable of.

New California does not yet have a single inhabitant[2] in spite of its fertility; a few soldiers married to Indian women, who live in the forts or are spread out like squads of mounted constables in the various missions, represent so far the total Spanish population in this part of America, which would certainly be on a par with Virginia, on the opposite side of the continent, if it were not so far from Europe; but its proximity to the East could make up for it, and I believe that good laws, and especially freedom of trade, would soon bring it settlers; for the possessions of Spain are so extensive that one cannot foresee a large population spreading in any of her colonies, particularly in view of the relatively high number of celibates of both sexes who have taken up that state out of devoutness, and of the unwavering policy of that government of allowing no other religion and using the most violent methods to maintain it.

[1] Kiakhta (today K'achta) played a similar role in eastern trade to Canton: it was the only other town where China allowed its people to trade with foreigners. Situated south of Irkutsk on the Mongolian frontier, it had a parallel Chinese establishment, Mai Mai-Cheng. From 1744, apart from times when the frontier was arbitrarily closed, roughly a thousand Russian merchants annually converged on Kiakhta to barter furs from Siberia and Alaska for silk and tea; but until William Coxe drew attention to this important trading centre in his *Account of the Russian Discoveries between Asia and America*, London, 1780, Europeans were largely unaware of it. As La Pérouse foresaw, the fur trade on the Northwest Coast had a disastrous effect on Kiakhta as English, American and, occasionally, French traders took their wares to Canton. What he did not foresee was that the rush for furs was bringing about a collapse in prices, which was shortly to affect his own expedition. On trade between China and Russia, see M.N. Pavlovsky, *Chinese-Russian Relations*, New York, 1949.

[2] Inhabitants (*habitants*, a term long used in French Canada) refers to a permanent settler or colonist. The Spanish equivalent was *poblador*.

I have already made known my opinion that the way of life of the people who have been converted to Christianity would be more favourable to a growth in population if the right of property and a certain freedom formed the basis of it; however, since the ten mission stations were set up in Northern California, the Fathers have baptised 7701 Indians of both sexes and have buried only 2388. But it must be stressed that this calculation does not indicate, as in European cities, whether the population is growing or not, because they baptise Independent Indians every day; the only consequence is that Christianity is spreading, and I have already said that the matters of the next life could not be in better hands.

The Franciscan missionaries are nearly all Europeans. They have a college[1] at Mexico under the control in America of the general of their Order; this house is not a dependency of the Franciscan Provincial in Mexico, and its superiors are in Europe.

The Viceroy is today the sole judge of the missions' contentious issues, and they do not recognise the authority of the Governor of Monterey; the latter is merely required to give them assistance when they need it; but as he has rights over all the Indians, and mainly those of the *rancherias*, and moreover commands the cavalry squadrons that reside in the missions, these various matters very often result in friction between the military and the religious administrations, the latter disposing of powerful influences in Spain to ensure they do not lose their case. Disputes used to be referred to the Governor of the interior provinces, but the new Viceroy, Don Bernardo Galves,[2] has reserved all the powers for himself.

The King grants 400 piastres to each missionary, the number of which is fixed at two per parish; if there is a supernumerary, he is not paid a salary. Money is not necessary in a country where there is nothing to buy: beads are the Indians' only currency, so the college in Mexico never sends any allowances in cash, but in goods, such as candles for the church, chocolate, sugar, oil, wine, with a

[1] Marginal note: 'That is the name they give to their convent.' The reference is to San Fernando College. Its students and teachers, among whom is numbered the great Junípero Serra were called *Ferdinandos*, a term which became synonymous with Franciscans in Alta California.

[2] Bernardo, Conde de Galvez (1746–86), was sent to Florida with the rank of colonel, became its governor in 1776 and fought successfully against the British, distinguishing himself in particular at Pensacola. He was appointed Viceroy of Mexico in 1785, but died in November of the following year. Galveston, Texas, is named after him.

few lengths of cloth which the missionaries cut into small belts to cover what modesty no longer allows the converted Indians to show. The governor's salary is 4000 piastres, his lieutenant's 450, a captain-inspector of the 283 cavalrymen scattered in the two Californias 2000, each cavalryman 217, but he has to see to his subsistence, supply horses, clothes, weapons and generally speaking all his own requirements. The King who owns horse-breeding establishments and cattle farms sells the soldiers horses and the beef they require for food. A good horse costs eight piastres, an ox five; the governor is the administrator of the breeding establishments and cattle farms which belong to the King; at the end of the year he supplies each horseman with a statement of what remains owed to him and scrupulously pays it to him.

As the soldiers had been most helpful to us,[1] I asked permission to give them a length of blue cloth, and I sent the missions rugs, cloth, beads, and iron utensils – broadly speaking all kinds of small items that could be of use to them and which we had not had the opportunity to hand around to the Indians of Port des Français; the Father in charge told the whole village that it was a gift from the King of France, a faithful ally, a close relative of their sovereign, whose subjects belonged to the same religion as the Spanish, which created an atmosphere of general goodwill so that everyone brought us on the next day a bundle of hay or straw for the cattle and the sheep we were to take on board. Our gardener gave the missionaries some potatoes from Chile, in perfect condition; I think this is not the least important of our gifts, and that this tuber will take perfectly in the light and rich soil of the Monterey district.[2]

We had started gathering wood and water as soon as we arrived; we were allowed to obtain wood from as close to our longboat as we wished. For their part, our botanists did not lose a minute before increasing their collections of plants, but the season was not

[1] Marginal note: 'There were only 15 in the Presidio.'

[2] Malaspina credits the French for the agricultural improvements which occurred at San Carlos and in the missions of Santa Barbara and San Diego where Fr Lasúen sent part of the seeds he obtained: 'Diferentes granos de la mejor calidad, que en el día han multiplicado mucho en la misión de San Carlos...merecen los majores elogios los rastros de humanidad que han dejado estos navegantes franceses en las misiónes de Nueva California.' Pedro de Novo y Colson (ed.), *Viaje político-científico alrededor del mundo por las corbetas* Descubierta *y* Atrevida *al mando de los capitánes de navío D. Alejandro Malaspina y Don José de Bustamente...desde 1789 a 1794*, Madrid, 1885, p. 438.

favourable – the summer heat had dried them out and their seeds were spread over the ground; those Mr Collignon was able to identify were the greater and the beach wormwood, the sagebrush, the mugwort, the Mexican tea plant, the golden-rod, the Michaelmas daisy, the milfoil, the black nightshade, the sea-fennel, the aquatic mint.[1] A multitude of vegetables grew in the gardens both of the missions and of the Governor, which were ransacked for us, and in no country did our crews obtain a greater quantity of vegetables.

Our lithologists were no less energetic than our botanists, but they were less lucky; all they came upon in the mountains, the ravines, the seashore, was a light and clayey crumbly stone, which is a kind of marl, some pieces of granit in which there were veins of crystallised feldspar, a few items of smoothed porphiry and jasper, but no trace of metal; shells are not more plentiful, apart from some superb sea ears[2] with a shell of the finest orient, measuring as much as 9 inches in length and 4 in width. All the rest is not worth the trouble of picking up. The eastern and southern coast of Old California is much richer in this branch of natural history. One finds oysters there, with pearls of a beauty and size equal to those of Ceylon or the Persian Gulf: it would be another highly valuable item with a guaranteed market in China, but the Spanish are unable to cope with their own various commercial needs.

On the evening of the 22nd everything was on board. We took our leave of the Governor and the missionaries; we were taking away as many provisions as when we left Concepción.[3] Mr Fages had had almost all his vegetables dug up; his poultryyard had also

[1] The first four belong to the *Artemisia* family: the *Artemisia tridentata*, *A. californica*, *A. arbuscula*, *A. vulgaris*. Mexican tea is the *Chenopodium ambrosioides*, the golden rod the *Solidago canadensis elongata*, the Michaelmas daisy the *Aster tripolium*, the milfoil an *Achillea millefolium*, the black nightshade the *Solanum nigrum*, the sea-fennel is a samphire, *Chrithmum maritimum*, the aquatic mint the *Mentha aquatica*.

[2] The sea ear is the ormer (Latin *auris maris*) or abalone of which there are several varieties: *Haliotis splendens*, *H. rufescens*, *H. cracherodii* of which the *rufescens* is the most common on the Californian coast. It is widely used in jewellery and ornamentation.

[3] Reporting to the Viceroy, Fagés listed what he had supplied to the frigates: 44 oxen, 51 lambs, 200 hens, 30 bushels of wheat, 32 of oats, 8 tunny fish, 80 large sacks of vegetables, 1 barrel of milk, wood and dried grass. *Gazetas de Mejico, compendido de noticias de Nueva España que se comprehenden los años 1786 y 1787*, Mexico, 1787, II, p. 287. He then forwarded a detailed report on the French visit on 28 September 1786 which was sent on to Spain, *Archivo histórica nacional*, Madrid: A.H.H. Estado, 1788.

been transferred to our hen-coops. The religious had not been any less generous, and had kept in the way of beans, peas and grain only what was strictly necessary for them; they were not prepared to take the slightest payment, and gave way to our protests only on the grounds that they were merely the administrators and not the owners of the mission's property.

On the 23rd the winds were contrary. and on the morning of the 24th we set sail with a W. breeze. Mr Don Esteven Martinez had come on board my ship at dawn; his longboat and crew had been constantly at our disposal and helped us in our work; I can only inadequately express the feelings of gratitude which his help deserves, and similarly in respect of M. Vincent Vasadore y Vega, a young man full of intelligence and merit, who is shortly to leave for China to sign a commercial treaty relative to the sealskin trade.

CHAPTER XI

Astronomical observations, comparisons of the results obtained by lunar distances and by our chronometers by which we drew the American coast. Justified belief that our work deserves to be trusted by navigators. Vocabulary and new remarks on the language of the various people who live in the neighbourhood of Monterey and comments on their pronunciation.

SEPTEMBER 1786

While our crews were busy on land gathering the wood and obtaining the water we needed, Mr Dagelet had his quadrant taken ashore in order to determine more accurately the latitude of Monterey, and he regretted that circumstances did not permit a longer stay, so that he could have continued his comparisons of our timekeepers; the theft of the observations logbook by the natives at Port des Français left him still uncertain about the daily loss of No. 19 which we had used to determine all the features of the coast of America. This astronomer even felt he should consider as void the comparisons he had made on Coenotaph Island, and preferred those of Talcaguana in Chile, although they were too far back in time to warrant our total confidence, but one must not forget that we compared their result with lunar readings taken on board both frigates, and it was from the perfect concordance of the two methods that we concluded to the accuracy of our observations.

People who work in the exact sciences may be interested to know the extent of possible errors in such work; they will know that the problem of longitudes is solved by finding, within the same mathematical moment, what difference in hours, minutes and seconds exists between a known meridian, taken as the basis of comparison, and the locality whose position is to be determined. Astronomy offers several methods of varying simplicity and precision, but the distance from the moon to the sun is generally favoured at sea, although all the efforts of geometry and arithmetic have not so far resulted in tables that are strictly accurate. Those used by navigators can, in extreme cases, differ by forty to fifty seconds from observed longitudes, which leaves 15 to 20′ of uncertainty in respect of the geographical longitudes that are calculated from distances observed on board and compared with those of the tables.

The second source of errors, related to the accuracy of the instruments and the precision of the observer, is much more difficult to pin down. It is closely related to the skill, the wisdom and the accuracy with which the sextants and circles are used. Without going into the detail of all the precautions we took to assess the degree of error of our instruments, the work of the most talented makers in London and Paris, Mr Dagelet believes that the sextants could not have been more than thirty seconds out, and the circles fifteen only, on account of the extreme difficulty there is in finding the formers' point zero, giving the circles a distinct advantage, as moreover they were much less well finished than Ramsden's sextants;[1] they were as well graduated, but less well finished as to the detail. However, the median of our results never left any uncertainty greater than fifteen seconds, which, added to the thirty seconds of the tables, could produce at the most an error of half a degree on the geographical longitudes: but if one bears in mind that these errors very often cancel each other out, it will be appreciated that it is all but improbable that we ever made a mistake of that extent, and since we combined several results of distances obtained under different circumstances and on board both ships, in order then to compare them with those of our chronometers – which provided evidence of their regularity since our departure from Talcaguana – it can be concluded that the various points of the American coast we determined by means of these chronometers deserve the utmost confidence, and errors (if there are any) must be attributed to the compasses used when taking bearings; these did however have sight-vanes and were the best available for use on board ships.

The usefulness of marine chronometers is now so widely recognised and so clearly explained in Mr de Fleurieux's Voyage that we

[1] Jesse Ramsden (1735–1800), born near Halifax, Yorkshire, worked for a London instrument maker before setting up on his own in 1762. He supplied instruments for James Cook's voyages. Elected to the Royal Society in 1786, he received the Copley Medal in 1795. The finish of his instruments was remarkable and today they are regarded as true works of art.

TRACK
OF THE EXPEDITION

9. Part of North America from Mt St Elias to Monterey, showing the track of the expedition, with a table of longitudes drawn up by Bernizet and Dagelet. AN 6 JJ1:34B.

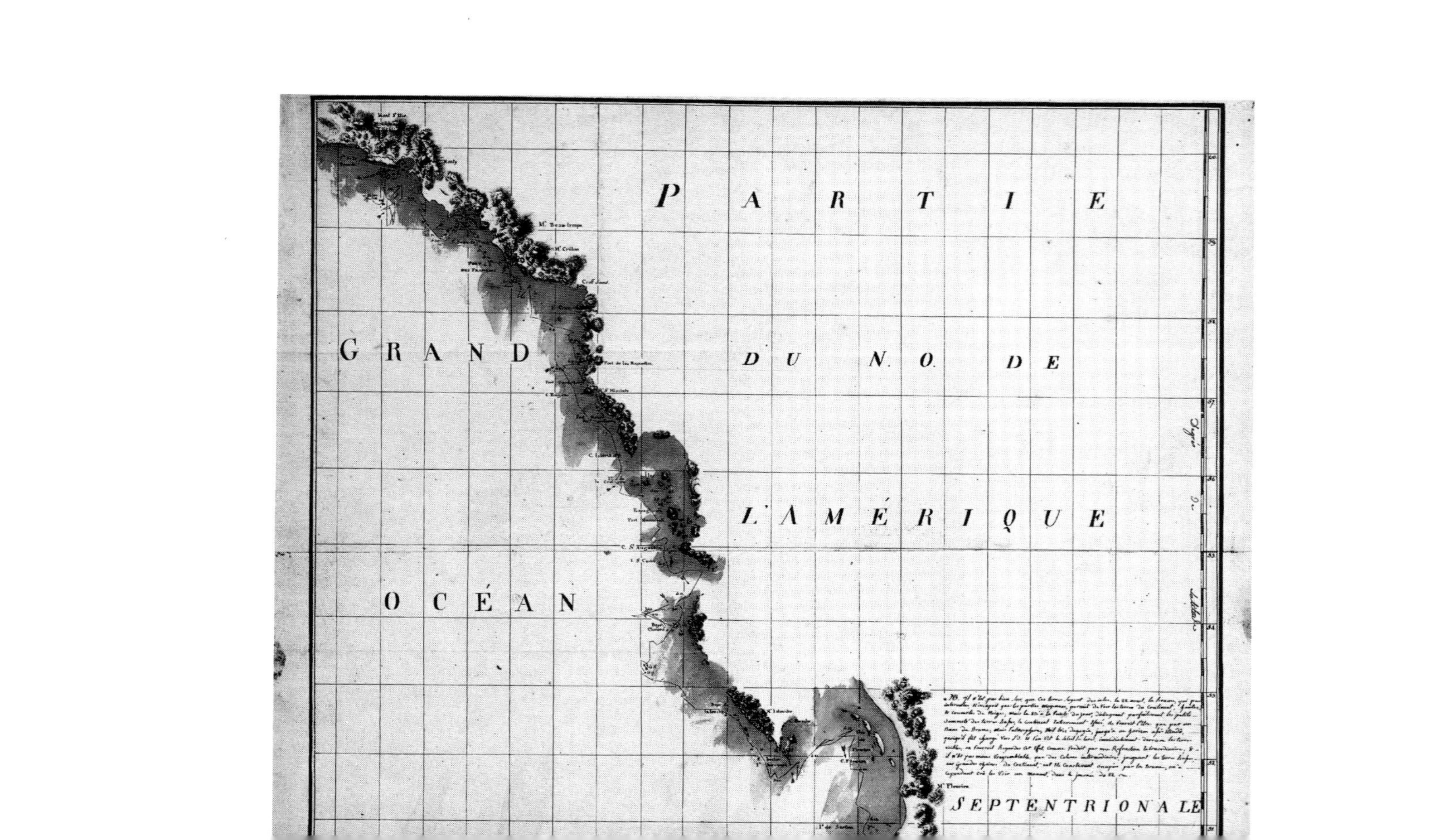
PARTIE
DU N.O. DE
L'AMÉRIQUE
SEPTENTRIONALE
GRAND
OCÉAN
Mt. Beau-temps
Mt. Crillon
Port des Français
Port de los Remedios
C. S.t Augustin

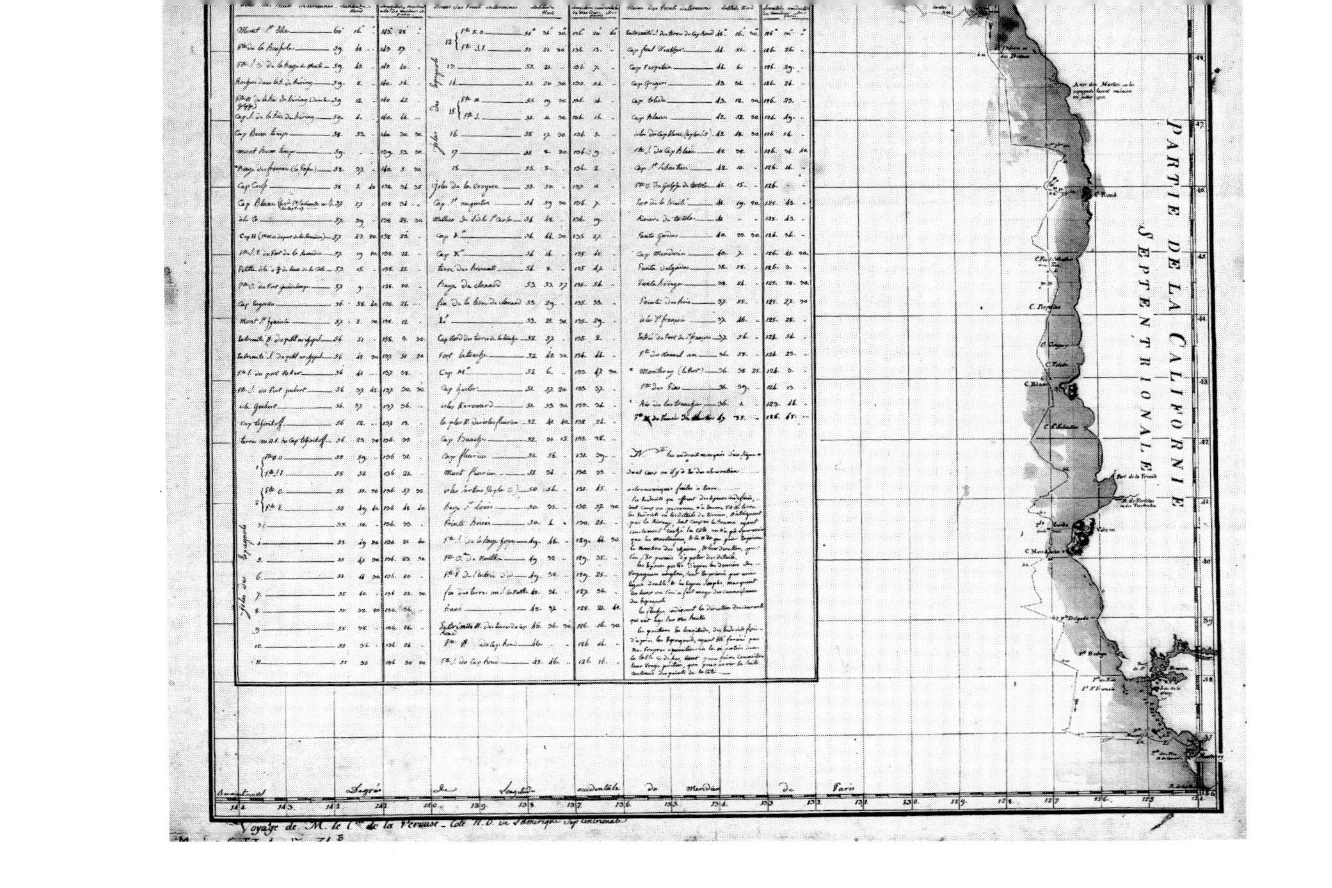

PARTIE DE LA CALIFORNIE
SEPTENTRIONALE
Degrés de Longitude occidentale du Meridien de Paris
Voyage de M. le Cte de la Perouse _ Cote N.O. de l'Amerique Sep. Septentrionale

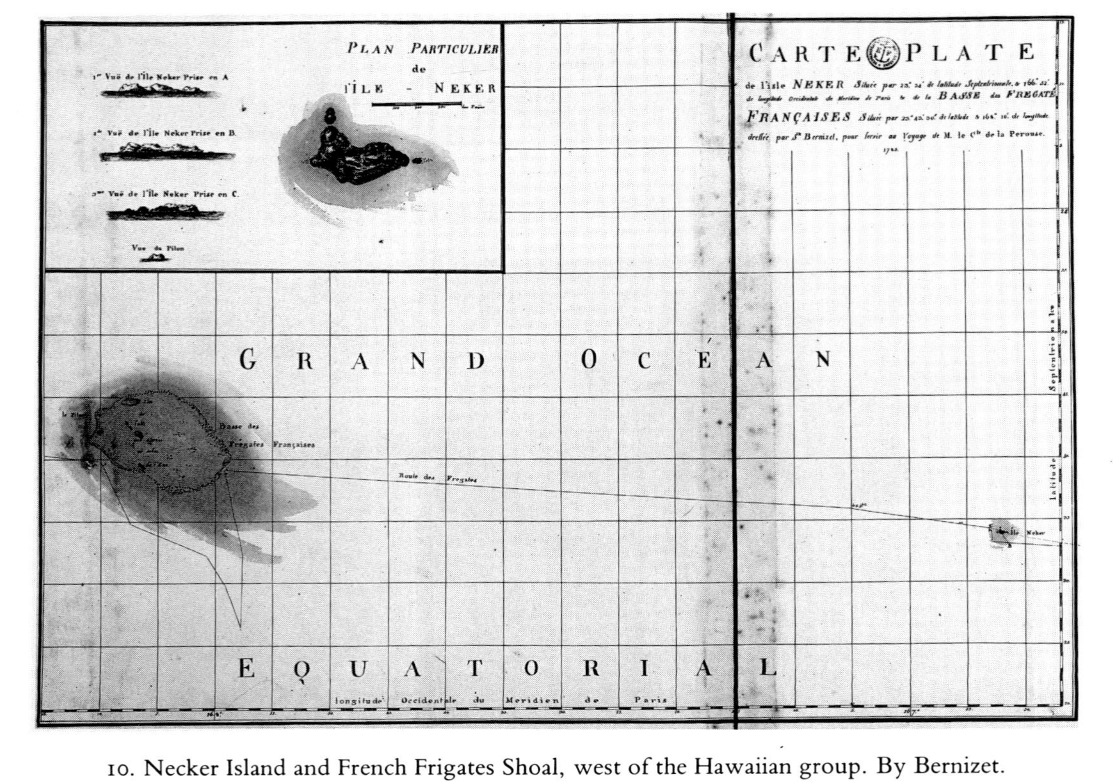

10. Necker Island and French Frigates Shoal, west of the Hawaiian group. By Bernizet. AN 6 JJ1: 25A.

will mention the advantages we obtained from them merely to stress how Mr Berthoud has exceeded himself, since, after 18 months on board, his No. 19 and No. 18 gave results that were as satisfactory as at the time we sailed, and enabled us to determine, several times a day, our precise longitude, following which Mr Bernizet has drawn up a chart which deserves the full confidence of navigators.[1]

One should not however overlook the fact that this chart leaves much to be desired in respect of details; we sailed too fast along the coast to have seen everything and we are answerable only for the features we determined with precision and the trend of the coast, excluding the contours of the bays and the various opening of which we did not sight the end. It struck us as quite safe and without any other dangers than the rocks visible above the water line; but this is a mere conjecture based on the fact that we did not see breakers anywhere out to sea, and it is quite possible that we have omitted shoals in the space between the coast and our frigates, which we have no reason to suspect – but I do not want to inspire in those who will come after us a sense of security which might prove deadly to them if they were to neglect the precautions which prudence requires in these almost unknown seas.

We could strictly be less circumspect in our remarks on the dialects of the various people who live in the neighbourhood of Monterey; such errors have lesser consequences, and although they can mislead etymologists who deduce the identity of two peoples out of the similarity of a few words, the results of these conclusions, often too hastily made, cannot be fatal; but I have made it a rule not to inspire in my readers, even in the most minor of subjects, a greater confidence than I have myself, and I would not hide from them that travellers who stay less than several months are very easily mistaken on the true meanings of words.

Although Mr de Lamanon is the author of the following notes, he shares my view that it is extremely difficult to record an exact vocabulary, and he is only answerable for the trouble and the care he has taken to avoid errors. He might himself have very little faith in his own observations, if he had not found at the missions, where he

[1] Marginal note: 'I must point out that the astronomical observations and the work on the charts were carried out on both ships, and as Mr Monge had left at Tenerife, the task of directing all this work fell upon Mr the Vicomte de langle, who is an excellent astronomer; he was helped by Messrs de Vaujuas, de Lauriston and Blondelas; the latter drew charts from information supplied to him.'

spent four days, two Indians with a perfect knowledge of Spanish who were of the greatest assistance.

After this outline, which may be too long, I will add that, according to Mr de la Manon, there is perhaps no country where there are more dialects than in northern California; this country is divided among several nations who, although quite close to each other, live in isolation and have their own language. It is the difficulty of knowing them all which consoles the missionaries for not knowing any of them, and they need an interpreter for their sermons and their exhortations at the hour of death.[1]

Monterey and its dependency, San Carlos Mission, is the country of the Achastla and the Eccelemachs;[2] the languages of these two people, who are partly brought together in the same mission, might perhaps create a third if the Christian Indians stopped communicating with those of the rancherias from which they come. The language of the Achastlians is proportionate to the feeble development of their intelligence; since they have few abstract ideas, they have few words to describe them; they did not appear to have distinctive names for all the various species of animals: they have the same word *ouakeche* for toads and frogs; nor do they make any greater distinction between vegetables they put to a similar use. The qualifying words they use for moral values are nearly all borrowed from sensations of taste, which is the sense they like to satisfy the most. Thus they use the word *missich* to refer to a good man and to tasty food, and they describe as *keches* a bad man and tainted meat.[3]

[1] La Pérouse's assessment of the language situation is correct. Dialects derived from dozens of languages were spoken by quite small groups, known to anthropologists as triblets, rather than tribes. These languages belonged to various families, such as Athabascan, Algonquin, Yokutsan, Wintun, Yukian and Uto-Atzecan; A.M. Gibson, *The American Indian*, Lexington, 1980, p. 81.

[2] The Coastanoans or coastal people belong to the linguistic group referred to as Penutian (from *pen* and *uti*, meaning 'two' – found in Lamanon's list as *outis*). See C.A. Callaghan, *Lake Miwok Dictionary*, University of California, 1965. Other identifications from the list provided by the French have been made, e.g. S.M. Broadbent, *Southern Sierra Miwok Language*, University of California, 1964, p. 341, and S. M. Broadbent, *International Journal of American Linguistics*, 23–4 (1957), pp. 275–80. The Ecclemachs or Esselens were a tribe of the Hoka family, linguistically linked to the present-day Yuman; thus *peke* for 'one' can be identified with *paka*, *oulach* for 'two' with *rwak*, 'night', with *tumas*, etc. See A. Campbell Wares, *A Comparative Study of Yuman Consonantics*, The Hague, 1968.

[3] The efforts made by the French during their brief stay to report on local dialects, with the help of the Franciscans who had themselves been in the country for only fifteen years, are quite impressive; but neither could hazard a guess at the complexities of Indian society and the use of abstract notions which they could not discern,

They make a distinction between the singular and the plural, and conjugate some verb tenses, but have no declensions.

Their nouns are much more numerous than their adjectives, and they never use the labials F.B., nor the letter X. They have a *chr* like the people of Port des Français: *chrskonder*, bird, *chruk*, hut; but their pronunciation is generally softer.

The diphthong *ou* occurs in more than half the words: *chouroui*, to sing, *touroun*, skin, *touours* fingernail; and the most common initial consonants are T. and K. Endings change most of the time.

They use their fingers for counting up to ten. Few of them can do it from memory and without any gesture. If they want to express the number which follows eight, they start by counting one, two, &c on their fingers and stop when they reach nine; it is rare that they can reach the number five without the assistance of their fingers.

Their numerical terms are:

one .... moukala
two .... outis
three .... capes
four .... outiti
five .... is
six .... etesake
seven .... kaleis
eight .... ouloumasakhen
nine .... pake
ten .... tonta.

The Ecclemachs live E. of Monterey, and their territory extends for twenty leagues; their language is totally different from all those of their neighbours, and even has more links with our European tongues than those of America: this grammatical phenomenon, the strangest yet seen on this continent, may interest savants who endeavour to trace the history of the transplantation of peoples by a comparison of languages. It seems that the American tongues have a distinctive character totally separating them from those of the old

---

any more than they could make allowance for the metalanguage of signs and traditional behaviour which did not need words to be understood within a tribe or between triblets. It can also be easily argued that referring to a person or to food as 'good', or to a man as 'bad' and to food as having 'gone bad', is not unusual in European society!

continent; by comparing them with those of Brazil, Chile, Port des Français, of part of California, as well as with the many vocabularies provided by travellers, it is noticed that American languages generally lack several labials, and more especially the letter F. which is pronounced as in Europe; this dialect is moreover richer than those of other Californian people, although it cannot be compared with the languages of civilised nations. If one drew the hasty conclusion that this nation is foreign to this part of America, one would have to admit that it has lived here for a long time, because it does not differ in any way in respect of the colour or features and generally speaking the whole external appearance of the other people of this country.[1]

Their numerical terms are:

one	peke	beard	iscotre
two	oulach	to dance	mefpa
three	oulef	teeth	aour
four	amnahou	seal	opopabos
five	pemala	no	maal
six	pekoulana	yes	ike
seven	houlakaolana	father	aoi
eight	koulefala	mother	atzia
nine	kamakoualane	star	aimoulas
ten	tomoïla	night	toumanes
friend	nigefech	[hapeau]	sekfes[2]
bow	pagounach		

[1] Lamanon's vocabulary was first used by Johann Christoph Adelung in his encyclopaedic work on general philology, *Mithridates, oder allgemeiner Sprachenkünde mit dem Vater unser als Sprachprobe in bey nahe funf hundrert Sprachen*, Berlin, 1806–17. The third volume, featuring American Indian languages, was completed after Adelung's death by Johann Severin Vater. The differences which had developed within the main languages indicate a slow and lengthy period of migration: using the technique of glottochronology, according to which a language loses approximately one-twentieth of its vocabulary every thousand years, it has been estimated that the coastal Indians arrived from Asia some 15,000 to 20,000 years before the birth of Christ and, behind the natural barriers of mountains and deserts, split into distinctive tribes and triblets.

[2] This last word so puzzled Milet-Mureau that he left it out altogether of the published 1797 edition. It is probably *chapeau* (hat), but might be *hameau* (hamlet). It should be noted that the transcriptions of Indian words have been left as they appear in La Pérouse's manuscript, and that they are the French's own renderings of the sounds they heard: an English listener would have transcribed them differently; thus *peke* for 'one' might have been recorded as 'pecka(y)'.

CHAPTER XII

Departure from Monterey & plan for a new route crossing the western ocean to China; fruitless search for the island of Nostra S^{ra} de la Gorta. Discovery of Necker Island. Encounter at night with French Frigate Shoals on which we were almost wrecked; description of this shoal; determination of its latitude & longitude. We continually found variable winds in regions we did not believe to be outside the limits of the trade winds. We set our course for the islands of la Mira and Gardens; we cross the position on which they appear on our charts without seing any sign of land. We sight the island of Assongssong in the Marianas. Description of this island; anchorage to leeward ¼ of a league from land: our boats have a great deal of trouble landing, and brought back a few coconuts, with a fair collection of plants & various other items of natural history. True position of this island in latitude & longitude. Errors on the old maps of the Marianas published by the Jesuits and copied by most geographers. We sight the Bahée Islands whose longitude we determine, and at last drop anchor in the anchorage at Macao on 3 January.

The western ocean which we needed to cross to reach Macao is an almost unknow sea in which we hoped we might discover a few new islands. The Spanish, who today are the only ones to sail this ocean, have long since lost that desire for discoveries, which possibly the yearning for gold had aroused, but which led them to brave all sorts of dangers: the old enthusiasm has been replaced by a cool evaluation of the risk involved: their route from Acapulco to Manila is restricted within a range of 20 leagues, between the 13th and 14th degrees of latitude.[1] On the return journey they keep roughly to the 40th degree with W. winds – very frequent in this area – quite confident as a result of their long experience that they will

[1] La Pérouse is here referring to the route of the Manila galleon, linking the Philippines with Spanish South America.

meet neither rocks nor shoals. They can sail at night with as few precautions as in European waters, their crossings are much shorter, and the interests of their principals much less exposed to be lost in a shipwreck.

Since the only purpose of our campaign was to make new discoveries, or at least to advance the progress of navigation in little known seas, we avoided frequented routes with all the determination the galleons put into keeping to the track of the vessel that had preceded them; we were nevertheless constrained to sail in latitudes where the trade winds prevail: we could not without their assistance hope to reach China within six months and consequently be in a position to pursue the later part of our programme.

When we left Monterey, I proposed to sail S.W. up to the 28^{d} of latitude, a parallel along which certain geographers have placed the island of Nostra S^{ra} de la Gorta.[1] All my attempts to discover which traveller had in earlier times made this discovery have been fruitless; I went through my notes and all the printed Voyages on board both frigates without any success, and I think that it was only on account of the map taken by Admiral Anson[2] from the Manila galleon that geographers have continued to place it in the western ocean.

I had obtained at Monterey a manuscript Spanish chart of that same ocean which was practically similar to the one the editor of Admiral Anson's Voyage had engraved, and one can rest assured that since the day that admiral captured the Manila galleon and even for two centuries knowledge of this sea would have made no progress had it not been for the fortunate discovery of the Sandwich Islands, the *Resolution and the Discovery* being with the *Boussole* and the *Astrolabe* the only ships which for two hundred years have followed a track other than that of the galleons.[3]

[1] There are few Pacific islands about whom geographers were more suspicious than Nuestra Señora de la Gorta (found occasionally as Santa Maria de la Gorta). Vaugondy, who drew a detailed map for Charles de Brosses' comprehensive *Histoire des navigations aux terres australes*, Paris, 1756 and did not hesitate to include islands whose existence or placing was open to question, balked at La Gorta. It may be a confused echo of Quiros' Virgen Maria (or Santa Maria) whose native name is Gaua, but this can only be a guess.

[2] As La Pérouse found when seeking Las Mojas, Anson's Spanish chart was quite unreliable.

[3] Marginal note: 'Admiral Anson and various buccaneers whose sole aim was the taking of prizes always followed the traditional route.'

Contrary winds and calms held us back for two days within sight of Monterey; but they soon veered N.W. and allowed me to reach the 28th parallel along which I planned to sail for 500 leagues up to the longitude assigned to the island of Nostra S^{ra} de la Gorta, less in the hope of coming across it than to erase it from the maps, because it would be desirable for the benefit of navigation that such islands, whose latitude and longitude are badly determined, were forgotten and ignored until such time as precise observations, at least in respect of their latitude, have placed them correctly on some parallel, even if observed longitudes did not enable them to be allocated a precise location on the globe. I then proposed to sail towards the S.W. and cut across Captain Clerke's route in 20^{d} of latitude and 179^{d} of longitude west of Paris; this is roughly the place where this English capt^{n} was forced to abandon this route to sail to Kamchatka.[1]

My crossing was very fortunate to begin with. The N.E. winds were followed by N.W. winds, and I had no doubt that we had reached the region where the winds are regular; but as early as 18 October they veered W. and were as persistent from that point of the compass as in the high latitudes, varying only from N.W. to S.W. I struggled for 8 or 10 days against these obstacles, taking advantage of various wind changes to progress W. and finally get to the longitude I intended to reach.

Storms and rain stayed with us almost continually; our 'tween-decks were soaked; all the sailors' clothes were wet, and I was very much afraid that scurvy might be the consequence of these troubles: but we were only a few degrees from our destination, and we reached it on 27 October. The only indications of land we saw were two birds of the *coulomb* variety[2] which we caught on the *Astrolabe*, but they were so thin that it seemed very likely that they had lost their way over the sea for quite some time and that they might have come from the Sandwich Islands which were only a hundred and

[1] After the death of James Cook, Charles Clerke took over command of the *Resolution* and of the expedition. Following Cook's plans, he sailed from the Hawaiian Islands to Kamchatka along the latitude of 20–21°N, intending to reach 170°E before veering towards the north; unfavourable winds made him change course when he reached 180°.

[2] The term *coulomb*, more properly *coulon-chaud*, was used to refer to the *Arenaria*. See M.J. Brisson, *Ornithologie, ou méthode contenant la division des oiseaux en ordres, sections, genres, espèces, et leurs variétés* (Paris, 1760), V, pp. 132–40. The *Arenaria interpres* turnstone, is quite widespread, but the birds caught by the French, which they also called sea-larks, were of the ash-grey variety, the *A. tringa morinella Linn.*

twenty leagues away. As the island of Nostra S^{ra} de la Gorta appeared on the Spanish chart 45′ further S. and 4^{d} further W. than on Admiral Anson's map, I altered course to reach this second location, with no more success: as the W. winds were continuing to blow in this region, I attempted to get closer to the tropic in order to find those trade winds that would at last take us to Asia, and where the temperature seemed to me to be more favourable to the good health of our crews: we still had no sick on board, but our voyage, although already quite extensive, had hardly begun, in relation to the immense distance we still had to cover. Our vast programme of navigation did not frighten anyone, but our sails and our rigging reminded us daily that we had been at sea for sixteen months. Our ropes broke time and again, and our men could not manage to repair sails that were worn out; admittedly we had spares on board, but the expected length of our voyage required us to exercise the utmost caution – almost half our ropes were already unusable, and we were far from having completed half our navigation.

On 3 November in 23^{d} 56′ of latitude and 165^{d} 2′ of longitude we were surrounded by birds of the booby, frigate and sea-swallow varieties[1] which generally do not venture far from land; we sailed with increased precautions, lessening canvas during the night, and on the evening of 4 November we sighted an island bearing 4 or 5 leagues W. It seemed small, but we suspected that it was not isolated. I gave signal to keep to and tack during the night, awaiting dawn with the greatest impatience to continue our discoveries. At 5 a.m. on 5 November we were only 3 leagues away and I approached, sailing before the wind, to examine it; I called out to the *Astrolabe* to move slowly ahead, ready to drop anchor should the coast offer an anchorage and a bay where it would be possible to go ashore.

This island, very small, is only some kind of rock some 500 *toises* in length and at most 60 in height; not one tree could be seen, but there was a great deal of grass on the top. The bare rock is covered in bird droppings and has a white appearance, which makes a contrast with various red patches where the grass has not grown; I

[1] Found in these latitudes are the boobies *Sula dactylatra personata*, *S.d. granti*, *S. Leucogaster plotus*, the frigate birds *Fregata minor* and *F. magnificens*, and sea-swallows or terns, of the *Sternidae* family.

came up to within a third of a league; the shore was as steep as a wall, and the waves broke angrily everywhere, so that it was out of the question to think of landing. As we sailed almost all around it, the appended chart is quite accurate, as are the drawings. Its latitude and its longitude, determined by Mr Dagelet, are 23^{d} 36′ and 166^{d} 52′ west of Paris. I have named it Necker Island, so that this famous name may save it from being overlooked – a fate to which its barenness might well consign it – which could be fatal to navigators.[1]

I sailed quite close to the S. part, without taking soundings so as not to slow down the frigate; everything suggested that this island is very steep: everywhere the waves broke against it, except at the S.E. point where a small line of rocks extended maybe two cable-lengths to sea, but I wanted before continuing on my way to satisfy myself about the depth; I took soundings, as did the *Astrolabe* which was almost a league to leeward, while the *Boussole* was at about half that distance; each frigate found only 25 fathoms, broken shells, and Mr de Langle and I were far from suspecting such a small depth. It seemed obvious to me that Necker Island is today no more than the summit, or in a way, the kernel, of a much larger island which the sea has eroded away presumably because it consists of soft or soluble matter, but the rock we see today is very hard and will survive for many centuries the attacks of time and the efforts of the sea: we felt it very important to assess the extent of this bank, and we continued to take soundings on both frigates, while sailing W. The depth increased gradually, as we left the island, and at about ten miles away a sounding-line of 150 fathoms could no longer reach the bottom; but along this space of ten miles we found only coral and broken shells.[2]

We constantly kept look-outs atop our masts; the weather was squally and rainy; there were however from time to time some very fine breaks in the weather, when our horizon extended to 10 or 12 leagues. Especially at sunset, it was as fine as could be hoped and

[1] Necker Island lies in 23°35′N and 164°39′W of Greenwich (166°59′W of Paris). It is a volcanic island 90 metres high with a crater on the summit. A dangerous bank, as La Pérouse states, extends to the south. As occurred with the Necker group off the American coast, Milet-Mureau eliminated all references to the politician and financier in the French 1797 edition.

[2] Necker Island is part of an deep undersea chain which links it to the Hawaiian Islands and by the Marcus Necker Ridge to Wake Island in the west.

we could see nothing around us, but the number of birds did not diminish and we saw flights numbering hundreds going in various directions, which put out our observations relative to the point of the compass where they seem to be going. It was so clear at nightfall and the moon which was almost full lit up the scene so well that I thought I could set off; on the previous day I had seen Necker Island in the light of this same moon 4 or 5 leagues away; I nevertheless ordered the studding-sails furled and a maximum speed of 3 to 4 miles an hour for the frigates: the winds were E. We steered W. We had not had so fine a night or such a moderate sea since we sailed from Monterey, and it was the calmness of the waters that almost caused our loss: at around one thirty in the morning we saw breakers two cablelengths ahead of our frigate; the sea was so fine, as I already pointed out, that they made almost no sound, breaking only from time to time and very slightly; the *Astrolabe* sighted them at the same time – she was a little further off than the *Boussole*. We both veered to starboard and made for the S.S.E. and since the frigate made headway during this manoeuvre I do not think our distance from these breakers could have been more than a cablelength; I had soundings taken right away: we found nine fathoms, rocky ground, soon after, 10 fathoms, 12 fathoms, and after a quarter of an hour no bottom at 60 fathoms: we had just escaped from the greatest danger in which navigators can find themselves, and I owe it to my crew to state that there has never been in similar circumstances less disorder or confusion; the slightest carelessness in carrying out the manoeuvres required to get away would inevitably have led to our loss: we saw the line of these breakers for another hour, but they were disappearing to the W. and by 3 o'clock we had lost sight of them. Nevertheless I kept to a S.S.E. course until dawn. It was quite fine and very clear and we saw no sign of breakers although we had covered no more than 5 leagues since altering course. I am convinced that if we had not examined this danger so carefully, there could still remain doubts about its existence; but it was not enough for me to be sure and to have avoided the danger, I still wanted sailors not to run any risk; consequently, at daybreak, I gave a signal to veer back in order to find it again; we saw it to the N.N.W. at 8 a.m. I crowded on sails to come up closer and we soon saw an islet or split rock, 50 *toises* in diameter at the most, and 20 or 25 in height; it was situated at the N.W. end of the reef whose N.E. point, which had so nearly caused our loss, extended more than four leagues in that direction. We saw, between the islet and the S.E. breakers, three sandbanks not four feet above sea level; they are separated from each other by gaps of greenish water that did not seem to be a fathom in depth; and rocks that are awash and on which the waves break angrily surround this reef, just as a circle of diamonds surrounds a medallion, and thus shield it from the fuy of the sea. We sailed along it, less than a league away, on the E., W., and S. sides. The only uncertainty left concerns the N. side which we saw only from the topmasts, in a bird's eye view, so that it may be more extensive than we think, but its S.E. to N.W. length, i.e. from the point that was so nearly fatal to us up to the islet, is four leagues. The latitude and longitude of this islet, which is the only conspicuous feature, were determined by Mr Dagelet at 23^{d} 45′ and 168^{d} 10′, 23 leagues W.¼ N.W. of Necker Island, but one should not overlook the fact that its E. point is 4 leagues nearer. I named this danger *Basse des frégates françaises*, because it so very nearly marked the end of our voyage.[1]

Having determined the geographical position of these shoals with all the precision we could muster, I set course for the W.S.W. I had noticed that all the clouds seemed to be gathering in that direction and I had hopes of at last finding land of some importance in the area; a heavy swell coming from the N.N.W. led me to assume that there was no island to the N. and I found it difficult to believe that Necker Island and French Frigate Shoals were not the forerunners of an archipelago that might be inhabited or which was habitable, but my theories were without foundation: soon the birds vanished and we abandoned hope of discovering anything.

I did not alter my plan to cut across Captn Clerke's route at the 179th degree of western longitude, and I reached this point on 16 November, but although we were more than two degrees S. of the tropic, we did not find those trade winds which in our own ocean vary only slightly and momentarily in this latitude, and for a distance of more than 800 leagues, up to the neighbourhood of the Mariana Islands, we followed the parallel of 20 degrees with winds

[1] French Frigate Shoals was another discovery. It consists of a steep rock, fairly attractive in appearance, 40 m. high, surrounded by reefs and sandbanks. The lagoon and nearby sea have a bad reputation, more because of the sharks which are common in the area, than on account of the danger to shipping they represent. It lies in 23°46′N and 168°36′W of Paris (166°10′W of Greenwich).

that were as changeable as those one finds in June and July on the French coast: the N.W. winds, causing high waves, then veered N. and then N.E. The sky became clear and fine: they soon veered E. to S.E. Then the sky became whiteish and dull, and there was heavy rain a few hours later, when these winds turned S.W., then W. and finally N.W., which cleared the horizon. This succession of changes went on for three or four days, and not once did the S.E. winds change back to E. and N.E.

I have spent some time on this repeated wind change, during this time of year and in this latitude, because it seems to contradict the views of those who explain the constancy and the regularity of the wind between the tropics by means of the rotation of the earth: it is somewhat extraordinary that in the largest sea on earth, over a space where the reaction of the land could not have any effect, we came upon variable winds for almost two months, and that it was only when we neared the Marianas that the winds settled as easterlies.

Although we followed only one track across this ocean, this does not mean it was an isolated sequence of events, because our crossing lasted almost two months. I agree however that one should not deduce from this that the zone lying between the northern tropic and the 19th degree falls outside the trade winds band during the months of November and December. One navigation is not enough to change widely accepted opinions. But it can be asserted that these laws are not so inflexible that they allow for no exception, and consequently they not bend before the explanations of those who think they have guessed all the secrets of nature.

Mr Halley's theory on magnetic variations would not have been any more successful, if this astronomer, famous in other respects, had sailed from Monterey in 124^{d} of western longitude and had crossed the Great Ocean as far as 160^{d} of western longitude – he would have noticed that, over a distance of 74^{d} or close on 1500 leagues, the declination does not vary by two degrees, and that in consequence it is difficult to draw any conclusion in respect of longitudes: but the method of distances, especially when linked with the use of marine chronometers, leaves so little to be desired that we made our landfall on the island of Assomption in the Marianas[1] with

[1] Asunción, where La Pérouse is about to anchor, is effectively north of Tinian, discovered by Samuel Wallis on 19 September 1767. Asunción might be the island

the utmost accuracy, assuming that the island of Tinian, of which Captain Wallis determined the position from his observations, lies approximately S. of Assomption, a direction which every geographer and traveller has agreed upon for the Mariana Islands. We sighted it at two in the afternoon on 14 December; I had set my course so as to pass through the middle of Mira Island and the desert islands of the Gardens,[1] arguable names that fill on the maps spaces where there has never been any land and thus mislead sailors who may come upon them several degrees to the N. or S. The island of Assomption itself, which belongs to a well-known group of islands[2] about which we have a multi-volume history,[3] appears on the Jesuits' chart – which has been copied by every geographer – 30′ too far N. Its true position is 19^d 45′ and 143^d 15′ east of Paris.

As from the anchorage we sighted the Mangs[4] bearing N. 28^d W. distant some 5 leagues, these three rocks are also placed 30′ too far N. and it is fairly certain that the same error affects Urac,[5] the last of the Mariana Islands which would seem to extend only up to 20^d 20′, the Jesuits having fairly well estimated the distance that separates them but been very inaccurate in their astronomical observations;[6] they

which Magellan called Magrague. The Mariana group however was explored by Luis de Morales in the 1680s, as Charles de Brosses, La Pérouse's main source of information, stated in his *Histoire des navigations aux terres australes*, II, pp. 512–13.

[1] This was an attempt to settle the question of islands reported in 1542 by Juan Gaétan as 'green islands with numerous palm trees' and which accordingly he named Los Jardínes; they were understood to lie in 9°30′N and 179°20′E (De Brosses, *Histoire*, I, p. 170). As for La Mira, it appears on some Spanish charts, but may be a copyist's error for La Mesa which led to consequential errors in longitude.

[2] Marginal note: 'I felt it necessary to inform navigators that these so-called rocks are in fact small islands, because this wrong description confused me for several hours.'

[3] The reference is to C. Le Gobien, *Histoire des isles Marianes nouvellement converties à la religion chrestienne*, Paris, 1700.

[4] The three Maug Islands surround a lagoon which is the crater of an ancient volcano. They are uninhabited.

[5] The small islands at the northern extremity of the Mariana group often confused geographers. Uracas is Farallon de Pájaros, the northernmost; it consists of a 350 m high volcano which is still active. Farallon can be found on certain charts north of Uracas which then is shown either north of the Maugs or as one of the three Maugs.

[6] The exploration of these islands goes back to 1668. In June of that year, Fr Diego Luis de Sanvitores set up a missionary station on Guam, and soon after began visiting the islands by canoe. His longitudes and latitudes were naturally approximate, and the Spanish policy of exclusiveness did not encourage the publication of accurate charts even if precise information had been available. In addition to Fr Le Gobien's *Histoire* of 1700, accounts of the missionaries' work appeared in F. Garcia,

were no luckier when it came to estimating the size of Assomption, because it is likely they would have had no other method available than dead reckoning: although they give it a circumference of 6 leagues, the angles we took reduce it to half that, and its height to 200 *toises*. The most vivid imagination would have difficulty in conjuring up a more horrible spot; after such a long crossing, the most ordinary appearance would have seemed delightful to us, but a perfect cone,[1] the entire side of which, up to 40 *toises* above sea level, is as black as coal, could only depress us and make us rue our expectations, because for several weeks we had been talking of the turtles and coconuts we were confident of finding on one of the Mariana Islands.

To be fair, we did see a few coconut trees which hardly took up a fifteenth part of the island's circumference to a depth of 40 *toises* and were, so to speak, huddled together, sheltering from the E. winds in the only part where ships can anchor, in a depth of 30 fathoms, black sand, which extends for less than a quarter of a league. The *Astrolabe* had reached this anchorage, I had also dropped anchor within a pistol shot of that frigate, but having dragged our anchor for half a cablelength, we lost the depth and were compelled to raise it with a hundred fathoms of cable and tack twice to come back to the land. This small misfortune did not worry me too much because I could see the island did not warrant a long stay. My boat was ashore, under the orders of Mr Boutin, lieutenant, as well as the *Astrolabe*'s in which Mr de Langle himself had gone, with Messrs de la Martiniere, Father Receveur, de Vaujuas, Prevôst; I could see, with the help of my glass, that they had had a great deal of trouble landing; the waves broke everywhere and they had taken advantage of a lull to jump into the water up to their necks. I was concerned that getting back into the boats might prove even more difficult, as the swell could worsen at any moment, and this was the only reason why I might drop anchor, as we were all as much in a hurry to leave as we had been to get here.

Vida y martirio de El Venerable Padre Diego de Sanvitores, Madrid, 1683, of which extracts appeared in the *Guam Reporter* in 1937–9, and W. Barrett (ed.) *Mission in the Marianas: an account of Father Diego Luis de Sanvitores and his companions 1669–1670*, Minneapolis, 1975.

[1] Asunción is a volcanic cone approximately 800 m. in height. It is uninhabited, and La Pérouse's comment about the western side being the only one with substantial vegetation is accurate.

Fortunately at 2 o'clock, I saw our boats coming back, and the *Astrolabe* set sail. Mr Boutin told me that the island was a thousand times less attractive than it had seemed from a quarter of a league away. The lava, running down, has formed ravines and precipices lined by a few stunted and sparse coconut trees, in a tangle of creepers, with a few plants, through which it is impossible to walk a hundred *toises* in an hour: fifteen or sixteen people had been employed from nine in the morning to midday taking coconuts to the two boats, which had needed only to be picked off the ground, but the real trouble was carrying them to the shore, although the distance was quite small. The lava pouring down from the crater has taken over the entire side of the cone up to about 40 *toises* from the sea: the whole summit looks, as it might be, vitrified, but into a black, sooty-coloured glass. We were unable to see the top of the cone; it was always hidden by clouds, and although we did not see it smoke, the smell of sulphur it emitted up to a half-league at sea led us to suspect that it was not quite extinct, and that its latest eruption was possibly fairly recent as there was no sign of any decomposition of the lava in the middle of the mountain.

All indications are that no human, no quadruped, has ever had the misfortune of having no other place of refuge than this island, on which we saw only the largest of crabs which could prove very dangerous at night should one fall asleep: one was brought back to our ships, which Mr de la Manon will describe: it is likely that this crustacean has driven away seabirds who always nest on land and whose eggs would have been eaten; all we saw were 3 or 4 boobies, but when we came near the Mangs or the island of St Lawrence our ships were continually surrounded by a multitude of birds. Mr de Langle shot on the island a bird resembling a blackbird which did not enlarge our collection as it fell into a precipice.[1] Our naturalists came across some very fine shells in the hollows of rocks; Mr de la Martiniere also made a fine collection of plants and brought back three or four bunches of a type of banana that I have not seen anywhere else; he will describe it and I have had it drawn by Mr Prevôt; the only fish we saw were a red cavally, some small sharks and a sea snake possibly three feet long by three inches in

[1] The land crab is probably the *Birgus latro* which feeds on coconuts and attains a size of 40 in. across. The bird might be an ordinary blackbird, *Turdus merula*, found in China Seas, but it was more probably a *T. paliocephalus*, sometimes called an island thrush.

diameter.[1] But the hundred coconuts and the small number of natural history specimens we had hurriedly taken from this volcano (for that is the real name of the island) had exposed our boats and crews to quite real dangers; Mr Boutin, forced to jump into the sea to land and get back, suffered several gashes to his hands, having been forced to cling to the sharp rocks that surround the island. Mr de Langle had also run some risks, but they form part of any landing on such small islands, especially those that are so round; the sea, driven by the winds, slides so to speak and creates an undertow that makes coming ashore very hazardous.

Fortunately we had sufficient water to reach China, for it would have been difficult to take any on at Assomption – if there was any, but our travellers only saw it in the hollows of a few rocks where it lay as in a vase, the largest of which did not amount to the equivalent of six bottles.

At 3 o'clock, the *Astrolabe* having got under sail, we continued our route for the W. ¼ N.W., coasting along the Mangs 3 or 4 leagues off; they bore from us N.W.¼ N. I would have liked to determine the position of Urac, the last of the Mariana Islands, but it would have caused me to lose a night and I was in a hurry to reach China for fear that all the European ships might have left before we arrived; I was very anxious to send to France details of our work along the coast of America, as well as the Relation of our voyage as far as to Macao, and in order not a lose a moment I went on all sails set.

During the night the two frigates were surrounded by a multitude of birds whom I believed to be residents of the Mangs and of Urac which are mere rocks. It is clear that these birds only fly to leeward, because we saw hardly any E. of the Marianas, but they followed us W. for 50 leagues. Most were frigate birds and boobies, with a few gulls, sea-swallows and tropic birds.[2] The winds were very strong in the channel which separates the Marianas from the Philippines, with very high seas, and the currents

[1] The cavally was probably a *Priacanthus hamrur*. The sea snake belonged to the *Hydrophiidae* family, but the variety cannot be identified from the information provided.

[2] The frigate birds more commonly found in this part of the Pacific are the *Fregata minor* Gmelin and the *Fregata ariel* Gray. The boobies would have included the brown *Sula leucogaster*, the red-legged *S. sula*, the blue-faced *S. dactylatra*. The gulls may have been *Larus novaehollandiae*. There are a number of sea-swallows, and the tropic birds could have been the *Phaeton lepturus* or the *P. rubricauda*.

continually bore us S. – their speed can be estimated at half a knot an hour.

The frigate made a little water for the first time since our departure from France, but I put this down to a few seams along the water-line where the oakum had rotted; our caulkers who worked along the side of the ship during this crossing found several seams quite empty of oakum and they suspected that those that were near the water were in the same condition; they had not been able to work on them at sea, but it was their first task when we arrived at the Macao roadstead.

On the 28th we sighted the Bahée Islands to which Admiral Byron allocated an incorrect longitude;[1] Captain Wallis was closer to the truth. We passed one league off a couple of rocks that are the most N. They must be called islets, in spite of what Dampierre states, because the largest[2] has a circumference of half a league, and although there are no trees on it, a great deal of grass grows on the E. side. The longitude of this island, determined when it lay one league to the S., was fixed by the median of 60 observations of distance made under the most favourable circumstances at 119^{d} 41′ and its latitude at 21^{d} 9′ 13″. Mr Bernizet also traced the direction of all these islands relative to each other and drew a plan which is the result of over two hundred bearings. I did not intend to land there, as the Bahées have already been visited several times, and there was nothing likely to interest us once we had fixed their position; I therefore continued on my way to China, all sails out. And on 1 January I found ground at 60 fathoms; the next day we were surrounded by a great number of fishing boats out at sea in spite of very bad weather; they seemed to pay no attention to us, but their method of fishing does not allow them to turn away in order to come alongside vessels: they trawl along the bottom with nets maybe of two hundred fathoms and which could not be raised in a couple of hours.

On 2 January we sighted the White Stone; we dropped anchor

[1] Byron estimated for Grafton Island in the Bashee Islands (the Batans) a latitude of 21°8′N and a longitude of 118°14′E of Greenwich. R.E. Gallagher, *Byron's Voyage of his Circumnavigation 1764–1766*, Cambridge, 1964, p. 125. The actual position is 21° 25′N and 122°E.

[2] These islets represent the southern point of the Bashee (Bashi) Channel between the Batans and the Kotoshos south-east of Taiwan. The largest, Y'ami, was accurately determined by La Pérouse: its position is 21°9′N and 119°32′E of Paris.

that evening N. of Long-ting Island, and the next day in Macao anchorage, having followed a channel[1] which I believe is not much used although a very good one; we had taken on board some Chinese pilots leeward of Lemas Island.[2]

[1] Marginal note: 'The navigators who wish to know this channel will have to obtain Mr Dalrimple's chart engraved in Mr Daprez's *Neptune*; we left the Great Lema, the island of Long-ting, Chichon, Laf-samu, Long-shi-low, Chong-chow, & to the S. and left to the N. or sailed S. of the island of Socko-chow and the large island of Lan-tao.'

[2] Macao, at the mouth of the Canton River, the Zhujangkou, is surrounded by islands, including the five Lemas. La Pérouse passed south of the islands that surround modern Hong Kong, the Po Toi group and Pok Liu Chau, and proceeded south of the small Cheung Chau and Shek Ku Chau, as well as the larger Lan Tao, before crossing the estuary to Macao. The references in the marginal note are to Alexander Dalrymple (1737–1808) whose 1769 *Plan for Extending the Commerce of this Kingdom* included a chart by Jean-Baptiste Nicolas-Denis d'Après de Mannevillette (1707–80), whom Dalrymple called 'the ingenious Author of the *Neptune Oriental*'. Mannevillette's *Neptune oriental, ou Routier général des côtes des Indes orientales et de la Chine*, Paris, 1745 was re-iussed in a revised and enlarged edition in 1775.

CHAPTER XIII[1]

Arrival at Macao. Stay in the bay of Typa. Courteous welcome by the Governor. Description of Macao. Its government. Its people. Its relations with the Chinese. Departure from Macao. Landfall on the island of Luzon. Uncertain position of the shoals of Bulinao, Mansiloq and Marivelle. Description of the village of Marivelle or Mirabelle. We enter Manila Bay by the southern pass; we had unsuccessfully tried the northern one. Observations for tacking safely in Manila Bay. Anchorage at Cavite.

The Chinese who had piloted us in front of Macao[2] refused to take us to the anchorage of Typa; they displayed the greatest eagerness to get into their boats, and we since learnt that, if they had been seen, the Macao mandarin would have required from each one half of the amount they had received. These kinds of taxes are fairly usually preceded by several beatings with cudgels; these people, whose laws are so much praised in Europe, are perhaps the unhappiest, the most harassed and the most arbitrarily governed on earth, if at least one can judge the Chinese government by the despotic behaviour of the Macao mandarin.

The weather, which was very cloudy, prevented us from seeing the town; it cleared at midday and we saw it bearing West one degree South distant about three leagues. I sent a boat ashore, commanded by Mr Boutin, to advise the governor of our arrival and tell him that we planned to stay a little while in the roadstead to refresh and rest our crews.

[1] This chapter is missing from the MS in the Archives Nationales, Paris. Five sheets have been cut away, for reasons that cannot be ascertained. The text that follows is the Milet-Mureau version, published as Chapter XIV in the 1797 edition.

[2] The present-day port of Macao does not exactly correspond to the anchorage in use in the eighteenth century. Tai Pa is one of the four islets situated at the south of the town, which formed a natural roadstead known to sailors as the Typa.

Mr Bernardo Alexis de Lemos,[1] governor of Macao, received this officer in the most courteous manner; he offered us all the help at his disposal and at once despatched a pilot to lead us to the Typa anchorage; we sailed the following morning at daybreak, and dropped anchor at eight o'clock in the morning in three and a half fathoms, muddy ground, the town of Macao bearing from us North-West distant five miles.

We anchored next to a store ship commanded by Mr de Richery,[2] *enseigne de vaisseau*, coming from Manila; it had been sent by Messrs d'Entrecasteaux and Cossigny[3] to sail along eastern shores and protect our trade. So we had at last, after eighteen months, the pleasure of of meeting, not only compatriots, but even comrades and acquaintances. Mr de Richery had accompanied the Moorish pilot the day before, and had brought us a very large quantity of fruits, vegetables, fresh meat and generally everything he felt could please sailors after a long crossing.

Our healthy appearance seemed to surprise him; he gave us the latest news about European politics, where the situation was absolutely the same as when we left France; but all his endeavours to find someone in Macao who had our mail were fruitless; it was more than likely than no letter had arrived for us in China, and we began to fear that we had been overlooked by our families and friends. Sorry situations create unfairness: it was possible that these letters which we were so saddened about had been handed over to the company ship that had missed its departure – only its consort had arrived that year and we learnt from its captain that most of the

[1] As La Pérouse indicates later, he had met both Lemos and his wife at Goa on a previous occasion.

[2] Joseph de Richery (1757–98) was born in Allons, Provence, and first joined the navy in 1766; he entered the naval school at Le Havre in 1773. Enseigne (sub-lieutenant) in 1778, he was actually promoted to lieutenant, first-class, in late 1786. The storeship was the *Marquis-de-Castries* which he commanded from March 1785 to April 1789. He received several other commands from 1789 to 1793 when he was dismissed and arrested by revolutionary forces at Brest; he survived however, and in 1794–5 was in command of the warship *Montagnard*, formerly the *Jupiter*.

[3] David Charpentier de Cossigny (1740–1809) served in the army from 1757, taking part in a number of battles in Germany and being twice wounded. He was appointed to the Ministry of Marine in late 1772 and in 1777 was sent to the Ile de France (Mauritius) as lieutenant-colonel of the colonial regiment. He fought in India from 1778, was raised to the rank of brigadier-general in 1784, and in 1790 succeeded D'Entrecasteaux as governor of the French territories east of the Cape of Good Hope. Joseph-Antoine de Bruny d'Entrecasteaux (1737–92) would command the expedition sent to look for the lost expedition of La Pérouse in 1791–2.

funds and all the letters had been taken by the other vessel. We were perhaps more affected than the shareholders by the setbacks which had prevented that ship from completing its journey; and we could not overlook the fact that, out of the twenty-five English vessels, five Dutch, two Danish, one Swedish, two American and two French ships, the only one to fail to complete the voyage belonged to our nation. Since the English only entrust these commands to extremely well trained sailors, such an event is almost unknown to them; and if when they arrive too late in the China Seas they find the north-east monsoon has started, they struggle with determination against such an obstacle; they often go up to the east of the Philippines and, sailing north into that much vaster sea which is less affected by currents, they come back south of the Bashée Islands to seek Piedra-Blanca and, like us, pass to the north of the Great Lamma. We witnessed the arrival of an English vessel which, having followed that route, dropped anchor ten days after us in Macao roadstead and sailed without delay up to Canton.

My first care, after seeing to the mooring of the frigate, was to go ashore with Mr de Langle to thank the governor for the kind welcome he had extended to Mr Boutin, and ask his permission to set up an observatory on land, and enable Mr Dagelet, who had been greatly exhausted by the crossing, to rest there, together with our chief surgeon, Mr Rollin, who had protected us from scurvy and all other illnesses by his care and his advice, but who would himself have succumbed to the fatigue of our long voyage if our arrival had been delayed for another week.

Mr de Lémos received us as though we were compatriots; every request was granted with a courtesy that is beyond description; his house was placed at our disposal; and as he did not speak French, his wife, a young Portuguese lady from Lisbon, served as his interpreter; she added to her husband's replies a grace, a friendliness that were particularly hers, and which travellers can only rarely hope to find in the main cities of Europe.

Dona Maria de Saldagna had married Mr de Lémos at Goa twelve years earlier, and I had arrived, commanding the store ship *Seine* shortly after her wedding;[1] she was kind enough to remind

[1] Lemos was Governor of Goa where La Pérouse called there, in command of the *Seine*, from 18 to 25 December 1774. Relations were not quite as cordial as this chapter implies: Lemos had tried to send his customs inspector on board the French warship, and La Pérouse flatly refused: 'He told me that he was following his

me of this event, which I had certainly not forgotten, and to add courteously that I was an old acquaintance; then, calling all her children together, she told me that she acted in this way with all her friends, that their education was her greatest concern, that she was proud to be their mother, that she should be forgiven for being so proud, and that she wanted people to know her with all her faults.

Nowhere in the world, maybe, has such a charming picture ever been offered to one's eyes; the handsomest of children surrounded and embraced the most charming of mothers; and the goodness and gentleness of the mother reached out to all who surrounded her.

We soon learned that she had, in addition to her attractions and personal virtues, a firm character and noble ideals; that at various times when Mr de Lemos had found himself in delicate situations vis-à-vis the Chinese, he had been strengthened in his noble decisions by Mrs de Lémos, and that both agreed that they should not, like their predecessors, sacrifice the honour of their nation to any other interest. Mr de Lémos' tenure would have marked an era had they been enlightened enough at Goa to keep him here for more than three years, and give him enough time to get the Chinese accustomed to a resistance which they have forgotten about for over a century.

As one is as far from China at Macao as one is in Europe, owing to the extreme difficulty of entering into that empire, I shall not imitate those travellers who have spoken of it without having been able to know it; and I shall restrict myself to describing the relations between the Chinese and the Europeans, the depths of humiliation which the latter suffer, the weak protection they can expect from the Portuguese establishment on the China coast, and the important role that could be played by the town of Macao for a nation

---

master's orders; I replied that I was following mine in not allowing any clerk on my ship and that the first ones to appear would become the victims of their obedience. After this conversation, none was bold enough to try.' (*Précis de ma dernière campagne à la côte de Coromandel et à celle de Malabar jusqu'à Surate*, AN.M B4:125.) Lemos's powers at Macao were more circumscribed; the settlement was merely tolerated by the Chinese and a wall surrounded it to prevent contact between Chinese nationals and the outsiders who were considered barbarians with little good and much evil to offer. The English, on the other hand, were rapidly developing their trade, buying mostly tea – La Pérouse mentions this in his correspondence with occasional ironical comments – but Chinese goods and curios had become popular in Europe and there was a growing demand for porcelain, silk, furniture and knicknacks, such items being known as *chinoiseries*.

which would behave justly, but firmly and with dignity, in the face of a government that is possibly the most unjust, the most oppressive and at the same time the most cowardly anywhere in the world.

Chinese trade amounts to fifty millions, two-thirds of which are paid for in silver, the rest in English cloth, linen from Batavia or Malacca, cotton from Surat or Bengal, opium from Patna, sandalwood, and pepper from the Malabar coast. Some luxury items are also brought in from Europe, such as very large mirrors, watches from Geneva, coral, fine pearls, but these latter items can hardly be taken into account and can only be sold profitably in very small quantity. All that is taken back in exchange for all these riches is green or black tea, with some cases of raw silk for European manufacturers; because I do not include in this reckoning the porcelain used as ballast for the ships and the silk cloth that return almost no profit. Certainly no country enjoys such a favourable commerce with foreigners, and yet none imposes harsher conditions, multiplies so boldly all kinds of vexations and annoyances: not one cup of tea is drunk in Europe that was not paid by some humiliation suffered by those who bought it in Canton, loaded it on their ship and sailed half-way across the world to bring that leaf to our markets.

I must report that, two years ago, an English gunner, firing a salute in accordance with his captain's instructions, killed a Chinese fisherman in a sampan that had incautiously come under the gun's range and whom he could not see. The santoq or governor of Canton asked for the gunner to be handed over, and finally had this request granted only when he promised that no harm would come to him, adding that he was not unfair enough to punish an involuntary homicide. On the basis of this assurance, the unfortunate man was handed over, and two hours later he was hanged. National honour would have required a prompt and drastic revenge, but merchants ships do not have the means for it; and captains of such vessels, accustomed to correctness, good faith and a moderation which does not endanger the interests of their owners, could not undertake a bold act of resistance that would have led to a loss of forty millions to the company whose ships would have sailed home empty: but no doubt they condemned this insult, and believed that they would receive satisfaction. I will be so bold as to say that every employee of the European companies would together give up a considerable part of their fortunes in order to teach those cowardly mandarins that there is a limit to injustices and that their behaviour had gone beyond all such limits.[1]

The Portuguese have even more cause to complain about the Chinese than most nations; we know their reasonable claim to Macao. The site was gifted as a token of his gratitude by Emperor Camhy; it was given to the Portuguese because they had rid the islands around Canton of the pirates who infested the seas and were ravaging the entire Chinse coastline.[2] It is pointless to claim that

[1] Visitors to Canton or Macao often lost their illusions, and La Pérouse's realistic approach comes out strongly in these remarks; but the trend in Europe was highly favourable towards Chinese culture. In his *Dictionnaire philosophique portatif* (London, 1764), Voltaire included an article on China which read in part: 'the constitution of their empire is still the best in the world'; Diderot in an article on China written for the *Encyclopédie* described the Chinese as 'people superior to all the nations of Asia through their antiquity, their mind, their progress in the arts, their wisdom, their politics, their taste for philosophy'. The Abbé Raynal expressed the view that China must be a country where more humanity is shown than anywhere else, *Histoire philosophique et politique des Deux Indes* (ed., Yves Benoit, Paris, 1981), I, pp. 29–30. Rousseau was impressed by China where 'a knowledge of literature leads to the highest positions in the land'. The economists of the Physiocrat movement, François Quesnay, A.R.J. Turgot, the Count de Mirabeau, expressed particular interest in what they perceived to be China's economic system. The works of Confucius, known in Europe since the seventeenth century (see, e.g., Fr Couplet's *Confucius Sinorum Philosophus*, of 1687), had influenced a number of thinkers and writers, such as Matthew Tindal in England (*Christianity as Old as Creation*, London, 1730, regarded as the bible of deism), and Leibniz in Germany. Reports of persecution and corruption, however, had begun to percolate from missionaries and traders; thus Fr de Marsy wrote in his *Histoire moderne des Chinois, des Japonais, des Indiens et des Persans*, Paris, 1754–78 that there were few countries where poverty was so great, and J.F. de La Croix in his *Dictionnaire historique des cultes religieux*, Paris, 1770 that the sciences had progressed faster in three centuries in Europe than in four thousand years in China. The tug of war between sinophily and sinophobia is described in L. Dermigny, *La Chine et l'Occident: le commerce à Canton au XVIIIe siècle, 1719–1833*, Paris, 1964.

[2] Macao's history is a little more complex, although the transfer of the territory in exchange for services rendered has a basis of truth. Trade in the China seas was in a deplorable state as a result of unrest in Japan and piracy which led in the 1540s to the virtual end of trade between China, Taiwan and Japan. Canton became a centre for trade with the Portuguese of Malacca who helped to put down pirates along the southern coast. In 1554 Leonel de Sousa received formal permission to trade – in effect, a monopoly which the Portuguese struggled strenuously to hold against other European powers for over a century. The Portuguese paid a tribute to China for the growing settlement they had established and which did not gain the extra-territoriality status until 1887. See Tien Tse-Chang, *Sino-Portuguese Trade from 1514 to 1644*, Leyden, 1934 and C.R. Boxer, *South China in the Sixteenth Century*, London, 1953. The Emperor 'Camhy' mentioned by La Pérouse was Kang Hsi (Kangxi) who issued a decree in 1684 allowing wider contacts with foreign merchants, but with strict conditions.

they lost their privileges because they abused them: their crime is the weakness of their administration; every day the Chinese subject them to new insults, they continually make new claims; the Portuguese government has never put up the least resistance, and this spot, from which a European nation that had a little energy could inspire the Chinese emperor's respect is no more than, as it were, a Chinese town where the Portuguese are tolerated, although they have the undeniable right to govern it, and the means of inspiring fear if only they kept a garrison of two thousand Europeans with two frigates, a few corvettes and a galiot carrying bombs.

Macao, situated at the mouth of the Tigre,[1] has room in its roadstead at the entrance to the Typa for ships of sixty-four guns, and in its port, which is below the city and communicates with the river on the eastern side, for ships, half-laden, of seven to eight hundred tons. According to our observations, its latitude North is 22^{d} 12′ 40″, and its longitude east 111^{d} 19′ 30″.[2]

The entry to this port is defended by a fort with two batteries, which one must pass as one enters, within a pistol shot. Three small forts, two of them equipped with twelve guns and one with six, defend the southern side of the town from any Chinese attack: these fortifications, which are in a very poor state, would instill little fear in Europeans, but can impress all the sea forces of China. In addition, a hill dominates the beach, on which a detachment could stand a very long siege. The Macao Portuguese, inclining more towards religion than towards military matters, have erected a church[3] on the ruins of a fort that stood on this hill and was an impregnable post.

The land side is defended by two forts; one is equipped with forty guns and can hold a garrison a thousand strong; it has a cistern, two springs of fresh water, and casemates for munitions and food supplies; the other fortress in which there are thirty guns cannot hold more than three hundred men; it has an abundant perennial spring. These two citadels command the bay. The Portuguese boundaries extend for little more than a league from town; they are marked by a wall guarded by a mandarin with a few soldiers; this mandarin is Macao's real governor, the one whom the

[1] The Bocca Tigris, or mouth of the Tiger, at the entrance to Canton River.

[2] The position given for this area is accurate, Macao being situated in 22°10′N and 111°14′E of Paris.

[3] This is a reference to the church of the Jesuit college at Macao.

Chinese obey: he does not have the right to sleep within the boundaries, but he can visit the town and even the fortifications, inspect the customs &c. On those occasions, the Portuguese must grant him a five-gun salute: but no European can step into the Chinese territory beyond the wall; such an indiscretion would place him at the mercy of the Chinese who could hold him prisoner or inflict a heavy fine on him: a few officers from our frigates did however run this risk, and this slight carelessness did not have any serious consequences.[1]

The total population of Macao can be estimated at twenty thousand souls, including a hundred Portuguese-born, and two thousand half-breeds or Indian Portuguese; the same number of kaffir slaves employed as servants; the rest are Chinese, and engage in trade and the various crafts that make those same Portuguese dependent on their work. The latter, although overwhelmingly of mixed blood, would feel dishonoured if they engaged in artisan's work and fed their families by such means; but their self-respect is not affected by their solliciting and importuning passers-by.

The Viceroy at Goa makes all the civil and the military appoinments for Macao; the governor is chosen by him, as are all the senators who share in the civil administration; he had recently decided that the garrison should consist of one hundred and eighty Indian sepoys and one hundred and twenty militiamen: the purpose of this body is to carry out night patrols; the soldiers are armed with sticks, only the officer is entitled to a sword, but under no circumstances may he use it against a Chinese. If a thief belonging to that nation is found breaking into a house or carrying off some property he must be arrested with the utmost precautions; and if the soldier, defending himself against the thief, has the misfortune of killing him, he is handed over to the Chinese governor and hanged in the middle of the market place, in the presence of the body of guards to which he belonged, of a Portuguese magistrate

[1] Louis Dermigny's great study, *La Chine et l'Occident*, referred to above, gives numerous examples of the difficulties encountered by European traders – and the situation was no better in the north, where Russian merchants faced the same problems. Essentially, the Chinese government did not feel that there could be any benefit in trading with other powers, and it knew that trading posts in India had gradually turned into quasi-colonial possessions. China was difficult enough to govern, with its numerous ethnic groups and distant provinces, without having to deal with foreign outposts. Given the problems that arose in the nineteenth and twentieth centuries, this attitude was not unreasonable.

and two Chinese mandarins who, after the execution, are given gun salutes as they leave the town, just as they were when they came in: but on the contrary if a Chinese kills a Portuguese, he is handed over to the judges of his own nation who, after robbing him, pretend to follow the other formalities of justice, but let him escape, quite indifferent to the protests that are made and which have never been acted upon.

Recently, the Portuguese carried out an act of firmness that will be graven upon brass tablets in the records of the Senate. A sepoy having killed a Chinese, they had him shot themselves, in presence of the mandarins, and refused to hand over this matter to the judgment of the Chinese.

The Macao Senate consists of the governor, as presiding officer, and three *vercadores*[1] who are the controllers of the town's finances which draws its income from the duties charged on goods entering Macao on Portuguese ships alone: they are so unenlightened that they would not allow any other nation to unload trade goods in their town, even paying the prescribed charges – as though they were afraid of increasing their fiscal income and reduce that of the Chinese at Canton.

There is no doubt that if Macao became a free port, and if that town had a garrison that could protect items of commerce stored there, the revenue produced by the customs would double and would certainly be enough to meet all the costs of government; but a small personal interest raises itself against an arrangement which common sense would justify. The Goa Viceroy sells Portuguese warrants to the merchants of the various nations who carry out the Indies trade; these merchants make gifts to the Macao Senate in proportion to the importance of their expedition; and this mercenary arrangement is a probably insurmountable obstacle to the establishment of a freedom that would transform Macao into one of the most flourishing cities in Asia, and a hundred times superior to Goa which will never be of any value to the mother-country.

After the three *vercadores* I have mentioned come two orphans' magistrates, in charge of property in abeyance, wills, the appointment of trustees and guardians, and generally of all issues relating to estates; there is a right of appeal from their decisions to Goa.

[1] The three *vercadores* were members of the Senato da Camarra or town council and elected by the leading Portuguese citizens of Macao.

Other civil or criminal matters are referred in the first instance to two senators appointed as magistrates. A treasurer collects the customs duties and pays, in accordance with the Senate's instructions, salaries and expenses, although these can only be authorised by the governor if they exceed three thousand piastres.

The most important magistrate is the procurator of the town; he serves as intermediary between the Portuguese and the Chinese governments; he deals with all the foreigners who winter over at Macao, receives and transmits to their respective governments the mutual complaints of the two countries, which are recorded, as are all the Senate's deliberations, by a registrar who is not entitled to speak or vote. His is the only permanent position; the governor is appointed for three years, and the magistrates are replaced annually. Such frequent changes, which nullify any chance of a coherent policy, have played a considerable part in the loss of Portugal's ancient rights, and the practice is no doubt continued because the Goa Viceroy finds it profitable to have numerous posts to allocate or sell – for customs and practices in the East lead one to hazard such a guess.

All the Senate's judgments are subject to an appeal to Goa; the known incompetence of these so-called senators makes such a provision highly necessary. The colleagues of the Governor, a man of great merit, are Macao Portuguese, very vain, very proud and more ignorant than our country schoolmasters.

The town has a very pleasing appearance. Several fine homes remain from its earlier opulence, now rented to supercargoes of the various companies, who are forced to spend the winter at Macao, because the Chinese force them to leave Canton[1] when the last ship of their nation has sailed and allow them to return only with ships arriving from Europe with the next monsoon.

Life in Macao is very pleasant during the winter season because

[1] European merchants had long attempted to trade in Canton itself. In 1637, John Weddell and Nathaniel Mountney arrived with several trading vessels, but were sent back to Macao. In the late seventeenth century, English and French merchants were allowed to set themselves up in the area of the 'Thirteen Factories', or *Chie-san Hang*, but only from October to January – the rest of the time they were forced to stay in Macao. The few French agents and employees who lived in Macao found it dull and depressing; a report on life in the town at the time of La Pérouse's visit appeared in Hervé du Halgouët, 'Pages coloniales: Relations maritimes de la Bretagne et de la Chine au XVIIIe siècle. Lettres de Canton', *Mémoires de la Société d'histoire et d'archéologie de Bretagne*, XV (1934), pp. 331–433.

the various supercargoes are mostly very worthy people, highly educated and paid a salary adequate for the maintenance of an excellent household. The purpose of our mission earned us their most courteous welcome; we would have almost been orphans had we been known merely as French, because our company still has no agent at Macao.

We must pay a public tribute to Mr Elstockenstrom, the head of the Swedish company,[1] whose courteous helpfulness was like that of an old friend and of a compatriot anxious to promote our country's interests. Upon our departure he agreed to organise the sale of our furs, the proceeds of which were to be shared among our crews, and was good enough to transmit the money to the Ile de France.

The value of these furs was a tenth of what it would have been when captains Gore and King arrived at Canton, because during the year the English had made six voyages to the north-west coast of America; two ships planning to trade there had sailed from Bombay, two from Bengal and two from Madras. Only the last two had returned, with a fairly small complement of furs, but the news of these expeditions had spread through China, and one could get only twelve to fifteen piastres for fur of the same quality which, in 1780, would have fetched more than a hundred.

We had a thousand furs which a Portuguese dealer had bought for nine thousand five hundred piastres, but as we prepared to sail for Manila and the money had to be paid out, he created some difficulties under various pretexts. Since the conclusion of our deal had caused all the other traders to return to Canton, he hoped no doubt that our embarrassment would result in our accepting whatever we were offered for them; and we have grounds to suspect that he sent on board new Chinese dealers who offered us a much lower price: but, although we were not used to such manoeuvres, they were too obvious not to be identified for what they were; and we totally refused to sell.

There was no problem in unloading our furs and storing them in Macao. The Senate, whom our consul, Mr Viellard,[2] contacted,

[1] The Swedish company had been established for many years in Canton and was one of the best organised; engaged in legitimate trade or contraband, as circumstances changed, they manoeuvred efficiently and skilfully among Chinese and Europeans.

[2] Philippe Vieillard, originally chancellor of the French consulate set up in 1776, was appointed consul in 1782; his previous position was then taken up by Paul-

declined permission; but the Governor, advised that they were our sailors' property, who were working for an expedition which could be of value to every seagoing nation of Europe, felt he was carrying out the wishes of the Portuguese government by waving the prescribed regulations, and behaved on this occasion, as on others, with his usual helpfulness.[1]

It is not necessary to add that the Macao mandarin did not ask us for anything in respect of our stay in the Typa which, like the various islands, is no longer a Portuguese possession; had he done so, his claims would have been rejected with contempt: but we learnt that he had insisted on the payment of a thousand piastres from the *crompador*[2] who supplied our food. This sum was modest relative to the dishonesty of this *crompador* whose accounts for the first five or six days amounted to over three hundred piastres; but convinced of his bad faith, we dismissed him. Our commissariat officer went daily to the market, as he would have in a European town, to buy whatever we needed, and our total expenditure was less in a whole month than it had been in the first week.

In all likelihood, our measures of economy displeased the mandarin; but this was only our guess – we had no dealings with him. The Chinese customs are only involved with Europeans over the trade goods that come from within China on Chinese vessels, or that are taken on these same vessels to be sold inside the empire; but

---

François Costar; other members of staff included Jean Galbert, interpreter, and Chrétien-Louis de Guignes, secretary. All found life in the East depressing and both Costar and Vieillard asked in 1785 to be allowed back to France. Vieillard was still waiting for a replacement when La Pérouse arrived. Vieillard's influence with the Chinese and the Portuguese was negligible, and he showed little interest in La Pérouse's expedition. La Pérouse kept his views out of his journal, but stated them to the Minister in a letter of 7 April 1787, criticising Vieillard, Costar and de Guignes, as well as Fouqueux des Moulins, in Macao, 'who had committed certain acts which, in Europe, would have seen him interned'. Moulins suffered from severe depression and had retired to Macao where, a few years later, it was reported that he was trying to join the Capuchin order. See Dermigny, 1964, p.110. This would not necessarily have suggested mental imbalance, but the strain under which the few Frenchmen lived in the East was quite severe, and a few months before La Pérouse's arrival, François Terrien, a supercargo who had been sent to Canton at the age of twenty-one and spent fourteen years in this 'Chinese prison', had shot himself.

[1] La Pérouse is probably concealing out of modesty a favour done to him by Lemos, as it seems unlikely that a Portuguese nobleman would have been overly worried about the remuneration of ordinary seamen.

[2] The word is *comprador* (purchaser).

what we bought in Macao, to be taken to our frigates in our own longboats, was not subject to any inspection.

The climate in Typa roadstead is very changeable during this season of the year; the thermometer varied by eight degrees from one day to the next; we nearly all suffered from fevers with heavy colds which were cured by the excellent temperatures in the island of Luzon. We sighted it on 15 February. We had left Macao on the 5th at eight o'clock in the morning with a northerly breeze that would have enabled us to sail between the islands if I had had a pilot; but wishing to avoid this expense, which is quite considerable, I took the ordinary route and passed south of the Great Ladrone.[1] We had taken on six Chinese seamen on each frigate, to replace those we had been unfortunate enough to lose when our boats were wrecked.

These people are so wretched that, in spite of the laws of this empire, which forbid anyone, under penalty of death, to leave it, we could have signed on two hundred men in a week, had we needed to.

Our observatory had been set up at Macao in the Augustinian convent, where we determined the longitude of the town at 111^{d} $19' 30''$ east, by means of the median of several sets of lunar readings; our timekeepers were also verified and we found the daily loss of No. 19 to be $12' 36''$, far more than we had previously observed: it should be said however that we had forgotten to wind up this chronometer for twenty-four hours, and that, as it had stopped, this interruption was probably responsible for this variation: but assuming that, until we reached Macao and before the oversight we were guilty of, No. 19 was as slow as we had worked it out to be at Concepción, this chronometer would have given a longitude for Macao of $113^{d} 33' 33''$, i.e. $2^{d} 14' 3''$ more than our observations had determined; and consequently the error of this timekeeper, after ten months of navigation, would not have exceeded forty-five leagues.

The northerly winds allowed me to sail east, and I would have been able to sight Piedra-Blanca[2] had they not soon veered East-South-East. The information I had been given at Macao on the best

[1] The reference is not to the Marianas originally called the Ladrones, but to a small group of islands to the south and east of the Canton River.

[2] Piedra Blanca or Pedro Blanco is an islet south-east of Hong Kong, with a white peak which made it a useful landmark for navigators bound for Canton or Macao.

route to take to Manila had not included advice on whether it was better to pass north or south of the Pratas shoal;[1] but I drew the conclusion, from the range of opinions, that either route was satisfactory. The easterlies blew wildly, which made me decide to sail close to the wind on the starboard tack and to leeward of that shoal which was badly marked on the charts prior to Cook's third voyage. Captain King, when he determined its precise latitude, rendered a great service to sailors engaged on the coastal trade between Macao and Manila and who used to follow confidently Mr Dalrymple's chart copied by Mr Dapres. These two authors, so worthy and so precise when they drew their maps from their own work, were not always able to obtain reliable information; and the placing of Pratas shoal, the tracing of the western coast of the island of Luzon and that of Manila Bay, are not to be trusted. Since I wished to make my landfall on Luzon in the 17th degree of latitude, so as to pass north of Bulinao bank,[2] I ranged along Pratas as closely as I could; I even sailed at midnight over the position shown for it on Mr Daprès' map, who extended this danger 25′ too far south. The position he gives for Bulinao, Mansiloq and Marivelle[3] is not any better. Ancient practices have shown that one runs no risk with a landfall to the north of 17^{d}, and this has seemed adequate for the various governors of Manila who, over two centuries, have not found a spare moment in which to send a few small vessels to seek these dangers and at least determine their latitude and their distance from Luzon which we sighted on 15 February in 18^{d} 14′. We thought that all we had to do was to sail down the coast with north-easterlies as far as the entrance to Manila: but the monsoon winds do not affect the coastal breezes; for several days they varied from North-West to South-West: the currents also bore North at a speed of a knot an hour, and until 19 February we did not make one league a day. Finally the North winds having freshened, we sailed along the Illocos coast[4] two leagues off,

[1] Pratas Shoal consists of several small islets, the Dongshaqun Dao, south-east of Macao, in 20°42′S and 116°43′E.

[2] Bolinao is the northernmost head of the large peninsula on the west coast of Luzon.

[3] Mariveles, at the southern end of the peninsula, marks the entrance to Manila Bay. It appears variously on old charts as Mirabela and Mirabelle.

[4] Ilocos is the name given to Luzon's west coast. On 19 February, the French had reached the latitude of present-day Vigan and were sailing rapidly south and east to turn Bolinao. Although there is now a town called Santa Cruz on the Ilocos coast, La Pérouse is probably referring to the bay in which was situated the old town of Santa Cruz, south of Bolinoa on the Zambales coast. What La Pérouse calls Capones is probably Sampaloc Point.

and sighted, in the port of Santa Cruz, a small two-master which we assumed to be loading rice for China. We were unable to match any of our bearings with Mr Daprès' map; but we can indicate the trend of this coast which, although quite frequented, is very little known On the 20th we rounded Cape Bulinao and sighted Point Capones on the 21st, bearing East exactly in the wind's eye: we tacked to get near it and reach the anchorage which extends only a league from the shore. We saw two Spanish vessels that seemed unwilling to make the entrance to Manila Bay, from which the East winds were blowing strongly; they kept to the shelter of the land. We continued our route up to south of Marivelle Island, and in the afternoon, the winds veering East-South-East, we directed our course to between this island and Mouha, and we were hopeful of entering by way of the northern pass: but after several tacks near this entrance, which is hardly half a league wide, we realised that the currents were running fairly violently West, and were totally unfavourable to our plan: we then decided to put into the port of Marivelle, one league to leeward, in order to await better winds or a more favourable current. We dropped anchor in eighteen fathoms, muddy bottom; the village bore from us North-West a quarter West, and the port South a quarter South-East 3^{d} South. This harbour is only open to south-westerlies, and the ground holds so well that I believe that one would run no danger during the monsoon when they predominate.

As we were short of firewood and I knew that it was very expensive in Manila, I decided to spend twenty-four hours at Marivelle to get a few cords, and the following day at daybreak we sent ahore all the carpenters of the two frigates with our longboats; at the same time I despatched our smaller boats to take soundings in the bay: the rest of the crew, with the large longboat, was sent fishing in the village cove which seemed to be sandy and convenient to put out the net, but this was a false impression – we came upon rocks and such a flat bottom two cablelengths from shore that it was impossible to fish. All we got for our trouble was a few spiny beaks in fairly good condition which we added to our collection of shells.[1] At around midday I went down to the village; it consists of

[1] The term used is *bécasse de mer* – strictly a bird, such as the oyster-catcher. The term, however, was in use in the eighteenth and early nineteenth centuries to refer to shells, or pieces of shell, having the appearance of a seabird's head and beak.

about forty bamboo houses, roofed with leaves and raised about four feet above the ground. These houses have bamboo floors, with gaps, that make one think of bird cages; one goes up by a ladder and I do not believe that the entire house including the roof timbers weighs two hundred pounds.

Facing the main street is a large stone building, which however was in ruins; one could nevertheless still notice two cast-iron guns at windows used as embrasures.

We learnt that this hovel was the priest's house, the church and the fort; but neither of these titles had impressed the Moors from the southern Philippines who had captured it in 1780, burnt down the village, set on fire and destroyed the fort, the church and the presbytery, enslaved all the Indians who had not had time to flee and had left with their captives without any difficulty. This event had frightened the natives so much that they do not dare to engage in any activity: nearly all the land is fallow, and this parish is so poor that we were only able to buy a dozen hens and one piglet. The priest sold us a young calf, assuring us that it represented the eighth of the only herd in the parish, whose land is ploughed by buffaloes.

This pastor was a young Indian half-breed who quite listlessly lived in the hovel I have described: a few earthenware pots and a straw litter were his only possessions. He told us that his parish contained approximately two hundred people of both sexes and of all ages, ready at the least alert to disappear into the woods to escape from these Moors who still frequently raid this coast; they are so bold and their enemies so incautious that they can often get right inside Manila Bay; during our brief stay at Cavite, seven or eight Indians were carried off in their canoes, less than a league from the entrance to the port. We were assured that boats on their way from Cavite to Manila were captured by these same Moors, although the journey is comparable to a sea crossing from Brest to Landerneau.[1] They carry out these expeditions in very light oar-propelled vessels; the Spanish put up against them a small armada of galleys that do not go and they have never caught any.

The chief official after the priest is an Indian with the pompous title of alcade who enjoys the supreme honour of a silver-knobbed

[1] Landerneau is a small town 20 km (12 miles) up the Elorn River from Brest. It was still a prosperous cloth and leather market centre when La Pérouse was writing.

walking stick; he seems to have considerable authority over the Indians: none was entitled to sell a chicken without his permission and his fixing the price; he also enjoyed the baneful monopoly of selling, on behalf of the government, the tobacco of which the Indians smoke a great deal and almost continually. This impost is fairly recent; the poorest members of the population can hardly bear this burden: it has already caused several rebellions, and I would not be surprised if one day it led to the same outcome as the tea and stamp duties had in North America. We saw at the priest's three little gazelles which he had reserved for the Governor of Manila and which he refused to sell us: anyhow, we had no hope of keeping them – this small animal is very delicate, its size is no more than that of a large rabbit; the male and the female are absolutely miniature deers and does.[1]

Our hunters saw in the forest the most delightful of birds, of all kinds of bright colours; but this forest is impenetrable on account of the creepers tangled around the trees, so that their hunt was not very successful since they could only shoot along the edge of the wood. We bought some stabbed turtle doves[2] in the market – we gave them this name because they have a red stain in the middle of their chest that looks exactly like a wound made by a knife.

Finally, at nightfall, we returned to the ships and made all the necessary arrangements to sail on the morrow. One of the two Spanish vessels we had seen on the 23rd off Point Capones had decided like us to anchor at Marivelle and wait for a more moderate breeze. I asked them for a pilot; the captain sent me his boatswain's mate, an elderly Indian who did not impress me: we nevertheless agreed that I would give him fifteen piastres to take us to Cavite; and at dawn on the 25th we set off for the southern pass, having been assured by the old Indian that attempts to go in by the northern one would be fruitless as the currents always run West. Although the distance from Marivelle to Cavite is only seven leagues, we took three days to cover this distance, dropping anchor in the bay each night in good muddy ground. We had the opportunity to note that

[1] A rabbit-size gazelle that looks like 'miniature deers and does' suggests that these may have been chevrotains – which are not antelopes, but rodents.

[2] This is the Bleeding-heart Pigeon of Luzon, *Gallicolumba luzonica*. The *Columba luzonica* Scopoli had its type locality inferentially restricted to the vicinity of Manila by K.C. Parkes, 'New Subspecies of birds from Luzon, Philippines', *Postilla* 67 (1962). Information supplied by S. Bartle, Museum of New Zealand, Wellington.

Mr Daprès chart is not very accurate; the islands of Fraile and Cavalo, which make up the southern pass, are badly placed; it is generally full of errors: but we would still have done better to follow that guide than the Indian pilot who almost grounded us on St Nicholas Shoal; he wanted to continue his tack towards the South, in spite of my protests, and we fell in less than a minute from seventeen fathoms to four; I altered course at once, and I am certain we would have struck bottom if I had gone another pistol shot further. The sea is so calm in this bay that nothing indicates the shallows; but a single observation makes this navigation quite easy: one must keep Mouha Island in sight by the northern pass of Marivelle Island and change course as soon as this island begins to be hidden. Finally, on the 28th, we reached the port of Cavite and dropped anchor in three fathoms, ooze, two cablelengths from the town. Our crossing from Macao to Cavite had lasted twenty-three days, and it would have been longer if, following the practice of the old Portuguese and Spanish sailors, we had set our minds on trying to pass North of Pratas shoal.